WOMEN AND THE
MESSIANIC HERESY OF SABBATAI ZEVI
1666–1816

THE LITTMAN LIBRARY OF
JEWISH CIVILIZATION

Dedicated to the memory of
LOUIS THOMAS SIDNEY LITTMAN
who founded the Littman Library for the love of God
and as an act of charity in memory of his father
JOSEPH AARON LITTMAN
and to the memory of
ROBERT JOSEPH LITTMAN
who continued what his father Louis had begun
יהא זכרם ברוך

'Get wisdom, get understanding:
Forsake her not and she shall preserve thee'
PROV. 4:5

The Littman Library of Jewish Civilization is a registered UK charity
Registered charity no. 1000784

Women and the Messianic Heresy of Sabbatai Zevi
1666–1816

ADA RAPOPORT-ALBERT

Translated from the Hebrew by
DEBORAH GRENIMAN

The Littman Library of Jewish Civilization
in association with Liverpool University Press

The Littman Library of Jewish Civilization
in association with Liverpool University Press
4 Cambridge Street, Liverpool L69 7ZU, UK

www.liverpooluniversitypress.co.uk/littman

Managing Editor: Connie Webber

Distributed in North America by
Oxford University Press Inc., 198 Madison Avenue,
New York, NY 10016, USA

First published 2011
First published in paperback 2015

Catalogue records for this book are available from the
British Library and the Library of Congress

ISBN 978-1-906764-80-7

Publishing Co-ordinator: Janet Moth
Copy-editing: Philippa Claiden
Proof-reading: Bonnie Blackburn
Index: Bonnie Blackburn
Designed and typeset by Pete Russell, Faringdon, Oxon.

Printed in Great Britain by
CPI Group (UK) Ltd, Croydon, CR0 4YY

Preface

THIS BOOK has its origin in a lecture, which I first delivered at the international symposium in memory of the late Gershom Scholem, held at the Hebrew University of Jerusalem and at Haifa University in December 1997. By 2001, when a much-enlarged version of the symposium's proceedings was published in Jerusalem in two volumes, my lecture, which had in the meantime developed into an extensive Hebrew monograph, was included in it as an article—arguably the longest ever published in any collective work.[1] I would like to thank the editor, my friend Rachel Elior, for agreeing to publish it in full without a moment's hesitation. Admittedly, she was at least in part responsible for the undue expansion of the piece, having shared with me, at the time of writing, Fania Scholem's manuscript Hebrew translation of Jacob Frank's Polish-language *Words of the Lord*, which she had just produced in typescript as 'an interim edition'. It was this translation that first introduced me to the full scope of the work, which turned out to provide many crucial pieces of the puzzle I was trying to assemble.

I have subsequently given guest lectures and seminars on the topic of the book at various universities, including Ben-Gurion, Tel Aviv, Munich, Stanford, Harvard, Columbia, and Brandeis, where comments by members of the audience often prompted me to refine or to enrich my arguments with additional details. I am deeply grateful to all those—too numerous to acknowledge here by name—who have shared with me their insights and knowledge with unstinting generosity. A number of colleagues and friends do, however, deserve special thanks for providing key items of information, facilitating access to otherwise inaccessible source materials, or pointing me in directions I had not considered before. They include Chimen Abramsky, Jan Doktór, Immanuel Etkes, Michael Honey, Yosef Kaplan, the late John Klier, Tuviah Kwasman, Yehuda Liebes, Paweł Maciejko, Jonatan Meir,

---

[1] Ada Rapoport-Albert, 'On the Position of Women in Sabbatianism' (Heb.), in Rachel Elior (ed.), *The Sabbatian Movement and its Aftermath: Messianism, Sabbatianism and Frankism* [Haḥalom veshivro: hatenu'ah hashabeta'it usheluḥoteiha: meshiḥiyut, shabeta'ut, ufrankizm], Jerusalem Studies in Jewish Thought 16 (Jerusalem, 2001), i. 144–327.

César Merchan Hamann, Ronit Meroz, Michal Oron, Michael Silber, Sara Sviri, Chava Turniansky, Piet van Boxel, Joanna Weinberg, Erna Weiss, and Noam Zadoff. Other, more specific, debts of gratitude are acknowledged in the footnotes ad loc.

My Hebrew monograph, which lies at the core of the present book, was skilfully translated into English by Deborah Greniman. Her ingenuity in dealing with extensive quotations from difficult seventeenth- and eighteenth-century Hebrew texts, themselves replete with quotations from or allusions to biblical, rabbinic, and kabbalistic sources, has been truly remarkable. Although I have updated and extensively revised the original text for this English edition, she is largely responsible for the present shape of Chapters 1–8, while the Introduction and the Conclusion (Chapter 9) are new and were originally written in English. The Appendix, which is an abridged version of a paper I wrote in collaboration with César Merchan Hamann, was first published in full and in English in 2007.[2] I am grateful to my indispensable collaborator, and to the Hebrew University's Department of Jewish Thought and Mandel Institute of Jewish Studies, for permission to republish the bulk of this paper here.

The Littman Library of Jewish Civilization bore with patience and good will my failure to submit the manuscript of the book by the deadlines I broke time and again over several years. When I finally submitted it, in November 2007, they provided the services of a production team whose meticulous care for every detail has spared me, and the reader, any number of errors, inconsistencies, infelicities of style, and the occasional slip into plain gobbledegook. The team included my copy-editor, Philippa Claiden, whose sharp eye, erudition, and subtle wit I valued and thoroughly enjoyed; the highly professional Janet Moth, who oversaw the editorial work in her capacity as publishing co-ordinator; George Tulloch, who ensured that all the Slavonic bibliographical references, phrases, and place-names were correctly spelled throughout; the designer Pete Russell; and Ludo Craddock, the chief executive officer.

---

[2] Ada Rapoport-Albert and César Merchan Hamann, '"Something for the Female Sex": A Call for the Liberation of Women, and the Release of the Female Libido from the "Shackles of Shame", in an Anonymous Frankist Manuscript from Prague c.1800', in Joseph Dan (ed.), *Gershom Scholem (1897–1982): In Memoriam* [Sefer zikaron legershom shalom bimlot esrim veḥamesh shanim lemoto], Jerusalem Studies in Jewish Thought 21 (Jerusalem, 2007), ii, English section, 77–135.

Above all, I benefited from the constant support and friendship of Connie Webber, Littman's managing editor. I am extremely grateful to them all.

University College London ARA
January 2010

Contents

Note on Transliteration and Conventions Used in the Text

THE transliteration of Hebrew in this book reflects consideration of the type of book it is, in terms of its content, purpose, and readership. The system adopted therefore reflects a broad approach to transcription, rather than the narrower approaches found in the *Encyclopaedia Judaica* or other systems developed for text-based or linguistic studies. The aim has been to reflect the pronunciation prescribed for modern Hebrew, rather than the spelling or Hebrew word structure, and to do so using conventions that are generally familiar to the English-speaking reader.

In accordance with this approach, no attempt is made to indicate the distinctions between *alef* and *ayin*, *tet* and *taf*, *kaf* and *kuf*, *sin* and *samekh*, since these are not relevant to pronunciation; likewise, the *dagesh* is not indicated except where it affects pronunciation. Following the principle of using conventions familiar to the majority of readers, however, transcriptions that are well established have been retained even when they are not fully consistent with the transliteration system adopted. On similar grounds, the *tsadi* is rendered by 'tz' in such familiar words as bar mitzvah, mitzvot, and so on. Likewise, the distinction between *ḥet* and *khaf* has been retained, using *ḥ* for the former and *kh* for the latter; the associated forms are generally familiar to readers, even if the distinction is not actually borne out in pronunciation, and for the same reason the final *heh* is indicated too. As in Hebrew, no capital letters are used, except that an initial capital has been retained in transliterating titles of published works (for example, *Shulḥan arukh*).

The letters *alef* and *ayin*, are generally indicated by an apostrophe in intervocalic positions as a failure to do so could lead an English-speaking reader to pronounce the vowel-cluster as a diphthong—as, for example, in *ha'ir*—or otherwise mispronounce the word. In cases of possible ambiguity, *alef* and *ayin* are also marked by an apostrophe at the beginning of internal syllables to clearly distinguish which word is intended.

The *sheva na* is indicated by an *e*—*perikat ol, reshut*—except, again, when established convention dictates otherwise.

The *yod* is represented by *i* when it occurs as a vowel (*bereshit*), by *y* when it occurs as a consonant (*yesodot*), and by *yi* when it occurs as both (*yisra'el*). In forms like *biyhudah* and *liyrushalayim* the *sheva* following the *yod* is not indicated.

Wherever the name of a Hebrew journal, or the title of a book or article in Hebrew, exists in a published English form, this form has been used, even when it is inconsistent with the overall system. Personal names have generally been left in their familiar forms.

Note on Sources

UNLESS otherwise stated, the quotations that appear in Chapters 1–8 from Aramaic, Yiddish, German, French, Italian, and Polish sources were translated into English by Deborah Greniman on the basis of my own Hebrew renderings as they first appeared in the Hebrew monograph that gave rise to the present volume. I have checked them all against the original sources to eliminate such minor inaccuracies of translation as were liable to occur as a result of mediation through Hebrew. All other translations of non-English sources are my own.

The English translation of quotations from the collection of Jacob Frank's dicta, *Words of the Lord*, is based on a comparison of Fania Scholem's unpublished Hebrew translation of the original Polish text contained in the Kraków manuscripts entitled *Zbiór Słów Panskich w Brünnie mówionych* (A Collection of the Words of the Lord Spoken at Brünn) (Jagiellonian University Library 6968, 6969/1, 2, 3), which was produced in a typescript 'interim edition–working draft' (*mahadurat beinayim–teyutat avodah*) by Rachel Elior under the title *Divrei ha'adon* (Jerusalem, 1997), with Jan Doktór's two-volume Polish edition of the work, *Księga Słów Panskich* (Book of Words of the Lord) (Warsaw, 1997), which was based, in addition to the Kraków manuscripts, on supplementary material drawn from a second Polish manuscript (Lublin, Łopacinski Public Library) containing further dicta 'spoken' by Frank at Brünn and at Offenbach, as well as a collection of what the manuscript refers to as *Widzenia Panskie* (The Lord's Visions). I did not consult Harris Lenowitz's limited access online English translation of the entire work, as it did not become accessible to me until after I had completed the bulk of the work on the present volume.

Additional records of Frank's dicta were available to Alexandr Kraushar, who quoted from them in his two-volume *Frank i frankisci polscy, 1726–1816* (Kraków, 1895) out of an apparently more extensive manuscript of *Words of the Lord*, now no longer extant. He also had access to a later Polish manuscript, emanating from the circle of sectarians at Offenbach in the period following Frank's death, known by the title of *Proroctwa Izajaszowe* (Isaiah's

Prophecies). This, too, is no longer extant, but Kraushar published extensive excerpts from it in his book. All quotations from Frankist sources preserved by Kraushar alone are based, with some minor modifications, on the English edition of his work, *Jacob Frank: The End to the Sabbataian Heresy* (Lanham, Md., 2001).

Another important Polish source for Jacob Frank's life, his teachings and his associates, is preserved in the same Lublin manuscript (Łopacinski Publichis associates Library 2118) of which some sections were incorporated in Jan Doktór's Polish edition of *Words of the Lord*. This particular section of the manuscript is entitled *Rozmaite adnotacje, przypadki, czynnosci i anekdoty panskie* (Various Notes, Events, Activities, and Anecdotes Concerning the Lord) and was published with an introduction under this title by Jan Doktór (Warsaw, 1996). The same text had already been published by Hillel Levine, under the title *The Kronika: On Jacob Frank and the Frankist Movement* (Jerusalem, 1984), where it was accompanied by an introduction in both Hebrew and English and an annotated Hebrew translation. References to both editions are provided in the notes throughout.

Moses Porges' memoirs of his stay at the Frankist court in Offenbach towards the end of the 1790s were first reported (but not fully published) by Leopold Stein in his 'Mittheilung über die Frankistensekte' (*Achawa*, 3, 1870). The memoirs were published in full, from a copy of the original manuscript, in a Yiddish translation by Nathan Michael Gelber (*YIVO—Historishe shriftn*, i, 1929), three years prior to their first publication in the original German as 'Eine Wallfahrt nach Offenbach' in the journal *Frankfurter israelitisches Gemeindeblatt* (6–7, 1932), and a full English translation appeared as an appendix in Arthur Mandel's *Militant Messiah* (Atlantic Highlands, NJ, 1979). In addition, under the same title, 'Di zikhroynes fun moses porges' (Memoirs of Moses Porges), Gelber published not only his Yiddish version of the memoirs themselves (cols. 265–88), but also his own introduction (cols. 253–64) and three appendices (cols. 289–96) containing his Yiddish translation of the manuscript accounts—originally recorded in Hebrew but extant only in Judaeo-German—submitted on 24–25 November 1800 to the rabbinical court of Fürth, reporting the testimonies of Moses Porges, his brother Leib-Leopold, and their friend Jonas Haufsinger who, while fleeing Offenbach a few months earlier, had been arrested in Fürth and interrogated by local rabbis about their sectarian involvement. While the Yiddish version of the memoirs is referred

to throughout by the English title 'Memoirs of Moses Porges' and appears
under Moses Porges' name, Gelber's introduction to this version, as well as the
three testimonies published in his appendices, are referred to by the Yiddish
title 'Di zikhroynes fun moses porges' under Gelber's own name.

Apart from one reference to the Revised Standard Version (RSV) of the
Bible, all other biblical quotations in English are taken from the Authorized
(King James) Version of the Bible.

Introduction

IN A PAPER first published almost twenty years ago, I set out to refute the notion that the hasidic movement brought about something of a feminist revolution in Judaism.[1] It was the early twentieth-century historian of hasidism S. A. Horodetsky who first claimed that the movement endowed women with 'complete equality in the religious life'[2]—a radical departure from the norm— which he found expressed in a variety of hasidic innovations. These ranged from women's direct, personal relationship with the charismatic leader—the rebbe or tsadik—which established a new equality between the sexes within the family and the community; through the breakdown of the educational barrier of Hebrew—the language of traditional scholarly discourse in the male world of Torah learning—by virtue of an outpouring of hasidic books in Yiddish, the women's tongue; to 'the rise of the Jewish woman even to the level of tsadik; if she showed herself worthy of it, nothing could stand in her way'.[3]

Against these far-reaching claims I argued that, from its inception until the early twentieth century, hasidism was and remained predominantly the preserve of men. Far from granting women equal access to the rebbe, the sabbath and festival assemblies at his 'court', and above all at his 'table'—the focal point of the hasidic gathering, where he delivered his personal *torah*—regularly excluded women. The male hasidim who travelled to the court would normally leave their women behind, thus periodically 'dropping out' of matrimony and its mundane obligations. The pilgrimages to the court offered them instead the spiritually invigorating experience of communal life within an emotionally charged, exclusively male fraternity, which functioned symbolically as an alternative to ordinary family life. Moreover, contrary to Horodetsky's claim, hasidism never embarked on a programme of Yiddish publications designed to create an educated female readership. The speculative literature of hasidism, with which, during the 1780s and 1790s, the movement first launched itself in print, was

---

[1] See Rapoport-Albert, 'On Women in Hasidism'.
[2] Horodetsky, *Hasidism* (Heb.), iv. 68.   [3] Ibid. 69.

published exclusively in Hebrew and remained totally inaccessible to the Yiddish-reading female (and uneducated male) public. Only the later, popular but never fully sanctioned hasidic hagiographical writings were published in both Hebrew and Yiddish.⁴ Women could read this type of literature, which was, at least in some cases, expressly directed at them (alongside other categories of readers who were not proficient in Hebrew—uneducated men and children),⁵ and may well have done so, but the evidence that they actually read it—perhaps surprisingly—is extremely sparse.⁶ Nor did hasidism lend any support or

⁴ For the questionable status of the hagiographical tales within hasidism, see Dan, *Hasidic Story*, 189–95; Shmeruk, *Yiddish Literature*, 210–11; Nigal, *Hasidic Tale*, 65–74.

⁵ See e.g. the introduction to the 1816 Korets Yiddish edition of *Shivḥei habesht*, 1b, which addresses the translation to 'all those people who do not know the Holy Tongue—men, women and children'. See also, on the same page, Naphtali Hirsch Hakohen's approbation, in which he recommends the edition 'especially since most women, and members of their households, are eager to read this book, to peruse its saintly narratives and miracle tales at leisure on the holy sabbath'. Similarly, the title pages of the 1816 Novy Dvor and the 1817 [Żółkiew] Yiddish editions (reproduced in both Shmeruk, *Yiddish Literature*, 215–16, and Mondshine, *Shivhey Ha-Baal Shem Tov*, 29–30), address the translation to 'men and women' (Novy Dvor) or 'especially righteous women' ([Żółkiew]) who cannot read Hebrew.

⁶ Notably, a pioneering study of the reading habits of east European Jewish women during the 19th century—the period in which hasidism was becoming a dominant force in much of the region—contains not a single reference to a woman reading a hasidic book, not even the popular *Shivḥei habesht* (In Praise of the Ba'al Shem Tov—the earliest hasidic hagiographical work, first published in Yiddish in 1815, only a few months after the publication of the first Hebrew edition at the end of 1814) or any of the subsequent collections of hasidic tales, which were being published in both Hebrew and Yiddish from the 1860s on. See Parush, *Reading Jewish Women*. The devotional Yiddish reading repertoire of all the women mentioned in the book, whether or not they were associated with hasidism, appears to have consisted of collections of women's prayers (*tkhines*), traditional ethical (*musar*) tracts, and the anthology of homilies on the weekly Bible readings known as *Tsenerene*, to which might be added a small number of popular history books and medieval or early modern romances translated into Yiddish (see ibid. 59, 66–7, 137–8). More recently, however, in a personal communication subsequent to the publication of her book, Prof. Parush supplied me with the only reference she has discovered so far to a woman—a midwife and herbal healer—who is described as regularly reading on the sabbath, together with her two daughters, *Shivḥei habesht* in addition to the *Tsenerene* and the usual range of devotional and ethical works available in Yiddish—a small 'library' in which all three women are said to have become 'well versed, from cover to cover' (Schwarz, *Ḥayai*, 162). The author—a Hebrew teacher born in 1860 in the Ukrainian town of Balta—is describing his childhood in the agricultural colony of Helbinova, which would place the woman and her daughters in the 1860s or early 1870s. However, even if the author's list of titles faithfully represents the contents of their 'library' rather than what he considered to be the standard set of pious works in Yiddish (notably, his list concludes with 'etc.'), the incorporation of *Shivḥei habesht* in the list does not in

legitimacy to the phenomenon of female tsadikim. The claim that it did was based on some late local rumours and oral traditions, which portrayed a small cluster of women as charismatic spiritual leaders, equal in status and power to the male tsadikim. As I argued in my paper, it is probable that, at grass-roots level, the hasidic movement did occasionally bring to the fore a type of woman whose spiritual powers were widely acknowledged in public. Such women may have attracted, at least for a while, a hasidic following of their own, but the very tradition that attests to the existence of the 'Maid of Ludmir'—the most remarkable of them all[7]—suggests that in 'official', exclusively male, hasidic leadership circles, a woman who conducted herself as a full-fledged tsadik in her own right was viewed as an aberration and was quickly, vigorously, and apparently thoroughly suppressed.[8]

itself necessarily suggest that the women who supposedly read it were thereby expressing their hasidic identity. In fact, there is no indication in Schwarz's account that the women and their family were associated with hasidism. On the other hand, Shmarya Levin, when describing his childhood in the small Belorussian town of Svisloch (Svislovitch) during the same period, reports that his mother, who came from a hasidic Habad family (but married a mitnaged, an Orthodox opponent of hasidism), used to tell her children hasidic 'stories and legends' (Levin, *Childhood*, 6). It is not impossible that hasidic stories were circulating among the women as oral lore, without being read in the hasidic books that were becoming available to them in Yiddish. This would seem to apply even to a prominent woman in the ruling Habad dynasty, the *Rebbetsn* Rivkah (1837–1914, wife of the fourth Rebbe, Shmuel). Her grandson—Yosef Yitshak, the sixth Rebbe—describes her as a rich source of oral traditions and tales about the early history of hasidism, but when referring to her reading habits, he makes no mention of any hasidic book, listing only the Yiddish *Tsenerene*, *Sheyres yisroel* (*She'erit yisra'el*), and *Yosippon*, from which apparently she used to read out every sabbath to a group of female relatives and associates. See Schneersohn, *Divrei yemei harabanit*, 105–8. The Galician Jewish Enlightenment activist (maskil) and staunch opponent of hasidism Joseph Perl has one of his fictional female characters not only reading but even studying *Shivḥei habesht* in Yiddish (see his *Revealer of Secrets* (*Megaleh temirin*, first published in Hebrew in 1819), p. 191, §112), but this is one of his satirical ploys, designed to expose the recently published book as fanciful nonsense fit only for feeble-minded women, and it cannot be taken as evidence that real women were actually reading the book. See, however, Werses, 'Women in Hasidic Courts', 37–8, 46–7, where the maskilic portrayal of women as avid readers of the Yiddish *Shivḥei habesht* is taken to be reliable and wholly realistic.

[7] For a critical analysis of the Maid of Ludmir tradition, see Rapoport-Albert, 'On Women in Hasidism'. For the latest attempt to construct her biography out of fragments of historical information, fleshed out by memoiristic-hagiographical accounts of doubtful historical value, see Deutsch, *The Maiden of Ludmir*.

[8] The Maid of Ludmir's adoption of the ascetic, celibate life, which gave rise to a popular perception of her 'holy virginity', was the most syncretistic aspect of her anomalous conduct,

In reality, up until the early decades of the twentieth century, when the entire Orthodox sector, hasidic and non-hasidic alike, woke up to the potential for engaging its womenfolk in the struggle against modernity and secularism,[9] hasidism had no message of its own for women. In fact, in the opinion of at least one nineteenth-century hasidic leader—Meir Rottenberg of Opatów (d. 1827)—who in 1824 was interrogated by the Polish authorities about the doctrines and practices of hasidism, 'women generally are not hasidim'.[10]

and can account for the hasidic leadership's endeavours to suppress it. By contrast, there were some hasidic women who acquired spiritual authority by intimate association, through family ties, with the most famous charismatic male leaders of their day. They all conformed, through marriage and childbearing, to their primary gender role, so that such extraordinary spiritual powers as they derived from their male relatives could be safely acknowledged without posing a threat to the traditional order of society. On this category of women as a successful, if more limited, alternative mode of female leadership in hasidism, see Polen, 'Miriam's Dance', 11–15; Loewenthal, 'Women and the Dialectic', 12–15; Rapoport-Albert, 'Emergence of a Female Constituency', 56*–59*. Nevertheless, if such women ever held their own 'table' and delivered their own '*torah*', as has been claimed in some 20th-century hagiographies, then the hasidic movement did not choose to preserve any of their speculative teachings, and the pre-20th-century hagiographical literature, to the extent that it mentions them at all, never depicts any of them as tsadikim in their own right. Horodetsky was the first to focus on the phenomenon and to present it in this light, clearly providing the impetus for the celebration of female rebbes in subsequent literature. I have, however, come across one reference (for which I am grateful to Dr Rivka Dvir-Goldberg) to a woman likened to a rebbe in an early 20th-century source, published some five years prior to Horodetsky's initial publication of his findings in 1909 (on which see below, at n. 13). This was the widow of Israel Abraham of Cherny Ostrov (1772–1814), Tsizye Hannah, of whom it was said by her grandson that 'she conducted herself as a rebbe after her husband's death, and the hasidim flocked to her as they had done to her husband in his lifetime. Once the holy man of God . . . Mordecai . . . of Chernobyl spent the sabbath in Cherny Ostrov and attended the third sabbath meal at her table' (from the approbation by Israel Abraham's grandson to the collection of his grandfather's teachings, in Donner, *Menorat zahav*, 7, reproduced in id., *Butsina kadisha* (hagiographical tales about Meshulam Zusya of Hanipoli, Israel Abraham's father), 54). In the course of the 20th century, references to this type of female leadership in hasidism begin to proliferate in a variety of hagiographical, memoiristic, journalistic, and belletristic publications.

[9] It was against this background that the Beit Ya'akov network of Orthodox schools for girls was established. Initiated by Sarah Schnierer, it gained the approval of both the hasidic and the non-hasidic leadership of Agudat Yisrael in inter-war Poland. On this and other Orthodox attempts to mobilize women during this period, see Rapoport-Albert, 'On Women in Hasidism', 523–5 n. 82. See also Loewenthal, 'Women and the Dialectic', 26–41; Weissman, 'Bais Yaakov'. For the debate about the Jewish education of girls, and early attempts to establish it in Galicia, see Manekin, 'Development of the Idea' (Heb.).

[10] This was in answer to the question: 'If a wife unaccompanied by her non-hasidic husband

The movement possessed no ideology aspiring to equalize women's religious or social status to that of men, nor did it set out to educate them in Yiddish, or to elevate them to positions of authority as rebbes. The evidence for this can be found, not least, in the thundering silence of all the eighteenth- and nineteenth-century hasidic sources, both speculative and hagiographical, on

or his son, who was still a juvenile, were to come to your congregation, would they be accepted?' His full answer was: 'They are free to come to the synagogue, but women generally are not hasidim. What is more, women and children fall under the authority of the father; if the father does not wish them to be hasidim, they cannot be accepted.' The text of the interrogation was published in the original Polish in Wodziński, 'Sprawa chasydymów', 237–9 and in French translation in 'L'Affaire des "Chasydymów"', 50–3. Meir of Opatów's reply to the question on women appears on p. 239 of the Polish edition and on p. 53 of the French. I am grateful to Prof. Wodziński for bringing this text to my attention. Reference to the same interrogation, quoting Meir of Opatów's view on the question of the hasidic affiliation of women, appears also in Dynner, *Men of Silk*, 44 and 182. However, Dynner takes Meir's exclusion of women from the category of hasidim to be 'patently false' (ibid. 44) or 'not accurate' (ibid. 181), presumably reading it as the tsadik's endeavour to refute the claim, made by some of hasidism's opponents (both mitnagedim and maskilim), to the effect that women were 'the primary victims of the zaddikim' and often visited and brought them donations without their husbands' consent (ibid. 44). This charge may well underlie the Polish interrogator's question regarding the wife and child of a non-hasid. The maskil Abraham Stern, who reported on hasidism negatively to the Polish officials, claimed that 'they would attempt to beguile and ensnare the younger and less sensible, particularly . . . the female sex' (ibid. 158), and at least one of the government reports giving rise to the investigation of hasidism in 1824 was probably inspired by Stern, and accused the hasidim of enticing 'the naïve and most deficient in reason' to join their ranks (Wodziński, 'Sprawa chasydymów' 231–2; 'L'Affaire des "Chasydymów"', 41). Nevertheless, Meir's replies to the interrogator's questions generally ring true, if defensive, and Dynner's conclusion from his anti-hasidic sources that 'women constituted a large proportion of Hasidic adherents' (*Men of Silk*, 182) is misleading. While some women did visit some (though by no means all) of the courts either with or without their husbands' permission, often under certain constraints that denied them direct access to the rebbes (see Rapoport-Albert, 'Emergence of a Female Constituency', 17*–32*), it is impossible to gauge their numbers or to guess what proportion they might have constituted of the total number of Polish hasidim—a figure which is itself at best contested and at worst elusive (compare Dynner, 'How Many *Hasidim*' to Wodziński, 'How Should We Count *Hasidim*'). Moreover, quite a few of the anti-hasidic writings penned by both mitnagedim and maskilim suggest the opposite picture when they accuse the hasidim of abandoning their women at home when they travel to visit their rebbes in the courts (see e.g. Wilensky, *Hasidim and Mitnagedim* (Heb.), i. 103; ii. 107, 151, 159–60, 173, 315; Maimon, *Autobiography*, 168; Perl, *Uiber das Wesen*, 125). Be that as it may, women's affiliation with the courts—the exceptional case, as Dynner himself admits, of the wealthy hasidic patroness Temerl Bergson notwithstanding—was much more restricted than the men's, and was considered problematic or even undesirable by at least some of the hasidic masters.

every one of these supposed innovations.[11] Most notably, throughout this period, the hasidic sources contain not a single reference to the Maid of Ludmir or to any other female tsadik of her type.[12] The latter-day interest in such remarkable women would seem to have sprung entirely from an oral tradition first recorded by Horodetsky in 1909 as a mere curiosity,[13] but which, by the early 1920s, when preparing for publication his four-volume history of

---

[11] I do not accept Nehemia Polen's interpretation of a certain homily by the hasidic master Kalonymus Kalman Epstein (*c*.1751–1823) as representing an agenda of 'radical egalitarianism' that provides the theoretical underpinnings, as it were, for hasidism's alleged promotion in practice of women's spiritual powers (See Polen, 'Miriam's Dance', 3–6, 8, and see the discussion below, Ch. 5 n. 65).

[12] A possible and, so far as I know, unique allusion to the Maid of Ludmir does, however, occur in one hasidic hagiographical work, published in the last decade of the 19th century, which mentions 'a woman of propriety' or 'a pious woman' (*ishah kesherah*) in the town of Ludmir who was able to foretell the future. See I. Landau, *Zikaron tov*, pt. 2, 15*a* [29] §4. For the book and its author, see Rapoport-Albert, 'On Women in Hasidism', 513–14 n. 21.

[13] This was a short article in Russian, based—as he noted—on the 'tales of old people in Volhynia'. See Horodetsky, 'Ludmirskaya deva', 219–22. I have encountered so far only one explicit reference to the Maid of Ludmir in a published source that pre-dates Horodetsky's initial report by two and a half decades. Significantly, however, this is not a hasidic source but rather a maskilic polemic, directed against a certain Barukh Esman of Kiev and his book of casuistry, *Ḥad veḥalak*, published in Vilna some two years earlier. Employing the language and literary conceits of Joseph Perl's satire, *Revealer of Secrets*, the polemicist ridicules Esman's daughter, portraying her as a famous rabbinic scholar and kabbalist, 'almost on a par with the Maid . . . of the town of Ludmir, who was subject in her day to the authority of the rebbe of Trisk. The only difference between them is that the Maid of Ludmir wore a *talit* and laid *tefilin* . . . paying no attention to the rabbis of her time, who had put her under *ḥerem* [a ban of excommunication] . . . because they feared that everyone would be misled into following her, taking her to be a tsadik, and all the hasidim would be drawn to her. About the present daughter, on the other hand . . . the rabbis will never say such a thing . . . Without a doubt, she, too, will soon don a fringed *talit* and lay *tefilin*, as befits her stature . . . and her uncle will no doubt soon find for her a lucrative rabbinic appointment . . . in Vilna' (Weissberg, *Ga'on vashever*, 44–5; I am grateful to Jonatan Meir for bringing this passage to my attention). Providing independent corroboration of Horodetsky's oral tradition, this account of the Maid of Ludmir confirms that her career as a rebbe attracted the opposition of the hasidic leaders of her day, which accounts for the eradication of her memory from all the literary sources of hasidism prior to Horodetsky's 1909 publication. For an early (and fully acknowledged!) infiltration of Horodetsky's Maid tradition into 20th-century hasidic hagiography, see Walden, *Nifle'ot harabi*, 88, which reads: 'the girl Hannah Sarah [this should be Rachel] of Ludmir, known as *dos ludmirer meydl*, became famous for her holy spirit and miracles (her entire story has been published in a periodical journal by Shmuel Abba Horodetsky of Bern)'. I am grateful to Prof. David Assaf for this reference.

hasidism (the first ever to feature a short chapter entitled 'The Jewish Woman in Hasidism'), he had come to regard as evidence for the unprecedented empowerment of women in hasidism—an eruption of fresh spiritual energies that could be harnessed to the project of Jewish national revival, with its own distinct, if never fully realized, female-liberationist strand. Horodetsky now presented the women he had first described as occupying a 'modest' or a 'passive' role, and only 'very rarely in the history of hasidism [becoming] active female characters who have influence on their surroundings',[14] in terms that celebrated them as full-fledged tsadikim—harbingers, as it were, of the new, egalitarian society being created in Palestine by the Zionist movement, for which he believed hasidism offered a viable traditionalist model.[15] But this was never substantiated by evidence from the literary sources of hasidism, and—grass-roots oral traditions apart—it would seem to be far removed from the genuine doctrines and gender norms of pre-twentieth-century hasidism.[16]

I had framed my arguments in that paper in the context of the fundamental divide between women and men, which is a built-in feature of both the halakhic and kabbalistic traditions. Hasidism had emerged from within these traditions, and in respect of gender did not stray from them at all. The movement subscribed to the selfsame construction of female nature as the one that had led to the exemption of women from much of Judaism's formal cult of ritual obligations, and to their exclusion from all the institutional frameworks for the attainment of its intellectual and spiritual goals.[17] That hasidism should have persisted in this exclusion of women may not be surprising in itself, but it is worthy of note in contrast to the prominence—well attested in a rich canonical literature—of holy women and female saints in the mystical traditions of both Christianity and Islam. Both had shared with rabbinic

---

[14] See Horodetsky, 'Ludmirskaya deva', 219, and see the discussion in Rapoport-Albert, 'On Women in Hasidism', 504–5.

[15] For Horodetsky's background, his intellectual development, his exposure to both Zionism and feminism, and his evaluation of hasidism as a forerunner of both, see ibid. 497 and 510 n. 12; Deutsch, *The Maiden of Ludmir*, 23–33. But cf. Rapoport-Albert, 'Emergence of a Female Constituency', 13*–14*, n. 15.   [16] See more on this below, Ch. 9.

[17] I refer here and throughout to the frameworks generated by rabbinic Judaism, which came into existence in the early centuries of the Common Era and continued, in one form or another, to shape traditional Jewish life from then on. I exclude from the discussion the entirely different landscape of biblical and Hellenistic Judaism, where gender norms operated quite differently.

Judaism the ontological divide between the female and the male, a distinction that led all three religions to deny women formal education, and generally to bar them from all positions of clerical, intellectual, and spiritual authority. Yet a considerable number of Christian as well as Muslim women were nevertheless deemed to have transcended the limitations of their sex. Viewed as women who had become like men, or who had shed altogether the earthly garb of sexuality, they were revered and held to be just as holy and as spiritually enlightened as any man could be. It was the sublimation of their carnal nature, achieved—for the most part—by embarking on a life of rigorous ascetic practice, and above all sexual abstinence, that enabled these women to rise to a plane of existence perceived as being purely spiritual, one in which there was no longer any meaningful distinction between the female and the male.[18]

This singular avenue to spiritual perfection on an equal footing with men, which lay open to the female mystics of both Christianity and Islam, was closed to their Jewish sisters, whose religious tradition knew no plane of existence that lay above or beyond the duality of male and female. For even the notion of the cosmic union of the female and the male within the kabbalistic godhead did not entail the obliteration of the sexual disparity between them, not even if it was perceived as the incorporation of the female within the male in a state of androgyny.[19] Rather, the 'matrimonial' union between them highlighted sexual disparity, and it was precisely from this that it derived its significance and meaning.

[18] See Rapoport-Albert, 'On Women in Hasidism', 520–1, at nn. 68–70.

[19] For this interpretation, see Wolfson, *Circle in the Square*; id., 'Constructions of the Shekhinah'; id., 'Gender and Heresy'; id., 'Engenderment of Messianic Politics', and the bibliographical references to his other writings on the same subject, ibid. 212 n. 27. Wolfson argues that, from the ontological point of view, the incorporation of the female in the male is her effective obliteration, and he thus regards the androgynous mating within the godhead as 'androcentric'. The logic of this is problematic, since the androgynous state is bisexual by definition. Wolfson agrees that, logically, obliterating the independent existence of the female necessarily deprives the male of its distinct existence, and so in effect, the very distinction between the sexes is thus obliterated. Nevertheless, he argues, one cannot deny the presence of a concept of 'masculine androgyny' in the literature of the kabbalah, where the female is subsumed and nullified in the male without this nullifying the male's distinctive masculinity. See 'Constructions of the Shekhinah', 60–1 n. 153, and 80–2. See also Elqayam's reservations in 'To Know Messiah' (Heb.), 662–6. To be sure, Elqayam admits that the kabbalistic sources do occasionally suggest the notion of an asexual divine or purely spiritual androgyny—devoid of masculinity and femininity alike, as it was conceived in the writings of Philo, Paul, and the early Gnostics. He pro-

To be sure, in Jewish scholarly and mystical circles men would not uncommonly resort to ascetic practices, often including a regime of strict, if intermittent, sexual abstinence, as a means—problematic from the halakhic point of view, but well tried and true—of exercising their intellectual, spiritual, or magical powers in what was usually referred to as a state of 'holiness' or 'purity'. When adopted for this purpose by women, however, these selfsame practices were not only seen as devoid of religious merit; they were condemned out of hand as a false posture or a self-delusion that threatened to undermine the natural world order and the foundations of society.[20] The religious ethics prescribed for women confined them to the sphere of material existence, where their engagement, within marriage, in practical affairs, and the satisfaction of all 'corporeal' needs, was viewed as wholly legitimate. It was their primary function, the purpose for which they were made, and it freed their husbands and their sons to pursue the intellectual or spiritual ideals that the system held out to men. Moreover, sexual abstinence was often forced upon the wives of scholars and mystics, as a consequence of their husbands' protracted sojourns away from home for the purpose of study, or the regime of peregrination in conditions of material deprivation and physical discomfort, which they would take upon themselves as an ascetic discipline designed to curtail their bodily needs in order to enhance their intellectual and spiritual capacities. These involuntarily celibate wives were recognized for their willingness to forgo

vides several examples of this: a passage from the Zohar, which implies an androgynous mating that transcends the distinction between the sexes; the medieval kabbalist David b. Judah Hehasid, who does away with the distinction between the bisexual countenances of the divine at the highest level of the emanation; and the 16th-century Simon [ibn] Lavi, who disposes of the same distinction within 'the depths of the divine *ayin* [naught]'. However, these formulations derive from the fundamental kabbalistic notion that the root of all being lies within the Ein Sof—that infinite, undifferentiated energy of the divine as it exists above or beyond the creation, transcending all distinction and separation while bearing within it the potentiality for both. Thus, even at this level, the polarization of the sexes exists as a potential if not in actuality, and its existence exerts itself at the very outset of the process of creation. See also Wolfson, 'Constructions of the Shekhinah', 59–62, for a discussion of the Sabbatian theologian Abraham Miguel Cardozo on the 'Cause of Causes' as that stage of the creative process that precedes sexual division.

[20] For the condemnation in the classical rabbinic sources of the 'female ascetic' or 'female celibate' (*ishah perushah*) as one of the categories of 'world destroyers', see, for the time being, Rapoport-Albert, 'On Women in Hasidism', 521 n. 72. The tradition and its historical implications are the subject of my forthcoming *Female Bodies—Male Souls*.

their halakhic entitlement to regular conjugal relations. It was a noble self-sacrifice that enabled their husbands to fulfil the highest religious ideals, from which they were themselves precluded by dint of their female sex. Their abstinence, therefore, was a regrettable consequence of their husbands' religious endeavours—unavoidable, but pointless in itself as a means of enhancing their own spiritual capacities.

This strict differentiation of gender roles, coupled with the indissoluble correspondence between gender and sex (in terms of normative conduct if not in the kabbalists' flights of mystical imagination),[21] was perceived as God-ordained and insurmountable. As a result, even if historically some Jewish women may have experienced mystical revelations and led a richly productive spiritual life, rabbinic tradition did not possess the conceptual tools that would equip it to acknowledge their achievement. Apart from the chance survival of a handful of references to female visionaries—some so fragmentary as to be obscure, others extant in a unique manuscript never intended for print or public dissemination[22]—it preserved no memory of such holy women or any literary record of their mystical experiences.[23]

It is against this background that the Sabbatian movement emerges as a unique and remarkable anomaly, striving to transcend the intransigent polarity of the prevailing gender paradigm by overturning the halakhic norms that set the ritual, social, and—most sensationally—the sexual boundaries dividing male from female.

Sabbatianism, a messianic movement of unprecedented duration and scope, was centred on, and derived its name from, the charismatic personality of Sabbatai (or, as pronounced in Hebrew, *shabetai*) Zevi—a seventeenth-century kabbalist from the Ottoman port town of Smyrna, who, at the height of his international celebrity as the long-awaited Jewish messiah, abruptly converted to Islam in the autumn of 1666. While this might have been regarded a shameful act of betrayal, as indeed it was instantly denounced by

---

[21] On which see e.g. Mopsik, *Sex of the Soul*, 5–52.   [22] See below, Ch. 2, at n. 56.

[23] An issue that lies beyond the scope of the present discussion is the spiritual energy that is capable of transforming any physical act, ritual or mundane, and of course also private prayer, into an intensely personal mystical experience, quite apart from any formal framework of religious life. Through the ages, this possibility may well have sustained the spiritual lives of many Jewish women, but as a private experience which, by its very nature, lacked outlets for expression in the public arena, it has left barely a trace on the historical record of rabbinic Judaism.

some, Sabbatai's conversion did not put an end to his remarkable messianic career. Rather, it was quickly and persuasively explained in kabbalistic terms as the messiah's most difficult and trying task—preconceived as an integral part of his redemptive mission. Many of the 'believers', as his mass following was called, held on to their faith in the apostate messiah, and in some quarters he was also believed to be an incarnate aspect of the kabbalistic godhead. But the messianic frenzy that at first surrounded him subsided gradually with the passage of time, as it became increasingly evident that he had failed to accomplish his mission. When he died, in relative isolation, in the autumn of 1676, his death was interpreted as a mere 'occultation' and gave rise to the expectation of his imminent return. Some groups of 'believers', who had followed him into Islam, continued to maintain a secret but distinctive Sabbatian identity as an Islamic sect within the Ottoman empire and subsequently in modern Turkey, where their tradition apparently survives to the present day. In east-central Europe, too, the movement persisted at least until the second decade of the nineteenth century. Some of its adherents converted to Catholicism in the second half of the eighteenth century, and formed around their leader, Jacob Frank, a syncretistic sectarian–messianic cult that eventually assimilated into Polish society. But the majority of 'believers' did not apostatize. For them Sabbatianism became an underground current of kabbalistic Judaism. They operated clandestinely, in diverse sectarian groupings, each headed by its own charismatic 'prophet', who was often considered at the same time to be a fresh embodiment of the messiah's soul, and in some cases, as in Sabbatai Zevi's, also a human incarnation of the divine.[24]

One of Sabbatianism's most distinctive and persistent features was the high visibility of women within its ranks. They were among the movement's earliest and most ardent supporters—championing the messianic cause,

[24] Gershom Scholem's monumental *Sabbatai Sevi* remains the most exhaustive study of the messianic movement during Sabbatai's lifetime. Scholem's collected papers on the subsequent developments of Sabbatianism appeared in two Hebrew volumes, *Studies and Texts* and *Researches*. The Ottoman context in which the movement originated, and its persistence as a Judaeo-Islamic sect, are the subject of 'A Jewish Messiah in the Ottoman Court', an unpublished doctoral dissertation by Cengiz Sisman. Other histories of the movement, or of particular aspects of it, include Barnai, *Sabbatianism* (Heb.); Goldish, *Sabbatean Prophets*; Lenowitz, *Jewish Messiahs*, 149–97; Liebes, *On Sabbatianism* (Heb.). See also the two collections of Sabbatian documents translated into English by Halperin: *Sabbatai Zevi* and Cardozo, *Selected Writings*. Freely's *Lost Messiah* is a popular and largely derivative work.

proclaiming its gospel, and from time to time emerging as its chief protagonists. Admittedly, the evidence for this is fragmentary, and much of it
is drawn from polemical sources, which are naturally marked by an anti-
Sabbatian bias. Hostile authors were liable to exaggerate the involvement of
women in the movement precisely in order to denigrate it and to besmirch its
character. For the very mention of women's involvement was enough to imply
that Sabbatian messianism was far removed from the rabbinical world and its
values, while at the same time suggesting, as a matter of course, its proclivity
for sexual impropriety.

   In spite of this, the extant documentation, problematic though it is, points
to the conclusion that if the seed of any revolutionary 'feminism' ever ger-
minated in a pre-modern Jewish milieu, it was in the Sabbatian and not in the
hasidic movement. Horodetsky who, as we saw, had characterized hasidism
as gender-egalitarian,[25] also drew attention to women's active involvement
in Sabbatianism. He saw both movements as belonging together in the
'mystical–messianic' strand of Judaism, which he perceived to be 'emotional'
and thus instinctively more accessible to women than the legalistic rationality
of male-dominated 'rabbinism' or 'official Judaism'. On the strength of this, he
proceeded to trace the course of women's apparent progression to ever higher
degrees of integration in the mystical spirituality of Judaism, a Judaism that
was becoming increasingly 'emotional' under the combined impacts, on the
one hand, of what he termed 'the kabbalistic movement', and on the other
hand a succession of messianic movements, with Sabbatianism at its peak:

Emotional religion, which transcends all rules and regulations, emotional Judaism,
which knows no limitation or differentiation, accommodated the Jewish woman and
allowed her much scope for direct involvement. Messianism, from its first stirrings in
the diaspora ... until Sabbatai Zevi, that popular movement that arose not only to liberate the people from material enslavement but also from spiritual enslavement, to
free pure faith and religious sentiment from the yoke of the innumerable laws and
restrictions that surrounded and threatened to suffocate them—in this religious
movement we see the Jewish woman taking part with the full warmth and ardour of
her emotions. She played an especially important role in the messianic movement of
Sabbatai Zevi, in which there were Jewish women who led the movement and wielded
immense influence. As the kabbalistic movement gained strength, and began gradually to descend from its esoteric heights to affect directly the spiritual lives of the
people, it affected also the life of the Jewish woman. Lurianic kabbalah in particular

---

[25] See above, at nn. 2–3.

had a great impact on the Jews of Poland in the sixteenth and seventeenth centuries, and the Polish Jewish woman was emotionally receptive to it in full.[26]

The convergence of Sabbatianism and Lurianic kabbalah, especially in Poland—the birthplace of hasidism—had prepared the ground, according to Horodetsky, for the culmination of the process in hasidism, with the 'complete equality in the religious life' that it allegedly granted women.

In the paper in which I refuted Horodetsky's assertions about the equality of women in hasidism, I also rejected his observations on their special receptivity to the emotional spirituality of both 'the kabbalistic movement' and Sabbatianism.[27] I pointed out that there was no evidence to suggest that women—in Poland or elsewhere—were ever drawn to Lurianic kabbalah, and that moreover it was hard to imagine how they might have been exposed to, or affected by, its esoteric doctrines. As for women's engagement with Sabbatianism—admittedly, I noted the existence of evidence on the numerous prophetesses that the movement had brought forth; on Sabbatai Zevi's wives, of whom at least one was said to possess a messianic dimension of her own; and on Eva Frank, who became the messianic figurehead in her father's circle of 'believers' (on all of which more will be said in the chapters that follow below). However, at the time of writing I did not regard these phenomena as indicating any significant reconceptualization of women's status in society. In this I had followed Scholem, who tended to belittle the importance of women's involvement in Sabbatian messianism, even though he observed it more than once, collected its principal attestations, and found in it 'a striking and very revealing sign of the messianic transformation of the old order'.[28]

It was only in the course of assembling the material for the present study that I came to realize the full scope and implications of the evidence before me. It pointed to what I now believe to have been the veritable gender revolution that the Sabbatian movement envisaged, and in no small measure put into effect. Admittedly, the 'female-liberationist' ideology that underlay it, drawing on ancient eschatological traditions and authentic kabbalistic doctrines, never achieved coherence or full articulation. Once the messianic faith was abandoned by the masses to become—whether within or without the traditional borders of Judaism—a covert, syncretistic, fragmented sectarian

---

[26] Horodetsky, *Hasidism* (Heb.), iv. 67–8.

[27] See Rapoport-Albert, 'On Women in Hasidism', 495–6.

[28] Scholem, *Sabbatai Sevi*, 403–5, and cf. his qualifying remarks, ibid. 192, 274 n. 220, 419, etc.

cult, what was left of its initial gender-revolutionary thrust found expression in divergent outlets, ranging from the extravagantly transgressive to the plainly bizarre. Nevertheless, the original vision and its tantalizing possibilities were discernible everywhere and throughout, surviving, in one form or another, right through to the movement's final stages of decay.

This realization raised afresh the question of hasidism's attitude to women. Against Horodetsky's claim of radical egalitarian innovation, I originally argued that the hasidic masters were simply conforming to the traditional gender paradigm, which rendered women the corporeal object of men's desire, and thus a constant threat to their spiritual integrity. Where Horodetsky saw women's progression, from Lurianic kabbalah through Sabbatian messianism to the pinnacle of their spiritual achievement as full-fledged charismatic leaders in hasidism, I saw no more than the perpetuation of an age-old construction of gender, which excluded women by definition from the spiritual life of the community. However, my subsequent findings on the revolutionary nature of women's involvement in Sabbatianism have led me to modify my position on this score. While I still reject Horodetsky's notion of women's alleged spiritual ascent through ever more powerful expressions of what he called their 'emotional Judaism', I do now see a certain connection between the Sabbatian and the hasidic orientation towards women. But far from presenting harmonious continuity or progression, as Horodetsky imagined, the connection appears to constitute a dialectical reaction. In other words, hasidism consciously broke away from a tradition of female spirituality, which reached its climax in Sabbatian messianism, but was inextricably linked to the unbridled sexuality that had become one of the movement's most notorious hallmarks. It was from this that hasidism shrank with horror, reclaiming instead the old gender paradigm that enabled it to contain the Sabbatian eruption of spiritually driven illicit sexuality by excluding women altogether from its own spiritual enterprise.

In the following pages I shall attempt to assemble the evidence for women's active involvement in the Sabbatian movement and its offshoots; to place this extraordinary phenomenon in a number of historical and ideological contexts; and to return finally to a fresh consideration of the relationship between the Sabbatian and the hasidic movements in regard to the status and function of women in society.

ONE

Female Prophets in Sabbatianism

THE ACTIVE PARTICIPATION of numerous women in the phenomenon of Sabbatian prophecy is beyond doubt. In a variety of sources that complement and corroborate each other, women are described as having visions and prophesying about the messianic mission of Sabbatai Zevi. To be sure, their status as prophets and the nature of their prophecies are to be distinguished from those of the great exponents of Sabbatian kabbalah, who were also regarded as prophets, such as Nathan of Gaza or Abraham Miguel Cardozo. Most of the accounts of prophesying by women appear in the context of mass outbursts of prophetic frenzy, in which unlettered men and children also took part—that is, precisely those segments of the population that ordinarily would have had nothing to do with prophetic revelation or religious tidings of any kind.[1] Under these circumstances, the prophecies of women, like those of the other mass prophesiers, were not perceived and certainly were not preserved as ordered speculative teachings, and we may assume that in many instances they did not even amount to any coherent, personal verbal expression. Sometimes they are described as mechanical repetitions of a series of enthusiastic exclamations or scriptural verses; at other times they appear as ecstatic states that reach their climax in total oblivion.[2]

---

[1] Jacob Sasportas, who reports on prophesying by women in such contexts, emphasizes repeatedly that if this had been true prophecy, it would have been given to men steeped in religious learning, and only in the Land of Israel, not to 'women, children, and servants', and not 'outside the Land'. See below, at nn. 9–13.

[2] For a selection of testimonies in this vein see Scholem, *Sabbatai Sevi*, 417–23, where he evaluates the phenomenon as follows: 'Nowhere did it articulate itself in orderly, literary form, or produce new kabbalistic insights, namely, "mysteries"' (p. 423). For a complete transcription of such a prophecy, preserved in the writings of Barukh of Arezzo, see ibid. 342; but cf. below, nn. 17–20. For a psycho-anthropological analysis of this type of prophetic phenomenon, particularly in relation to women, see Bilu, 'Dybbuk and Maggid', esp. pp. 362–6.

Thus, for example, the Dutch clergyman Thomas Coenen, whose testimony is critical and hostile but generally taken to be reliable,[3] gives the following description of the wave of mass prophesying that swept the Jews of Smyrna on 9 Tevet 5426 (17 December 1665):

In order for everyone to recognize his [Sabbatai Zevi's] true nature, prophecies were required in support. And indeed, to this end, a great number of prophets came to light at that time, men and women, youths and young girls, and even children. All these claimed and even demonstrated publicly that the spirit of prophecy had descended upon them. The Jews displayed remarkable gullibility, putting their faith in the phenomenon, even though nothing came out of these pseudo-prophecies but silly cavorting and vain chatter. All that was to be heard were cries of 'Long live the sage Sabbatai Zevi, our messiah, who has already been accepted in heaven and upon earth and has now also received his crown' . . . When the Jews saw the great number of people of every stripe and allegiance who betook themselves to prophecy, they declared—and I heard this more than once with my own ears—that the time had arrived for the fulfilment of the prophecy in Joel 2: 2–9,[4] where God declares by way of the prophet: 'Afterward . . . I will pour out my spirit on all flesh; your sons and your daughters shall prophesy.'[5]

Having cited the prophet Joel's vision of the end of time, Coenen notes that the Jews 'knew how to adapt all these prophecies to the Scriptures'.[6] Indeed,

---

[3] For an evaluation of Coenen's testimony see Scholem, *Sabbatai Sevi*, 372 and 388; and Yosef Kaplan, in the introduction to Arthur Lagawier and Efraim Shmueli's Hebrew translation of Coenen's *Ydele verwachtinge der Joden*, entitled *False Hopes*, 16–21.

[4] 'And it shall come to pass afterward, that I will pour out my spirit on all flesh; your sons and your daughters shall prophesy, your old men shall dream dreams, and your young men shall see visions. Even upon the menservants and maidservants in those days, I will pour out my spirit.' According to the division and numbering of the verses in the Hebrew Bible, the reference is to Joel 3: 1–2.

[5] Coenen, *False Hopes* (Heb.), 58–9. These verses are mentioned often in descriptions of the messianic age in rabbinic literature. See e.g. *Num. Rabbah*, end of §15; *Deut. Rabbah*, end of §6; *Lam. Rabbah*, 2: 11, 4: 14; and many other places. See also Even-Shemuel, *Midrashim of Redemption* (Heb.), 350. The same verses were cited frequently also in Christian millenarian circles, particularly in relation to prophecy by women. See e.g. the justification of the prophetic powers of women by Mary Cary—a member of the Fifth Monarchy sect in 17th-century England—in her *A New Mappe*, 236 ff., quoted in O'Faolain and Martines, *Not in God's Image*, 265. See also Thomas, 'Women and the Civil War Sects', 326, 328, 332. Joel's prophecy, which is reproduced in the New Testament (Acts 2: 17–18), was read out loud as a prelude to the prophetic trance experienced collectively by men, women, and children at the gatherings of the Russian Orthodox sect of the Khlysty (on which see below, Ch. 8). See e.g. Heard, *The Russian Church*, 258.   [6] Coenen, *False Hopes* (Heb.), 58.

Joel's description of the descent of the spirit of God 'on all flesh', which Coenen invoked in his characterization of the outburst of messianic prophecy in Smyrna, was fulfilled on that occasion to the letter; the spirit prevailed upon both sexes and all age groups, and even 'upon the menservants and maidservants'. This is precisely how a non-Jewish, Flemish observer in Liège, drawing upon various writings by eyewitnesses from Smyrna, described these events in a letter, written in French, to one of his noble acquaintances. In it he referred to 'some prophecies by the female prophets of Smyrna, most of them in Hebrew, and all of them composed of scriptural verses. And there was one little girl who prophesied in Spanish.' He reported further:

The spirit of prophecy descended even upon a Christian servant girl, who later said that she remembered nothing of what she had said. Nevertheless, a priest came to exorcize the spirit from her, and she reviled him in the presence of the Christians and the Turks and declared that Lord Sabbatai Zevi is the messiah. Later on she denied having said anything, but she felt a great fire in her heart; and so it is with many of our female prophets—after the melody stops playing, they remember nothing of what they said.[7]

The testimonies collected by Jacob Sasportas also corroborate this description. Drawing upon 'letters from Smyrna', he reports:

More than two hundred male and female prophets, women, men, and children, stood there, and all of them prophesied in unison according to the prophecy of Nathan [of Gaza], that Sabbatai Zevi is the Messiah son of David, and anyone who doubts him will lose his place in the World to Come.[8]

It would seem Sasportas, too, had seen the same letter to which the Flemish correspondent referred. In a further diatribe against the 'troop of prophets who prophesy from Smyrna, women, infants—both male and female—youths and maidens', he adds furiously:

The sap of prophecy has dried up; it rests upon dry branches, women, children, and servants; for I have seen a letter that came from Smyrna attesting to a non-Jewish maidservant who saw what no great scholars of Israel have ever seen, and she, too, fulfilled the promise [in Joel] concerning the prophecy of women and children.[9]

Like Coenen, Sasportas, too, views these prophecies as fabrications; as he sees

---

[7] Aescoly, 'Flandrian Newsletter' (Heb.), 234; for the original French see p. 227.

[8] Sasportas, *Tsitsat novel tsevi*, 60.   [9] Ibid. 147–8.

it, they cannot be valid because they fail the criteria set down for prophecy by the Sages:

There is no prophecy outside the Land of Israel, or in those unworthy of it, according to what our Sages have declared: 'prophecy can rest only upon a man who is learned, mighty and wealthy';[10] and in *Mo'ed katan*[11] [the Sages] said: 'our rabbi [Rav Huna] would have been worthy of having the Divine Presence rest upon him, but [his dwelling in] Babylonia prevented this.'[12]

Sasportas is clearly infuriated by the phenomenon of women prophesying, and he denounces it over and over again:

For who has gathered the spirit that goes forth from the domain of truth in order to prophesy [*lehitnabe'ot*] in the spirit of Naboth [cf. BT *Shab.* 149*b*], if not these women, who are bereft of any of the conditions of prophecy, since there is no wisdom, no might, and no wealth in an impure land [namely, outside the Holy Land]. They bow themselves and fall, naming their master and proclaiming him messiah; and they bring forth their young ones [cf. Job 39: 3], their male and female infants, to pry into the mysteries that lie in the cracks and orifices of the city of David [cf. Isa. 22: 9], in order that it will be rebuilt by their king. They cast out their sorrows [*ḥevleihem*] [cf. Job 39: 3]—bevy [*ḥevel*] upon bevy of prophets who see his form imprinted on the seventh heaven, and the whole heavenly host standing and proclaiming: 'Make way and render sovereignty, might and glory to your master.' ... And so the spirit of holiness and prophecy has taken leave and gone far from the side of the male to the side of the female, nay, to the female of the lowest abyss.[13]

---

[10] BT *Shab.* 92*a*: 'The Divine Presence prevails only upon a man who is wise, mighty, wealthy and of good stature'; and similarly in *Ned.* 38*a*: 'The Holy One, Blessed be He, lets His presence prevail only upon a man who is mighty, wealthy, wise and humble.'

[11] 25*a*.   [12] Sasportas, *Tsitsat novel tsevi*, 147.

[13] Ibid. 96; and cf. ibid. 162: 'And lo, one and then two women come forth from among them, with the spirit of prophecy filling their wings—and they have wings like the wings of a stork [*ḥasidah*], to lift up with pious words [*milei ḥasiduta*] the measure of prophecy between the earth and the heaven, in the defiling air of foreign lands, to build it a house in the land of Shinar [cf. Zech. 5: 9–10]. And I set my face against these daughters of my people prophesying, and against those who sew pillows to the sides of their garments [cf. Ezek. 13: 17–18]: the spirit of God abhors them, and yet with them is the word of God, apart from the male and female infants and the fools looking on—they see visions of God: here says a man that our king and saviour reigns over the Upper and Lower Worlds, and here declares a woman, "He sits upon his throne in the firmament, and all the kings have taken the crowns from their heads and placed them on his head." ... What I report is no exaggeration, for I have seen a letter saying that a non-Jewish servant girl, one of impure soul, has seen what was not given to the Sages of Israel to see, for all their intellectual and moral fitness and their precious souls. And if this be the fulfilment of the prophecy of Joel, according to which "I will pour out My spirit on all flesh" [Joel 3: 1], then let

The phenomenon spread rapidly from Smyrna to other Jewish communities throughout the Ottoman empire and even beyond:

Apart from this, prophets and prophetesses arose in Smyrna, in Chios, in Rhodes, in Germany, in Morea and in the West [North Africa], from the four corners of the earth, little boys and little girls, old men and old women, all crying out loud together after they had fallen, swooning, to the earth, possessed by great and wonderful prophecies, saying: 'Sabbatai Zevi is the true redeemer; he is our righteous messiah; salvation is near at hand', and so on. In this fashion five hundred prophets and prophetesses went forth in Constantinople.[14]

Barukh of Arezzo confirms all this in his memoirs and even gives the names of several prophesiers, about half of them women, who were known to him in Smyrna and Aleppo:

Afterwards prophecy came to a great number of men, women and children in Smyrna, in Constantinople, in Aleppo, and in other places, and a single recitation was in the mouths of all: they all testified and declared that Sabbatai Zevi was the messiah of the God of Jacob. And this is how prophecy used to come upon people in those days: a great swoon would come upon them, and they would fall to the ground as dead. . . . And after about half an hour a breath would issue from their mouths, though their lips did not move, and they would utter verses of praise and verses of consolation, and all would declare: 'Sabbatai Zevi is the messiah of the God of Jacob.' And afterwards they would rise to their feet, and they would be ignorant of what they had done and said. In the city of Smyrna there were more than a hundred and fifty prophets, among whom were these whose names are known: the wife of our lord;[15] the wife of Jacob Peña; the wife of Wana; the wife of Jacob Serano; the wife of Jacob Benveniste; the wife of Jacob Capua; the sage Daniel Pinti; Joseph Halevi; Solomon, son of his honour, our teacher Daniel Valencin; Joshua Morelito; Samuel Bomuano; Moses Safami; Elijah Bonsenior; and a certain orphan. And these are the names of the prophets of Aleppo: Rabbi Isaiah Hakohen; Moses Galati; Daniel Pinto; the wife of Yom Tov Laniado; the

God be so good [*yo'il*, a play on the name of the prophet Joel] as to devolve his spirit and impart of his glory to those who fear him, so that illumination will appear upon them. That he should give of his spirit to just any man or woman, youth or maiden—for this the elders in the gates ought to garb themselves in shame and wear it as a cloak. For women who are at ease have found the leisure to speak "right things", and complacent daughters have shed their ordinary clothes to gird themselves [cf. Isa. 32: 9–11], to serve in holy garments and don cloaks of light . . . while troops of holy persons cringe in shame and are silent, wearied by the feminine power; and today is a day of good tidings [cf. 2 Kgs 7: 9].' 　　　　　　　　　　　[14] Ibid. 156; see also p. 182.

[15] This was Sarah, Sabbatai Zevi's Ashkenazi third wife. See below, at nn. 48–54.

wife of Rabbi Nissim Mizrahi; the daughter of Abraham Tammon; and some twenty other prophets and prophetesses.[16]

The same phenomenon is described by Leib ben Ozer:[17]

This is one of the greatest things that occurred in those days, things that were supernatural and were the cause of the great faith people had in Sabbatai Zevi. For in the year 5426 since the creation of the world, in the month of Tevet [December 1665], it happened everywhere, in Izmir, which is Smyrna, and in Constantinople and also in Adrianople and in Salonica, that prophets arose by the hundreds and thousands, women and men, youths and maidens, and even small children. All of them prophesied in the Holy Tongue [Hebrew] and in the language of the Zohar [Aramaic], and none of them knew a word of the Holy Tongue, not to speak of the language of the Zohar. And thus it was: they would fall to the ground as though smitten with epilepsy; foam would issue from their mouths, and they would convulse, and they would utter mysteries of kabbalah on many subjects in the Holy Tongue. But the formula that would issue from all of them, each in his own words, was this: 'The kingdom of Sabbatai Zevi, our lord, our king, our messiah, has been revealed in heaven and upon earth, and he has received the royal crown from heaven.' . . . And all that one heard was that so-and-so had become a prophet and so-and-so a prophetess, and that here had arisen a troop of prophets. Some prophesied one way and some prophesied another way, but what arose from the utterances of all was that Sabbatai Zevi is our messiah and our righteous redeemer.[18]

[16] Barukh of Arezzo, 'Memorial' (Heb.), 49–50.

[17] See the comments of Zalman Shazar in the introduction to his edition of Leib b. Ozer, *Story of Sabbatai Zevi* (Heb.), 14–17. He points out Leib b. Ozer's genuine amazement at these marvellous events and notes the tendency of Jacob Emden, who included an abridged version of this work in his book, *Zot torat hakena'ot*, to tone down the writer's enthusiasm and moderate his testimony, because 'some of his statements seem exaggerated'. Scholem, in *Sabbatai Sevi*, 423 n. 204, accepts Emden's evaluation.

[18] Leib b. Ozer, *Story of Sabbatai Zevi* (Heb.), 53–4. For additional testimonies on the spread of this phenomenon see Scholem, 'Notes from Italy' (Heb.), 495–6 and 504–5. These testimonies include the disclosures that 'there are today in Aleppo twenty prophets . . . and four prophetesses', and that in Gaza, Nathan the prophet and a certain prophetess announced the destruction of all the 'abominations' in 'the Holy Land'. The prophetess from Gaza, who is mentioned in this report alongside Nathan of Gaza and represented as collaborating in his prophecy, seems to go beyond the phenomenon of mass prophesying, and she apparently drew a great deal of personal attention; see ibid. 505 n. 58. A further account of prophets and prophetesses in Aleppo appears in a pamphlet in English printed in London in 1666, based on a letter sent from Gaza to Cairo on 17 Kislev 5426 (25 November 1665): 'Know, That Letters are come hither from *Aleppo* and *Damascus*, which give us good News, that in *Aleppo* are discovered Twenty Prophets men, and as many women' (Wilensky, 'Four English Pamphlets' (Heb.), 165–6).

Leib ben Ozer notes that 'many of their prophetic statements have been recorded in writing',[19] and Jacob Emden elaborates, making a point of stressing the kabbalistic content of the prophecies:[20]

And the doings of the prophets and prophetesses who multiplied at that time in the country of Turkey, in every city, have already been widely publicized, in writing and particularly in print. Men and women who had never read a book fell to the ground in convulsions, heaven forfend, and began uttering passages from the Zohar and interpreting them by way of kabbalah and of deep mysteries. And those who related this, trustworthy men, said that they knew that over ten thousand pages of mystical secrets had been recorded from the issue of their mouths.[21]

Further on, Jacob Emden relates the testimony of his own father, who in his childhood saw female messianic believers clad in white—after the custom of the kabbalists—demonstrating in public their complete mastery of supernatural powers:

And even more remarkably than this, my late father and mentor, the great sage [Hakham Tsevi], who was a child in the time of Sabbatai Zevi,[22] related that there were women at that time who would say: 'let us go and kill some evil spirits'. They would dress themselves in white linen garments and guide their outstretched hands to and fro in the air, one to one side and one to the other, and they would spread out their dresses to receive and catch from the air large quantities of blood in their clothes, as though they had spilled great amounts of blood with their own hands, by stretching them high into the air, so that it looked like the flow of blood from the slaughter of an animal. One woman said, 'Who would like me to give them the scent of Paradise?' And she caught from the air with her hands that were raised towards heaven and bestowed a most wonderful scent upon anyone who wished.[23]

[19] Leib b. Ozer, *Story of Sabbatai Zevi* (Heb.), 57.
[20] Scholem was dubious about the credibility of the accounts of women prophesying in 'the language of the *Zohar*', which he attributed to Leib b. Ozer's tendency to exaggerate. See Scholem, *Sabbatai Sevi*, 256 n. 161. But Emden appears to have drawn in this regard on other sources as well, since uncharacteristically, his version of Leib b. Ozer's account (see above, n. 17) expands upon his statements here rather than curbing them. See also the account of Abraham Rovigo, who reported: 'Some children, maidservants and unschooled persons fell to the ground of a sudden and uttered lofty kabbalistic matters, and all of them concluded their utterances by declaring, "Sabbatai Zevi is the Messiah of the God of Israel"' (Sonne, 'Notebook of Abraham Rovigo' (Heb.), 49).   [21] Emden, *Zot torat hakena'ot*, 9.
[22] Emden, who spells the name 'Shabetai Tsevi' here as an acronym preceded by the definite article (namely הש״בץ), clearly does so in order to mock and denigrate the messiah by alluding to the Hebrew noun שבץ, which means apoplexy or convulsion.
[23] Emden, *Zot torat hakena'ot*, 9. The white garments and also the technical terminology

The 'apparition of Elijah', which had been viewed as the lot of the chosen few, also became widespread in this period among both women and men.[24] The same non-Jewish Flemish observer who had reported in French on the events in Smyrna relates, for example:

One woman whose mother and brother live in Amsterdam wrote to them that she and her husband were visited by Elijah the Prophet, who told them that a son would be born to them, and that she should call him Elijah. On the day of the birth, he returned

('guiding' the imaginary knife 'to and fro' through the air, and 'receiving' the blood while performing the act of slaughter) in the description of the women killing the evil spirits are drawn from the ritual performed by the High Priest on the Day of Atonement (see e.g. BT *Yoma* 49a and 60a–b) and from the laws of ritual slaughter (see e.g. Maimonides, *Mishneh torah*, 'Hilkhot sheḥitah', 2: 7–9 and 3: 11) and must have been meant to evoke this association. My thanks to Dr Joanna Weinberg, who drew my attention to this. The ability to exude 'the scent of Paradise' from his body is attributed to Sabbatai Zevi in several sources, and according to him it was a consequence of his having been anointed with oil by the Patriarchs Abraham, Isaac, and Jacob, who appeared to him in a vision while he was fully awake. See Coenen, *False Hopes* (Heb.), 85–6; and Scholem, *Sabbatai Sevi*, 139 and 654. It was also said of Nathan of Gaza that he exuded 'a very goodly and perfumed scent, like "the smell of the fields that the Lord has blessed"', and that this scent 'came from that spark of spiritual holiness that had entered Rabbi Nathan' (Barukh of Arezzo, 'Memorial' (Heb.), 47). For another source on the scent that came forth from Nathan's room while he was at prayer see Scholem, *Sabbatai Sevi*, 924–5 n. 266. The ability to exude a goodly scent from their bodies was also attributed to several other messianic prophets in the Sabbatian movement, and it had already been said of Isaac Luria that 'the scent of Paradise arose from his bed', following the Zohar (ii. 'Beshalaḥ', 44a), which attributes this quality to the prophet Elisha. See e.g. *Sefer toledot ha'ari*, 157. The women, then, were able to control this 'scent of Paradise', which originated in a holy source and had been the possession of a chosen few, but which they could now bestow upon whomsoever wished it. This, in addition to their ability to defeat the powers of impurity by means of the ritual slaughter of evil spirits portrayed as sacrifices that do not fight back, reflects the perception of these women—even as preserved in the hostile testimony of Hakham Tsevi—as driven by the power of holiness and acting on its behalf, apparently in the context of the rise to dominance and ever abundant effluence of the powers of holiness with the dawning of the messianic era. In another context they would most likely have been considered witches or madwomen.

[24] Avraham Elqayam distinguishes between the apparition of Elijah in the kabbalistic tradition, where Gershom Scholem describes it as a means of diffusing the tension that necessarily springs up between fresh mystical experience and traditional religious authority, and the apparition of Elijah in Sabbatianism, in which Elqayam discerns a striving for liberation from traditional religious authority, and which he defines as an antinomian experience (Elqayam, 'Sabbatai Zevi's Zohar' (Heb.), 370). The 'cheapening' of the apparition of Elijah in Sabbatianism—its transformation into a commonplace affair of the masses, and even, or perhaps especially, of women—may be interpreted as an additional aspect of the same phenomenon.

and appeared to her in the company of two personages whose names he did not divulge, and no one could remain in the room in which they received this annunciation because of the splendour that filled it.[25]

Coenen, too, reported on apparitions of Elijah to women:

A certain Jewish woman got to be the first to have the honour of a sighting; she said that she had seen Elijah in a dream, and she told the others about it as something of great importance. Another woman immediately joined her and related that she had seen him when awake. Yet another woman, neighbour of a certain Jew, who hitherto had taken no part in this monkey play, related that on the eve of the sabbath she had met a pauper who begged her for a handout. She testified that she had never seen that pauper before, and she swore in the name of their God that he was Elijah.[26]

The miraculous dimension of these phenomena, their 'supernatural' quality, endowed them with great persuasive power. Leib ben Ozer saw this as 'the cause of the great faith people had in Sabbatai Zevi'.[27] Indeed, it would seem that the very appearance of women as prophets, who, moreover, prophesied in the Holy Tongue and in the Aramaic of the Zohar, was so extraordinary that it could not but be seen as proof of the truth of their prophecy. Thus, these women often were the most effective propagandists of Sabbatai Zevi's messianic gospel, and they succeeded in convincing even those men who had at first doubted or explicitly rejected it. Several mutually corroborative and complementary sources tell, for example, of the daughters of the Smyrna notable Hayim Peña, who had denied Sabbatai Zevi and was one of his most ardent opponents[28]—until his daughters' prophecies convinced him that Sabbatai Zevi was the messiah:

Among the first women prophets were the daughters of this Hayim Peña . . . When he saw the new ways of his daughters and the resemblance between the prophecies of each, he became very excited, nay, inflamed to the point of losing his good sense. He now wholeheartedly accepted what he had previously so firmly opposed. He openly declared his new faith, that is, that Sabbatai Zevi was the true messiah. Sabbatai Zevi himself visited his home and saw with his own eyes how those girls shook and trembled as though seized by a frenzy—like all the other prophets. He was most gratified

[25] Aescoly, 'Flandrian Newsletter' (Heb.), 235–6; the original French text is on p. 228.

[26] Coenen, *False Hopes* (Heb.), 71. See also the versions of Leib b. Ozer, *Story of Sabbatai Zevi* (Heb.), 68, and Emden, *Zot torat hakena'ot*, 29.

[27] Leib b. Ozer, *Story of Sabbatai Zevi* (Heb.), 53.

[28] On Hayim Peña's opposition to Sabbatai Zevi and its background see Scholem, *Sabbatai Sevi*, 395 ff.

that none other than the daughters of this man, who had turned away from him so stubbornly, had prophesied to their father, before his own eyes and in front of a great crowd. They said that they were seeing the sage [Sabbatai] Zevi seated upon a high and lofty throne in heaven, with a crown upon his head. When they had finished this narration, while still in the throes of their derangement, they called out one after the other, 'crown, crown'.[29]

The version of Leib ben Ozer is fuller and emphasizes the power of the event to attract new believers to the cause:

This Hayim Pekhina[!] came to his home and found a large gathering there, and he had no idea what had occurred to draw such a great number of people to his door. He asked what was going on . . . and people told him that his two daughters had become prophets, and they were prophesying like the other prophets. When this Hayim entered his house, he saw his daughters trembling and convulsing and uttering great things. They said that they were seeing the sage Sabbatai Zevi seated on a royal throne in heaven with a royal crown on his head, and a great many other things. When they had finished their narration, they called several times, one after the other, 'crown, crown'. When their father, Hayim Pekhina, saw his daughters in this state, he was most astonished and confounded, and he did not know what to say, for he was one of Sabbatai Zevi's most outspoken opponents. . . . When word of this came out, everyone was eager to hear the prophecies of his daughters, even though there were many other prophets. They all wanted to see for themselves whether it was true that the daughters of Hayim Pekhina were prophesying about Sabbatai Zevi, because everyone knew that he was an obstinate man who opposed Sabbatai Zevi, and now his own daughters were prophesying about Sabbatai Zevi. This caused a great stir in Smyrna and was considered a great wonder.[30]

This testimony is echoed also in the French report of the Flemish non-Jew, who relates tersely that 'with most of those who did not put their faith in the king [the messiah Sabbatai Zevi], their daughters prophesied, to the mortification of their fathers'.[31]

It would seem that Abraham Cardozo, too, was influenced by the prophetic visions and miraculous experiences of the women of his household in finally becoming persuaded that Sabbatai Zevi was the messiah. According to his letter to the rabbinic judges of Smyrna, written in Tripoli in the month

---

[29] Coenen, *False Hopes* (Heb.), 58.

[30] Leib b. Ozer, *Story of Sabbatai Zevi* (Heb.), 55–6. See also Emden, *Zot torat hakena'ot*, 9.

[31] Aescoly, 'Flandrian Newsletter' (Heb.), 234; for the original French see p. 227.

of Sivan 5429 (the summer of 1669),[32] he saw in these wondrous events, which occurred in the first few months after the coronation of Sabbatai Zevi as the messiah in 1665, the hoped-for response to his prayers that he be granted a sign from heaven conclusively confirming the truth of the messianic revelations vouchsafed him:

Thereafter, in the month of Shevat in the year 5426 [the beginning of 1666], during the last watch [of the night], a great light was revealed in my home to an old woman[33] who has suffered for thirty-one years from the ailment called paralysis, so that her left arm dried up and remained as dead, without any movement. And nine years ago the ailment recurred, with the result that the bone of her lower left leg became dislocated. The tendons contracted, and the lower leg and foot were left without movement, like her arm. And when she saw this great light, she thought that the sun had already risen. Afterwards she went back to sleep, and when she awoke and saw that the whole house was dark, she was afraid and said, 'Lord of the Universe, isn't it enough that I am as dead; I've lost my sight as well.' For she thought that she had suddenly lost her sight. Then the madman [i.e. the *muezzin* in the mosque] began calling according to his custom, and she was relieved, for she realized that it was still night. In the morning she told the story and we laughed at her. Afterwards the same lights were revealed to her three or four times within fifteen days, and even then I did not take account of what she said. But one night it was hinted to me that a star as large as the full moon would be displayed in the firmament of heaven. In the morning this same woman told me that during the third watch she had seen a star like the sun or the moon, and it had illuminated the whole house, and from this I realized that what she said was right. . . . And on the third day, around the time of the afternoon prayers, this old woman was near the entrance to the courtyard when she cried out that a star as big as the sun had been revealed to her four times, and she had almost been blinded by its splendour and brilliance. . . .

In the months of Shevat and Adar, too, I saw in a dream seven Sages of the Mishnah sitting and discussing the Torah . . . and the Patriarch [*Nasi*] commanded them to call upon a certain man, and the man came, and I was there. And I heard the Patriarch telling the seven Sages, 'Give honour to the King!' They all rose to their feet, and the Patriarch cried aloud, 'Bring a throne for the King!' . . . In the morning, the old woman told me that she had been shown, within the light that was revealed to her, a great throne as white as snow. It said, 'May it be your will, Lord my God, that I be shown who is to sit upon this throne.' And the cloud was revealed, and it covered the

---

[32] See Scholem, 'Letter of Abraham Cardozo' (Heb.), 300.

[33] An earlier letter, evidently written in 1668 (see ibid.), contains a shorter version of the same story, from which it would seem that this 'old woman' was in fact Cardozo's sister-in-law; he refers to her as 'the sister of my wife Judith'. See Cardozo, 'Letter' (Heb.), 87.

throne. Then I began to believe beyond any doubt that this elderly woman was speaking the truth. Thereafter, one night, I besought the blessed God all night, in prayer and supplications, that he have mercy upon me and give me a faithful sign, in that this old woman would be healed. . . . For if the people were to see this great miracle, they would be strengthened in faith, repentance, and good works. And lo, in the morning watch, the light was revealed to her; her hand opened and her big toe stretched out, and the bone of her lower left leg returned to its place, and her mouth and her left eye were righted. Her right eye remained a bit sunken, but not as it had been. And her left shoulder, too, rose up to its place. Her arm was stretched out from her body and her leg was extended, but not so much that she could stand upon it, for the blessed God did not desire that the sign be obvious to all; but it was shown to me so that I would believe in his emissary.[34]

This same mysterious light was revealed also to Cardozo's wife, for whom it took the form of a human figure:

After these things, my wife Judith, too, began to experience revelations of this light, and when I commanded her to speak thus and so, it appeared to her in the form of a man. He spoke to her many times while standing within the light, pure and gleaming.[35]

Even Cardozo's small daughter saw the man who spoke from within the light and heard him utter messianic revelations:

Moreover, one day as I was sitting at my desk, pondering deeply the significance of three visions that had come to me during the night, my little daughter Rachel, who was 3 years old, came up and told me clear and wondrous things about what was in my heart, including the significance of the visions. When I said to her, 'Who told you all these things?' she laughed and said, 'Don't you see the man above your head? Look: it's him who's speaking to me.' Then she ran out of the room, and later she didn't remember any of what she had said.[36]

As a consequence of all these signs and revelations, which appeared to him and were confirmed by the prophetic experiences of the female members of his

---

[34] Scholem, 'Letter of Abraham Cardozo' (Heb.), 321–3.   [35] Cardozo, 'Letter' (Heb.), 87.

[36] Ibid. 88. Another version of the same account appears in a letter written in 1669, about a year later, in which the little girl is described as being about 4 years old. Here Cardozo emphasizes a different miraculous aspect of the event, noting that 'she revealed the secrets of my heart, not in ordinary words but in a wondrous way, as though she were giggling. In a few words she revealed to me unfathomed matters in my heart, and all of my messianic musings. She revealed wondrous things to me and then left the room' (Scholem, 'Letter of Abraham Cardozo' (Heb.), 323).

family, Cardozo at that time came to the conclusion that 'the true messiah is Sabbatai Zevi'.[37]

From a report sent by an anonymous Italian Christian observer to his patron, who served as archbishop of Aix-en-Provence between 1650 and 1685, it would seem that the prophecy of a young girl was once again the trigger that set off the messianic movement, this time among the Jews of Galata, the European quarter of Constantinople:

This prophecy about the messiah began in Galata (that quarter of Constantinople in which most of the Christians and Jews lived) by way of a Jewish girl of about 16 or 17—a virgin, so it is said—who had a mighty talent for supernal contemplation. She told her parents how God had shown her astonishing things. Among other things, she related that an angel had appeared to her, garbed in light and [holding] a shining sword, and he had told her of the messiah for whom they so hoped, and that they must prepare to welcome him and go down to meet him on the bank of the Jordan, where he would soon appear in order to bring about the advent of the joyous and glorious redemption of the Jews. The girl's father informed several wise men of these revelations, and, in consultation with them, he arrived at the conclusion that faith in this heavenly voice must on no account be denied, and that they must go to Jerusalem as quickly as possible in order there to await the fulfilment of the angel's promise. This news spread quickly throughout the land, but many Jews did not believe in it, until they saw many others selling up their property and going off to Palestine.[38]

According to this account of the events, the girl's prophecy was fully confirmed by Nathan of Gaza,[39] and the writer attached so much importance to it as to report in his conclusion (and this rumour is unsupported by any other source) that 'as for the girl from Galata and Nathan of Gaza—the Jews put both of them cruelly to death'.[40] However this may be, another Christian observer reported that at the height of the messianic fervour in Galata, for a period of several months, no fewer than seven or eight hundred women filled with this new spirit of prophecy could be seen in that quarter of the capital. They were so deranged by its influence that several had to be tied down and beaten in order to calm their frenzy.[41]

[37] Scholem, 'Letter of Abraham Cardozo' (Heb.), 324.

[38] Méchoulan, 'Au dossier du Sabbatisme', 188. The manuscript published by Méchoulan is undated, but it must have been written between 1680 and 1685, since the death of Nathan of Gaza, which occurred in 1680, is mentioned at the end of the letter, and Archbishop Grimaldi, the addressee, died in 1685, as Méchoulan notes in his introduction (ibid. 185).

[39] Ibid. 189.   [40] Ibid. 195.   [41] See Scholem, *Sabbatai Sevi*, 606.

In Corfu, too, the messianic fervour that arose in 1666 turned on a young and beautiful virgin, the daughter of a wealthy Venetian merchant, Hayim ben Aharon, who had been bankrupted before moving to Corfu. The girl's prophetic activity was described by the Corfu nobleman Andrea Marmora in his Italian treatise on the history of the island, printed in Venice in 1672. To be sure, this treatise is notable for its hostility towards both Jews and women. The writer attacks the Jews for refusing to acknowledge Jesus as the messiah because he was born of woman, while now—so he claims—putting their faith in a girl from whom the messiah was to be born (this 'Christian' belief is not attributed to the Jews in the description of the events themselves, and the author would seem to have contrived it in the heat of his religious polemic against Judaism).[42] However, his account of the girl's messianic prophecy is credible in itself, relying as it does, among other things, on the testimony of a young Christian from a noble family who had witnessed the events with his own eyes and so brought them to light. Marmora wrote:

In Corfu there are about five hundred Jewish families that have become wealthy through extortion and commerce with east and west . . . Among these people . . . was a man by the name of Caim d'Aron who had once been wealthy, among the most prominent of his nation's merchants. . . . He had a very beautiful daughter, if someone with a blemished soul can be called beautiful, and he thought by means of her to improve his situation and recover his good name, at least among his own people. The girl was intelligent and clever like her father . . . Closeting herself in a room with her father, she spent many a day learning how to look as though she had been overcome by the holy spirit, which would whisper to her what she was supposed to transmit to the crazed people of the community. . . . The first lessons taught his pupil by Caim, who sought to exploit the naivety of his brethren . . . were how to wriggle all her limbs, inflame her eyes, shake her breast, foam at the mouth and change colours. Broken words, half-prophecies, promises of redemption, congratulations on the coming of the messiah and hundreds of like follies. Women will do as they wish. They and pretence were born together, and that is why these are viewed by the world as twins. . . . Such was this Hebrew girl, who was so well trained that she was able to deceive the elders of her community, and had the thing not come to light by chance, it might have caused great harm to the Christians as well. In the year 1666 Caim began to spread word among the Jews about something exceptional that had appeared amongst the Jewish people[43] . . . And he asked what they thought of the fact that a pure young girl, holy in

---

[42] See the remarks of Mizrahi in his introduction to 'Messianic Agitation on Corfu' (Heb.), 538.

[43] Sabbatai Zevi is not mentioned in this account, but the rumours of his messianic mission are undoubtedly its subject. See also Mizrahi's remarks, ibid.

her ways, should do supernatural deeds and prophesy extraordinary events, and [he told them] that he believed that some easement would come about in the tribulations of the Jews, and that the messiah surely would not be long in coming, on account of the signs that he had discerned in one of his daughters, who was imbued with divine wisdom.[44]

The sages of the community interrogated the girl rigorously, came to the conclusion that her words were true, and 'enjoined her to stay at home, with all the requisite comforts, at the expense of the community'. From that moment on, 'everyone kept running to the home of that woman, worshipping her like a goddess and bringing her gifts'. On how this affair became known to the island's Christian inhabitants—an eventuality which the community sages apparently had feared, and rightly so—Marmora relates:

The affair came to light, though such a thing is unfit to be made public, on account of the curiosity of a Christian youth from a noble family. He saw that a great crowd gathered daily in Caim's chamber, and he wanted to know the reason. Since it was difficult for someone who was not a Jew to gain entrance, he donned worn-out clothes, wrapped himself well in a tattered cloak and put on a hat bearing the mark of the Jews, and in this way he was able to deceive the guards and get in. He saw a peculiar sight. The woman, dressed in white, sat grandly on a splendid throne, surrounded by those fools, who were honouring her with songs of praise. A lamp brought from the synagogue hung above her head, while the rabbis, with Torah scrolls in their arms, encircled her and paid her homage. They would not have done more even for the Temple and the Ark of the Covenant than they did for this worthless woman.[45]

The Christian youth who had infiltrated the crowd of Jews was discovered and ignobly expelled from the house,

and thus did the affair become known as quick as a wink throughout the city, and [the Christians], for scorn and anger [at the Jews], prepared to wreak their ire upon them, but the more knowledgeable ones urged that the whole matter be overlooked, so that the fraud would come to light by itself—as indeed happened, to the embarrassment of all those who saw that the whole business ultimately came to naught.[46]

The power of prophecy was attributed also to Sarah, Sabbatai Zevi's third wife, who was among the first to prophesy that he was the messiah.[47] She

---

[44] Ibid. 538–9.   [45] Ibid. 539–40.   [46] Ibid. 540.

[47] For the evidence on Sarah's life, see Scholem, *Sabbatai Sevi*, 191–7. For a discussion of Sarah as prophetess in the context of the wider phenomenon of Sabbatian prophecy, see Goldish, *Sabbatean Prophets*, 89–97.

appears at the top of a list of six prophetesses and eight prophets identified by name among the 'more than a hundred and fifty prophets' of Smyrna, and three prophets and three prophetesses among the 'twenty prophets and prophetesses' of Aleppo.[48] It was said of her that she had 'foretold future events' even when she was still living in Livorno, before leaving for Egypt and marrying Sabbatai Zevi. During that period, according to the reported testimony of Isaac Valle, 'He, too, went to speak with her, and he asked her to reveal to him the root of his soul and other things that cannot be transcribed, and she answered his query, and he knew clearly that what she had said was genuine and true.'[49] Revealing to individuals the roots of their souls and the series of transmigrations they had undergone through history was known to be one of Isaac Luria's supernatural gifts, and the same gift was later attributed to the most eminent male kabbalists and mystics of their day, including the charismatic leaders of the hasidic movement.[50] The attribution of such an extraordinary gift to a young woman of mysterious origin and dubious virtue was no small matter. It evinces a surprising readiness to see in her—apparently even before her messianic marriage and the eruption of mass prophecy that fol-

[48] See above, at nn. 15–16.

[49] Barukh of Arezzo, 'Memorial' (Heb.), 46. This account is corroborated by Immanuel Frances' comment on one of his own anti-Sabbatian poems, in which he describes Sarah as 'rising briskly in the very middle of the night; all her deeds are most furtively concealed' (I. and J. Frances, *Tsevi mudaḥ*, 126). He notes regarding this verse: 'I suggest here that she was a sorceress while I was still living in the city of Livorno' (ibid. 127 n. 8). The epithet 'sorceress' was almost surely meant in condemnation of the kind of prophetic activity that Isaac Valle had described as genuine and true.

[50] As regards Luria, see e.g. Vital, 'Book of Visions', 156 ff. (*Sefer haḥezyonot*, pt. 4, p. 134 ff.) and *passim*. The gift of revealing the historical roots of individual souls was similarly attributed, for example, to the scholar and mystic Moses Suriel, one of the first Sabbatian prophets in Constantinople, who began prophesying as soon as Sabbatai Zevi revealed himself as the messiah (on him see Scholem, *Sabbatai Sevi*, 435–8). Leib b. Ozer relates that 'this R. Moses Suriel was able to tell any person the root of his soul, what kind of soul he had, and all the prophecies of this R. Moses Suriel were found to be true' (*Story of Sabbatai Zevi* (Heb.), 59); moreover, 'He told R. Isaiah Halevi, son of the [famous Polish scholar, David b. Samuel Halevi, author of the] *Turei zahav*, that his soul was that of Caleb ben Yefuneh' (ibid. 80). These details appear also in Jacob Emden's version of this source (*Zot torat hakena'ot*, 17). For the attribution of the same gift to Jonathan Eybeschuetz see Nigal, *Magic, Mysticism and Hasidism*, 18. On the disclosure of the roots of souls and its significance in hasidism see Rapoport-Albert, 'Hasidism after 1772', 126–40.

lowed Sabbatai Zevi's proclamation as messiah—one acquainted with divine mysteries, and conversant with the supernal realms.[51]

Sarah herself was clearly imbued with a sense of her own messianic mission, seeing herself from her early youth as destined to become the messiah's bride.[52] Indeed, there were those who claimed that it was she who had awakened her husband's messianic self-awareness,[53] and even if this is not entirely true—since we have credible testimonies regarding the initial stirring of Sabbatai's own messianic consciousness in Smyrna in 1648, many years before he met Sarah in Egypt[54]—there is some truth in it: undoubtedly, his encounter with Sarah, his 'predestined' messianic bride, like his encounter with his prophet, Nathan of Gaza, who recognized the messiah in him, galvanized his unstable messianic identity, confirmed and constantly reinforced it.

All these prophetic manifestations, including the numerous displays of prophecy by women, did not desist even when, in the month of Elul 5426 (the summer of 1666), news began to reach the 'believers' that Sabbatai Zevi had converted to Islam.[55] Barukh of Arezzo records accounts from Adrianople of a prophetess who had seen a vision of the messiah 'in Ishmaelite garb':

While he was there, delegates arrived to greet him from distant lands, sixteen months' journey from Constantinople, from the land of Lazbek [variant reading: Lubeck], near the kingdom of Kinah, and from Great Tartaria. They said that people had come

---

[51] The reports of Sarah's prophetic gifts may be read in the context of Hayim Vital's descriptions, in *Sefer haḥezyonot*, of many prophetically gifted women in the Jewish communities of Safed, Jerusalem, and Damascus at the turn of the 16th and 17th centuries. All these accounts similarly exhibit no hesitation about the attribution of such gifts to women. See below, Ch. 2, at nn. 16–55.

[52] For a survey of the sources on her biography prior to her marriage to Sabbatai Zevi see Scholem, *Sabbatai Sevi*, 192–7.

[53] So asserts Immanuel Frances in 'Sipur ma'aseh', 133: 'Sarah, the wife of Sabbatai Zevi, instigated her spouse to proclaim himself King of Israel.' See also his comment on one of his poems: 'An Ashkenazi woman by the name of Sarah, the wife of Sabbatai Zevi, instigated him to proclaim himself the messiah' (*Tsevi mudaḥ*, 127 n. 7). See also Scholem, *Sabbatai Sevi*, 192.

[54] See ibid. 138–42.

[55] This conflicts with Jacob Emden's assertion that 'all these prophets and prophetesses were active from the beginning of the month of Tevet 5426 [December 1665] until 16 Elul 5427 [September 1667(!)], on which date Sabbatai Zevi deserted his faith and they ceased their prophesying' (Emden, *Zot torat hakena'ot*, 10). Elsewhere he contradicts himself; see below, n. 62. For the circumstances of Sabbatai Zevi's apostasy in September 1666, see Scholem, *Sabbatai Sevi*, 679–86.

from Pamos [Phamos?] to Praga [variant reading: to Mergezeh (Margazah?)] in the month of Elul 5465 [summer of 1665] and related that they had prophets and prophetesses. One prophetess, whose name was Rebecca, had given numerous signs, all of which came to pass, and she said that she had seen Elijah and Rabbi Nissim, and with them the Messiah son of David, and the two of them had told her: 'this is the Messiah son of David'. She also said that on the sabbath before Passover she had been shown the Messiah son of David, dressed in black clothes, and she also said that the messiah would remain alone, bereft of his devotees, and he would be dressed in Ishmaelite garb. They sent five messengers out into the world, and prophets and prophetesses gathered in several other places, and they all prophesied that the messiah was present in the world. Then four more delegates arrived from the land of Cush to greet our lord, and when they learned that our lord was wearing this garb, they, too, donned the same garb, and they came to our lord, may his honour be exalted, inside the mosque, to kiss his hands . . . and they said that in their country, too, there were a number of prophets and prophetesses.[56]

Even in the years following Sabbatai Zevi's death in 1676, as the Sabbatian movement began to disintegrate and split up, women apparently continued to see visions of the redemption. Their credibility as prophetesses was unshaken among the faithful, although the episodes of mass prophecy seen in 1665/6 necessarily died out with the growing hostility towards the discredited messianic movement, which was now in the process of going underground and becoming a clandestine sectarian organization.

Thus, for example, we learn of the prophetic authority of a certain woman from Adrianople, about whom Abraham Cardozo complains in one of his autobiographical letters. The letter apparently was written early in the first

[56] Barukh of Arezzo, 'Memorial' (Heb.), 63–4. The place names as printed in Freimann's edition are hopelessly corrupt, and it is difficult to determine the messengers' supposed lands of origin from them, particularly since even the original names would have been no more than distant rumours to the author. 'The Kingdom of Kinah' would seem to be China; 'Lazbek' might refer to the region inhabited by the Uzbeks in central Asia, while 'Lubeck', if this is the correct reading, is a German city north-east of Hamburg; 'Great Tartaria'—a region whose political boundaries in this period are rather hazy—was, in all events, the land of the Tatar tribes, north-east of the Black Sea and beyond that, east of the Caspian Sea, up to the borders of Mongolia and China to the east and Siberia to the north. 'Pamos' (or perhaps Phamos) is unidentifiable, as is 'Mergezeh' (or possibly Margazah), given the ambiguities of the vowel-less Hebrew, while 'Praga', which could refer to Prague, is also a small town near (and eventually a suburb of) Warsaw on the right bank of the Vistula river, where the Jews were permitted to settle in the period when they were not allowed to reside in the city of Warsaw itself. 'The land of Cush' is probably the North African region of Nubia.

decade of the eighteenth century,[57] and it describes, among other things, the bitter disappointment ensuing from the redemptive hopes that had arisen again in 1682, only to be proven false. Cardozo, who had been one of the foremost prophets of this date for the redemption, had become a butt of scorn and criticism; he and his disciples had 'suffered such tribulations and persecutions, such humiliation and shame as the mouth cannot relate, nor the pen record'.[58] During this difficult period, in which he was embroiled in controversy and quarrelled with circles of the faithful whose doctrines he could not accept, as well as with the 'deniers' who had abandoned their Sabbatian faith, this woman spread a slanderous accusation against him on the strength of her prophetic revelations. According to his account, she approached him—apparently towards the end of the period of his residence in Constantinople—in the company of two of her woman friends, and declared:

Moses and Aaron the priest appeared to me in Adrianople, and they sent me to speak with your honour about making a repair in your circumcision, and this will be the occasion for the salvation of Israel to begin, for it depends upon you.

Cardozo recounts the medical particulars that gave rise to this false suspicion that his circumcision did not conform to the requirements of Jewish law, and he endeavours unsuccessfully to repudiate the woman's prophecy:

And because I told her that these apparitions of Moses and Aaron the priest who had sent her to me were just big husks [*kelipot*—evil forces] that had adhered to her since 1666, she went to the sages of Istanbul, and I suffered great humiliation. . . . Later, when I went to Adrianople, I found her there saying marvellous things. In the middle of a marketplace she shouted at me, 'How long are you going to keep the nation of Israel in exile? Be circumcised and have mercy upon this nation!' . . . And I went away shamefaced from this event.[59]

This prophetic activity of women, which had accompanied Sabbatianism

---

[57] At the beginning of the letter Cardozo mentions Mordecai Ashkenazi's book, *Eshel avraham*, which was printed in Fürth in 1701; the book had recently reached his hands, and he already had some criticisms regarding Ashkenazi's interpretations of the Zohar. See Molkho and Amarillo, 'Autobiographical Letters' (Heb.), 202.   [58] Ibid. 220.

[59] Ibid. 220–1. Elijah Hakohen, too, refers to Cardozo's flawed circumcision, calling him 'uncircumcised and impure, a man with a foreskin' and claiming that 'he, too, admits to part of this allegation that he is uncircumcised and was not circumcised from the day he fell on the birthing stones' (Hakohen, *Sefer merivat kodesh*, 11 and 32). For the problematics of circumcision among the Conversos returning to Judaism during this period, see Kaplan, 'Attitudes towards Circumcision' (Heb.).

from its inception, did not desist with the movement's decline, and continued right up to its very last phases. There are attestations of prophecy by women throughout the eighteenth century and even at the beginning of the nineteenth, though its content and modes of expression are not entirely clear. They include rumours of prophetic 'fits' that continued to occur among simple folk and women. According to Abraham of Shargorod, 'speaking with no ulterior motives' and recorded by Jacob Emden, youths and young girls prophesied regularly in the Częstochowa fortress, where the incarcerated Jacob Frank held court during the 1760s and early 1770s:

> Whenever the abominator [Frank] so wished, he would tell some foolish, ignorant youth or some simple girl who didn't know anything about anything that he was honouring them with the tremors. Then the spirit would overcome them and throw them forcefully to the ground, and they would lie there in a fit for an hour or two, and, lying there like corpses, they would mutter mysterious things in the language of the Zohar. Those who heard them would write down everything they said, and when they rose from the ground they would remember nothing of what they had said while they were lying there, writhing in fits; they remained as ignorant as before. They had never read a book and knew not a single letter of the Holy Tongue.[60]

This description—whose credibility we have no reason to suspect[61]—is reminiscent in all its details of the descriptions of mass prophecy at the height of the Sabbatian movement, during the lifetime of Sabbatai Zevi. It, too, emphasizes the miraculous dimension of the phenomenon: the prophecies of ignorant youths and young girls in the language of the Zohar, and about profound kabbalistic mysteries, which were recorded by their astonished listeners.[62] Here, too, the extraordinary nature of the phenomenon itself would seem to have served

---

[60] Emden, *Ma'aseh nora*, quoted here from the appendices to Balaban, *Frankist Movement* (Heb.), pt. 2, 304.

[61] Although it clearly is not eyewitness testimony; moreover, the testimony of Abraham of Shargorod regarding the Ba'al Shem Tov's participation in the Lvov disputation with the Frankists was disproved by Balaban; see ibid. 305–20.

[62] See above, at nn. 17–21. Emden himself points out the continuity of the phenomenon of prophesying by women and unlettered folk, from the time of Sabbatai Zevi through that of Jacob Frank: 'And as for the uttering of esoteric and kabbalistic matters in the idiom of the Zohar by unlettered folk and ignorant women, by way of falling and lying on the ground, possession by demons, vain declamations and enticements to sin . . . a phenomenon attested from when Sabbatai Zevi, may his evil name rot, arose to wreak evil and confusion upon the world— this filth never lost its hold on the apostates of Salonica, and they sent the Frank [a derisory allusion to Frank's Oriental/Sephardi background, which became his name] to Poland' (ibid. 305).

as proof that the messianic message was true, but while the mass prophesying of the 1660s was marked by its spontaneous and public character, in Frank's time—about a century later—it occurred at his instigation, under his direction, and within the closed confines of his sectarian circle of 'believers'.

In addition to the prophesying by youths and young girls who had been 'honoured with the tremors' at Frank's whim, a number of women—daughters of elite Sabbatian families—became known during those years as independent prophetesses who wielded a great deal of influence within their sectarian milieu. They included Rosa and Merle Schotten, daughters of Arieh Leib Schotten, the Sabbatian rabbi of the Jewish community of Mattersdorf in western Hungary; Hayah Schor, daughter of the well-known Sabbatian preacher Elisha Schor and sister of Solomon Schor, a well-known Sabbatian from Rohatyn, south-east of Lvov; and Roesel Eger, sister of Jonas (Yonah) Wehle, head of the Sabbatian fellowship in Prague at the end of the eighteenth century and in the first two decades of the nineteenth.[63]

Rosa and Merle Schotten, daughters of Rabbi Arieh Leib Schotten (originally of Frankfurt am Main), together with their brother, Rabbi Nathan Neta Schotten, were all identified with Sabbatianism. A local tradition in Mattersdorf had it that the sisters were 'elderly spinsters', reputed to command extensive biblical and talmudic learning, and known as *newietes*—'prophetesses', although the historian and folklorist Max Grunwald, who recorded this information in his comprehensive article on the history of the Mattersdorf community, acknowledges that 'nothing has come down to us on the nature of their prophetic gifts'.[64] He apparently was unaware of the significance of the prophetic title in the Sabbatian context.[65] The spinsterhood of these two women, particularly taken together with their scholarly and prophetic demeanour, may well be no mere biographical quirk (a rather rare one in traditional Jewish society[66]), but rather silent evidence that they rejected the normative Jewish framework of married life.

---

[63] See Scholem, 'Information on Sabbatians' (Heb.), 614 n. 23; id., 'Sabbatian Will', 168 and 356 n. 5. See also Balaban, *Frankist Movement* (Heb.), 107, 115, and 117; and see below on each of these women.

[64] Grunwald, 'Mattersdorf', 427. See also Moses, 'Inschriften', 312–13. I am grateful to Dr Michael Silber for this last reference.   [65] See Scholem, *Researches* (Heb.), 614 n. 23.

[66] In the course of the 18th century, economic constraints imposed by the civil authorities began inducing the Jews, at least in the German lands, to marry as late as possible, which made the phenomenon of remaining single for extended periods much more widespread in Jewish

Rejection of the marital state meant that these women must have opted for lifelong sexual abstinence—the route that always led to the enhancement of spiritual experience in Christian society, and one that was also recognized by the Jewish tradition, albeit under certain constraints. As we have seen, Judaism normally kept sexual abstinence within the marital framework, limiting it to particular stages in life and to particular types of men, while denying altogether its value to women, in whom it was viewed as a deviation to be repressed.[67] However, in the context of sectarian messianic heresy during the first half of the eighteenth century, the life-long spinsterhood of these two Sabbatian prophetesses may well have amounted to nothing less than their holy virginity. This would represent a breaching of traditional bounds, not in the direction of the sexual licentiousness more usually associated with Sabbatianism (and particularly with its female adherents), but rather in the opposite direction of celibate chastity, which was also a grave deviation from the norms of womanhood in Jewish society. It would seem to betray the assimilation of a Christian ideal into the sectarian consciousness of the women, a process in keeping with the syncretistic tendency characteristic of Sabbatianism, particularly in its later stages.

Eva Frank, who also never married and was never characterized as sexually profligate, was called the Virgin in her father's court, at which his doctrine of the female redeemer also hinted (on this, see below, Chapter 7), and her virginity was clearly viewed as a mark of sanctity.[68] The daughter (or granddaughter) of Berukhyah, head of the Salonican sect of Sabbatian converts to Islam, was similarly called the holy Maiden (though there were rumours of a plan to marry her to Wolf, the son of Jonathan Eybeschuetz).[69] Perhaps the many references to 'young girls', 'maidens', and even 'little girls' who prophesied, some of which specifically mention that they were virgins, should be viewed as belonging in the same syncretistic context.[70] They may point to a recognition—never stated explicitly—that the virgin state made these girls especially receptive to the flow of spiritual energies and prophetic revelations.[71]

---

society. However, 'we do not hear of the single state as a lifelong choice' (Shohet, *Beginnings of the Haskalah* (Heb.), 160).

[67] See above, Introd., and below, Ch. 2, at nn. 7–11.   [68] On Eva's status see below, Ch. 8.

[69] See Emden, *Sefer hitabekut*, 19*b* and 35*a* (and see below, at n. 131).

[70] See above, at nn. 28–31, 38–46, and below, Ch. 2, at nn. 7–11, 61–3.

[71] This idea was prevalent in Christianity from its inception, and it is expressed in other reli-

By contrast, accounts of other Sabbatian prophetesses active in the same period feature not sexual abstinence or virginity, but rather sexual licentiousness, and this specifically within the framework of marriage. Regarding the prophecy of Hayah Schor of Rohatyn, for example, Emden writes:

One reliable informant swore to me that he knew how that accursed woman made herself a prophet (like Sibylla to the Romans and Venus to the Aramaeans[72]), by falling on the ground in a fit, like one possessed by a demon, and reciting passages from the Zohar by heart while in this trance.[73] All the members of this accursed fellowship knew how to do this, as a kind of sorcery. Even their children pranced like goats; 7- and 8-year-olds fell down in fits, speaking in tongues and reciting long passages from the Zohar.[74]

To be sure, this description accords with all the accounts surveyed so far of ecstatic spells of prophecy, in which not a word was ever said of orgiastic ceremonies, or adulterous or wanton practices. However, most of the evidence we have about the prophetess Hayah attests that she 'whored' with the knowledge of her husband—and also without his knowledge—with all of her brothers and brothers-in-law and with several other Sabbatians. She would also seem to have been the central figure in the infamous incident that took place in Lanckorona in the course of Jacob Frank's visit there in 1756. On that occasion she was seen through cracks in the wall of the home of her brother-in-law, Leib Shabses, dancing naked with a 'Torah crown' on her head, and with members of the fellowship of believers carousing around her and falling upon her to embrace and kiss her.[75] She clearly enjoyed a position of power and authority within her Sabbatian circle, acting independently, of her own accord

gions as well. For a discussion of its development in early Christianity see Brown, 'Notion of Virginity', 427–43. See further on this subject below, at nn. 85–7, and at the beginning of Ch. 3.

[72] Emden is referring to the Sibyl, the priestess-prophetess in Graeco-Roman (and Hellenistic Jewish) literature, and to the goddess Venus (spelt Fenus on the wrong assumption that the letter *v* here should be pronounced *f*, as is usually the case in German), who in German folk culture took the form of a seductive female demon, enticing men to sin. 'Aramaeans' no doubt refers to the Romans or to other pagan peoples. See Jastrow, *Dictionary*, s.v. *Arami*.

[73] On the instruction of women in the Zohar in Sabbatian circles, which may explain the descriptions of them prophesying in trance in the language of the Zohar, see below, Ch. 5.

[74] Emden, *Sefer shimush*, 20a.

[75] The accounts of Hayah Schor and her Sabbatian family are surveyed in Balaban, *Frankist Movement* (Heb.), 107, 114–18, and 120–2. The principal source for them is Emden's *Sefer*

and not only at the behest of her husband. Here is what the repentant former Sabbatian Samuel ben Solomon Segal had to say about her in his confession, delivered 'while weeping copious tears' before the rabbinic court convened in Satanów on 13 Sivan 5516 (11 June 1756):

Hayah, the wife of Hirschl Shabses, I embraced and kissed about six times. But in terms of real activity, I didn't do anything with her. She said to me, 'you are not worthy of taking up with me, for I am a believer in Sabbatai Zevi, and my father and also my grandparents and uncles are all believers. You still have not learned much Torah. You lack this merit.' Once I demanded of her that she sin with me, and she responded, 'have you learned the Song of Songs today, as I have?[76] How can you be permitted to perform such a holy act?' Once her husband Hirsch heard from me that his wife Hayah had whored with his brother Leibush while they were travelling to the fair in Tarnopol. He became angry with her because she had done this without his knowledge. He said, 'after all, I would not have objected. But you knew that this commandment is one that must be fulfilled by permission.'[77]

The testimony from Satanów goes on to relate in the name of the same witness that Hirsch's will was subordinated to his wife's in a clear, dramatic, and public display of Sabbatian antinomianism:

Rabbi Samuel, the son of Rabbi Solomon, told me several times . . . how he wanted to kiss the wife of Rabbi Hirsch Shabses. She did not wish to allow him to kiss her. He approached her husband, Hirsch. He [Hirsch] gave him permission to whore with

shimush. See also the testimonies given in the Satanów synagogue, printed by Emden at the end of his edition of *Seder olam rabah, Seder olam zuta* and tractate *Ta'anit* (unpaginated), and the account by Abraham of Shargorod, as transcribed by Emden at the end of *Sefer hapedut vehapurkan*, in Balaban, *Frankist Movement* (Heb.), 298. Cf. the version given by Dov Ber Birkenthal of Bolechów in *Divrei binah*, 214–16, and see also Kraushar, *Frank and his Following* (Heb.), 71–2 (English version in id., *Jacob Frank*, i. 84).

[76] On the status of the Song of Songs in the Sabbatian library see e.g. Emden [David Avaz], *Petaḥ einayim*, 15*b*; and Emden, *Akitsat akrav*, 13*a*. See also Kraushar, *Frank and his Following* (Heb.), 57 (English version in id., *Jacob Frank*, i. 70); Elmaleh, *Sabbatai Zevi in the Present Day* (Heb.), 35; Galanté, *Nouveaux documents*, 74; Kahana, *History of the Kabbalists* (Heb.), 139 (on the special sanctity attributed to the Song of Songs in the circles of the Doenmeh in Salonica); and Liebes, *On Sabbatianism* (Heb.), 157 (on Jonathan Eybeschuetz's kabbalistic commentary on the Song of Songs, which is not extant).

[77] Emden, *Sefer shimush*, 5*b*. On the speculative underpinnings in the Sabbatian kabbalah for these adulterous practices, which were viewed as holy deeds to be performed with the knowledge and permission of the husband and even at his behest, see Liebes, *On Sabbatianism* (Heb.), 124–7.

her. Nevertheless, she did not oblige. He went to her husband. He suspected her of not being a believer. She took a knife, cut some forbidden fat and ate it.[78]

According to another repentant former Sabbatian, Joseph, who testified about his activities before the rabbinic court in Satanów and confessed them again before 'the entire holy community in the holy synagogue', it was Hayah who initiated him into the secret practices of the Sabbatian fellowship. She would seem to have performed initiation rites like these for other young people who wanted to join the sect:

First of all, you should know that I have already been in the fellowship of Sabbatai Zevi, may his name be blotted out and his lineage uprooted, for nine years. My first act of sin took place when I expressed my wish to join them and be among them. There was a woman there, a whore and a heretic, the wife of Tsevi [Hirsch], son of Rabbi Shabses. She is the daughter of Elisha of Rohatyn. This is what she said to me: 'If you pass the test that I am about to show you, you will be worthy of joining us.' She took a knife and cut a piece of forbidden fat from the fat-burning candle and ate it, and she enjoined me to do the same. I took a piece of the fat as well and ate it. Then they took me among them and revealed their secrets to me.[79]

Immediately after this account, the confessing penitent describes Hayah's acts of harlotry with her brother Leib Shprintses (the Leibush mentioned above). His confession was recorded in its entirety by Emden, who translated it 'from Yiddish into the Holy Tongue, so that the Sephardim and all the rest of the people, whatever their language, could understand it'.[80]

These accounts, like the others transmitted to us by Emden, are credible but problematic: his writings on the Sabbatians are fiercely polemical, and consequently, his presentation of the evidence he collected on their activities tends to be one-dimensional.[81] He condemns them universally for rejecting the yoke of the commandments and wallowing in filth, and this applies particularly to the women, who are all portrayed in his writings as wanton harlots. It is certainly true—and Emden understood this all too well—that the

---

[78] Emden, *Sefer shimush*, 6*b*.   [79] Ibid. 20*a*–*b*.   [80] Ibid. 20*a*.

[81] Only rarely, with evident reluctance, does Emden admit: 'Even if the believers in Sabbatai Zevi, may the name of the wicked rot, are divided into sects, so that some of them even keep the Torah, as we have heard people say . . . but even if they do not transgress the Torah, they have repudiated the redemption, and they turn the hearts of the Jews astray and make them despair of the righteous redeemer; and all of them certainly make a pagan idol of him. So how can we believe that they keep the Torah, when we know that Sabbatai Zevi, may the name of the

conceptualization of the new, messianic Torah as a break with the halakhic system of prohibitions, particularly those relating to illicit sexual unions, was a prominent feature of Sabbatianism from the outset. The requisite kabbalistic acts of *tikun*—the restoration of the world to a state of perfection—were often understood by the Sabbatians to mean the inversion of ritual law, to be accomplished through ceremonial acts of transgression, above all sexual transgression.[82] However, not all the currents of Sabbatianism took this route, or called on all their adherents to follow it. There were many Sabbatians who observed the commandments strictly and led a life of pious asceticism, on the assumption that the time had not yet arrived for the new Torah to come into effect, and there were some circles in which both approaches were present simultaneously.[83]

wicked rot, transgressed the whole Torah and considered this a *tikun*?' (Emden, *Zot torat hakena'ot*, 142, and see also p. 61). This attitude, leading Emden to condemn all expressions of the Sabbatian faith with equal severity and thus to blur the distinctions between moderates and radicals, derived not only from the heat of his polemic but also from the nature of his understanding of Sabbatianism. He saw Sabbatai Zevi and all those who followed him as representing the anti-messiah, the 'Messiah of Impurity', who wielded great power. It was thus not enough to expose him as an impostor or an empty shell; his heresy had to be confronted seriously and fought to the point of eradication. For this convincing interpretation of Emden's position see Liebes, *On Sabbatianism* (Heb.), 198–211.

[82] On the accuracy of Emden's evaluation in this regard, which is becoming even clearer with the publication of previously unknown Sabbatian documents that confirm and buttress his claims, see Liebes' remarks in *On Sabbatianism* (Heb.), 79, and also his article on the relationship between Emden's own messianic conception and his attitude towards Sabbatianism, ibid. 198–211. For further accounts transmitted by Emden of the licentiousness of the Sabbatian women see below, Ch. 4, at nn. 5–8.

[83] See Scholem's comments on the alternation between 'the extremes of an ethic of pious asceticism, on the one hand, and an ethic of licentiousness, on the other', in *Studies and Texts* (Heb.), 107 and 113. See also Elqayam, 'To Know Messiah' (Heb.), 637–70. This kind of alternation, and the coexistence of the two opposing norms of sexual morality, have many precedents and parallels in the history of religions. On the phenomenon within Islam, in the circles of the Sufi dervishes, see Karamustafa, *God's Unruly Friends*, 14–23 (I am grateful to Prof. Cornell Fleischer for referring me to this work). For a discussion of this issue in relation to the medieval Cathar heresy see Nelli, 'La Continence cathare', 139–51. See also Lacombe, 'Ascèse de chasteté', 61–9, and several other essays in the same volume. Norman Cohn, in *Pursuit of the Millennium* (esp. chs. 8 and 9), discusses conflicting testimonies on the sexual morality of the heresy of the 'free spirit', which swept through Europe at the end of the Middle Ages and in the early modern period. See on this also Lerner, *The Heresy*, 10–34, 82–4, 86, 92, 109, 143–7, 150, 158–61, 176. In this movement, too, prophesying women played a prominent role (See Cohn, *Pursuit of the*

Emden regarded all the Sabbatian women as possessed of a wantonness born as much out of spite against religious law as of sheer lust,[84] but there is also, as we have seen, a certain amount of contrary evidence pointing to the practice of celibate chastity among them, some of it even more explicit and broader in scope than the incidental remarks on the lifelong 'spinsterhood' of the two Sabbatian prophetesses in Mattersdorf, or the unique designation of Eva Frank as the messianic holy Virgin. For example, a code of sexual abstinence may be inferred from the memoirs of Moses Porges, son of a Prague Sabbatian family, who was sent by his parents to spend some time at the Frankist court in Offenbach at the end of the 1790s, when the court was headed by Jacob Frank's children, his daughter Eva, and her two brothers, Josef and Rochus. Porges attests quite unambiguously to the strict separation between the sexes at the court, the absolute ban on marriage,[85] and the regular flogging of light-headed youths who admitted to desiring 'a female':

Millennium, 229–30, and Lerner, *The Heresy*, 18), and it paralleled the Sabbatian messianic–prophetic outbreak in several other ways as well. See more on this below, Ch. 2, at nn. 70–4.

[84] See below, Ch. 4, at nn. 5–8.

[85] The ban on marriage at Offenbach may be an echo of Frank's command: 'Take care to observe all that I shall command you, so as not to transgress any of it, heaven forbid. Thus, it is my will that your children, your daughters and sons, not marry among themselves; let them wait until the Jews arrive, and they shall marry them. This will happen as it will happen, and you will go with them to the Faith (*Das*), and only then will you be under my wings, and I will be able to declare: "Until now you have been what you have been; from now on you will be gathered under my shadow, and Satan will have no more to say where you are concerned"' (Jacob Frank, *Words of the Lord*, §961). Clearly, 'the arrival of the Jews' and their mass entry into 'the faith'—that is, Frank's apostate religion—refer to the conclusion of the redemptive process as envisioned by Frank, and it was only then that the sons and daughters would be permitted to marry. It could even be that the ban should be interpreted in light of Frank's hazy references to future couplings of another kind (which—as Frank was clearly aware at the time of addressing his followers on this topic—had failed to materialize), namely, the alliance he had envisaged between the members of his circle, 'brothers' and 'sisters' of the flesh (for the use of these designations in Frank's court see below, Chs. 4 and 6), with the 'brothers' and 'sisters' from 'there', that is, mythical ethereal beings, masculine and feminine, inhabiting the divine realm. As a consequence of this projected mating, children would have been born endowed with 'immense power', of a nature that lies somewhere between the human and the divine, and Frank himself would have performed their marriages: 'Then our brothers would have mated with the sisters from there, and those brothers with our [sisters] . . . for we are water and they are fire, and they would have become one, for they ardently desire embodied beings, and we, too, need them. Therefore I told you several times that I myself would perform the wedding ceremonies for your sons and your

The youths, especially my roommates, were, as they often declared, loyal believers, but—as usual with young people—light-headed. Notwithstanding the strict morality generally [practised there] [in the German original: *trotzt der allgemeinen strengen Sittlichkeit*; in the Yiddish version: *nisht gekukt oyf der arumiker shtrenger moralisher prishes*], they were not very rigorous in this regard. No contact with the opposite sex was permitted, and marriage was strictly prohibited.[86] One morning we were even commanded in a 'vision' [German: *in einer Vision*; Yiddish: *als a ḥezyon*][87] that anyone who had desired a female must agree to receive ten lashes—and almost all the young men agreed to the lashes. Furthermore, I must mention that 'visions' like this were proclaimed almost every day by one of the three masters [Jacob Frank's three offspring], and they were written down in a book, of which several copies were made.[88]

daughters. This was my intention: the children that would have been born would have possessed immense power; their cry would have felled a whole city' (ibid., §1275). On the couplings between this world and 'there' see further ibid., §418, and below, Ch. 6, at nn. 16–20. The ban on marriage may also have been inspired by the Russian sectarians who had abolished marriage, and with whom Frank was in contact, on which see below, Ch. 8.

[86]   This reference to the ban on marriage is corroborated by another testimony on life at the Offenbach court, delivered before the rabbinic court of Kollin on 24 (or 29) Sivan 5560 (June 1800) and published in Judaeo-German, liberally sprinkled with Hebrew, by Dr Samuel Back in 'Aufgefundene Aktenstücke', 410–20. The witness, a repentant ex-Frankist, reported that 'no matches were made among them' (ibid. 419). Further confirmation appears in a report on the Frankist court at Offenbach prepared by a representative of the Prussian government in Frankfurt, which states: 'It is also well known that, since their arrival [in 1788], none of them got married' (quoted in Mandel, *Militant Messiah*, 117).

[87]   This would seem to refer to one of the prophetic revelations regularly experienced by the Frank siblings, by which they dictated the activities of their followers, as described in the same testimony before the Kollin rabbinical court: 'Everything that was done there was done by decree (these were the visions [*maros* in Ashkenazi pronunciation, Heb. *mar'ot*], which were taken as prophecy). These visions were always proclaimed at the morning assemblies. It was the accursed daughter of Jacob Frank with her two brothers, Josef and Rochus, who saw the visions. So it was that they went to church on their holy day [i.e. Sunday], but when this was forbidden in a vision, and they were told not to go, they did not go' (Back, 'Aufgefundene Aktenstücke', 419). The prophetic command designated as *mar'eh* in this witness's testimony would seem to be the same as the *Vision* mentioned in the original German version of Porges' memoir, and the *ḥezyon* of Gelber's Yiddish translation.

[88]   The original German text of Moses Porges' memoirs is in the hands of the Porges family in Israel (on this see Liebes' note in Scholem, *Researches* (Heb.), 677, and Liebes, *On Sabbatianism* (Heb.), 423), but it was published in two instalments under the title 'Eine Wallfahrt nach Offenbach' in *Frankfurter israelitisches Gemeindeblatt*, nos. 6–7 (Feb. and Mar. 1932), 121–3 and 150–1. I would like to thank professors Yehuda Liebes and Tuviah Kwasman for providing me with copies of this German edition. The original German text, including an addi-

This eyewitness testimony is credible and convincing, though we may suspect that it does not necessarily reveal the whole truth. It could well be that the rigorous discipline of sexual abstinence practised by the believers was broken at Offenbach from time to time by clandestine orgiastic rituals. These would take place around the 'masters', Frank's offspring (and apparently only around them), at those times, such as the Day of Atonement, which had always been the occasions for Sabbatianism's practice of transgression by inversion of ritual law. We learn of an event of this kind from the account of Rabbi Wolf Lipmann Hamburger, the representative of the rabbinic court of Fürth (Fiorda). Rabbi Hamburger testified before the rabbinic judges on 7 Kislev 5561 (24 November 1800) on the findings of his interrogation, conducted some

tional paragraph which is missing from the printed edition, was translated into Yiddish, apparently from the manuscript version, by N. M. Gelber, and published even before the publication of the German edition as 'Di zikhroynes fun moses porges' (hereafter referred to as 'Memoirs of Moses Porges'). An English translation of the full German text appears as an appendix to Mandel, *Militant Messiah*, 155–70. The passage quoted above appears in Porges, 'Eine Wallfahrt', 123, col. 1; in 'Memoirs of Moses Porges', cols. 276–7; and in Mandel, *Militant Messiah*, 162. Gelber's Yiddish translation is marked by terminological modifications of the original German text, which he clearly borrowed from the world of hasidism and saw fit to introduce wherever he sensed a strong resemblance between the hasidic doctrines and customs he knew well, and the Frankist practices described in the account of the court at Offenbach. Thus, for example, he uses the hasidic term *shirayim* in rendering the description of the sect's adherents grabbing scraps of leftover food from the table of the 'three masters' ('Memoirs of Moses Porges', col. 276). This term does not appear in Porges' original German text (p. 123, col. 1: 'Die Speisen, die übrig bleiben'), and there is no way of knowing whether it was already in use among the Frankists at that time or whether it was a later coinage of the hasidim (on the relative lateness of references to this custom in the hasidic movement see Rapoport-Albert, 'A Maskilic Defence' (Heb.), 101–4, n. 24. Another example is Gelber's use of the term *hirhurei ishah* to render the German phrase 'eine Neigung für die Frauensperson' (literally: 'an inclination towards the female', translated above as 'anyone who had desired a female'), thus creating an implicit association with the hasidic doctrine of *maḥashavot zarot* (extraneous thoughts). Similarly, in his translation of the testimony of the three youths who had escaped from Offenbach and were interrogated by the rabbinical court in Fürth (on which see directly below), he translates the German term *Opfer* (sacrifice) or *Opfergabe* ([sacrificial] offering), used to denote the sum of money demanded from visitors to the Offenbach court, as the Hebrew/Yiddish *pidyon* (ransom [money]), which is the technical term for the comparable institution in hasidism. The existence of ideological and institutional affinities of this nature between hasidism and Frankism is an open question that should be given due consideration (on this see e.g. Liebes' interesting observations in *On Sabbatianism* (Heb.), 97–100, and his additional references on p. 359 n. 4), but it should not be foisted on a Frankist text as though it could be taken for granted.

three months earlier, of three youths, Moses Porges (the author of the above memoir), his younger brother Leib-Leopold, and their friend Jonas Hauf-singer of Dresden. They had fled in a panic from the Offenbach court and stopped off in Fürth on their way home, where they were arrested by the police for interrogation on behalf of the town's rabbinic court. Rabbi Hamburger's account of their statements was translated into Yiddish by N. Gelber from a German copy in the possession of the Porges family (the Hebrew original apparently has not been preserved[89]) and was published as an appendix to his translation of Moses Porges' memoir:

the Day of Atonement, 5560, that is, 1800 [in fact, October 1799]. Ruah[90] committed grave sins and indecent acts. Three women, including the daughter of Mendel Itschin [Jičín], were ordered, following various rituals and preparations, to come to him and remain with him in his room. The three youths were ordered to stand guard with weapons drawn outside the door. Thus were harlotry and all kinds of obscene acts committed, on the pretext that he [Rochus] had seen by the holy spirit that this was what must be done in order to avert harsh divine decrees in that year. Mendel's daugh-ter wrote afterwards to her father that she was very happy to have been chosen for this purpose. The three youths have many other stories to tell of adultery and acts of folly.[91]

The description of the events of that the Day of Atonement is corroborated in the account of another investigator on behalf of the rabbinic court in Fürth, Rabbi Baer Simon Eichenhäuser, whose testimony gives details provided by Jonas Haufsinger, one of the three young fugitives from Offenbach who had stood guard at Rochus Frank's door. This testimony was recorded before the rab-binic court in the following day's session, on 8 Kislev 5561 (25 November 1800):

They were shocked by the abominations committed by the scions of Jacob Frank on the Day of Atonement. Just then they were standing guard at the door, and they heard various indescribably shameful acts. Mendel Itschin's daughter wept bitterly, but she later wrote in a letter to Prague that she was very happy.[92]

[89] See Gelber, 'Di zikhroynes fun moses porges', col. 262. The German version of this testi-mony from Fürth was also published, after deletion of the names of the people involved, by Samuel Back—see Back, 'Aufgefundene Aktenstücke', 189–92, 232–40.

[90] This name, meaning 'spirit', 'evil spirit', or 'demon' in Hebrew, is used throughout the text to denote Jacob Frank's son Rochus.

[91] Gelber, 'Di zikhroynes fun moses porges', appendix 1, col. 290, §4. In the German version published by Samuel Back (see n. 89 above), this paragraph appears on p. 192.

[92] Gelber, 'Di zikhroynes fun moses porges', appendix 2, col. 293, §1. In Samuel Back's German version this testimony appears on p. 235.

The two additional details in this testimony—the shocked reaction of the youths who were guarding the door, and the bitter weeping of the girl (before she reported her great joy to her family)—strengthen the impression that activities of this kind were spontaneous and clandestine. They certainly were not a part of everyday life in the Offenbach court, which, as we have seen, was distinguished by a strict separation between the sexes, sexual abstinence, and a ban on marriage.

We thus cannot rule out the possibility that there existed alongside each other two opposing norms of sexual morality: pietistic abstinence on the one hand, and antinomian licentiousness on the other, each applying to a different category of believers at all times, or to all categories of believers at different times.[93] Consequently, we cannot rule out the possibility that some Sabbatian prophetesses were lifelong 'holy virgins', while others regularly practised 'harlotry' within marriage.[94] In general, however, it would appear that the sexually transgressive norm, even if it remained mandated in theory as part and parcel of the eschatological doctrine, was gradually abandoned in practice as the movement was approaching its final stage.[95] Roesel Eger, for example, sister of

[93] For example, Elisha Schor, father of Hayah the prophetess, notwithstanding his Sabbatian beliefs and the conduct of the other members of his household, did not have adulterous relations until the advent of a certain stage, which apparently coincided with the visit of Jacob Frank to his town of Rohatyn. This, at any rate, is what transpires from the testimony of Shmuel Segal before the rabbinic court of Satanów, as transcribed by Jacob Emden: 'Even old Elisha whored after the arrival of the Frank' (Emden, *Sefer shimush*, 5*b*). This testimony is corroborated by the account of another witness: 'We asked him whether Elisha himself had also done this, and he responded that up to then Elisha himself had never done this. But after the arrival of the Frank, he, too, performed the commandment with his above-mentioned daughter-in-law' (ibid. 7*a*).

[94] This twofold propensity was already evident in Sabbatai Zevi's own biography; as we know, in some periods his lifestyle was one of asceticism and abstinence, while in others he surrounded himself with women and apparently committed sexual transgressions. See below, Ch. 5.

[95] See Scholem, 'Redemption through Sin', 136, and see also Appendix below. By the second half of the 19th century, among those descendants of the messianic sectarians for whom affiliation with Sabbatianism had become no more than a distant family tradition, the movement could be described as 'a blameless way of life, strict morality, honesty, and charity; in fact all the virtues of a good citizen' (Scholem, 'Sabbatian Will', 174). Thus did Gottlieb Wehle of Prague (nephew of the well-known Prague Sabbatian Jonas Wehle), who emigrated to America in 1849, characterize his family tradition in his last testament to his children, written in 1863–4. His description is corroborated by 'Dr Klein', who served as rabbi of the Stolpe community in eastern Germany. In 1848, Klein wrote of the Sabbatians of the previous generation in Prague

Jonas Wehle, the head of the Sabbatian fellowship in Prague, was another pilgrim to the Offenbach court in the last decade of the eighteenth century.[96] In 1848, less than two decades after her death, it was said of her that 'she lived in Prague and was known as a prophetess of the Sabbatians, and she died in 1831 without arousing much notice'.[97] This wording would seem to indicate that the writer, who had put some effort into gathering information on Prague's Sabbatians, had heard of no aberrant activity—sexual or otherwise— connected with this prophetess, though he did relate of her niece that, as a young girl at the Offenbach court, 'she was said to be a prophetess, but she was really Frank's concubine'.[98] An anti-Frankist satire published anonymously in

that, although they were known for their Christianizing tendencies, 'they maintained their own synagogue and study house, and were distinguished for their erudition in the Bible and the Zohar'. Of the Sabbatians of his own generation, he wrote: 'The members of the Wehle and Bondi families are new Jews, and we may say in their favour that they are people of high morality; those with whom I was personally acquainted were experts in Scripture' (Klein, 'Zuschrift an Moses Mendelson', col. 540).

[96] See Gelber, 'Di zikhroynes fun moses porges', appendix 1, col. 292, §11 (in Samuel Back's German version, p. 233, but without divulging any names), where Wolf Lipmann Hamburger, in his testimony before the Fürth rabbinic court on 24 November 1800, reports on the large sums of money that the believers who visited the court had to pay over to Frank's scions. Roesel Eger (whose husband is never mentioned in this context and apparently was not a party to her sectarian affiliation; see below, Ch. 4, at nn. 30–2) was also ordered to pay. She refused but was ultimately made to hand over the money.	[97] Klein, 'Zuschrift an Moses Mendelson', col. 528.

[98] Ibid. Klein presents the niece's concubinage as necessarily incompatible with her being a prophetess, while with regard to her aunt, Roesel Eger, he has no such information that might—in his own terms—undermine her status as a reputable prophetess. For him, sexual licentiousness clearly could not be reconciled with prophecy. It is hard to know whether this sensibility was based on any real familiarity with the nature of female prophetic activity in the Sabbatian movement of his day, or whether it was a naive assumption, unrelated to the true state of affairs.

As for the niece, she was the 'daughter of Mendel Itschin' mentioned in the two eyewitness accounts of events at Offenbach on the Day of Atonement in 1799. The fact that the girl was related also to the prophetess Roesel Eger can be inferred from her father's name, Itschin, indicating that he came from the town of Jičín, north-east of Prague, which was the home of 'Emanuel Wehle of Gitschin', the well-known Sabbatian brother of both Jonas Wehle and Roesel Eger (see Scholem, 'Sabbatian Will', 168). Emanuel of Gitschin and Mendel Itschin are one and the same (see the genealogical information supplied by his nephew, Gottlieb Wehle, in Scholem, 'Sabbatian Will', 172–3). Support for this may be drawn from the fact that Wolf Lipmann Hamburger's account of the high payments exacted from the believers who had come as pilgrims to the court of Offenbach (see above, n. 96) mentions Mendel Itschin, together with

Prague in 1800, apparently written by the maskil Barukh Jeiteles,[99] also mentions an important Prague prophetess, evidently alluding to Roesel Eger. Even this description, which was thoroughly hostile, contains no echo of illicit sexual conduct: 'There is among them a woman who prophesies just like one of the [classical] prophetesses, and they go to her to hear her dreams, her visions, and her mysteries.'[100] On the other hand, Rabbi Eleazar Fleckeles, who attacks the Sabbatians of Prague in a work also written at the end of the eighteenth century and published in 1800, associates—like Emden, and as something he took for granted—the prophesying of Sabbatian women with sexual licentiousness: 'And a lascivious harlot that doth speak, what is this speaking? She has had intercourse with a man, and "she keeps secret the fact that she has defiled herself";[101] such is the one who says, "Such did I see in a vision".'[102]

brother and sister Jonas Wehle and Roesel Eger, as constituting a single group, of which Mendel Itschin is clearly the third sibling. Since Roesel Eger's niece was that daughter of Mendel Itschin with whom Rochus Frank committed his 'abominations' on the Day of Atonement 1799, she must have been the 'concubine' of Rochus Frank and not—as Dr Klein has it—of his father Jacob who, by 1799, was no longer among the living. Some confusion on this point in the tradition as it came down to Dr Klein may be the result of the efforts apparently made by Jacob Frank's offspring to obscure the fact of their father's death (in December 1791). They seem to have tried over a long period to create an impression among the believers that Frank had not really died but, rather, had 'disappeared', and that he would reappear among them at least once a week, in the course of the Sunday visits to the church near his palace in Offenbach. Frank had instituted these ceremonial visits to the church during his lifetime, and they continued in great pomp and splendour long after his death. This, at any rate, is what transpires from the short German version of his memoirs that Moses Porges related orally to Dr Leopold Stein of Prague before writing them down himself (see above, n. 88). Stein published this short version in the original German as 'Mittheilung über die Frankistensekte' in 1870. On p. 158 we find a description of the weekly visit to the church. A guard of honour escorted the carriage in which sat a well-concealed figure purported to be 'Baron Frank' and called 'the Lord' by the believers. Dr Stein was much concerned, in the 'Editorial Afterword' that he appended to his version of Porges' memoirs, with the identity of the mysterious figure in the carriage; see ibid. 161–6. On the doubts concerning the death of Frank, who was still regarded as alive in an anonymous Polish pamphlet published in 1819, see Duker, 'Polish Frankism's Duration', 290.

[99] On this composition and its background see Werses, *Haskalah and Sabbatianism* (Heb.), 74–81, and the author's bibliographical references on p. 74 n. 45.

[100] *A Conversation between the Year 1800 and the Year 1801* (Heb.), 27.

[101] Based on the interpretation of Num. 5: 13 in BT *Ket.* 13a: 'She was seen speaking with a man . . . What does "speaking" mean? Ze'iri said, "in secret"; Rav Assi said, "she had intercourse with him".' See also below, Ch. 5, at n. 136.   [102] Fleckeles, *Ahavat david*, 25b.

In order to grasp the full significance of the prophesying by women in the later stages of Sabbatianism, we must take into account a further dimension of the phenomenon of Sabbatian prophecy. It is clear that the term 'prophecy' was not always used in the same way.[103] As we saw above, from the earliest stages of the movement, those who enounced its redemptive message and were called its prophets could be divided into several classes. There were the handful of learned, kabbalistically informed men, of the rank of Nathan of Gaza and Abraham Cardozo, whose prophecies were recorded, redacted, and diffused, becoming the building blocks of the Sabbatian doctrine; there were also the masses of men, women, and children prophesying in episodes of ecstatic frenzy, whose messages were garbled or banal, their principal significance lying in the phenomenon having taken place at all. Most of the accounts of women prophesying, from the outbursts of mass prophecy in 1666 to the resting of the 'spirit' on Hayah Schor or on the girls 'honoured with the tremors' by Jacob Frank a century or so later, assign them to the latter category, and at any rate, despite the oft-repeated claims that profound mysteries in the Holy Tongue or in the Aramaic language of the Zohar were revealed and recorded from the lips of these women during their fits of prophecy, no prophetic or kabbalistic revelations attributed to any Sabbatian women have ever been found.[104]

Sabbatian prophecy, including that of women, found yet another mode of expression in apparitions of Elijah, Moses, Aaron, and other such heavenly heralds, imparting coherent messianic messages to men and women, who encountered them awake or in a dream, and thereby acquired a measure of authority among their fellow believers. Furthermore, as we have seen, Sabbatian prophecy was associated also with mastery of supernatural powers and magical prowess ('sorcery' or 'fakery', as the hostile accounts put it).[105] The

---

[103] For a recent phenomenology of Sabbatian prophecy, see Goldish, *Sabbatean Prophets*. This lucid exposition does not, however, address the issue of the fluid boundaries between the roles of prophet, messiah, and divinity incarnate, which became a hallmark of Sabbatianism, and on which see below.   [104] But see below, Ch. 5, at nn. 103–50.

[105] This, for example, is how Emden describes the 'false prophet' Daniel Israel: 'Several years after the demise of Sabbatai Zevi, may the name of the wicked rot, there arose a charlatan by the name of Daniel Israel. He declared that Sabbatai Zevi still lived on in a secret place, and that he would remain there for forty-five years and then reveal himself to redeem Israel.... This impure man was no scholar, merely a cantor from Smyrna and a conniver versed in fakery, knowing well how to delude the people with his works of sorcery... Once he sat upon a table and said, "I have

display of such capabilities was similarly attributed to both men and women, although in men it would have been perceived by the believers as the exercise of powers traditionally associated with *ba'alei shem* (masters of the [divine] name) and other practitioners of esoteric kabbalah, while in women—who are mentioned far less frequently in this context—it must have registered as miraculous in itself.

A further connotation accrued to the prophetic title in the years that followed the messiah's death: prophets who were active during this period, experiencing visions of the oft-delayed redemption, sometimes emerged as messianic figures in their own right. They were viewed as new incarnations of the messianic soul—Sabbatai Zevi's heirs or surrogates—and were expected to bring to successful conclusion the messianic project he had begun. An outstanding example is Abraham Cardozo, who began prophesying even before Sabbatai Zevi was proclaimed messiah,[106] and later became one of the most prominent exponents of Sabbatian kabbalah. His doctrines were inspired and regularly confirmed by the prophetic visions that continued to visit him right up to the end of his life, and in this respect he remained a prophet in the classical sense of the term. At a certain stage, however, he began to identify personally with Messiah son of Ephraim, who was to accomplish what had been withheld from Messiah son of David—Sabbatai Zevi.[107] As Messiah son of Ephraim, revealed after the death of Messiah son of David (contrary to the ancient tradition whereby Messiah son of Ephraim or of Joseph would appear first and die in battle, paving the way for the final advent of Messiah son of

heard, and my innards are inflamed", and he stood up in great agitation, so as to deceive those who were with him, or to make them think that he had been visited by prophecy and believe in him. He walked around the room with a fireball following after him. Then he turned towards the people who were standing around him and proclaimed, "The Master is King! The Master is King! The Master will reign forever!" The fireball moved from its place and came to rest upon his chest, and the four-letter name of God appeared upon him.… And people believed that he was a prophet, and that he performed such miracles and wonders by virtue of the holy spirit which prevailed upon him' (Emden, *Zot torat hakena'ot*, 55). For an analysis of the convergence of prophecy and magic in Sabbatianism, and its sources in earlier strands of kabbalah, see Idel, 'On Prophecy and Magic', esp. 36–47.

[106] In a letter to his brother Isaac, as transcribed by Jacob Sasportas, Cardozo relates: 'In the year 5424 [1664] I was told from heaven that in the year 5425 [1665], a little after the middle of the year, the King Messiah would be revealed' (Sasportas, *Tsitsat novel tsevi*, 289).

[107] On Cardozo's messianic consciousness see Wolfson, 'Constructions of the Shekhinah'; and Elqayam, 'The Absent Messiah' (Heb.). See also n. 109 below.

David[108]), Cardozo believed that he was destined to complete the abortive mission of his predecessor and bring about the redemption in Nisan 5442 (the spring of 1682). It would seem that he confided the secret of his messiahship to some of his disciples (though he denied it at the end of his life),[109] and there is no doubt that his promise of the redemption became the focus of excited anticipation. That Cardozo's personal messianic status was gaining wider recognition at this time is suggested by the fact that in Tevet 5442 (December 1681/January 1682), when expectations of the redemption were reaching their peak, Sabbatai Zevi's widow approached him with the proposal, pregnant with messianic promise, that he should marry her, as she claimed, at the behest of her deceased husband. Cardozo related this in a letter to his disciples written many years after the event, probably in 5461 (1701):

And as if that were not enough, shortly before his death, he [Sabbatai Zevi] told his wife that she must seek me out and tell me secret things that would be a sign for me to take her as my wife. This was told to me, and I arose from Rodosto to go to Constantinople. Three days later, she came to Rodosto with Joseph Karillo and a woman who waited upon her. When she did not find me there, she wept and sent a messenger to me in Constantinople, asking me to permit her to come there and tell me all that the messiah had commanded her, or to come myself to Rodosto to hear it from her, for these were things upon which the advent of the redemption depended.[110]

Neither the meeting nor the marriage ever took place, but the very proposal of such a union with Cardozo, and its presentation as the command of the dying messiah, as well as the widow's promise to reveal, in the name of Sabbatai Zevi, 'secret things' upon which the advent of the final redemption depended, imply recognition of Cardozo as the messiah's heir. Meir Benayahu surmises[111] that it was this event that prompted Cardozo to propose, in his *Derush kodesh yisra'el lashem* (the homily on 'Israel was holy to the Lord'), which was written during the very same period, the extraordinary possibility that the advent of the redemption would be heralded by a woman. Cardozo incorporates this idea in his discussion of the roles played by the two Messiahs, son of Ephraim and son of David, whose complex interrelationship stems from their origins in different kabbalistic *sefirot*, a concept which, in itself,

---

[108] See e.g. BT *Suk.* 52*a*; Even-Shemuel, *Midrashim of Redemption* (Heb.), 57–142.

[109] See Scholem, 'Cardozo' (Heb.), and Liebes, 'Michael Cardozo' (Heb.), 43–4.

[110] Molkho and Amarillo, 'Autobiographical Letters' (Heb.), 200–1.

[111] Benayahu, 'Great Apostasy' (Heb.), 80–1.

reflects Cardozo's ambivalent attitude towards Sabbatai Zevi.[112] In the course of the discussion, he invokes the symbol of the four sources of 'the river that goes forth from Eden', derived from a verse (Gen. 2: 10) which features in the Zohar as a key phrase alluding to the flow of the creative divine influx.[113] Cardozo identifies the four sources of the river with four distinct messianic figures:[114] son of David, son of Ephraim, Moses, and 'the fourth herald, who is Elijah, but there is some doubt as to whether the redemption will be proclaimed by him or by a woman, the "[female] herald of good tidings to Zion" [*mevaseret tsiyon*]'.[115] Scholem, who edited and published the homily, noted the oddity and distinctiveness of this statement:

This veiled hint . . . that Elijah's role of proclaiming the redemption will be assigned to *a woman*, who is called by the symbolic name of the 'herald of good tidings to Zion', is unprecedented in the messianic doctrine. . . . This is the first allusion of which I am aware in Sabbatian literature to the fulfilment of such a role by a woman, an idea that was to resurface and gain importance in Frankist doctrine a century later.[116]

Benayahu conjectures that this possibility took shape in Cardozo's mind in response to the promise of Sabbatai Zevi's widow that by marrying her and being apprised of the secrets in her possession, he would be able to fulfil his

---

[112] On the relations between the two see Scholem, *Researches* (Heb.), 427, and Liebes, *On Sabbatianism* (Heb.), 43–4.

[113] See on this, Melila Hellner-Eshed, *A River Issues* (Heb.), 268–96; ead., 'A River' (Heb.).

[114] In some of his esoteric writings, the 18th-century Italian kabbalist Moses Hayim Luzzatto (Ramhal) employed precisely the same symbol in discerning four distinct messianic figures, by contrast with the messianic triad that more commonly features in his work. It is not impossible that he drew both the idea and the symbol from Cardozo's homily, of whose influence on him in other respects there is very little doubt. For a discussion of Luzzatto's use of the symbol of the four sources of the river in this context, see Tishby, *Messianic Mysticism*, 203–4, 255. For the influence of Cardozo's writings on Luzzatto, see ibid. 76–9, 471 n. 58).

[115] Scholem, *Researches* (Heb.), 449. See also Cardozo, *Selected Writings*, 249–51, 264–6. The expression *mevaseret tsiyon* is drawn from Isaiah 40: 9: 'Get you up to a mountain, O herald of good tidings to Zion; lift up your voice with strength, O herald of good tidings to Jerusalem', but Cardozo's source must be the exposition of this verse, itself probably influenced by *Sefer zerubavel* (on which see below, n. 118), in Zohar, iii. 173*b*: '"Get you up to a mountain, O herald of good tidings to Zion" etc. . . . "Herald of good tidings to Zion"—this is Heftsi-bah, wife of Nathan, son of David, mother of the messiah Menahem, son of Ami'el; she will go out and herald, and she is included in the "herald of good tidings to Zion".' This zoharic passage features in Nacht, *Symbolism* (Heb.), 206. I am grateful to Prof. Zeev Gries for these references.

[116] Scholem, *Researches* (Heb.), 427. Emphasis in original.

messianic ambition. He thus developed the notion that the woman who had been the wife of the deceased Messiah son of David (Sabbatai Zevi), and who was now to marry the living Messiah son of Ephraim (Cardozo himself), was the one who might be destined to proclaim her husband the final redeemer, and thus to trigger the advent of the redemption.

The substitution of Elijah the Prophet, Judaism's quintessential herald of redemption,[117] with a female heraldic figure, as surprising and unprecedented as this may be in the long tradition of Jewish messianic speculation,[118] accords well with the inner logic of Cardozo's complex homily, which attributes distinct sefirotic values to each of the four messianic figures it features. The fourth figure, that of the female herald, fittingly symbolizes the feminine *sefirah* Malkhut (Sovereignty), which was, in fact, identified with several wives of the Sabbatian messiahs, who had each been given symbolic kabbalistic names alluding to the divine female.[119] If Benayahu's conjecture is correct, it

[117] The role of Elijah as herald of the redemption derives from Mal. 4: 5 (3: 23 in the Hebrew Bible): 'Behold, I will send you Elijah the prophet before the coming of the great and dreadful day of the Lord.' This verse serves as the point of departure for an array of legendary traditions. See e.g. *Pesikta rabati*, 35, end; and see Even-Shemuel, *Midrashim of Redemption* (Heb.), 29–54, and J. Klausner, *Messianic Idea*, 451–7.

[118] An exception to this rule is Heftsi-bah, the mother of Menahem b. Ami'el, who is the Messiah son of David. According to *Sefer zerubavel*, she does battle with the enemies of God and kills them with the 'staff of salvation' that she received from Nehemiah b. Hushiel—who is the Messiah son of Joseph. See *Sefer zerubavel*, 71–88. This female messianic figure is unparalleled in the Jewish apocalyptic tradition, and most scholars are inclined to think that its origin lies in Christian traditions (though Israel Knohl proposes that the messianic figure of Menahem b. Ami'el, which occurs in the talmudic and midrashic sources, may derive from the period of the Second Temple; see his 'The Friend of the King' (Heb.), 258, and especially *The Messiah*). She is rarely mentioned again in later literature (but see n. 115 above for the reference to her in the Zohar). On *Sefer zerubavel* see e.g. Speck, 'Apocalypse of Zerubbabel', and Dan, 'Armilus'.

[119] On this see below, at the beginning of Ch. 7. The surprising presence in this homily of a feminine redemptive figure identified with the feminine *sefirah* of Malkhut–Shekhinah may belong in the kabbalistic context of the intensification of the feminine powers in the messianic era, expressed at its height in the rise of this *sefirah* from the bottom to the top of the sefirotic hierarchy. This eschatological inversion of the gender hierarchy has been presented as one of the central themes in Cardozo's thought, which—including the explicit parallel he draws between Malkhut–Shekhinah in Judaism and Mary, the mother of Jesus, in Christianity—was clearly influenced by the Mariological tradition that was part of his Catholic–Converso heritage. See Wolfson, 'Constructions of the Shekhinah', 29 ff.

would seem that the messianic and the prophetic vocations were intertwined in the consciousness of Cardozo, not only in regard to his own status as one who was both the prophet of the redemption and the redeemer who would bring it about, but also in regard to his messianic spouse, who was destined to become its herald.

This dual status of prophet-cum-messiah was by no means unique to Cardozo. It can be discerned in other Sabbatian prophet-messiahs, including some who, unlike Cardozo, believed also that they were elevated to the point of being incorporated in the divinity itself, or who were taken to be no less than the flesh-and-blood incarnations of the divine. One of the latter was Berukhyah, head of the apostate Sabbatian community in Salonica, who appeared as a prophet and was acknowledged as the messiah 'in whom the divinity has garbed itself'. He is described in the Doenmeh tradition as being simultaneously 'a messiah and a prophet',[120] and his son, too, was made out to be 'a prophet and Messiah son of Joseph'.[121] The same was said of the Sabbatian prophet Mordecai of Eisenstadt, who began prophesying in Prague in the heyday of Sabbatai Zevi, but after the latter's death, came to view himself, while also being seen by others, as Messiah son of Ephraim, or Messiah son of David, or both.[122] Similarly, Leibele Prossnitz was a Sabbatian prophet who claimed the title of Messiah son of Joseph,[123] and according to one account, he saw himself as the son of Joseph, while ascribing to Jonathan Eybeschuetz the title of son of David.[124] Wolf Eybeschuetz, too, the younger son of Jonathan Eybeschuetz—himself a leading rabbinic and kabbalistic authority, who was suspected of involvement in the messianic heresy—was presented by his father, and viewed by others, as both a prophet possessed of the holy spirit and the messiah in whom the redemption would be fulfilled.[125]

[120] See Scholem, *Researches* (Heb.), 335, 340, and Rosanes, *History of the Jews in Turkey* (Heb.), 469. [121] Scholem, *Researches* (Heb.), 378.

[122] Ibid. 536–8, 544–54, and the bibliographical appendix by Yehuda Liebes on p. 562.

[123] Emden, *Zot torat hakena'ot*, 71–2, 81. On Leibele Prossnitz see also Liebes, *On Sabbatianism* (Heb.), 70–6.

[124] On this see Liebes, *On Sabbatianism* (Heb.), 333 n. 3. On the messianic status of Jonathan Eybeschuetz in his own view and that of others see also Emden, *Akitsat akrav*, 7b–8a.

[125] See the account of Jacob Emden in *Sefer hitabekut*, 19b–20a, 24b. On Wolf Eybeschuetz see Liebes, *On Sabbatianism* (Heb.), 77–102, 137–97. For a discussion of the messianic consciousness of Jonathan Eybeschuetz and his son see esp. pp. 83–6.

Even the famous kabbalist and prophet Heshel Tsoref, who remained a pious Jew all his life and concealed his Sabbatian leanings, clandestinely identified himself with Messiah son of Joseph.[126]

This blurring of the boundaries between prophecy, messiahship, and divinity would seem to be a natural cognitive progression, capable of reasserting itself time and again in the context of mystical messianism.[127] We have even witnessed it in our own time, in the eruption of high messianic tension within the Habad-Lubavitch hasidic community, where it centred on the figure of its charismatic leader, the late Menachem Mendel Schneerson.[128] What distinguishes Cardozo's position, however, and makes it effectively unique, is the apparent projection of the same dynamics—albeit in a single and rather surprising sentence—onto a female figure. To be sure, this sentence might be seen as no more than a singular, eccentric deviation from conventional patterns of thought, but it might also be viewed as a milestone along the path that leads from Sabbatai Zevi's special message for women at the outset of the messianic movement, to what ultimately turned, as Scholem observed, into the cult of

[126] On him see Scholem, *Studies and Texts* (Heb.), 84–96; id., *Researches* (Heb.), 591–9, and ibid., the bibliographical appendix by Liebes; and Scholem, *Kabbalah*, 452–3. In contradistinction to all these, see Elqayam's insightful observation ('The Absent Messiah' (Heb.), 34–5) that Nathan of Gaza rejected the possibility of claiming for himself the status of Messiah son of Joseph, while nevertheless replicating the binary structure of the messianic figure, by construing himself—the messianic prophet—as a complementary counterpart of the messiah—Sabbatai Zevi—which can be seen as an alternative to the traditional split between Messiah son of Joseph and Messiah son of David.

[127] Abraham Abulafia's prophetic–messianic consciousness is a prime example of this, as is the integration of prophetic insight and personal identification with Messiah son of Joseph in both Isaac Luria and Hayim Vital. This blurring of boundaries is discernible also in Nahman of Bratslav's perception of himself as the herald of the messiah, the father of the messiah, and even, apparently, as the messiah himself, although the exploration of this theme lies beyond the scope of the present discussion. See, however, Moshe Idel's analysis of the relationship between prophecy and messianism in *Messianic Mystics*, 61–5, 295–307. See also Dan (*On Sanctity* (Heb.), 448–51), who sets this phenomenon in the context of the rise in the early modern period of a group of mystical leaders who integrated the elements of prophecy, messianism, and divinity into a new concept of earthly leadership. On similar processes that transpired, around the same time, among the European heretics of the 'free spirit', see Cohn, *Pursuit of the Millennium*, 172–6; and in the context of the charismatic leadership of the schismatic sectarians of the Russian Orthodox Church, see Scholem, *Researches* (Heb.), 105–6. For more on these sects in relation to the prophetic–messianic–divine status of Jacob Frank, see below, Ch. 8, at nn. 33–7.

[128] See e.g. Elior, 'The Lubavitch Messianic Resurgence', 397–8.

the redemptive messianic Virgin in the circle of believers surrounding Eva Frank (on which see further below, in Chapters 5 and 7 respectively). An inkling that Cardozo's notion of the redemptive 'female herald' was not merely the passing flicker of an idea, but rather the articulation, however hesitant, of a principle that was to be carried forward (though not necessarily in a straight or consistently central line of thought), appears in a poem composed in Ladino by a member of Berukhyah's apostate circle in Salonica, apparently in the 1720s, towards the end of his life:

> *Por mano de la seniora, mandamos buena besora*
> (By the hand of the Lady he has sent us good tidings.)[129]

Isaac Ben-Zvi, who prepared the critical edition of this text, notes: 'This evidently refers to Berukhyah's wife, whose status within the Salonican sect was similar to that of Eva Frank in Offenbach.'[130] Indeed, it is known that Berukhyah's wife was called the Lady in his circle, and their daughter (or possibly their granddaughter) was known as the holy Maiden and the Matronita (alluding to the *sefirah* of Malkhut),[131] just as Eva, Frank's daughter, was known as the holy Virgin and, after her mother's death in 1770, was bequeathed her mother's title of the Lady.[132] There is no doubt that these titles were charged with messianic connotations; they reflect a bisexual conceptualization of the redeemer, opening up the way for the 'heraldic' women who bore them to become the objects of redemptive hopes, and we shall return to this subject further on.

Women began prophesying with the inception of the Sabbatian movement, and they continued to do so right up to its demise. As we have seen,

---

[129] Ben-Zvi, 'Kabbalistic Tracts from Berukhia's Circle' (Heb.), 372.   [130] Ibid., n. 101.

[131] See Emden, *Sefer hitabekut*, 35a. See also Scholem's discussion in *Researches* (Heb.), 378–80.

[132] According to Moses Porges' memoir of his stay in Offenbach at the end of the 1790s, upon Jacob Frank's death, the leadership of the believers was transferred to his daughter Eva, who was known by the title of the Lady (*Gevira* in Hebrew), as Porges indeed refers to her throughout the memoir, offering the Hebrew term in transliteration. See Porges, 'Memoirs of Moses Porges', trans. Gelber, e.g. col. 267, corresponding to the second column on p. 121 of the German edition ('Eine Wallfahrt'), and col. 268, corresponding to the first column on p. 122 of the German edition. It would seem that Frank had originally bestowed this title upon his wife and, after her death, upon his daughter (who previously had been known as the Virgin). See Scholem, *Researches* (Heb.), 644–9, and see further below, Ch. 7, at nn. 28–34.

their prophetic activity was manifested in virtually all the forms that marked the experience of Sabbatian prophecy as a whole: fits of ecstatic frenzy that were wiped from the memory as soon as they were over; receipt of pertinent messages from a range of other-worldly figures; the ability to work magic; and, finally, incorporation in the messianic personality itself (with the exception, apparently, of the enunciation of original, coherent, kabbalistic messianic teachings, for which, at any rate, there is no trace of literary evidence). The continuity and breadth of this phenomenon demonstrate that it was an essential feature of Sabbatianism and not merely a matter of incidental circumstance. Moreover, the unqualified acknowledgement of women's prophetic power—perceived as marking the dawn of the messianic age—bore within it a re-evaluation of the nature and status of the female in relation to the male, and this enabled the female prophets of Sabbatianism to acquire positions of authority. Admittedly, the limited and problematic evidence for this, as surveyed above, does not enable us to document the phenomenon fully, but it suffices to establish the unprecedented character of this development in the history of Jewish messianism.

TWO

Historical Precedents and Contexts

THE RABBINIC TRADITION inherited from Scripture four women who were called by the title of prophetess: Miriam, Deborah, Huldah, and Noadiah.[1] While the Bible itself recognizes the phenomenon of the prophetess without pondering its validity (at least not expressly, but we shall leave that issue aside), rabbinic literature views it as problematic. The status of the Bible's prophetesses conflicts with the Sages' fundamental exclusion of women from public activity and from positions of ritual, spiritual, or scholarly leadership.[2] To be sure, the classical rabbinic sources increased to seven the number of biblical prophetesses known by name, and they certainly acknowledged the authenticity of their prophetic powers. However, they tended simultaneously to deprecate their character by means of an exegesis that cast aspersions on their moral integrity, or put them in their proper place—in the shadow of their husbands.[3] This sense of discomfort with female prophets also came to

[1] See Exod. 15: 20; Jud. 4: 4; 2 Kgs 22: 14; and Neh. 6: 14. Also mentioned is the unnamed prophetess to whom Isaiah 'went' and who subsequently bore the son named 'Maher-shalal-hash-baz' (Isa. 8: 3). In the context, she may well have been no more than a prophet's wife.

[2] The literature on this subject is constantly growing. Much of it serves the causes of Orthodox apologetics on the one hand, and of feminist polemic or creative reinterpretation on the other. For discussions of the status of women from a historical point of view see e.g. Azmon, *Women in Jewish Societies* (Heb.); the articles in the first section consider the attitudes of the Sages towards public activity by women.

[3] See e.g. BT *Meg.* 14*a*–15*a*. For a short discussion of the Sages' interpretations of the phenomenon of biblical prophetesses see Kuzmack, 'Aggadic Approaches', 259–61. For a large and varied selection of rabbinic traditions on these prophetesses see Ginzberg, *Legends of the Jews*, following the relevant entries in the index. And see, more recently, Levine Katz, 'Seven Prophetesses' (Heb.), 123–30, which discusses the body of midrashic traditions on the biblical prophetesses and traces the kabbalistic tradition that identifies them with the seven lower *sefirot*. Levine Katz pinpoints the beginning of this tradition in the commentary of Bahya ibn Pakuda on the Torah. Although Bahya extols the spiritual and theological gifts of the prophetesses, his very effort to explain the phenomenon of prophecy in women attests to his

expression in later traditions, though attestations of the phenomenon are extremely rare and rather obscure.

Prophecy as such, and not only by women, was problematic, since according to rabbinic tradition, it had ceased with the demise of the last of the minor biblical prophets, near the time of the destruction of the Second Temple.[4] Nevertheless, messianic hopes, erupting in different places, under differing circumstances and at different times, were instrumental in stirring the resurgence of prophecy, and they were even able temporarily to endow it with renewed legitimacy. Admittedly, the traditional disapproval of all attempts to calculate the time of the redemption or to hasten it also constrained the willingness of the faithful to credit the truth of messianic prophecies. *Sefer ḥasidim*, for example, rejects in principle the possibility of post-biblical prophecy and sees any redemptive tidings as ill-starred, though it preserves in passing a rumour of women who prophesied consolation 'in the Land of Canaan'[5]—no doubt a muted echo of the messianic awakening that occurred in response to the Mongol conquests in Europe and the Middle East in the thirteenth century. The book's principal aim in the following passage was to dismiss the augury of redemption, whether it was borne by men or by women:

If you should see someone prophesying about the messiah, know that he is dealing in sorcery or divination of demonic spirits . . . And there were women in the land of Canaan who recited all the consolations of Isaiah, and the ignorant folk knew by heart all these consolations, but they will be the cause of a harsh persecution, for no man knows of the coming of the messiah.[6]

consciousness of its problematic nature: 'And as for how prophecy can rest upon a woman, it seems to me that this is no cause for wonder; for after all, she belongs to the human race [*min ha'adam*], and she is explicitly named human [*adam*], as we learn in the verse: "And [He] named them [i.e. male and female] *adam*" [Gen. 5: 2].' And further: 'You will find that great theological principles of the Torah are expounded by women, like the World to Come, which is called "the bundle of the living", by Abigail [1 Sam. 25: 29]; the resurrection of the dead and the modes of supplication, by Hannah [1 Sam. 1]; and the transmigration of souls, by the woman of Tekoa [2 Sam. 14]; and all this shows that woman is not an entirely subsidiary thing, but she has [spiritual] substance' (quoted in Levine Katz, 'Seven Prophetesses' (Heb.), 124).

[4] See BT *Yoma* 9a; BT *BB* 12a. On this tradition and the exceptions to it see Urbach, *The Sages*, 577–9.

[5] This designation refers to the Slavic lands, and in particular, in the period when *Sefer ḥasidim* was composed, to the regions of Bohemia-Moravia and Slovakia. See Jakobson and Halle, 'The Term *Canaan*'.   [6] *Sefer ḥasidim*, 76–7, §212.

On the other hand, it did happen that prophesies of a coming redemption gained public recognition and were capable of generating messianic ferment, at least for a time and on a local basis. Very occasionally, such tidings would be borne by women.

Thus, for example, we learn from a document recovered from the Cairo Genizah of the expectations of redemption among the Jews of Baghdad in 1120–1, which centred on a girl, 'daughter of Joseph, the doctor's son'. It was told of her that she 'declared that she had seen Elijah, peace be upon him, of blessed memory, in a dream, saying to her: "Go down to these people and tell them in my name that God, may he be exalted, has already drawn nigh the deliverance."' These tidings seem to have stirred excited activity within the local community. When word of it reached the non-Jews, 'the Caliph snickered and guffawed, and said: "The intelligence of the Jews has surely deteriorated if they trust the wit of a woman. Tomorrow I'll have the woman burnt, and I'll permit the blood of the Jews."' But then Elijah the Prophet appeared to the Caliph himself, and he cancelled his decree in fright.[7]

The document has not survived in its entirety, and several parts are missing, leaving its precise meaning and context in some doubt. However, one interesting detail that was preserved points to a connection—perhaps fundamental—between this affair and the handful of extant references to Jewish women endowed with extraordinary spiritual powers, which belong to literary traditions and historical circumstances that are quite remote from the girl in Baghdad:

They saw that the girl behaved like her father, [continuously occupied with] fasting, prayer, and charity. A marriage was proposed to her, but she refused it, saying: 'I will not change my ways; for marriage would distract me from these things.' Then our lord

[7] The original document is in Judaeo-Arabic. It was first published and translated into Hebrew by S. D. Goitein in 'Messianic Troubles'; the passages quoted here are on pp. 74 and 76. Moshe Gil republished the document in a new Hebrew translation, incorporating several minor corrections, which is the basis of the English translation of the excerpts quoted here. See Gil, 'In the Kingdom of Ishmael' (Heb.), i. 419–20 (discussion) and ii. 228–34 (text); the excerpts are from vol. ii, pp. 229–30 and 233. Gil differed with Goitein regarding the nature of the event described in the document: Goitein saw it as a messianic awakening, while Gil sets it in the context of the deliverance of the Jews from a cruel local edict. This disagreement has little bearing on the issue at hand, as will presently become clear. I am grateful to Prof. Daniel Frank for bringing Gil's publication of the document to my attention.

Daniel, may God preserve him, son of our lord Hasdai, may the memory of the righteous be a blessing, intervened in the matrimonial negotiations and married her off.[8]

The girl prophet, given to fasting, praying, and charitable works, had adopted a pious, ascetic way of life such as a man might do, and accordingly preferred celibacy to marriage. She explicitly recognized the role of her celibacy in advancing her spiritual activity. It was surely a factor in her ability to prophesy, and was seen as such by others as well. But this type of behaviour was intolerable in a woman, and so the girl was constrained to marry, as a result of the intervention—apparently at the request of her family—of a leading male member of the community. She remained with her husband 'for a few months, until the month of Elul', but then she seems to have withdrawn from him to 'go down' to the people and continue to preach redemption.[9]

Now, this is exactly what is related of the hasidic 'Maid of Ludmir', who was also noted for her ascetic way of life, her celibacy, and her remarkable intellectual and spiritual capacities. She too, and for similar reasons, spurned the wedded state but had it foisted upon her by the most prominent male hasidic leader in her vicinity, and this, in spite of her refusal to consummate the marriage, apparently put an end to her charismatic leadership.[10] In the same vein, an early nineteenth century tradition emanating from the circle of the chief opponent of hasidism, Elijah the Gaon of Vilna, also relates: 'There was a virgin who performed wonders, said great things, and learned the Zohar and other profound mystical matters with scholars. The Gaon, Rabbi Elijah of Vilna, of blessed memory, said that the spirit would desist from her when she married, and so it was.'[11]

To be sure, these traditions cannot be taken as verifiable historical evidence, but they may be seen as reflecting an authentic and near-universal sensibility. However widely disparate their provenances and historical settings, they give expression to precisely the same sense that ascetic piety and sexual abstinence—traditionally acknowledged by Jewish society as the means to

---

[8] Gil, 'In the Kingdom of Ishmael' (Heb.), 229–30; cf. Goitein, 'Messianic Troubles', 73.

[9] Gil, 'In the Kingdom of Ishmael' (Heb.), 229–30. The matter of her staying with her husband for a certain period and then 'going down' from him is not altogether clear.

[10] For a summary of the tradition of her life story, see Rapoport-Albert, 'On Women in Hasidism', and appendix 4 to the expanded Hebrew version of the same article. For a full study, see Deutsch, *The Maiden of Ludmir*.

[11] Asher Hakohen, 'Keter rosh' ('All this was recorded for posterity here, in the holy community of Volozhin, may God protect it, in the year 1819'), 29.

spiritual enhancement and a mark of holiness in men (or at least in some men)—are to be repudiated as a perversion and suppressed when it comes to women who seek in this way to exercise their spiritual powers. In every such instance, the most authoritative man in the vicinity is called upon to act, and he solves what is clearly perceived as a problem by forcing the woman to marry. This solution is simple and effective. The woman's connection to the supernal worlds and the spiritual forces emanating from them had been purchased at the price of muting her sexuality and suppressing her bodily needs. That connection would wither away with her entry into the framework of marriage, which defines her by way of her sexuality, and imposes upon her the myriad of mundane burdens that 'distract' her from inappropriate and undesirable spiritual preoccupations. Against this background, the full legitimization of women's prophecy in Sabbatianism is quite remarkable, as will be shown below.

Further surviving accounts of messianic prophecies by women, prior to the outbreak of mass prophecy in the Sabbatian movement, are few in number and rather obscure. Another document from the Cairo Genizah gives an account of a redemptive prophecy espoused, in an uncertain historical context, by an anonymous woman in Sicily. The time and circumstances of her prophecy are a subject of debate: some scholars have placed it in the twelfth century, others in the thirteenth, fifteenth, or sixteenth century.[12] This time the woman in question was married and even pregnant, but 'the nine months had passed, [and she had not yet given birth]'. Instead,

she lay in fear and trembling, and she thrust forth her left hand . . . and bore. On that hand appeared the image of a man, and from it dripped [something like] saffron, and all of us who were standing there partook and tasted thereof, and the taste of it was like the taste of fresh oil [cf. Num. 11: 8], and it had a pleasing smell, like pure myrrh [cf. Exod. 30: 23].

---

[12] The document was first published, with an introduction and explanatory notes, by Jacob Mann in 'Messianic Excitement'. A. Z. Aescoly republished it in his *Jewish Messianic Movements* (Heb.), 286–9, with references to discussions by other scholars (ibid. 289). His introduction, and the supplementary notes by Y. Even-Shemuel, who prepared the book for press, summarize their divergent views on the nature and provenance of the document (ibid. 240–7). For a more recent edition, and a 15th-century dating, see, Zeldes, 'A Magical Event' (Heb.). See also Palermo, 'The Settlement' (Heb.), 127–33, who proposes a 16th-century date, and Bowman, 'Messianic Expectations'.

The woman's fingers, too, 'flowed with something like oil, and her husband took [of it] and gave some to each, and we ate, and it had the taste of honey and the smell of pure myrrh'. The woman asked to be covered with prayer shawls, and these immediately were marked by combinations of letters. At the conclusion of this 'birth', she prayed: 'Hear O Israel, the Lord our God, the Lord is One [Deut. 6: 4], God long-suffering and abundant in goodness [and truth; cf. Exod. 34: 6] . . . [and afterward] she raised her hands [as do] the priests [when they rise to bless the congregation], and blood rose up on the prayer shawl.' The content of her prophecy was as follows:

'Woe to the wicked, and woe to those who do not repent, for thus did the Holy One swear to me before the angels and before Moses, that the end is nigh, and if the wicked do not repent, many will die by the sword, by starvation, and by religious persecution. But if they repent, they will be spared, for My salvation is near at hand. And him that I did eat . . . will the Holy One, Blessed be He, give to Isra[el].' And she said to us, 'Go to the synagogue [and say the] prayers', and we went and prayed.

Following her prophecy, others, too, had visions of 'a fire that entered the synagogue' and 'an angel with [a sword in his hand, and in] his other [hand] a great fire'. Soon afterwards, her pronouncements were buttressed by tidings brought to the island by 'a foreigner from Morea'[13] about messianic ferment that had broken out in other places, upon the appearance of 'those who were concealed'—the ten lost tribes—who were threatening to vanquish 'the king of Spain, the king of Germany, the king of Hungary, and the king of France'. The account is broken by several indecipherable passages, some of which were reconstructed by J. Mann. It is full of oddities, including the description of the peculiar 'parturition' by which the woman becomes the 'mother' of the messiah, and the ingestion of the wondrous flesh of the messianic 'image of a man', which evokes Christian associations upon which we shall not dwell in the present context. It also contains several details reminiscent of the descriptions we have already encountered in the wondrous visions and deeds of the Sabbatian prophetesses, such as the ability to emit or impart to others a goodly smell from a heavenly source, lifting the hands in the manner of the priests, and blood dripping out of the air.[14] But these motifs all derive from ancient literary traditions, so that we cannot draw conclusions from their appearance here regarding a possible historical continuity between the phenomenon of

[13] The name given by the Venetians to the Peloponnese region of southern Greece.
[14] See Ch. 1, at nn. 22–3.

female prophecy in Sabbatianism and the event described in this bizarre document of uncertain provenance.

On the other hand, there does seem to be a relationship of historical continuity between the Sabbatian outbreak of prophecy by women in the second half of the seventeenth century, and the many accounts appearing in Hayim Vital's autobiographical work, *Sefer ḥaḥezyonot* (Book of Visions), of the messianic visions and magical practices of women in the communities of Safed, Jerusalem, and Damascus in the second half of the sixteenth and the early seventeenth centuries.[15] Vital describes women's prophetic visions and dreams alongside those of men, including his own. He is equally attentive to all of them—as they almost all revolve around himself and his exalted messianic status—and has no doubt of their credibility. It would seem that women, whether married or not, were viewed in his milieu as no less capable than men of seeing true visions. In fact, certain types of prophetic activity, such as foretelling the future by means of 'oil-drop divining', which Vital attributes primarily to women, evidently were seen in that milieu as women's special province. Thus, for example, he records:

The same year.[16] I saw a woman who was an expert in divining by dropping oil into water and she said to me: I was very frightened by what I saw in this oil—you will undoubtedly rule over all of Israel in the future. . . . I never saw anyone, in my practice of oil divination, on such a high level in this whole generation.[17]

---

[15] I am grateful to Dr Ronit Meroz for first drawing my attention to these accounts and allowing me to read the chapter of her work in progress, 'Isaac Luria and Hayim Vital—A Biography' (Heb.), which discusses this phenomenon. Joseph Chajes devoted a penetrating and exhaustive discussion to the same subject in a chapter of his doctoral dissertation, which reached me only after I had penned the discussion in the following paragraphs, and whose conclusions accord largely with my own. Chajes places the women whose 'magical–mystical' activity is described in *Sefer ḥaḥezyonot* within their cultural and comparative context, and supplies numerous bibliographical references to scholarly studies treating women's activities of this kind from several disciplinary perspectives. See Chajes, 'Spirit Possession', 198–244, and *Between Worlds*, 97–118, as well as his 'City of the Dead'. An annotated English translation of Vital's *Sefer ḥaḥezyonot*, 'Book of Visions', appears in Faierstein, *Jewish Mystical Autobiographies*, pp. 43–263. With some modifications, all excerpted citations from the work follow this English edition.

[16] Going by the book's immediately preceding section, this refers to the year 5325 (1565), when Vital was living in Safed.

[17] Vital, 'Book of Visions', 44 (*Sefer ḥaḥezyonot*, pt. 1, §5). The practice of divining in oil described here seems related to the magical practice of divining the 'spirits of oil' or the 'spirits of eggs', mentioned already in the Talmud (BT *San.* 101*a*) and widespread in different variations

Further on, he describes how, about five years later, he again had recourse to the services of a Safed woman endowed with similar powers:

In the year 5330 [1570] there was a wise woman who foretold the future and was also expert in oil-drop divination. She was called Soniadora.[18] I asked her to cast a spell over the oil, as was customary, concerning my comprehension of kabbalistic wisdom. She did not know what to answer me until she assumed a "spirit of jealousy" [Num. 5: 30], which strengthened her incantations. She stood up, kissed my feet, and said:

Forgive me that I did not recognize the greatness of your soul—the importance of your soul is not that of the sages of this generation, but that of the generation of the early *Tannaim*, according to what I saw in this oil.

In response to your question, I was shown in the oil the following, written in square letters: Concerning this man who asks, the Talmudic Sages z"l [of blessed memory] gave an analogy through the parable mentioned in *Midrash Song of Songs* concerning King Solomon a"h [peace be upon him]: "Very sweet waters bubble forth from a very deep well. Nobody knows how to draw the waters up until an intelligent person comes and ties together several ropes and descends to drink."[19] You have a desire and thirst to know a discipline called *Kabbalah* and you are asking about it; know that you will comprehend, as in the parable about King Solomon mentioned above, that which none of the scholars who preceded you were able to comprehend. A great sage will come this year to Safed from the south, e.g., from Egypt, and he will teach you this wisdom.

So it was, for in that year my teacher z"l [i.e. Isaac Luria] came from Egypt.[20]

The woman described as 'wise' can read square letters, cites the Midrash on the Song of Songs, reveals to Vital the supernal root of his soul, and correctly predicts Luria's arrival from Egypt and the consequent progress made by his student Vital in the attainment of kabbalistic wisdom.

In the Damascus community, where Vital spent the last twenty-two years of his life and clashed with Jacob Abulafia, rabbi of the city's Sephardi community,[21] he also encountered women endowed with similar gifts. In an entry for the new moon of Elul 5369 (1609), he describes at length his visit with 'the

('cup spirits', 'thumb spirits', 'mirror spirits', etc., all of which were otherworldly entities that appeared on the shiny surface of the oil, the water, or the polished mirror, and showed the diviner portents of the future while also being harnessed to his or her service) among both Jews and non-Jews. See Dan, 'Archons of the Cup' (Heb.), 34–43; Trachtenberg, *Jewish Magic*, 218–22; Daiches, 'Babylonian Oil Magic'.

[18] Female dreamer in Spanish.

[19] Cf. *S. of S. Rabbah*, I: 8.

[20] Vital, 'Book of Visions', 44–5 (*Sefer haḥezyonot*, pt. 1, §6).

[21] See ibid. 121 (pt. 3, §16).

sister of Rabbi S. Hayati, [who] was an expert in incantations with drops of oil in a goblet of water':

I asked: Will I succeed in causing the people of Damascus to repent? She responded: It is from God to implant penance in their hearts. Many people will repent, but not all of them, since their source is bitter and the evil inclination has been implanted in their hearts. Nonetheless, it is appropriate to cause them to repent, since it is not my obligation to finish the work. There will be great disputes between the *Mustarabs* [Jews from Arab lands] and the *Sefardim* and they will lose much money....

I asked further: Where is my fortune? She said to me: So long as I am outside the land of Israel or here in Damascus, I will not find any satisfaction, not for my soul, not for my body, and not for my money. If I go to Safed, I shall have many times the satisfaction that I have in Damascus. Indeed, my fortune, in all of its details, exists only in Jerusalem, in my life, in this world and in the World to Come. God, all the souls, and all the angels are angry with me that I am living here. Previously, I lived there, but I left because of the controversies and slander that occurred there. If I had not left, perhaps the redemption would already have come in my days.[22]

Further on, the woman prophesies that Vital will return to Jerusalem and take action to rebuild it 'on the path to redemption' (all of which evidently proved false). However, she could not predict the actual date of the redemption, because 'these spirits'—presumably the spirits of the oil that she had seen in the cup—did not have 'the power to know when it would occur'.[23]

A little more than a week later, on 9 Elul, Vital once more sought the counsel of a woman: 'Mazzal Tov, who divines over drops of oil', and who 'also hears voices speaking to her'. She, too, prophesied that 'all the greatness of my zodiac sign is only in Jerusalem, in all respects—with regard to my complete comprehension of the wisdom, with regard to my livelihood, with regard to power and honour'. She also declared that he would reach the apex of his wisdom at the age of 75 and would die at the age of 89 or 100 (in fact, he died at the age of 78).[24] Although not all their prophecies came true, Vital had complete faith in these women who divined in oil, and their prophetic statements, as he recorded them, reflect their honourable and authoritative status.[25]

[22] Ibid. 143–4 (§53).   [23] Ibid. 144.   [24] Ibid. 145 (§54).

[25] In 'Archons of the Cup' (Heb.), 35–6, Dan cites several examples of oil divining drawn from *Sefer haḥezyonot*. In two of them, Vital attributes this practice to Muslim sorcerers (the third example is the one given above, at n. 18, of 'a wise woman who foretold the future and was also expert in oil-drop divination'). On this basis, Dan hypothesizes that the practitioners of this art 'apparently were non-Jews; however, the Jews did not forbear to approach them'. To be

Apart from descriptions of 'oil divining' and the female seers who practised it, *Sefer haḥezyonot* is full of accounts of women who may not have been professional diviners, but who had prophetic dreams, saw waking visions, and heard other-worldly voices. It is clear that their milieu was so highly charged with messianic tension that it could elicit visionary revelations from anyone, man or woman, whether they practised magical techniques or not. Thus, for example, it is related of Mira, the sister of Rabbi S. Hayati—the same woman who, as we have seen, was skilled at 'incantations with drops of oil in a goblet of water'[26]—that even without recourse to divining, she 'saw in a dream R. Mordecai . . . R. Moses Cordovero, R. David ibn Zimra, and R. Moses Baruch, her husband', all of whom were dead, and she was commanded to tell Vital in their name that 'Until now we have endeavoured to find merit for the inhabitants of this city [Damascus]. Look at the sweat that is pouring from us, which testifies to our exertions. Yet, our prayers are not able to defend them from the abundance of sins that are in its midst.'[27]

Mira's sister-in-law Merhavah, Hayati's wife, who was never described by Vital as a diviner, also had visionary dreams. They included oblique instructions to Vital, referring to his dispute with Rabbi Jacob Abulafia and his efforts to rouse the Damascus community to repentance in order to prepare it for the coming redemption.[28] Of another woman, Rachel, sister of Rabbi Judah Mashan, who also was not a diviner, it is related that she saw wondrous visions and uttered true prophecies throughout her life:

5338 [1578]. I was preaching publicly in Jerusalem one Saturday morning. Rachel, the sister of R. Judah Mashan, was there, and she told me that the whole time I was preaching she saw a pillar of fire over my head, with Elijah z"l to my right supporting me. They both disappeared when I finished preaching.

She also saw a pillar of fire over my head[29] when I led the *Musaf* service on *Yom Kippur* in the synagogue of the Sicilian community in Damascus, in 5362 [1601]. The

sure, the Jews, including Vital, had no hesitations about approaching Muslim 'sorcerers', who are represented as well versed in the art and as true seers, but it cannot be doubted that all the women described in Vital's memoirs as experts in oil divining were Jewish, and they, too, are represented as highly skilful practitioners who spoke the truth.

[26] See above, at nn. 21–3.   [27] Vital, 'Book of Visions', 138 (*Sefer haḥezyonot*, pt. 3, §47).

[28] See ibid. 137 (§46), and 142 (§50).

[29] On the significance of this as a sign that Vital was destined to become Luria's successor, see Faierstein, *Jewish Mystical Autobiographies*, 309 n. 20.

above-mentioned woman was used to seeing visions, demons, spirits, and angels, and most of what she said was correct from the time of her youth and through adulthood.[30]

In Safed, too, Vital heard the prophecies of a woman who had been known all her life for receiving revelations from a heavenly 'voice'. Her prophecy buttressed his messianic expectations:

5354 [1594]. I was in Safed and I arranged study times for them and I preached for them on the day of the *mishmarah*.[31] A woman was there, Francisa Sarah, a pious woman, who saw visions in a waking dream and heard a voice speaking to her, and most of her words were true. The daughter of Rabbi Solomon Albakez [Alkabetz] z"l said to her: Is it possible that such a holy mouth, someone so eloquent, should die? She responded: Do not worry about this, for the Messiah will undoubtedly come in his lifetime.[32]

To the list of female visionaries, dreamers, and prophetesses mentioned in Vital's memoir, we may add his own wives: Hannah, who, on her sickbed, saw visions of Paradise and Hell and described them 'in a low voice that sounded like a ghost's from the ground' [Isa. 29: 4], but afterwards the event was wiped from her memory,[33] and Jamilla, who was told and even commanded in a prophetic dream about her future marriage to 'Rabbi Hayyim the Kabbalist'.[34] Similarly, Vital's diary notes describe the prophetic visions of Sa'adat, the wife of Jacob Nasar;[35] Simhah, the sister of Zabda, wife of Cuencas;[36] Nehamah, the daughter of Joseph Sajjah;[37] Rachel the Ashkenazi woman from Safed;[38] his wife's aunt;[39] the older wife of Rabbi Benjamin Saruk;[40] and the wife of Uziel, beadle of the Sicilian synagogue.[41] All would seem to have been worthy and respectable women, some of them Vital's own relatives, neighbours, and

[30] Vital, 'Book of Visions', 47 (*Sefer haḥezyonot*, pt. 1, §12).

[31] This is the term used in the Sephardi tradition for the commemorative meal partaken of on the anniversary of the death of a relative. See Faierstein, *Jewish Mystical Autobiographies*, 309 n. 27.

[32] Vital, 'Book of Visions', 50 (*Sefer haḥezyonot*, pt. 1, §18). In *Sefer haḥezyonot*, ed. Aescoly, p. 10 n. 25 (and in Faierstein, *Jewish Mystical Autobiographies*, 309 n. 28), the editor notes the mention, in the chronicle of Joseph Sambari, *Sefer divrei yosef*, of 'a wise woman and worker of great deeds, in Upper Galilee, in Safed, may it be rebuilt speedily in our days, whose name was La Franciza, and she had a *magid* [heavenly mentor] to tell her and announce to her what was to happen in the world' (see Neubauer, 'Excerpts' (Heb.), 152, and more recently *Sefer divrei yosef*, ed. Shtober, 364–6). The reference would seem to be to the same woman, whose name evidently went before her.

[33] Vital, 'Book of Visions', 49–50 (*Sefer haḥezyonot*, pt. 1, §17).

[34] Ibid. 120–1 (pt. 3, §15).

[35] Ibid. 73 (pt. 1, §26), and 115 (pt. 3, §8).

[36] Ibid. 73 (pt. 1, §27), and 153 (pt. 3, §66).

[37] Ibid. 116 (pt. 3, §10), and 122 (§18).

[38] Ibid. 89 (pt. 2, §12), and 133–4 (pt. 3, §38).

[39] Ibid. 122–3 (pt. 3, §20), and 128–9 (§28).

[40] Ibid. 122 (§19).

[41] Ibid. 140–2 (§49).

acquaintances. It is evident that he did not consider their experiences in any way odd or problematic. Rather, they served him as legitimate channels of communication with the supernal worlds, and he found confirmation in them of the validity of his messianic path.

Alongside such incidents of legitimate female prophecy, Vital also reports events pertaining to the prophetic pathology of spirit possession, where a departed soul that has not attained its proper 'rectification' (*tikun*) returns to inhabit the body of a living person. Usually the body was that of a virgin girl, to which the spirit would transmit important messages from the world of the dead—such as might expose sinful or erroneous acts that required rectification.[42] On the strength of hearsay, Vital recorded: 'They also told me that in Aleppo, literally during the same time,[43] a spirit entered a young girl and preached to them concerning repentance, on the eve of *Rosh Hashanah*. They instituted fasts and repentance, and after several months the girl died.'[44] By the power of the spirit that had taken hold of her, the girl called for repentance and actually succeeded in eliciting a response from the community—but at the price of her life. By contrast, Vital devotes a lengthy passage to another spirit possession story from the end of the year 5369 (1609), revolving around his own struggles with Rabbi Jacob Abulafia and his supporters in Damascus. At its centre is a young girl, the daughter of Raphael Anav, who at first draws her power from the spirit speaking through her throat, but ultimately, once the spirit has lost its grip on her, prophesies on her own account and becomes a remarkably authoritative figure. She manipulates the power struggle between the rival camps in the community and even takes upon herself Vital's mission of inducing the Jews of Damascus to repent.[45] The prophetic revelations of the girl and of the spirit that spoke through her—that of the Jerusalem sage Jacob

[42] On the phenomenon of spirit possession (dybbuk) as reflected in Jewish sources see Nigal, *"Dybbuk" Tales* (Heb.). On the particular propensity of dybbuks to enter the bodies of young girls see ibid. 35. See also Bilu, 'Dybbuk and Maggid', 346–7, 348 n. 21, 354, and 364, and see the comprehensive studies of Chajes, 'Spirit Possession' and *Between Worlds*.

[43] By the context, this must refer to the end of 5369 (1609), when Vital himself was involved in a dybbuk affair in Damascus, on which see below.

[44] Vital, 'Book of Visions', 257 (*Sefer haḥezyonot*, 'Tosafot vetikunim', §18).

[45] This affair, which spans §§22–4 in pt. 1 of *Sefer haḥezyonot*, was copied in different versions and published in several places, on which see the editorial comment in Aescoly's edition (p. 19 n. 36), and in Faierstein, *Jewish Mystical Autobiographies*, 310 n. 41. One of these versions was published by Nigal in *"Dybbuk" Tales* (Heb.), 74–6. Meroz, in her work in progress on Luria and Vital (see above, n. 15), and Chajes (in 'Spirit Possession', 215–34, and *Between Worlds*, 104–13)

Peso, who had died thirty-five years before—are suffused with messianic tension and were meant to stir Vital to take action so as to hasten the redemption. This is what the spirit said through the mouth of the girl:

For I have been sent by Heaven to reveal to him Heavenly secrets which he did not learn from his teacher z"l, in order that he should cause the world to repent. Everything depends on him, to repair the world. I have come to reveal to him matters concerning the Messiah. He is on the verge of coming. He always preaches that they should repent so that the Messiah will come. R. Jacob Abulafia, because of jealousy, says to the people: He speaks lies, since the Messiah is not coming in this generation, and he makes fun of him. Woe to him, for his sin is great, since because of his words and because of the great sins in this city, the Messiah has been bound with heavy iron chains and will be delayed another twelve years. During this time, many troubles will befall Damascus; it will be overturned like Sodom, and Jerusalem will also be burned. Only Safed will be saved. Afterwards, Gog and Magog will come, and then the Messiah will come with 'eight princes of men' [Mic. 5: 4]. The sage preached three sermons last year, before the plague, and the people repented somewhat. Because he refrained from preaching further, his beloved daughter, who was a great soul, died in the plague, although his small son will be a great rabbi in Israel. He has lost the opportunity to hear divine secrets, because I was sent from Heaven for this. When he seeks me, he will not find me because I have been given permission to speak only on this day, and tomorrow I must return to my place.[46]

On the departure of the spirit from the girl's body, and her resumption of prophetic activity in her own right, Vital reports somewhat doubtfully—and no wonder, since at this point she was castigating him in public for the neglect of his duty while taking upon herself the task of calling on the people to repent:

I have written in section twenty-two what occurred concerning the spirit which entered the daughter of Raphael Anav, what I saw for myself and what was told to me by Raphael and R. Jacob Ashkenazi. All this occurred on the Sabbath, *Rosh Ḥodesh Ab*. On Sunday morning, he [the spirit] undoubtedly left and ascended to his place. Afterwards, other things happened which were not caused by the above-mentioned spirit while still in her guise. He had already left, and the girl had been restored to complete health, but she said that she sometimes has visions, both while awake and dreaming, of souls and angels and on rare occasions of that spirit. I am uncertain if what she says is true or is a mixture of good and evil, because of the above-mentioned

analyse this affair in detail, emphasizing how the girl's power and authority were enhanced by the spirit that possessed her.

[46] Vital, 'Book of Visions', 61–2 (*Sefer haḥezyonot*, pt. 1, §22).

reason. There is also another reason. I did not see this with my own eyes as I saw it the first time. However, what amazed me was that all her words were only about repentance, fear of God, and moral rebuke. Therefore I will not refrain from writing them down as they were reported by truthful people.

She said that now that the spirit has left her, she always sees an angel who in her dreams leads her to Paradise and *Gehenna* and shows her the places of the righteous. In the majority of these visions, they tell her that she should caution me to cause the people of Damascus to repent—perhaps God will relent in his anger against them....

The night of the seventh of *Ab*: She was told to tell me that previously the soul of a *Tanna* [mishnaic sage] would always appear to me by means of a Unification through which I would connect with him. Yet now, for a long time, two and a half years to be precise, he has not revealed himself to me, for two reasons. First, because I have desisted from the above-mentioned Unifications. Second, because I have desisted from preaching my sermons to rebuke the people and cause them to repent as previously. Because of these two reasons, my daughter died in the plague. The night of the eighth of *Ab*: Elijah z"l told her in a waking dream, during the Sabbath *kiddush*: Tell R. Hayyim and the other sages of the city that they are neglecting [to act on] everything they have heard. Great evil will befall the inhabitants of Damascus because of this, and particularly R. Hayyim. They also told her: ... Does he not believe what we told him through the above-mentioned spirit? His teacher z"l also told him before his death that he only came into the world to cause the people to repent. The angel that he brought down also told him this, yet he still is uncertain and does not believe at all![47]

The girl, speaking in the name of an angel revealed to her in a glass mirror, had no compunction about chastising Abulafia for 'always mocking the coming of the Messiah';[48] denouncing the grave sins of the sages of Egypt, which she saw as 'scandals';[49] uttering wrathful prophecies about the Venetian community;[50] or naming one by one the sinners with whom she was acquainted in the Damascus community, rehearsing their sexual offences in detail.[51] Abulafia proclaimed in response, on penalty of the ban of excommunication, that 'all those standing there ... should not reveal a thing, out of respect for his honour and the honour of the others mentioned by the spirit ... and [he] publicly excommunicated the above-named spirit because he had defamed righteous people'. The girl thereupon notified him 'in the name of the spirit ... that the spirit stands daily in the Heavenly Academy and excommunicates him and everyone who agrees with what he did'.[52]

[47] Vital, 'Book of Visions', 65–6 (§24).   [48] Ibid. 68.   [49] Ibid. 69.
[50] Ibid.   [51] Ibid. 69–71.   [52] Ibid. 72–3.

The intensive prophetic activity described in *Sefer haḥzyonot*, in which, judging by all the testimonies cited above, women took a full and at times even a focal part, was accompanied by a call for repentance. This was Vital's main concern and what he saw as his public mission. The call to repent emanated from the mystical circles of Safed and was driven, as we have seen, by their messianic expectations, whose early fulfilment was viewed as depending upon the degree to which people responded. The practice of repentance, in this circle, took a decidedly ascetic cast,[53] and this is reflected in the penitential activities described in *Sefer haḥezyonot* itself: protracted and frequent fasting, weeping, sleeping on the ground, sexual abstinence, seclusion, 'sackcloth and ashes', rending of garments, and leaving the hair unkempt.[54] In this context, we note a certain 'Jewish woman' mentioned in one of Vital's entries for the year 5339 (1579)—about two years after he moved from Safed to Jerusalem— who also was among the prophets of redemption. She dreamed that she saw a Muslim sheikh giving Vital the keys to the gates of the Temple, and Vital, accompanied by 'many Jews', overseeing the Temple's reconstruction, its purification, and the resumption of the sacrifices in it. This woman is described as having 'fasted all her life',[55] and, notwithstanding the traditional repudiation of women who took extraordinary pieties and extra fasts upon themselves,[56] Vital saw no reason to make any disparaging comments about her ascetic inclinations. On the contrary, he seems to have valued them as a positive expression of the kind of mass penitential movement for which he was calling in his sermons.

[53] Much has been written about this ascetic penitential movement in Safed. See e.g. Schechter 'Safed in the Sixteenth Century'; Dan, *Ethical Literature* (Heb.), 202–29; Pachter, 'Concept of Devekut'; Fine, *Physician*, index, s.v. 'asceticism', 'ascetic rituals'.

[54] See Vital, 'Book of Visions', 64, 72 (*Sefer haḥezyonot*, pt. 1, §§23 and 24); ibid. 87, 109 (pt. 2, §§10 and 53); ibid. 130 (pt. 3, §30(29)); ibid. 160, 161, 167, 172–3 (pt. 4, §§6, 7, 11, 17, and 18); ibid. 253–4 ('Tosafot vetikunim', §14).   [55] Ibid. 113 (pt. 3, §3).

[56] See e.g. the definition of an abstinent woman in JT *Sot.* 3: 4: 'A virgin who fasts a great deal [*betulah tsaimanit*]—because of her fasting she will lose her virginity.' See also Tosafot on BT *Sot.* 22a: '"A virgin who fasts a great deal [*betulah tsaimanit*]—because of her fasting she will lose her virginity"... Rabbi Judah Hanasi explained: "because of her fasting she will lose her virginity"—all that fasting will make her hymen wither away. But my teacher and brother, R. Moses, explained: "She acts as though she is very pious and constantly at prayer, following our reading of the word in the Talmud: *tsalyanit* [i.e. a woman who prays a great deal], and as though she were fasting and performing acts of abstention in order to afflict herself at prayer, but she does it only as a pose in order to escape supervision, and so she goes whoring and loses her virginity."' See also Introd., at nn. 18–23 and above, at nn. 10–11.

Sefer haḥezyonot concludes with a series of reports entirely devoted to documenting messianic–visionary activity among the Conversos, the Jews of Spain and Portugal who had been forced to convert to Christianity. Vital obtained his information from personal acquaintances, Conversos who had left the lands of their birth and returned to Judaism, such as Abraham ben Yaish, a doctor, who said of himself that he had once 'served the King of Spain'.[57] He also drew upon travellers' reports and letters from Spain and Venice telling of Conversos who prophesied the destruction of these king- doms, the approaching demise of the leaders of the Inquisition, the advent of 'a descendant of David who will return the kingdom and the Jewish religion to their former place', and the manifestation in the New World of 'the kingdom of Daniel the Jew',[58] rumours of which were threatening the king of Spain.[59] There can be no doubt, then, that Vital's circles not only were aware of the sufferings of the Conversos and their expectations of redemption, but were in continuous, vital contact with them. In light of this, it seems reasonable to assume a direct historical connection between the prophetic–messianic movement that arose among the Iberian Conversos and the outbreak of prophetic–messianic activity in the same period in Palestine and the Levant, whose communities were absorbing at that time considerable numbers of Iberian refugees seeking to return to Judaism. It should come as no surprise, then, that prophesying women not only make frequent appearances in Safed, Jerusalem, and Damascus, as we learn from Vital's accounts, but also play a central role in the Iberian messianic awakening. This phenomenon, too, was a precedent for the emergence of female prophecy in the Sabbatian movement in the second half of the seventeenth century, and it may be seen as forming part of its immediate historical context.

We have some fairly rich information about prophesying women in the Converso communities of Spain at the time of the expulsion and shortly thereafter, at the turn of the fifteenth and sixteenth centuries.[60] This concerns

---

[57] Vital, 'Book of Visions', 258 (*Sefer haḥezyonot*, 'Tosafot vetikunim', §20).

[58] The source of this tradition is the popular account of the 9th-century traveller Eldad Hadani. For bibliographical references, see Faierstein, *Jewish Mystical Autobiographies*, 331 n. 30, and Aescoly's edition of *Sefer haḥezyonot*, p. 246 n. 20.

[59] Vital, 'Book of Visions', 258–63 (*Sefer haḥezyonot*, 'Tosafot vetikunim', §§20–4).

[60] This information is drawn mainly from the files of the Inquisition. Parts of it were first published in an anthology of sources on Spanish Jewry assembled by Yitzhak Baer in *Die Juden im christlichen Spanien*, ii. 528–34. See also id., 'Messianic Movement' (Heb.), and Aescoly,

a number of girls and women who reported seeing apparitions of Elijah and Moses, wondrous lights, souls of the departed, and angels who led them on heavenly journeys, being instructed by all these to herald the redemption that was to occur in the year 1500. Their prophecies inspired a mass movement of return to the Jewish faith, with special emphasis on fasting 'according to the custom of the Jews', charity, and rigorous observance of the sabbath, all in anticipation of the advent—so imminent as to call for the donning of holiday garments—of the messiah, who would lead the Conversos to the Holy Land and a promised life of joy and prosperity.

This messianic movement lasted for a few years before being suppressed by the Inquisition. The best known of the prophetesses was Inés of Herrera, a shoemaker's daughter who began prophesying in 1499, when she was just 12 years old. She was arrested and interrogated less than a year later and was burnt at the stake in 1500. Another prophetess whose name we know was Mari Gómez of Chillón. There was also a group of women in Córdoba, which included two daughters of the Converso Juan de Córdoba, a Moorish servant girl who had been converted to Judaism and began to prophesy about the coming redemption of the Jews, and a Christian woman who had no Jewish forebears but nevertheless prophesied the return of the Conversos to the Holy Land. There appear to have been quite a few prophesying women among the Conversos in this period, although their names and the contents of their prophecies were not always preserved.[61] It would also seem that many more women than men were swayed by the prophetesses' tidings of redemption.[62] The prophecy of Inés of Herrera, for example, included a promise to the young, unmarried Conversas that if they put their faith in her message and carried out all her instructions, they would be met in the Holy Land by Jewish young men who were awaiting their arrival in order to marry them.[63]

Jewish Messianic Movements (Heb.), 300–5. Haim Beinart has devoted several studies to the phenomenon of messianic stirrings and female prophets among the Conversos in the period of the expulsion. See e.g. 'The Prophetess Inés' (Heb.), 'Conversos of Chillón' (Heb.), 'Almadén' (Heb.), 'The Prophetess Inés in Herrera' (Heb.), 'Conversos of Agudo' (Heb.), 'A Prophesying Movement in Cordova' (Heb.), and 'Conversos of Halia' (Heb.). See also Sharot, *Messianism, Mysticism and Magic*, 76–85.

[61] See Beinart's note in 'Almadén' (Heb.), 31.

[62] See Beinart, 'The Prophetess Inés in Herrera' (Heb.), 471.

[63] See ibid. 487. For an analysis of Ines' prophetic activity stressing its syncretistic Jewish–Christian character, see Koren, 'Christian Means'.

One should not, therefore, ignore the extraordinary prominence of women in the prophetic–messianic movement that arose among the Iberian Conversos in the aftermath of the expulsion. The imprint of this phenomenon on the collective memory of the Conversos may well have contributed to the prophetic inspiration of women, and the evidently unquestioned credibility of their prophecy, as we encountered them in Vital's accounts of prophesying women in his predominantly Sephardi milieu.[64] The same factor very likely was at work in the milieu of Sabbatai Zevi, which was similarly suffused with the influence of Iberian Jewry. The Smyrna community, into which he was born, and the other Jewish communities in the Ottoman empire, from which the Sabbatian movement spread in all directions, had in the course of the sixteenth and the first half of the seventeenth centuries absorbed many Conversos seeking to return to Judaism.[65] In Smyrna itself—a new community, founded only at the end of the sixteenth century, which quickly developed into a flourishing mercantile centre in the course of the seventeenth century— former Conversos comprised an important, wealthy, and influential economic and cultural sector.[66] Sabbatai Zevi personally, and the messianic movement that formed around him, were on close terms with them, as studies by Jacob Barnai have newly clarified.[67] Their connections with contemporary millenarian Christian circles, and the long tradition of messianic expectations that was part and parcel of their Iberian cultural legacy, must have contributed to the formulation and speedy acceptance of the Sabbatian tidings in Smyrna.

A special affinity with Sabbatianism is also evident throughout the Converso diaspora communities in Europe and the Levant,[68] which maintained

[64] For the tide of Iberian immigrants that flooded into Palestine and the Levant during the 16th and early 17th centuries, see e.g. David, 'Safed as a Centre for the Resettlement of Conversos' (Heb.); id., *Immigration and Settlement in Erets Israel* (Heb.), 7, 12, 15, 72–8, 91, 99, 112–18, 126, 135. [65] See Beinart, 'Exodus' (Heb.).

[66] See Barnai, 'Origins' (Heb.), and id., 'Portuguese Marranos' (Heb.). The designation of the Conversos who arrived in Smyrna as 'Portuguese', as opposed to 'Sephardi' (i.e. Spanish), refers to their land of origin rather than to any kind of cultural distinctiveness from the Spanish Conversos as a group. Many of the Portuguese Conversos had spent lengthy periods in Spain on their way out of the Iberian peninsula, and the political unification of Spain and Portugal also contributed to the blurring of the distinction between the two communities of Conversos. On this see Beinart's remarks in 'Exodus' (Heb.), 69–70, 87. [67] See Barnai, 'Christian Messianism'.

[68] Gershom Scholem pointed out the special appeal of Sabbatianism to the Sephardi Jews, particularly the former Conversos. He attributed it to their unique susceptibility to the paradoxical Sabbatian ideology of conversion, which reflected and gave expression to their own his-

family and economic connections among themselves. They also kept in contact with their Christian relatives who had remained in the Iberian peninsula and its subordinate territories, despite the perils of the Inquisition and the efforts of the Jewish community to prevent, at all costs, the return of the former Conversos to the 'lands of idolatry'.[69] The messianic heritage of the Conversos in Iberia, which was suppressed as heretical by the Inquisition, could well have borne within it the memory of the women who prophesied the redemption in the aftermath of the expulsion. It is also likely to have played a part in the emergence of various Christian mystical—messianic heresies in the course of the sixteenth and early seventeenth centuries, born of the wars of the Reformation and the triumph of Catholicism in Spain. All these phenomena were taken, rightly or wrongly, as belonging to the single heretical movement of the 'Alumbrados' (Illuminated), and the Inquisition, in its efforts to stamp it out, tended to identify it with the 'New Christians'. The prophetic activities of women were notable in all the diverse currents of this movement, and some of these women indeed were of Converso origin. Most were nuns or women who had otherwise vowed to devote their lives to their religious vocation. They were accused, among other things, of sexual licentiousness, because of their belief that they had been purified of original sin by virtue of their mystical union with God, and of antinomian acts—deliberate flaunting of church law and ritual, use of satanic powers, and fits of ecstatic prophesying, which were discredited as fakery.[70]

In a broader context, these phenomena may be related to the wave of prophetic 'enthusiasm' that was sweeping not only through Catholic Spain and its dominions, but elsewhere in the Catholic world, as well as in Protestant Europe—Holland, Germany, England, and Switzerland—where various

torical experience. See Scholem, *Studies and Texts* (Heb.), 24, and id., *Sabbatai Sevi*, 485–6. Y. H. Yerushalmi, on the other hand, emphasizes the continuity of messianic tension in the Iberian peninsula, which the Conversos who returned to Judaism brought with them to their lands of resettlement, and which made them particularly susceptible to the messianic message of Sabbatianism. See Yerushalmi, *Spanish Court*, 302–12. On this see also Kaplan, *From Christianity to Judaism*, 373–5, and Sharot, *Messianism*, 101–4.

[69] See Kaplan, 'Travels', and id., 'Struggle' (Heb.).

[70] On all this see Hamilton, *Heresy and Mysticism*, and Sharot, *Messianism, Mysticism and Magic*, 76–85. For a variety of phenomena involving female prophecy in late medieval and early modern Spain, see also Kagan, *Lucrecia's Dreams*, and Christian, *Apparitions*. I am grateful to Dr Javier Castaño for these last two references.

radical Reformation sects, such as the Anabaptists, the Mennonites, the 'Family of Love', and the Quakers, were active in this same period. Various affinities between these Protestant sects and the Jewish Sabbatian movement have already been noted by a number of scholars.[71] Some viewed them as indicating no more than parallel religious phenomena, or, at most, as reflecting the impact of Jewish messianic fervour at its height upon Protestant observers who had their own millenarian agendas,[72] while others interpreted such affinities as suggestive of mutual influence and cross-fertilization between Christian millenarianism and the outbreak of Sabbatian messianism.[73] It seems, however, that as yet no one has considered the possibility that influence of this kind may also have contributed to the unqualified readiness, unprecedented in its scope, of the Sabbatian movement to recognize and confer full legitimacy on the prophetic spirituality of women. For most of the radical Reformation sects, in much the same way as Sabbatianism, viewed women as fully capable of receiving the freely flowing 'spirit', and created frameworks that enabled women to emerge as renowned apocalyptic prophets and preachers.[74]

[71] Even contemporary observers were aware of the connections. A journal penned by an Italian Jew early in 1666, assembling pieces of information and documents on the expectation of the coming redemption and the excitement it was generating among both Jews and non-Jews, includes a detail attesting to the great interest taken by English Quakers in the Jewish messiah: 'A sect called the Quakers in London sent a ship to Jaffa without any cargo, in order to find out the truth of the matter so that they would know what to do' (cited in Scholem, *Researches* (Heb.), 508). Thomas Coenen, who took a hostile view of all these displays of ecstatic messianic prophecy, remarked in his treatise on Sabbatianism: 'all this was just the work of Satan, who took pleasure in striking that stiff-necked people with massive blindness, or should we say, delusion mixed with massive chicanery. It could well be sensed that there was something artificial here, as with the Quakers in England' (Coenen, *False Hopes* (Heb.), 59). On Coenen's antagonism towards the Christian 'enthusiasm' of his time, both Catholic and Protestant, see Kaplan's introduction to the Hebrew edition of *False Hopes*, 18–20. Michael Heyd's lecture, 'Thomas Coenen's Critique of "Enthusiasm"', is entirely devoted to this subject, and I thank him for giving me a copy of it in manuscript. Heyd points out a parenthetical comment by Coenen indicating his awareness of the central place occupied by women in all these prophetic movements—Catholic, Protestant, and Sabbatian: 'It should be noted that women are fanatical; they will easily, and often, put their faith in anything, and they have great influence upon the men' (Coenen, *False Hopes* (Heb.), 54). See also Heyd, 'The "Jewish Quaker"'.

[72] See Scholem, *Sabbatai Sevi*, 99–102, 332 ff., 545–8, and 868.

[73] See Sharot, *Messianism, Mysticism and Magic*, 106; Popkin, 'Three English Tellings'; id., 'Jewish–Christian Relations'; id., 'Jewish Messianism', esp. 79 ff.; id., 'Christian Interest'; Barnai, 'Christian Messianism'.

[74] See e.g. Thomas, 'Women and the Civil War Sects'; Wyntijes, 'Women in the Reform-

Moreover, a certain factor within the Muslim context, in which Sabbatianism first emerged, and which continued to shape its contours even in the forms it later took within the domains of Christianity,[75] may similarly have fostered the movement's remarkable openness to women as active participants both in its rank and file and among its prophets. This was the presence of the Bektashi order of Sufis in close proximity and probable contact with the Sabbatians. Gershom Scholem, in several studies,[76] pointed to the likelihood that the Bektashis had exerted an influence both upon Sabbatai Zevi himself and, after his death, upon the circles of Sabbatian converts to Islam, which existed side by side with the Bektashi communities in Asia Minor and the Ottoman regions of the Balkans. He based the probability of such an influence on several striking and unique features that were common to both sects: clandestine organization, the principle of dissimulation, syncretism, the doctrine of divine

ation'; O'Faolain and Martines, *Not in God's Image*, ch. 10, pt. 5: 'The Protestant Promotion of Women', 262–9; Williams, *The Radical Reformation*, s.v. 'women'; Hamilton, *Family of Love*; Cohn, *Pursuit of the Millennium*, 261; P. Mack, *Visionary Women*; and Jelsma, *Frontiers of the Reformation*, 40–90. For the phenomenon of religious 'enthusiasm' in general, see Knox's classic study, *Enthusiasm*, where women's prominent involvement is observed (somewhat dismissively, as one might expect in a work first published in 1950) on pp. 30, 55, 68, 162, and 319. It is worth noting in this connection the intriguing relationship between the 16th-century French Orientalist and millenarian Christian kabbalist, Guillaume Postel, and the prophetic virgin, the nun Zuanna (Giovanna or Johanna)—'the divine Mother', as he refers to her—whom he encountered during his sojourn in Venice. He identified her with the female aspect of the kabbalistic godhead, the Shekhinah, apparently proclaimed her a female messiah, and attributed to her his initiation into the mystery of the eschatological 'restitution of all things'. According to his testimony, although she knew no Latin, Hebrew, or Aramaic, she was able to explain to him difficult passages in the Zohar (a work he first acquired, and began to translate, only on arrival in Venice, possibly under her influence). It is not clear where or how she may have acquired her knowledge of Jewish esotericism, and it has often been speculated that she was of New Christian origin, although there is no conclusive evidence for this. See Kuntz, *Guillaume Postel*, 69–99; Williams, *The Radical Reformation*, 856–60; Idel, *Messianic Mystics*, 155, 379 n. 70, and 381 n. 3, with additional bibliographical references.

[75] The conduits for this influence included Berukhyah—or Barukh—Koniyo in Salonica, and the sect of Sabbatian converts to Islam in Turkey, with whom Hayim Malakh and other evangelists of Sabbatianism in Poland were in contact, and in whose circles Jacob Frank, too, had sojourned at the outset of his mission. On these relations see Scholem, *Studies and Texts* (Heb.), 100–20.

[76] See Scholem, *Researches* (Heb.), 116, 328, 347, and 353–5; id., *Messianic Idea*, 150–4; and id., *Kabbalah*, 329. See also Attias, Scholem, and Ben-Zvi, *Songs and Hymns* (Heb.), 61, and Fenton, 'Shabbetay Sebi and his Muslim Contemporary', 81–8. On the transmission of Sufi influence to

incarnation, Trinitarianism, and antinomian and libertine tendencies. But Scholem, and all subsequent historians of Sabbatianism, would seem to have overlooked an additional and equally striking common feature: the unique status of women as full and active participants in the spiritual life of the sectarian community.

The independence and prominence of the Bektashi women had apparently distinguished the order—which admitted both married and celibate members—from its inception at the end of the thirteenth or the beginning of the fourteenth century. This feature drew the sharp criticism of the Orthodox Muslim establishment, which accused the order of sexual licentiousness. According to the hagiographical traditions about its founder, Haji Bektash, the order's unique rituals were already established in his lifetime, and they included secret initiation ceremonies and communal meals in which women took a full and equal part alongside the men. One such tradition has it that Haji Bektash taught his entire doctrine to a woman, and it was she who disseminated it to his disciples. Another Bektashi tradition tells of a woman by the name of Husnaya ('the beautiful') who outwitted the spokesmen of Orthodox Islam and won a theological debate about the roots of evil. The status of the Bektashi women, who wore no veils and mixed freely in male company, was unique in Ottoman history. It attracted a good deal of attention and is mentioned as one reason for the secrecy of the order's rituals and the

Jacob Frank and his followers by way of the apostate sect of Berukhyah in Salonica see Levine, *Kronika*, 44–5 nn. 64–5, and 52 nn. 97 and 100. To this might be added the ritual referred to in the *Kronika* as the 'secret act' ('czynność taiemna'), ibid. 54–6, §46; the Polish text of the entire *Kronika* was subsequently republished by Jan Doktór as *Rozmaite adnotacje*, where §46 appears on pp. 60–1), in which Frank and his wife locked themselves up in a guarded room together with their circle's 'brothers and sisters'. They proceeded to take off all their clothes, and, after extinguishing the lamps lit at the outset of the ritual, all together performed 'the act of love'. The 'extinguishing of the lamps' was said to have been one of the Bektashis' most notorious rituals, on account of which they were charged with sexual depravity; see the bibliographical references in n. 77 below. It is perhaps no coincidence that Frank, according to the *Kronika's* account, performed this ritual in the small Podolian town of Iwanie immediately after his return from Kamenets-Podolsky, where he had spent two days in the company of 'Othman Chelebi', one of the heads of the Berukhyah sect in Salonica, and 'Our Othman', Israel Czerniewski, one of Frank's Polish disciples, who had just arrived from Salonica; see *Kronika*, 52–4, §45 (*Rozmaite adnotacje*, 60). On the ritual 'extinguishing of the lamps' performed among the Doenmeh at the conclusion of their 'Festival of the Lamb' see Galanté, *Nouveaux documents*, 50, 77. My thanks to Prof. Michal Oron for providing me with a photocopy of Galanté's book, which I was not able to locate in a UK library.

isolated locations in which they chose to settle, far from the prying eyes of strangers.[77] If indeed there were personal contacts between Sabbatai Zevi and the head of a certain order of dervishes in Constantinople, and between the Doenmeh in Salonica, or at least one of their factions, and the Bektashi cloister adjoining the lot where they buried their dead, it may well be that the Sabbatian sectarians had absorbed, among other things, the Bektashis' unique attitude towards women.

The anomalous participation of women as prophets, which marked the Sabbatian movement from the start, belongs in these wider historical and religious contexts. Even if they could not on their own have brought about the Sabbatian revolution in the status of women—of which the outbreak of female prophecy was but one expression, as we shall see—they may well have functioned in particular localities as a catalysing or conducive factor. There is little doubt, however, that in its Jewish context, the phenomenon was quite unique. The difference between this eruption of prophecy and all previous manifestations of prophetic powers in women was not only quantitative—and there were hundreds or even thousands of prophetesses at the peak of the messianic frenzy, while prophetic activity on the part of women continued within the sectarian frameworks in which Sabbatianism persisted for another century and a half—but also qualitative. This latter difference may be inferred from the testimonies about Sabbatian women who prophesied, although it scarcely finds explicit expression or acknowledgement in any of them. Nevertheless, once this qualitative difference is recognized, it will offer a solution to the riddle of the quantitative difference, which is clearly evident and spectacular in its dimensions.

[77] On the unique status of women in the Bektashi order see Birge, *Bektashi Order*, 38, 45–6, 49–50, 85, 126–7, 159, 164–5, and 171; Schimmel, *Mystical Dimensions*, 341 and 432; Mélikoff, 'La Cérémonie du Ayni-i-Djem'; ead., 'Recherche sur une coutume', 75–6; Dankoff, 'An Unpublished Account'; and *Encyclopaedia of Islam*, i. 1161–3, s.v. 'Bektāshiyya'.

THREE

Sabbatian Women as Religious Activists

THE SENSE that the dawning messianic age, as characterized by the biblical prophet Joel, had brought the 'spirit' to rest 'upon all flesh', including
women—a sense that was common, as we have seen, to Sabbatianism and a
diversity of early modern Christian religious 'enthusiasm' movements[1]—
broke down the barriers by which rabbinic tradition had always marked the
inherent difference between the sexes, and accordingly assigned them discrete
spheres of activity. This propelled the Sabbatian movement simultaneously in
two opposite directions. On the one hand, the messianic believers displayed an
unprecedented willingness to recognize as fully legitimate the phenomenon of
'spinster', 'maiden', or 'virgin' prophetesses, and in some circumstances even to
accord them priority and set them at the centre of the messianic stage.
Notably, we hear of no attempts to exorcize the 'spirit' that inspired so many of
them to prophesy, such as we do hear, by contrast, of some prophetic women
described as 'possessed' in Hayim Vital's *Book of Visions* or in later exorcism
accounts that proliferated in east European hasidism. Nor is there any evidence to suggest that such women were being married off in order to silence
them—that instinctive rabbinic establishment response to the 'aberration' of
prophetic chastity in women that we encountered in the handful of extant
sources on the efforts to suppress the phenomenon in diverse times and
places.[2] On the contrary, where the Sabbatian sources address the issue explicitly, we are told, for example, of the strict ban on marriage, and the rigid separation between the sexes, that were practiced in Jacob Frank's court at
Offenbach (a separation occasionally disrupted, as we saw, with secret licentious rites, such as those celebrated by Frank or his sons—but not, as far as we
know, by his virgin daughter Eva). The Offenbach regime of strict sexual

---

[1] See above, Ch. 1, at n. 5, and Ch. 2, at nn. 68–74.   [2] See above, Ch. 2, at nn. 7–11.

abstinence must surely be interpreted as the means by which the court was being sanctified in order to enhance the spiritual experience of its residents, both male and female.[3] Admittedly, it is unlikely that any more than a small minority of Sabbatian women took on celibacy as a way of life, and it is possible that most or some of them did so within marriage and for limited periods only (rather like the male pietists who practised sexual abstinence in traditional Jewish society); the problematic and sparse information at our disposal does not permit a full mapping out of the phenomenon. Yet there is no doubt that the celebration of the female virginal state, or the full legitimization of the practice by women of either temporary or permanent sexual abstinence, signified a shift in the conceptualization of the female sex. It released women from the inherently sensual, corporeal, material nature by which rabbinic tradition had always defined them, and made it possible for them for the first time to be perceived in terms of 'spirit' and 'form', terms that would normally apply exclusively to men. In this way, women's ontological status was implicitly equalized with that of the men, and the way was opened for them, as inspired prophetesses, to achieve positions of charismatic authority within their Sabbatian circles.

On the other hand, alongside this novel, revolutionary trend, which allowed women, or at least some women, to be incorporated in the framework of pious asceticism that Judaism had always reserved for the male elite,

---

[3] It is instructive, in this context, to compare the Frankist court at Offenbach with the gathering at the court of the tsadik or rebbe in the early stages of hasidism. The hasidic court, too, undoubtedly sanctified all its comers. Sojourning there was an intense, transformative spiritual experience, and it is not insignificant that it was achieved in conditions of sexual abstinence. This was never imposed explicitly, but it was the inevitable consequence of the all-male composition of the company assembled at the court of the rebbe or gathered around his table (*tish*) to hear his discourses. Most of its members were 'the youths' (*benei hane'urim*)—young men in the early years of marriage, who disengaged from their families for shorter or longer periods in order to attach themselves to their new spiritual masters. The hasidic court thus constituted a temporary but effective alternative to family life—an all-male fraternity from which the wives, who had been abandoned at home, were utterly excluded. By contrast, the court at Offenbach, which also functioned as an alternative spiritual 'family', and whose sojourners were referred to as 'brothers' and 'sisters' (on which see below, Ch. 4, at nn. 35–6, 47–54, and Ch. 6, at nn. 4–23), opened its doors to women, included them in all its mysteries, and explicitly demanded a regimen of sexual abstinence from men and women alike. On this difference between the affiliation of women with Sabbatianism and hasidism respectively, see further below, Ch. 4 n. 52, and at nn. 63–9.

Sabbatianism violated the bounds of tradition from precisely the opposite direction. It broke down the halakhic network of prohibitions and pre-scriptions—'negative' and 'positive' commandments—by way of adopting a-nomian or antinomian modes of religious conduct, or both, and this revolution, too, had egalitarian implications for the status of women.

From the very outset of Nathan of Gaza's propagandist activity on behalf of his messiah, Sabbatianism set out to dislodge the halakhic system of com-mandments and precepts from its traditional standing as the focus of Juda-ism's soteriological doctrine—the only means of vouchsafing the individual's 'share in the World to Come'. Faith in the messiah became a supreme value and replaced compliance with the commandments and precepts as the key to personal salvation. Thus, for example, Nathan of Gaza emphasized Sabbatai Zevi's power

to do as he pleases with the Israelite nation, to declare them righteous or—God forfend—guilty. He can justify the greatest sinner, and even if he be [as sinful] as Jesus he may justify him. And whoever entertains any doubts about him, though he be the most righteous man in the world, he [that is, the messiah] may punish him with great afflictions. In short, you must take it for absolutely certain that a Jew will have no [eternal] life unless he believes all these things without a sign or miracle.[4]

This message continued to reverberate in Sabbatian circles even after Sabbatai Zevi's apostasy and in the years following his death, when the ever-growing gap between, on the one hand, the dazzling vision of the redemption, and on the other hand, the mundane reality in which the movement persisted, could be bridged only by the paradoxical faith in the apostate, deceased messiah. Thus in the summer of 1672, some four years after Sabbatai's apostasy, in a letter written soon after his return to Poland from a visit to the community of messianic believers in Adrianople, the Volhynian Sabbatian rabbi, Solomon Katz, reiterated the same message forthrightly as a piece of advice to his brother: 'You must pray with the intention of becoming one of the believers in our lord, and you will thus attain great benefit, for faith in this regard is greater than the entire Torah.'[5] Some forty years later, long after the messiah's death, the Sabbatian kabbalist Nehemiah Hayon reportedly declared: 'Even if a per-

---

[4] From a letter sent by Nathan of Gaza to Raphael Joseph in Egypt in 1665, published in Sasportas, *Tsitsat novel tsevi*, 9–10. For an English translation (slightly modified here to reflect more faithfully the original Hebrew), and analysis of this letter see Scholem, *Sabbatai Sevi*, 268–90.　　　　　　　　　[5] Freimann, *Sabbatai Zevi* (Heb.), 65.

son should transgress the entire Torah, if he has faith in this regard, etc., he belongs to the holy elite and is devoid of any sin or iniquity.'[6]

Gershom Scholem pointed out the revolutionary nature of this 'emphatic stress on pure faith as a religious value', adding that 'this notion of faith as independent of, and indeed outweighing, all outward religious acts and symbols is distinctly Christian in character',[7] substituting as it does the promise of salvation by 'works' or 'deeds' with the promise of salvation by faith.[8] He admits, however, that it is difficult to identify such channels of Christian influence as may have been accessible to Nathan of Gaza, who was apparently the first to formulate this novel Sabbatian doctrine.[9]

The deflection of the centre of religious gravity from ritualistic action to pure faith had significant implications for the status of Sabbatian women. For the connection of women with traditional Judaism's complex network of positive commandments had always been limited and largely indirect. This may be illustrated by the example of the all-important commandment of Torah study, which alone could outweigh all others in its capacity for securing for the men who observed it their share in the World to Come. Since women were exempted from this positive commandment, and were usually held to be precluded from observing it, the Sages could do no better than to declare that their personal salvation was to be gained as a reward for the performance of their domestic duties, which facilitated the observance of the commandment by their husbands and sons.[10] By contrast, women's connection with the messiah—their belief in him, in his redemptive mission, and in his elevation to divinity—was not mediated by men or circumscribed in any way, since in

---

[6] Ibid. 133, from a statement apparently made in 1711, cited in a long letter, written two years later, by the Amsterdam *ma'amad* (Sephardi Community Council).

[7] Scholem, *Sabbatai Sevi*, 282. On the centrality of faith in the Sabbatian value system, and its affinity with the Christian notion of faith, see also ibid. 211–12, 282–4, 312, 487–9, 689–91, and 795–6. For a definition of Sabbatian doctrine as focused essentially, from the outset, on the problematics of faith rather than on the hope for concrete, political redemption, see Liebes, 'Sabbatean Messianism', 93–106; and Elqayam, 'Mystery of Faith' (Heb.), 1–6.

[8] See e.g. Rom. 3: 28, 4: 13–6, 5: 1; Gal. 3: 24; Eph. 2: 5–9; Jas. 2: 24.

[9] For a consideration of the possibility of Christian influence, see Scholem, *Sabbatai Sevi*, 282–4.

[10] See BT *Ber.* 17a. On the relationship of women to the commandments in rabbinic tradition see Ellinson, *Woman and the Mitzvot*; R. Biale, *Women and Jewish Law*, 10–43; and Meiselman, *Jewish Woman in Jewish Law*.

regard to personal faith, there existed no halakhic or institutional mechanism that would differentiate the women from the men. The more the Sabbatians stressed the value of faith as the test of redemptive Judaism, and the further they strayed from the system of the commandments, which they saw as a world order whose time had passed, the greater their women's capacity grew to become actively involved in the messianic revolution on an equal footing with the men.

Moreover, the most important, kabbalistically charged, religious act for the Sabbatians was *tikun*, the act of 'rectifying' or 'restoring' the world to perfection. Where Nathan of Gaza had seen *tikun* as an ascetic rite of penitence,[11] other Sabbatian circles transformed it into a range of antinomian acts of transgression, on the model of Sabbatai Zevi's 'bizarre acts'. These acts did not consist in breaking those positive commandments that have no bearing on women, but rather they tended to comprise transgressions of commandments that apply to the entire community, and in particular the negative commandments, which apply in their entirety to women just as much as to men. This broke the monopoly exercised by men over the full scope of religious activity, opening it wide to women, who were quite as capable as men—if not even more so—of 'rectifying' the world by way of transgression. For the quintessential Sabbatian 'restorative' transgressions pertained largely, and not accidentally, to the body, such as eating forbidden foods or at forbidden times, and, above all, breaking the code of sexual purity.[12] The body—the locus of this 'restorative' action—had long been identified in the medieval philosophical and kabbalistic traditions with the

[11] On Nathan's penitential acts of *tikun* see Scholem, *Sabbatai Sevi*, 236–40, and Elqayam, 'To Know Messiah' (Heb.), 640–50.

[12] See e.g. the detailed list of transgressions appearing in the testimonies of the repentant Sabbatians given before the rabbinic court of Satanów on 13 Sivan 5516 (1756) and reproduced in Emden, *Sefer shimush*, 5b–7b. Most of the transgressions consisted of adultery, incest, and whoring, while the rest had to do with trespassing the limits placed on the pleasures of the body, such as smoking on the sabbath, breaking fasts, eating non-kosher meat, or imbibing spirits distilled from grain on Passover. According to one of the witnesses, he was asked to prove his loyalty to the sect by transgressing the prohibition on sexual contact with another man's wife. This transgression was clearly meant to serve as the test of his Sabbatian orientation: 'R. Joseph once said to me: "Kiss my wife, and then I'll know that your faith is truly sincere"' (ibid. 6b, §20). Emden himself gives the following definition of the essence of Sabbatianism:

> From what is known of the evil opinions of the sect of Sabbatai Zevi, may the name of the wicked rot, which is worse than any kind of idol-worship, their corrupt and loathsome goal is to upend the words of the living God. They turn day into night, making of transgression, commandment—and of commandment, transgression—and they turn all the prohibitions

feminine realm as opposed to the masculine realm of spirit or soul.[13] The physical body with its sensual appetites, and particularly its sexuality, were considered the natural habitat of women, whose very creation and existence marked out the sexual tension between male and female. In this habitat women were viewed as naturally able not only to act, but also to take charge, and to activate the men around them.

No wonder, then, that the Sabbatian prophetess Hayah Schor, according to the testimonies surveyed above,[14] excelled at using her body not only to per-

in the Torah, *particularly those against whoring and adultery*, into great acts of *tikun* for their souls, which are hewn from the rootstock of filth. They take great pleasure in any opportunity to lure others into an act of transgression. (Emden, *Akitsat akrav*, 7*a*; emphasis added)

Elsewhere he reports: 'The most terrible sins are commandments to them, and acts of *tikun* for their souls, such as sexual contact with another man's wife, adultery, and onanism' (Emden, *Sefer hitabekut*, 42*b*). To be sure, there might be grounds to suspect that Emden exaggerated the sexual transgressions of the Sabbatians on account of his own preoccupation with sexual matters and with the pathology of the bodily organs involved, as disclosed by his autobiographical work, *Megilat sefer*. On this book and its surprisingly confessional quality in this respect see Schacter, 'Autobiography of Jacob Emden', 441–2; Moseley, *Jewish Autobiography*, 369–79; id., *For Myself Alone*, 288–312. Mortimer J. Cohen, in his biographical work, *Jacob Emden*, does present Emden as having projected his own sexual psychopathology on to the Sabbatians, whom he accused of utter sexual corruption; and see Scholem's critique of this interpretation in *Researches* (Heb.), esp. pp. 655–8. However, Emden's charges are confirmed not only by the testimonies of penitent Sabbatians that he himself collected, and by other anti-Sabbatian reports (see e.g. Fleckeles, *Ahavat david*, 14*b*, 19*a–b*, 27*b*, and many other places; Fleckeles, too, characterizes the Sabbatians mainly by their sexual transgressions), but also in the writings of the Sabbatians themselves, such as the book *Va'avo hayom el ha'ayin*, which makes abundant use of wild, flagrant sexual symbolism. On this see Liebes' remarks in *On Sabbatianism* (Heb.), 79, 107, and 336 n. 5. See also Perlmutter, *Jonathan Eybeschuetz* (Heb.), 49, 53, and 326–7. Emden thus would seem to have been correct in his evaluation, and it is further confirmed by reports about the activities of the Salonican Sabbatians after their mass conversion to Islam; see Scholem, *Researches* (Heb.), 346–51; and Benayahu, 'Great Apostasy' (Heb.), 99–100.

[13] On the association of woman with body and man with soul, paralleling the conceptualization of the female as matter and the male as form, which has its roots in Greek philosophy, see Buchan, *Women in Plato*; Horowitz, 'Aristotle and Woman'; R. Baer, *Philo's Use*; Allen, *The Concept of Woman*; Maimonides, *Guide*, i. 'Introduction to the First Part', p. 13, and ch. 17, p. 43; Zohar, i. 124*b*, *Midrash hane'elam*; *Tikunei hazohar*, §21, 61*a*, and §70, 134*a*. And see Klein-Braslavy, *Maimonides' Interpretation* (Heb.), 198–9, 202–6; Robinson, 'The Source of Maimonides' Plato'; Schwartz, *The Philosophy* (Heb.), s.v. *ḥomer* and *tsurah*; Boyarin, *Carnal Israel*, 57–60; Liebes, 'Sections of the Zohar' (Heb.), p. 171, §14, s.v. *gufa*. Even the female *sefirah* of Malkhut is called 'body', as against her male partner, Tiferet, which is called 'soul'; see ibid., p. 178, §33; Green, 'Shekhinah', 41 n. 163.   [14] See above, Ch. 1, at nn. 72–80.

form transgressive acts of *tikun* on her own behalf, but also to initiate men in her milieu who were making their way into the Sabbatian circle. Reading between the lines of the testimonies that Emden collected from repentant Sabbatians, and from Emden's own sarcastic comments about the nature of their activities, we learn of the dimension of messianic *tikun*—that is, of religious activism—that the Sabbatians attributed to the licentious sexual activities in which their wives took a central and active part. Thus, for example, Emden recorded an account of the 'restorative' adulterous activities of Jonathan Eybeschuetz and his wife:

And he [the witness] said that the old man's [Eybeschuetz's] wife, who had died about six years before, also used to commit adultery with others, as he did and still does with the wives of other men, all for the sake of *tikunim*, 'he with a pumpkin and she with a marrow'.[15] And she, too, received her just deserts: she got her punishment by way of affliction with cancer of the breast, and the doctors amputated her breasts, heaven forfend.[16]

He records a similar testimony regarding the activities of another woman, the wife of Wolf Akives, who, together with her spouse, belonged to the circle of Jonathan Eybeschuetz's son Wolf, and whose adulteries involved the noted Sabbatian Moses David of Podhajce:[17]

Whenever he ran into the wife of Wolf Akives, he would curse her to her face and call her the wanton whore of Moses David. . . . And he said that that Satan, Moses David, may the name of the wicked rot, used to pride himself on having committed adultery with the wife of Wolf Akives, (cavorting with her) possibly as many as ten times. He would joke that he'd gone many a time in her company 'with the pumpkins'. He [i.e. the witness] said that in principle, 'You should know that whatever you suspect about Eybeschuetz and his wicked circle is but the thousandth part of all the wicked, filthy, abominable things that they do, all in the name of *tikun*.[18]

These acts of *tikun*—the positive commandments of Sabbatianism, however perverse they may have seemed from a halakhic point of view—shifted the women from the margins to the centre of the arena of religious performance. Thus, they, too, in their way, reflect the egalitarian disposition of the Sabbatian revolution.

[15] Cf. BT *Meg.* 12*a* (and also *Sot.* 10*a*); that is, they are both iniquitous in the same way.

[16] Emden, *Sefer hitabekut*, 43*a*; see also ibid. 18*a*.

[17] On Moses David of Podhajce, Wolf Akives, and this circle as a whole see Wirszubski, 'Sabbatian Kabbalist' (Heb.).   [18] Emden, *Sefer hitabekut*, 42*b*–43*a*.

Women in Sectarian Sabbatianism

FROM THE VERY OUTSET, it was evident that Sabbatianism held a special attraction for women. All the evidence on the eruption of messianic prophecy during this early period[1] suggests that women responded en masse to Sabbatai Zevi's tidings. As we have seen, they were often the first to acknowledge his messiahship on the strength of their prophetic visions—themselves a phenomenon deemed remarkable enough to invest the redemptive tidings with the ring of truth, and so to convince even the most eminent and persistent male sceptics. We shall return below to the question of women's particular receptivity to the Sabbatai Zevi's messianic call, to examine it in light of the promises he made specifically to the female sex.[2]

However, in those early stages, at the height of the movement's popularity, the Sabbatian faith, enthusiastically embraced by men and women alike, had not yet begun to divide the 'believers' from the bulk of the Jewish community, nor did it clash, either overtly or covertly, with its traditional institutions and values. On the contrary; the community itself was rapidly being transformed into a fellowship of messianic 'believers', and it marked off as 'heretics' the minority who dared to voice their opposition or doubts.[3] Adherence to the messianic faith did not, as yet, demand that the restraints of Jewish law be cast off or subverted; rather, the movement initially called for repentance in entirely traditional terms. Even the first antinomian acts being ordered by Sabbatai Zevi, such as the abolition of the fasts of 10 Tevet, 17 Tamuz, or 9 Av, did not split the believers or generate any tension between their self-perception as pious Jews and the integrity of their Sabbatian faith.[4]

Only after Sabbatai Zevi's apostasy, and increasingly in the years following his death, when Sabbatianism—now discredited, proclaimed a heresy, and

---

[1] See Ch. 1 above.　　　　　　　[2] See below, this chapter and Ch. 5.

[3] On this see, Scholem, *Sabbatai Sevi*, 475, 515, 518–21; id., *Kabbalah*, 260.

[4] See e.g. Scholem, *Sabbatai Sevi*, 466–7, 532, 577, 599, 615–33, 643–4, 658.

hounded by the rabbinic authorities—was forced underground to find its out-lets in a variety of clandestine sectarian groupings, did the messianic faith of the secret believers assume its subversive character, explicitly and consciously pitting halakhic Judaism against a creed committed to its demolition from within, as a necessary stage in the realization of the redemptive vision. Among other things, this subversive Sabbatianism undermined the gender boundaries rooted in halakhah, which had traditionally governed the social and religious order of Jewish society. As a result, it was precisely within the sectarian organizations in which Sabbatianism persisted throughout the eighteenth century and until at least the first quarter of the nineteenth, that the tradi-tional barriers between men and women also crumbled, both in theory and in practice.

The testimonies Emden collected on Sabbatian women—whether or not they were known as prophetesses—who were active in the sectarian organiza-tions of his time focused, as we have seen, on their sexual profligacy, which he tended to dissociate from its antinomian–religious context and denounce as mere debauchery and the desire to cast off the burden of religious law. An ex-ample of this is his treatment of Schöndl-Katharina Hirschl, wife of Solomon Zalman Halevi Dobruschka, mother of the Frankist Moses Dobruschka, and a cousin of Jacob Frank, whom Scholem describes as 'the best-known benefactor of the Moravian Sabbatians, especially in the 1760s'.[5] Emden consistently refers to her as 'the whore' or 'the strumpet of Brünn (Brno)', reporting on her antics in the company of the young Sabbatian messiah Wolf, son of Jonathan Eybeschuetz, as nothing more than wanton depravity:

In Brünn, Wolf took up lodgings with Dobruschki, who was married to a flagrant whore. She rode out to meet him: 'And lo, a woman meets him, dressed as a harlot, wily of heart' [Prov. 7: 9–10]. She went with him in a covered wagon and brought him to her home, and this youth lived with her as a man with his wife. He stayed with her for many a day, even when her husband was not at home. He even went riding with her several times in a covered wagon, the two of them alone, and once they returned home on sabbath's eve, several hours after nightfall. That accursed woman held him fast, liberally endowing him with money and with beautiful garments that she had made for him.[6]

---

[5] Scholem, *Studies and Texts* (Heb.), 144–5. On her, and especially on her financial activities, see Krauss, 'Schöndl Dobruschka', although Krauss did not fully grasp the nature of her connec-tion to Sabbatianism and to Jacob Frank, and his information on this is rather confused.

[6] Emden, *Sefer hitabekut*, 19b. On fo. 24a he again writes: "And lo, a woman meets him, dressed as a harlot, wily of heart'"—a well-known strumpet came out to meet him at Dresden

Another example is Meir Prossnitz's wife, who served as the cook in the home of Wolf Eybeschuetz, of whom both she and her husband were ardent followers. Emden had this to say about her:

The festive meal[7] was cooked by the wife of Meirl Prossnitz. It is said of her that she is a beautiful but coarse woman [cf. Prov. 11: 22] who sits in the street spreading her legs to any passer-by, her underskirts exposed, her legs made bare [cf. Jer. 13: 22] up to the crotch while people in numbers promenade past her house.[8]

Even if Emden was right—and as we have seen, he probably was—in consistently ascribing such conduct to the Sabbatian women he describes, and in presenting this conduct as the very hallmark of their Sabbatian affiliation, it is difficult to penetrate beyond his exposés into the significance the women themselves may have attached to their sexual licence, and what part it played in determining the texture of their sectarian religious experience. Though there are several reports of women who were coerced or lured into committing sexual transgressions by their Sabbatian husbands, fathers, or brothers,[9] in

by arrangement of the procurer Nathan Erholtz, who was his [i.e. Wolf Eybeschuetz's] herald and made him a big name. He brought the whore to Dresden, and they transported this youth, Eybeschuetz's son, alone with her in a carriage. They travelled together to her home in Brünn, and she bestowed upon him liberally her earnings from the proceeds of the imperial tobacco trade in the province of Moravia. And so she prospered and became wealthy, and she held on to the youth, kissed him, provided for him, and dressed him in silks.' See also ibid. 30*b* and 45*b*.

[7] The 'festival', on this occasion, was the fast-day of 9 Av—an allusion to the group's antinomianism.   [8] Emden, *Sefer hitabekut*, 30*a*–*b*. See also ibid. 28*a* and 38*b*.

[9] See e.g. ibid. 44*a*, on a woman 'whose husband used to try to seduce her and also to rape her and force her into having sexual relations with him when she was menstruating, and she, being a pious woman, refused to obey him', until finally he sent her, on pain of being beaten to death, to Jonathan Eybeschuetz, who permitted her to have sexual relations with her husband while she was menstruating. For a similar instance see Emden, *Zot torat hakena'ot*, 70. Apparently there were even some instances in which covert Sabbatians were unmasked by their wives, who refused to transgress the commandments of sexual purity at their behest. Thus, for example, Emden reports: 'In Podhajce, too, their shame was disclosed by a woman whose husband had demanded of her that she sin with him [in the context, by demanding that she have sexual relations with him while menstruating]. Her husband had assured her that several great scholars were in agreement that doing this was a great *tikun* and a *mitsvah* in this time, and that their *magid* [preacher], R. Issachar, whom they considered a great and pious man, had thus commanded. This clever woman slyly told him that if this were so, then she would surely comply.' However, she arranged a dinner for the Sabbatian *magid*, to which she also invited 'the pious heads of the community', and that was how his shame came to be exposed; 'the matter came to light, and these sectarians were punished by the [civil] authorities with an enormous fine' (ibid.).

most cases they seem to have been quite compliant, and in some they initiated such acts of their own free will.[10] We may well suppose that their active involvement with Sabbatianism gave these women a new sense of power and self-worth. This can perhaps be read between the lines of Emden's account of Jacob Frank's marriage:

Someone here said that a man called R. Tuvyah[11] gave his daughter as wife to that accursed Frank, of whose activities he had been unaware. She was a very beautiful woman. When her father later heard about his wicked deeds . . . he counselled his daughter to separate from him and obtain a divorce. However, she did not heed her father, because she had already begun whoring with [Frank's] wicked company, who made him wealthy on her account, for it was by her means that he acquired all this wealth, and he used to parade her around in jewels like a queen, 'he with pumpkins and she with marrows'.[12] She prostituted herself with priests and nobles as well. She was also a great sorceress, entrapping souls in a pit: 'her guests are in the depths of She'ol' [Prov. 9: 18].[13]

Admittedly, this rumour may be somewhat inaccurate. Hannah's father Tuvyah would actually seem to have maintained cordial relations with Frank; at any rate, he welcomed Frank into his home when the latter paid a return visit to Nikopol in 1756, and he even went to see Frank while he was imprisoned in Częstochowa,[14] which is hard to reconcile with an attempt to sever his daughter's marital union upon learning of the 'wicked deeds' of his son-in-law. However, Emden connects the daughter's refusal to oblige her father by divorcing her husband not only with her enjoyment of high status as Frank's wife, but also with her craving for the sexual profligacy obtaining in his circle, her relations with the higher echelons of the Christian nobility and priesthood, her capacity to amass wealth for herself and her husband, her talents as a sorceress (a synonym, in Emden's terminology, for a Sabbatian prophetess[15]), and her power to 'entrap' other souls. All this points to her willing and complete identification with the 'wicked company' and hints at her motives: the deviant sectarian framework threw open to her, as a woman, a new, wide-

[10] An example is Hayah Schor, who chose her own partners, not always with the knowledge and agreement of her husband; see above, Ch. 2, at nn. 77–80.

[11] On Frank's father-in-law, the merchant Tuvyah of Nikopol, whose daughter Hannah married Frank in 1752, see Kraushar, *Jacob Frank*, i. 42, 69; see also below, at n. 14.

[12] See above, Ch. 3 n. 15.   [13] Emden, *Sefer shimush*, 83a.

[14] See Frank, *Words of the Lord*, §1257, and Levine, *Kronika*, 68, §69 (Doktór, *Rozmaite adnotacje*, 70).   [15] Cf. above, Ch. 1, at nn. 72–4.

ranging field of activity, infinitely enhancing her social, economic, sexual, and spiritual power. Whether or not the rumour cited by Emden derives from a genuine residual memory as regards the early period of Frank's marriage, it seems to preserve a true impression of the attraction the sectarian fraternity held specifically for women.

This impression is reinforced by the testimony of Rabbi Eleazar Fleckeles of Prague, who refers to the presence of women, and their active participation, in the conclaves of the Sabbatians, their study sessions, and the full range of their activities—a phenomenon which he, too, singles out as a hallmark of the sectarian heresy:

And if you ask, how shall we know them, these worthless men who are unclean by [dint of coming in contact with] the dead body of a wicked man [cf. Num. 9: 6–7], I shall give you clear signs. They who are unlearned in the Talmud and halakhic works but occupy themselves with rabbinic legends and the Zohar . . . and they among whom the women, too, sit in study . . . 'They all [erroneously] make substitutions [for that which is sanctified], men and women alike' [Mishnah *Tem.* 1: 1; cf. Lev. 27: 10], 'they have all gone astray, they are all alike corrupted' [Ps. 14: 3] by vain pursuits.[16]

He returns to the same subject a little further on:

It is this to which Moses our teacher, may he rest in peace, was referring when he declared: 'Beware lest there be among you a man or woman or family or tribe, whose heart turns away this day from the Lord your God ...' [Deut. 29: 18]. A clue lies in the words 'lest there be among you a man or woman', for in that wicked faith, men and women come together—the women, too, dabble in their vanities. The women sit 'weeping for Tamuz' [Ezek. 8: 14] and Av, because we do not believe that that corpse Sabbatai Zevi, may his name be obliterated, was the messiah, 'and all who believe that he is a strong redeemer'[17] . . . are glad and happy, and they make these days 'for gladness and feasting and a good day' [Esther 9: 19]. And the reason he specified 'or family' etc. . . . is that most of the time He smote the entire family[18] with this evil plague, and this is one of the clearest signs of this vile leprosy, 'of Merari were the family of the Mahlites' [Num. 3: 33], 'it is the gall of asps within [it—i.e. the family]' [Job 20: 14].[19]

Again and again, Fleckeles emphasizes the full participation of women in the life of the sect:

---

[16] Fleckeles, *Ahavat david*, 6*b*.   [17] From a hymn for the High Holy Days liturgy.

[18] A play on the words *safaḥ* (smote) and *mishpaḥah*, 'family', following Isa. 3: 17.

[19] Fleckeles, *Ahavat david*, 7*a*. The word *merorat*, 'gall', in the verse from Job is used to make a play on the name of Merari in the verse from Numbers, while the name 'Mahlites' is taken alliteratively to invoke the word *maḥalah*, 'disease'.

Thus do they commit together all these deeds of folly, men and women, youths and infants, and so lamented the prophet: 'but hear, all you peoples, and behold my suffering; my maidens and my young men have gone into captivity'[20] [Lam. 1: 18]. 'All are fouled by afflictions' [Mishnah *Neg.* 3: 1]; all must fulfil the obligation to show their faces[21] in the town where he is buried:[22] the young man and the sullied girl [cf. Deut. 32: 25[23]], 'the grey-haired and the aged' [Job 15: 10].[24]

According to the documentation in our hands, not only were women full participants in the Sabbatian practices of their male relatives; they could also join the movement independently—of their own accord, in their own right, and at times even in defiance of their husbands. For example, while the aforementioned Schöndl-Katharina Hirschl-Dobruschka most certainly was an active sponsor and propagandist of the young Sabbatian messiah-prophet Wolf Eybeschuetz, nothing is known of any involvement with the Sabbatian movement on the part of her husband, Solomon Zalman Halevi Dobruschka, a wealthy tobacco contractor who died as a Jew in 1774.[25] We do know that ten of the couple's twelve children left the Jewish faith as Frankists, most of them, including the second son, Moses Dobruschka, in the year after their father's death (the eldest son had already been baptized in 1769, while three sisters did not do so until 1791).[26] Scholem, in his comprehensive study of Moses Dobruschka and his family, surmised that 'her [i.e. Schöndl's] husband was almost certainly a member of the sect, though he was not active in it, as far as

[20] The word *shevi*, 'captivity', playing on the name of Sabbatai (Heb. *shabetai*) Zevi.

[21] This passage is a play on Mishnah *Ḥag.* 1: 1.

[22] The reference is to the pilgrimages made by sect members to Offenbach, where Frank had died on 10 December 1791. This obligation of course fell equally upon men and women.

[23] The verse reads 'young man and virgin [*betulah*]'; the word *pesulah*, 'sullied girl', is a play on *betulah*, which these Ashkenazi Jews would have pronounced *besulah*.

[24] Fleckeles, *Ahavat david*, 25*b*; see also ibid. 26*a*. For further evidence on this, including the instruction of women in the Zohar, see below, Ch. 5, at nn. 103–50.

[25] See Scholem, *Studies and Texts* (Heb.), 145 and 147. On him and his family see also Krauss, 'Schöndl Dobruschka', 144–6.

[26] See Scholem, *Studies and Texts* (Heb.), 149–51. Scholem supposed that Schöndl Hirschl herself must also have converted to Christianity at the end of her life, when she changed her name to Katharina; see ibid. 151 and n. 31. However, Arthur Mandel argues that the name change was not necessarily a consequence of baptism but rather 'was done in compliance with the imperial order issued on 23 July 1787, according to which all the Jews in Austria had to take German names'. He asserts that there is no evidence for Schöndl-Katharina having been baptized before her death in 1791; see Mandel, 'Marginalia' (Heb.), 72. See also id., *Militant Messiah*, 84.

we can tell for the moment'.[27] However, we could equally well conclude from the utter lack of evidence to suggest any form of engagement by Solomon Dobruschka in Sabbatian activity of any sort, as against the wealth of attestations regarding his wife's flagrant, independent Sabbatian pursuits, that it was she who maintained the family's affiliation with Sabbatianism, guiding all her sons and daughters along the same path.[28] This conclusion is compatible with the appearance of Schöndl's name, but not that of her husband (who was still alive at the time) in one of the lists of the Sabbatian heretics whom Emden set out to expose in his writings. The names of other women, too, occasionally appear in his lists in their own right and not as appendages of their husbands. Emden's list of Wolf Eybeschuetz's supporters reads as follows: 'These were his supporters in Prague: Zerah Eidlitz, Zalman Karov, Nathan Yerushalmi, and the widow of Simon Frankel. In Holleschau [Holešov] his relatives gave aid to the wicked. In Prossnitz and Brünn there was the whore Dobruschka [i.e. Schöndl Hirschl].'[29]

Moreover, we learn from Moses Porges' memoir of his sojourn among the Frankists at Offenbach of the presence at the court of groups of women who had arrived without male companions, and who clearly functioned as members in their own right of the circle of its postulants and supporters. Some were married, like Roesel Eger, the Sabbatian prophetess from Prague, while others were single, like her niece, who was probably the 'daughter of Mendel Itschin [or Jičín]', chosen to offer her services in the bed of Frank's son Rochus on the Day of Atonement in 1799.[30] Roesel Eger had strong family connections with the Sabbatian movement: her brothers, including Jonas Wehle, were the leaders of the Sabbatian circle in Prague and its environs at the time. However, most of the reports about her and her involvement with Sabbatianism make

[27] Scholem, *Studies and Texts* (Heb.), 145. Scholem suggested this tentatively in his 1970 article on Moses Dobruschka; it would appear that he had fruitlessly searched for evidence of Solomon Zalman's Sabbatianism. Some thirty years earlier, in 1939–40, when his critique of Mortimer Cohen's *Jacob Emden* was published, he was still quite certain that 'the wealthy Zalman Dobruschka in Brünn, and most of his partners in the tobacco business, were Sabbatians' (Scholem, *Researches* (Heb.), 674).

[28] This looks all the more likely since her children were still minors when her husband died in 1774, except for the eldest son Karl, who was born in 1751. See Krauss, 'Schöndl Dobruschka', 143.

[29] Emden, *Sefer hitabekut*, 45*b*. The list appeared in the first edition of the work, published in 1762, while Schöndl's husband, Solomon, did not die until 1774.

[30] See above, Ch. I, at nn. 92–4 and 96–8.

no mention at all of her husband, whose existence may be inferred only from the fact that she was called by his surname, Eger, rather than by her maiden name of Wehle. For example, her husband clearly did not accompany her on her visit to the court at Offenbach, since, according to the testimony given by Wolf Lipmann Hamburger to the rabbinical court of Fürth, the Frankists exacted of her, personally and directly, the same sum that they collected from all the other Sabbatian pilgrims arriving from Prague. These included her brothers Jonas Wehle, Mendel Itschin, and other 'intimates', but her husband's name is conspicuously missing from the list, and he is not mentioned anywhere else throughout Hamburger's testimony. On the contrary; according to the investigator who recorded the witnesses' accounts, it was Roesel herself who objected to the size of the sum demanded of her, and who ultimately had to submit to the order of Frank's sons and pay up: 'Mendel Itschin, too, was made to pay thousands of guilders. Roesel Eger, too, was made to do the same; at first she even refused to obey the order, but they compelled her to do it.'[31]

In the single source where her husband, Simon Eger, is mentioned by name, it is explicitly said of him that he withstood all of his wife Roesel's efforts to draw him into her family's Sabbatian tradition and firmly refused to donate any of his money to the sect's funds, which were meant to maintain the court at Offenbach. The marital stress this occasioned ultimately led to a total separation, whereupon the couple embarked upon a protracted dispute regarding the division of their property, which climaxed in a vocal, public quarrel in July 1799.[32] It would seem, then, that Roesel Eger's commitment to the sect took precedence over her loyalty to her husband, and her marriage to a man who objected to her Sabbatian activities not only failed to put a stop to them, but, on the contrary, was treated as an obstacle to be removed.

Another example of this is Jacob Goliński, an erstwhile Polish supporter of Jacob Frank, who eventually recanted his Sabbatian faith and became his sworn enemy. He, too, was married to a woman—her name has not been preserved—who appears to have belonged to a long-standing Sabbatian family, and is likely to have been the one who introduced him to the heretical messianic faith. When he changed his stripe, in 1770, she remained faithful to the doctrines of the sect, abandoned her husband and, on her own, joined

---

[31] Gelber, 'Di zikhroynes fun moses porges', appendix 1, col. 292, §11.
[32] See Žáček, 'Zwei Beiträge', 363–4 and 405.

Frank's coterie in Brünn, where he settled with a group of his adherents in 1773, following his release from imprisonment in Częstochowa.[33]

According to the Polish *Kronika*, a group of fourteen women was brought to Brünn on 27 September 1777. They stayed for some ten days, until 7 October, during which period Frank subjected them to a certain 'secret', 'humiliating', and 'shameful' experience. He subsequently sent them a note (described by the *Kronika*'s author as 'amusing'), promising that 'because they obeyed me, and I had humiliated and shamed them in front of everyone, when my time comes I shall raise and place them above everyone'.[34]

Groups of women, apparently acting on their own initiative, had already been joining Frank's court at Częstochowa. An explicit reference to this appears in the *Kronika*'s account of a period marked by feverish activity in 1767/8, in the course of which Frank sent emissaries to Moravia, Prague, Podolia, Chernovtsy, Germany, and Hungary, apparently in order to rouse his supporters to action. At the height of this period, 'on the 20th [of June 1768], Pawłowski and Franciszek Wołowski arrived *with the women who had come from Ruhatyn*'.[35] The same source tells us of the presence at the court of married 'sisters' whose husbands were considered 'aliens'—that is, they did not share their wives' Sabbatian faith. Frank instructed them to divorce those husbands and marry 'brothers', who were similarly ordered to divest themselves of their 'alien' wives:

At Częstochowa, when the old men and the women sat down to table with the Lord . . . after the luncheon meal, he called upon them together to reveal his intention, namely, the utter necessity that the brothers whose wives were aliens should leave them and take to wife those sisters whose own husbands were aliens, not brothers.[36]

A similar picture emerges from the Polish documents examined by Balaban:

---

[33] See the discussion ibid. 355–7, and the formal complaint lodged by Jacob Goliński against Jacob Frank with the Austrian authorities in the summer of 1776, ibid., appendix 1, pp. 401–3. See also Rabinowicz, 'Jacob Frank in Brno', 443–4. Rabinowicz, unaware of Žáček's earlier publication in Prague, published Goliński's complaint from another copy of it that he found in Brünn. Substantial portions of Goliński's complaint appear in English translation in Kraushar, *Jacob Frank*, ii. 262–8.

[34] Levine, *Kronika*, 84, §97 (Doktór, *Rozmaite adnotacje*, 79–80). Cf. Levine's comment on this, on p. 85 n. 206. See also Kraushar, *Jacob Frank*, ii. 270.

[35] *Kronika*, 72, §71 (*Rozmaite adnotacje*, 71); emphasis added.

[36] *Kronika*, 96, §105 (*Rozmaite adnotacje*, 87).

In 1752, things of this nature [i.e. Sabbatian sexual transgressions] also happened in Brody, where the Jews had enacted, as it were, the practice of confession. Those who came to confess would recount to the 'confessors' the sins of various Jewish women, so much so that their husbands and mothers forsook them and expelled them from their homes; not only did their husbands banish them from married life, but their fathers and mothers, too, would not let them set foot in their houses. The '[Jewish] Council of the Lwów District', which dared to issue a grave condemnation of these foolish women's activities, was harshly punished for this. The women who were to suffer punishment turned for assistance to the lord of the city, Joseph Potocki, who dispersed the Jewish elders and harshly punished the most eminent of them.[37]

It was clearly the women who were exposed in these confessions as Sabbatians practising their faith by transgression, while the husbands who divorced them were responding to their actions in accordance with the demands of Jewish law. That is to say, they were halakhically observant Jews who did not identify with their wives' heresy.[38]

[37] Balaban, *Frankist Movement* (Heb.), 72. On this see also Gelber, *History of the Jews in Brody* (Heb.), 106–7.

[38] Dov Ber Birkenthal of Bolechów also tells of Sabbatian women who entertained men in their homes when their husbands were away, put them to the Sabbatian test of eating fat from the candle, and if they ate it, thus proving their Sabbatianism, offered them their sexual services as well. See Birkenthal, *Divrei binah*, 212. Birkenthal implies that their husbands, too, were Sabbatians but were out of the house when these acts were committed:

> It is said that they were also permitted to swap wives. If one of them came to the home of another sect member and did not find the husband at home, he would tell the wife that he, too, belonged to their group, as described above. Then she would give him a piece of fat from candles made for lighting, and if he ate it without fear of breaking the prohibition on eating forbidden fat, which is punishable by excommunication, then she would be willing to fulfil any of his desires; she would debauch herself.

However, the Sabbatians saw 'making a bed for a guest' as a holy act that was to be performed with the express knowledge and permission of the woman's husband; compare, for example, the angry response of the Sabbatian prophetess Hayah Schor's husband, Hirschl Shabses, to her 'whoring' in his absence and without his knowledge (above, Ch. 1, at n. 57). Thus, the women referred to by Birkenthal may have been married to husbands who either objected to their wives' Sabbatian affiliation or who did not involve themselves in it, such as the women in Brody who were divorced by their husbands, expelled from their homes, and ostracized by the community. In considering all these cases, an important practical factor must be taken into account, that may have enhanced the women's loyalty to the sect, or at least would have stopped them from taking the same path of repentance as the men who confessed their sins in Brody. Reverting from sectarian Sabbatianism to halakhic Judaism was extremely difficult for women who had been exposed as adulteresses, since Jewish law mandated divorce without financial compensa-

Women whose husbands shared in their Sabbatian faith are also some-times described as taking an independent, daring, public stand on issues relat-ing to their sectarian views. They were clearly acting without fear of conflict with the community's leaders. Thus, for example, Emden relates of the wife of Wolf Akives in Altona (with the intention, of course, not of praising but of denigrating her bold personal initiative):

In the year 1766 a 'chased deer' [*tsevi mudaḥ*, a play on the name of Sabbatai Zevi (Heb. *tsevi*, meaning deer); cf. Isa. 13: 14], Aharon Teomim of Horodenka,[39] was caught here. He was banished in disgrace, and a special broadsheet was published about him. When he came here, he immediately enquired after the address of Wolf Akives, and in the women's synagogue (after the scandal of this abomination had already been told around the town), his wife[40] declared publicly that she supported him, disregarding the authority of the rabbi and the rabbinic court.[41]

The women of the Wehle family in Prague—Jonas Wehle's wife Eva and her two married daughters, Judith Frankel and Rebecca Wiener—were also known in their community as active Sabbatian heretics in their own right. They (and not their husbands, though the latter were also known as Sabbatians) clashed publicly with the sect's opponents in the city, headed by the rabbis, and they were at the centre of a brawl the broke out in the famous Altneuschul on 10 October 1800. In the course of this incident, Judith Frankel was denounced for 'poisoning' her husband—that is, for goading him into Sabbatianism—a charge that was also levelled at her on other occasions, apparently with justification.[42] The same accusation was made against Jonas

tion from their husbands, and this had severe social and economic consequences, as is evident from the fate of the banished wives in Brody. This factor may have left them no other choice but to retain their sectarian identity, out of a sense of having 'burned their bridges', in contrast to the men who, once they had confessed and returned to the fold, could be reintegrated into Jewish society.

[39] On him see Scholem, *Studies and Texts* (Heb.), 136–7.

[40] I believe this refers to the wife of Wolf Akives.   [41] Emden, *Sefer hitabekut*, 73b–74a.

[42] See Žáček, 'Zwei Beiträge', 363, 376–7. Among the official documents from the archive of the Czech Ministry of the Interior upon which Žáček based his study, some of which he pub-lished as appendices, was the testimony of Löw Enoch Hönig Edler von Hönigsberg, the hus-band of Judith's sister Deborah. In his complaint to the municipal police against the city's zealous rabbis for their persecution of the innocent Frankists, von Hönigsberg described the events that took place in Prague. Scholem published this document in his 'Frankist Document'; see p. 806 there. See also below, Appendix, at n. 37.

Wehle's two sisters, Roesel Eger, who, as we have seen, had failed in her efforts to draw her husband Simon into the faith, and separated from him on this account,[43] and her sister, who married Markus Simon Porges, inducing him to embrace the heresy. Markus Simon's mother, the widowed Malkah Porges, never desisted from her desperate efforts to distance her son from his wife's family, and these included, on one occasion, accosting the heretics on the city's streets.[44] In the satirical *A Conversation between the Year 1800 and the Year 1801*, composed in Prague in the very same period,[45] a certain family—and this most certainly was meant to be the Wehle family—is denounced as the core of the city's heretical foment. The Haskalah-inspired author emphasizes that the Sabbatian arrogance and effrontery of this clan's women rival only the 'overweening pride' of its men:

Many of this new sect's adherents in the principal Jewish community of P— [i.e. Prague] belong to one family . . . The outstanding quality of the members of this family is their overweening pride, their pursuit of fancied honour and grandeur. Both the men and the women of the family share the same trait of 'speaking with insolent necks' [cf. Ps. 75: 6]; they are arch of brow and brazen of visage. . . . And truth be told, not to bury it under my tongue: they are not lacking in sense and cunning, nor are they ignorant of the Torah and Jewish lore. They are most famous for this—that their men are lovers of learning and science, while their women are valiant and by no means unspirited.[46]

That the Sabbatian women belonged to the sect personally, individually, and in their own right is also implied by the very use of the term 'sisters', which is what they were consistently called in Frank's court, just as the men were called 'brothers'.[47] This designation was bestowed indiscriminately upon married and single women alike,[48] and it was clearly intended to create a 'familial'

---

[43] See above, at n. 32.   [44] See Žáček, 'Zwei Beiträge', 364 and 406.
[45] See above, Ch. 1 n. 100.   [46] *A Conversation* (Heb.), 8–9.
[47] The term 'sisters' first appears in the period of Frank's sojourn in Iwanie, in 1758. At that time, 'he chose these first seven women and designated them as his sisters' (Levine, *Kronika*, 48, §39; Doktór, *Rozmaite adnotacje*, 57). A few months later, Frank chose seven more women (*Kronika*, 50, §42; *Rozmaite adnotacje*, 58), and after that he picked out twelve men, to whom he added two more, and he called these fourteen men 'brothers' (*Kronika*, 50, §43; *Rozmaite adnotacje*, 58–9). For the use of the terms 'brothers' and 'sisters' see also *Kronika*, 52, §44; 54, §46; 56, §§47 and 49; 92, §104; 96, §§105 and 106; and 104–6, appendix (*Rozmaite adnotacje*, 59–60, 60–3, 84, 87, 94). These terms appear dozens of times throughout Frank's *Words of the Lord*.
[48] See e.g. *Kronika*, 48, §39 (*Rozmaite adnotacje*, 57), which lists 'Jakubowski's wife and

relationship that would link them to one another, to the 'brothers', and to Frank himself on a totally fresh basis. It obliterated their previous identities and status, displaced all their former familial ties,[49] and above all released them from exclusive accountability to their husbands.[50] The women's affiliation with Frank's court introduced them to an alternative egalitarian framework made up of individual 'brothers' and 'sisters' who were all—men and women, together and apart[51]—directly and equally subject to Frank's authority.[52] It is very probable that he adopted these designations by direct

Henryk Wołowski's wife' among the first seven sisters. Henryk Wołowski was among the relatives of Elisha Schor of Rohatyn—father of the prophetess Hayah Schor—who changed their family name to Wołowski (a literal translation into Polish of the Hebrew Schor, i.e. 'ox') when they converted to Christianity. See also n. 50 below.

[49] See e.g. Frank, *Words of the Lord*, §267: 'I have appointed you to be my brothers and sisters, and I have not asked you, "My children, who are you?"' My translation is based on Doktór's Polish edition; Fania Scholem's Hebrew rendering is ambivalent here.

[50] According to the *Kronika* (p. 50, §42; *Rozmaite adnotacje*, 58), a few months after choosing the first seven 'sisters' in Iwanie, Frank chose seven more women. That they were also 'sisters' seems to be implied both by the appendix to the *Kronika* (p. 106; absent from *Rozmaite adnotacje*), which lists the two groups as 'the first seven women' and 'the other seven women', making no other distinction between them, and by the text itself (p. 92, §104; *Rozmaite adnotacje*, 84), which speaks of 'those fourteen women whom the Lord chose as his sisters'. At the time of their appointment, however, he referred to the second group as 'seven girls' or 'seven maidens', so it could be that he at first assigned them to his wife or his daughter, as he had designated the first seven women for himself. This may be the implication of his allusion to Esther 2: 9, which speaks of 'seven maidens which were meet to give her out of the king's house'. At any rate, their designation as 'girls' or 'maidens' might also have effaced the women's relationship to their husbands. At least four of them were married; they were listed as 'the first wife of Pawłowski of sacred memory . . . the wife of Dębowski . . . the wife of Franciszek Wołowski . . . and the wife of Michał Wołowski'. (Franciszek Wołowski was either the former Solomon Schor, Elisha Schor's son, who was called Łukasz-Franciszek after his conversion, or Solomon's son, who was called Franciszek; Michał Wołowski was Nathan-Lipmann, another son of Elisha Schor; see Duker, 'Polish Frankism's Duration', 317.) The designation 'girls' or 'maidens' also blurred the distinction between the married women, who are called by their husbands' names, and the three women listed only by their own names ('Cimcia . . . Eva Jezierańska was first . . . old Lewińska'), who may have been single, or they may have joined Frank's court without their 'alien' husbands. It also clearly had nothing to do with their age, since one of them is actually described as 'old'.

[51] On separate but equal activities for women see below, Ch. 6.

[52] S. A. Horodetsky made a similar claim about hasidism, namely, that the status of women within its ranks became equal to that of their husbands by virtue of the couple's shared connection to the tsadik:

A shared faith, and their common yearning for the tsadik, united the hasidic husband and his

inspiration from the Christian milieu—either Catholic monastic or Orthodox schismatic—with which we know him to have had some contacts.[53] There, too, the terms symbolize the displacement of physical, familial ties by the mutual relations among individual men and women who are bonded together as a spiritual 'family', either within the framework of a sectarian cell or in a convent, a monastery or a monastic order, headed, as in Frank's case, by an all powerful, single authority figure. Moreover, the Christian 'sisters' are dedicated to their Christ as his brides (albeit in a sublimated, spiritual way), in much the same way as Frank—quite concretely—claimed the 'sisters' who were dedicated to him.[54]

Another phenomenon may also belong in the context of women's independent affiliation with the sectarian frameworks of Sabbatianism. Among the liturgical poems composed by the apostate Sabbatians of Salonica, apparently towards the end of the first half of the eighteenth century, are a great many necrologies—hymns commemorating the community's departed notables—which are devoted specifically to women.[55] Some of them are referred to by their full names while others are designated by first names only. The assumption that

hasidic wife, making them as one. Here there was no distinction between the 'scholar' and the 'ignoramus', between the grand and the lowly; both together were devoted to the one, both as one were bound only to him, to the figure of the tsadik towering high above them, protecting them and mediating between them and God. (Horodetsky, *Hasidism* (Heb.), iv. 69)

This claim has no basis in the social reality of hasidism. The relationship of the wives of the hasidim to the tsadik was limited, and it differed considerably from that of their sons and husbands. Some hasidic leaders refused to see women and did not allow them to visit their courts at all. On this see Rapoport-Albert, 'On Women in Hasidism', 497–8 and n. 21; ead., 'Emergence of a Female Constituency', 17*–32*. Comparison between the status of women in the hasidic movement and the Frankist court only highlights the conservative posture of the former as against the latter's revolutionary innovations. On this see also above, Ch. 3 n. 3, and below, at nn. 63–9.

[53] Frank's language in this respect, as preserved in different versions of his statements, is somewhat hazy, making it difficult to determine whether he intended the designation of the women to mean 'nuns' or 'sisters', although he certainly was aware of the ambiguity of the term 'sisters' in the languages of Christian countries; on this see Levine, *Kronika*, 85 n. 206. Frank left his daughter Eva in the care of Dominican nuns in the town of Góra Kalwaria (Gor, Gur, or Ger in Jewish parlance); on this and on his contacts with both monks and nuns see ibid. 76–8, §83 (*Rozmaite adnotacje*, 74–5). On his contacts with the Russian schismatic sectarians active in his Polish surroundings, which also operated as egalitarian fraternities whose male and female members were designated 'brothers' and 'sisters', see below, Ch. 8.

[54] See e.g. *Kronika*, 92–4, §104 (*Rozmaite adnotacje*, 84–5).

[55] See Attias, Scholem, and Ben-Zvi, *Songs and Hymns* (Heb.), 18.

these women, in their own right, enjoyed a high standing within the sectarian community, and that they played an active part in its clandestine activities, accords with an early twentieth-century description of the Doenmeh women of Salonica:

The Doenmeh women have an attractive, pleasant manner of speaking. They are not strict in their observance of the Muslim laws of *ḥarem*. Though they veil their faces when they go out, and their windows are shuttered like those of the Muslim homes, the harem is not observed among members of the sect. Women often visit their friends and let themselves be seen by the men with unveiled faces. They take part in the life of the community and are not shut in behind lock and key in their own homes, like the Muslim women.[56]

The perception that women could choose to join, and play an active part in, sectarian Sabbatianism, not only by virtue of their familial connections to men of Sabbatian leanings, but also in their own right and on their own initiative, is further strengthened by the *ḥerem* (excommunication) formulae employed, time and again, in the proclamations issued against the messianic heretics:

The following [categories of people] are excommunicated, ostracized, proscribed, and set apart from the domain of Israel's holiness; they are to be expelled from the assembly of the diaspora, and have no share in the consolations forecast by the prophets for the entire congregation of Israel. Whoever they may be, Sho'a or Ko'a [cf. Ezek. 23: 23, probably understood, following the medieval commentators, as high-ranking officials and dignitaries], master of hundreds, even if he is a scholar, or one of the pious and the chaste; leader, official, or governor, *man or woman*, whoever they may be.[57]

The formula employed for the most severe *ḥerem* proclaimed in the holy communities of Lvov, Lutsk, Brody, and Dubno and in all of the [surrounding] districts, as set out in the book *Kol bo*, shall apply to any *man or woman* who belongs to this wicked band, or

[56] Elmaleh, *Sabbatai Zevi in the Present Day* (Heb.), 28, and see also ibid. 35: 'Only the married men and the women are allowed to worship.' These observations on the exceptional status of the sectarian women within their Muslim milieu are corroborated by Bali ('Memoirs', 318), where the 20th-century Salonican memoirist Münevver Ayaşlı notes the 'strange atmosphere' prevailing in a certain Doenmeh household whose old women were, unusually, all unveiled. These descriptions also reflect the similarity between the status of women among the Doenmeh and in the Bektashi Sufi order (see above, Ch. 2, at n. 77), where their active participation in all the sect's rites alongside the men was regarded as extremely unusual.

[57] Wilhelm and Scholem, 'Proclamation' (Heb.), 103; from the writ of excommunication issued against the Sabbatians in Altona on 28 Elul 5485 (1725). Cf. Emden, *Sefer hitabekut*, 41a. Emphasis added here and in the following quotations.

who arranges a marriage with them, or who engages in any dealings with them, or who eats of their food; all these shall be banned like them.[58]

[This is the version of] the *ḥerem* proclaimed in the great synagogue of Brody, on the fast-day called on 20 Sivan, and also proclaimed at the meeting of the Council of the Four Lands held in the synagogue of Kostantin [Starokonstantinov]. It reads as follows. The well-known formula of the *ḥerem*, as set out in the book *Kol bo*, with the customary blowing of the ram's horn and the extinguishing of the lamps, is to be applied to anyone who believes that Sabbatai Zevi is the messiah, and to those who believe in Berukhyah, may the name of the wicked rot, or in their false prophet Nathan of Gaza—polluted abomination, canine congregation, impious sons—and it goes without saying that the *ḥerem* applies to all those who pervert the words of the living God . . . and to anyone who knows of any *man or woman* that they belong to this wicked band but nevertheless arranges a marriage with them, engages in dealings with them, or eats of their food—he shall be banned just like them.[59]

To be sure, the formula of the *ḥerem* set out in the book *Kol bo*—that is, the grave rite of excommunication drawn from the medieval collection of customs and laws known as *Kol bo*, which served as the model for all the bans proclaimed against the Sabbatians—includes the wording: 'any son of Israel or

---

[58] *Records of the Council of the Four Lands* (Heb.), 416, §752; cf. Emden, *Sefer shimush*, 2b.

[59] *Records of the Council of the Four Lands* (Heb.), 417, §753; cf. Emden, *Sefer shimush*, 7b. See also the formula used in the ban proclaimed shortly after Sabbatai Zevi's apostasy by the 'Sages of Constantinople', as quoted by Emden from Leib b. Ozer's *Story of Sabbatai Zevi* (Heb.):

As of today, we declare on pain of a great ban, the ban of Joshua bin Nun, that no Israelite, minor or adult, *man or woman*, shall henceforth invoke the name of the aforementioned man, and—it goes without saying—all the more so is it forbidden to associate with his sect, or to speak with them, for good or for ill. (Emden, *Zot torat hakena'ot*, 20)

However, Scholem rightly doubted the authenticity of this text. Although it does appear in the memoir of Leib b. Ozer (*Story of Sabbatai Zevi* (Heb.), 113–15), who apparently drew upon the same letters from Constantinople cited by Thomas Coenen (*False Hopes* (Heb.), 95–100), Leib did not have before him the text of the proclamation itself, nor, certainly, did Emden (see Scholem, *Sabbatai Sevi*, 699 and 705). It may well be, then, that Emden's reconstruction of it was influenced by the formulae used in the bans proclaimed against the Sabbatians closer to his own time and place, as quoted above. On the other hand, note the wording of the ban cited in the authentic letter by Samuel Aboab, written in the name of the General Academy of Venice about eight years after Sabbatai Zevi's apostasy. It was published in the volume of Aboab's collected responsa, *Devar shemu'el*, and is quoted in Emden, *Zot torat hakena'ot* (p. 52): 'We, the undersigned, do hereby, in the name of the Sages of our General Academy . . . ostracize, ban, and excommunicate any *man or woman*, adult and of sound mind, who, being in good health, shall disdain the fast of the fifth month, which is the month of Av.'

daughter of Israel who transgresses any of the agreed regulations'.[60] Clearly, this formula was meant to cater for all events and circumstances, allowing, in principle, for the ban to apply to any Jewish woman who had attracted the penalty of the *ḥerem* under Jewish law. In practice, however, the *ḥerem* was hardly ever used against women. The usual versions of the prescribed text refer explicitly only to men, placing them under the *ḥerem* either individually or as specifically targeted categories of offenders. Women, on the other hand— whether or not they are meant to be included implicitly—are neither named as individuals nor denounced as a distinct category. I have found the phrase 'man or woman' employed only in rabbinic ordinances (*takanot*) prohibiting, on pain of the *ḥerem*, the initiation by Jews of legal proceedings in the non-Jewish courts, particularly in divorce cases.[61] By contrast, in the bans proclaimed against the Sabbatians, the phrase 'man or woman' appears repeatedly, with 'woman' clearly signifying a distinct category of female offenders who are themselves to be placed under the ban and ostracized for their affiliation with the messianic heresy, or who are included explicitly among the categories of offenders with whom the community is admonished, on pain of the *ḥerem*, to sever all contacts and dealings. We may well take this to indicate that, rather unusually, women were identified as a distinct class of Sabbatian affiliates,

[60] *Kol bo*, 98*b*, §139.

[61] The issue of specific ordinances prohibiting husbands and wives from suing each other in non-Jewish courts might seem to be superfluous, since for Jews to resolve their internal disputes by resort to the non-Jewish courts was prohibited in any case. Nevertheless, such ordinances were indeed promulgated, explicitly and on pain of excommunication by *ḥerem*, for reasons explained by the Spanish/North African halakhic authority Simon b. Tsemah Duran (Rashbats; 1361–1444) as follows:

> Since, as is well known, the husband holds the wife in his power [under Jewish law], it happens at times that the wife will cast her fate in the hands of idolaters, preferring to litigate in their courts—that is why this ordinance has come to prevent them from doing so on pain of the *ḥerem*. (Duran, *Tashbets*, quoted in Elon, *Jewish Law*, ii. 651 n. 94)

The formula 'man or woman' appears in this context in Ashkenazi halakhic sources as well, in an ordinance derived from the rulings of the tosafist Jacob b. Meir (Rabbenu Tam; *c*.1100–1171):

> We have hereby resolved, decreed and condemned to ostracism and excommunication by *ḥerem*, any man or woman, near or far, who shall sue his fellow [Jew] in the courts of the idolatrous gentiles or shall subject him to judgement by idolatrous gentiles, whether he [the gentile judge] be noble or lay, ruler or soldier, unless it be by agreement between the two [litigants] and before witnesses who are fit according to Jewish law. (cited in Elon, *Jewish Law*, i. 17)

See also *Kol bo*, 89*b*, §117.

alongside the classes of the wealthy, the scholars, the 'pious and the chaste', etc.[62]

   This supposition is further strengthened by comparison of the bans issued against the Sabbatians with the numerous proclamations of the *ḥerem* against the 'sect' of the 'new hasidim'—the followers of Israel Ba'al Shem Tov, who were being ostracized by the communal authorities only a few decades later. As is often stated explicitly in the opening lines of these proclamations, they were derived from the same *Kol bo* version of the *ḥerem* as the one used against the Sabbatian heretics. They similarly list various classes of adherents and discern distinct degrees of affiliation with hasidism, placing every category thus specified under the ban of excommunication.[63] Notably, they never mention hasidic women as a separate category, and the formula 'man or woman' is conspicuously absent from all of them.[64] This makes the repeated appearance of

[62] To be excluded from consideration in this context are the bans on arranging marriages with Sabbatian families:

> We hereby condemn, by decree of the holy angels [cf. Dan. 4: 17], anyone who should arrange a marriage between his son or daughter and the offspring of this wicked company . . . for we have declared their wives and daughters to be whores, and their sons and daughters to be entirely unfit for marriage [*mamzerim gemurim*]. ('A Double-Edged Sword', ban issued in Brody in 1756, published in the Hebrew translator's 'addenda' to ch. 4 of Kraushar's *Frank and his Following* (Heb.), 79, but not included in the English version of the work)

While this is again a specific reference to the wives and daughters of the heretics, the reason for the prohibition on marriage with them had to do with the Sabbatians' flaunting of the laws of sexual purity. The designation of their wives and daughters as whores, like the designation of their children as unfit for marriage, was demanded as a matter of course by Jewish law, but did not in itself imply that the women were viewed as heretics in their own right. The same is true of the references to women in the bans on the use of amulets distributed by R. Jonathan Eybeschuetz, as in the proclamation issued by R. Ezekiel Landau of Prague: 'I hereby condemn, by the ban of Joshua bin Nun, anyone who wears these amulets, man or woman . . . let them put away their amulets and turn them in to the rabbinic court . . . even infants, male and female, who wear these amulets' (quoted in Emden [David Avaz], *Petaḥ einayim*, 4*b*).

Such proclamations cannot be cited as evidence that the women in question were viewed as heretics in their own right, since women had always been among the primary users of amulets.

[63] On the various distinct categories and degrees of association with the early hasidic movement, which did not solidify into a shared consciousness of belonging to a coherent movement until and on account of the campaign launched against hasidism by its rabbinic opponents, see Rapoport-Albert, 'Hasidism after 1772', 131–3.

[64] The only document, from 1778, to specifically mention women—and even here their association with hasidism is neither clear nor explicit—is probably a forgery. See Wilensky, *Hasidim and Mitnagedim* (Heb.), i. 328–9.

the formula in the proclamations of the *ḥerem* against the Sabbatians seem all the more extraordinary and significant.[65] To be sure, women do make an occasional appearance in the polemical writings of the opponents of hasidism, but this is mainly in the context of the accusation that the hasidim abandon their wives and children during their extended sojourns in the courts of their leaders, the tsadikim.[66]

Indeed, at the beginning of hasidism, and throughout the period of its rapid expansion and spread, the movement operated as an exclusively male fraternity. Most of the recruits to its ranks were youths in the early years of marriage, and their affiliation with one or another of the groups that were forming around the new charismatic leaders amounted to flight from marriage and family life, for which the emotionally charged framework of the hasidic court provided an effective alternative.[67] This was clearly how the movement was perceived by its adversaries in the 1770s and 1780s, and it is no wonder that when they set out to uproot it by placing the new 'heretics' under the most severe form of the *ḥerem*, carefully listing them by distinct classes of affiliation—the heads, their adherents, those who abet them, those who identify with only some of their deeds, etc.—it never occurred to them to include 'their women' as one of the categories to be banned. The wives, mothers, sisters, and daughters of the hasidim, who were not seen as an active hasidic constituency at that time, were implicitly excluded from all the proclamations directed against the movement. As time went on, however, affiliation with hasidism ceased to be a voluntary or even rebellious act by individual males who were thereby cutting themselves off from their native familial surroundings; instead it gradually came to define the abiding,

[65] The Jewish community of Amsterdam issued comparable bans during the 17th and 18th centuries, which were meant to quash various manifestations of heresy, insubordination, and deviance in the Spanish and Portuguese community, such as the reversion to the semblance of Christianity that would be required of them if they were to return to the Iberian peninsula, or the challenge to rabbinic theology referred to as 'Karaism'. These also did not specify women among the categories of banned sinners, an impression confirmed in a personal communication by Prof. Yosef Kaplan, who plans to publish a comprehensive study on the use of the *ḥerem* in these communities. Meanwhile, see Kaplan, 'Travels'; 'Struggle' (Heb.); 'Social Function of the *Ḥerem*'; and 'Karaites'.

[66] See e.g. Wilensky, *Hasidim and Mitnagedim* (Heb.), i. 102–4; ii. 46–7, 107–8, 151, 159–60, 173. For a discussion of this issue and of the relationship of women to the hasidic courts, see Rapoport-Albert, 'On Women in Hasidism', 497–8 and 510–14; and see above, n. 52.

[67] See Rapoport-Albert, 'On Women in Hasidism', 497; above, Introduction, at nn. 9–10, and below, Ch. 9.

collective, hereditary identity of entire families and even whole sections of the population.[68] Only then did women effectively become an integral part of the hasidic camp, and even so, their access to its leadership and institutions was usually indirect or restricted.[69] By that time, however, from the early decades of the nineteenth century, the traditionalist opposition to hasidism had abated. No one clamoured any longer to ban the movement or to include in the ban—as by this time they might have done—the large female constituency that hasidism now encompassed. This subtle difference between the two versions of the *ḥerem*— the one repeatedly proclaimed against the Sabbatians, which was inclusive of their women, as is evident from the fact that it almost invariably contained the rarely invoked formula 'man or woman', and the other directed at the followers of hasidism, which appears to have been exclusive of their women, since it never resorted to the 'man or woman' formula or referred to them in any other way— can serve as a further indication that, unlike the passive, indirectly affiliated, almost invisible women of early hasidism, the Sabbatian women were rightly perceived to be an active constituency of the heretical sect, held to be as culpable as the men, and fully deserving of punishment in their own right.

[68] On this see Rapoport-Albert, 'Hasidism after 1772', 137–9.

[69] See e.g. the accounts of Sarah Schnirer and Ephraim Shmueli describing the exclusion of women from the hasidic courts of Poland in the early decades of the 20th century, despite the long-standing association of their families with the same courts (cited in Rapoport-Albert, 'On Women in Hasidism', 514, end of n. 21). Women were forbidden to visit the courts of various hasidic leaders, including e.g. the third Habad-Lubavitch Rebbe, Menahem Mendel (the Tsemah Tsedek), his grandson Shalom Dovber (the fifth Lubavitcher Rebbe), as well as R. Nahman of Bratslav, R. Isaac of Nezkhis, and R. Meir of Peremyshlyany (see Rapoport-Albert, 'On Women in Hasidism', 513–14 n. 21, and 'Emergence of a Female Constituency', 17*–32*). To be sure, the polemical tracts of hasidism's opponents, dating from the end of the 18th century, contain a number of references to the presence of women in the courts, especially childless women who were seeking the rebbe's blessing for fertility. They insinuate all manner of indecency in this context, hinting that the rebbe may have himself undertaken the impregnation of the barren women he 'blessed'. See e.g. the statements by David of Maków quoted in Wilensky, *Hasidim and Mitnagedim* (Heb.), ii. 46, 66–9, 105, and 137; and see also Dubnow, *History of Hasidism* (Heb.), 366. However, the credibility of these reports is dubious; they are belied by the many complaints about the wives of the hasidim being left alone at home, and it could well be that they arise from misrepresentation of the hasidic doctrine of 'elevating alien [i.e. distracting, usually erotic] thoughts', or from the failure of hasidism's adversaries to distinguish between the new hasidic 'sect' and the more familiar perversions of the Sabbatian–Frankist heresy. On this see Rapoport-Albert, 'On Women in Hasidism', 513, beginning of n. 21.

FIVE

The Egalitarian Agenda: Sources of Inspiration and Modes of Implementation

T HE ATTRACTION that sectarian messianism held for women was certainly not incidental. Something inherent in Sabbatianism must surely account for their active involvement with both the overt and the clandestine frameworks in which the movement persisted. Women continued to be drawn to the sectarian fellowships not only as messianic prophetesses—a capacity in which they had distinguished themselves from the start—but also as full-fledged members in their own right, personally and even prominently engaged in all the fellowships' activities alongside or together with the men.

As we have seen,[1] where Judaism traditionally had stressed a religious life bounded by the commandments—that dense web of gendered prescriptions and rituals which segregated the sexes and assigned them different spheres of activity—Sabbatianism shifted the emphasis towards a faith-based religiosity. As a meta-halakhic value, faith transcended the gender boundaries that were built into the halakhic system, and thus it could open a single arena of action to both sexes. That, coupled with the gradual transition from penitential asceticism to antinomian transgression as the quintessential mode of *tikun*, enabled women to take a more active part in the sect's spiritual, organizational, and ritual life than had ever been allowed them within the traditional frameworks of Jewish religious practice. But all this was no more than a by-product of the shifts that more generally marked the evolution of Sabbatian doctrine; it did not in itself represent the implementation of any ideological agenda designed to address the issue of the status of women.

That such an agenda existed, its egalitarian tendency part and parcel of the world-turned-upside-down vision of the Sabbatian redemption, is attested

[1] See above, Ch. 4.

from the very outset of the messianic movement. It seems to have originated in Sabbatai Zevi's own mind, and its basic outlines can be reconstructed from a report of his public, direct address to women, recorded by Thomas Coenen, who was, as we have seen, a hostile but close observer:

As for you wretched women, great is your misery, for on Eve's account you suffer agonies in childbirth. What is more, you are in bondage to your husbands and can do nothing small or great without their consent; and so on and so forth. Give thanks to God, then, that I have come to the world to redeem you from all your sufferings, to liberate you and make you as happy as your husbands, for I have come to annul the sin of Adam.[2]

Gershom Scholem has pointed out just how remarkable this declaration was for its time and place:

These were revolutionary words indeed for a Jew of Smyrna in the year 1665. A new *Lebensgefühl* and utopian vision of the equality of the sexes seem to have taken root in Sabbetai's heart . . . The notion that Adam's sin would be repaired by the messiah was current in Lurianic writings . . . In spite of the commonplace premise, Sabbatai seems to have been the first to draw the conclusion in terms of the emancipation of women.[3]

Indeed, the redemptive tidings addressed specifically to women was a major new departure. Annulment of the original sin implies the abrogation of its punishment. The messiah is thus proposing to release all women from the punishment of Eve, under which they had laboured on her account ever since the expulsion from Eden. He promises to abrogate both parts of the sentence, namely, the tribulations of childbirth and subservience to men, as proclaimed in Genesis 3: 16: 'I will greatly multiply your pain in childbearing . . . yet your desire shall be for your husband, and he shall rule over you.' This latter re-doubles the affliction of women, and dooms them not only to physical pain but also to the wretchedness of subjugation. The vision of their release from Eve's punishment thus portends not only their liberation from suffering but also, explicitly, their discharge from bondage to men. Not only will the messiah transform the misery of women into a condition of pure joy, but this transformation is designed to render them equal to their husbands, as the promised state of joyous existence will be the lot of men and women alike. There seems little doubt that this egalitarian notion had become an integral element of Sabbatai Zevi's vision of the redemption.

[2] Coenen, *False Hopes* (Heb.), 54–5, and cf. Scholem, *Sabbatai Sevi*, 404.

[3] Scholem, *Sabbatai Sevi*, 404–5.

His message to women clearly implies a challenge to the hierarchical relationship between the sexes, a relationship set down in Jewish law and tradition while also prevailing in the wider, non-Jewish society. The originality and boldness of his message are, therefore, intriguing: where could Sabbatai Zevi have found the inspiration for his remarkable vision of the equality between the sexes, and what might have prompted his surprising sensitivity to the poor lot and wretchedness of women? The literary sources that could have spurred his imagination are considered in some detail below, but first, a number of historical factors must be taken into account, that might have heightened his awareness of the problematic status of women while at the same time providing conditions that were conducive to the propagation of his message of liberation, which promised to resolve it.

The seventeenth-century Jewish community of the Ottoman empire—the environment into which Sabbatai Zevi was born and in which he operated for most of his life—had been subject to successive currents of migration that, for at least a century, had been flowing both into the empire and within it. This constant movement of Jewish migrants gave rise to an unprecedented diversity of ethnic origin, conflicting halakhic traditions, organizational bifurcation, openness to the non-Jewish society—which itself was extremely heterogeneous, inter-communal tensions, and altogether a considerable measure of demographic, social, and economic instability.[4] All this was even truer of Sabbatai Zevi's native community of Smyrna—a relatively new city, established at the end of the sixteenth century. In the course of its rapid development as a commercial port during the first half of the seventeenth century, it absorbed large numbers of Jewish immigrants from the Iberian peninsula and from other places all over the empire and beyond. The accelerated growth and ethnic complexity of the city's Jewish population led to internal divisions, tensions, and discord among its diverse congregations.[5] Inevitably, in the absence

---

[4] For surveys of the Ottoman Jewish communities during this period, all emphasizing the presence of these conditions, see Barnai, 'Jews in the Ottoman Empire' (Heb.); id., 'Jews of the Ottoman Empire in the Seventeenth and Eighteenth Centuries'; Hacker, 'Sephardim in the Ottoman Empire' (Heb.); id., 'Sephardim in the Fifteenth through Eighteenth Centuries' (Heb.); id., 'The *Sürgün* System'; Bashan, 'Political and Economic Crisis' (Heb.); Gerber, *Economic and Social Life* (Heb.); Geller, 'Inter-Ethnic Relations' (Heb.); Bornstein-Makovetski, 'Social Relations' (Heb.).

[5] On the Jewish community of Smyrna, its ethnic complexity, and the internal tensions that prevailed within it in this period, see Barnai, 'Origins' (Heb.), 'Portuguese Marranos' (Heb.),

of any long-established and authoritative local tradition, this heterogeneous, dynamic Jewish community could provide fertile ground for the cultivation of revolutionary ideas.

Moreover, in a series of studies of the Iberian exiles and their descendants who settled throughout the Ottoman empire from the end of the fifteenth to the beginning of the seventeenth century—a great wave of migration which left its mark on all the Jewish communities that absorbed it—Joseph Hacker has pointed to an acute sense of crisis, and the destabilization of values and norms, that characterized the immigrants' long-drawn-out resettlement process.[6] This stemmed not least from the encounter of the émigrés with local traditions and customs that were very different from their own, the difference turning often enough on questions relating to the status of women in society.[7]

'Christian Messianism', 'Yosef Escapa (Heb.)', 'Congregations in Smyrna' (Heb.), 'Hayim Benveniste (Heb.)', *Sabbatianism* (Heb.), 61–6; Tamar, *Studies* (Heb.), 119–35, and 148–53.

[6] See Hacker, 'Sephardim in the Ottoman Empire' (Heb.), 'Sephardim in the Fifteenth through Eighteenth Centuries' (Heb.), 'The *Sürgün* System', and 'Pride and Depression' (Heb.).

[7] See e.g. Hacker, 'Jacob b. Solomon Ibn Habib' (Heb.), esp. pp. 119–20, where Hacker discusses the response of Ibn Habib, a Sephardi rabbi in Salonica, to the local Romaniot custom of allowing women to retain possession of their dowries instead of transferring them to their husbands, thus endowing them with independent economic power. This conflicted with the Castilian tradition, which Ibn Habib sought to conserve. For a discussion of this matter and of other Romaniot traditions relating to the status of women, principally with regard to marital relations and inheritance—traditions that were criticized for their divergence from accepted practice among both Sephardim and Ashkenazim—see Fishman, 'A Kabbalistic Perspective', 204–8. See also Lamdan, *A Separate People*, 224–61; and Geller, 'Inter-Ethnic Relations' (Heb.), 37–9. The conflict between different approaches to the question of women's economic independence may have been exacerbated by the encounter of the immigrants with a local phenomenon that was strikingly unique. This was the prominence, in the capital city, of a number of powerful Jewish women, known by the Greek title of 'Kiera' or 'Kira' (Lady). They ingratiated themselves with the royal palace by virtue of their employment as exclusive providers of goods and services to the women of the harem, who were not allowed any direct contact with the outside world. The Jewish 'ladies' enjoyed substantial economic benefits and even positions of authority and influence, which they sometimes exploited in order to advance the interests of the Jewish community. This phenomenon persisted throughout the 16th century and at least to the beginning of the 17th, when it may have suffered a setback with the abrupt fall from grace and assassination of one of the most notable 'kieras' of her time. On this see *Encyclopaedia Judaica*, x., cols. 990–1, s.v. 'kiera', and the bibliographical references there. For a recent review of the subject, pointing to a certain confusion in the sources that has resulted in the amalgamation of several 'kieras' into one, see Rozen, *The Jewish Community of Istanbul*, 204–7.

It also had to do with the shocks to family structure that began with the expulsion and continued through all the further waves of migration that followed in its wake. The separation of close relatives—parents and children, brothers and sisters, even married couples—was commonplace in this society of émigrés, often leading to the total collapse of established family units, and the reconfiguration of their scattered remnants into improvised alternative structures. This upset the traditional balance of power and undermined conventional norms of conduct in the realm of family life.[8]

The Iberian exiles had some political and economic advantages over the indigenous populations of the Ottoman empire, by virtue of which they succeeded quickly in rehabilitating themselves. They re-established their social and communal institutions, ultimately imposing their own culture on the local traditions with which they had at first come into conflict. Hacker shows, however, that despite the rapid stabilization of their existential conditions, the sense of crisis and its attendant anxieties remained acute and lingered on among the descendants of the emigrants for several more generations. This subjective perception of dislocation and trauma was prone to produce a frame of mind that would be critical of the existing order and give rise to yearnings for radical change. Indeed, messianic tension soared within the Iberian diaspora communities in this period, and with it proliferated instances of prophecy that foretold the imminent transformation of the world by way of the redemption.[9]

These phenomena were considered above in relation to Sabbatai Zevi's personal contacts with the Converso community in Smyrna, the special receptivity to his messianic tidings generally displayed by the Iberian exiles and the Conversos returning to Judaism, and the spate of Sabbatian prophesying by women, which may well have evolved from the older tradition of messianic prophesying by Iberian Conversas in the aftermath of the expulsion.[10] However, in the present context, not only the attestations, throughout the Converso diaspora, of this striking messianic tension and prophetic activity must be taken into account, but also the impression that among the Conversos who remained in the territories subject to the jurisdiction of the Inquisition,

---

[8] See Hacker, 'Sephardim in the Fifteenth through Eighteenth Centuries' (Heb.), 48–9; id., 'Pride and Depression' (Heb.), 542–7; Lamdan, *A Separate People*, 130–1, 136–8, 192–3, 203–10, 218–20; and Rivlin, 'Jewish Family in Greece' (Heb.), 79–104.

[9] See above, Ch. 2, at nn. 57–9.   [10] See above, Ch. 2, at nn. 60–70.

it was chiefly the women, in the course of the sixteenth and seventeenth centuries, who were preserving the clandestine connection to the Jewish tradition. Since the public, institutional presence of Judaism on Iberian soil had become outlawed, and since the Conversos were denied access to all the Hebrew textual sources of their old religion, the only way by which their memory of Judaism could be passed from one generation to the next was through oral transmission, in the privacy of the home and the intimate family circle. Under these circumstances, where allegiance to Judaism was expressed primarily within the domestic sphere that had always been dominated by women, it is hardly surprising that in contrast to the marginal involvement of women in the public rituals of Jewish life, the Conversas were becoming central to the observance of Judaism in private. There is evidence for this throughout this period in the numerous suits brought by the courts of the Inquisition specifically against 'Judaizing' women.[11] The question should, therefore, be asked, whether this shift from the periphery to the centre of ritual practice, at least for as long as the public observance of Judaism continued to be proscribed, may not have led to a radical reappraisal of the position of women in relation to the practice of Judaism once the Conversos were free to embrace it openly in the lands of their resettlement. To the best of my knowledge, this question has not been addressed so far in the scholarly literature on the resettlement of the Conversos and their gradual resumption of the open practice of Judaism. For the time being, therefore, it is impossible to provide any more than a speculative answer.

In this connection, it may well be recalled that Hayim Vital, in his *Book of Visions*, attributes intensive visionary activity to a significant number of women, some of whom, on the authority of their visions, also take strong, independent, public stands on matters relating to morals, repentance, and redemption.[12] Admittedly, not all of these women were themselves of Iberian origin, but all were living in an environment—in Safed, Jerusalem, and Damascus—that had been exposed to powerful Iberian influences during the second half of the sixteenth century and the beginning of the seventeenth.

[11] On this see Levine Melammed, 'Women in Crypto-Jewish Society' (Heb.), and *Heretics or Daughters of Israel?*. A similar suggestion has been made with regard to the Morisco women of Iberia, who were often brought before the Inquisitorial courts on suspicion of being involved in crypto-Islamic activities. See Hasenfeld, 'Women's Roles in a Marginal Community' (Heb.).

[12] See above, Ch. 2, at nn. 15–52.

Throughout this period, all three communities not only were inundated with the overwhelming numerical presence and cultural impact of the Iberian exiles,[13] but they also maintained close contacts with the remaining Conversos in Iberia, as well as with other individuals and communities returning to Judaism throughout the Converso diaspora.[14] On the basis of Vital's evidence, incidental though it is, and apparently never intended for public dissemination, there is room to suppose that the prominence he ascribes to women in the spiritual lives of all three communities may be an indication that at least in this milieu, one of the legacies of the Converso experience may have been a shift in the perception of women's status within the Jewish faith. It follows that even if the Converso women had been integrated into Judaism in the lands of their resettlement, we need not assume that they were always and everywhere returned to the margins of religious life. And even where they were, the process of reintegrating the Conversos, which is known to have generated considerable tension over several other issues, might at the very least have prompted misgivings regarding the position of women in society. Sabbatai Zevi's liberationist promise to women had emerged against this historical background. His message was thus conceived in conditions that not only could inspire it, but may well have been particularly conducive to its reception and rapid propagation.

As for the literary stimuli to which Sabbatai Zevi may have been responding when he displayed such an unusual concern for the plight of women— his recognition of their inferiority and subjugation to their husbands, his acknowledgment of the physical suffering to which they are doomed, and his promise to rectify this state of affairs by putting women on an equal footing with men—he may well have found all these in the two works that first introduced him to the world of kabbalah. When he embarked, at around the age of 20, on the study of the esoteric 'wisdom of truth', as kabbalah was traditionally known, he did not take a teacher, but rather unusually studied entirely on his own. According to a friend of his youth, Rabbi Moses Pinheiro, the only

---

[13] On the overwhelming influence of the Iberian exiles and former Conversos on the Safed and Jerusalem communities during this period see David, 'Spanish Exiles', 'Safed as a Centre for the Resettlement of Conversos' (Heb.), and *Immigration and Settlement in Erets Israel* (Heb.), 72–8, 112–18. On p. 126 of the latter, David quotes statistics on the population of the Spanish and Portuguese communities in Safed, which indicate their substantial growth during the 16th century. On the censuses from which these statistics are drawn see Cohen and Lewis, *Population and Revenue*.   [14] See above, Ch. 2, at nn. 57–9.

kabbalistic works he studied were the Zohar and *Sefer hakanah*.[15] In both these works he could have found ideas to provoke a critique of women's status in Jewish law, together with some of the literary underpinnings for his vision of their liberation in the messianic age to come.

Sefer hakanah, an anonymous work that gives mystical rationales for the commandments, sets out to prove that the law, taken literally, is irrational and open to perverse interpretations running counter to its true intention. The book seems to have been written at the end of the fourteenth or the beginning of the fifteenth century, within the borders of the Byzantine empire, perhaps in northern Greece,[16] that is, in the realm of Romaniot Jewish culture, which fell under Ottoman rule in the second half of the fifteenth century. *Sefer hakanah*, along with *Sefer hapeliah*—a kabbalistic interpretation of the first chapters of Genesis that was composed in the same region and probably by the same anonymous author—was not printed until the end of the eighteenth century, but it was widely circulated in manuscript and exerted a great deal of influence in kabbalistic circles.[17] *Sefer hakanah* is constructed as a dialogue between a pupil and his father, who is also his mentor.[18] Among other things, the book is distinguished by the attention it pays to the issue of women in relation to the bulk of Judaism's ritual commandments, a subject to which the author returns time and again throughout the work. Over and over, the pupil protests against the arbitrariness of the Sages' legal arguments and the injustice of their consequent exemption of women from positive time-bound commandments, including the study of Torah, which is said to outweigh them all. Not only are women denied the reward, in this world and the next, for keeping these commandments, but the Sages also humiliate them 'to the ground' by likening their status to that of non-Jewish slaves:

Anyone who heeds the words [of the Sages] must raise his voice to God and ask him why he created this lowly woman, who has neither reward nor punishment, since they

[15] See Freimann, *Sabbatai Zevi* (Heb.), 95; and see Scholem's discussion in *Sabbatai Sevi*, 116–17.

[16] And not, as most scholars, including Scholem (ibid. 116 n. 40), used to think, in Spain. On this see Kushnir-Oron, 'The *Sefer ha-peli'ah* and the *Sefer ha-kanah*' (Heb.), 1–30, and Ta-Shma, 'Where Were the Books *Hakanah* and *Hapeliah* Composed?' (Heb.).

[17] See Scholem, *Sabbatai Sevi*, 116, and Kushnir-Oron, 'The *Sefer ha-peli'ah* and the *Sefer ha-kanah*' (Heb.), 31–70.

[18] On the dialogic structure of the book and the fictional identity of the speakers see Kushnir-Oron, 'The *Sefer ha-peli'ah* and the *Sefer ha-kanah*' (Heb.), 337–43.

have exempted her from some of the commandments, such as those which are time-bound. [Women] can have no reward for fulfilling the commandments from which they are exempt, nor any punishment for failing to do so, since it has been declared that 'he who is commanded [and fulfils the commandment is greater than he who fulfils it even though he is not so commanded'].[19] The Holy One [i.e. Scripture] obligated her in the commandment of Torah study, which outweighs all the other commandments combined, but the Sages exempted her because they encountered the word 'sons' in the text of the commandment to study Torah [*velimadetem otam et beneikhem*, 'You shall teach them to your sons',[20] Deut. 11: 19], and though they might have said that this is not a time-bound commandment, and women are therefore obligated to perform it, they did not. As if that were not enough, they drew an analogy between phylacteries [*tefilin*] and the study of Torah and exempted her from laying phylacteries as well, and then they extrapolated from the case of phylacteries to the whole category of time-bound commandments, from which they declared women exempt . . . And harshest of all, as if it were not enough for this lowly woman to be humiliated to the ground by being exempted from the most important of God's commandments, is that they liken her to a slave, declaring that any commandment that is binding upon a woman is also binding upon a slave.[21] For God's sake, tell me, my teacher, what does a slave have in a common with a woman, who is a free person of the seed of Israel, while the Canaanite slave is of the worthless seed of a non-Jew?!![22]

Regarding the exemption of women from the commandment to recite the Shema ('Hear O Israel'), the pupil argues:

The recitation of the Shema is a time-bound commandment, and women are exempt. Who would not fear thee, O Holy King?[23] If so, they are laid open to apostasy, for if they do not proclaim God's unity, whose shall they proclaim—the sun's or the moon's? Lord of the Universe, proclaiming the unity of God is the foundation of all your commandments, and you have exempted women! Yet you cursed Eve, in the Garden of Eden, for not proclaiming your unity, and you endowed her with a grim heritage of pain.[24] You wrote in your Torah that [the commandment of proclaiming God's unity must be performed] 'when you lie down, and when you rise' [Deut. 6: 7, 11: 19], making it a time-bound commandment and so exempting the lowly woman. If so, is it your will that she be lost altogether to the World to Come?[25]

---

[19] BT *Kid.* 31a and its parallels.

[20] The word *beneikhem*, which is masculine, can mean either 'your children', referring to both sons and daughters, or, more narrowly, 'your sons'.   [21] BT *Ḥag. 4a.*   [22] *Sefer hakanah, 5b–6a.*

[23] After Jer. 10: 7: 'Who would not fear thee, O King of the nations?'

[24] In reference to Gen. 3: 16: 'I will greatly multiply thy sorrow and thy conception; in sorrow thou shalt bring forth children.'   [25] *Sefer hakanah, 15a.*

The pupil rails in a similar vein against the exemption of women from the commandments of circumcision, wearing ritual fringes, erecting a sukkah on the festival of Tabernacles, hearing the call of the ram's horn on New Year's Day, and so on. The teacher, in response, resolves all of his difficulties by way of mystical explanations that are meant to elucidate and justify the decisions of the Sages, though they simultaneously jettison the rational basis of those determinations as elaborated in the Talmud's legal debates.

Michal Kushnir-Oron has examined *Sefer hakanah*'s attitude towards the restricted application to women of the bulk of Judaism's ritual commandments. She points out the sources for this attitude in classical rabbinic literature, where the need to justify women's exemption had already arisen in various contexts, and she clarifies *Sefer hakanah*'s mystical grounds for upholding this exemption. Rejecting the evaluation of several scholars, who had seen *Sefer hakanah* as an expression of both rebellion against the halakhic system, and protest against its unfair treatment of women, she concludes that the book's approach to the two issues is fundamentally conservative. Its arguments against the halakhah reflect no real desire to overthrow it, nor any genuine sense of the injustice it has allegedly done to women; rather, they constitute a pedagogic or rhetorical strategy whose sole aim is to reinforce, not to undermine, the edifice of Jewish law (perhaps, as she suggests, in response to contemporary misgivings as to its continued viability, the arguments of the pupil reflecting what might have been a live cultural issue) by way of underpinning it with mystical explanations. These, in the anonymous author's opinion, provide the law's only sense and validity.[26]

More recently, Talya Fishman has analysed anew the attitude of *Sefer hakanah* toward the limited applicability of Judaism's ritual commandments to women.[27] Among the main points of the pupil's 'protest' against the unfair treatment of women in Jewish law, she lists the frustration of their efforts to secure their portion in the World to Come, since they are deprived of the opportunity to counterbalance their sins with the merits that accrue only to men, through the performance of the many ritual commandments that apply exclusively to them; their ignorance, which stems from their exclusion from Torah study, as a result of which they cannot properly perform even those commandments that do apply to women; and their exposure, like Eve in her

---

[26] See Kushnir-Oron, 'The *Sefer ha-peli'ah* and the *Sefer ha-kanah*' (Heb.), 241–5.

[27] Fishman, 'A Kabbalistic Perspective'.

day, to the danger of heresy: Eve 'cut down the plants' of the Garden of Eden[28] and so brought divine retribution upon women through the ages, all because she had not learned to proclaim the unity of her Creator by reciting the Shema—a commandment that did not apply to her as a woman. Fishman shows how the book exposes the numerous internal contradictions, and the blatant deviations from Scripture's plain meaning, that characterize the rabbinic legal debates resulting in these conclusions. But she also points out that the author's own arguments are inconsistent and even contradictory, sometimes condemning precisely the opposite view to the one the pupil purports to challenge. Thus, for example, he appears to dispute the inclusion of women among those who are obligated to perform certain time-bound commandments, such as eating matzah on the first night of Passover, despite the fact that, as a rule, rabbinic tradition exempts women from the commandments that fall into this category. The true thrust of the book is clearly not the call for an equal application of the commandments to both sexes, ostensibly in order to rectify the injustice that the halakhah has done to women. Rather, the author is out to challenge the validity of the Sages' method of reasoning in determining the law, and the arbitrariness of their rulings on women's relationship to the commandments furnishes his case with particularly poignant illustrations.[29] In fact, *Sefer hakanah*'s anonymous author is fully committed to upholding the Sages' rulings; only the rationale they provide to account for them is the target of his attack. His rejection of their arguments, for which he substitutes a mystical rationale of his own, serves only to make him exceptionally rigid in his application of the rule of law, and in the case of women, to preclude them altogether from the performance of commandments from which the Sages had simply exempted them.

The author's mystical rationale for the commandments derives from the kabbalistic doctrine that endows their punctilious performance with the power to influence the state of the divine *sefirot*. In addition, he postulates a tripartite correlation between every commandment, the individual who performs it, and the *sefirah* that is affected by it. This correlation is based, among other things, on the categorization of all three parties by gender, and it obtains

---

[28] The phrase connotes belief in heretical doctrines that run counter to the monotheistic principle of Judaism. See BT *Ḥag.* 14b, where it is used of *aḥer* (the 'altered' one)—Elisha b. Avuyah, the classical rabbinic prototype of the heretic.

[29] Fishman, 'A Kabbalistic Perspective', 215–24.

so long as there exists among them harmonious gender compatibility. It follows that if a commandment which has been categorized as 'masculine' is performed by a woman, to whom it does not apply, her action is not just an empty theurgic gesture but has the power to exert a destructive influence on the entire sefirotic world.[30] It is on this principle that *Sefer hakanah* bases its strict preclusion of women from performing any of the commandments that rabbinic law did not apply to them.

The rabbinic tradition had always vacillated over the relationship of women to the commandments, never arriving at an unequivocal conclusion as to whether they were permitted to perform those acts from which the law had declared them exempt, and whether, if permitted, they would gain a reward for doing so. As we have seen, this vacillation provided *Sefer hakanah*'s author with a convenient means of demonstrating the faults he believed to be inherent in the traditional method of determining rabbinic law.[31] However, as Fishman shows to be patently obvious from his own style of argumentation, not only does he share some characteristic features of the same method himself, but he also quite clearly subscribes to the same traditional value system that under-girds it: 'The power of the pupil's criticisms stems largely from the fact that they are drawn from *within* rabbinic culture. They are systemically referential, reflecting fidelity to substantive and methodological elements found within the tradition.'[32] Fishman accepts Kushnir-Oron's conclusion as to the halakhic conservatism, even severity, which *Sefer hakanah*'s author bases on his mystical rationale for the commandments, but she qualifies this conclusion with an important observation: 'Though the teacher's kabbalistically detailed responses serve as a counterpoint, muting the pupil's criticism, the latter have a life of their own *precisely* because they draw upon categories indigenous to rabbinic literature. If the pupil's motives and animus place him outside the pale of tradition, his observations alone clearly do not.'[33]

Sabbatai Zevi was reared in the same rabbinic methodology and conceptual framework that underlay *Sefer hakanah*'s kabbalistic exposition of Jewish law.[34] By the logic of Fishman's observation, this would have made him receptive to the influence of the book's major topics and themes, quite independently of the direction to which its final conclusions pointed. Moreover, since he encountered *Sefer hakanah* in his youth, while taking his first steps in the

---

[30] Fishman, 'A Kabbalistic Perspective', 238–40.   [31] Ibid. 209.   [32] Ibid. 225.
[33] Ibid. 226.   [34] On Sabbatai Zevi's rabbinic education see Scholem, *Sabbatai Sevi*, 110–12.

study of kabbalah, its impact on Sabbatai's developing consciousness is likely to have been profound. That the book's critique of the methods of Jewish law was centred specifically on the inferior status of women would have been sufficient to impress the issue on his young mind. Admittedly, as we have seen, while raising subversive questions, *Sefer hakanah* ultimately delivers an unequivocally conservative message: it defends the preclusion of women from all the ritual obligations prescribed only for men, advocates the dependence of wives on their husbands, who discharge those obligations on their behalf, and robs the halakhic decision-making process of the flexibility that had occasionally allowed it not only to permit the fulfilment by women of at least some of the men's obligations, but also to invest their actions with positive religious value. Nevertheless, it was precisely *Sefer hakanah*'s ploy of reinforcing the halakhic disabilities of women while appearing to denounce them as irrational, humiliating, and unjust, that could have fired Sabbatai Zevi's eschatological imagination inversely: the overturn of the book's extraordinary strictures on the status of women in Jewish law might well have featured as an attractive option in his world-turned-upside-down vision of the dawning messianic age.

The conceptualization of the messianic future, and similarly of the World to Come,[35] as the antithesis of familiar everyday realities springs from ancient literary sources. The biblical prophets had already envisioned the End Time that would follow the violent upheavals associated with the Day of Judgement as an age governed by a radically different natural world order. Dramatic transformations would occur simultaneously on the personal, national, universal, and cosmic levels, with the result that the emergent future world would be a new creation, or one both new and primeval, but at any rate a world that is totally incongruous with the familiar conditions of the present. The prophetic depiction of the End of Days thus relates dialectically to present-day reality and displays the tendency to weave together both restorative and utopian strands of thought.[36]

---

[35] On the close affinity, amounting to overlap, between the concepts of 'the Time to Come' (*le'atid lavo*) and 'the World to Come' (*ha'olam haba*), both of which are used to denote, on the one hand, the age of messianic redemption, and on the other, life after death, see e.g. Klausner, *Messianic Idea*, 408–19; Urbach, *The Sages*, 651–2; and Ginsburg, *The Sabbath*, 145–6 n. 46. The blurring of the distinction between these two eschatological concepts stems from the fact that both are conceived as antithetical to the familiar reality of this world.

[36] For surveys of prophetic eschatology in the Bible that emphasize these issues see e.g. Klausner, *Messianic Idea*, 7–236, and Uffenheimer, 'From Prophetic to Apocalyptic Eschatology' (Heb.).

Rabbinic speculations on the nature of the messianic future—which are by no means all of a piece—also occasionally envisage the overturn of the existing world order.[37] Here, too, the End Time may be conceived as both a return to the glorious primordial past and progression to an unknown future, with memories of the dawn of creation interlaced with fanciful depictions of novel situations and realities.[38] This type of speculation has given rise to the question of the status of the Torah and its commandments in the messianic age: will the Torah retain its present structure and validity even after the transformation of the created order—especially after human nature has been sublimated through the eradication of the evil inclination,[39] when it would no longer be necessary to restrain it by means of the ethical framework of the commandments? The answers to this question are also not all of a piece. Many rabbinic dicta invest the Torah with everlasting validity, insisting that even the commandments associated with the Holy Land and the Jerusalem Temple will be resumed in the messianic age, with the return from the exile, the reconstruction of Jerusalem, and the restoration of the Temple service. Other traditions, however, anticipate the bestowal of a new messianic Torah that will abrogate some, most, or all of the old commandments.[40] Gershom Scholem has placed this idea in the context of the utopian strand of messianic speculation, pointing out its anarchic and even antinomian potentialities:

The greater the assumption of changes in nature or of revolutions in man's moral character—which latter were determined by the extinction of the destructive power of the Evil Inclination in the Messianic Age—the greater did the modification also have to become which under such circumstances affected the operation of the law. A positive commandment or a prohibition could scarcely still be the same when it no longer had for its object the separation of good and evil to which man was called, but rather arose from the Messianic spontaneity of human freedom purely flowing forth. Since by its nature this freedom realizes only the good, it has no real need for all those 'fences'

[37] See e.g. R. Joshua b. Levi's son's famous depiction of the World to Come as a world turned upside down in which hierarchies are inverted, according to BT *Pes.* 50a and its parallels. For a discussion of this theme in medieval Hebrew literature see Gutwirth, 'The "World Upside Down" in Hebrew'.

[38] See Scholem, 'Toward an Understanding of the Messianic Idea', 3–4, 12.

[39] On the rabbinic traditions concerning the 'killing', 'slaughtering', or 'eradication' of the *yetser hara* (the evil inclination) in the Time to Come, see e.g. BT *Suk.* 52a; *Exod. Rabbah*, end of ch. 41; *Num. Rabbah*, 15: 12; and *Midrash tanḥuma*, 'Beha'alotekha', §10.

[40] See Klausner, *Messianic Idea*, 513–14; Urbach, *The Sages*, 279–314; Rosenthal, 'Abrogation of the Commandments' (Heb.), 218–19.

and restrictions with which the *Halakhah* was surrounded in order to secure it from the temptations of evil. At this point there arises the possibility of turning from the restorative conception of the final re-establishment of the reign of law to a utopian view in which restrictive traits will no longer be determinative and decisive, but be replaced by certain as yet totally unpredictable traits. . . . Thus an anarchic element enters Messianic utopianism. . . . Finally, the anarchic element is also joined by the antinomian potentialities which are latent in Messianic utopianism.[41]

Medieval scholars were uncomfortable with the notion of the abrogation of the commandments in the messianic age, and some of them struggled to deflect it, endeavouring to reconcile its undeniable presence in several normative rabbinic texts with the conflicting rabbinic principles of the eternal validity and immutability of the Torah. The issue became particularly fraught under the pressure of the polemic with Christianity, which saw in these ancient rabbinic traditions a Jewish corroboration of its own doctrine, whereby the New Testament had superseded the Old, rendering its archaic commandments obsolete and proclaiming the freedom to abrogate them with the advent of Christ.[42] Even a number of modern historians found it difficult to accommodate these anarchic traditions within any 'authentic' rabbinic conception of the messianic future. This led them to the view that these traditions were forgeries contrived by apostates or Christian theologians who were engaged in the religious polemic against Judaism.[43] Nevertheless, there is no doubting the authenticity of such rabbinic statements as the following:

The commandments will cease in the Time to Come.[44]

The Holy One declared: 'A new law will go forth from me' [see Isa. 51: 4]—A recreation of the Law will go forth from me. R. Berakhyah said in the name of R. Isaac: 'The Holy One will make a great feast for his righteous servants in the Time to Come, and all who abstained from eating unclean flesh in this world shall be privileged to eat of it in the next, in accordance with the verse: "The fat of an animal that dies of itself, and the fat of one that is torn by beasts, . . . on no account shall you eat it" [Lev. 7: 24]— so that you may eat of it in the Time to Come.'[45]

[41] Scholem, 'Toward an Understanding of the Messianic Idea', 3–4.

[42] See e.g. Abravanel, *Sefer yeshu'ot meshiḥo*, pt. 2, 'Fourth Consideration', ch. 1, 67*a*–69*a* (I am grateful to Professor Zeev Gries for directing me to this reference); Lieberman, *Sheki'in* (Heb.), 80–1; Rosenthal, 'Abrogation of the Commandments' (Heb.), 222–33.

[43] See Yitzhak Baer, 'Forged *Midrashim*' (Heb.), and Lieberman, 'Raymond Martini'.

[44] BT *Nid.* 61*b*.   [45] *Lev. Rabbah*, 13: 3.

All the Torah that you learn in this world is as nothing compared with the Torah of the World to Come.[46]

'The Lord unbinds the bound' [*matir asurim*, Ps. 146: 7[47]]—What does this mean? Some say it means that all the animals that were declared unclean in this world will be declared clean by the Holy One in the Time to Come ... and in the Time to Come He shall permit [*matir*] all that He had forbidden [*asar*] ... And what else is meant by *matir asurim*? There is no greater prohibition than that of a menstruant woman, who, when she sees [her] blood, is forbidden by the Holy One to her husband, but in the Time to Come He will permit her to him.[48]

The literature of the Zohar in its later strata—the *Ra'aya mehemna* and *Tikunei hazohar*—develops these utopian motifs in its own way. It distinguishes between the Torah that was revealed at the time of the creation, called *torah diberiah* (the Torah of Creation), and the hidden Torah, called *torah de'atsilut* (the Torah of Emanation), which will be revealed in the messianic future. The Torah of Creation is identified with the Tree of Knowledge of Good and Evil, that is, with the framework of commandments and laws that demarcates evil from good, and sets out all the requisite prohibitions and permissions. The Torah of Emanation, by contrast, is identified with the Tree of Life, and exists in a sublime realm that transcends all distinctions, limitations, and restrictions. Within that utopian realm, the constraints of the halakhic system become totally devoid of meaning. In the messianic future, therefore, which will be governed by this Torah, the current system of commandments and laws will be transcended and come to an utterly new expression.[49]

Notions such as these have the power to induce the eschatological imagination to conjure up startling images of life in the World to Come, where the order of reality is inverted, and the strictest religious taboos may be broken, such as the prohibition on ritually unclean meat or on sexual relations with the menstruant. It is precisely from this inversion of right and wrong, from the tantalizing prospect of transgressing boundaries, that these traditions derive

[46] *Eccles. Rabbah*, 2: 1. Similarly, ibid. 11: 8 declares: 'All the Torah that a man learns in this world is as nothing compared with the Torah of the messiah.'

[47] Unvocalized, the words *matir asurim* can be read as *matir isurim*, 'permits the forbidden'.

[48] *Midrash tehilim*, ed. S. Buber, p. 535. For a list of fifteen statements in this vein see Rosenthal, 'Abrogation of the Commandments' (Heb.), 219–22. For a discussion on the origin and development of this theme in Sabbatian literature, see H. Mack, 'The Source' (Heb.).

[49] See Scholem, 'Meaning of the Torah'; id., 'Toward an Understanding of the Messianic Idea', 22–4; Tishby, *Wisdom of the Zohar*, iii. 1101–8; Liebes, *On Sabbatianism* (Heb.), 164, 312 n. 90.

their force and fascination. Admittedly, the purpose of all this wild speculation is to reinforce, not to break, the halakhic constraints, since it focuses attention precisely on the divide between mundane reality and the fantasy of the future. This, indeed, would seem to be the function of the 'anarchic' or 'antinomian' traditions cited above. Nevertheless, there is no doubting their power to shape the messianic vision of a man like Sabbatai Zevi, who believed himself capable of bringing about the full realization of the utopian future—a fantasy which would turn, in his own hands, into the actual reality of the present.

Among the eschatological traditions inverting the familiar conditions of the mundane reality of the present there is one, standing almost alone, that concerns the status of women in the World to Come, and it, too, was capable of stirring Sabbatai Zevi's imagination. This was the vision of the heavenly *heikhalot* (palaces) peopled by myriads of righteous women, as revealed, according to the Zohar, to Rabbi Simeon bar Yohai[50]—and it should be recalled that the Zohar was one of the two works to which Sabbatai Zevi devoted his exclusive attention when he first embarked on the study of kabbalah in his youth. The Zohar locates the women's *heikhalot* in what it calls the Other World (*alma uhra*) (in contradistinction to this world—*hai alma*), while the late 'midrash' known as *Seder gan eden* (the Order of Paradise)[51]—which

---

[50] See Zohar, iii. 167*b*. Chava Weissler has drawn attention to this source in her pioneering study of the Yiddish *tkhines* literature. See Weissler, *Voices of the Matriarchs*, 76–85; and see also her earlier version of this chapter: Weissler, 'Women in Paradise'. Weissler analyses the imprint of this unique zoharic tradition on popular Yiddish works which were either addressed to or written by Ashkenazi women, and were thus accessible to Ashkenazi women who were literate in Yiddish but not in Hebrew or Aramaic (and also to uneducated Ashkenazi men, who were in the same position). Yiddish adaptations of the Zohar's description of righteous women in Paradise appear in a variety of works of this type, mostly dating from the 17th and 18th centuries. These works tend to credit the righteous women with greater spiritual force than does their zoharic source, skirting the limitations imposed on it in the original Aramaic text. Comparing these versions to the original, Weissler concludes that once the zoharic account had been lifted from its arcane kabbalistic context to be set in the context of women's devotional literature—a context that gave it fresh prominence and put it directly before a female readership—it could convey to women a sense of self-worth and enhanced religious empowerment.

[51] See Jellinek, *Seder gan eden*, 136. In his German introduction to this 'midrash' (ibid., pp. xxvi–xxviii), Jellinek suggests that the work was written around the middle of the 11th century and was probably based on ancient sources. However, Ginzberg, in *Legends of the Jews* (v. 32–3 n. 97), sees in it evidence of the influence of 'speculative mysticism' and therefore presumes a later dating, at the end of the 12th century, while Scholem, in 'Rabbi Gadiel' (Heb.) (pp. 274–83),

exists in more than one version and offers, as far as I am aware, the only parallel source to this zoharic description—locates them in the 'Northerly Paradise' (where they are called *medorot* or *dirot*—'dwellings'—rather than *heikhalot*). That is, both sources situate the righteous women in the World to Come, where the souls of the righteous live on after death, rather than in the messianic future as such. However, we have already noted the effective overlap between these two eschatological domains,[52] which have in common precisely that fanciful inversion of the familiar conditions of reality, and there is no question that we may read what is said of the one as also referring to the other.

The Zohar places its description of the righteous women in the context of certain wondrous sights revealed to Rabbi Simeon bar Yohai by two heavenly 'messengers', who had been granted permission by the head of the supernal academy to bestow this esoteric knowledge upon him: 'Rabbi Simeon said, "There is one thing I would like to know, if you can tell me. Regarding women in that world: are they considered worthy of ascending to the supernal realm— or how is it that they are there?"'[53]

Rabbi Simeon's question is somewhat surprising. In asking whether (righteous) women are considered worthy of ascending to the 'supernal realm'— presumably from the lower to the higher level of Paradise—he pretends to wonder, naively, whether they have a full share in that part of the World to Come which is reserved for the perfectly righteous. This seems to flout a rabbinic tradition anchored in the verse, 'Rise up, women who are at ease, hear my

dates it even later, to the end of the 13th century. Scholem observes the close relationship between the Hebrew *Seder gan eden* and its parallel in the Aramaic Zohar, going so far as to speculate that they were written by the same person, namely, Moses de Leon. The affinity between the description of the women's 'dwellings' in the 'midrash' and their 'palaces' in the Zohar certainly leaps to the eye, although the names of the women mentioned in the two works do not entirely coincide, and there are some slips in both works in the numbering of their heavenly residences. The most significant difference between them, however, lies in their respective accounts of the qualities that distinguish the righteous women in Paradise, and the type of activities in which they engage. In *Seder gan eden*, the women are praised for no more than their traditional womanly virtues of ensuring that their sons study the Torah, being hospitable to scholars who come to visit their husbands, practising charity, and so forth, as well as for the illustrious men—Joseph and Moses—whom they have brought into the world or cared for and raised. The Zohar's version, in addition to all this, has them performing commandments that, as women, they were unable to fulfil during their lifetimes in this world, and even discussing the reasons for the commandments, on which see below, n. 58.

[52] Above, n. 35.   [53] Zohar, iii. 167a.

voice; you complacent daughters, give ear to my speech' (Isa. 32: 9), which was interpreted as a promise vouchsafed to righteous women—though they had amassed no reward for fulfilling the commandments that do not apply to them—that they would gain the World to Come by virtue of having facilitated their sons' and husbands' fulfilment of the commandment of Torah study. The Sages had declared this promise 'greater' than the promise vouchsafed to men, who are obligated to perform all of the commandments in order to secure their share in the World to Come.[54] Admittedly, implied in this rabbinic declaration is the acknowledgement that doubts might indeed be raised with regard to women's very entitlement to a share in the World to Come, since their exemption from most of the ritual commandments would deny them much of their reward, but the Sages refute all such doubts unequivocally: the women are at least as deserving as the men, though they obtain their share of the World to Come by different means. The Zohar proceeds from this tradition to a detailed description of the righteous 'women at ease' in the heavenly palaces reserved exclusively for them. In response to Rabbi Simeon bar Yohai's question, one of the messengers reports:

Ah, Rabbi, they showed me six palaces, each with its pleasures and luxuries, in the place where the curtain is drawn in Paradise beyond which men never enter. Bitya, the daughter of Pharaoh,[55] is in one palace, along with thousands and myriads of righteous women, each of whom has her own place of light and luxuries, so that they are not at all crowded. Three times a day, the heralds call out: 'Here comes the figure of Moses, the faithful prophet.' Then Bitya goes forth into a certain screened-off place that she has and sees the figure of Moses, bows down before it, and declares, 'Happy is my lot, to have raised this luminary.' This is her [particular] pleasure, beyond all the rest. She returns to the women, and they occupy themselves with performing the commandments. All of them look as they did in this world and wear garments of light,[56] like those of the males, except that they do not shine in the same way. In that Other World they busy themselves with performing the commandments that they were not able to perform in this world, and elucidating the reasons for them. All the women who dwell with Bitya, Pharaoh's daughter, are called 'women at ease', for they never suffered any of the torments of Hell. In another palace is Serah, the daughter of Asher,[57] together

---

[54] See BT *Ber.* 17a.   [55] On her see *Lev. Rabbah*, 1: 3.

[56] For the concept of 'garments of light', and its association with Adam and Eve's 'coats of skin' (Gen. 3: 20), which is based on the Hebrew homonyms *or* meaning light and *or* meaning skin, see Kimelman, *Mystical Meaning* (Heb.), 134–84.

[57] The Bible provides no details about Serah, daughter of Asher, who is mentioned several times in the lists of Jacob's descendants (Gen. 46: 17; Num. 26: 46; 1 Chron. 7: 30), but midrashic

with thousands and myriads of other women. Three times a day [the heavenly herald] calls out before her, 'Here comes the figure of Joseph the Righteous.' And she is joyous, and she goes forth into a screened-off place that she has and sees the luminous figure of Joseph, and she rejoices and bows down before him, declaring, 'Happy is the day on which I brought word of you to my grandfather.' Then she goes back to the other women, and they occupy themselves with praising the Lord of the World and acknowledging his name. There are other such places and such joys, of which each of the women has her particular one. Afterwards they go back to busying themselves with the commandments of the Torah and the elucidation of their rationales.[58]

The passage goes on to describe the remaining palaces of the women. In the palace of Jochebed, mother of Moses, 'there is no herald's call', but the tens of thousands of women who surround her thank and praise the Lord of the World three times a day and even sing, under her direction, the song that was sung at the parting of the Red Sea (Exod. 15: 1–18), while the righteous men in Paradise listen to her voice (presumably from the other side of the curtain that demarcates the women's dwellings), and the angels 'acknowledge and praise the Holy Name along with her'. In Deborah's palace, the women give thanks to God, chanting 'the same song that she declaimed in this world' (Judg. 5: 2–31). The description concludes by mentioning the four hidden palaces of the Holy Matriarchs, which have never been seen and 'have not been imparted for revelation'.

As Chava Weissler points out,[59] these descriptions may place the righteous women at the heart of the heavenly scene, waxing eloquent in their praise and unstinting in their glorification, but they still reflect the traditional sense of the inferiority of women to men: though the women wear garments of light, just like the men, they 'do not shine in the same way', and both Bitya and Serah bow down to the two male figures whose association with them is the sole source of their own glory. Nevertheless, these nods in the direction of the reality of this world cannot obscure the essential point of the narrative, which is to emphasize the diametrically opposed conditions in which the women operate in that Other World. In their heavenly palaces they are relieved of all

tradition calls her a woman of valour and praises her for her beauty, piety, wisdom, and musical talents, relating that she entered Paradise while she was still alive. Among other things, it is said that she was the one who informed her grandfather Jacob, in song, that his son Joseph was not dead. See Targum Pseudo-Jonathan to Gen. 46: 17, and the index to Ginzberg, *Legends of the Jews*, s.v. 'Serah bat Asher'.

[58] Zohar, iii. 167*b*.   [59] Weissler, *Voices of the Matriarchs*, 79.

their earthly duties and obligations. Not a word is said of the traditional female burdens of tending a husband, bearing children, feeding a family, and other mundane chores. On the contrary, the righteous women devote all their time to spiritual 'pleasures and luxuries': prayer, songs of praise, and the performance of commandments—precisely those commandments that, in the normal run of things, would be beyond their reach as the exclusive prerogative of the men. Moreover, they converse about the reasons for the commandments (and in the context of the Zohar, this would probably be a reference to the mystical rationale of the commandments), engaging in just that kind of speculation from which women on earth have been specifically precluded.[60] From all this it follows that, in stark contrast to their situation in this world, women in the World to Come participate fully, with equal rights and obligations, in all the intellectual and spiritual pursuits of the men.

Notably, the matching of women's religious status to that of the men in the World to Come is accompanied by a strict separation between the sexes. As one of the heavenly 'messengers' reports: 'All day long, [the women] are by themselves, as I told you, and so are the men'; and even the 'messengers', who had received special permission to look upon the women's palaces so as to be able to bring their report to Simeon bar Yohai, do so from without, beyond the boundary of a 'curtain' that males are forbidden to cross. That the separation of the sexes is so strictly observed in this eschatological fancy would seem to represent yet another 'concession' of messianic time to the reality of the present, where men and women are kept apart for fear that they are liable to be led astray by the evil inclination, which may entice them into sexual misconduct.[61] In fact, the persistence of the practice of separation in eschatological time is in line with the rabbinic tradition whereby 'men apart and women apart' even in the time of the messiah, 'when the evil inclination no longer exists'.[62] Clearly, then, though the Zohar goes a considerable way towards transforming the status of women in the World to Come, it does not entirely discard the

[60] See ibid. 79–80 and 219 n. 8, based on *Sefer ḥasidim*, §835: 'A man is required to teach his daughters the commandments, that is, the conclusive requirements of the law. As for the statement, "If one teaches his daughter Torah, it is as though he taught her *tiflut*" [Mishnah *Sot.* 20: 1; *tiflut* has been interpreted variously as denoting frivolity, triviality, or sexual licentiousness], this refers to the deeper study of the Talmud, the rationale of the commandments, and the esoteric meanings of the Torah, which may not be taught to a woman or a minor.'

[61] See Ellinson, *Woman and the Mitzvot*, ii: *The Modest Way*, 1–41.

[62] Cf. JT *Suk.* 5: 2 and BT *Suk.* 52a.

traditional norms that regulate the relationship between the sexes. Nevertheless, it should be noted that even under normal, earthly conditions, the rabbinic definition of women as 'a separate people'[63] bestowed a certain degree of freedom upon those women who wished to engage, within their own segregated quarters, in the intellectual, spiritual, or ritual pursuits from which they were excluded in the public domain of men.[64] The Zohar exploits this traditional leeway to the full, allowing the righteous women in Paradise to occupy themselves with activities that are traditionally set aside exclusively for men, so long as they remain strictly confined to their own quarters.

It is clear, moreover, that the separation of the women from the men in Paradise applies only to the daytime hours, which are devoted to prayer,

---

[63] BT *Shab.* 62a.

[64] Thus, for example, women in the Ashkenazi milieu might worship separately in the 'women's synagogue', where they prayed under the direction of a *firzogerin* or *zogerke* who was versed in the prayer service. On this see Weissler, *Voices of the Matriarchs*, 9 and 194–5 n. 12, and the bibliographical references given there; and see Abrahams, *Jewish Life*, 25–6. There are also some references to learned women—usually belonging to the households of well-known halakhic scholars—who were expert in the laws concerning women and who made halakhic decisions in response to women's inquiries. For example, Abraham Grossman (*Early Sages of Ashkenaz* (Heb.), 224 n. 62) notes that Bellette, sister of R. Isaac b. Menahem, one of the sages of northern France in the mid-11th century, issued halakhic decisions to women. For more information on this type of activity see id., *Pious and Rebellious*, trans. Chipman, 162–6, and the somewhat fuller version in id., *Pious and Rebellious* (Heb.), 282–9. According to Lamdan (*A Separate People*, 110), 'the Ari [Isaac Luria] himself instituted separate classes for women'. She bases this on a certain passage in *Sefer toledot ha'ari*, where the wives of Luria's disciples in Safed are said to have studied his esoteric teachings at the same time as, but apart from, their husbands. In fact, *Sefer toledot ha'ari* reports that when it was revealed to Luria that he was soon to die, he assembled the 'companions' and promised to explicate several mysteries to them before his departure. 'Then the Rabbi set up a study house [*hesger*] for them, and he arranged rooms in his court for the women and children, with a separate room for each woman and her children.' While the published text contains no reference to the women in their rooms engaging in kabbalistic study, some of the manuscript versions, cited by the editor in his notes (*Sefer toledot ha'ari*, 201 n. 3), go on to say: 'And so they did, and they set aside a room for the men by themselves and a room for the women by themselves, and they studied by day and by night'; or: 'And so they did, and they allocated a special court with separate accommodations for men and for women.' These variant readings may support Lamdan's unequivocal assertion, but they remain ambiguous, since it is hard to tell whether the 'they' who studied 'by day and by night' were the men, who were simply being separated from their families in order to be free to devote themselves to study, or whether 'they' included the women, who did not only occupy separate quarters but studied in them apart, in parallel sessions.

contemplation, and study. The hours of the night, on the other hand, are devoted—in the World to Come as in they are this world—to the mating of males and females, although this heavenly mating is construed as being spiritual rather than physical:

But every night they all come together, for the hour of mating is at midnight, in that world as in this one. Mating in that world consists in the cleaving of soul unto soul, of light unto light, as the mating of this world is of body with body. Each goes to its appropriate counterpart: species to species, mate to mate, body to body, and in the mating of that world, light to light. . . . Happy is the lot of the righteous, men and females, who walk the straight path in this world and are found deserving of the pleasures of that world! Ah, Rabbi, ah, Rabbi, were you not Bar Yohai, it could not be imparted. [From] the mating of that world is born a fruit greater than the fruit of this world's mating. In the mating of that world, which is by their mutual will, when the souls cleave to one another, they bear fruit, and the lights that issue from them become lamps. These are the souls of those who convert to Judaism, and they all enter into a single palace.[65]

---

[65] Zohar, iii. 167*a*–168*a*. This zoharic promotion of righteous women to the remarkable spiritual and intellectual heights that become accessible to them in the eschatological domain of the Other World may provide the key to the rightful evaluation of other such exaltations of righteous women—often the mythical heroines of the Bible—that occur here and there in the homiletical literature of hasidism and kabbalah. Every depiction of a messianic future or an afterlife in which women's spiritual power is held to be supreme and to exceed even the power of the greatest men of their time is based on the conceptualization of the World to Come as the antithesis of present-day reality. This kind of flight into the far reaches of the male eschatological imagination does indeed liberate women from the traditional bonds of their earthly existence—the bonds of physicality, sexuality, and materiality—but at the same time it also emphasizes the unyielding nature of the conventions that confine them to their material existence in the here and now. Such fanciful explorations of the utopian future do not, in themselves, suggest any agenda of 'radical egalitarianism' in the minds of their authors. It is in this light, I believe, that we should read the sermon of the hasidic master, Kalonymus Kalman Epstein (*c*.1751–1823), in which Nehemia Polen, in an article that takes issue with some of the views I expressed in 'On Women in Hasidism', finds the theoretical underpinnings for what he regards as hasidism's unprecedented acknowledgement of the spiritual authority of women. Polen cites R. Kalonymus Kalman's sermon on the 'Song of the Parting of the Red Sea' (Exod. 15), which describes Miriam the Prophetess as follows: 'She had all the women follow her and performed circle dances [*hakafot*] with them, with the intent implicit in the verse "a woman shall encircle a man" [*nekevah tesovev gaver*, Jer. 31: 22], in order to draw upon the supernal light from the places where the categories of masculine and feminine do not exist. Now Moses said, "I will sing unto the Lord" [Exod. 15: 1]. This was because Moses spoke while still under the categories of masculine/feminine, for the light of supernal clarity had not yet appeared. . . . For this reason he

The potential for this unique zoharic tradition to be detached from its original kabbalistic context and to function as a message addressed specifically to women may be deduced from all its independent appearances in the devo-

adopted the future tense: When I attain [to that state], then "I will sing". But Miriam, through her circle dance, drew down the supernal light. Then they came to such realization than which no greater realization is possible. So she said, "Sing ye" [Exod. 15: 21]—now. For their realization was such that no greater realization is possible' (Epstein, *Ma'or vashemesh*, i. 178; with some minor additions and modifications, the English translation is Polen's in 'Miriam's Dance', 4).

This 'supernal light' which transcends the distinction between male and female is the light that is to be revealed in the Time to Come: 'In the [eschatological] future, however, all will restore their souls to their [metaphysical] roots, and the holy sparks will rise, and the forces of evil will cease altogether. At that time the bright light of the Divinity will shine throughout the worlds, the line and the circle will be equal, and there will no longer be the categories of masculine and feminine' (Epstein, *Ma'or vashemesh*, i. 178). Miriam clearly succeeds, in her own historical time, in drawing down the light that is to be revealed only in the messianic future. She and the women who join in her cry of 'Sing ye!', in the imperative voice, are acting in the eschatological dimension—actualized for them at that moment within the concrete reality of the present. Moses, on the other hand, correctly distinguishes between the two dimensions, the eschatological (future beyond time) and the historical (present), and so he consciously chooses to employ the future tense. His declaration, 'I will sing', refers to the ultimate redemption that is yet to come: 'that is to say . . . in the masculine, *shir* (song), and not [in the feminine variant of the same word] *shirah*, and therefore he said "I will sing", meaning that at that time, at the time of the future redemption, then we will sing unto the Lord' (ibid., i. 177). As Polen emphasizes, Miriam's spiritual achievement, by which, in that moment, she attains and causes the other women to attain a 'taste' of the ultimate redemption, exceeds the achievement of Moses, who remains bound by the limitations of the present. Even so, it is no accident that the feminine achievement is placed in an eschatological setting, highlighting the radical difference between the utopian future and the conditions of present-day reality. Moreover, in the very same homily, Miriam—whose grasp of the divine was inherently limited by her being 'in the state of the female'—is disparaged for her impatience, as a result of which she was able to sing no more than one verse of her song, while the male Moses was able to sing his 'to its conclusion': 'Even though Miriam was a prophetess, she was in the state of *nukba* [the female] and did not attain the conception of awe for the divine. Had she waited for Moses, she would have been able to sing the entire song; but she did not wait. As soon as she saw the Egyptians enter the sea, when the water closed in on them while the Israelites were walking on dry land in the midst of the sea, she immediately "took the timbrel in her hand" [Exod. 14: 20]. That is to say, she attained the conception of love [of the divine] alone [without the mitigating conception of awe] by which to utter her song. She did not wait for Moses, and that is why she was only privileged to say that [first] verse alone. Afterwards, when Moses and the [male] Israelites uttered it, the women repeated the song with them to its conclusion' (Epstein, *Ma'or vashemesh*, i. 177; partial English translation in Polen, 'Miriam's Dance', 3).

Moses' recitation, which alludes to the final redemption in the messianic future while retaining awareness of the limitations of the present redemption, is complete and appropriate for its

tional writings in Yiddish directed at women.[66] In much the same way it could have gained an independent life in Sabbatai Zevi's eschatological imagination, serving as a stimulus and stirring him to envision the liberation of women from their earthly constraints. That vision, first articulated in the revolution-ary statement of his egalitarian agenda as recorded by Thomas Coenen,[67] aspired to realize, in the here and now, the conditions of women's existence in the World to Come. In Sabbatai Zevi's view, that utopian Other World was becoming reality in the circumstances of the present. Consequently, women were now poised to be relieved of the historic burden of their sex's affliction: to be liberated from their subservience to their husbands, set free to engage in spiritual 'pleasures and luxuries', and to share equally in the state of un-bounded joy that was about to embrace the entire universe, just as the righteous women of the Zohar were free to rejoice in their heavenly palaces.

True, as Scholem points out, 'Sabbatai . . . lacked the capacity to give this ideal of emancipation definite form and contents. His ideal, which found

time, and it is no wonder that it is enunciated by a man. The homily highlights the inferior char-acter of Miriam's endeavour in the here and now, precisely by placing it in sharp contrast to the superiority it will gain in the messianic future. This can hardly be viewed as a prime source for the 'radical egalitarianism' that Polen found in it, particularly since R. Kalonymus Kalman's homilies are generally devoid of any immediate messianic tension. He clearly did not expect, and certainly did not advocate, that the hierarchical relation between the categories of male and female should be transcended or reversed in the concrete hasidic reality of his own time. The same can be said of at least two other hasidic homilies—both by R. Shneur Zalman of Lyady— of which one is discussed briefly by Polen ('Miriam's Dance', 6) as a possible source for the theme of R. Kalonymus Kalman's homily, and the other is elaborated by Yael Levine Katz ('Voice of the Bride' (Heb.)). Both make use of the same verse, 'a woman shall encircle a man' (Jer. 31: 22), to develop the common kabbalistic motif of the inversion of gender hierarchies in the messianic future. In the second homily, focusing on the wording of the sixth and seventh marriage benedictions, R. Shneur Zalman distinguishes between the diaspora reality (alluded to in the wording of the sixth benediction), where the joy of the bride is secondary to the groom's and utterly dependent on it—a state of affairs which, at the present time, reflects the status of the female on both the human and the divine plane—and the messianic future (alluded to in the wording of the seventh benediction) in which the hierarchy on both planes will be inverted. At that time, 'the essence of the groom's joy will come from the bride's', for 'it is in the [messianic] future that the aspect of "voice of the bride" will be supreme'. Here, too, in the absence of any indication that the final redemption was anticipated within the foreseeable future, the emphasis is being placed at least as much on the persisting inferiority of the female in the present as it is on the ultimate supremacy she will achieve at some distant point in the future, beyond foreseeable time.

[66] See above, n. 50.   [67] Above, at n. 2.

such noble expression in the sentence reported—albeit with a disparaging intention—by Coenen, remained vague and ephemeral.'[68] Indeed, this egalitarian, liberating agenda never crystallized into a coherent policy, either during Sabbatai Zevi's lifetime or in the various transmutations of the movement that followed. Nevertheless, its existence can account for several of the messiah's most 'outlandish' or 'bizarre' acts, and some flickerings of his original vision can still be detected in the doctrines of his successors and in all the clandestine, sectarian organizations in which the movement persisted long after his death.

We learn from a number of discrete sources of Sabbatai Zevi's fondness for women, the special interest he took in them, and his tendency to surround or even sequester himself with them in various and sundry circumstances. He was not necessarily motivated in this by the desire to indulge in sexual relations; in fact, he appears to have experienced sexual intercourse as an acutely problematical act, and it would seem that he abstained from it altogether during several periods of his life.[69] His relations with women are often mentioned in ritualistic–symbolic contexts,[70] and in the context of intimate social contact which, though it flew in the face of both the letter and the spirit of Jewish law, and was seen as 'alien', 'bizarre', or even scandalous, did not necessarily amount to sexual depravity. Such was his behaviour towards the wives of other men and his own ex-wives, who were all halakhically prohibited to him, and also towards the maiden daughters of some of his followers, who were placed at his

[68] Scholem, *Sabbatai Sevi*, 405.

[69] On the radical swings in Sabbatai Zevi's sex life between strict, ascetic abstinence (which led, among other things, to his divorces from his two first wives, with whom he never fulfilled the commandment of marital consummation) and antinomian, deviant sexual activity, and their relationship to the mood swings between depression and manic elation that characterized the mental illness from which he is said to have suffered, see Elqayam, 'To Know Messiah' (Heb.), 650–6; and Scholem, *Sabbatai Sevi*, 127–38.

[70] On Sabbatai Zevi's penchant for inventing new rituals that were at once solemn and bizarre, Scholem remarks (*Sabbatai Sevi*, 389): 'Sabbatai's ritualistic longings were not satisfied by brief antinomian outbursts. They also sought expression in the invention of new cultic procedures in which the sublime and the ridiculous were curiously mingled. The secret satisfaction of transgressing the Law was merely one factor among others. Sabbatai seemed to derive a particular pleasure from the invention of new rituals. However grotesque and pathetic these may have been, there was nothing positively forbidden about them.' Sabbatai's fondness for newly made-up ceremonials and rituals may perhaps be placed in the wider context of the ritualization of Jewish life generally during this period, on which see Bar-Levav, 'Ritualisation'.

disposal by their fathers for various purposes. For example, Coenen reports:

[Sabbatai Zevi] also did not refrain from honouring his supporters by making personal visits to their homes. Thus it happened that he lingered on three or four occasions in the company of the wives he had abandoned, or rather—for the reason mentioned above—had been taken from him.[71] He met them affectionately and sat beside them in conversation, though this is expressly forbidden by Jewish law, which states that a man who has been divorced of his wife may not have any converse with her, nor may he remain with her under the same roof.[72]

Jacob Sasportas also knew of such incidents. He records a rumour that reached him in a letter from Kraków: 'As for his dancing with married women and sequestering himself with his first ex-wife, these are recorded in a book, as you will see below.'[73] Further on, quoting a letter of his own to Rabbi Raphael Sofino in Livorno, he adds more details:

He jested and danced [*vayehi kimetsaḥek vekhimeraked*; cf. Gen. 19: 14 and 1 Chron. 15: 29], filling his mouth and his tongue with shouts of joy [Ps. 126: 2], leaping and dancing [2 Sam. 6: 16] amidst maidens playing timbrels [Ps. 68: 26] and women making merry [1 Sam. 18: 7], but all his crooning could hardly be likened to that of David,[74] for the latter made light of himself before the Lord who had chosen him, before the ark of God [2 Sam. 6], and not with the kind of laughter and light-headedness that accustom people to debauchery. But what will all these dancing women have to say upon seeing God's messiah leaping and bounding as lightly as a gazelle [*tsevi*, cf. S. of S. 2: 8–9, alluding to the messiah's name], yet never stopping[75] his mouth [Ps. 107: 42] from singing and dancing [cf. 1 Sam. 18: 6] with the married daughters of Israel.[76]

---

[71] Coenen was referring to Sabbatai Zevi's first two wives, having related the story of these ill-fated marriages at the outset of his exposition: 'When he was about 22 or 24 years old, he took a Jewish woman to wife. However, he did not have relations with her—or so rumour tells it— due to physical weakness or a fancied sense of holiness and purity (an explanation I heard frequently), or for other undisclosed reasons. Since she did not arrive at consummation of the marital union with him, the girl was taken from him in accordance with the laws of the Jews, because he had rejected her. After some time he again married a Jewish woman, also from Smyrna, of a very distinguished Jewish family in that city. But what had happened in his first marriage happened again in this second marriage, and therefore his second wife was taken from him just like the first' (Coenen, *False Hopes* (Heb.), 39).   [72] Ibid. 54.

[73] Sasportas, *Tsitsat novel tsevi*, 80.

[74] To whom most of the verses invoked in these lines refer.

[75] *Kofets*, 'stopping', is a play on *mekapets*, 'bounding', in the previous line.

[76] Sasportas, *Tsitsat novel tsevi*, 89, and see ibid. 98, on how he sequestered himself with his ex-wife.

All this would seem to have amounted to 'the kind of laughter and light-headedness that accustom people to debauchery' rather than to debauchery as such, though Immanuel Frances does call Sabbatai Zevi an 'adulterer' in one of his polemical poems, going on to spell out: 'He cuddled and kissed women who were forbidden to him, to one putting out his hand, to another his breast.'[77]

A different type of relationship to women, one that was evidently ritual or ceremonial in nature, is reported by Abraham Cuenque—a Sabbatian who lived in the Holy Land, and whose memoirs were transcribed and preserved by Jacob Emden. Cuenque describes the messiah's adoption of royal pomp and ceremony during his period of incarceration in the fortress of Gallipoli. This included 'seventy beautiful virgins, daughters of aristocratic Jewish families, dressed in royal finery, who waited upon him'.[78] Virgins who were given over to Sabbatai Zevi for unclear but apparently non-sexual purposes are again mentioned in two Armenian sources, composed shortly after the messiah's apostasy, according to which he was presented by his adherents with 'three virgins whom he kept in his company for a time, and afterwards he let them go'.[79] A letter sent by Abraham Yakhini, a prominent Sabbatian kabbalist and preacher, to Nathan of Gaza in the summer of 5433 (1673) speaks of a mysterious episode in connection with a girl whom Sabbatai Zevi seems also to have taken into his custody without making sexual use of her. During the last of his sojourns in Constantinople, according to this source, he took to himself 'by way of his supernal acts of *tikun*' a girl who was betrothed to and apparently even pregnant by another man. He 'dressed her in the wrap of the Ishmaelites' and wed her in a Muslim ceremony while still being married to his wife Sarah, despite the 'hue and cry' that this affair aroused within the community of the faithful in that city. According to Abraham Yakhini, Sabbatai Zevi told him 'that it should not occur to him [Yakhini] that he [Sabbatai] had laid a hand on so much as the little finger of this betrothed girl, and he swore to this by the God of his faith'.[80]

The Ladino manuscript containing the doctrines of Judah Levi Tovah, a member of the eighteenth-century apostate Doenmeh sect,[81] also credits

---

[77] Frances, *Tsevi mudah*, 125.

[78] Emden, *Zot torat hakena'ot*, 41, cited in Scholem, *Sabbatai Sevi*, 670.

[79] Galanté, *Nouveaux documents*, 85 and 97. See also Scholem, *Sabbatai Sevi*, 434 and 670.

[80] A. Epstein, 'Abraham ha-Yakhini', 212, cited in Scholem, *Sabbatai Sevi*, 878–80.

[81] Rivka Schatz-Uffenheimer, who studied the manuscript and translated part of it together

Sabbatai Zevi, apparently on the strength of a reliable tradition, with an odd symbolic act having to do with a virgin girl. The girl, who was the daughter of Abraham Yakhini, was told to open a 'sealed pouch', into which Sabbatai Zevi had secreted forty-two slips of paper bearing the names of forty-two of his adherents, 'chosen by lot'. When the girl opened up the pouch 'in great purity' and laid out the slips in rows on a sheet spread out before her, they formed ten lines of text setting forth some decidedly antinomian statements:

> The texts resembled those of the 613 commandments of Moses, such as 'thou shalt not uncover the nakedness' [Lev. 18, enumerating forbidden sexual relationships], but what was written there was the opposite. And where [Moses] had commanded, 'There shall be no cult prostitute of the daughters of Israel' [Deut. 23: 18 in the Hebrew Bible (verse 17 in the Old Testament)], it was written otherwise there. And where he had commanded, 'You shall not approach a woman to uncover her nakedness while she is in her menstrual uncleanness' [Lev. 18: 9], the opposite was written there. All ten texts came out like these, but no more can be said; let this suffice.[82]

These associations with women, in a variety of circumstances whose common element was the deliberate, public flaunting of the restrictions of law and tradition, all hint in one way or another at the dissolution of the boundaries of sexual morality in the dawning messianic age, and the radical transformation in male–female relations that this has brought about. It is no wonder, then, that Sabbatai Zevi's irregular interactions with his own ex-wives, with other men's wives, or with virgin girls could be interpreted as signifying nothing more than his sexual depravity and proclivity to commit adultery (which is how they indeed were interpreted by Immanuel Frances, by the Armenian and Greek sources published by Galanté, and by Jacob Emden)[83]—or, as Coenen saw them, as subtle ploys to gain the affection of his adherents by wooing their

with Isaac Molkho, believed that it was written soon after the year 5459 (1699); see Schatz-Uffenheimer, 'Sabbatian Sect' (Heb.), 397. Scholem argued that it should be dated to the end of the 18th or the early 19th century; see Scholem, 'Dönmeh', 161–2, and id., *Researches* (Heb.), 305 n. 2. More recently, Aharon Telenberg suggested that it was written between 1720 and 1725; see Telenberg, 'The Sabbatian Theology' (Heb.), 152–3.

[82] Schatz-Uffenheimer, 'Sabbatian Sect' (Heb.), 408.

[83] For Frances' interpretation see above, at n. 77. The Armenian sources say of Sabbatai Zevi that 'he had relations with women' and express their disapproval of 'his way of life with women and with his associates [possibly referring to sexual relations with men]' (Galanté, *Nouveaux documents*, 94 and 106; and see Scholem, *Sabbatai Sevi*, 669). In a similar vein, a contemporary Greek source remarks: 'The Jewish nobles gave him their daughters in order for him to debauch

naive wives: 'He further sought to lure the friendship of women and to make himself appealing to them (it should be noted that women are zealous and often gullible enough to believe anything, and they have much influence upon the men).'[84]

However, by dint of detaching his relations with women from their proper ideological context—however hazy and fragmentary it may have been—all these interpretations fall short of explaining the messiah's motives and aspirations. Whether or not he had sexual relations with the women whose company he sought out (and we may suppose that he was as inconsistent in this regard as in others), there is little doubt that Sabbatai Zevi was motivated neither by unbridled sexual lust nor by the tactical considerations attributed to him by Coenen, but rather by his belief in the abrogation of original sin and the release of women from the burden of its penalty, which seemed to him an integral part of the revolutionary process of redemption. This can be seen from a series of strange acts which, though they did not amount to a coherent policy, signalled the intention to liberate women in one of two ways: either by demonstrating that, with the messianic advent, the halakhic lines of gender demarcation were rapidly fading away, or else by creating a segregated but egalitarian equivalence between the sexes, in much the same way as the sexes

himself with them, and for them to be impregnated by his seed' (Galanté, *Nouveaux documents*, 109). Emden, in one of the barbed asides with which he peppered Abraham Cuenque's memoirs, interprets in this vein Cuenque's reference to the seventy virgins who waited upon Sabbatai Zevi (above, at n. 78): 'Here, too, the informant [Cuenque] contradicts his own words above, where he wrote that he [Sabbatai Zevi] abstained from all the pleasures of the world, and so he did display himself at first, so as to mislead the masses, but ultimately he proved himself a "pokey ascetic" [*parush nikpi*; cf. BT *Sot.* 22*b*], and "he sought a multitude of wives" [2 Chron. 11: 23]. Why did he not have manservants? For surely, the Sages have declared, "One should not have a woman as a personal servant" [BT *Kid.* 70*a*]—let alone seventy beautiful virgins in regal attire' (Emden, *Zot torat hakena'ot*, 41).

He makes a similar comment about Cuenque's descriptions of Sabbatai Zevi's extreme asceticism: 'He was entirely hypocritical in making himself out as a "pokey ascetic", even as his heart poked him on to excesses even greater than one might speculate; he was suffused with all kinds of evil lust and could not satisfy the cravings of his soul and the covetousness of his heart . . . for he was a pursuer of sensual pleasure—needless to say, by way of the sense of touch. He appears to have been a well-equipped steed [cf. Rashi's comment on BT *Ket.* 61*b*: 'His [male] beast [*behemto*]—a horse or an ass well-equipped and eager to copulate [with a woman]']. He loved many women, dallied with his divorced ex-wives, and danced on the holy sabbath day with beautiful young married women in the "lesser Temple" [i.e. the synagogue]' (ibid. 34).

[84] Coenen, *False Hopes* (Heb.), 54.

were segregated but equal in the zoharic Paradise scene, where spiritually empowered righteous women were engaged in activities traditionally reserved for men.

Both these strategies, which also gave vent to Sabbatai Zevi's antinomian and ritualistic propensities,[85] were already at work in the dramatic events that transpired on the sabbath, 4 Tevet 5426 (December 1665), in the Portuguese Synagogue of Smyrna, where many of those who repudiated Sabbatai Zevi's messianic claims were concentrated. According to the testimony of Samson Bacchi, an Italian emissary from Casale,[86] the messiah used an axe to break down the synagogue doors, which had been locked in order to keep him out. He interrupted the service that was in progress and delivered to the congregation 'a blasphemous sermon'.[87] After that,

He took a [printed] copy of the Pentateuch from his bag, declaring that it was holier than the Torah [manuscript] scroll. He read the Pentateuchal lesson, calling his elder brother [Elijah] first as [if he were] a priest and making him King of Turkey. His second brother he appointed emperor of Rome. He called none of the many priests and Levites present in the synagogue to the reading of the Torah, but he called many [other] men *and even women*, and he forced all of them to pronounce the Ineffable Name.[88]

A shorter account of the same incident appears in the memoirs of Barukh of Arezzo, though the reference to women being called up to the Torah occurs in only one of the manuscript versions: 'he began the reading of the Torah by calling upon his elder brother . . . and he called upon many men [and women too]'.[89] A further echo of this incident, implying that it had become Sabbatai Zevi's regular practice to call women to the Torah, can be detected in a comment by Rabbi Moses Hagiz on Abraham Cuenque's memoir, as quoted by Emden in one of his parenthetic asides. Referring to Cuenque's testimony regarding the 'seventy beautiful virgins' who waited on Sabbatai Zevi in Gallipoli,[90] Emden remarks: 'Rabbi Moses Hagiz adds the following: "On the

---

[85] See above, at n. 70.

[86] On his identity see Scholem, *Sabbatai Sevi*, 376 n. 101.

[87] For a reconstruction and analysis of his address see ibid. 396–405.

[88] Brüll, *Sabbatai Zevi* (Heb.), 15, following Scholem's translation in *Sabbatai Sevi*, 397. Emphasis added.

[89] Barukh of Arezzo, 'Memorial' (Heb.), 49. In note 1 on that page, the editor, Freimann, notes the variant reading appearing in the manuscript furnished to him by Abraham Epstein.

[90] See above, at nn. 78 and 83.

sabbath he would call seven virgins to the Torah."'[91] Although calling women
to the Torah was only one gesture among many others comprising a series of
transgressions and newly devised rituals that commenced on that sabbath day,
its significance should not be overlooked, as Gershom Scholem was fully
aware:

> A striking and very revealing sign of the messianic transformation of the old order,
> and of the substitution of a messianic Judaism for the traditional and imperfect one,
> was Sabbatai's innovation of calling women to the reading of the Torah. Sabbatai evi-
> dently envisaged a change in the status of women . . . The truth of the matter is that
> Sabbatai, in whose life the love or favor of women never played any ascertainable role,
> dreamed of a radical reform of the status of women.[92]

Some two days after the eventful sabbath service in the Portuguese synagogue, there was a gathering of the faithful—apparently in the same
synagogue (or possibly in Sabbatai Zevi's home)[93]—to declare their allegiance
to the King Messiah. This time the women were separated from the men,
in keeping with Jewish tradition, but they were assigned a solemn, splendid
ceremony of their own, which resembled in every detail the ceremony assigned
to the men:

> Once Nathan had declared the messiah . . . all those who believed in him as the mes-
> siah began demonstrating their subservience to him. Young and old, men and women,
> maidens and youths went forth to behold him, hail him as the new messiah, and kiss
> his hands. All this came to pass, attended by great displays of reverence, on 7 Tevet for
> the men, and on 8 Tevet for the women, in the Portuguese synagogue.[94]

True, in contrast to the calling of women to the Torah in the presence of the

[91]   Emden, *Zot torat hakena'ot*, 41.
[92]   Scholem, *Sabbatai Sevi*, 403.   [93]   See ibid. 412 nn. 177–8.
[94]   Coenen, *False Hopes* (Heb.), 45. In Emden's Hebrew version, Coenen's description is given
as follows: 'After the declaration of the futile messiah . . . those who believed in him prepared
themselves to demonstrate the submissiveness appropriate to the King Messiah, to hail and
welcome him joyfully with gifts and offerings. This took place on 7 Tevet in the synagogue of
the Sephardi community. [First] came the men, bringing gifts to him who is to be feared [cf. Ps.
76: 12], and the women did the same on the following day, 8 Tevet, coming before his presence
with blessings, gifts, and offerings' (Emden, *Zot torat hakena'ot*, 27). On the separation of the
female believers from the male, in which framework they acquire a comparable standing, see
above, at nn. 61–4, where this phenomenon is discussed in connection with the Zohar's description of righteous women in the World to Come. See also below, Ch. 6, at nn. 24–40, for a discussion of a similar phenomenon in Jacob Frank's circle.

entire community of worshippers—a gesture which constituted flagrant defiance of a gender boundary deeply rooted in Jewish law—the holding of identical but separate ceremonies for men and women respectively still conformed to the traditional segregation of the sexes in the context of public worship. Nevertheless, it too, in its own way, reflected the egalitarian tendency of Sabbatai Zevi's project: it forged a direct, personal connection between the messiah and his female adherents, while creating for them a framework of involvement in precisely that kind of public ceremonial from which Jewish tradition had always preferred to distance women.

This egalitarian tendency, which became evident at the start of Sabbatai Zevi's messianic 'reign', not only did not wane after his apostasy and death but grew more and more pronounced, ultimately constituting a veritable hallmark of the messianic heresy. One of its manifestations is associated with the Polish Sabbatian Judah Hasid ('Judah the Pious'), who headed the large group of Sabbatian devotees that set off for the Land of Israel in 5460 (1700).[95] On their way, the prospective settlers stopped over in various German towns where they hoped to obtain funds for the journey and recruit supporters. Judah Hasid, whose Sabbatian belief was expressed, among other things, in his call for penitence by means of ascetic mortifications, used to preach in this spirit in all the synagogues of the communities through which they passed. Jacob Emden describes his activities, on the basis of the eyewitness testimony of his father, the Hakham Tsevi:

After that, R. Judah Hasid would go into synagogues and give sermons of admonition, arousing great fervour and much weeping, and he made a great impression upon the masses, though he was really no scholar, as I heard from the holy lips of my late father and teacher . . . And this Rabbi Judah Hasid not only admonished the men with his sermons, but he went to the house [synagogue] of the women as well. He would take out a Torah scroll and carry it in his arms into the women's synagogue, there to preach admonitory sermons to the women. Many people found this outlandish and peculiar, but the masses were deceived into viewing it all as a matter of consummate holiness and spirituality, as though the women were [no more alluring to him than] white geese.[96] But of course this is mere arrogance; such a thing has never been heard of in Israel. Even in the time of the prophets, we find that Jeremiah and Zephaniah were

<hr/>

[95] On him see Benayahu, 'Holy Brotherhood' (Heb.).

[96] BT *Ber.* 30*a*: 'To me, [the women] are like white geese'; that is, they arouse no sexual desire.

sent by God to prophesy to the men, while Huldah was sent to the women.[97] Nay, even in the Time to Come, after the evil inclination has been slain, it is said that 'The land shall mourn, each family by itself' [Zech. 12: 12].[98] For this alone, he deserved to be ostracized. Nevertheless, the rabbis did not find the strength to protest this thing, because the masses of the people, both men and women, followed him devotedly and deemed him a man of God. However, in the matter of taking out the Torah scroll without good cause, my late father and teacher, the rabbi, protested forcefully and decreed that he should be banned for this . . . and he obeyed him and desisted from it.[99]

Emden does not expand upon the Sabbatian beliefs of Judah Hasid, nor does he attribute to him any transgressive or sexually debauched behaviour, as he so often does in his denunciations of many other messianic heretics. On the contrary, he acknowledges that 'he did some good in stirring the people to penitence by bringing them to tears'. At most, he disparages him for being 'really no scholar', observing that, for all his piety, 'the end of the matter showed that his assemblage was not truly for the sake of heaven, and so it was not to endure'.[100] What really bothered him (and his father) were Rabbi Judah's appearances in 'the women's synagogue'—the special sermons he preached to the women, and the Torah scrolls he brought them in his arms, apparently in order to read to them, or possibly even to call them to the reading from the Torah, as Sabbatai Zevi had done before him (albeit from a printed Pentateuch). Emden refers to these activities as 'outlandish and peculiar . . . never hitherto . . . heard of in Israel', and he denounces them on the basis of rabbinic traditions that unequivocally disallow any activity which might be construed as blurring the gender distinctions set down by the halakhah. He clearly understood, and utterly rejected, the association of the messianic heresy's egalitarian leanings with the eschatological rabbinic notion of a new Torah, which alluded to the collapse of gender boundaries and the establishment of novel relations between the sexes in the messianic era. It is no accident that he chose

[97] Cf. *Pesikta rabati*, ch. 26, ed. Friedmann, 129*b*.

[98] BT *Suk.* 52*a*: "'The land shall mourn, every family apart; the family of the house of David apart, and their wives apart" [Zech. 12: 12]. [The Sages] said: This may be understood *a fortiori*. If in the Time to Come, when they will be occupied with mourning and free from the power of the evil inclination, Scripture declares that the men and the women will be apart, how much more so now, when they are occupied with joyful matters and subject to the power of the evil inclination.' The context of this discussion in the Talmud is the 'upper level' location of the area in the Temple set apart for women, which was meant to keep them out of sight of the men so as not to arouse the latter's evil inclination.   [99] Emden, *Zot torat hakena'ot*, 56–7.   [100] Ibid.

to cite a rabbinic pronouncement ruling out this possibility 'even in the Time to Come, after the evil inclination has been slain'.

Throughout the eighteenth century, this same egalitarian tendency was discernible wherever the Sabbatian movement persisted in the Ottoman empire, central and eastern Europe. Sabbatai Zevi's 'female liberationist' message, addressed to women as early as 1665,[101] still resonated, for example, in the Doenmeh doctrine of the apostate Salonican, Judah Levi Tovah, who wrote, apparently at some point during the 1720s:

Come and see: before Adam sinned, Scripture said of him: 'And they were both naked, the man and his wife, and were not ashamed' [Gen. 2: 25]. From this it is clear that she was not yet in the state of ritual uncleanliness, of which she was ashamed, and they still strolled in the Garden of Eden, Adam to one side and Eve to the other, each his[/her] own master ... But after they sinned, when Eve was cursed—as Scripture says: 'And he shall rule over you' [Gen. 3: 16]—she came under the authority of her husband, until the sin of Eve, which had caused this, was mended. Concerning this, Rabbi Nathan [of Gaza] said that when the sin of Adam is mended, everything will revert to how it was in the beginning, as if the sin had not occurred. Then, he will be his own master and she her own mistress, as if they had not sinned.[102]

One of the most remarkable expressions of the egalitarian tendency was the novel practice of instructing women in Zohar and kabbalistic doctrine—a radical departure not only from the usual rabbinic restrictions on the religious education of women,[103] but also from the traditional limitation of access to the esoteric discipline of kabbalah.[104] Most of the evidence on this extraordinary innovation relates to the Sabbatians of Bohemia-Moravia and Germany—that is, to the western Sabbatians—but some of it originates in the Ottoman empire, and one cannot rule out the possibility that it was adopted also by the Sabbatians and Frankists in Poland, at least in the first generation or two after

[101] See above, at nn. 2–3.

[102] Telenberg, Avayou, and Elqayam, 'A Translation' (Heb.), 350. For the original Ladino version, see Avayou and Elqayam, 'A Critical Edition' (Heb.), 262. For the presumed time of composition, see above, n. 81.

[103] On these restrictions, as set forth in rabbinic tradition, see e.g. Ellinson, *Woman and the Mitzvot*, i. 240–72; R. Biale, *Women and Jewish Law*, 29–41; Meiselman, *Jewish Woman in Jewish Law*, 34–42.

[104] On the restricted access to kabbalistic study, see e.g. Idel, *Kabbalah*, 253–6, 'Interdiction' (Heb.), and 'Particularism and Universalism'. On the instruction of women in the Zohar as part of the general Sabbatian policy of disseminating esoteric mystical knowledge as widely as possible see below, at nn. 151–64.

the conversion of the latter to Christianity, before they abandoned altogether the use of Hebrew, Aramaic, and Yiddish.

It was already reported of Abraham Cardozo, who roamed widely in various cities in Italy, North Africa, Turkey, and the Land of Israel, that he taught his mystical doctrine to women. In his *Merivat kodesh*, a rhymed, acerbic polemic against Cardozo, written in Constantinople in 5467 (1707), about a year after his death, Rabbi Elijah Hakohen[105] speaks derisively of the presence of women in Cardozo's audience:

He gathered a crowd of 'worthless and reckless persons' [Judg. 9: 4], billy goats, ravers, mockers . . . 'and they came, both men and women' [Exod. 35: 22], 'the stork and the heron' [in Hebrew, both feminine gender nouns, suggesting females; cf. Lev. 11: 19 and Deut. 14: 18, in the lists of abominated and forbidden fowl], and all manner of affianced serving-women [cf. Lev. 19: 20], and the woman who lifts the *efah* [measure of corn; cf. Zech. 5: 6–11].[106]

Further on, Hakohen again remarks: 'and they came, both men and women, in synagogues and study halls',[107] and he mocks the prophetic utterances of these devotees, which came to them by way of heavenly 'mentors', such as were known to have revealed esoteric knowledge to some of the most illustrious kabbalistic masters: 'For he [Cardozo] had bestowed a heavenly mentor [*magid*] upon each and every man and wife, and so had he assigned heavenly mentors to all his disciples.'[108] Invoking the talmudic tradition that associates teaching Torah to women with *tiflut*—a term understood as denoting unbridled sexual lust— Hakohen censures as wanton Cardozo's very instruction of women in his faith:

He began doing all these things in the open—'a leaning wall, a tottering fence' [Ps. 62: 4, referring here to the brazen lack of any attempt to conceal these activities behind a more effective shelter]—and he sought to bring women into his faith and teach them his Torah. Thus he 'made naked their fountain' [cf. Lev. 20: 18], discounting as mere foolishness the statement that 'whoever instructs a woman in the Torah, it is as though he taught her *tiflut*'.[109]

Cardozo himself corroborates this testimony in one of his autobiographical letters.[110] Written early in the first decade of the eighteenth century, it

---

[105] On this writer, who is not to be identified with the famous preacher R. Elijah Hakohen 'Ha'itamari' of Smyrna, see Scholem, *Researches* (Heb.), 453–7.

[106] Hakohen, *Sefer merivat kodesh*, 4.   [107] Ibid. 8.   [108] Ibid. 19.

[109] Ibid. 26. Cf. Mishnah *Sot.* 3: 4, which reads: 'whoever instructs his daughter in the Torah, it is as though he taught her *tiflut*'; on the rabbinic restrictions on teaching Torah to women see above, at n. 103, and below, at nn. 138–40.   [110] See above, Ch. 1, at n. 57.

contains a long, bitter complaint about the torments inflicted upon him by the 'Sages of Constantinople'. Among other things, he claims that they persecuted him merely for disseminating to the masses—including women—the 'matter of the Shekhinah', that is, 'her actuality and origin' (*metsi'utah veshorshah*) and 'the unity of her holiness which is utterly divine' (*yiḥud kedushat hashekhinah shehu elohut gamur*):

> Ultimately, they said that they were persecuting me only because I told this to every man, woman, and child, for I should have kept this matter of the Shekhinah to myself. But I was only doing my duty, for though I am not the messiah, I am that man of whom the Faithful Shepherd [i.e. Moses] said to R. Simeon bar Yohai and his companions, 'Righteous is he who endeavours in the latter-day generation to know the Shekhinah, to honour her by way of the commandments of the Torah, and to suffer tribulations on her account',[111] and if I do not declare the unity of the Shekhinah's holiness, which is utterly divine, how should these trials and tribulations come my way?[112]

We hear more about the novel Sabbatian practice of instructing women in the Zohar from the writings of Moses Hagiz, an ally of the Hakham Tsevi, who devoted many years of his life to fighting the messianic heresy:[113]

> One must take care not to take instruction from anyone who confounds his thoughts with this new evil—ideas instigated by those who are crazed in mind, in faith (may the Merciful One save them), and in learning.[114] For they have set aside the mainstays of Torah learning, and where in former times, even among the elders and the men of [good] deeds, there might not have been one from a town or two from a clan who were familiar with the Zohar, now every worthless and reckless know-nothing youth takes

---

[111] Zohar, iii. 239*a*.

[112] Molkho and Amarillo, 'Autobiographical Letters' (Heb.), 221–2. By emphasizing the pure divinity of the Shekhinah, Cardozo was explicitly contesting both the rationalist philosophical tradition of the Middle Ages, which conceived the Shekhinah as a divinely created entity rather than being itself divine (see e.g. ibid. 233, and see Wolfson's remarks in 'Constructions of the Shekhinah', 27), and those Sabbatians, led by Samuel Primo, who held that the messiah became divine by way of the *sefirah* of Malkhut donning his body (see Cardozo's citation of Primo in Scholem, *Studies and Texts* (Heb.), 286–7; and see the discussion of Yael Nadav in 'Kabbalistic Treatise' (Heb.), 324–5). These Sabbatians were the 'Sages of Constantinople' who, according to Cardozo's letter, and other sources as well, were making his life a misery. On Cardozo's campaign against Primo and the doctrine of the messiah's divinity see Scholem, *Studies and Texts* (Heb.), 276 and 285–8. On his conceptualization of the Shekhinah, in this and other contexts, see Wolfson, 'Constructions of the Shekhinah'.

[113] On Hagiz's anti-Sabbatian activity see Elisheva Carlebach's comprehensive study, *Pursuit of Heresy*.

[114] I interpret 'this new evil—ideas instigated by those who are crazed in mind, in faith ... and in learning' as referring to the Sabbatian heresy, though Hagiz does not say so explicitly.

it to hand, spouts it in public, and boasts about town that he can interpret, correct, and translate it. He sits reading it aloud to women and children, in the vernacular for those who so require. I am astounded at the great scholars of the generation, who fail to rebuke them, especially in a great city of sages and scribes, whose name I shall not invoke here so as to preserve its honour, for it is famed in the eyes of God and man, a fount of Torah for the Jews, and all the greatest scholars of the law have come from there![115] How can they allow this holy book of the Zohar to be taught in the academies in the company of women,[116] in public, and on top of it all in the vernacular?[117]

According to Jacob Emden, the Polish Moses David of Podhajce was another Sabbatian who taught the Zohar to women. Known as a kabbalist,

[115] Hagiz's travels make it hard to determine which 'great city of sages and scribes' he had in mind. He battled Sabbatianism mainly during his sojourns in Amsterdam, London, and Altona, so that he may have been referring either to the three sister communities of Altona, Hamburg, and Wansbeck (see below, n. 121) or to Amsterdam. Both the former and the latter were famed in the Jewish world for their scholarship and were tainted by the Sabbatian heresy during the period of Hagiz's anti-Sabbatian activities, in the first half of the 18th century. Benayahu, on the other hand, has no doubt that Hagiz was referring to Salonica, where the Zohar, or parts of it, was translated into Ladino, so that it could be imparted even to women and children 'in the vernacular'; see Benayahu, 'Great Apostasy' (Heb.), 182 and 271. Zeev Gries, in a personal communication, has suggested to me the possibility that the reference to Zohar instruction in the vernacular may have been to the book *Naḥalat tsevi* by Tsevi Hirsh Khotsh. Published in Frankfurt am Main in 1711, this was a popular Yiddish adaptation of selected 'moral teachings, tales, and the more straight-forward, exoteric passages' of the Zohar. On the book and its author see Liberman, 'The Book *Naḥalat tsevi*' (Heb.); Gries, *Conduct Literature* (Heb.), 69, 76, 96; and Weissler, *Voices of the Matriarchs*, s.v. '*Nakhalas Tsevi*'. There were a few other Yiddish translations of selected passages from the Zohar, produced at the turn of the 17th and 18th centuries. These included *Abir ya'akov* by Simon Akiva b. Joseph Hanokh of Schnaittach, covering the Zohar on Genesis and published in Sulzbach in 1700 and again in Amsterdam in 1716, as well as the still unpublished *Be'er sheva* by the Sabbatian rabbi Ber Perlhefter (in collaboration with his wife!), which is extant in several manuscripts and was composed between 1699 and 1702. Notably, the zoharic account of the righteous women's chambers in Paradise (see above, at nn. 50–64) appears in *Naḥalat tsevi* (on Numbers, fo. 13*b*), in some of the manuscripts of *Be'er sheva* (on which latter work and its author, see Riemer, 'Beer und Bila Perlhefters Schrift'; id., 'Zwischen', and Tishby, *Paths of Faith* (Heb.), 85–99, 91–107, 296–8, 300–5), and in several other anthologies of zoharic passages which appeared in Yiddish during the 17th and 18th centuries. Hagiz could have been referring to either the Yiddish or the Ladino translations of selected portions of the Zohar, or indeed to impromptu verbal translations into either (or any other) vernacular. For a comprehensive review of vernacular Zohar translations published during the 17th and 18th centuries, and the evident Sabbatian involvement in this project, see Huss, 'Zohar Translations' (Heb.), 38–52.

[116] It seems likely that the Hebrew word *anashi*[*m*] (men) here should be amended to read *nashim*, 'women'.

[117] Hagiz, *Mishnat ḥakhamim*, 56*b*, §240. See also the testimony of R. Jacob ibn Na'im, who

magician, and faith healer (*ba'al shem*), Moses David was ostracized on account of his heretical Sabbatian beliefs, for which he was expelled from several Polish communities. He thenceforth wandered far and wide through Moravia and Germany, maintaining close contact with the sect's leaders there.[118] Emden has the following to report concerning Moses David's sojourn in his own city of Altona, where he allied himself with Rabbi Jonathan Eybeschuetz and the latter's son Wolf:

Woe! 'How the faithful city has become a harlot' [Isa. 1: 21]—the holy community of Altona, which formerly raised a barricade against those who would breach every fence, the abominable sect of Sabbatai Zevi, may the name of the wicked rot! ... And that boy [Wolf], spurred by his foolish, ignorant old father [Jonathan Eybeschuetz], established a temple for the Sabbatian abomination, and all the cronies of that accursed sect would gather there. From Moravia came Meirl Prossnitz, Nathan Erholtz, may the name of the wicked rot, and some boorish youths, and they set at their head [ראש] ([which can be read as] the acronym of רשע [wicked], ארור [cursed], ש״ץ [an acronymic reference to Shabetai Tsevi]) the loathsome Moses David of Podhajce, who was banned in Poland, for that land could not tolerate him ... He was on intimate terms with young wives[119] in Altona and taught them the Zohar and the mysteries of his faith.[120]

From the continuation of this passage it emerges that the city was suffering at the time from

an epidemic of young women dying in childbirth, several of them in the same period, and the hand of the Lord was striking young men down as well, four of them within

was chief rabbi of Smyrna until his death in 1714. In his collection of sermons, *Mishkenot ya'akov*, he attacked the imparting of mystical knowledge, particularly of the messianic brand, to the masses—specifically including women:

> For there is no greater disgrace to the messiah, son of David, than for him to be blabbered about by worthless and reckless persons, delinquents, and women polluted by menstruation' (quoted in Spiegel, 'R. Jacob ibn Na'im' (Heb.), 202).

[118] On him see Wirszubski, 'Sabbatian Kabbalist' (Heb.), 189–209.

[119] Emden seems to have coined the Hebrew expression *nashim yeladot* as a calque of the Yiddish *vayblekh*, 'young wives', i.e. recently married women, a meaning that cannot be conveyed in any single Hebrew word. This must be his intention in using the same expression in the texts quoted below, at nn. 124–9, which clearly refer to married women, whence the gravity of the teacher's intimacy with them during the Zohar lessons. Cf. also Emden's use of this expression in his book *Beit yehonatan hasofer*, 20b, where it clearly refers to a young married woman: 'In this way he ordered [to speed up] the death of the young wife of R.L.P. [Reb Leibele Prossnitz], peace be on her' (*ha'ishah hayaldah eshet rl"p a"h*). [120] Emden, *Sefer hitabekut*, 20b.

thirty days, all of them called Jonah, so that the city's cry rose to heaven—and this was in Hamburg alone.[121] The heads of the three communities therefore bestirred themselves to establish a court charged with investigating the matter and removing the hindrances from these communities.[122]

The court's findings, based on statements taken from 'those decent young men who know all about the loathsome deeds that have been committed in the home of the old rake [Jonathan Eybeschuetz] and his son [Wolf], and in the homes of some of the established householders as well', linked these instances of untimely death to the Sabbatian activity in the city, and this led to the decision to expel the heretics.

Notably, Emden's characterization of the Sabbatians' principal activities resulting in this decision was that 'under the direction of their loathsome spokesman, Moses David [of Podhajce]', they 'incite and lead astray the simple-minded folk', and 'learn Zohar in the company of young wives, with whom he [Moses David] meets daily on intimate terms'.[123] This suggests that Zohar instruction to women was viewed as one of the most outrageous hallmarks of the Sabbatian heresy, particularly since it involved intimate encounters between the teachers and their female pupils. That the attractive young pupils were married women cast the sessions of Zohar instruction under the grave suspicion of adultery, and contributed to the reputation of the heretics for sexual licence.[124]

Indeed, once the hunt for the city's Sabbatians was on, according to Emden, a young man by the name of Solomon Leib, formerly among the most enthusiastic supporters of Jonathan Eybeschuetz, recanted his heretical views in the following way:

---

[121] Altona is a suburb of Hamburg. From the second half of the 17th century, the three neighbouring Jewish communities of Altona, Hamburg, and Wansbeck united to form a single communal authority, which was known by its initials, AHW.

[122] Emden, *Sefer hitabekut*, 20*b*–21*a*.

[123] Ibid. 21*a*, and see also ibid. 57*a*: 'He did many loathsome things here in Altona, meeting intimately with young wives and teaching them the Zohar.' Similarly, Emden writes in *Beit yehonatan hasofer*, 17*b*, §115: 'And this loathsome Moses David, may the name of the wicked rot, sojourned in Altona for many a day, meeting intimately with young wives and learning the Zohar with them.'

[124] The association, which was perceived as self-evident, between instructing women in the Torah and sexual licentiousness is already implied in the ancient rabbinic tradition formulated in Mishnah *Sot.* 3: 4 and its subsequent interpretations. See the references cited in n. 103 above.

He stood in full public view under the window (of his former mentor, the Eybe-schuetzer, may the name of the wicked rot), calling out: 'Jonathan, you are an apostate! A heretic!' . . . There was also a certain young wife (who had learned the Zohar with that sorcerer [*ba'al shed*—'master of demons', a play on *ba'al shem*—'master of the (divine) name'], the aforementioned loathsome Moses David, who had met with her intimately) whom he called an adulterous harlot in the street, and he was sued on this account in a non-Jewish court, and he lost his money over it.[125]

Elsewhere Emden relates how the same Moses David of Podhajce taught the Zohar to the Sabbatian wife of Wolf Akives.[126] Here, too, he associates this type of instruction with the breach of sexual boundaries:

And here in Altona, his [Jonathan Eybeschuetz's] friend, Moses David, may the name of the wicked rot, behaved in just the same way. It is well known that he had intimate meetings with pretty young wives, at which he taught them kabbalah. It has been testified that he was seen standing next to Wolf Akives' wife, holding the book of the Zohar open in front of her and reading it along with her. 'And they looked after him' etc.—indicating that they suspected him of adultery.[127] To be sure, a man falls under such suspicion only in a place where he has no enemies,[128] but he had publicly expressed his sanction of sexual liberties.[129]

---

[125] Emden, *Sefer hitabekut*, 21a. The reference to the suit which the 'young wife' brought in a non-Jewish court accords with similar reports of Sabbatian women in Poland who were denounced as adulterous and divorced by their husbands as a consequence of their association with the messianic heresy. They, too, brought their complaint, with some degree of success, to be adjudicated by the local Polish noble. See above, Ch. 4, at n. 37.

[126] On her see above, Ch. 3, at nn. 17–18.

[127] Cf. Exod. 33: 8: 'Whenever Moses went out to the tent, all the people rose up, and every man stood at his tent door, and looked after Moses, until he had gone into the tent.' On the interpretation of this verse as 'indicating that they suspected him of adultery' (cf. BT *San.* 110a), and on Moses David's intimation, in the Sabbatian sermon he gave in Wolf Akives' home, that the verse referred to himself, see Emden, *Sefer hitabekut*, 36b–37a. See also Wirszubski's discussion in 'Sabbatian Kabbalist' (Heb.), 202–3.

[128] Cf. BT *MK* 17b: 'A man falls under suspicion of such a thing only if he did it. . . . Go and learn: "When men in the camp were jealous of Moses and Aaron, the holy one of the Lord" [Ps. 106: 16]. . . . This indicates that every man was jealous of his wife on Moses' account! But on that occasion, this arose out of enmity . . . and it [i.e. the assumption that the rumours upon which the suspicion is based have some foundation] applies only where a person has no enemies. But if he has enemies, it was presumably they who spread the rumour.'

[129] Emden, *Edut beya'akov*, 45a (quoted with some errors in Wirszubski, 'Sabbatian Kabbalist' (Heb.), 205).

Emden had accused Jonathan Eybeschuetz, too, of suspicious activities among the womenfolk, invoking the verse 'And they looked after him' to press a similar innuendo. However, it appears that Eybeschuetz got together with women not necessarily in order to teach them the Zohar, but for the sake of imparting the holy spirit to them joyfully and at ease, as his 'mentor' Sabbatai Zevi had done before him:

That heretic, may his name be obliterated, as it were by way of divulging profound, esoteric, kabbalistic mysteries, said that it was incumbent upon him to meet behind closed doors with women in order to gladden them with music and dancing, so that he could impart the holy spirit to them expansively and at ease, for it can be imparted only with joy. It had now been made manifest to him why his master's master, the apostate Sabbatai Zevi, may the name of the wicked rot, danced with married women in the synagogue at the outset of his activities in Smyrna, as is well known. And this was entirely true, and according to him it was good and right, though he only came to teach licentiousness to those whose spirits had gone astray. And he continued in his wicked ways, meeting and speaking with women behind closed doors, where even his master had done so only in the open.[130]

From Eleazar Fleckeles' *Ahavat david* (1800), we learn that it was also customary among the Sabbatians of Prague in the late eighteenth century to teach the Zohar and kabbalah to women. Unlike Moses David of Podhajce, who, according to Emden's sources, taught his female pupils in private, the instruction in Prague seems to have taken place in groups in which both women and men participated: 'They study the *agadot* and the Zohar . . . and the women do so along with them.'[131] Further on, we read:

Children and women come to hear the kabbalistic teaching of Jacob [Frank] the impostor, and all together they study the mysteries of the unclean chariot [the demonic forces], 'sweeping away moist and dry alike' [Deut. 29: 18]. Young men and sullied girls,[132] old men and youths, discuss and expound the mysteries of Isaac Luria's writings and those of 'the antelope' [*tsevi*] and the mountain-sheep' [cf. Deut. 14: 5], gathered together in heaps.[133] [They take their instruction] from that cadaver of a teacher [Jacob Frank?],[134] guide in deception, and from other utterly vile new ones

---

[130] Emden, *Edut beya'akov*, 45a.   [131] Fleckeles, *Ahavat david*, 6b.

[132] Cf. Deut. 32: 25 and Ch. 4 n. 23 above; the word *pesulos*, 'sullied girls', is a play on *besulos*, virgins, in the Ashkenazi Jewish pronunciation of the Hebrew *pesulot* and *betulot*.

[133] *Ḥomarim ḥomarim*, 'in heaps' (Exod. 8: 14 in the RSV Bible, 8: 10 in the Hebrew Bible), is a play on *yaḥmur*, 'mountain sheep', in the phrase from Deut. 14: 5.

[134] By the time that *Ahavat david* was published in 1800, Frank had been dead for some nine

who have come in of late [cf. Deut. 32: 17], cadavers all of them,[135] and from the lascivious harlot [Eva Frank?] who [was seen] speaking [to a man]—'what does this speaking mean? She has had intercourse with a man and keeps secret the fact that she has defiled herself'[136]—'thus and so', says she, 'did I see in a vision'.[137]

Several times Fleckeles reiterates his objection to the improper practice of teaching kabbalah to women and children:

And I ask you another question: If men come to learn, why do women and children come along as well?[138]

Youths who have barely learnt any Talmud or any of the major halakhic works, sit in study, endeavouring to discover all the Lord's esoteric mysteries. And not only this, but even light-headed women[139]—who want but their measure of *tiflut*,[140] of mirth and revelry, which is why our Sages of blessed memory declared that 'whoever instructs his daughter in the Torah (even in non-esoteric matters), it is as though he taught her *tiflut*'[141]—sit and study along with them. They are all a herd of ewes, talebearers,[142] revealing what should be kept secret and wrecking the foundations. . . . And the reason why the Torah refers to 'both young man and virgin, the suckling child with the man of grey hairs' [Deut. 32: 25, referring to those who will be destroyed by God's vengeance], is that all of them come to suck it up together, the young man and the virgin with the man of grey hairs.[143]

Fleckeles' evidence is fully corroborated in the allegorical satire, *A Conversation between the Year 1800 and the Year 1801*, written in Prague in precisely the same period. In it, the year 1800 makes the following complaint:

So they have been conducting their clandestine affairs for years, and even though they are wise and resourceful people, it is known that they learn the Zohar, as well as dipping into the writings of Rabbi Isaac [Luria], studying nothing but the kabbalistic books; both the males and the females have the same practice of studying esoteric matters for an hour or two every day. The chit-chat of these women is not like that of other women, for they are touched by the spirit of the Zohar and the kabbalah, and

years, but at his court in Offenbach every effort was being made to conceal this fact. However, rumours of Frank's death must have reached Prague, whose Sabbatian sectarians maintained regular contact with the Offenbach court. On this see above, Ch. 1 n. 98.

[135] *Ḥadashim lapegarim* is a play on *ḥadashim labekarim*, 'they are new every morning', in Lam. 3: 23.   [136] See above, Ch. 1 n. 101.

[137] Fleckeles, *Ahavat david*, 25*b*.   [138] Ibid. 26*a*.   [139] Cf. BT *Shab.* 33*b*.

[140] Cf. Mishnah *Sot.* 3: 4.   [141] Ibid.; cf. n. 109 above and the text there.

[142] The author seems to be playfully conflating the Hebrew *raḥel* meaning 'ewe' and *rakhil* meaning 'tittle-tattle' or 'gossip'.   [143] Fleckeles, *Ahavat david*, 27*a*.

regularly spout mystical terms, like *sefirot, sitra [de]dukhrei venukba* [the male and female sides], *shekhinta ila'ah vetata'ah* [the Upper and Lower Shekhinah], and so on.

The year 1801 responds: "'Like a gold ring in a swine's snout' [Prov. 11: 22] are esoteric mysteries revealed by women!'"[144]

Further on, the author connects these women's kabbalistic expertise with their prophetic talents:

There is another great and evil malady about this sect, namely, that they have women who prophesy and declare the advent of the messianic age on the basis of their dreams and visionary experiences. They foretell signs of what is to come to pass, and disclose profound mysteries from the kabbalistic books—these virgins who serve the Queen [cf. Esther 1: 10].[145]

Fleckeles, too, associates the kabbalistic proficiency of these women with their prophetic skills.[146] Indeed, as we saw above, there are numerous attestations— beginning with the earliest days of the messianic movement and continuing right up to its end—of women who prophesied in the language of the Zohar, recited extensive passages of it from memory, or even disclosed new and remarkable kabbalistic doctrines while in a prophetic trance.[147]

To be sure, it was often remarked that with the passing of the prophetic trance, all these things were wiped from their memory, and they returned to the usual ignorance natural to a woman, thus emphasizing the miraculous character of the phenomenon, which was taken as proof of its authenticity. Furthermore, though some of these new kabbalistic doctrines were reportedly written down over dozens or hundreds of pages, they have all vanished without a trace. No wonder, then, that scholars have tended to discredit such reports and to dismiss them as the exaggerations of enthused believers.[148] Nevertheless, the notion that women could have transmitted kabbalistic doctrines may not be entirely far-fetched. There is no reason to reject out of hand the possibility that Sabbatian women, who, as we are told, regularly studied Zohar and kabbalah, should have prophesied in the language of the Zohar,

---

[144] *A Conversation* (Heb.), 11–12; also quoted in Werses, *Haskalah and Sabbatianism* (Heb.), 77. The full verse in Proverbs reads: 'Like a gold ring in a swine's mouth is a beautiful woman without discretion.'   [145] *A Conversation* (Heb.), 24

[146] See above, at n. 137.   [147] See above, Ch. 1, at nn. 18–21, 60, 62, and 73.

[148] See above, Ch. 1, at n. 20. However, Jacob Emden, who certainly was no impassioned believer, took these testimonies entirely seriously and referred to those who transmitted them as 'reliable men'; see above, Ch. 1, at n. 21.

cited passages from it, or even delivered new expositions of it during their bouts of prophecy. That no such original expositions by women have survived in their names does not put them beyond the realm of possibility, given that the movement's opponents denounced all the writings it produced as heretical (unless they failed to recognize their Sabbatian character) and not only made no effort to preserve them, but did their utmost to suppress, proscribe, and destroy them. The Sabbatians, on their part, also hid away their writings and sometimes even destroyed them in response to persecution.[149] As a result, their literature has been preserved only in random fragments, and the identity of its authors is often uncertain, particularly since, from the very beginning, it was common for Sabbatian texts to be written either anonymously or pseudepigraphically.[150] Under these circumstances, the lack of any literary trace of kabbalistic texts composed by Sabbatian women should elicit no surprise.

Furthermore, with the waning of clandestine Sabbatianism over the course of the nineteenth century, its last adherents—apostates and Jews alike—were gradually assimilated into the regular frameworks of Jewish, Christian, or Muslim society. Whether these frameworks were traditionalist in character or whether they were in process of modernization and secularization, they certainly did not share Sabbatianism's posture as regards the involvement of women in kabbalistic messianism. Consequently, little value was set on the tradition of women's kabbalistic prophecy, and there was no interest in preserving any literary output it might have left behind. Moreover, in the course of the nineteenth century, the gradual decline throughout all sectors of Jewish society in the status and study of kabbalah as such (to which we shall return in the Conclusion) further diminished the chances for the preservation of any kabbalistic writings that might have survived in the name of the Sabbatian prophetesses.

The instruction of women in the Zohar must be set not only in the context of the Sabbatian tendency to establish an egalitarian equivalence between the sexes or to blur the gender distinction between them, but also in the context of another, broader, and equally controversial Sabbatian agenda: the dissemination of kabbalistic knowledge, particularly the Zohar, to all sectors of the population, so as to speed up the process that would culminate in the final redemption. This conflicted with the traditional restraints on the dissemina-

[149] See Scholem, 'Redemption through Sin', 79–82.   [150] See id., *Sabbatai Sevi*, 230–3.

tion of kabbalistic lore, driven by the belief that its mysteries were not to be disclosed until after the redemption.[151] But the force of Sabbatianism's messianic thrust was enough to turn this tradition on its head, making the widest possible dissemination of kabbalah instrumental in effecting the messianic advent.[152] This is the context of Moses Hagiz's remonstrations to the effect that 'every worthless and reckless know-nothing youth takes it [the Zohar] to hand, spouts it in public, and ... sits reading it aloud to women and children, in

[151] See above, at n. 104.

[152] Already the zoharic composition *Ra'aya mehemna* had attributed to the Zohar itself the capacity to bring about the messianic redemption: 'Because Israel shall taste of the Tree of Life, which is this book of the Zohar, by this means shall they go forth from the exile in mercy' (Zohar, iii. 124*b*). On this inversion, in the context of escalating messianic tension, of the relationship between the disclosure of kabbalistic mysteries and the messianic advent, see Abraham Azulai's remarks in the preface to *Or haḥamah*, his commentary on the Zohar:

> I have found it written that the heavenly decree prohibiting the study of kabbalah in public was valid only until the end of the year 250 [1490 CE]. Thereafter it [the generation living at that time] would be called the last generation [before the final redemption]. The decree was abrogated and permission was granted to study the Zohar. From the year 300 [1540 CE, the beginning of the kabbalistic movement in Safed] onward it will be accounted an end of special merit to both old and young to study [kabbalah] in public, as it is stated in *Ra'aya mehemna*. And since the messianic king will appear through the merits [of this study] and through none other, it behoves us not to be remiss.'

Scholem cites these remarks in his discussion of the growing popularity of kabbalah in the aftermath of the expulsion from Spain (*Sabbatai Sevi*, 21–2), and in particular the currency of Lurianic kabbalah in the generation preceding the outbreak of Sabbatianism (ibid. 22–6 and 66 ff.). Moshe Idel has since challenged Scholem's assumption of a historic connection between the trauma of the expulsion from Spain and the spread of Lurianic kabbalah, disputing also the claim that Lurianic kabbalah was inherently messianic and had therefore become particularly widespread during this period (see e.g. Idel, *Kabbalah*, 256–60, and id., 'One from a Town'). Zeev Gries has similarly concluded that it was not Lurianic kabbalah that prepared people for the message of Sabbatianism, but, on the contrary, it was Sabbatianism that impelled the dissemination of Lurianic kabbalah, or at least the popular Lurianic literature of *hanhagot* ('conduct' tracts) and *tikunim* (kabbalistic penitential rites) (Gries, 'The Fashioning of *Hanhagot* Literature (Heb.)', 563 and 570–2; id., 'Copying and Printing of Kabbalistic Books' (Heb.), 206). Be that as it may, and regardless of whether or not Lurianic kabbalah was a critical factor in preparing the ground for the spread of Sabbatianism, there is no shortage of evidence to show that the Sabbatians promoted the spread of kabbalah in the second half of the 17th century and throughout the 18th. For a fresh examination of the relationship between Sabbatianism and the dissemination of the Zohar and kabbalah from the end of the 17th century, including a discussion of the Sabbatian practice of teaching Zohar even to women, see Huss, 'Sabbatianism and the Acceptance of the Zohar' (Heb.).

the vernacular for those who so require'.[153] According to him, under the influence of the heretics, who have 'set aside the mainstays of Torah learning', study of 'esoteric lore' is usurping the study of the revealed Torah, to the point that

I fear they are leading the congregation astray, and, if I see aright what is coming, I am afraid that this will spread even further if it is not put right, so that they will ultimately forget the Torah itself, heaven forfend, over and above various wrongdoings that have proliferated among the masses. For I swear that I have seen and talked with quite a number of people who are viewed by the masses as being proficient kabbalists and magicians, and they did not even have a proper knowledge of the laws governing recitation of the Shema and the ritual washing of one's hands.[154]

It is to this situation that Fleckeles alludes in his aforementioned complaints,[155] deprecating the improper study of Zohar and kabbalah not only by women but even by 'children', 'old men and youths', and 'youths who have barely learnt any Talmud or any of the major halakhic works'—that is, the ignorant and unlettered, including women, whose exposure to the mysteries of kabbalah he denounces as scandalous. Similar complaints are reiterated elsewhere in his writings: 'I have seen yet another evil malady, I, "the man whose eye is opened" [Num. 24: 3], and this, for our many sins, is a malignant growth: men unversed in the Talmud and the major halakhic works sit in groups and study the Zohar and the Lurianic writings.'[156] He cites a long list of early and latter-day halakhic authorities who forbade the public dissemination of mystical lore, and links the study of kabbalistic texts with the sin of the Sabbatian heresy:

Lift up your eyes and see: If this was dealt with as an outrage in those days, how much more so [should it be] nowadays, when we see with our own eyes and hear with our own ears of so many wrongdoings on account of this kind of study. Many have cast aside their dignity and gone to keep company with evil men who transmit impurity

[153] See above, at nn. 113–17.

[154] i.e. the most basic daily observances; Hagiz, *Mishnat ḥakhamim*, 56b–57a, §240. Hagiz reversed his own position regarding the dissemination of esoteric writings. At one time he advocated it and even embarked on the publication of several kabbalistic treatises, in the belief that this might heal the spiritual ailments of his generation. However, when the Sabbatian movement took up this stance, embracing the teachings of kabbalah and harnessing itself enthusiastically to the task of disseminating the kabbalistic texts as widely as possible, Hagiz changed his mind and began fighting to restore kabbalah to its former esoteric status. On this reversal see Carlebach, *Pursuit of Heresy*, 75–80.

[155] See above, at nn. 131–43. [156] Fleckeles, *Teshuvah me'ahavah*, introduction, 8b.

before God, like the adherents of that abomination, that wicked, loathsome creature, Sabbatai Zevi, may his bones be ground to dust, . . . One should take great care to distance oneself from this kind of study.[157]

Jacob Emden cites corroborative evidence. He transcribes a letter sent from Hamburg on 13 Kislev 5520 (1759) by a certain 'Pesah, son of the late Joshua of Lithuania', to Rabbi Ezekiel Landau in Prague, reporting that the same Moses David of Podhajce who taught women the Zohar and the mysteries of the Torah 'studies kabbalah here with youths and ruffians who are not students of the Torah'.[158] Landau himself railed furiously against the same phenomenon:

How incensed I am against those who busy themselves with the Zohar and kabbalistic books in public! They remove the yoke of the revealed Torah from their necks, and talk and mutter about the Zohar, and are able to master neither, so that the Torah becomes neglected in Israel. And this is not all, for in our own time the followers of the sect of Shabbetai Zvi, may his bones be ground to dust, have increased in number, and we ought therefore to limit the study of the Zohar and books of kabbalah.[159]

Similarly, the ban declared against the Sabbatians by the rabbis of Lvov (Lemberg) in 5515 (1755) contains a whole paragraph denouncing the heretics' instruction of the unlettered in Zohar and kabbalah, and imposes severe restrictions upon the study of mystical doctrines:

Secondly, we have seen fit to raise a barrier and call to order those who would break through and come up to God [cf. Exod. 19: 24] and strive to climb onto the chariot. They see themselves as duty-bound to set aside the study of Talmud and major halakhic works, and go out in search of illumination in the mysteries of the Torah, though they have not yet learned to read the Pentateuch itself, nor have they the wit to understand the plain sense of Scripture or Talmud. Yet they beat a path to peruse and penetrate the secret doctrines; they grasp at the mysteries with all ten fingers, so that this hindrance comes about by their own hands. . . . And they anchor their own foolish notions in the Zohar and the writings of Isaac Luria of blessed memory, even daring to

---

[157] Fleckeles, *Teshuvah me'ahavah*, introduction, 9a.

[158] Emden, *Sefer hitabekut*, 28b. Emden himself was prompted to criticize the Zohar on account of the extensive use made of it, and of kabbalistic literature in general, by the Sabbatian heretics. See e.g. Emden, *Mitpahat sefarim*, in the 'proposal' on the back of the title page, fos. 2a–b, and 30b, and *passim*.

[159] Landau, *Noda biyhudah*, i. 'Yoreh de'ah', §74. Quoted in Tishby, *Wisdom of the Zohar*, i. 39.

'innovate' by making erroneous emendations to the text. We have therefore decreed, on pain of the curses inscribed above, that no man may study any of their writings, not even their versions of those [texts] that are known to be the authentic, unadulterated writings of Luria himself. It is absolutely forbidden for any man to study these texts until the age of forty. . . . Not everyone who wishes to partake of the Lord may just walk up and take—only one who has first filled his belly with the Talmud and major halakhic works.[160]

The Sabbatian policy of teaching kabbalah to all strata of the population, and particularly to those who, in ordinary times, were denied all access to it, would also seem to be the context of the rumours that the heretics were teaching Zohar to non-Jews. One such case was reported to Jacob Emden by a 'veteran' student of his in the community of Halberstadt, in the name of a reliable witness from the community of Neustadt: 'He told me that these evil men are divulging the secret doctrines and the Zohar to non-Jews, especially those of the noble classes, to the point that one such nobleman is able to recite several pages of the Zohar by heart.'[161]

It had already been told of Sabbatai Zevi that in the final years of his exile in Albania, he 'taught non-Jews the Zohar in Turkish',[162] and various sources mention non-Jews joining the ranks of the Sabbatian faithful.[163] If there is truth to these rumours—which seems perfectly possible—they must surely indicate the presence of certain universalistic elements in the Sabbatian doctrine of the redemption. Not only were (Jewish) women deemed fit to study the esoteric lore on whose public disclosure depended the conclusion of the redemptive process, but even non-Jews were being invited to join in the same enterprise! The implicit attribution of positive, 'restorative' value to the study of the Zohar by non-Jews stands in stark contrast to the particularistic character of the kabbalistic vision of the redemption, which anticipates the destruction of the non-Jewish 'husks' (*kelipot*) once the last sparks of holiness

[160] Kraushar, *Frank and His Following* (Heb.), 79–80 (one of the Hebrew translator's addenda to ch. 4 of Kraushar's original Polish version, which does not appear in the English version of the work). Cf. *Records of the Council of the Four Lands* (Heb.), 418, §753.

[161] Emden, *Sefer hitabekut*, 83*b*, quoting a letter dated the eve of the new moon of Elul, 5529 (1769).

[162] Emden, *Zot torat hakena'ot*, 41. Emden makes this remark in a parenthetical aside, attributing it to Moses Hagiz.

[163] See Scholem, *Researches* (Heb.), 115, and *Sabbatai Sevi*, 830–2.

trapped within them have been released—as envisaged even by those who invoked kabbalistic justifications for the Sabbatian conversions to Islam or to Christianity.[164]

[164] On the coexistence of both these redemptive visions within Sabbatianism, their roots in earlier kabbalistic literature, and their interplay, in various versions, in Sabbatai Zevi's own mind, as well as among the apostate Sabbatians and those who justified their apostasy, see Scholem, *Sabbatai Sevi*, 801–2, 830–5, 864–7, and 869; Liebes, *On Sabbatianism* (Heb.), 29 and 58; Idel, 'Particularism and Universalism'; and Schatz[-Uffenheimer], 'Mystic Visions' (Heb.), 222–5.

In the Egalitarian 'Family' of Jacob Frank

THE EGALITARIAN IMPULSE which disposed Sabbatianism to pro-mote women to the status of men—either on an equal but separate basis, or by breaking down traditional gender barriers—found one of its most spec-tacular expressions in the messianic doctrine of Jacob Frank.

It was the kabbalistic conceptualization of bisexuality as a cosmic principle, which Frank took, quite literally, to be operative at every level of existence,[1] that stirred him to a fresh mode of mythical thinking, and turned his mes-sianic project into a series of remarkable applications and manipulations of this principle. The resultant shifts in the balance of power and scheme of rela-tions between the sexes applied simultaneously to the divine sphere and to the earthly circle of his adherents. This followed from his belief that the earthly scheme was to be constructed in conformity with the layout of the divine, since it was precisely the correspondence of the one to the other that made it possible to establish a relationship between them.[2] The process of redemption, as Frank conceived it, was to culminate in the actualization of this relationship by way of the two schemes merging into one.

The kabbalistic tradition had equipped Frank with the basic structure of his mythical universe, but he made idiosyncratic, innovative use of its stock of conventional symbols. In his anthropomorphic imagination, a set of personi-fied metaphysical forces, both comprising and surrounding the godhead in its supernal realm, took the form of a heavenly 'family', at whose head stood a cer-tain 'Big Brother'[3]—the 'One who stands before God'[4] or who 'is within God'.[5]

---

[1] Frank attributed male or female sexuality and the ability to copulate even to rocks and statues; see e.g. Frank, Words of the Lord, §§145 and 1005.

[2] On the relationship between Frank's corresponding worlds of mythical entities and earthly beings see Elior, 'Jacob Frank and his Book' (Heb.), *passim*.

[3] *Words of the Lord*, §410.   [4] Ibid., §338.   [5] Ibid., §410.

By his side—but sometimes also replacing him on her own—stood a female consort called, variously, 'Queen',[6] 'the Queen of Sheba', or 'Bathsheba',[7] 'the Queen of Heaven', 'She', 'Daughter of Zion', 'the Virgin', the supernal 'Maiden', and so on.[8] The Big Brother is always surrounded by a fixed, symbolic number of powerful entities. These are divided into two groups, paralleling each other in every detail but consistently differentiated by their sex. The males are referred to as 'brothers', 'companions', or 'friends', while the females—half of whom are 'wives', and the other half 'virgins'—are variously called 'maidens' or 'sisters': 'The name of the One who stands before God is not known to the world … He has twelve brothers and seven women and seven virgins.'[9]

Accordingly, Frank—the earthly counterpart of the Big Brother—selected from among his associates a fixed number of men and women whom he named 'brothers' and 'sisters'. Their numerical, sexual, and functional correspondence to their celestial counterparts is explained as follows:

I wanted to accomplish a certain thing by your means, and so I lifted up from your midst twelve brothers and fourteen sisters;[10] for you have long had it that there is a an upper and a lower *sefirah*.[11] This *sefirah* is called *Thaira*[12] in Hebrew, but I have said

---

[6] *Words of the Lord*, §418.   [7] Ibid., §420.

[8] For all these designations, see Ch. 7. In so far as the development of Frank's ideas over time can be reconstructed from the collection of his statements recorded in *Words of the Lord*, it would seem that the image of the Big Brother standing at the head of the system with his wife, the Queen, at his side, was displaced at some stage by the appearance of another consort, the all-powerful, supernal Virgin or Maiden, who became the central divine–redemptive figure, swallowing up her companion's powers as well. Almost certainly, this process took place after the death of Frank's wife Hannah, towards the end of the period of his incarceration in Częstochowa. On this see Ch. 7, at nn. 94–100.   [9] *Words of the Lord*, §338.

[10] On the shift from a set of twelve brothers and fourteen sisters to one of fourteen brothers and fourteen sisters see below, n. 25.   [11] The Polish original has the word *sfera* here.

[12] Although the context clearly calls for a Hebrew or Aramaic word here, Fania Scholem's Hebrew version, as printed in the 'interim edition' that was available to me, has *Thieren*, which looks like the Yiddish-German word for 'doors' or 'gates'. I have preferred the version of the Polish edition, *Thaira*, which would seem to be the reading of the original manuscript. Even Fania Scholem's version attests this reading indirectly: in parentheses, with a question mark, she surmises that the word intended here was *tahiro*, *torah*, or *atarah*; thus, every one of her suggested readings ends, like *Thaira*, with a vowel, and not, like *Thieren*, with a consonant. It could be that the typescript of the Hebrew version is erroneous here; I was not able to examine Fania Scholem's own manuscript. The word *Thaira* may reflect the Aramaic word *tar'a*, 'gate' (as it was indeed interpreted by the Polish editor Jan Doktór in *Księga Słów Pańskich*, i. 88, note a), which is one of the kabbalistic appellations of the *sefirah* of Malkhut (see Cordovero, *Pardes rimonim*,

simply that there are upper *thieren*[13] and lower *thieren*, that is, doors and gates. For there are seven kingdoms in the hidden worlds ... But above the seven kingdoms are seven higher kingdoms, and these are called kingdoms which are above the kingdoms ... That is why I have set up twice seven, and I have called them my sisters, my friends ... Similarly, there is here one who is my counterpart, and he has twelve brothers, and that is why I have set up twelve here and called you by the name of my brothers, my friends.[14]

Neither the supernal 'family' nor its earthly counterpart is entirely self-sufficient; each suffers from a very particular shortfall but has the capacity to complement the other. Consequently, the two 'families' are in need of each other and must come together in order to compensate for their mutual deficiencies:

Just as we need them, so do they need us. They confidently expect that those who are

pt. 23: 'Appellations', ch. 21, s.v. *sha'ar*), to which the continuation of the passage also alludes, although Frank derives from it a second set of seven *malkhuyot* (royal dominions), and it may have been his intention to also include the seven *heikhalot* (palaces) that are below Malkhut, according to the Zohar (ii. 260*b*, iii. 251*a*; and see also Liebes' discussion and references in *On Sabbatianism* (Heb.), 145–6, and 370 n. 68), or the six *sefirot*—the *ketsavot* (ends)—that are above Malkhut, which are similarly called 'gates' (*she'arim*; see *Pardes rimonim*, pt. 23: 'Appellations', ch. 21, s.v. *sha'ar*), and whose appellations and symbolic colours are also evoked in the continuation of the passage. At any rate, these *sefirot*, in contrast to their usual sexual identity, are clearly stamped with Malkhut's femininity, as emerges from the continuation, in which all the *malkhuyot* are analogized to Frank's flesh-and-blood 'sisters', in contradistinction to both the supernal and the lower male 'brothers'.

[13] Fania Scholem's version has the word in its correct German form, *Türen* (doors). I have again favoured the reading of the Polish edition, which reflects the Yiddish that would seem to be the language of the original version.

[14] *Words of the Lord*, §305. Elsewhere, Frank relates a dream in which, 'in a Jewish synagogue ... twelve Jews' appeared to him:

whose countenances glowed with a singular brilliance, full of insight ... and they said, 'We have been sent to you by God himself, so that you will allow us to be your brothers.' I answered them, 'This cannot be, for I have already chosen my brothers at Iwanie.' ... And on the other side I saw twelve women whose countenances expressed beauty and virtue, and they, too, said, 'Behold, God himself has sent us to you to be your sisters.' But I answered them, too, as I had answered the men. (ibid., §7)

In his dream, Frank rejects the attempt of these emissaries to break through from the divine realm into his own. Their desire to join together with him, the earthly Big Brother, is a trespass that might confound the order of both domains. To be sure, the heavenly domain and the earthly one are meant to unite at the conclusion of the redemptive process (see directly below), but their ability to do so depends upon their existence, for the time being, as two parallel domains.

called brothers and sisters will come to them. . . . Were you there, each one of you would recognize his very self, for he would see his own image.[15]

[The supernal beings] desire . . . union with the human beings of this world . . . for they lack one thing that we have here, and we lack what they have. We are waiting for it, and we must unite with them.[16]

The deficiency of the supernal brothers and sisters is their disembodied state of existence. In the absence of a flesh-and-blood body, their differentiation as males and females is insubstantial. They will achieve corporeality only at the redemption, by way of sexual mating with their corresponding earthly humans. The latter, on their part, lack and yearn to acquire the supernatural powers of their celestial counterparts, powers whose nature is alluded to here but amply illustrated elsewhere:[17]

Then our brothers would mate with the sisters from there, and those brothers with our sisters . . . for we are the water, and they are the fire, and with great eagerness, these would become one, for they ardently desire embodied beings, and we, too, need them. Therefore I have told you several times that I myself will perform the weddings of your sons and your daughters. . . . Only then would you have seen that the children to be born would have great power; at their cry a whole city would topple.[18]

The union of the supernal brothers and sisters with their earthly male and female counterparts was thus to take place by way of cross-mating supernal brothers with earthly sisters and supernal sisters with earthly brothers. The realization of this union depended entirely upon Frank: not only was he guiding the earthly 'brothers' and 'sisters' to the encounter with their heavenly partners, but he will also provide the supernal Big Brother with the essential directions he requires in order to break through the bounds of his own domain and lead his 'family' to the earthly domain of Frank's 'family' below. The union between the two 'families' would lead to such rejoicing 'as there has never been', and it would be sealed with the chiastic blessings of the Big Brother for the earthly world and of the earthly Frank for the supernal one:

[15] *Words of the Lord*, §305.   [16] Ibid., §338.

[17] The powers of the supernal beings include inestimable wealth, unrivalled wisdom, unimaginable beauty, the ability to overcome the limitations of time and space, and above all eternal youth. See e.g. ibid., §§326, 377, 418, 978, 1023, 1301, 1302, 1303, and many other places. And see Ch. 7, at nn. 249–53.

[18] *Words of the Lord*, §1274 (§1275 in Fania Scholem's Hebrew version). On the possibility that this prospect of the matings between the supernal and the earthly beings is what led to the ban on marriage in the earthly world see Ch. 1 n. 85.

I say to you that all goodness resides with this Big Brother.... From the beginning of creation, all goodness has been concealed within the bounds of his realm ... He desires continually to see and unite with the people who dwell in this world. He knows of me, that I have appeared here in this world, and that I am toiling in pursuit of some good thing. It is also known to him that I, too, have brothers and sisters as he has, but nevertheless, even if he is within God, the way for him to pass through the boundary and join with us here is unknown to him, for that partition of the realms has existed since the beginning. Were you perfect brothers, I would send him a word of counsel from myself, so as to reveal to him that a good thing is concealed within him, but he himself cannot apprehend it on account of the grandeur of his thoughts. But I am a simple man; I would counsel him about how to take [that good thing] in such a way that the partition will not hinder him, and meanwhile, until he goes beyond his bounds, I would prepare my household and yourselves, brothers and sisters. I would be provided with all the signs possessed by his own brothers and sisters. As soon as he arrived with his household at my household, such rejoicing would break forth as there has never been. For the brothers would unite with those sisters, and the sisters with those brothers, never to be parted. He would bless you as Jacob blessed his sons; and I, conversely, would bless them.[19]

The rejoicing at the union of 'his household' with 'my household'—the mating of the divine males with flesh-and-blood females and of the divine females with flesh-and-blood males—celebrates the perfection of the world and its redemption, conceived as the concrete, literal fulfilment of the kabbalistic myth of redemptive sexual unions. The supernal brothers and sisters

all hope that this thing will be fulfilled in its entirety, and that this will lead to their own rectification as well. For there will be a conjunction with this world, and they will take women from this world, and men from here will take women from there. There will be hospitality from us to them and from them to us.[20]

The egalitarian structure of this mythical family of supernal brothers and sisters—differentiated from each other by their sex but not in their status,

---

[19] Ibid., §410, slightly emended on the basis of Doktór's Polish edition.

[20] Ibid., §418, and see also §1402 in the original Polish version of *Księga Słów Pańskich*, which has not survived in the version of the work that has come down to us, but was available to Kraushar, who quoted it in his *Jacob Frank*, ii. 307 and n. 21. Needless to say, the ancient pagan myth of the matings between gods and humans is echoed in Scripture, in the Midrash, and especially in the Zohar's representation of Moses as having withdrawn from his wife to mate with the Shekhinah from the time of his meeting with God at the burning bush. For a discussion of the Sabbatian evolution of this concept in the doctrines of Nathan of Gaza see Elqayam, 'To Know Messiah' (Heb.), 666–70.

powers, or functions—was reflected in the equality of 'brothers' and 'sisters' that prevailed in Frank's earthly court. This is implied in the very adoption, discussed in a different context above, of the titles 'brothers' and 'sisters',[21] which establish, in both dimensions of existence, the equality between 'siblings' of either sex in relation to their Big Brother. Thus, it is said of the 'sisters' who are subject to the authority of the supernal Big Brother that 'they may not take husbands, because they belong wholly to him'; and, likewise, 'all the men who are there belong wholly to him ... and so his brothers, too, have no wives', even though 'his' wives 'are permitted to them, and they have sexual relations with them'.[22] The same applied to the 'brothers' and 'sisters' subject to Frank's authority in his court: 'You are not siblings in relation to me, but among yourselves, you must be called brothers and sisters.'[23] In Frank's earthly court, the unconditional personal loyalty and subservience he demanded from his company of intimates were enough to displace all existing familial, social, and legal bonds between the women and the men. Thus, as we have seen, the exclusive claim on each other between husbands and wives was annulled, giving way to Frank's lordship equally over both; so, too, were confounded the distinctions between married and single, young and old, as, in certain contexts, was the gender division between them.

The equivalence of status between the 'brothers' and 'sisters' found expression in various rituals and ceremonies which Frank devised—as Sabbatai Zevi had done in his day—for women and men on a separate but equal basis, rigorously emphasizing the symmetry and balance between the two sexes.[24] Thus, for example, after choosing fourteen 'sisters' at Iwanie, he picked out an equal number of 'brothers'[25] and bade them all to stand in a circle for three continu-

---

[21] On the selection of the 'brothers' and 'sisters' at Iwanie in 1758/9 see above, Ch. 4, at nn. 36, 47–54, and below, n. 25.   [22] *Words of the Lord*, §418.   [23] Ibid., §417.

[24] See above, Ch. 5, at nn. 93–4. As described in the last chapter (Ch. 5, at nn. 61–4), the Zohar also created a parity between men and women in Paradise, while insisting on the separation between the sexes within their segregated quarters.

[25] This process began on 11 December 1758 with Frank's selection of the first seven 'sisters'. Five months later, on 10 May 1759, he chose seven more 'girls' or 'maidens', alluding to the number's symbolic significance by citing Esther 2: 9: 'he quickly provided her ... with seven chosen maids from the king's palace' (Levine, *Kronika*, 48–50, §§39 and 42; Doktór, *Rozmaite adnotacje*, 57–8); on Frank's interpretation of the symbolic meanings of the number seven and its multiples in this context see also *Words of the Lord*, §§305, 377–8, and 604; and see also below, at n. 35, and Ch. 7, at nn. 71, 118–19). From then on the two groups of seven women were combined into a single unit of fourteen, always referred to as 'the sisters'. About a month later, on 6 June 1759, Frank

ous days and nights—the men on 8, 9, and 10 June, and the women on 23, 24, and 25 June 1759.[26] A few weeks later, on 14 July, he again presided over a ceremony in which fourteen women and fourteen men took part in two separate groups, performing exactly the same actions by turns:

In the evening he bade the fourteen women to stand in a circle, and he ordered the men to stand behind them. The Lord himself sat down, and the men passed through a gate made by [the outstretched hands of] two women. This took place outdoors, in the open. Afterwards the men stayed in the middle, and the women passed through a gate which the men made by [stretching] their hands.[27]

After the whole company had left Iwanie to take up residence in Lvov, there to engage in a public disputation with the rabbinic spokesmen of

chose twelve 'brothers' (*Kronika*, 50–2, §43; *Rozmaite adnotacje*, 58–9)—a number which did not match that of the 'sisters' but was loaded with symbolic associations of its own that Frank may well have found difficult to resist. These included the twelve sons of the scriptural Jacob, with whom, and with whose kabbalistic symbols, he was wont to identify in a variety of contexts (see e.g. *Words of the Lord*, §§779 and 1158; and see also Elior's comments in 'Jacob Frank and his Book' (Heb.), 495–7), as well as Jesus and his twelve disciples. (On Frank's identification with Jesus in this connection see e.g. *Words of the Lord*, §1291, and *Kronika*, 38–40, §23 (*Rozmaite adnotacje*, 52), where it is said of Frank that already in 1756, following a revelation of the holy spirit, 'He declared: I shall go to the Christian religion with twelve of my men.' It is quite likely, as Levine suggests, that he had in mind Jesus' twelve disciples. For more on this see below, Ch. 8, at nn. 51–7.) At any rate, two days later, on 8 June, 'the Lord joined unto them two more men' (*Kronika*, 52, §43; *Rozmaite adnotacje*, 59); the event is mentioned again in the appendix to the *Kronika*, 106 (*Rozmaite adnotacje*, 94)). He thus raised the number of men to fourteen, creating a full numerical equivalence between the male group and its female counterpart. The desire to achieve perfect balance between males and females, with its associated eschatological significance, would seem to have prevailed over the attraction of the symbolic number twelve. In *Words of the Lord*, however, the fourteen 'sisters' are said to correspond to twelve 'brothers' (see e.g. above, at nn. 9–14). It could be that both symbolic numbers were used, or that unlike the number of 'sisters', the number of brothers never stabilized.

[26] *Kronika*, 52, §43 (*Rozmaite adnotacje*, 59). In fact, already on 21 March, the first seven 'sisters' (the second group had not yet been chosen, nor had the group of 'brothers') were bidden to 'stand on their feet in a circle for three days, that is, on Tuesday, Wednesday, and Thursday, and they stood there day and night' (*Kronika*, 48–50, §40; *Rozmaite adnotacje*, 57–8). For rituals involving parallel groups of men and women standing still for lengthy periods see also *Words of the Lord*, §§456 and 459.

[27] *Kronika*, 54, §45 (*Rozmaite adnotacje*, 60). See also the description of the cross-bearing procession in which fourteen women marched in two columns to the right and left of Frank, who marched between them leading a column of men (*Kronika*, 52, §44; *Rozmaite adnotacje*, 59–60).

Poland's Jewish community,[28] Frank devised a further ritual in which the women and the men were again assigned identical motions, performed in parallel but separately:

The Lord went up with the brothers and sisters, and, picking up twelve new ducats, he first placed them in a pile and stepped on them with his right foot, after taking off his winter boots. After that he spread them out with his foot and again stepped [on them], and then he again put them in a pile and stepped [on them] again. After that he bade the Lady of blessed memory to do the same. After her he bade all the women, each in turn, [to do the same], and after them all the men, also each in turn; he [bade them] to perform [these actions] in the same sequence in which he had performed them first.[29]

A similar event took place in Częstochowa:

The Lord went up the ramp with Hanneleh [his wife] of blessed memory, and two men and two women, of the brothers and the sisters, went up after him. He told them to hold on to each other and follow him, and so he ran fourteen times, as fast as he could, up and down a ramp situated to the right of the Santa Barbara [church].[30]

The numerical balance and symmetrical correspondence between the 'brothers' and the 'sisters' are again conspicuous in an imaginary ritual which, according to Frank, would have taken place in the real world if several of his associates had not betrayed him by refusing to follow him in converting to Christianity:

Three days after I arrived in the prison [at Częstochowa], six men who were loyal to me and six women who did not agree to what they [i.e. those who had refused to convert to Christianity] had done would have been with me there ... and I would have shown you the window where she always sits.[31] And three of you men and three women would have stood for three hours with hands upraised to your faces, so as to look upon that place, and the three other [men], and the three [other] women, would have stayed in the room, and we would have done there what was necessary. After three hours we would have changed places . . . repeating this over and over for twenty-four hours.[32]

In contrast to all the other ceremonies and rituals described above, where the corresponding groups of men and women were kept apart, albeit perform-

[28] On the disputation at Lvov (Lemberg) see Balaban, *Frankist Movement* (Heb.), 209–66. See also below, Ch. 8, at nn. 10–19.   [29] *Kronika*, 56–8, §49 (*Rozmaite adnotacje*, 63).
[30] *Kronika*, 96, §106 (*Rozmaite adnotacje*, 87–8).
[31] This is a reference to the divine, redemptive Virgin or Maid, of whom Eva Frank was the earthly counterpart, and with whom *Words of the Lord* is much concerned. See Ch. 7 below.
[32] *Words of the Lord*, §456.

ing identical motions, in this instance doing 'what was necessary' alludes to a stage of the proceedings in which intimate contact does take place between the two groups. It appears to refer to sexual intercourse between the 'brothers' and the 'sisters' who were to remain in the room—all three pairs in turn. Such matings would surely have been conceived as a ritual enactment of the redemptive cross-matings that were due to unite the 'brothers' and 'sisters' with their supernal counterparts at the Maiden's manifestation. Nevertheless, here, too, we are presented with a rigorous adherence to the principle whereby males and females must always be maintained in perfect balance, obliging both sexes to perform the same tasks in parallel with each other.

This symmetrical correspondence between the two sexes, whose paradigmatic status is reflected in all the rituals described above, is formulated as an explicit principle in *Words of the Lord*:

We need both sexes, the male sex and the female sex. . . . We need to say to one male: 'You do this', and to another, 'You accomplish that'. And the same goes for the women.[33]

There must everywhere be both brothers and sisters.[34]

I wished to establish you as brothers and sisters, for there are brothers and sisters everywhere, as there are with the aforementioned Big Brother. Seven and seven are to be found even in the air, and they are brothers and sisters.[35]

Although this principle has egalitarian implications that subvert the tradition of differentiating the sexes by their respective functions, ritual status, and spheres of religious activity, nevertheless it is consciously rooted in precisely the same tradition, from which it derives the impulse to locate men and women in parallel but separate frameworks: "'Abraham converted the men, and Sarah the women",[36] by drawing them towards what they themselves toiled at. So must you and your wives do as did your forefathers and foremothers.'[37] In issuing to his followers the instruction to do 'as did your forefathers and foremothers' Frank was ostensibly doing no more than calling upon them to preserve their ancestral tradition. In fact, however, he was demanding that they 'draw' their sons and their daughters towards 'what they themselves toiled at', which signified, as is evident from the context, the total demolition of the ancestral tradition and release from the constraints of its laws: 'Jacob honoured his Lord in a place of a foreign god. So we, too, must honour our Lord—in

[33] Ibid., §143.   [34] Ibid., §679.   [35] Ibid., §768.
[36] *Gen. Rabbah*, 39: 21.   [37] *Words of the Lord*, §218.

what way? By casting off every law and every creed, and so on, and following me step by step.'[38]

The practice of separating women from men within the traditional frameworks of Jewish society was a response to the sense that the 'evil inclination' was everywhere and always liable to lead to instances of sexual transgression.[39] In light of this, the ritualized separation between the sexes in Frank's circle might seem to be devoid of meaning, since within that circle, the sexual codes were in any case being violated on a regular basis.[40] Nonetheless, the apparent licentiousness of the Frankist court should not be viewed as wanton anarchy, unregulated and unchecked.[41] On the contrary, the sexual contraventions practised there, which Frank endowed with symbolic, sacramental meanings,[42] were always performed at his own dictate, in carefully prescribed man-

[38] *Words of the Lord*, §219. On this aspect of Frank's teachings see Elior, 'Jacob Frank and his Book' (Heb.), 487–94.   [39] See Ellinson, *Woman and the Mitzvot*, ii. 1–41.

[40] For explicit descriptions of such activities see e.g. *Kronika*, 54–6, §46; 66, §64; 68, §67; 72–4, §74; 92–4, §104; and 96, §106 (*Rozmaite adnotacje*, 60–1, 68, 69, 72, 84–5, 87–8).

[41] For such a definition see Scholem, *Studies and Texts* (Heb.), 129.

[42] Frank knowingly and pointedly presented his own copulations with the 'sisters', and the copulations of the 'sisters' with the 'brothers', as incestuous sexual acts. This was clearly implied in the sibling status they had adopted to define the relations between them. Frank was quite open on this score:

> In Warsaw, when we were being tested, I was asked: 'If you call them sisters, how can you have intercourse with them?' (*Words of the Lord*, §375)

> King Solomon said: 'Open to me, my sister' [S. of S. 5: 2] ... How can it be that his lover was called his sister? (ibid., §377)

He was also fond of referring to Abraham and Sarah who posed as brother and sister in Egypt. This provided him with a biblical 'precedent' for legitimate incestuous intercourse:

> Abraham said to Sarai, 'Say you are my sister' [Gen. 12: 13]. Had he called her 'my wife', no man could have taken her from him. But when he ordered her to be called sister, did he not thereby give her permission to lie with others? ... Here are words of wisdom, for Abraham did not speak at his own behest, but at the behest of the One who led him [God]. 'Say you are my sister'—this is the right thing, in the same way as the verse in the Song of Songs [5: 2] that says 'Open to me, my sister' is the right thing. (ibid., §614)

See also ibid., §§407, 674, 796, 1222, and 1236. Elsewhere, Frank compares the violation of the prohibition against incest between the 'brothers' and the 'sisters' at his court to its violation at the court of a legendary king 'of the family of the children of the sun', whose son defiles the virginity of one of his father's wives. In the parable, the king absolves his son of punishment, arguing that 'he is not one of the simple folk but is destined to be king'. Frank concludes: 'So also have I called you brothers and sisters, so that you cannot be judged like the rest of humanity'

ners, and at particular times and places. They bore the hallmarks of antinomian activity—meaningful precisely because it recognizes the authority of the laws it sets out to violate. The transgressions instigated by Frank thus became a subversive cult of 'other gods', whose envoy, 'Jacob'—identified with Frank himself—was guiding his believers 'step by step' in the ways of a new religion. For all his quest to demolish 'every creed' and 'trample all the laws that ever were',[43] for all his insistence that 'the place to which we are going cannot bear the laws', since the laws originate 'in death, and we are going towards life',[44] Frank was imperious in his demands for meticulous observance of his newly devised customs and ritual 'commandments'.[45] Not unlike the halakhah that he repudiated so savagely, he produced his own sets of 'prohibitions and permissions', severely punished all those who disobeyed him,[46] and generally sought to imprint on his surroundings a highly structured, ritualistic, personal mark.

As we have already seen, it is quite possible that the ritualized violations of sexual prohibitions practised at Frank's court were interspersed with periods of total separation between the sexes. During these periods, a strict regimen of chastity was imposed on both males and females, as emerges from several accounts, including Moses Porges' description of life in the court at Offenbach after Frank's death.[47] It seems reasonable to suppose that this way of life was established during Frank's lifetime and at his behest. It accords well with his 'traditional' insistence, in most of his statements that have come down to us, upon a strict, symmetrical balance—in parallel but separately—between the 'brothers' and the 'sisters'. Thus, he repeatedly differentiates between the men

(ibid., §722). See also Elior, 'Jacob Frank and his Book' (Heb.), 517, 521–32; Elior links Frank's statements in this regard to his conceptualization of his band of 'brothers and sisters' as the earthly reflection of the world of the *sefirot*, in which incestuous copulations take place because 'on high [the prohibition on] incest does not apply', as the *Tikunei hazohar* (§56, 90*b*) puts it. For a discussion of the incestuous relations between the male and female powers within the godhead in the medieval kabbalistic work *Sefer habahir* see Wolfson, 'Hebraic and Hellenic Conceptions', esp. pp. 155–63.

[43] There are dozens of equally outspoken statements in this vein throughout *Words of the Lord*: see e.g. §§96, 130, 219, 397, 421, 450, 513, 708, 735, 746, 798, 803, 805, 813, 890, 937, 953, 977, and 1240.　　　　　　　　　　　　　　　　　　　　　　　　　　　[44] Ibid., §805.

[45] See e.g. ibid., §§327, 329, and many other places.

[46] For descriptions of a flogging see *Kronika*, 76, §81, and 80, §88 (*Rozmaite adnotacje*, 74, 76).

[47] See above, Ch. 1, at nn. 85–94.

and the women in all of his references to the identical tasks that he wishes to impose upon both sexes simultaneously:

If you had sought perfection while I was in prison, I would have commanded you to stand guard day and night, you on one side and the women on the other.[48]

When the time shall arrive and the Jews will come . . . I shall divide the company into groups . . . But over you, who were brothers, I shall place a man, Judah, who shall instruct you on how to serve God with all your hearts . . . and in the same way there will also be a God-fearing woman, wholehearted with God and with men. I shall place her over the women who were called sisters, and she shall teach them the virtues that I described earlier.[49]

I have stationed women to serve her[50] . . . I would have sent them to a certain place, where they would have bathed in the well . . . so would I also have sent you there, to the same two springs, and you would have served her. By her power I would have made you kings, and the women kings' wives.[51]

Not only in imaginary situations, as above, but also in the concrete reality of their communal life, men and women in Frank's court were kept apart even as they were undergoing precisely the same procedures at precisely the same time. Thus, when the faithful were brought to trial before Eva and Jacob Frank, the women and the men were judged separately: 'Her Honour [Eva] supervised as all the members of the company were brought to trial, women and men separately. The Lord stood to one side. So did they judge each one who was to attain [eternal?] life, and they probed his good deeds.'[52]

Similarly, such interaction as Frank envisaged—prior to the final redemptive union—between the mythical world of 'brothers' and 'sisters' and its earthly reflection in his court, was also marked by a strict separation between the two sexes, so that the mythical 'brothers' would be in touch only with their corresponding earthly males, and the mythical 'sisters' with their corresponding females:

If you were good . . . you would have palaces with many rooms, and your own servants, and you would see her great power. You would bring me great treasures from there, brothers from the brothers, sisters from the sisters.[53]

---

[48] *Words of the Lord*, §410.   [49] Ibid., §434.

[50] This is another reference to the divine, redemptive Maid or Virgin. On her see below, Ch. 7.

[51] *Words of the Lord*, §604.

[52] Ibid., §749 (the Hebrew version is deficient here and has been supplemented by the Polish version).   [53] Ibid., §801.

This is the Big Brother, who is the King of Kings ... Now all of his brothers are distressed, and they are angry with you, as are the sisters with the sisters.[54]

And the same principle applies to the anticipated appearance of the biblical Patriarchs among the male believers, and of the Matriarchs among the females: 'I made of you a garden covered with vines ... If you had been a good garden, then there would have come to you Abraham, Isaac, Jacob, Moses, David, Solomon, while our Matriarchs and other honest women would have come to the women.'[55]

There is no doubt that the equivalence-by-way-of-separation that was established between the sexes—as reflected in all the descriptions and statements cited above—was essentially subversive in its egalitarian implications, even though it preserved the traditional sexual tension inherent in the very juxtaposition of male and female. That separation and equality between the sexes went hand in hand is conspicuous in Frank's call to apostasy: 'All Jews must be baptized, *the men and women separately*. I will dress them in other clothes, *I make them all equal*, the tall and the short. I will convert them into another people.'[56]

Even when the gender distinction is peripheral to his concerns and not in the least necessitated by the logic of his argument, Frank takes pains to note, quite superfluously, that his statements apply equally to men and women:

When I set you up in Iwanie, a suit of clothes and a crown was ready for each one, along with some other precious items, *for the men and also for the women*.[57]

There would have been a banner ready for you to bear, and *another banner for the women* ... And had I seen that one was raised higher than another, I would have delayed the proceedings, if only for a short time, until the other, too, should be uplifted, so that all of them would be uplifted equally. *This would happen with the women as well*.[58]

[54] Ibid., §964.

[55] Kraushar, *Jacob Frank*, ii. 523, citing the Lublin manuscript of *Words of the Lord*, §2178, which appears in Jan Doktór's Polish edition of the text, *Księga Słów Pańskich* (ii. 128, §2171), but is not present in Fania Scholem's Hebrew translation.

[56] Kraushar, *Jacob Frank*, i. 219, citing §2097 in *Words of the Lord*—a section that appears neither in the Hebrew translation of Fania Scholem nor in the Polish edition of Jan Doktór. Emphasis added, here and in the following passages.

[57] *Words of the Lord*, §446.   [58] Ibid., §687.

When God shall help me . . . I will go around the whole company, from one to the next, and anyone on whom I shall see the sign of . . . two *Wuwen*[59] shall be fearless . . . I wish for all of you that I shall see this sign *upon you and upon the women*.[60]

And now, if you were wholehearted, I would send you out to the four corners of the earth, *you and your women* . . . And when you surrender to the authority of our Lord who has sent us to you, *you and your wives* will be rescued from suffering.[61]

This habitually 'inclusive' language, explicitly and constantly acknowledging the presence of the women, even when there appeared to be no material reason for doing so—when no special message for the women, or any clarification of their particular status was intended—stands in stark contrast to the discursive tradition of rabbinic Judaism, where women as a category are ordinarily ignored, unless the need arises to discuss them specifically—their character, legal status, unique concerns, and so on—by dint precisely of their being 'other' than the male norm.

Alongside the perfectly symmetrical comparability of men and women as distinct categories, the egalitarian impetus in Frank's circle expressed itself also in breaches of gender boundaries, blurring the very distinction between the categories of masculine and feminine. This entailed the overturn of traditional norms of behaviour that were considered appropriate for women and men in their separate spheres of activity. An example may be found in Dov Ber of Bolechów's account of a girl dressed in men's clothing, who accompanied Frank as his personal bodyguard on his travels through Poland: 'All these workers of iniquity went off to the town of Lanckorona, and with them was a virgin girl from Lvov, dressed in men's garb, like a boy.'[62]

Frank eventually said of this virgin that she served him as 'a guardian and protector', and she herself is said to have confirmed that 'she would go with him into the interior of Poland, to guard him and be his shield against all dangers'.[63] She was surely conceived by Frank as an earthly manifestation of the mythical supernal Maiden, whom he also saw as his bodyguard, protecting

---

[59] *Wuwen* appears in this form in the Polish version. It must reflect the Yiddish plural of the Hebrew character *vav*, whose name is spelt by repeating the same letter twice. The letter *vav*, sixth in the order of the alphabet, has the kabbalistic value of the sixth, male *sefirah* of Tiferet, with which the biblical Jacob, and hence also Jacob Frank, is associated.

[60] *Words of the Lord*, §342.   [61] Ibid., §1170; see also ibid., §1213, and many other places.
[62] Birkenthal, *Divrei binah*, 215.
[63] Kraushar, *Jacob Frank*, i. 83, citing *Words of the Lord*, §166 (missing from Fania Scholem's Hebrew translation, but cf. the slightly different wording of §166 in Jan Doktór's Polish edition,

him from the dangers of Poland: 'You saw me, an ignoramus, devoid of learning, literacy, and language, and nevertheless I wandered through Poland among the Edomite [Christian] magnates. Had she not protected me, nothing, God forbid, would have been left of me.'[64]

Frank thus associates the role of the armed guard—a plainly masculine role within the culture in which he operated—with the Maiden, the supernal feminine entity, 'into whose hands, since the time of the creation of the world, all the weapons have been given'.[65] There can be no doubt that Frank was drawing his inspiration from the Zohar's descriptions of the Matronita—the feminine *sefirah* of Malkhut—as having been appointed to the role of guardian of Israel and entrusted with all the Holy One's armaments and fighting forces.[66] This Maiden would extend her protection to his associates by virtue of their loyalty to him: 'I shall ask her to remember your youth, when you were the first to follow me, and to give you one maiden for protection, for without such a maiden one cannot get anywhere.'[67] At the same time, however, he upbraids them for failing to comply faithfully with his instructions: 'I told you long ago that all of the royal armaments had been given into her hands. You should have waited for her to clad you with these weapons . . . But you refused and said: "This armour is too heavy for us."'[68]

On other occasions, too, Frank surrounded himself with female guards. According to the Polish *Kronika*, when the sect's members gathered for one

Księga Słów Pańskich, i. 61) and §383: 'I shall go with you into the depths of Poland, protect you from all the dangers and be your shield.'

[64]   *Words of the Lord*, §434.

[65]   Ibid., §397. See also §565: 'for all the weaponry is in her hands'.

[66]   See Zohar, ii. 50*b*–51*a*, which says, inter alia: 'The King issued the following proclamation: "From now on, all that belongs to the King will be delivered into the hand of the Matronita." He entrusted her with all of his armaments: spears, swords, bows, arrows, daggers, catapults, towers [or perhaps: metal armour], planks, stones, all the warriors . . . The King said, "From now on, my warring is delivered over to you; my armaments and warriors are in your hands. From now on you shall be my guardian, as Scripture has it, 'the Guardian of Israel' [Ps. 121: 4]."' On the probable relationship in Frank's mind between this image of the supernal Virgin and that of the Black Madonna of Częstochowa as a valiant warrior for Poland see below, Ch. 7, at nn. 48–52. The parallel between the image of the Matronita of the Zohar and that of the Virgin Mary, mother of Jesus, as leader of the divine host was already noted by Raphael Patai in *Hebrew Goddess*, 199–203. On this see further below, Ch. 7 n. 51.   [67]   *Words of the Lord*, §607.

[68]   Ibid., §492. See also §826: 'When the time comes she will gird each one with a sword. . . . She will gird with a sword everyone whom she wills.'

of their secret (and apparently unchaste) ceremonies in a locked room in Lanckorona—an event that spawned a host of rumours and a great deal of official censure[69]—Frank was ringed, among others, by the 'women guardians and protectors'.[70] Although the text does not say so explicitly, we may assume that these female bodyguards were armed, in light of Frank's declaration on the subject: 'Scripture plainly states: "By your sword you shall live" [Gen. 27: 40] . . . Women, too, should bear swords.'[71] And towards the end of his life, during his period of residence in Offenbach, he expressed his disappointment with his followers on this as on many other scores: 'Had there been no disturbance among the believers a long time ago, I would have told the women to learn horseback riding and warfare, but what was I to do? Yet there will come a time when everyone sells their clothing to buy a weapon.'[72]

Indeed, Moses Porges relates in his memoir of the Frankist court at Offenbach that in the entrance to the 'holy chamber', which held the departed Frank's bed and clothes, and served the faithful as a place of prayer throughout the day, 'several maidens stood guard, most of them beautiful, dressed in the garb of Amazons and armed with rifles and sabres'.[73] Local German observers also mentioned that at Frank's grand funeral procession on 12 December 1791, his daughter Eva's carriage was surrounded by 'twenty young women' of her 'Amazon guards',[74] while a German journal published in Weimar in February 1800 reproduced two accounts of the Frankists in Offenbach, describing their colourful processions through the city, which included 'groups of young women dressed as Amazons and decked in silver breastplates'.[75]

On the other hand, Frank aspired—at least according to one of his

---

[69] See above, Ch. 1, at n. 75.

[70] Kraushar, *Jacob Frank*, i. 84, quoting the version of the *Kronika* that was at his disposal, which differs in several places from the extant version. This particular detail is missing from §17, where it clearly belongs, in both Levine's and Doktór's editions; see Levine's discussion on p. 37 n. 35.   [71] *Words of the Lord*, §821.

[72] Kraushar, *Jacob Frank*, ii. 338, citing the Lublin manuscript version of *Words of the Lord*, §2188, which appears in Jan Doktór's Polish edition of the text, vol. ii, appendix 2 (the Offenbach *Words*), 129, §2181.

[73] This is my own rendering of the passage in the manuscript of Porges' memoir (see above, Ch. 1 n. 88). It appears on p. 123 of the published German version (Porges, 'Eine Wallfahrt'), in col. 278 of the Yiddish version ('Memoirs of Moses Porges', trans. Gelber), and on p. 163 of the English translation in Mandel, *Militant Messiah*.

[74] Cited in Mandel, *Militant Messiah*, 112.   [75] Ibid. 106.

dreams—to take upon himself, as a man, one of the ritual roles traditionally reserved for women:

On 5 November[76] the Lord saw in a dream: I entered a room, and in it was a mirror reflecting six small wax candles standing in a circle, with the seventh candle in the middle. I wished to light the candles and make the blessing over them. Someone came up to me and said, 'Jacob, what are you about to do? That is a woman's job; she must light [them], and she must make the blessing.' I replied: 'Once it was done that way, but now I myself will light them and make the blessing.'[77]

The blurring of gender boundaries in Frank's circle is also intimated by the account of how the believers were flogged in punishment for abandoning him during the Russian siege at Częstochowa: 'on 18 November 1771 they were all flogged, men and women alike.'[78] Admittedly, Jewish law prescribes flogging as a penalty for both women and men,[79] but the flogging of women was extremely rare in Jewish society—particularly, it seems, in the Ashkenazi communities[80]—in contrast to the prevalent practice in the surrounding

---

[76] 1784, according to the context. See *Words of the Lord*, §1092.   [77] Ibid., §1094.

[78] *Kronika*, 76, §81 (*Rozmaite adnotacje*, 74). See also Kraushar, *Jacob Frank*, i. 239, in reference to the same incident, and ii. 521, citing *Words of the Lord*, §2151 (which appears as §2144 in Jan Doktór's Polish edition, ii. 125): 'Through you, I can see how to manage the Jews who are all of a stubborn nature. Whoever dares to open his mouth against baptism or to say anything bad about it, women as well as men, I will march to the street corners and squares under the threat of the whip.'

[79] See e.g. Maimonides, *Mishneh torah*, 'Laws of Prohibited Sexual Relations', 17: 5: 'In every case in which he would be flogged, so would she; and in every case in which he would not be flogged, neither would she, since there is no distinction between men and women with regard to penalties.'

[80] See e.g. the well-known objection of R. Abraham b. David of Posquières—'I have never heard of women being chastised with the lash'—in response to Maimonides' pronouncement in *Mishneh torah*, 'Laws of Sexual Intercourse', 21: 10, that 'If a woman should balk at doing any of the labours that she is obliged by law to do [for her husband], she may be compelled to do it, even with the lash.' See also Rashi, *Responsa* (Heb.), 371, §373; and see the discussion in S. Assaf, *Penalties* (Heb.), 78, §75, which notes the fact, observed occasionally in the responsa literature in the context of the punishments appropriate to women, that the ruthless physical mortifications of 'commensurate penitence' demanded by Eleazar b. Judah of Worms in the section on 'Laws of Repentance' in his *Sefer haroke'aḥ* make no mention whatsoever of the female penitent and appear to apply only to men, from which it may be concluded that 'penitance by way of flogging' was never prescribed for women. To be sure, there were rabbinic authorities who did prescribe severe bodily affliction, including flogging, to women as well, especially for the sin of adultery (see e.g. Elbaum, *Repentance* (Heb.), 19, 24–5, 230–7), but this stance was considered problematic

Christian society. In Frank's milieu, the flogging of women would surely have been considered unconventional, as implied by the *Kronika*'s emphasis on the flogging of 'men and women alike' as something not to be taken for granted. From the point of view of Jewish tradition it represented, in practice if not by the letter of the law, the crossing of a covert gender boundary.

and elicited considerable misgivings. In a forthcoming study I deal extensively with this reluctance to prescribe physical penalties or penitential mortifications to women.

SEVEN

The Redemptive 'Maiden'

T HE MOST RADICAL EXPRESSION of Frank's predilection for inverting conventional gender norms was the reversal of sexual identity in the figure of the messianic redeemer. As we saw above, a pointer in this direction may already be discerned in the early stages of the Sabbatian movement, in Abraham Cardozo's tentative stipulation of a female 'herald of good tidings to Zion'.[1] Another seems implicit in the fact that, among the Sabbatian apostates in Salonica, whose decisive influence on Frank is indisputable,[2] both Berukhyah's daughter, the Holy Maiden, and his wife, the Signora—the Noble Lady or Matronita, who was referred to by this appellation of the Shekhinah[3]—enjoyed a certain messianic–divine status of their own, paralleling and at the same time complementing Berukhyah's status of messiah in whom divinity had become incarnate.[4] According to the testimonies collected by Jacob Emden, the Noble Lady of Salonica continued to maintain 'diplomatic' relations with Jonathan Eybeschuetz and his sons even after Berukhyah's death,[5] and we may well suppose that she was imbued with a sense of messianic mission in her own right.

The beginning of this process may be traced back to the status of Sarah, Sabbatai Zevi's messianic spouse, who, as attested by Sasportas, 'used before his apostasy to write to her women friends and promise them favours, and she would sign by the name of "Queen Rebecca, the Matrona"'.[6] Scholem, who downplayed her importance to Sabbatai Zevi's messianic endeavour, argued that 'there is no evidence that Sarah ever took any initiative in the movement.

---

[1] See above, Ch. I, at nn. 115–19.   [2] See Scholem, *Researches* (Heb.), 355 ff.

[3] See above, Ch. I, at nn. 129–32.

[4] For a discussion of the incarnation of the male and female aspects of the divinity in the messianic couple see below, at nn. 259–72.

[5] See Emden, *Sefer hitabekut*, 34*a* and 59*b*. See also Scholem's discussion in *Researches* (Heb.), 378 and 384–5.   [6] Sasportas, *Tsitsat novel tsevi*, 4.

As a rule, she merely followed the example of her husband,' and he cited her letters to her female friends, signed 'with the symbolic name that Nathan of Gaza had bestowed upon the messiah's wife', as the sole evidence of any independent action on her part.[7] Nevertheless, we should not overlook the rumours that, long before her first meeting with Sabbatai Zevi in Egypt, Sarah believed herself to be the predestined spouse of the messiah, and it was apparently this independent self-awareness that eventually led to their marriage.[8] Moreover, her signing herself by the symbolic name of Rebecca may well be viewed as a surreptitious challenge to Nathan of Gaza,[9] who was at pains to distinguish, in at least one of his prophetic pronouncements, between Rebecca, 'the daughter of Moses'—the Matronita who was to be the messiah's ultimate spouse—and his present wife, who was merely the former's handmaid:

At that time, the aforementioned rabbi [Sabbatai Zevi] will return from the river Sambatyon, together with his predestined mate, the daughter of Moses. It will be known that today it was fifteen years since Moses was resuscitated, and that [today] the aforementioned rabbi's predestined wife, whose name is Rebekah, blessed among women, was thirteen years of age.[10] His present wife will be the handmaid, and the wife which he will marry shall be the mistress [the Matronita]; but as long as he is [still] outside Jerusalem, may it be rebuilt speedily in our days, the handmaid is mistress [Matronita].[11]

---

[7] Scholem, *Sabbatai Sevi*, 192.   [8] Ibid. 192–3; and see Sasportas, *Tsitsat novel tsevi*, 4–5.

[9] Relations between her and Nathan would appear to have been strained from the start. It is probable that the rumours of her sexual promiscuity, before and also after her marriage (on which see Scholem, *Sabbatai Sevi*, 194–8; and Emden, *Zot torat hakena'ot*, 53), did not sit well with the strict code of sexual morality, which formed an integral element of Nathan's mystical piety (see Elqayam, 'To Know Messiah' (Heb.), 640–50). If he moderated the rigour of his ascetic norm in relation to his messiah's own deviations from it, for which he made haste to contrive mystical explanations, it may have been harder for him to do so when it came to the messiah's wife, particularly since his personal relationship with Sabbatai Zevi had about it a powerful, though evidently sublimated, homoerotic tone (on which see ibid. 670), and it is not to be ruled out that on a certain level he saw Sarah as an undesirable (if unavoidable) rival for his love. On Nathan's antipathy towards Sarah see also Scholem's comment in *Sabbatai Sevi*, 850–1, and see also n. 15 below.

[10] According to a comment by Isaiah Tishby, who edited this text, the consonants of the word *mibat* (i.e. 'of age'), are to be understood as an acronym, alluding to the scriptural phrase *minashim ba'ohel tevorakh* (Judg. 5: 24), 'of tent-dwelling women most blessed'.

[11] Sasportas, *Tsitsat novel tsevi*, 11–12; English translation, with some minor alterations, in Scholem, *Sabbatai Sevi*, 273–4. On the kabbalistic basis for the conception of the status, respec-

By signing her name as Rebecca, Sarah assimilated into her own person the mythical figure of the superior messianic bride, implicitly rejecting Nathan's distinction between the two women: Moses' daughter, Rebecca, who was to be revealed as the Matronita in Jerusalem—that is, at the end of the redemptive process—and Sarah, who might for the moment be occupying her place but who would ultimately revert to being her humble 'handmaid'. Sarah thus emphasized her claim to the title of the messiah's one and only spouse, which evoked much more than the mere fact of her marriage to Sabbatai Zevi, since he made her his consort not only as messiah but also as messiah clad in divinity. This might be inferred from the very title of Matrona or Matronita—one of the common kabbalistic appellations of the female aspect of the godhead, the *sefirah* of Malkhut—Shekhinah[12]—which was the title she adopted and the one by which Nathan had referred to Sabbatai Zevi's messianic bride. Moreover, in the years following his apostasy, Sabbatai Zevi used to sign himself in Hebrew as *Turko*, which as it stood meant simply 'the Turk' but could also be interpreted as a mystical appellation meaning 'Mount of God' or 'Divine Mount',[13] apparently alluding to the messiah's elevation to the rank of incarnate divinity. His wife, similarly, was known as *Turkah*, which again could be understood simply to mean 'the female Turk' but could also be read as 'Mount of the Shekhinah' or the 'Female Divine Mount'.[14]

Symbolic names alluding to the divine dimension of the messianic spouse were given also to Jochebed, daughter of the Salonican rabbi Joseph Filosoff,

tively, of the Matronita and the handmaid during the exilic and in the redemptive time, formulated as an interpretation of the 'handmaid' of Prov. 30: 23 who 'succeeds her mistress', see e.g. Zohar, iii. 69*a* and 277*b*. See also n. 15 below, and Appendix, p. 343, n. 18.

[12] See above, Ch. 1, at n. 131, and Ch. 6 n. 66, and below, n. 15.

[13] *Tur* is the Aramaic equivalent of the Hebrew word *har*, i.e. mountain, while the last two letters of *Turko*, *kaf vav*, have the numerical value of 26, which corresponds to the numerical value of the letters of the ineffable divine name YHVH.

[14] *Kaf heh*, the last two letters in *Turkah*, is an appellation of the Shekhinah in kabbalistic literature. On these names see Freimann, *Sabbatai Zevi* (Heb.), 96, based on the testimony of Moses Pinheiro. See also Scholem, *Sabbatai Sevi*, 835–6; id., *Researches* (Heb.), 101; Benayahu, 'Great Apostasy' (Heb.), 292; and Liebes, *On Sabbatianism* (Heb.), 279–80 n. 68, although Liebes suggests that the appellation *Turkah* may have referred to Sabbatai Zevi himself, in his direct relationship, as the messiah, to the *sefirah* of Malkhut–Shekhinah. On the framing by Nathan of Gaza of the connection between the messiah and the Shekhinah—which already appears in the classic kabbalistic literature—see e.g. his letter regarding Sabbatai Zevi's apostasy, in Scholem, *Studies and Texts* (Heb.), 244–5 and n. 73.

who was married to Sabbatai Zevi after Sarah's death in 1674, becoming (as it seems) his fourth and last wife. He called her Michal, wife of David; Esther–Hadassah, redeemer of her people; and the beloved of the Song of Songs, who, according to the Song's standard allegorical interpretation, was identified with *keneset yisra'el* (the Community of Israel), which is one of the Shekhinah's most common mystical appellations: 'My wife Michal Hadassah, blessed among women, is Esther, my sister, my love, my dove, my perfect one.'[15] Abraham Cardozo attests that Jochebed, her personal messianic consciousness unfazed after she was left a widow by Sabbatai Zevi, sought to marry him on account of his status as the messiah's successor and heir, and even promised to transmit to him messianic secrets that her husband had vouchsafed her in

[15] Freimann, *Sabbatai Zevi* (Heb.), 68, quoting Sabbatai Zevi's letter to his father-in-law, Joseph Filosoff. See also Scholem, *Sabbatai Sevi*, 888–9. There are conflicting traditions regarding the name of Joseph Filosoff's daughter, but according to the Sabbatian tradition she was known as Jochebed. On this see Benayahu, 'Sabbatai Zevi's Marriage' (Heb.), 27–32. Nathan of Gaza reports in a letter from 1672 that already in 1671, before Sabbatai Zevi's marriage to this Jochebed, he had temporarily divorced his apostate wife Sarah, after their relationship had deteriorated to the point that she twice attempted to poison him:

> Because she had been overcome by the power of the serpent, causing her to hound him and seek his demise with all her might, to the point that she twice cast a deadly potion into his food, though the saintly man came to no harm, and she remained all the while steadfast in her rebellion—on this account he divorced her. (Amarillo, 'Sabbatean Documents' (Heb.), no. 7, pp. 263–4).

It was then that he made up his mind to get married again to a Jewish woman, and he became engaged to the daughter of R. Aaron Majar of Sofia. However, the woman died shortly thereafter, while still in Sofia, so the marriage never came to pass. According to Nathan, Sabbatai Zevi intimated a symbolic analogy between his divorce from Sarah and the Holy One's divorce of the 'handmaid', the servant girl who, according to Zohar, iii. 69a, had usurped the position of her mistress, the divine Matronita, that is the *sefirah* of Malkhut or Shekhinah. He had cleaved to the handmaid—Sarah—for as long as 'he had to have a mate in a place not his own', that is, in the realm of the *sitra ahra*, the Other Side, which is the realm of the handmaid. Now that the completion of the redemptive process was imminent, however, he would divorce her so as to mate with her mistress, the Matronita, who would be restored to her proper place as Queen at the side of the supernal King. He had this to say about the messianic status of his new wife: 'This taking [to wife] will be of great benefit to the Jews; she will be as Esther unto Ahasuerus, and she will not be made to apostatize, but only to wear Ishmaelite garb, symbolizing what R. J[oseph] Taitatsak was told by his heavenly teacher, that the Shekhinah will be dressed in Ishmaelite garb' (Amarillo, 'Sabbatean Documents' (Heb.), no. 7, pp. 263–4). On the heavenly teacher of R. Joseph Taitatsak see Benayahu, *Azulai* (Heb.), 291; and Scholem, *Studies and Texts* (Heb.), 244.

his lifetime.[16] Jacob Emden, quoting the Salonican scholar Moses Habib, relates that she initiated and figured centrally in the messianic revival that followed Sabbatai Zevi's death, engendering the Doenmeh sect among the apostate Sabbatians in Salonica:

Sabbatai Zevi's wife came after his death, declaring that Sabbatai Zevi had appeared to her in a dream and told her that she was pregnant with the soul of the righteous Joseph. Six months later, she took her brother, who was 15 years old, and closeted herself with him in a room apart for three days and three nights, and when he came out she said of the youth that he had died, and not even a bone the size of a barley grain had remained of him. Then Sabbatai Zevi had come and had relations with her in the ordinary way, and she had given birth to the youth and suckled him, and he had instantly grown up to his former age. He was thus the messiah, the son of Joseph; that is, his father was a descendant of David, namely, Sabbatai Zevi, may his name and memory be blotted out, and his mother a descendant of Joseph.[17]

These diverse traditions regarding the consorts of the Sabbatian messiahs indicate that they were all conceived of as messianic figures in their own right. Precisely by virtue of being female, they were construed as necessary complements to the figures of the redeeming males—a concept that appears to be rooted in kabbalistic tradition. The Zohar already alludes to the idea of a male and female messianic pair by joining the circumstances and protagonists of the original sin to those of the future redemption:

When the serpent perverted Adam and his wife, by approaching the woman and casting filth into her,[18] and causing Adam to be tempted, then the world was defiled and the earth cursed on his account, and he brought mortality upon the whole world. The world was about to punish him, until the Tree of Life came and atoned for Adam, subduing that serpent so that he would not govern the seed of Jacob in perpetuity . . . On this account, the world will continue to exist until a woman comes who is like Eve, and a man who is like Adam, and they will pervert the evil serpent and outwit it and him who is mounted upon it,[19] as all this has been told.[20]

---

[16] See above, Ch. I, at nn. 110–11.   [17] Emden, *Zot torat hakena'ot*, 54.

[18] According to a rabbinic *midrash*; see BT *Shab.* 146a and parallels.

[19] The 'him who is mounted upon it' is Samael (Satan). See *Pirkei derabi eli'ezer*, ch. 13. See also Zohar, i. 35a, 263b.

[20] Zohar, i. 145b–146a. Cf., however, Daniel Matt's English translation of the same passage, and his comments ad loc. (*The Zohar* (Pritzker edn.), ii. 314–15), whereby the appearance of the Adam-and-Eve-like couple does not refer to the messianic future but rather to the biblical Jacob and his mother Rebecca, who 'outwitted' Esau, identified with the evil serpent, in their

Just as the primordial pair, Adam and Eve, had jointly brought the curse upon the world, so would it be redeemed jointly by their latter-day counterparts, the messianic couple, 'a woman who is like Eve and a man who is like Adam'.[21]

This idea was developed further in Isaac Luria's doctrine of the transmigration of souls.[22] The first redeemer, Adam, and his consort, Eve, are reincarnated over and over again down through the generations, until their final reincarnation as the ultimate redemptive couple. The chronicle of these reincarnations with their attendant matings is quite elaborate and convoluted. According to ancient legend, Adam had two mates: the first Eve—Lilith— also known as 'the wife of fornication', and the second, pure Eve, who deposed the first. Their counterparts were Eve's own two mates: the impure serpent,

own historical time. This, together with the sefirotic values, Malkhut ad Tiferet, to which the redemptive couple alludes, is probably the correct interpretation of the passage in its zoharic context, but the passage can also be, and certainly was, understood by some as referring to the final redemption in the Time to Come, on which see below, at nn. 264–71. Elsewhere kabbalistic literature invests Adam with a redemptive dimension, linking him not only to the messianic King David but also to the very title of messiah, by interpreting the name 'Adam' as the acronym of all three, Adam–David–Messiah (see below, n. 25). Here, however, the focus is clearly not on the single male figure of Adam but on the messianic Adam-and-Eve-like couple, who were prefigured in the original couple of the Genesis narrative, and who will be charged with the task of subduing the evil to which the original couple succumbed. It is not impossible that underlying this zoharic idea is the Christian conception of Christ and his mother Mary as 'the second Adam' and 'the second Eve', prefigured in the Adam and Eve of Genesis, and credited with the power to free the world from the legacy of their sin. If this assumption is correct, then the passage may be added to the growing body of evidence suggesting the possibility of underlying Christian influence on the development of certain zoharic ideas, not least the conceptualization of the divine female. On this, see below, nn. 51 and 54. For Jesus and Mary as the new Adam and Eve in the history of the Christian doctrine of salvation, see e.g. Pelikan, *Mary through the Ages*, 39–52; Warner, *Alone of All Her Sex*, 59–67; Anderson, *Genesis of Perfection*, 2–8, 35–6, 84–5, 102–3; Hahn, *Hail Holy Queen*, 31–45, 84–5. For the prevalence of this theme, and especially the conceptualization of Mary as the second Eve, in the Slavonic and Balkan tradition, see Badalanova, 'The Virgin Mary in Slavia Orthodoxa'. See also Schäfer, *Mirror*, 164–8, 170, 229. Surprisingly, Schäfer, who highlights the probability of Christian influence on the development of the kabbalistic notion of a female element in the godhead, and who considers it in the context of the flourishing Mariological cult of 12th- and 13th-century western Christianity, where Mary was celebrated as her son's full consort and, as such, as second Eve to his second Adam, does not mention this particular zoharic passage as a possible site of Christian influence.

[21] For the use that Jacob Frank was to make of this zoharic passage see n. 141 below.

[22] The following discussion of the messianic consort in Luria's doctrine is based on Meroz, 'Redemption in Lurianic Teaching' (Heb.), 315–21.

who was the first to have relations with her, and her husband Adam, who was the second. It follows that each member of each of the couples in the subsequent chain of reincarnations will experience a defective first coupling, with a wicked or non-Jewish mate, by means of which they will be purified and become suitable for a second coupling that will be perfect and pure. However, the remains of the *kelipah*—the impure 'shell' scattered throughout creation at the primordial 'breaking of the vessels'—still adhere to the members of the couple even after they have found their pure mates, necessitating further processes of purification and rectification, by way of a succession of impure and pure couplings stretching down through the generations in a long series of reincarnations. These transmigratory cycles and their attendant couplings—defective and perfect, sullied and pure—are expressed in history, as narrated by rabbinic tradition, not only in the reincarnations of the redeeming male, Adam, in the form of various twice-espoused messianic figures, including King David, who was married to Abigail and Bathsheba, and Rabbi Akiba, who was married to the wife of the wicked Turnus Rufus and to Rachel, the daughter of Kalba Savua. They also take form in the reincarnations of the redeeming female, whose identity was split in two from the start. The first Eve reappears in such figures as Dinah, who was married to Shechem and then to Job, and Abigail, who was married to Nabal and then to King David; while the second Eve recurs in the figures of Bathsheba, King David's second wife, and Rachel, the second wife of Rabbi Akiba. Ronit Meroz, who has analysed these passages and determined their status in the Lurianic doctrine of redemption, concludes:

The same things that happened to Adam, the first redeemer, and his mate will go on happening to the various messianic figures in which he is reincarnated, up to the ultimate messiah, and to their female consorts. In the same way that Eve, Adam's true mate, deposed her predecessor, the wife of fornication, so will her future reincarnations depose their rivals. And as the wife of the first redeemer was mounted by the serpent before she could mate with her husband, Adam, so, too, will this recur in the future. . . . [23] These passages intimate a female redemptive figure alongside the male figure. The former rectifies the defects of Eve, the latter those of Adam. . . . According to the *midrash*, 'One who has no wife . . . is not a complete man . . . both together are

---

[23] Meroz points here, in a footnote, to the possibility that this understanding of the Lurianic doctrine is what led Sabbatai Zevi to take a 'wife of fornication'—his wife Sarah—whose promiscuity was widely rumoured (see Scholem, *Sabbatai Sevi*, 192–7).

called man/Adam.'[24] Adam, then, was incomplete without a wife, and so we find that the cosmic soul, too, comprises the soul of Adam and that of Eve. But if Adam is to be read as an acronym, representing Adam, David and messiah,[25] then the latter-day messiah, too, will be incomplete without a wife. As far as I know, this setting of a consort beside the messiah was a Lurianic innovation—one quite in keeping with the Jewish belief in the importance of marriage.[26]

The traditions regarding the consorts of the leading Sabbatian messiahs, which seem likely to have drawn upon these kabbalistic doctrines, may be taken as precedents heralding the gender transmutations that transpired in Jacob Frank's mind, which were reflected in the government of his court at the end of his life and in the years following his death. To be sure, these precedents were all confined to the addition of a discrete feminine element to the personality of the redeeming male. With Cardozo, this was expressed in the inclusion of a female figure in the quartet of mythical messianic entities; with Berukhyah and Sabbatai Zevi, it meant that the spouse of the man in whom the soul of the messiah had been reincarnated, allowing him to rise to the level of divinity, was herself conceived of as embodying and complementing this very dimension of his figure. Frank himself, at the outset of his career, was no exception to this rule. Already in his childhood, by his own testimony, he had conceived of the bisexual divinity as being compounded of 'the Daughter of God', 'the Wife of God', and God himself:

> My uncle Jacob told me that when I was 2 years old he took me with him to his bed to sleep with him. I would not let him go to sleep until he had finished saying 'Good night' with me to every creature, from the largest to the smallest.... After that, he said with me: 'Good night, Daughter of God! Good night, Wife of God! Good night, God!' Only then would I let him go to sleep.[27]

Later, the title of Lady that he conferred upon his wife Hannah,[28] the royal homage paid her and her daughter at his court,[29] and her regular participation

---

[24] *Gen. Rabbah*, 17: 1.

[25] On this acronym and its sources in kabbalistic literature see Scholem, '*Gilgul*', 214.

[26] Meroz, 'Redemption in Lurianic Teaching' (Heb.), 320–1.   [27] *Words of the Lord*, §479.

[28] She is consistently called by this title throughout the Polish *Kronika* (Levine, *Kronika*; Doktór, *Rozmaite adnotacje*).

[29] Thus, for example, the Lady sat at Frank's side during the performance in Giurgiu (Bulgarian Gyurgevo, in the Polish sources Dziurdzy or Dziurdzowa) of the 'line of kingship' ceremony, whose significance is not quite clear, but its interpretation as having to do with their 'acknowledgement as God' seems to indicate the divinization of the couple. Its contrivance may

at his side in various and sundry rituals[30] all derived from her status as his consort. Admittedly, this must have endowed her with something of his aura of messianic divinity in the eyes of the believers, but there seems little doubt that her position remained secondary, her function little more than ceremonial, and that Frank subjected her to his erratic will no less—and perhaps even more—than his other associates.[31]

Only after Hannah's death on 25 February 1770,[32] with the transfer of the title Lady to her daughter,[33] did Frank begin to express himself in a new way regarding the primary status of the divine Maiden and to hint at the embodiment of this Maiden in his virgin daughter Eva.[34] This novel turn, which was to lead to the cult of the redemptive Virgin in Frank's court, seems to have

have been influenced by the Sufi rituals with which Frank became acquainted by way of his contacts with the sect of Berukhyah in Salonica. On this see *Kronika*, 42–4, §30 (*Rozmaite adnotacje*, 54) and Levine's n. 64 on p. 44. See also *Kronika*, 50, §41 (*Rozmaite adnotacje*, 57–8), which describes the festive preparations for the arrival from Giurgiu of the Lady, accompanied by her children and entourage, at Iwanie, where Frank had established his court in April 1759. Furthermore, it would seem that Frank, after choosing the first group of seven women at Iwanie, whom 'he designated as his sisters' (*Kronika*, 48, §39; *Rozmaite adnotacje*, 57), designated for his wife the seven women who were added to them shortly thereafter. He alluded in this context to her status as his royal consort: 'In so doing, he quoted a passage from Esther: "he quickly provided her ... with seven chosen maids from the king's palace" [Esther 2: 9]' (*Kronika*, 50, §42; *Rozmaite adnotacje*, 58). On the regal status of Frank's daughter Eva, who was then still a child, see below, at nn. 115–16.

[30] See e.g. *Kronika*, 42, §30; 50, §41; 52–4, §45; 54, §46; 56–8, §49; 66, §64; 68, §§67–8; 72–4, §74; 74, §78; and 96, §106 (*Rozmaite adnotacje*, 54, 57–8, 60, 61, 63, 68, 69, 72, 73, 87–8).

[31] See e.g. *Kronika*, 92–4, §104 (*Rozmaite adnotacje*, 84–5), according to which Frank ordered the fourteen 'sisters' to choose one of their number to be dedicated to him, so that he could 'comport himself with her seven times a night and six times a day' until she bore him a daughter. His wife responded 'with a request to be that woman', but she was rejected with a rebuke: 'This has nothing to do with you. It must be done by one of the sisters. You already have what belongs to you, and now you must have sons, not a daughter.'

[32] See *Kronika*, 74, §78 (*Rozmaite adnotacje*, 73).

[33] The transfer of the title may be inferred from the *Kronika*. The text consistently refers to both women by the title of Lady, but in most of the references to Frank's wife Hannah, the title is followed by the abbreviation ś.p. (*świętej pamięci*), 'of sacred memory', indicating 'the late', 'the deceased' (*z.k.* for *zikhrah kodesh* in Levine's Hebrew translation), making it clear that the account was recorded after her death. Eva, Frank's daughter, who was still alive, is simply called Lady throughout. See *Kronika*, 42, §30; 50, §41 (*Rozmaite adnotacje*, 54, 57), and *passim*, as against pp. 32, §§3 and 5; 66, §66 (*Rozmaite adnotacje*, 47–8), and *passim*.

[34] On this see below, at nn. 91–129.

aroused great astonishment in the circles of the faithful. This is attested in passages from a Frankist letter, written partly in Hebrew and partly in German (in Hebrew characters), which appears to have been composed in Prague at the end of the eighteenth or the beginning of the nineteenth century:[35]

Finally, he [Frank] spoke of the Virgin, though he did not speak explicitly of her, saying that she is a shepherdess,[36] and she is the messiah, which has never occurred to anyone before—[namely] that the Virgin, who is the Lady, is the redeemer![37]

The main thing is that first of all, the Virgin must be the redeemer, and one must hold fast to her.[38]

Elsewhere in the same letter, the reference to the Virgin is accompanied by a note of disappointment that hopes for redemption by her hand had not yet been fulfilled: 'The Lady has not yet revealed herself by a whit to be that same Holy One of whom the Holy Father [as Frank was called by the last of the Frankists[39]] told all, and to whom he drew attention!'[40]

There are numerous parallels in *Words of the Lord* that echo this shifting of the messianic focus from Jacob Frank to his daughter Eva. Thus, for example, Frank, clearly alluding to his daughter, gives the following interpretation of the verse in Genesis describing Rachel as a shepherdess, the same verse which, in the letter cited above, was specifically interpreted in his name as referring to the Lady Eva: 'How could you have failed to understand that primacy in the leadership is to be hers? Is it not written of Rachel that "she is a shepherdess"?'[41]

As we have seen, the cult of Eva Frank seems to have already begun taking shape in Frank's lifetime and at his initiative, evidently in the early 1770s, following the death of the Lady Hannah towards the end of Frank's incarceration in the fortress of Częstochowa.[42] He undoubtedly drew his inspiration from the local Christian cult of the Holy Virgin Mary, whose dark-faced icon, known as the Black Madonna, was famed for its miracle-working power and had for generations drawn pilgrims in great numbers to the Pauline convent of

[35] This letter was edited and published by Scholem in *Researches* (Heb.), 634–50; and see his comments on p. 644 n. 67, and in id., *Studies and Texts* (Heb.), 125. On the manuscript containing this letter, see also below, Appendix.

[36] Gen. 29: 9, referring to Rachel—a frequent sobriquet of the Shekhinah in kabbalistic literature, and also of Eva Frank.   [37] Scholem, *Researches* (Heb.), 644.

[38] Ibid. 645.   [39] See Scholem's remarks, ibid. 643 n. 53.   [40] Ibid. 645–6.

[41] *Words of the Lord*, §671.   [42] See Kraushar, *Jacob Frank*, i. 204, and below, at nn. 94–104.

Jasna Góra, which is within the fortress compound. Frank spoke explicitly and respectfully of the cult of the Holy Virgin in Częstochowa, rebuking his associates for not being clever enough to discern in it the path to the true divine Maiden:

Is it for naught that kings and nobles make their way, in fear and trembling, to the portrait of the Virgin in Częstochowa? They are wiser than you, for they can see that all the power is concentrated in her hands. Just as it is said of Christ that he was resurrected, so will she, too, rise from the earth, and all the kings of the world will bow down to her.[43]

Frank saw the portrait of the Virgin, her concrete 'black' icon at Częstochowa, as representing the hidden essence of the supernal Maiden: 'Why did you not ask me how it is that the Maiden is concealed in a painted board?'[44] His comparison of the supernal Maiden to a princess posing as a dark-skinned Gypsy alluded to the dark colour of the image, which quite likely connected in his imagination with the black colour of the kabbalistic *sefirah* of Malkhut 'in its waning phase':[45]

No one recognized her, because of her black skin—no one but he [the King's son]. . . . His tutor said, 'Why do you want to start up with a black one like her?' . . . So also here; how is it that you had no heart to see and to recognize things as they are even in that black colour, and to say: 'I shall love you even more as you are'—and only afterwards to ask her to show herself to you all as she really is?[46]

It was in the power of the Virgin's portrait to proffer a direct approach to the 'other' divine Maiden: 'Had you gone with me wholeheartedly during the time in Częstochowa, that Maiden who was there would have led you to the other Maiden.'[47]

It is quite possible that the militaristic image of the supernal divine Maiden, 'into whose hands . . . all the weapons have been given', and who was

---

[43] *Words of the Lord*, §778.   [44] Ibid., §614.

[45] See Cordovero, *Pardes rimonim*, pt. 10: 'The Colours', ch. 4. The verses in the Song of Songs describing the beloved as 'dark, but comely' or 'swarthy' (S. of S. 1: 5, 6), which the kabbalistic literature interpreted as allusions to the *sefirah* of Malkhut, were interpreted in Christian tradition as referring to the 'Black Madonnas' whose dark icons have been venerated for centuries in many places throughout the world. On this see Warner, *Alone of All Her Sex*, 274–5, and Pelikan, *Mary through the Centuries*, 25–6 and 78. On the connections between Mary, mother of Jesus, and the *sefirah* of Malkhut in kabbalistic and Sabbatian tradition see below, n. 51.

[46] *Words of the Lord*, §545; and see also ibid., §§215 and 370.   [47] Ibid., §597.

capable of 'girding each one with a sword' and serving as a 'shield and body-guard',[48] was influenced not only by the zoharic image of the Shekhinah, but also by that of the 'Black Madonna', who was famed throughout Poland as a seasoned warrior, a heroine in battle, and a symbol of the political freedom of the Polish Commonwealth. During a Hussite raid on the fortified monastery at Częstochowa in 1430, the portrait of the Virgin had been slashed with a sword and stabbed with a dagger. Even after its restoration, her cheeks were left with 'scars', attesting to her heroism. In 1655, when the Swedish army laid siege to Jasna Góra, the Virgin 'in a shining robe' was spotted 'on the walls, priming the canons and tossing shells back in the direction from which they came'.[49] The vanquishing of the Swedish army in this battle, which ultimately led to the liberation of Poland from foreign occupation, was credited to the Virgin and her miraculous powers. In the last two years of Frank's sojourn at Częstochowa, which ended with the first partition of Poland and his release from imprisonment by the invading Russian army, the 'Black Madonna' was again identified with the forces of the Confederation of Bar, which heroically defended the fortress of Jasna Góra until its final defeat by the Russian armies in August 1772.[50] There can be no doubt that Frank, having lived for over twelve years at the epicentre of the cult of the 'Black Madonna', was familiar with these traditions. It is reasonable to suppose that her image as a warrior, which melded so well with that of the kabbalistic 'Matronita', commanding general of the divine legion,[51] captured his heart and integrated neatly with his

[48] See above, Ch. 6, at nn. 63–8.

[49] From Wespazjan Kochowski, *Annalium Poloniae Climacter Secundus* (Kraków, 1688), as translated by Norman Davies in *God's Playground*, ii. 452.   [50] See ibid. 520.

[51] See above, Ch. 6 n. 66. The characterization of the Black Madonna at Jasna Góra in Częstochowa as an intrepid Polish warrior had a number of parallels in the tradition of the medieval church, in which the image of the Virgin, mother of Jesus, incorporated overtly militaristic motifs that were associated with her designation as the 'valiant woman' (*eshet ḥayil*) of Prov. 31: 10. On this see Pelikan, *Mary through the Centuries*, 91, and Patai, *Hebrew Goddess*, 202–3. It is not impossible that this Christian characterization of the valiant Virgin inspired the medieval kabbalistic attribution of a militaristic character to the *sefirah* of Malkhut. Dark colour and a militaristic disposition are not the only affinities between the images of Mary, mother of Jesus, and the *sefirah* of Malkhut, on which see ibid. For a presentation of all these affinities as a likely Christian influence on the kabbalistic conception of the female aspect of the divinity see also Idel, 'Attitude to Christianity' (Heb.), 88–90, and see especially the recent and comprehensive treatments of the subject by Arthur Green, 'Shekhinah', and Peter Schäfer, 'Daughter' and *Mirror*. It is worth noting that Abraham Cardozo, who was born into a Converso family and trained in Christian theology before leaving Spain and returning to Judaism in Livorno, was

own militaristic inclinations on the one hand,[52] and with the gender revolution that was taking place in his mind on the other.

Frank saw the Holy Virgin, who in the course of the Middle Ages became the focus of Catholic worship and whose power to absolve and save the faithful came to rival that of her son,[53] as the essence of Christianity and the secret of its advantage over both Judaism and Islam.[54] It was precisely the Virgin, in her manifest femininity, who served as the path to the hidden, supernal Maiden—the redemptive female—who began in Frank's mind to rival the Big Brother, his own alter ego 'within God'.[55] It was for this reason, he claimed, that he had led his followers into the embrace of Christianity. Their conversion was required on account of the absence of the Virgin in Jewish worship:

Why, then, did you become Christian? Because in that status, on the level of Jewishness, you could neither hear nor see any trace of a Virgin in any synagogue. But in this religion you hear that the whole world is filled with her and believes in the

well aware of the affinities between the Virgin Mary and the kabbalistic *sefirah* of Malkhut and discussed them explicitly in his homiletical writings. Thus, for example, he asserts in a description of the faith of the Christians: 'Most of their prayers, entreaties, and cries are to Jesus, who is always the object of their effusive praise, but they also laud his mother Miriam, entreat her and pray to her, for she parallels the holy Shekhinah' (transcribed by Scholem in *Studies and Texts* (Heb.), 291). See also Wolfson's discussion in 'Constructions of the Shekhinah', 29–35, of the Mariological conception of the Shekhinah evident in Cardozo's homilies and perhaps also reflected in a work originating in Berukhyah's circle in Salonica.

[52] On these inclinations see Scholem, *Studies and Texts* (Heb.), 129–30.

[53] On this historical process in the Catholic Church see E. Johnson, 'Marian Devotion', and the bibliography on pp. 413–14. Pelikan, in *Mary through the Centuries*, 125–36, shows how this process developed out of the ancient Byzantine tradition that placed Mary in a singular and central position, both in its theological literature and in its iconographic expressions, on which see ibid. 103–4. On the especial veneration of the Holy Virgin in Poland, where her cult was seen as representing the authentic tradition of Polish Catholicism as against such reformist Catholic trends as the papacy, in response to the Protestant threat, was trying to enact from its centre in Rome, see Davies, *God's Playground*, i. 171–2.

[54] This had been Abraham Cardozo's understanding of the Holy Virgin's status in Christianity: 'The Christians bow down to the female, Miriam, whom they call Maria, Queen of all the angels above and chief of all created beings, and they refer to her more than they refer to God. When I was still in Spain among the Christians, they used to say that when one entered the home of his fellow, he ought not to say *alabado sea Dios* (praised be God), so as to remove any doubt that he might be a Jew, but rather *Ave Maria*, that is, "Thine is salvation, O Mary". The Ishmaelites only ever mention the male, for they have no regard for the female.' See Scholem, *Studies and Texts* (Heb.), 294.

[55] See below for the relationship between the Big Brother and the Maiden.

Virgin, though she is not really a virgin, but nevertheless that name, of the Virgin, never leaves their mouths. That is why we have entered into this, so as to seek that Virgin of whom all the world knows naught, nor has it ever seen her.[56]

Elsewhere he again emphasizes this lack in Judaism, all of whose historical redeemers had been male:

The exodus from Egypt was not perfect, because the one who redeemed them [i.e. Moses] was male,[57] but the basis of redemption derives from the Maiden.[58] As I have told you, [King] David and that First One [Sabbatai Zevi] were of the mystery of the female,[59] and they called themselves saviours. There [in Judaism] the mystery was concealed in words,[60] while here [in Christianity] it is manifest. Therefore we proceed from that status in which there are only words, to enter into the religion that is the shell surrounding the fruit. Here one says outright that salvation begins with the Maiden, and one prays to her.[61]

Judaism does acknowledge the femaleness of the redeemer, but it expresses this only by way of 'words', that is, by way of the kabbalistic appellations of the redemptive feminine *sefirot*, which were applied to the messiah and thence to the male persona of Sabbatai Zevi—the 'First One'. However, this course proved unsuccessful; the Maiden could not be made manifest in the world and bring about the redemption in her embodiment as a man: 'The Jews, too, believe in that word: Shekhinah–Lady,[62] and the faithful go so far as to say of

[56] *Words of the Lord*, §258.

[57] Apart from the biblical Moses being male by virtue simply of being a man, he is regularly identified in the kabbalistic literature with the quintessentially male *sefirah* of Tiferet. See Cordovero, *Pardes rimonim*, pt. 23: 'Appellations', ch. 13, s.v. *moshe*.

[58] At the bottom of this would seem to lie the kabbalistic linking of the King Messiah and his associated symbols with the *sefirah* of Malkhut, the daughter, who is the lower female, as well as the association of redemption with the *sefirah* of Binah, the mother, who is the supernal female. See ibid., ch. 3, s.v. *ge'ulah*, and ch. 13, s.v. *melekh* and *hamelekh*.

[59] The biblical David was of course male, but by virtue of his traditional identification with the King Messiah he was associated with the feminine *sefirah* of Malkhut (see ibid., ch. 4, s.v. *david*), and so he was 'of the mystery of the female'. The same applies to Sabbatai Zevi (to whom Frank often referred as the 'First One'; Berukhyah was the 'Second', and both were the predecessors of Frank, the *third* redeemer), who was also a male messiah 'of the mystery of the female'. Frank diagnoses in both the discrepancy between their overt masculinity and covert femininity as the defect that prevented them from fulfilling their messianic mission.

[60] That is, in the symbolic language of the kabbalah, in which, alone, could the femininity of these messiahs come to expression.   [61] *Words of the Lord*, §725.

[62] 'Shekhinah–*gevirah*', revising 'Shekhinah–*gevurah*' in the Hebrew version of Fania Scholem, which appears to be a misprint. The Polish version, '*Schina*–dama', seems preferable.

that First One that he was secretly of the female sex. But I shall reveal all: What was in spirit will be in flesh,[63] so that nothing will be concealed. The whole world will see openly and clearly.'[64] Frank mocks the 'First One', who 'was a man, but was said to have been of the female sex'[65]—by which he may

[63] Here, too, my English translation revises the Hebrew version of Fania Scholem, which has *vehayah baguf*—'and was in the body'; this, too, may well be a misprint. The Polish edition reads 'co było w duchu, aby zostało w ciele'.

[64] *Words of the Lord*, §552. Frank speaks scornfully of the kabbalistic symbols, which can do no more than allude to the 'concealed' truth. They are but empty 'words', obscuring the truth rather than making it concretely manifest. Thus, for example, he mocks the kabbalistic devotions:

> Whatever possessed your minds to throw yourselves into the place from which you had gone out and call out before me those two names, Tiferet and Shekhinah [the two Hebrew appellations are transliterated in the Polish source]? What are they to us? Thus did your fathers and forefathers cry out, but there was no response. (ibid., §421)

He scoffs at the Sabbatian version of kabbalah, too:

> When R. Mordecai revealed the secret faith to me, he told me that God was to be found among the *sefirot* in the [*sefirah*] of Tiferet [here, too, the words 'Tiferet' and '*sefirot*' are transliterated in the Polish source]. I asked him, 'How do you know who is to be found there? Perhaps he went to relieve himself and left there the very worst one.' (ibid., §527)

This negative attitude towards the kabbalah and its symbols belongs with Frank's rejection of all the books, religions, and laws 'that ever were' and his repeated calls for their total eradication (on which see above, Ch. 6, at n. 43, and below, Ch. 8, at nn. 43–50), although he admits to liking certain parts of the Zohar, which he apparently took to refer to himself:

> I showed you several times in the Zohar, and I told you that of the whole book I was most pleased with one chapter in which it is written: 'Who cast Joseph into prison? God. Who redeemed him from there? God. Who made him King of Egypt? God' [this perhaps refers to the zoharic passage on the Torah portion 'Mikets' (Gen. 41: 1–44: 17), Zohar, i. 193*a*–197*a*], and so on. Thus, too, have I said to you that I favoured another chapter in which it is asked, 'What does the embalmment of Jacob mean?' R. Simon replied: 'Go and ask a doctor' [ibid., i. 250*a*, at the end of the passage on the Torah portion 'Vayeḥi' (Gen. 47: 28–50: 26)]. . . . You should have asked me, and I would have answered and revealed the truth to you, that I do not like the Zohar altogether, and that we have no need of all the kabbalistic books. (*Words of the Lord*, §1088).

[65] *Words of the Lord*, §982. On the 'classic' Sabbatian conceptualization of Sabbatai Zevi as a female figure, identified, as the messiah, with the *sefirah* of Malkhut and even with the supernal mother, Binah—the *sefirah* of redemption, see Elqayam, 'To Know Messiah' (Heb.), 557 and n. 76. See also id., 'Bury My Faith' (Heb.), 5 n. 4, where Elqayam cites an explicit statement to this effect from the manuscript of a work entitled 'Sod ha'elohut hakadosh' (The holy secret of the divinity): 'And that Malkhut, which is the female [aspect] of the Holy King, is the soul of the King Messiah Sabbatai Zevi.' The female dimension of Sabbatai Zevi is also referred to explicitly in one of the necrological poems, written, probably in the 1720s, in the circle of the apostate Sabbatians of Salonica. It is dedicated to a certain 'Esther Levi', who is likened to

have been alluding, among other things, to the rumours of Sabbatai Zevi's homosexual activity.[66] However, it was not on account of this defect that Frank rejected him, but rather because his femaleness was no more than a 'mystery concealed in words'—a merely symbolic statement that had little to do with his true male nature, irredeemable by virtue simply of his being a man. Sabbatai Zevi's very maleness was thus the flaw that disqualified him as the messiah! Frank, on the other hand, had the ability to bring his believers to the redemptive Virgin, who was openly a woman, unlike the 'First One', who was merely 'secretly a woman'.[67] The abortive mission of Sabbatai Zevi—the 'First' male, whose association with the female amounted to no more than mystery and symbol—was merely a 'premonition' of the forthcoming redemption by way of the Maiden, who would be revealed to be genuinely female in every aspect of her being:

See for yourselves that that First One who was before, as it were pointed the way; and it was said of him that he was secretly a woman. You sang of him, in hymns and paeans, that all the kings of the earth would bow down to him. What made you think that kings would bow down to him? This was but a premonition of the present time; when

the biblical Esther as a saviour of her people. She is said to allude to the feminine *sefirah* of Binah, which signifies the redemption, and thus she points to 'the secret of Sabbatai the redeemer . . . who is surely both male and female'. See Attias, Scholem, and Ben-Zvi, *Songs and Hymns* (Heb.), 156, §162. And see also Scholem, *Studies and Texts* (Heb.), 244–5; and Tishby, *Paths of Faith* (Heb.), 321 n. 120. Frank's assertions about the covert female nature of Sabbatai Zevi are reiterated throughout *Words of the Lord*; see also §§215, 552, 609, 813.

[66] Emden, *Zot torat hakena'ot*, 54, cites the testimony of Moses Habib, a Salonican sage who travelled to Jerusalem around the turn of the 17th and 18th centuries: 'I heard from a certain man—one of those who had been lured into apostasy by Sabbatai Zevi but later returned to Judaism—that he himself had seen Sabbatai Zevi, may his name and memory be obliterated, wearing phylacteries while having sexual relations with a boy, and he said that this was a great *tikun*.' On the credibility of Moses Habib's testimony as preserved by Emden see Benayahu, 'Key to Understanding' (Heb.), 35–40. On homosexual acts in the tradition of the apostate Sabbatians in the Salonican circle of Berukhyah, and on the mystical allusions to this in the Sabbatian kabbalah developed in the circle of R. Jonathan Eybeschuetz, see Scholem, *Researches* (Heb.), 346–51; and Liebes, *On Sabbatianism* (Heb.), 117–18 and 165–6. For the prevalence of homosexuality in the Ottoman empire in general, and among the Sufi fraternities in particular, as well as within the Jewish communities throughout the empire, where the practice was tolerated in spite of being denounced by halakhists and moralists, see Ben-Naeh, 'Same-Sex Sexual Relations' (Heb.); id., 'Response' (Heb.); and Lamdan, 'Notes on Yaron Ben-Naeh's Article' (Heb.).   [67] *Words of the Lord*, §813.

she goes out into the world, you will see with your own eyes how all the kings of the earth shall bow down before her.[68]

In statements expressing a heady celebration of female power asserting its domination over the world—a world that, purified of its corruptions, she builds anew—Frank repeatedly emphasizes that the redeemer must be a real woman, female in both her inner essence and her openly visible physical appearance:

When this Maiden is revealed to the world, I shall have to send her to bathe in a certain place. By means of this bathing, all the faults that are the lot of every person will fall away from her. Furthermore, it will be necessary for this bathing to be attended by seven virgins and seven women. First she will bathe, and afterwards they will bathe. Similarly, it will be necessary for seven of the brothers to be with her. As it was said of the First One that he was secretly of the female sex, so you too would serve her, and the whole world would understand that you are women. That First One was secretly a female but not openly so, yet they nevertheless said of him, 'La Signora vino in Teivel'.[69] *But this one will really be a woman, openly a woman*', and she will build up the world. Without her no construction is possible. It will not be as you have said up to now, that the Shekhinah walks by night seeking sustenance for those who fear her.[70] Now everything will happen in the light of day.[71]

There can be no doubt that the Maiden will manifest herself in the figure of a flesh-and-blood woman, for she, too, will have to be purified of 'all the faults that are the lot of every person'. Nor can there be any doubt that this flesh-and-blood woman is really the messiah:

How could it have occurred to you that the messiah is a man? This is utterly preposterous, for the very foundation is the Maiden. It is she who will be the true messiah. She will direct all the worlds, for all the weapons are given into her hand.[72] Whatever was said of David and of that First One, they came only to show the way to her. However,

---

[68] Ibid.

[69] 'The Lady has come into the world'. The phrase appears thus in the Polish version. Frank evidently was citing one of the hymns composed by the apostate Salonican Sabbatians. For another mention of the 'Signora' in these writings see above, Ch. 1, at n. 129.

[70] Fania Scholem's Hebrew version has 'seeking salvation [*yeshu'ah*]', but the Polish edition's *żywność* (sustenance) clearly indicates that the source of this concept lies in the biblical praise of the Virtuous Woman who 'rises while it is yet night and provides food for her household' (Prov. 31: 15). The Zohar (ii. 18*b*) interprets this verse as a reference to the Shekhinah, which is the attribute of night; see Cordovero, *Pardes rimonim*, pt. 23 ('Appellations'), ch. 12, s.v. *lailah* (night).

[71] *Words of the Lord*, §609. Emphasis added.   [72] See above, Ch. 6, at n. 66.

they never completed anything. Note well: his religion is now being demolished. But her honour is not in the least touched.[73]

In Frank's view, Sabbatai Zevi's mission was forestalled not only because of his own maleness, but also because his activity took place in the domain of Islam, a religion of males that left no room at all for the cult of the redemptive female, the Maiden. True, Sabbatai Zevi had tried to overcome this problem and create a relationship with Christianity—and thereby with the Maiden— by marrying a Polish woman who had been brought up as a Christian.[74] But this indirect relationship was insufficient to create an opening for redemption:

[This applies] even to that First One, who did a good thing by shattering the laws of Moses and opening up that status [i.e. Christianity] . . . but in the country where he was, nothing could be accomplished, because there is no mention of the Maiden there. He did take a Polish wife, from that status, but this was a mere gesture, and so he, too, fell there.[75]

A mere 'gesture' directed at the Maiden could not but miss its target so long as it was made within the domain of Islam, nor could mere 'talk' or 'song' suffice to reach her, since, within the domain of Judaism, they could do no more than allude to her. The way to the redemptive Maiden could be found only by fully, openly entering into the domain of Christianity, her natural abode:

All the Jews are seeking something of which they have not the slightest inkling. They have a custom of reciting every sabbath: 'Come, my beloved, to meet the bride', calling out 'Welcome' to the Maiden. This is all mere talk and song. But we pursue her and try to see her in reality. How that First One pursued her; he pursued the Maiden for a whole night! He had intended to bestir a certain thing, but in his religion [i.e. Islam] nothing could be done, because nothing is known there of any Maiden. That is why there has never yet been anyone in the world who could go all the way in and proceed to enter upon the proper way, for without her, nothing can be accomplished.[76]

Frank repeatedly stresses the superiority of Christianity, in that it was a 'bareheaded' religion, as against the deficiency of Islam, the religion into which Sabbatai Zevi had converted, with its practice of 'covering the head', such that from within it, the Virgin could never emerge and show herself to the world: [77]

---

[73] *Words of the Lord*, §1051.

[74] He was referring to Sarah, Sabbatai Zevi's Ashkenazi wife, who, orphaned and left homeless by the Chmielnicki massacres in Poland, spent her youth in a convent. For the traditions on this see Scholem, *Sabbatai Sevi*, 192–5.   [75] *Words of the Lord*, §397.   [76] Ibid., §315.

[77] Muslim (and Jewish) custom demands the covering of one's head in token of humility and respect before God. Frank appears here to interpret this as a barrier between man and the divine

Wherever was your reason when you believed that anything could be made manifest to the world from the status of Ishmael? You can see for yourselves how in that religion all heads are covered, wrapped up in turbans, and the hands are let down. But in this religion the head is bare—a sign that there really is a head here[78]—and the hands rest proudly upon the rib,[79] indicating that it is from here that the thing will come out into the world.[80]

Maiden, whom he identified with the *sefirah* of Malkhut—the Shekhinah. This would have been a conscious inversion of the rabbinic tradition according to which 'Rav Huna b. Rav Joshua never walked more than four paces with his head uncovered, for he said, "the Shekhinah is above my head" [BT *Kid.* 31a]'. According to Frank, a head-covering occludes the Shekhinah, and one ought to remove it before her, as is the custom of men entering a holy place in Christianity.

[78] The 'head', in Frank's parlance, referred to the supernal Maiden: 'You wanted to go by your own wit, without a head. But without a head there can be nothing. Scripture explicitly states: "The wise man has his eyes in his head" [Eccles. 2: 14]. That Virgin is the head' (*Words of the Lord*, §766).

To be sure, *rosh*, 'head', on its own, is not often used as an appellation of the *sefirah* of Malkhut in kabbalistic literature. It ordinarily refers to the initial *sefirot*, Keter or Hokhmah, or, in expressions like 'the head of the righteous' or 'the head of things', to the masculine *sefirot* of Tiferet or Yesod. In this context, however, the focus is specifically on the conjugal relationship between these *sefirot* and Malkhut. See Cordovero, *Pardes rimonim*, pt. 23: 'Appellations', ch. 20, s.v. *rosh* (head). Moreover, in expressions such as *rosh pinah* ('the cornerstone', *Tikunei hazohar*, §18, 32b) or *rosh hashanah* ('the New Year', ibid., ch. 21, 45b and 56a; Zohar, iii. 257b), and particularly in certain contexts, as when she is called *rosh letata'ei* ('head of the Lower Worlds', Zohar, i. 20a) or *reshit lanivra'im* ('first of created beings', ibid., preface, 11b), the *sefirah* of Malkhut is indeed the 'head'. This is clearly the relevant context for Frank's identification of the redemptive Maiden with Malkhut, taken as the 'head', and it also hints at the association between Malkhut and the Virgin Mary, who was already described by Cardozo as 'head of all created beings' (see above, n. 54).

[79] I follow Fania Scholem here, who renders the Polish *bok*, meaning 'side', with the ambivalent Hebrew *tsela*, meaning both 'rib' and 'side', on the assumption that Frank would have had this ambivalence in mind. It was from the rib that woman emerged out of man, and *tsela*, 'rib', is also one of the appellations of the feminine *sefirah* of Malkhut in kabbalistic literature; see Cordovero, *Pardes rimonim*, pt. 23: 'Appellations', ch. 18, s.v. *tsela*. This, too, alludes to the fact that Christians place their trust in a woman, which, as Frank saw it, was the defining characteristic of the Christian faith.

[80] *Words of the Lord*, §1107; and see also §1307. Cardozo, too, while reaching entirely different conclusions regarding the identity and gender of the messiah, distinguishes between Christianity and Islam precisely on this point: 'The Christians bow down to the female, Miriam, whom they call Maria ... and they refer to her more than they refer to God ... The Ishmaelites only ever mention the male, for they have no regard for the female' (see above, n. 54). But while Frank categorizes Islam as a 'male' religion and Christianity as a 'female' one, on the basis of the objects of their respective devotions and their attitudes towards women, Cardozo makes an opposite distinction between the metaphysical roots of Christianity and Islam in the

Elsewhere, Frank berates the inferiority of women in Islam, as opposed to the chivalry displayed by Christian men, who show their respect for women, standing at the ready to serve them and curry favour with them:

Note well: among the Ishmaelites, there's no going near her or courting her, for to them a woman is an indentured servant, and no man pays her respect. But in this status [i.e. Christianity], the ladies and maidens are in charge. Even a great lord, when he stands before a lady, bares his head, stands before her like a servant, and pays her compliments.[81] Only here must we pursue her and take shelter under her wings.[82]

Christianity's superiority over both Islam and Judaism lies in the honoured and public place it allocates to women, and foremost among them the Holy Virgin—the Maiden—who is manifestly present within it, leading the faithful. Islam, on the other hand, imposes upon women, including the Maiden, the total concealment of their faces, while Judaism allows the Maiden to appear only as a kabbalistic symbol:

The Lord [Frank] cursed all those who considered the deeds of Ishmael, for there everything is covered and under wraps, and the women, too, cover their faces. But here, in the status of Edom [Christianity] . . . the women bare their hair and their breasts . . . and the name Shekhinah is not invoked, but rather the name Maiden [Holy Virgin], as is the practice of the people. And if, up to now, the name of the Maiden was whispered in secret, now it will be said in the open, and of a real Maiden, for the renewal of the world is to come from her.[83]

realm of the 'shells': Christianity, according to him, derives from the male Samael (Satan), while Islam derives from the snake, which the Zohar identifies with the female demon Lilith. On Cardozo's gendered conceptions of these two religions see Wolfson, 'Constructions of the Shekhinah', 29–34, esp. 31 n. 63.

[81] Frank became acquainted with the customs of Muslim society during his prolonged sojourns in various parts of the Ottoman empire. As for the chivalrous gestures displayed towards women within the Christian aristocracy, Frank became familiar with them through his personal contacts with the nobles and high-ranking clergy during his years in Częstochowa and in his courts at Brünn and Offenbach.   [82] *Words of the Lord*, §1175.

[83] Ibid., §1194 (§1195 in Fania Scholem's Hebrew version). In this context, 'the status of Edom' functions primarily in its usual Jewish sense as an allusion to Christianity, which Frank is pitting against Islam, referred to, again as usual, as 'Ishmael'. However, in other figures of speech used by Frank and his believers, 'Edom' becomes a reference to the particular 'religion' or 'knowledge' that he himself had initiated. This 'Edomite' religion found its abode within the domain of Christianity but did not entirely coincide with it and ultimately sought its demise. On the meaning of this term and its connections with the Sabbatian doctrines of Jonathan Eybeschuetz see Scholem, 'Redemption through Sin', 131–2 and 138–40; and Perlmutter, *Jonathan Eybeschuetz* (Heb.), 90–1 and 337–8.

In order to reach the Maiden, Frank had to bring his believers to the place where she took physical shape—the portrait of the Holy Virgin at Częstochowa—and do there as did the Christians, who openly, en masse, worshipped her icon: 'But we went to the place that is called hers, the place unto which almost half the world streams in order to bow down before her; there we sought her out and found her. She will direct all the worlds.'[84] Although his protracted sojourn at Częstochowa had been forced upon him arbitrarily, as a result of the decree of banishment and incarceration issued against him by the Polish authorities, he interpreted it after the fact as an act of will intended to draw him and his followers towards the divine Maiden concealed there within 'the painted board':

As you have it, *Puk haie ma amme daber*—'go out and take heed of what people are saying'.[85] So many lands and uncounted numbers of people speak of her. And you especially know what I told you already in Giurgiu,[86] that in Poland I would be locked up in prison. And who would undertake to be jailed for no reason? You also saw that I took all these trials upon myself, devotedly and without complaint. I did all this for the sake of her love. . . . I meant this for your own good, that I might bring you before her.[87]

In the years that followed the period of his incarceration, Frank gave vent more than once to his great regret at having missed the opportunity to bring about the Maiden's full manifestation during the time when he and his followers (who disappointed him by being of such little faith) stood at her very gates, that is, in the dwelling of the Virgin [Maiden] Mary, and her famous icon at Częstochowa:

Had you been with me wholeheartedly at Częstochowa, I would have dressed you in such garb as to astound the entire world. They would have known that these are not

---

[84] *Words of the Lord*, §982.

[85] This is how the Polish scribe transliterates the Aramaic saying cited in BT *Eruv.* 14*b* and elsewhere: *puk ḥazei mai ama devar*, 'Go out and see how the people conduct themselves.' Frank's translation is inaccurate, since *devar* in Aramaic means 'conduct', while he takes the word in the sense of the Hebrew *daber*—'talk'.

[86] Giurgiu is a town located on the border between Romania and Bulgaria, which was under Ottoman rule at the time. While resident in this region during 1757, Frank converted to Islam. See Balaban, *Frankist Movement* (Heb.), 193–4; and Levine, *Kronika*, 40–41 n. 50, and 42, §29 (Doktór, *Rozmaite adnotacje*, 54).

[87] *Words of the Lord*, §614. See also ibid., §776: 'At Częstochowa I ordered the whole group to come there. My intention was to bring them all before her.'

the works of men . . . The whole world would have feared you, and they would have declared that the Maiden, Mary, had clothed you in these garments. But now I don't know what to do with you. In order to bring you to her, I would need to go back to Częstochowa and spend days and years there. How is that possible?[88]

Nevertheless, Frank's very proximity to the icon at Częstochowa had brought some of the Maiden's power to rest upon him: 'She is the power of all powers. She is to direct all the worlds. Even now, though she [the supernal Maiden] is concealed beneath that other one [the Virgin Mary] whom I mentioned before, she nevertheless endows me with every power and guides me in all my paths.'[89] Again:

I commanded you and the whole group to journey to Częstochowa. Why did I do that? I'll explain it to you by way of a parable: once there was a king who had in his royal chamber a statue imbued with the power of the Virgin. When people arrived for judgement, the king would look at the statue, and she would indicate to him who was guilty and who was innocent. The whole land was astounded by his wisdom, but they did not know that all his actions derived from the statue at which the king always gazed. So I, too, brought all of you before her in Częstochowa, and she gave me signs as to who you are[90]

The collaboration described in the parable between the king sitting in judgement and the Virgin standing beside him in statuary form, intimating the verdict to be passed upon his subjects, seems to bear a relation to the description of Frank's collaboration with his daughter Eva, who 'saw that judgement was being passed upon the whole group' while 'the Lord stood aside'. It was said at the time of Eva herself, 'She needs no judgement passed upon her. She will be inscribed in the book of eternal life. And they said thrice to her: "To life, to life, to life".'[91]

Elsewhere, Frank sheds light upon Eva's appointment to the position of judge of the court, to whom all the faithful confessed their sins and who meted out punishment to each:

I set only Eva, your sister, over you, for you to confess before her and for her to punish you with two or three lashes . . . And when she would write that so-and-so had received his punishment, then that one would be free, for this was given into her hands.[92]

---

[88] *Words of the Lord*, §1217 (§1218 in Fania Scholem's Hebrew version).   [89] Ibid., §406.

[90] Ibid., §145.   [91] Ibid., §749; and see above, Ch. 6, at n. 52.

[92] Ibid., §1155. We cannot, however, be entirely sure that this Eva, here called 'your sister',

Indeed, there can be no doubt that the image of the Holy Virgin—the Madonna of Częstochowa and the divine Maiden who stood at her gate—gradually merged in Frank's consciousness with his virgin daughter Eva:

At Częstochowa, several Polish lords had gone to the chapel. Upon their return, they approached me. One of them was an honest man. He looked into the eyes of the Lady [Eva] and said to his companions, 'It seems much more reasonable to me that this is the Holy Mother and the true Virgin.' They thought he was merely joking.[93]

It could be that the merging of these feminine images, to the point of Eva's being conceived of as embodying them all, took place in response to a concatenation of circumstances that led to Frank's temporary isolation and, apparently, created a new, intense intimacy between him and his daughter. During the Russian siege of the fortress at Częstochowa and the battles that raged there until the forces of the Polish Confederation were defeated in August 1772,[94] most of Frank's followers fled the court in terror, notwithstanding Frank's strong disapproval. He did not forgive them their treachery: 'for a whole year, his people never saw the Lord. The Lord's wrath waxed ever greater.'[95] In the same period, his wife Hannah and his son Jacob died, and he sent his two remaining sons, Rochus and Josef, to safety in Warsaw, where

was the same as Frank's daughter Eva, who was ordinarily referred to as the Lady or the holy Maiden. It could be that the passage refers to Eva Jezierańska, one of the fourteen 'sisters' whom Frank chose at Iwanie. The *Kronika* (Levine, *Kronika*, 50, §42; 90–4, §§103–4 (Doktór, *Rozmaite adnotacje*, 58, 83–5), and p. 106, appendix) counts her among the seven 'additional' women who were chosen about a month after the first seven, and it states (on p. 50, §42) that 'Eva Jezierańska stood at their head'—that is, she enjoyed a certain seniority. On the other hand, both in the *Kronika* and in *Words of the Lord* (§§243 and 749), Eva Jezierańska is always referred to by her full name, and never, like the Eva in the present passage, by her first name alone. In all events, the notion of the Maiden as judge, whether embodied in the statue of the Virgin or in Eva Frank, with her ability to look into the hearts of the king's/her father's subjects and deliver their verdicts, almost certainly was inspired by the image of the kabbalistic *sefirah* of Malkhut as a righteous judge meting out reward and punishment to all created beings. On this see Tishby, *Wisdom of the Zohar*, i. 376. In *Sefer habahir* the lower divine female is described as 'the divine wisdom' bestowed by the Holy One upon Solomon, so that he could establish 'appropriate judgement' and 'judge [justly]'. See *Sefer habahir*, ed. Margaliot, 29–30, §§64–7; ed. Abrams, 141–3, §§44–5.

[93] *Words of the Lord*, §325. [94] On which see Kraushar, *Jacob Frank*, i. 237–42.
[95] *Kronika*, 76, §§80 and 81 (*Rozmaite adnotacje*, 73–4), which describes how the faithful who deserted Frank at that time were given the lash in punishment.

they were under the protection of his followers there.[96] Only his daughter Eva remained with him throughout the siege and the battles, and, as a comely young girl, she was apparently exposed to the danger of abduction by soldiers of the Confederation, who 'in November 1769 conceived a plot . . . against the Lady'.[97] Eva's unwavering loyalty transformed her status in Frank's eyes:

When Her Honour was in trouble in Częstochowa because of the Russians and the Confederacy, the Lord said to her: 'My daughter, everyone has deserted me: brothers, sisters, and the rest. Only you have remained to endure with me throughout all my years in prison. Therefore do I bless you that you will be the comeliest of women, and all of them will be as naught beside you.'[98]

But that appellation, 'the comeliest of women', is one of the appellations of the divine Maiden in Frank's parlance: 'Why were you not wholehearted and good enough for the comeliest of women to teach you, the way a mother teaches her children? Had the Maiden herself taught you, it would have been much better.'[99] The following commitment made by Frank also seems to belong in this context:

When my help shall come, I will purchase a lovely house and fit it out with lovely furnishings. I shall assign a lovely room to my daughter, may she live long; I shall garb her in regal clothing and precious stones. I shall let no one enter in unto me; I shall rejoice only with her, just she and I alone together. I shall walk about with her; we will dine together—perhaps when non-Jewish guests arrive they will eat with us—and I shall sit together with her day and night, and speak with her briefly about everything, so that she can come to know the greatness of our faith, for until today I have not spoken even one word with her. But during that time, I shall speak with no one but her, whether we are at home or on the road. I wish to make a human being of her, and she will undergo everything.[100]

---

[96] See *Kronika*, 74, §§77–9 (*Rozmaite adnotacje*, 73); and Kraushar, *Jacob Frank*, i. 238–9.

[97] *Kronika*, 74, §76 (*Rozmaite adnotacje*, 73), and see Kraushar's comments in *Jacob Frank*, i. 237.   [98] *Words of the Lord*, §60.

[99] Ibid., §481, and see also §§1066 and 1069. In kabbalistic, symbolic terms, 'the comeliest of women' is the *sefirah* of Hokhmah, 'Wisdom', as it manifests itself in Malkhut (see *Zohar ḥadash*, 'Song of Songs', 70b–71a). It is reasonable to suppose that Frank consciously invoked this appellation.

[100] *Words of the Lord*, §784. In light of these descriptions of the exclusive intimacy between Frank and his daughter Eva, and in the context of the incestuous conjugal relations that he instituted within the circles of the 'brothers' and 'sisters' at his court (above, Ch. 6, at n. 42), the possibility that Frank had intimate relations with her should not be ruled out, though there is no

Eva's identification with the 'true' Virgin, inspired by her connection to 'the Maiden Mary' and her icon, is implied, for example, in the distribution of Eva's portraits among the community of believers. The Polish *Kronika* reports that 'on 22 May [1777][101] the Lord ordered three portraits to be made of the Lady:[102] one for the brothers and the other two for Altona'.[103] One of those portraits was later described by Moses Porges in his memoir of the court at Offenbach as 'a portrait of the Lady, done up on the model of the Holy Virgin', which hung on the wall alongside 'various symbols of the Catholic Church'.[104] From Porges' account, it would even appear that the faithful called Eva, the Lady, by the oft-used designation of the Virgin Mary as the Holy Mother, and that it was she who stood at the centre of the court and was the focus of its cult.

The process by which the Eva to be seen in her portraits was merged with the depiction of Christianity's Holy Virgin-Mother,[105] with both of them conceived of as embodying the Maiden—the supernal redeemer—certainly began during Frank's lifetime. It was he who ordered the making and dissemination of the portraits of his daughter, and who promised his believers: 'I would have shown you the way . . . so that you could reach that Maiden. . . . And if I showed you the true portrait in which she will one day reveal herself to you, you would rejoice greatly.'[106]

explicit mention of this in the sources that have come down to us. On this see Rachel Elior's remarks in 'Jacob Frank and his Book' (Heb.), 530–40.

[101] According to the editor, the version of the *Kronika* that Kraushar had at his disposal included the missing notation of the year, during the period when Frank was living in Brünn. See Levine, *Kronika*, 84 n. 204.

[102] This certainly refers to Eva, and not to her mother who was referred to by the same title; these events took place some seven years after the death of the mother, Hannah, and the absence here of the Polish initials *ś.p* (indicating 'of sacred memory'), which follow most references to the mother Lady throughout the *Kronika*, indicates clearly that it was the living Lady Eva who was to be the subject of the portraits.

[103] *Kronika*, 84, §96 (*Rozmaite adnotacje*, 79).

[104] Porges, 'Memoirs of Moses Porges', trans. Gelber, col. 273 (in this version the portrait is likened to that of the Holy Mother's); Mandel, *Militant Messiah*, 161. This passage is omitted from the published German version ('Eine Wallfahrt'), perhaps for fear that the comparison of Eva's likeness to that of the Holy Virgin might be taken by Christians as offensive.

[105] Porges, 'Eine Wallfahrt', p. 122, col. 2; id., 'Memoirs of Moses Porges', trans. Gelber, col. 273; Mandel, *Militant Messiah*, 160.   [106] *Words of the Lord*, §327.

In several of his parables, Frank expressed the importance he attributed to the portrait in providing a concrete manifestation of the concealed Maiden and demonstrating her very existence:

As I have told you, the Maiden sits in a tower, but neither she nor the tower can be seen. So, when she desires to be visible to her lover, she shows him a portrait of herself through the window, and he, when he finds that picture, guesses and knows that the Maiden is there.[107]

Frank repeatedly emphasized that the Maiden, the tower, and the portrait should not be taken as allegorical references to abstract supernal forces, but that they existed in concrete reality, in this world, though they were concealed from those who lacked sufficient desire for them:

How could you have failed to understand what I said?! I told you that there is a tower where the Maiden conceals herself, and to anyone whom she sees toiling for her with all his might, she will toss her portrait. By this he knows where she is to be found, and he will not move until he reaches her. *And I did not relate all this to you in spirit or in heaven, but openly, on this earth. For there is a Maiden, and there is a tower, and there is a picture called a portrait*, but you did not heed my words, and now you will be sorry.[108]

This marvellous ability of the seemingly inanimate portrait to concretize the Virgin and exercise her power in the world could also be inferred from the stories told by Christians of the power of their Holy Virgin's portrait:

A lord once told me: 'If you wish to convert to Christianity, I will show you some amazing things here in Wallachia. In one place where that portrait is, when good people come to visit, the picture flies to meet them and makes them welcome. This marvel was shown to two Turks, and they immediately converted to Christianity.'[109]

Not only the portrait, but also the ritual of ceremonial gestures which the faithful were instructed to perform when they presented themselves to Eva demonstrate her regal status at Frank's court and hint at her amalgamation with the figure of the supernal Maiden, the Queen of Heaven who ruled all the worlds. Frank's instructions to his faithful, intended to prepare them for their future meeting with the concealed Maiden, included the following: 'Fall

---

[107] *Words of the Lord*, §507. Scholem, in a rare note to his wife's translation ('Sefer divrei ha'adon', n. 2 to §255), points out the resemblance between Frank's parable of the Maiden in the tower and the Zohar's parable of the Beloved concealed in her palace, who reveals her face for fleeting moments to her lover as he circles her house (Zohar, ii. 99*a*), referring to the revelation of the Torah to those who love her.

[108] Ibid., §1001. Emphasis added.   [109] Ibid., §1005.

upon your face, and without looking at her countenance, kiss the ground . . .
She will say, "Approach me." Approach and kiss her feet, but not her hands.'
Only at a later stage, once their credentials had been fully established, might
the faithful be permitted to proceed further: 'She will say to you, "Brother!"
Only then may you kiss her hand.'[110] Just so does Porges describe his first
encounter with the Lady Eva, soon after his arrival in Offenbach: 'I dared not
look at the Lady's face. I got down on my knees and kissed her feet, as I had
been directed.'[111] Only on the eve of his flight from the court, after he had won
her trust and affection, was he able to kiss her hand.[112] So, it transpires, did
the faithful behave towards Eva during Frank's lifetime. As he related, 'A rich
young lord once came to me in Częstochowa and sought permission to bow
down before Her Honour and kiss her feet.'[113]

Moreover, Frank said of the divine Maiden: 'Just as nobly born ladies and
maidens surround a queen to serve her, so too are her ladies and maidens in the
divinity; each of them is a queen, and they serve her.'[114] So, too, did Frank
surround Eva, when she was still a child, with 'the young maidens of the Lady
Hawaczunia [his Polish pet name for her, derived from Hava—Eva]', who
included not only little girls but also married women from among the noblest
of the Frankist families.[115] Even as a baby, Frank saw her as a queen:

The Lord spoke to Osman in Nikopol about Her Honour, who was then 1½ years old:
'Look at my daughter; know that she is a queen; nor should you take it into your head
that I have designated her as a queen on account of her beauty, no: she is actually, without any doubt, in her very essence—a queen.'[116]

At this early stage, it seems that he did not yet attribute to her the qualities of
the redemptive divine Maiden. Once she had come of age, however, he alluded
clearly to her unique status as the embodiment of the supernal Maiden by
attributing to her the same supernatural qualities that distinguished the
Maiden and her divine entourage: inestimable beauty, splendour like that of
the sun, the power of rejuvenation, and immortality. Thus, for example, in a

---

[110] Ibid., §314.

[111] Porges, 'Eine Wallfahrt', p. 122, col. 2–p. 123, col. 1; id., 'Memoirs of Moses Porges', trans.
Gelber, col. 274; Mandel, *Militant Messiah*, 161.

[112] Porges, 'Eine Wallfahrt', p. 123, col. 2; id., 'Memoirs of Moses Porges', trans. Gelber, col.
280; Mandel, *Militant Messiah*, 165.   [113] *Words of the Lord*, §329.   [114] Ibid., §378.

[115] *Kronika*, 67–8, §66 (*Rozmaite adnotacje*, 68–9).   [116] *Words of the Lord*, §9.

rebuke to his believers, he reminds them that had they adhered rigorously to his strictures,

That Maiden herself would have requested that you come to me. You would have con- ducted yourselves as I had instructed you earlier, until you were found worthy of seeing her face to face . . . I would have commanded you to ask three things of her, which she would have granted you: first, immortality; rejuvenation to the age of 20; and splen- dour of countenance like that of the sun.[117]

Frank made similar comments about the qualities of the fourteen supernal 'sisters' who surrounded the Holy Maiden in the divinity:

There are seven and another seven, and all are within the divinity. They call each other sisters, and death does not pertain to them. When they reach the age of 100, they bathe in water and go back to being 16. . . . But no one has ever attained her beauty.[118]

I appointed women to serve her, as in the time of Esther, who was given seven women from the king's palace [cf. Esther 2: 9], but I appointed seven and another seven women, as there are in the entourage of the Big Brother. [Had] I sent them to a certain place, they would have bathed there at the well and arisen from it as though they were 15 years old for beauty and for strength.[119]

She herself and all those who are with her will shine like the splendour of the sun.[120]

Similarly, he says explicitly of his adult daughter Eva: 'When my help comes, in another six weeks, you will see of my daughter, may she be well, how her years will be rejuvenated, and she will be like a girl of 15 and will shine like the splendour of the sun.'[121]

Eva herself had a dream about this which was recorded in *Words of the Lord*, affording us a rare, fleeting glimpse of what went on in her own mind. The dream reveals some of her misgivings about the lofty role designated for her by her father,[122] but she received reassurance from the mysterious figure of a

---

[117] *Words of the Lord*, §432.   [118] Ibid., §377.   [119] Ibid., §604.   [120] Ibid., §609.

[121] Ibid., §1024. Frank's association of the rejuvenation of the females—his daughter, the Maiden, and her female companions, both heavenly and earthly—with the coming of the redemption may have its origin in *Pirkei derabi eli'ezer*, ch. 45, where women are said to have been promised rejuvenation 'like the new moon' as their reward in the World to Come, for hav- ing refused to contribute their gold earrings to the construction of the golden calf (on this com- mon midrashic theme, see e.g. *Num. Rabbah*, 21: 11). See also *Tikunei hazohar*, §18, 36*b*, where the renewal of the moon, symbolizing the female *sefirah* Malkhut, in the messianic future is associated with the verse 'thy youth is renewed like the eagle's' (Ps. 103: 5).

[122] Among other things, she admits: 'I feared that I would never wed a man'—an innocent, touching concern for an aging virgin of about 30; Eva was born in October 1754 (see *Kronika*, 32,

heavenly old man who appeared in the dream and confirmed that all her hopes would be realized:

On 24 November[123] in the year [17]84, the Lady had a dream: 'I saw an old, bearded man lying down . . . half dead, half alive . . . "Be not abashed or afraid of me", he said. "Come hither." I approached . . . He declared his thanks to God: "Happy am I, that I have merited seeing you face to face. . . . You will renew your youth, and your beauty will glow like the splendour of the sun." I asked: "How many years will I live?" He answered me: "Though you will grow old, you will renew your youth and become young again."'[124]

Frank hints further at the assimilation of his daughter in the figure of the supernal Maiden when he projects Eva's dependence on the community of the faithful, who bore the burden of supporting the court and were expected to provide her with all her earthly needs, upon the situation of the Maiden, who was similarly dependent on their material support. According to him, the Maiden had not received all she needed from the faithful, and was therefore cast into a state of 'poverty and lowliness':[125]

I said to you, you will be the heralds; 'Rejoice greatly, O daughter of Zion!' [Zech. 9: 9],[126] 'him shall the nations seek' [Isa. 11: 10],[127] 'Let all the nations gather together'

§5; *Rozmaite adnotacje*, 48), and she had the dream in September or November 1784. Her fear was allayed by a promise that she would marry her heart's chosen, who had been designated for her 'from the creation of the world', and would bear him four sons, in whom she would take 'true joy'. These promises all proved false, for Eva remained a virgin until her dying day. They express natural hopes of marriage and motherhood; indeed, it is hard to believe that Eva, at least in her youth, had no longings for ordinary family life. Ultimately, however, she seems to have internalized her father's vision and taken upon herself the role of the messianic Virgin, as would appear from all the above-cited descriptions of her court at Offenbach.

[123] This is how the date appears in the Polish edition. In Fania Scholem's translation it is given as 21 September.　　　　　　　　　　　　[124] *Words of the Lord*, §1168.

[125] On the financial crises that struck Frank's court at various times as a result of waning donations, and on Frank's efforts to get out of them, see e.g. *Kronika*, 90–2, §103 (*Rozmaite adnotacje*, 83–4).

[126] Frank quoted this verse frequently (see e.g. below, at nn. 182–3 and 193), apparently following the Zohar, which sees in it an allusion to the *sefirah* of Malkhut (see e.g. Zohar, iii. 69*a*) and also following the Christian tradition that sees it as referring to the Holy Virgin Mary, who, precisely because she was a Hebrew woman, could symbolize the continuity between the Old and New Testaments and the transfer of the firstborn status from the Children of Israel to the Christian Church (see Pelikan, *Mary through the Centuries*, 28 and 34). 'Daughter of Zion' was one of Frank's most frequent appellations of the Maiden.

[127] Fania Scholem's translation paraphrases the Hebrew verse so that its biblical origin is no longer recognizable, but the Polish version (§1245) discloses it.

[Isa. 43: 9]—that is, unto me, since I am her guard. But I also wanted to make lords of you. . . . And that would have been quite natural, because you would have brought great treasures from the ends of the earth and purchased estates, and you would have been lords. But now she is in a state of poverty and lowliness. And I thought that you would provide for her.[128]

Similarly, he relates how he ordered two of his followers to pay off his daughter Eva's debts and save her from a financial crisis brought upon her by 'instigators'.[129]

The amalgamation of these feminine figures—the Virgin Mary, taken as the 'shell' that surrounds the fruit and gives access to it,[130] and the Maiden concealed within her, who is the embodiment of the divine *sefirah* of Malkhut —into the figure of one flesh-and-blood woman, Frank's virgin daughter Eva, said to be the messiah, was not so easily accepted as an article of faith. We have already noted the existence of testimonies showing that the believers regarded this as a rather peculiar and startling innovation. Even *Words of the Lord* contains echoes of the opposition aroused amongst them by the tidings of a female messiah: 'So you, too, accustomed as you are to your [Jewish] madness, even when you went over to another status [Christianity], you did not forget your folly. You said that the messiah would be of the male sex, and other such crazy things.'[131]

It is clear that even after their conversion to Christianity, the believers remained in the grip of the Jewish norms to which they had been raised to conform, and they had trouble digesting Frank's new concept of the messianic role of the redemptive Maiden, just as they had trouble transgressing their Jewish laws and customs, no matter how often Frank told them off for the sinfulness or 'craziness' of their adherence to traditional practice.[132] Even so, from the time that Frank conceived the idea that the redemptive Maiden was embodied in his daughter, her figure began to appear with great frequency in

---

[128] *Words of the Lord*, §1245 (§1246 in Fania Scholem's Hebrew version).   [129] See ibid., §1125.

[130] See below, n. 213 and the text there.

[131] *Words of the Lord*, §1210 (§1211 in Fania Scholem's Hebrew version).

[132] See e.g. ibid., §§420, 450, 477, 805, 820, 887, 923, 953, 977, and 1316. See also §2240, which is missing from Fania Scholem's Hebrew translation but which appears in Doktór's Polish edition (*Księga Słów Pańskich*, ii. 142), and is quoted in Kraushar, *Jacob Frank*, ii. 288, where Frank reports one of his dreams: 'On 7 February 1784, I saw that I was standing outside Adam Krępowiecki's door and heard him teaching Jewish prayers to a small child. When he saw me he jumped away to escape so I would not scold him.' Cf. Kraushar's discussion of this, ibid. 293.

his addresses to his followers, rivalling that of the Big Brother—the super-human, omnipotent male entity construed at the start of his career as his alter ego in the supernal realms, alluding to his own divinely messianic role. Although the compilation of his speeches that has come down to us was not edited methodically, and most of it is undated,[133] it certainly includes tradi-tions pertaining not only to Frank's last years in Brünn and Offenbach, dur-ing which the speeches were recorded and collected, but to his entire long career. We can thus chart the Maiden's first appearance and the progress of her increasing dominance in his mind, by comparing his early doctrines, apparently developed during the 1750s and 1760s—particularly during his stay in Iwanie in 1758/9, which is often mentioned as a significant point of depar-ture[134]—with the doctrines he began to formulate towards the end of the period of his incarceration at Częstochowa, in 1770–2.

Frank himself was aware of the novelty of the redemptive Maiden's appear-ance in his vision and even acknowledged her total absence from it during his earlier sojourn in Iwanie, when he still envisioned the advent of redemption as the manifestation of the male entity referred to as 'King' or simply 'God':

I said to you several times at Iwanie: 'Not by wind and not by fire, but by a still small voice after the fire—there comes the King.' . . . You should have understood the inti-mation that the King was about to arrive here. And so also did I tell you that I would show you God. *But it was never said that what I meant to show you was the Maiden.*[135]

Indeed, there are teachings scattered throughout *Words of the Lord* in which no mention is made of the supernal Maiden, Virgin, or Queen, and the redemp-tive process still focuses on the single male figure of the Big Brother, who is intimately connected to his human counterpart, Jacob Frank himself. In these teachings, the supernatural powers and the roles later ascribed to the divine Maiden are all attributed to the Big Brother or to his earthly embodiment, Frank. Thus, for example, he mentions to his associates that 'then', namely, in the Iwanie period, 'when I appointed you as brothers and sisters, the Big Brother rejoiced greatly, he and all his household';[136] the absence of the

[133] On the circumstances of the redaction of the various manuscripts, most of which seem to have their origin in the Brünn and Offenbach periods of the Frankist court, see the remarks (in English) of the editor of the Polish edition of *Words of the Lord*, Jan Doktór, in *Księga Słów Pań skich*, ii. 157–9; and see Shmeruk, 'The Peregrinations' (Heb.); Maciejko, 'The Literary Character', 175–95.   [134] On this period see Kraushar, *Jacob Frank*, i. 112–26.
[135] *Words of the Lord*, §1159. Emphasis added.   [136] Ibid., §415.

supernal Maiden from the household and from the whole event is glaring. In other traditions which are explicitly linked to the Iwanie period and before it, as opposed to the traditions dating to the later Częstochowa period, it was the manifestation of the Big Brother, not that of the Maiden, that Frank and his faithful anticipated:

Were I to send you to the Big Brother, he would come to me, as it is written, 'Lo, your king comes to you' [Zech. 9: 9];[137] he is half a mile tall, and the whole world would see that this is an awesome God. . . . Of him I declared to the faithful in Iwanie: 'As you can see the sun, so shall I show you God.'[138]

The redemptive figure is still in the male image of the King Messiah—'All the kings of the world shall bend their knees and declare: "Before thee, our King Messiah!"'[139]—identified, following the Zohar, with the primordial Adam or the biblical Jacob, whom the kabbalistic tradition associates with Adam and his messianic dimension,[140] and with whom Frank, as his namesake, often identified in his sermons:

A good thing was made ready for the First Adam, but on account of his sin he was not able to attain it. Someone must come in the form of Adam and attempt to achieve the level on which Adam [stood], and then he will arrive at that thing which was made ready for Adam, and all those who follow him will achieve this level, for the fear of them will fall upon all the wild beasts of the earth. But all this will not come to pass until a certain thing is in hand, as it is written, 'What have you in the house?' [2 Kgs 4: 2]. It is also necessary to don a garment with the help of which the beasts will become fearful. Look: Jacob had to don that garment just to obtain the blessing. All the more so [is it needed] now, when one must openly gain dominion over the beasts.[141]

---

[137] As we saw above, Frank was wont to cite the first part of this verse—'Rejoice greatly, O daughter of Zion!'—in connection with the messianic advent of the Maiden (see n. 126 above), but here he focuses rather on its second part as heralding the advent of the male King Messiah.

[138] *Words of the Lord*, §384.   [139] Ibid., §445.

[140] See Kimelman, *Mystical Meaning* (Heb.), 172–3.

[141] *Words of the Lord*, §518. This passage appears to be based on the vision of the End of Days in the seventh chapter of the book of Daniel and on Zohar, i. 145b–146a, which interprets the words 'and behold, with the clouds of heaven there came one like a son of Adam' (Dan. 7: 13) as a reference to 'the King Messiah'. This is the same passage in the Zohar that goes on to assert: 'On this account, the world will continue to exist until a man comes who is like Adam and a woman who is like Eve'; (cf. above, at nn. 20–1). Chapter 7 of Daniel is the vision of the four great beasts—the four great powers that rule the world, but which lose their dominion one after the other, until the End of Days, when dominion will be given over to the one who is 'like a son of

It was Frank himself, unaided by the Maiden's mediation, who would lead his believers to redemption: 'I wanted to bring you to eternal life, to take you out of the place to which Adam fell and bring you to the place to which Adam was told to go.'[142] Frank, not the Maiden, girds his sword to take on the role of the 'divine gatekeeper':

And furthermore, I say unto you: 'Without me, none can approach or enter before God. I shall allow whomsoever I wish to enter, and whomsoever I do not wish, will not go in.' The Lord said these things in Poland in the year 1756. And he added: I am the divine gatekeeper, and should I not wish to let someone enter unto God, then even if God desires him, I shall hurl him 400 parasangs away. And if I should desire someone and select him, even against God's will, I shall appease and entreat Him until He lets that person enter.[143]

Again: 'You heard me say already in 1756 that I am the divine gatekeeper. And when I arrived in Iwanie in [17]59, I said that I would show you God. You should have deduced from this that mine is the power and the dominion, and God has elected me.'[144] And yet, once he proclaimed the manifestation of the divine Maiden at Częstochowa, she became the gateway to God, and only by way of her could one reach His abode: 'How could you have failed to understand, when I told you that I would show you God, that it was necessary, first

Adam'. The Zohar's expansion of this theme connects it with the figure of Jacob, who outwitted his brother Esau (by means of a 'garment', as Frank put it), won his father's blessing, and postponed its complete fulfilment until the Time to Come—the time of the King-Messiah. If Frank did draw this amalgam of motifs—the advent of the redeemer 'in the form of Adam', the need to 'openly gain dominion over the beasts', and Jacob's deceit so as 'to obtain the blessing'—from Zohar, i. 145*b*–146*a* and the verses from Daniel woven into it, this would buttress the supposition that he had not yet thought of the female figure of the redemptive Maiden. If he had, the Zohar would have provided him not only with the male messiah in the form of Adam, but also with his female mate, 'a woman who is like Eve', who could easily have been identified with the figure of the Maiden. Had Frank already in that period envisioned the manifestation of a female messiah, one would have expected him to connect her with the Eve-like woman mentioned by the Zohar, but he pays no attention to this female messianic figure and looks only to the one who comes 'in the form of Adam'. For a similar combination of the same motifs see also ibid., §628. But cf. also ibid., §§666 and 1291, and below, at nn. 265–72, for other, presumably later, speeches by Frank that refer to the same passage from the Zohar and dwell explicitly upon the 'woman in the form of Eve'.

[142] *Words of the Lord*, §496.   [143] Ibid., §955.

[144] Ibid., §958. Cf. §§1105 and 1124, where Frank again refers to himself as the gateway to God or as having the ability to pass his believers through that gateway.

of all, to discover the Maiden! For it is she who is before God; she is the gate-way to God. Only by way of her can one arrive at and reach Him.'[145]

Early in his career, Frank also attributed exclusively to the Big Brother the ability to grant a person supernatural powers, including those of rejuvenation and immortality:

So would I ask of the Big Brother to bestow upon me the gift of a mountain from his land, three miles high, and for it to fulfil all my wishes, that the earth and the trees would be of pure gold. . . . And so would I ask of him a certain herb from his land which has the power to renew one's years, not such as to make you like a 15-year-old, but a herb that restores one to the age of 20. So would I ask of him a well in which a man of 100 who washes would have his youth renewed. . . . He would do this for my sake.[146]

From the Częstochowa period, however, Frank, as we have seen, attributes the very same capacity to the Maiden and her supernal entourage: 'I would have commanded you to ask three things of her: first, immortality; rejuvenation to the age of 20; and splendour of countenance like that of the sun.'[147] His vision of the egalitarian family of 'brothers' and 'sisters' in the supernal world, that mythical 'household' of the Big Brother corresponding to his own earthly 'family' of 'brothers' and 'sisters, first conceived in the beginning of his messianic career at Iwanie,[148] was now developing in a new direction, focusing on the status of the 'sisters': 'His retinue, the Lord said, consists of twelve brothers and fourteen sisters, and these sisters are bedfellows for the brothers. All the women are queens, because there, the women rule the kingdom.'[149]

From the time when the Maiden was first revealed to him at Częstochowa, a transformation occurred in Jacob Frank's conception of his messianic mission. Only then did it become clear to him that the embodiment of the divinity in flesh and blood, as the messiah had been conceived of from the earliest stages of the Sabbatian movement in several of its branches,[150] could come

---

[145] *Words of the Lord*, §620. See also ibid., §580 for the identification of the Maiden with the *sefirah* of Malkhut, one of whose appellations is 'gateway'.   [146] Ibid., §414.

[147] Ibid., §432, and see also §§605, 801, and 818.   [148] See above, Ch. 6, at nn. 25–6.

[149] *Words of the Lord*, §677, which has not survived in the versions that have come down to us but was available to Kraushar, who quoted it in his book. See Kraushar, *Jacob Frank*, ii. 307 and n. 21.

[150] On Sabbatianism's deification of the messiah, either by way of his rising to the level of divinity (apotheosis) or by way of the embodiment of the divinity in human flesh (incarnation), in connection either with the *sefirah* of Tiferet or with the *sefirot* of Yesod or Malkhut, see Scholem, *Sabbatai Sevi*, 608, 797–8, 835–6, 870–2, and 913–6; id., *Researches* (Heb.), 362–74;

about only by way of the manifestation of the feminine powers of the divine in a human female. The feminine powers of the godhead—particularly the female *sefirah* of Malkhut, the 'lowest' boundary of the divine realm,[151] from which the soul of the messiah was derived[152]—were much more closely and more directly associated with the physical world below than were the masculine powers situated 'above' her. This association was the key to redemption, for the redemption was envisaged as the merger of the Upper and Lower Worlds,[153] and the place where they touched was precisely the domain over which the divine female had charge. No wonder, then, that with the dawn of the messianic age, the divinity that was becoming embodied and manifest was the divinity in its feminine aspect. It had to take shape in a body that conformed to this aspect in every detail, for by this means alone could its inherent femininity come to full realization. The feminine powers thus had to be manifested in the figure of a real woman, in the same way as they did in the human manifestation of Christianity's Holy Virgin,[154] and not in the figure of a man who was only 'secretly a woman', in whom the feminine powers were merely intimated without coming to complete expression. Such, as we have seen, was that 'First One', Sabbatai Zevi, whose physical masculinity was incompatible with the feminine origin and nature of his messianic soul. This, combined with his turn towards Islam, a religion for males alone, is what prevented him from fulfilling his messianic promise.

The divine Maiden's first self-revelation—personal, tangible, and made exclusively to him in his own room in Częstochowa—was, for Frank, a formative, defining experience:

Wirszubski, *Between the Lines* (Heb.), 185–6; Nadav, 'Kabbalistic Treatise' (Heb.), 318–26; Liebes, *On Sabbatianism* (Heb.), 69, 88–91, 140–6, 190, and 289 n. 180; and Elqayam, 'Mystery of Faith' (Heb.), 33, 152–63, and 222–4.

[151] On the liminality of the *sefirah* of Malkhut and its implications regarding the special bond between Malkhut and the Lower Worlds see Scholem, 'Shekhinah', 164, 167–8, 171–3, and *passim*; and Tishby, *Wisdom of the Zohar*, i. 372.   [152] See above, nn. 58–9 and n. 65.

[153] On the tangible expressions of this merger in Frank's vision of redemption, in the form of a 'chiastic' sexual mating between the divine 'brothers' and the human 'sisters' and between the divine 'sisters' and the human 'brothers', see above, Ch. 6, at nn. 15–20.

[154] On the status of Mary, a flesh-and-blood woman who gave birth to God and so endowed him with the embodied, human dimension of his existence, making her a vital element in the Christian doctrine of the Incarnation, see e.g. Warner, *Alone of All Her Sex*, 15, 45, 59, 65–6, and 200–1; Brown, *Body and Society*, 175; Atkinson, *Oldest Vocation*, 102, 107–8, 110–11, 115, and 124; and Pelikan, *Mary through the Centuries*, 48–52, 55–65, 130–1, 145, and 157.

That is the meaning of the verse, 'from my flesh I will see God' [Job 19: 26], as is customary in the world and particularly in Edom [i.e. among the Christians].[155] She had never revealed herself to a soul, and her dwelling is unknown. Yet to me she appeared in my room at Częstochowa, and I showed her your likenesses.[156]

From here on Frank conceived of the supernal Maiden in her embodied human form as the true messiah of Israel, who must, of necessity, be of the female sex. Only in and through her could the kabbalistic *sefirah* of Malkhut actualize her messianic potencies. As we have seen, she was the 'gateway' to God.[157] According to Frank, 'every hue is to be found in her; each person will see her in a different colour';[158] she is the 'head',[159] and the highest judge;[160] 'she has dominion over all, even the depths of the sea';[161] 'she is the life of all the worlds,[162] and she shall lead the children of Israel';[163] 'she is the power of all powers,[164] and she will lead all the worlds';[165] she is the 'essence',[166] which is 'a Maiden—the one who will be the true messiah. She shall direct all the worlds, for all the weaponry is given into her hands.'[167] 'For she is the Matronita, guardian of Israel—armed commander of the army of the Holy One, Blessed be He.'[168]

'When the bloodshed commences, the verse "shake yourself from the dust" [Isa. 52: 2] shall be fulfilled. Then she will rise up with all her maids.'[169] This bloodshed, as Frank envisaged it, was simultaneously an apocalyptic echo of

[155] The translation here is based on the punctuation in the Polish edition rather than in Fania Scholem's Hebrew version, which distorts the meaning. Frank seems to interpret the verse from Job in the Christian sense of seeing God manifested in flesh and blood. That is how the Maiden was revealed to him in his room in Częstochowa. [156] *Words of the Lord*, §1175.

[157] See above, Ch. 6, at nn. 12–13, and this chapter, at n. 145.

[158] *Words of the Lord*, §847. This quality, too, distinguishes the *sefirah* of Malkhut. See Cordovero, *Pardes rimonim*, pt. 10: 'The Colours', ch. 4.

[159] See above, n. 78, and see also *Words of the Lord*, §1140. [160] See above, at nn. 91–2.

[161] *Words of the Lord*, §605. For the appellation 'sea' as an allusion to the *sefirah* of Malkhut see e.g. Zohar, i. 86a, 236b, 267b; ii. 56b, 226a; iii. 58a.

[162] On the designation of the *sefirah* of Malkhut as 'eternal life of the worlds [*ḥei ha'olamim*], for she gives life to all the worlds that emanate from her' see Cordovero, *Pardes rimonim*, pt. 23: 'Appellations', ch. 8, s.v. *ḥai/ḥei* (life), at the end of the entry. [163] *Words of the Lord*, §1118.

[164] For the designation of the *sefirah* of Malkhut as 'power' (*ko'aḥ*) see e.g. Zohar, i. 196b; iii. 220a–b. [165] *Words of the Lord*, §406.

[166] For the appellation 'essence' (*ikar*) as an allusion to the *sefirah* of Malkhut see e.g. Zohar, i. 154a. [167] *Words of the Lord*, §1051.

[168] See above, Ch. 6, at n. 66. [169] *Words of the Lord*, §782.

the coming wars at the End of Days and an allusion to the zoharic myth of the doe in the throes of an obstructed birth, whose womb was burst open by the bite of a snake. In the Zohar, the doe (*ayalta*) refers to the *sefirah* of Malkhut and the mystery of redemption, while the snake is a symbol of the *sitra aḥra*, the evil Other Side; but the Sabbatians, in frequent references to this myth from the movement's earliest stages, identified the snake with the figure of the messiah, as they inferred from the equivalent numerical values of the words *naḥash* (snake) and *mashiaḥ* (messiah).[170] In his apocalyptic vision of the Maiden's rise, which would take place 'after the bloodshed'—with the cessation of the wars of the End of Days—Frank stresses the critical difference between her messianic drive, which leads to enduring redemption, and the abortive endeavour of Sabbatai Zevi, in whose wake 'everything went back to being as it was before':

On the day when she shall arise, some thirty thousand lords will die, and many will go mad. Kings will collapse, and the soldiers will drop their arms in fright, for on that day their fortunes will change and collapse . . . After the bloodshed, when she shall arise, water will go forth, and the company will drink, and all the world will drink,[171] and the war will cease—not as you said [about what] the First One [did] in another land [Turkey], [which happened] while you suffered [the Chmielnicki massacres and their aftermath] in Poland. Is that how it should be? What benefit came of all those

[170] On this motif in the Zohar and its roots in the midrashic literature see Berger, '*Ayalta*', and see Liebes' discussion of its sources and the various forms it took in Sabbatian texts in *On Sabbatianism* (Heb.), 177–8. For an analysis of the same motif in Lurianic kabbalah see Meroz, 'Redemption in Lurianic Teaching' (Heb.), 306–15.

[171] The linkage of the bloodshed to the waters that will slake the world's thirst derives from the Zohar's account of the doe:

When the world is in need of rain, all the rest of the animals gather around her, and she ascends to the summit of a high mountain, lowers her head between her knees and bays, over and over, and that is the significance of the verse, 'like a gazelle thirsting for streams of water' [Ps. 42: 2]. What is the meaning of 'streams of water' here? These are the streams of water that have dried up, and the world is parched, and so she thirsts. She becomes pregnant, but she is blocked up. When the time comes for her to give birth, she bays and howls, over and over. . . . And the Holy One, Blessed be He, hears her and comes to her aid. He calls forth a huge serpent from deep within the mountains of darkness, and he advances through the mountains, licking the dust. He reaches that gazelle, draws nigh, and bites her twice in that certain place. The first time, blood spurts out, and he licks it up. The second time, water spurts out, and all those beasts that are in the mountains drink, and she opens up and gives birth. (Zohar, iii. 249*b*)

troubles? Everything went back to being as it was before. But you did not have anywhere to direct that thing, and so you turned it into a spiritual force. But here everything will happen in the open, and your own eyes will see it.[172]

The Maiden is thus the true messiah, and 'all know that they will be saved by her';[173] 'from her the world will grow'[174] and emerge in its new, redeemed state: 'Everyone will see the place from which the world will begin afresh—from her.'[175]

It might seem that Frank's conception of the Maiden as the incarnation of the divinity in a female messiah would clash with his own divine–messianic male self-awareness. One might even have expected that his allusions to the redemptive mission of his daughter would undermine his own standing among the believers and reduce him to the secondary, inferior status of mere messianic facilitator. But this did not happen. Frank saw himself, and presented himself to his court, as the exclusive mediator between the Maiden and her faithful, leading them gloriously on her behalf and at her command until such time as she would manifest herself openly to all. In a dated statement from the year 1784,[176] during his sojourn in Brünn, he recalled: 'Already when I was in jail,[177] she gave me signs to do with you what I intended to do.'[178] To be sure, the relationship between them was rather complex, since each was invested with both an overt human identity, as, respectively, Jacob Frank and his daughter Eva, and a currently covert divine identity, suggested by their respective associations with the Big Brother and the supernal Maiden. The hierarchical relations between the two worked themselves out on both levels,

[172] *Words of the Lord*, §831. See further §1254 (§1255 in Fania Scholem's Hebrew version), which also echoes the Zohar's account of the doe: 'By the time the cry of the bloodshed had spread abroad, the world would be filled with blood, for blood is required first of all; blood is required before she can come out into the world. As you know very well, the blood will spurt first from the doe, and afterwards... etc.'. The Aramaic word *ayalta*, doe, is transliterated in the Polish text.   [173] *Words of the Lord*, §102.
[174] Ibid., §1194 (§1195 in Fania Scholem's Hebrew version).   [175] Ibid., §849.
[176] Ibid., §410; Fania Scholem's Hebrew version reads: 'In the year 1784, on the first of April', while the Polish edition gives the date as 1 October in the same year.
[177] This is how Frank often referred to his years of incarceration in Częstochowa, and it is reasonable to suppose that here, too, he is referring to that period, though he had also been imprisoned briefly at several earlier times in his life. On his incarceration in Lanckorona, in Wielchowiec, and in Kopczyńce in 1756 see Levine, *Kronika*, 36–40, §§17, 18, 20, 21, and 23 (Doktór, *Rozmaite adnotacje*, 50–2); and see Kraushar, *Jacob Frank*, i. 85–6.
[178] *Words of the Lord*, §410.

so that each had a twofold relationship with the other. Thus, at times he is depicted as her faithful servant and emissary, subject in all ways to her command: 'I must do her bidding. . . . I have told you that I am her emissary, and what she tells me I must do.'[179] At others, however, he speaks as the master, giving her commands and dictating her actions: 'When this Maiden manifests herself, I shall have to send her to bathe in a certain place.'[180] At times he is described as sacrificing himself and suffering greatly on her behalf: 'I acquired a carriage drawn by six horses so as to drive around like a great lord, to demonstrate that for the sake of her love I am willing to forgo even this, to be like a lord, and it was pleasant for me to sit in jail. . . . I relinquished it all and went to prison for her sake.'[181] At still other times he emphasizes their common fate, in that they both suffer persecution and torment on account of their followers' paucity of faith:

When the verse 'Rejoice greatly, O daughter of Zion . . . Lo, your king comes to you' [Zech. 9: 9] shall be fulfilled, you will see how he always suffered and sacrificed himself, and she, too, suffered greatly.[182]

I shall tell only to you the verse 'Rejoice greatly, O daughter of Zion'. And I have something else to tell, but I cannot, and I am most bitter on this account. She, too, suffers great bitterness. If you knew how much she suffered, you would faint. When this thing will be revealed, you will know how great is her distress, and all because of you; how could you presume to follow your own minds?[183]

As I am persecuted, so she, too, is persecuted.[184]

And now that you have gone away, she said to me: 'Look! The people you chose have crumpled and not endured!' She wept, and I wept with her.[185]

Clearly, at any rate, the relationship between them was presented as being extremely close, and it was one of exclusive interdependence. It is to him alone that she manifests herself, and she clings to no one but him:

She had never revealed herself to a soul, and her dwelling is unknown. Yet she appeared in my room at Częstochowa.[186]

As from the world's earliest days, the Maiden has been given only to me, so that I should be her guardian.[187]

---

[179] Ibid., §215. See also §595: 'I had to come in order to perform a certain service for her.'
[180] Ibid., §609.   [181] Ibid., §635.   [182] Ibid., §622.
[183] Ibid., §566.   [184] Ibid., §668.   [185] Ibid., §1118.   [186] Ibid., §1175.
[187] Ibid., §629. The wording of this assertion in Fania Scholem's Hebrew translation, *malbushah* ('her garment', reflecting the Polish *strój* rather than *stroż*, as in the Polish edition),

As for him, all his power derived from her and from the revelations that she vouchsafed only to him:

Even now, though she is concealed ... she endows me with great power and guides me in all my ways.[188]

No one knows the place of the stump-legged men [*haba'alei kabin*],[189] but the Virgin informed me where their place is.[190]

Just as she protects and defends him,[191] so he also declares: 'I am to guard her.'[192] Frank pleads on behalf of his followers to the Maiden and readies them for her advent; only by virtue of him will she manifest herself to them as well:

When the verse 'Rejoice greatly, O daughter of Zion' shall come to fulfilment, she will come to my house, and I will ask her to take all the company under her wing.[193]

I would command you what to say and how to look upon her, and as soon as she revealed herself, you would have been readied by me and would know what to say at that moment.[194]

I wanted only to bring you unto her. I wanted to teach you what to do, to speak thus and so, and had I brought you unto her, you would have stayed there forever. I would

raises the possibility that he might have been speaking of the Maiden donning his own body, as a man, as she had previously attempted to don the male bodies of Sabbatai Zevi and Berukhyah of Salonica. This possibility gains credence, of course, from the gender instability of the *sefirah* of Malkhut, which under certain conditions can turn male, notwithstanding its distinctively female identity; on this see Tishby, *Wisdom of the Zohar*, i. 372, and see below, at n. 232. However, this possibility seems remote, given that Frank had found fault with the messianic achievements of his predecessors precisely because of the dissonance between their spiritual femaleness and their physical maleness, which prevented the Maiden from fully manifesting herself.

[188] *Words of the Lord*, §406.

[189] In the Polish edition, this term is transliterated as 'Baałakaben'. The doctrine of the *ba'alei kabin* ('the stump-legged persons'; see BT *Ḥag.* 4a) derives from an enigmatic story in the *Tikunei hazohar* (§69, 103a ff.) 'about a fellow who was one of those *ba'alei kabin*'. In the Sabbatian tradition, where this story was linked to the Mishnah's ruling that 'the stump-leg [*kite'a*] goes out [of his house on the sabbath] with his wooden leg [*kab*]' (*Shab.* 6: 8), it became a legend about the 102 (the numerical value of the word *kab*) true pupils of the 'stump-leg', Sabbatai Zevi. This tradition seems to have originated with the Doenmeh sect in Salonica, whence it travelled to the Sabbatians of central Europe. Frank may have picked it up during his sojourn in Salonica, by way of his contacts with the local apostate Sabbatians. In Frank's own further development of the tradition, the *ba'alei kabin* become esoteric, mythical creatures. They are the concealed leaders of the faithful, and only he knows the secret of how they can be reached. See Scholem, *Researches* (Heb.), 380–3.

[190] *Words of the Lord*, §1023.   [191] See above, Ch. 6, at n. 64.

[192] See above, n. 128.   [193] *Words of the Lord*, §607.   [194] Ibid., §456.

have recommended you to her, saying: 'These are the people who first recognized me and followed me', and she would have recommended you further, for without her good word you cannot get anywhere.[195]

In contrast to the plethora of statements by Frank proclaiming the supreme messianic leadership of the Maiden, this last reference to the possibility that she might have to 'recommend' the faithful even 'further' implies the existence in his imagination of a domain more sublime than hers, which is the believers' ultimate destination.[196] Indeed, the Maiden's manifestation in the world is at times represented as no more than the initial stage in the process of redemption; her role is to make way for the manifestation of the Big Brother, who continues to appear from time to time in Frank's later teachings. He is depicted as an un-knowable, exalted level of the divine, whose manifestation in the world is the goal of the redemptive process:

Until she goes forth from her place, the Big Brother cannot come out into this world . . . Had you imparted to him that she was made manifest in the world, he, too, would have appeared.[197]

Had you been wholehearted at Częstochowa, I would have brought you before her to bond with her, and I could then have sent you on to the Big Brother, according to what has been said.[198]

She has the power to bring you to the Big Brother, who is the King of Kings … so that all of the company can behold him, as I have promised you that I would show you God.… You would be redeemed from everything, from death, from slavery, and so on and so forth.[199]

Without her, one cannot seek God or approach him.[200]

She must teach what must be done in order to arrive at that thing, and after that at God himself.[201]

On the other hand, at times the Big Brother kneels before the Maiden, and she commands him, compensates for his lack, and is revealed to him 'by her great name', so that it is her revelation that appears to be the ultimate goal and object of hope:

She would command him to bring that thing which is lacking here, and she would

[195] Ibid., §565.
[196] In §580 Frank says this explicitly: 'Everything will begin with Malkhut—for she is the first gate to be entered—or the last, lowest level, since if one does not enter unto her, one can get no further.' [197] Ibid., §604. [198] Ibid., §1023.
[199] Ibid., §441. [200] Ibid., §516. [201] Ibid., §711.

give him, corresponding to it, that thing which he lacks[202] . . . and she would become eternally manifest among you, and would never more conceal herself from you.[203]

At the moment when she manifested herself, you would already have been made ready by me, and you would know what to say at that moment. She would no longer conceal herself from you, never moving from her place . . . And I would immediately approach her and take her hand, and she would reveal her name to me, and would lead us to her chambers, which she would allot us. I and she would sit down, and you would stand before her . . . and you would attain eternal life and absolute freedom, and no man in this world could stand against you . . . I would send these tidings to the Big Brother, informing him that she had manifested herself in the world, and that this is her name. For even though all the power is in his hand, he does not know her name, but only the appellation by which she goes, for no one knows her great name. He would rejoice greatly and immediately come unto us, in the company of his brothers and sisters. He would kneel before her, and you would stand there and behold what great honour he pays you.[204]

This ambiguity in Frank's statements about the relative status of the revealed Maiden is explainable on both the psychological and the mythical levels. On the psychological level, it may be interpreted as a consequence of the complex familial relationship between him and his daughter Eva. On the one hand, Eva was Queen and Lady—the incarnation of the redemptive divine Maiden—and as such she served as the focal point of the court's messianic cult and aspirations. Frank himself—the human counterpart of the Big Brother—repeatedly declared that he was but her agent and emissary, disseminating the tidings of her advent to the faithful and readying them for her ultimate manifestation. On the other hand, she was, after all, his daughter and protégée—a defenceless girl, pretty but apparently rather ignorant and devoid of any special talent. Having lost her mother at an early age, she yearned for marriage and a normal family life[205] but remained a virgin, evidently at her

[202] 'That thing which is lacking here'—in the Lower World—is the tremendous, supernatural power of the Upper Worlds, while 'that thing which he'—the Big Brother and his entourage in the Upper World—'lacks' is a body, on which see above, Ch. 6, at nn. 16–18, and below, at nn. 244–53. Nor is it incidental that the Maiden should be the one to make up for the Big Brother's lack of embodiment, since it was she who first manifested herself in the material world. Her relationship to that world, as a female, is closer and more direct than his, since the realm of the body clearly pertains to her.

[203] *Words of the Lord*, §604, in the same passage in which the manifestation of the Maiden is depicted as making way for the manifestation of the Big Brother.

[204] Ibid., §456.   [205] See n. 122 above and the text there.

father's bidding, leaving her under his control and entirely dependent upon him and his caprices. It was he who moulded her image and messianic consciousness; as we have seen, he promised to closet himself with her in 'a lovely house', there to sit with her 'day and night, and speak with her briefly about everything, so that she can come to know the greatness of our faith', and to 'make a human being of her, so that she will undergo everything'.[206] The cast of this ambiguous father–daughter relationship seems to have been extrapolated, by way of transference, to the fluctuations in the relative status of their supernal, divine counterparts.

In addition, on the mythical level, the ambivalence in the relationship between the Maiden and the Big Brother derived from the ambivalent status of the female in relation to the male aspects of the divine, both in kabbalistic literature in general and in the doctrines of the Sabbatians. This ambivalence is expressed, from the earliest stages of the kabbalistic tradition, in the splitting of the female into the 'upper Shekhinah' (the *sefirah* of Binah) and the 'lower Shekhinah' (the *sefirah* of Malkhut).[207] It is intensified in the characterization of the erratic nature of the *sefirah* of Malkhut herself, and in the transposition of her ranking in the sefirotic hierarchy that marks the dynamic of the processes of redemption.

On account of her fickle nature, the Zohar likens the *sefirah* of Malkhut to the Tree of Knowledge of Good and Evil and calls her

the place that changes, turning from one colour to another, from good to evil and from evil to good . . . and for this reason it is called the sword which turns every way [Gen. 3: 24]: it turns from one side to the other, from good to evil, from mercy to strict justice, from peace to war, turning in all ways, for good and for evil, as it is written: 'the Tree of the Knowledge of Good and Evil' [Gen. 2: 9].[208]

This distinction between the contrary natures of the *sefirah* of Malkhut is reflected in several of Frank's teachings about the Maiden (though not in all of them), in which he splits her image in two. One aspect, that of the 'strange' or 'foreign' woman, embodies the evil nature of the divine female; strongly related to the powers of the *sitra aḥra*, she ensnares the man who 'strays from

---

[206] *Words of the Lord*, §784.

[207] On this see Scholem, 'Shekhinah', 174–8, and id., *Origins of the Kabbalah*, 178–80.

[208] Zohar, i. 222*b*, and *passim*. On this attribute of the feminine *sefirah* of Malkhut see Tishby, *Wisdom of the Zohar*, i. 371–2, and Scholem, 'Shekhinah', 185–92.

the good way' and chastises him for it. The second aspect, the embodiment of the good, is the object of the soul's desire, the true redeemer: 'That strange woman who pursues men is the very trap into which they fall. But the Maiden for whom we strive, she whom we court, is the one in whose shade we would take shelter.'[209] The 'evil' *sefirah* of Malkhut is the serving-maid who rules the world in place of her mistress, the true, benevolent Matronita, who will soon show herself—with Frank's assistance—and depose her usurping rival:[210]

But when a man strays from the good way, he is quickly ensnared, and she brings him into her chambers. There are various chambers there—one for drinking, one for fasting, and others for dancing. She seduced you to fast in this status, and to study the niceties of the law for fear of her.[211] She lures people to her and then herself deals out their chastisement. She is the serving-maid who usurped the place of her mistress, as I have already told you: the true Maiden is also in great distress, and she is in hiding, while that woman has seized her power. And if she does manifest herself occasionally, she takes the form of a doe, so that she will not be recognized for what she really is. That serving-maid knows well that when the other woman resumes her reign, she herself is sure to fall. . . . God made the one over against the other . . . From the time when the world was created, all the weaponry has been placed in her hands—all distress, pain, and sorrow come from her. And all those who fell, it was there that they fell. . . . She is the best beloved of the tree of death, which is one of the three gods who direct the world.[212] His love for her is boundless. He chose her and charged her over diseases, sorrow, and all the means of death that exist in the world. Since all his weaponry is entrusted to her, she is called the strange woman, the evil woman, more bitter than death. She is the lowest abyss, but even so, there is something very good and very great in her, something hidden inside her, and

[209] *Words of the Lord*, §1135.

[210] On the image of the handmaid and her Lady, and the sources of that image, see above, nn. 11 and 15.

[211] As it would seem, she thwarts the believers by inducing them to practise the fasts and to study the laws that pertain to their old Jewish 'status' (see above, at n. 132). Frank was constantly upbraiding his followers for persisting in their commitment to traditional Jewish praxis despite their conversion to Christianity. It could be, however, that he was rebuking them for responding to her Christian seductions, that is, for inordinate devotion to the fasts and canon law of the Catholic faith, into whose domain they had entered for the purpose of subverting it from within, as part of Frank's vision of the ultimate demolition of all religions at the End of Days. He refers to this explicitly on several occasions, e.g. in the continuation of this passage: 'For I was given this thing, to enter into Christianity in order to break it down utterly, to demolish all of the laws that have existed until now' (*Words of the Lord*, §397).

[212] On these three gods see also *Words of the Lord*, §§98, 163, and 891. And see Scholem, *Studies and Texts* (Heb.), 54.

one cannot get close to that thing except by entering into her. She is the lowest door, the *sefirah* leading into Christianity (baptism). Therefore, because they knew that a great thing was hidden inside her, all the great men sought to approach her, but they did not enter into her, for she is as it were the shell guarding the fruit. . . .[213] Up to now she has been called the Queen, sovereign over all, because everything is in her hands. She is called by the name of Rachel, but she of whom it is written that she 'is weeping for her children' [Jer. 31: 15][214]—she spurred the construction of the two Temples, the First and the Second, and herself destroyed them. Had Solomon himself destroyed his

---

[213] Frank appears to identify this 'strange' or 'evil' woman, who nevertheless bears within her 'something very good and very great' and is 'as it were the shell guarding the fruit', with the Virgin Mary, 'the lowest door, the *sefirah* leading into Christianity', into which one must enter in order to reach the Maiden who is the true redeemer. He alludes to this elsewhere as well:

> It is well known that the shell comes before the fruit. You will see for yourselves that she is called the eternal Virgin. It is said of her that she is the Queen of Heaven, before whom they bow and prostrate themselves. It is said of her that she is the very Saviour. At first, she suffered together with him [apparently her son, Jesus], and she had no place of rest. She wandered with him and fled with him to Egypt [cf. Matt. 2: 13–15]. It is she who comes before the fruit that is about to go forth into the world, and before whom all the kings of the world shall bow. (*Words of the Lord*, §917)

The Queen of Heaven is a frequent designation of the Holy Virgin in Christian tradition; see Pelikan, *Mary through the Centuries*, 109, 140, 147, and 151; E. Johnson, 'Marian Devotion', 405–10; Warner, *Alone of All Her Sex*, 103–17. It would be interesting to probe the potentially problematical relationship between this positive image of the 'Queen of Heaven' as Mary and the unequivocal condemnation of the idolatrous cult of the 'Queen of Heaven' in Jer. 7: 18 and 44: 17–19, 25, where *malkat hashamayim* ('Queen of Heaven') has been modified in the Hebrew Bible to read *melekhet hashamayim* (as it were, 'the work of heaven') but where the original 'queen' was preserved in most of the early versions that fed into the Christian tradition.

This passage displays an essential continuity with the very earliest Sabbatian doctrines; Nathan of Gaza saw Jesus as the 'shell' of the true messiah (see Scholem, *Studies and Texts* (Heb.), 126–7, and Nathan's 'Treatise on the Serpents', in Scholem, *Footsteps of Messiah* (Heb.), 43). Frank, however, transfers this shell-and-fruit relationship from its original application to a pair of males—Jesus and Sabbatai Zevi—to a pair of females: the Virgin Mary and the Maiden, who is the true redeemer.

[214] In several other contexts, too, Frank represents the biblical Rachel—the *sefirah* of Malkhut in the kabbalistic literature—not as the redemptive Maiden herself but as her looka-like who 'died by the wayside' (cf. Gen. 35: 19, where Rachel is said to have died and been buried 'in the way to Ephrath'), thus exposing her impersonation of the true redeemer. Similarly, he represents the biblical Jacob as a man who was duped, not only for having been tricked by Laban into marrying Rachel's sister Leah, but for marrying his beloved Rachel herself:

> Only then did Jacob answer him: 'I will serve you for your younger daughter, Rachel' [Gen. 29: 18]. He kept his word and served for her sake. And after that, she died by the wayside! Is it

handiwork, he would have freed himself of her net and attained that good thing, and he would have lived. Though the Queen of Sheba imparted this to him, she lacked the ability to give him life, because she was a woman, and so on a lower level than a man. Had she manifested herself to a woman in this world, she could have granted her [eternal] life.[215] Moses, Aaron, and David also had hold of a certain thing, and they thought they had a good thing in their grasp, but it came from her. It was she who gave them the rose to hold, and so they fell, because none of them yet came close to the true rose.[216]

Along with her changeable nature, and as a consequence of it, the *sefirah* of Malkhut also inverts her position in the hierarchy of the sefirotic realm. The processes of redemption culminate in her rise from the bottom to the top of

fitting for him to have pursued a maiden who would die? If you had asked me, I would have answered you that he was pursuing a real Maiden, but this one was just the lookalike of the true Rachel upon whom all life depends, and who stands before God. (*Words of the Lord*, §107, and see also ibid., §§92, 132, and 370)

[215] This surprising assertion of woman's relative inferiority to man, reflecting traditional assumptions about power relations between the sexes (and also the inferior status—in her waning phase—of the *sefirah* of Malkhut, located at the bottom of the sefirotic system), seems to deviate from the spirit of the statements made by Frank throughout *Words of the Lord*, aggrandizing the power of the redemptive female and pressing for the equalization of the status of both sexes, which he saw as one of the clearest signs of the redemptive age. In this context, however, he seems to require the inferior rank of the woman for his explanation that the Queen of Sheba—that is, the divine Maiden—had to manifest herself 'to a woman in this world', and not—as in the historical event—to Solomon, a man, whose nature was incompatible with hers. That incompatibility is mentioned again when Frank declares: 'The Queen of Sheba gave Solomon a ring on which was the seal of the King ... Had Solomon received that ring from the first king, he would have had a long life. But he received the ring from a woman' (*Words of the Lord*, §331).

As we have already seen, the Maiden could manifest herself fully only to a woman, a real female, made just like her, who would have the capacity to assimilate her powers. From this point of view, there is no contradiction between Frank's statements here and those concerning the messiah as a flesh-and-blood female, and the direct relationship between the redemptive female and the *sefirah* of Malkhut in its phase of plenitude, of which she is the embodied manifestation. In another atypical, derisory statement about women, reflecting the traditional conception of their nature as derived from the sin of Eve, which brought mortality upon humankind (see JT *Shab.* 2: 6, and *Gen. Rabbah* 17: 8), Frank speaks bitterly of having been deserted by his followers (evidently referring to their flight from his court at Częstochowa before its fall to the invading Russian army): 'Had three or four of you only remained, and three or four women. ... But nothing can be accomplished with women, because woman brought death into the world, and I wish to bring life into the world' (*Words of the Lord*, §561).

[216] Ibid., §397.

this hierarchy, and this, too, is reflected in the fluctuating hierarchical relationship between the Maiden and the Big Brother. The kabbalistic literature likens the dawning of redemption to the arrival of the sabbath, which the Sages had already depicted as 'a taste of the World to Come'.[217] 'Sabbath' is one of the appellations of the *sefirah* of Malkhut—the lower divine female, who points to the existence of a higher female, the *sefirah* of Binah, which is identified with the 'big' or the eschatological sabbath, representing freedom and redemption.[218] The status of Malkhut in the realm of the *sefirot*, inverted temporarily on the weekly sabbath, is expected to be transformed permanently in the eschatological sabbath, when she will free herself from the hold of the evil powers and return from her exile; that is, she will rise from her inferior place on the periphery of the World of Emanation so as to come together with the male *sefirot* above her, to receive the flow of their vitality and to unite herself with them.[219] As the Zohar describes it, 'Once the sabbath has entered, that point [Malkhut] rises up, adorns herself, and takes hold on high, and they all [the *sefirot* that are above her] are enfolded within her.'[220] At this stage, the lower female—Malkhut—gathers strength, merges with the higher female—Binah—and rises up with her to mate with the very highest male levels within the godhead.[221] In Lurianic kabbalah, too, the messianic era is characterized by the growing power of the feminine forces—the 'female waters'—in the lowest *sefirah*, Malkhut, known in Lurianic terms as the countenance (*partsuf*) of the 'female [partner] of the Minor One'. These forces raise her up from her lowly rank at the outer limit of the godhead and position her in the place for which she was destined, at its head, allowing the perfect mating of the divine male and female to come to fruition—face to face, and equal in stature.[222]

---

[217] See BT *Ber.* 57*b*, and see also Zohar, i. 48*a*.

[218] For a discussion of the eschatological sabbath in classical kabbalistic literature see Ginsburg, *The Sabbath*, 95–100, 134.

[219] See ibid. 74 and 115–16; Tishby, *Wisdom of the Zohar*, iii. 1225; and Wolfson, 'Coronation of the Sabbath Bride'. [220] Zohar, ii. 204*a*.

[221] Ibid.; see also Zohar, i. 5*a*. Here, too, Wolfson, in 'Coronation of the Sabbath Bride', sees in the coronation of the sabbath—that is, the highest point in the ascent of the *sefirah* of Malkhut as she mates with the divine male—an integration of the divine female into the male, to the extent that she loses her separate identity as a female (see above, Introd., n. 19). Whether or not Wolfson is right, this is not how the process looked to Frank; he repeatedly emphasizes the Maiden's femaleness and envisions how the redemption would materialize through her, in fulfilment of the sexual duality existing at every level of being.

[222] On this see Scholem, *Sabbatai Sevi*, 276; and Jacobson, 'The Aspect of the Feminine', 252.

Sabbatian kabbalah, too, had recourse to this motif of the inversion of the sefirotic hierarchy at the conclusion of the redemptive processes. Thus, for example, Nathan of Gaza, using terms drawn both from the Zohar and from Lurianic kabbalah, describes the ascent of the divine female to the head of the male and her installation there as 'the crown of her husband' (cf. Prov. 12: 4). In this state, her power, likened to the light of the moon, intensifies to equal that of the male, which is likened to the light of the sun:

In the Time to Come . . . the power of the moon will intensify, with two kings sharing a single crown, which is alluded to in the verse: 'the crown of her husband', and the light of the moon will be like that of the sun—not like the light it has at present, but after the sevenfold intensification of its light . . . then the light of the moon will be like that of the sun.[223]

With the advent of the messiah, according to Nathan, the worlds are now 'on the eve of the sabbath', that is, 'No spark of the Shekhinah is within the [grasp of the] exterior [evil] forces . . . and in our time, with God's help, [all pure] things will be sorted [from the impure], and the great lights will spread, and Malkhut will be in the aspect of "the crown of her husband".'[224] On the basis of this belief, Nathan calls upon the faithful to stop practising the 'intentions' (*kavanot*) composed by Luria to guide the mystics through their meditative prayer. This was because the 'intentions' had become 'entirely irrelevant to our time, since the worlds are in a different state, so that one [who practises them] is like a person who engages in a weekday activity on the sabbath'.[225] Scholem interprets these statements in light of the redemptive inversion of the sefirotic hierarchy:

If the cosmic *tikun* was achieved, and if no sparks of the Shekhinah were left in the realm of the 'shells', then the present structure and order of the mystical cosmos corresponded to the 'new law' of redemption. The classic Lurianic devotions had lost their purpose, and hence their relevance. . . . All that remained to be done was to 'adorn the bride' and to beautify the Shekhinah; there was no more need to raise her from the

For a detailed discussion of how the Lurianic doctrine of redemption, at each stage of its development, describes the growing strength of the feminine forces that occurs with the advent of the messianic sabbath, see Meroz, 'Redemption in Lurianic Teaching' (Heb.), 119–27, 146–51, 171–6, 208–26, and 240–54.

[223] Nathan of Gaza, 'Treatise on the Lamp', in Scholem, *Footsteps of Messiah* (Heb.), 114–15.
[224] Nathan of Gaza, letter to Raphael Joseph in Egypt, in Sasportas, *Tsitsat novel tsevi*, 8.
[225] Ibid.

dust of exile, since she was already risen.... Of course, the ultimate state of perfection was not yet achieved. The Sabbath-day of the cosmos had not yet dawned, but at least the eve of the Sabbath had arrived. Until now the state of the world could be compared to the days of the week; now it was like unto the eve of the Sabbath with its distinct character and prayers. The purpose of every prayer was to lift the Shekhinah from her low position at the bottom of the divine pleroma, to her rightful and exalted place. At present she was still below the *sefirah* of Tiferet, known by the symbolic name of the Holy One Blessed be He, but soon she would rise not only to the level of Tiferet (the 'husband of the Shekhinah') but even to the very highest *sefirah*, Keter ('crown'). Kabbalists referred to this process as the Shekhinah's 'ascent' by which she was mystically raised to a realm where she would be 'the crown of her husband'.[226]

Abraham Cardozo, too, emphasizes the link between Malkhut, the last of the *sefirot*, and Keter, the first,[227] anticipating their union at the conclusion of the process of redemption, with the ascent of Malkhut to serve as the 'crown' upon the head of the supreme divine male.[228] In the Sabbatian mystical texts pertaining to the circle of Jonathan Eybeschuetz, whose demonstrable affinity with Frank's circle has yet to be fully investigated,[229] this motif takes on bold new terms. The upper, 'supernal Shekhinah', the *sefirah* of Binah, would in the Time to Come ascend, as is alluded to by the verse 'a good wife, crown of her husband', to a level above that of 'the God of Israel'—the countenance of *Atika kadisha*, 'the ancient Holy One', exalted and unknowable, thus named when it dwells or manifests itself within the male *sefirah* of Tiferet.[230] In this mystical doctrine, the mating between the male and the female takes place entirely within the realm of the Ein Sof, above and beyond the levels of the sefirotic emanations, and it is at times depicted as a mating between two male aspects of the divinity, in which the female serves only as an enticement to attract the aspect of 'the God of Israel' to the aspect of its 'root' (*shoresh*) within the Ein Sof.[231]

[226] Scholem, *Sabbatai Sevi*, 277–8.

[227] See e.g. Cardozo's 'Treatise on the Shekhinah', in Wolfson, 'Constructions of the Shekhinah', 96–7, 121–2, and *passim*.

[228] Wolfson devotes most of his 'Constructions of the Shekhinah' to this motif in Cardozo's writings, although he regards it, as we have seen, as an additional confirmation of his understanding that the ascent of the female to the head of the male represents her subsumption in him, to the point of ceasing to exist as a distinct entity. See n. 51 above.

[229] See Perlmutter, *Jonathan Eybeschuetz* (Heb.), 169 and 338; and especially Liebes, *On Sabbatianism* (Heb.), 77, 86–7, 89, 96–7, 143–7, and 193.

[230] See Perlmutter, *Jonathan Eybeschuetz* (Heb.), 96, and Liebes, *On Sabbatianism* (Heb.), 115 and 123.   [231] See Liebes, *On Sabbatianism* (Heb.), 123.

The long kabbalistic tradition that envisaged these shifts in the relative standing of the divine male and female, along with the centrality of the female to and her 'ascent' in the final stages of the redemptive process, may also shed light on the fluid hierarchical relations between the Big Brother and the Maiden, the ethereal counterparts in the Upper World of Frank and his daughter in the lower one. At times, as we have seen, he functions as her agent and the doer of her bidding, uniquely entrusted with the role of preparing the world for her full manifestation; at others, she, in manifesting herself, prepares the ground for his own manifestation, when his full, unknowable, and supreme divine stature will be revealed throughout the worlds.

Moreover, among her other metamorphoses in the kabbalistic tradition, the *sefirah* of Malkhut also inverts her gender. In relation to the *sefirot* above her, and also in her connection with the powers of impurity, she is a passive female with no vitality of her own, who can do no more than receive the flow of male powers spilling into her. In relation to the Lower Worlds, however, she functions as an active male, spilling the divine plenty down into them:

She [Malkhut] is a messenger [or angel] who at times is male and at times female. Thus, when she generates blessings for the world, she is male and is called male; like a male who generates blessings for a female, she generates blessings for the world. But when she stands in judgment over the world, then she is called female; like a pregnant female, she fills up with judgement, and then she is called female.[232]

These inversions in the gender identity of Malkhut opened the way for Frank to divert the hope of redemption from a messianic figure of the male sex, as it had been envisaged in Jewish tradition from time immemorial, to the female messianic figure of the Maiden, hinted at in Christianity's Holy Virgin and now embodied in his own virgin daughter Eva. The kabbalistic tradition, by linking the soul of Messiah son of David to the *sefirah* of Malkhut, had already bestowed a distinctly female dimension upon the male figure of the ultimate redeemer, but it still saw that figure, in all its historic incarnations, as a human male. Frank drew a logical but radical conclusion from this: in place of a redemptive male, endowed with a female dimension, he set a redemptive female—the Maiden or the Virgin—whose virginity admittedly may suggest that she possessed a certain aspect of active, creative maleness, but who, as the embodiment of the *sefirah* of Malkhut, the quintessential divine female, was

---

[232] Zohar, i. 232*a*; Tishby, *Wisdom of the Zohar*, i. 372.

of necessity bound to appear as an actual woman in her flesh-and-blood messianic manifestation.

This inversion served the advancement of the redemptive processes well: the association of Malkhut as a female with the realm of matter and the body—the female realm[233]—and her dominion over the Lower Worlds, which are entrenched in that realm, are what suited her, precisely in her embodiment as a woman, to fulfil Frank's mission. For that mission not only set out to expose the redemptive divine female 'openly and clearly',[234] 'truly . . . and openly . . . and actually . . . in the light of day'[235] (as opposed to the 'allusion', 'night', and 'concealment' by which it had been obscured in all the abortive redemptive missions previously undertaken by males); it was also distinctive in being presented as taking place in what had traditionally been construed as the natural domain of the female—'in the body', that is, in the concrete, earthly, physical, tangible plane of reality, rather than in the intellectual, spiritual dimension of existence, which was the exclusive domain of the male. Frank constantly derided the abstract, spiritual nature of earlier Sabbatian redemptive missions, which had failed in material reality, becoming a mere 'spiritual force' in the consciousness of the faithful: 'What benefit came of all those troubles? Everything went back to being as it was before. But you did not have anywhere to direct that thing, and so you turned it into a spiritual force.'[236] Of his own vision, on the other hand, he declared: 'But I have told you of all this not as [taking place] in spirit or in heaven, but in the open, on earth.'[237] Redemption that takes place 'in spirit' or 'in heaven' is no true redemption; what distinguishes Frank's messianic vision from those of all his predecessors is precisely the stress it lays on the redemption as a manifestation of spiritual forces in physical form—'what was in spirit will be in flesh'[238]—and this must take place 'on earth', 'in this world', and not in 'the world of the spirit', which, for Frank, lies beyond experience, since it cannot be perceived by the senses:

A king[239] commanded that after his death a sack of earth should be placed upon his coffin. In so doing, he signalled that he wished to turn the world of the spirit to flesh.

---

[233] On the association of the female—including the divine female—with this realm, in contrast to the male, who is identified with the realm of the spirit, the soul, or form, see above, Ch. 3 n. 13.   [234] *Words of the Lord*, §552.

[235] Ibid., §609; and see also §831.   [236] Ibid., §831.

[237] Ibid., §1001.   [238] Ibid., §552, and see above, n. 63.

[239] This word appears in Fania Scholem's Hebrew rendering as 'a certain king' (*melekh eḥad*),

And I say unto you that in this world, everything that is in spirit must be turned to flesh, just like ours, so that it can be seen by all as a visible thing can be seen.[240]

assuming the reading 'Khan'. The Polish edition has 'ów Ran', which the modern editor, Jan Doktór, interprets as reflecting a transliterated Hebrew acronym for Rabbi Nathan [of Gaza]; see further on this in the next note.

[240] *Words of the Lord*, §548. See also §564, where Frank delivers the following rebuke to his believers:

> How can you speak of that *yesod* ['Foundation', the *sefirah* of the divine *membrum virile*]? Can such an exalted thing be mentioned in the vile place where you now stand? Scripture explicitly demands: 'Remove the filthy garments from him!' [Zech. 3: 4, according to Fania Scholem's Hebrew translation. The Polish edition has 'Zdejm twoją zwalaną szatę', i.e. Gen. 35: 2: 'purify yourselves and change your garments', which seems more likely, especially since the preceding section, §563, cites a proximate verse, Gen. 32: 7, which, like Gen. 35: 2, concerns the relationship between Jacob and Esau.] This means that they want to set him up in such a place, and therefore he has first to shed his vile cloak and don a fine one in its place, even though that place has not the worth of the place to which I want to bring you. But the word *yesod*: it is a living thing, and who but she can bring it back to life? In her hands it will revive and live forever. By means of this *yesod*, the dead will revive. . . . Thus is it written in Scripture: 'Righteous and saved is he' [Zech. 9: 9]. The Righteous One [tsadik—one of the common designations of the *sefirah* of Yesod–Foundation], long having languished, is about to be helped [namely, 'revived']. But this cannot happen in the corrupt flesh. He must arrive at the level of Adam, and he must first of all arrive at this level. Not—as that *Khan* declared [again, Doktór's Polish edition has 'that *Ran*', on which see below]—that flesh should be made from spirit, but, rather, flesh will be made from flesh [Fania Scholem's translation reads *ye'aseh meruḥaniyut gashmiyut umigashmiyut lo kol sheken gashmiyut*, i.e. 'physical substance will be made from the spiritual, and all the more so will physical substance be made from physical substance', while the Polish edition reads: 'że z duchownego cielesne zrobi, ale z cielesnego dopiero cielesne zrobić']. How can you say that this *yesod* is a lovely thing? Can it be exposed before kings and great lords? Yet it is bigger on a horse, and what of it?

Frank seems to be arguing here for the corporeal substantiation of the divine *membrum virile*, which, as long as it lies concealed in the spiritual worlds, is as though dead, but, with the physical manifestation of the Maiden, will be stimulated ('touched' by 'her hands') back to life and manifest itself physically as well; that is, it too will be embodied and remain eternally vital.

The concept of 'the level of Adam' appears frequently throughout *Words of the Lord*. In the present context, it seems that it must be interpreted in light of its usage in §585: 'How can you dare to speak of *yesod* when you don't yet know what Adam is, and you have not seen any man on his level? Until now, there is no head and there are no legs or arms in the world.' (See also §588, where Frank contrasts the 'whole', redeemed man with the first man, Adam, who was created deficient.) 'The level of Adam' apparently refers to the full stature of the manifest divinity, substantiated in human form, with all its *sefirot* or limbs in place.

As for the discrepancy between the reading 'Khan', i.e. king or ruler, in Fania Scholem's translation and 'Ran'—reflecting the Hebrew acronym for Rabbi Nathan—in the Polish edition, it is

Sabbatai Zevi was by no means the only potential redeemer who failed on account of the 'spiritual' and 'otherworldly' character of his messianic project. According to Frank, King Solomon attempted to redeem the world by delivering mankind from the power of death; he was followed by Christ, who similarly promised the gift of eternal life. All this was worthless, since the ambitions of both could not be realized except in the World to Come, while the present, concrete, material world was the only arena in which the true redemption would unfold.[241]

According to a long-standing eschatological tradition that originated in the rabbinic literature of the first centuries CE and subsequently found numerous expressions in both philosophical and kabbalistic writings, redemption— whether it was utopian or restorative—would be experienced as the intellectualization or spiritualization of material reality, including the sublimation of the body and its physical appetites.[242] Frank turned this, too, on its head: his

difficult to determine which is correct without re-examining the Polish manuscript, which was not at my disposal. In all events, the identification made by Jan Doktór, the editor of the Polish edition, of 'Ran' with Nathan of Gaza is far from obvious. While Frank refers fairly frequently to Sabbatai Zevi ('that First One') and Berukhyah of Salonica ('the Second One'), I have encountered very few references to Nathan of Gaza in his 'words', and in all of these he is referred to by his name, Nathan, and not by the acronymic 'Ran' (see e.g. *Words of the Lord*, §39: 'A certain Nathan, who was held to be a prophet of the First One', or ibid., §40: 'And when I was there [in Skopje, where Nathan of Gaza was buried] in the year 1754, an old woman told me the history of Nathan'). Nor can the statements here attributed to 'Ran' [if this is indeed the correct reading] be immediately identified with any of Nathan's doctrines (although I did not have before me all of his doctrinal writings, most of which are still available only in manuscript). It could be that the acronym, if such it is, refers to the Rabbi Nathan described in *Words of the Lord*, §1199 (§1200 in Fania Scholems's Hebrew version) as the spiritual mentor of Frank's father. This R. Nathan, apparently a veteran Sabbatian who was in contact with the apostate Sabbatians of Salonica, is said there to have accompanied Jacob Frank on his journey to Salonica in 1753, around the time of Frank's marriage. He is mentioned several times in the Polish *Kronika* as 'Nussen' (reflecting the Ashkenazi pronunciation of Nathan), 'Rabbi Nussen', or 'Rabbi Nussen the Blind' (see Levine, *Kronika*, 32, §§4 and 7, and 34, §8; Doktór, *Rozmaite adnotacje*, 48).

[241] See Kraushar, *Jacob Frank*, ii. 279–81, on the basis of *Words of the Lord*, §1776, which has not survived and is missing from both the Polish edition and the unpublished Hebrew translation by Fania Scholem.

[242] See BT *Ber.* 17a: 'In the World to Come there is no eating or drinking, no reproductive activity or commerce ... but the righteous sit with crowns upon their heads, enjoying the splendour of the Shekhinah, as it is written [Exod. 24: 11]: "They beheld God, and ate and drank".' For discussions of this tradition in various contexts see e.g. Winston, 'Philo and the Rabbis'; Liebes,

vision of the redemption entailed the substantiation of the spirit and so, too, the materialization of the divine reality.[243] As we have seen, he declared that the supernal 'brothers' and 'sisters' had need of their human counterparts in the Lower World, whom they craved so as to make up for their own great lack—the want of a flesh-and-blood body.[244] Redemption, then, would be characterized by the embodiment of the ethereal supernal 'brothers' and 'sisters' through 'chiastic' sexual matings with their human counterparts in the Lower World.[245]

To be sure, the desire prevailing between the Upper and Lower Worlds was mutual; the denizens of the latter, too, sought to make up for their own lack by way of redemptive matings with their supernal counterparts. Indeed, in several places Frank describes the Lower World as suffering for want of a 'soul'— the logical converse of the want of a body suffered in the supernal world:

No one in the world has a soul; not even that First and that Second One [Sabbatai Zevi and Berukhyah of Salonica] had souls, and the Patriarchs, too, the pillars of the world, lacked souls, for the soul can be given only by God himself, and from one other place. Then shall the worlds have eternal existence, and everyone that has a soul shall live forever, and shall be able to gaze from one end of the world to the other, always farther and farther . . . for when Adam was created,[246] he lacked three things, and

'Messiah of the Zohar', 50–1; Idel, *Messianic Mystics*, 65–125; id., 'Redemptive Activities' (Heb.), 254–63; Safran, 'Rabbi Azriel and Nahmanides'; Halbertal, 'Nachmanides' Conception' (Heb.), 133–62; Schwartz, *Messianism* (Heb.), 104–11; Wirszubski, 'Sabbatian Theology' (Heb.), 183; id., 'On Spiritual Love' (Heb.).

[243] See also Scholem's comments in 'Redemption through Sin', p. 125, on the Frankist redemption as 'a process filled with incarnations of the divinity'. On Frank's messianism as an 'earthly' vision that was to be worked out within the concrete political and economic reality of his time and place see Levine, 'Frankism'.

[244] See above, Ch. 6, at nn. 16–18. See also *Words of the Lord*, §416, which describes 'the Queen of Sheba' and 'her great King' in their supernal realm as experiencing great desire for the 'lovely and comely' 'people of this world'. The Queen of Sheba made a gift to her divine mate of a flesh-and-blood girl who was snatched away from this world, passed through the 'partition' separating the Upper and Lower Worlds, was granted eternal youth, and 'ever since' has been the delight of the King. In return, the Queen of Sheba asked of the King 'that he give her the power to pass through the partition so as to copulate with a man of this world. Out of love for her, he sent one of his brothers to accompany her and pass her through the partition. That is how she came to Solomon, and he satisfied her desires in every way.'   [245] See above, Ch. 6, at nn. 19–20.

[246] Fania Scholem's version reads *etzel madregat ha'adam* ('on the level of man'); my reading is based on the Polish edition: 'przy stworzeniu Adama'.

where there is lack, life cannot last. . . . From this we learn that the true God has no part in the present creation.[247] That is why the vessels, up to now, are always being broken, for he who created them breaks them himself, so that they will come out finer and more pure . . . So it is not possible for a soul to subside in a body as crude and lowly as it is now. I wanted to bring you to a place where you would be cleansed and purified, so that you would be powerful enough to receive a soul.[248]

Humankind's lack of a soul, arising from its flawed creation, thus parallels the divine flaw of lacking a body, and both these lacks are to be filled with the advent of redemption: 'the true God', in the process of self-manifestation and bodily substantiation, will endow the human body with a soul—once that body has been cleansed of its 'crudity' and 'lowliness' to be granted eternal life. This conception of the ensouled body, purified in the course of its redemption, would seem to accord with the traditional conception of the spiritualization of the physical in eschatological time. In fact, however, and in contrast to the convention of juxtaposing the physical and the spiritual as a polarity by which the Lower and the Upper World, this world and the next, are distinguished from one another, most of Frank's statements regarding the lack which is inherent in the lower, physical world refer not to a lack of spirit or soul but rather to a lack of sheer power—the prodigious supernatural power enjoyed by the beings inhabiting the supernal worlds—and he describes this power in the bluntest of physical, mundane, material terms: '[It is a] power at least enough to uproot a tree . . . all the good things in the world, and the crowns of its dominions . . . power such as has never been in the world.'[249] Elsewhere he describes a fabulous journey that could be undertaken with the power he had acquired from the supernal world, at the end of which

You would have been set before the man of gold, and you would have talked with him face to face, not as it was with Nebuchadnezzar, where there was only a head of gold [cf. Dan. 2: 32], but here he is made up entirely of pure gold. And you would have seen with what especial, extraordinary power you would have returned from there.[250]

The product of contact with the supernal world is an incalculable accumulation of physical strength and material prosperity:

And when he shall return from there . . . he will be thirty cubits or more in height, and he will be capable of eating a whole ox every day, and his youth will be restored to the age

---

[247] For this 'gnostic' aspect of Frank's doctrine see *Words of the Lord*, §§205, 586, 637, and 980; and see Scholem, 'Redemption through Sin', 129, and 132–3.   [248] *Words of the Lord*, §578.
[249] Ibid., §305.   [250] Ibid., §307.

of 18 or 20, according to his wish; and he will have the strength to uproot the largest of trees, and his wealth will be boundless. . . . They could have as much wealth as they wished, even 10,000 million ducats would be given them, and three men would be allotted from there . . . and those three would lift up a mountain as quick as a wink, and they would put their hoard inside the mountain and take from it each day to spend it according to their need. And I would have the strength of seven oxen, and I would be capable of ripping out the hugest of mountains; they would also bring me precious stones, of a size never before seen in this world, and along with this I would command those three to build a bridge seventy miles long, and all this would be erected immediately.[251]

Had his associates only been fit for it, he would already have sent them over to the Big Brother and his supernal 'family':

If but one or two of you were to go to him, they [the supernal brothers] would see and acknowledge them as brothers, and they would bring you to their leader, and all your wishes would be granted, that is eternal life, wisdom, beauty, stature, power, limitless wealth, and no weapon would be strong enough to harm you. And not only for their own sake, but they could also endow their brothers with all these powers.[252]

Even the ensoulment of human beings—the fulfilment of the lack left by their defective creation—is expressed not in the spiritualization and refinement of the body, but, principally, in the immense invigoration of that body, achieved by overcoming death: 'All the world languishes in want. Nothing endures. Only when the time comes, and humans are fit to be created by God himself, will they receive from him a new soul, and at that time humans will become everlasting, like God himself.'[253]

This aggrandizement of physical, material power in Frank's vision of redemption may well lie at the bottom of two doctrinal features pointed out by Scholem: his 'territorialist ideology'—which broke away from Jewish messianism's traditional association with the distant, spiritualized Land of Israel to focus on the realm that lay at hand, that of Poland—and his militaristic penchant.[254] This was no mystical redemption; rather, the materialization of

[251] *Words of the Lord*, §309.

[252] Ibid., §326; cf. above, Ch. 6, at nn. 17–18, and the references given in Ch. 6 n. 17.

[253] *Words of the Lord*, §205; and see also §§578, 586, and 637, which similarly define the first creation as being defective on account of its susceptibility to death. This defect serves as proof that the first creator was of necessity evil and false, and that he himself will succumb to the power of death at the time of the redemption. Only when the true, good God reveals himself, and grants mankind a soul, will man and God alike enjoy eternal life.

[254] See Scholem, 'Redemption through Sin', 122–3; and id., *Studies and Texts* (Heb.), 121–2 and 129–30.

the spiritual forces at play within it brought about an enhancement of concrete reality, formulated in terms of augmented physical prowess and material abundance. The redeemed Jew—male or female—would be endowed with eternal youth, colossal strength, and fabulous wealth; and he would be a soldier, armed and trained in the stratagems of war upon his own soil—that of Poland! Scholem points to this blatant materialism of the Frankist vision of redemption:

In spite of its negative elements, this doctrine of Frank's was certainly more realistic, more concrete, cruder, and more primitive than the mystical Sabbatianism of the generation that followed Sabbatai Zevi's apostasy. It spoke of gold and of dominion, of the sword and of military might; it expressed the dreams of the poor and oppressed and an aspiration for a regime of the Jews, who would rise to greatness and wealth.[255]

Two revolutionary tendencies underlie Frank's doctrine of the messianic Maiden. The first, his flouting of traditional gender boundaries, expressed in

---

[255] Scholem, *Studies and Texts* (Heb.), 133. Liebes, 'Sabbatean Messianism', 101, argues that the Frankist understanding of the redemption follows the essentially religious conception expounded by Sabbatai Zevi and his apostate successors, finding in Frank's own doctrine no 'intimations of yearnings for political redemption'. But although Frank's conception does not comply with the conventional 'political' strand of Jewish messianic speculation—the one that anticipates the ingathering of the exiles and the establishment of the messiah as sovereign king specifically in the Land of Israel—it is nevertheless one of concrete, political redemption, played out in the arena of physical reality, albeit in Poland, and not in the realm of theology and religious faith. As appears from the writings left by the last of Frank's followers who remained Jewish, it was only after their hopes for physical redemption were scotched with his death, and with his daughter's failure to realize them subsequently, that his original vision was diverted to the spiritual realm, in line with Liebes' argument.

A contemporary parallel to the concrete, materialistic, physical character of Frank's redemption has recently come to light in the form of a late 18th-century messianic hymn, preserved in a mixture of Turkish and Ladino, and emanating from one of the circles of the Sabbatian converts to Islam. It depicts the redemption as taking place not in any unworldly or otherworldly domain but rather on earth, in this world (*dünya* in Turkish, derived from the Arabic), marked precisely by its material, physical nature. See Elqayam, 'Başım tacı Şabbetai' (Heb.), 232–4. Cf. also the Doenmeh tract published by Ben-Zvi ('Kabbalistic Tracts from Berukhia's Circle' (Heb.), 366, 371, and 382), where 'God intends to descend to corporeality', where 'there will be a manifestation, you have become embodied', and where 'On earth ['in *tevel*'] we shall have longevity, on earth we shall serve God', which seems to allude not only to the divine incarnation of Berukhyah, the messianic leader of the sect, but also to the earthly, corporeal nature of the redemption he will bring about. Given Frank's long-term relations with the apostate Sabbatians of the Ottoman empire, this particular feature of his messianic doctrine may well reflect the influence of a comparable development in theirs.

the parity of conduct and status he established between the sexes in his circle, had been one of the original features of the Sabbatian vision of the redemption.[256] Once the ontological difference between males and females had been abolished—as was implicit, on the one hand, in the creation of separate but identical devotional and ritual frameworks for each of the sexes respectively, and on the other hand, in the eradication of the barriers that Jewish tradition had set between them—the way was opened for the substitution of a male redeemer with the female messianic Maiden. The second tendency, inverting a long-established eschatological tradition, was to conceptualize the redemption as consisting not in the spiritualization of bodily existence but rather in the materialization and embodiment of the spirit, which was to take place not on some rarefied, unworldly or other-worldly plane of spiritual existence but rather in the realm of concrete reality, on this earth, and in the flesh—that is, in the domain traditionally identified above all with the female. It was the amalgamation of these two tendencies, inspired in the first instance at Częstochowa, by observation at close quarters of the popular Catholic cult of the Black Madonna, and perhaps also arising from other contacts between Frank and his Christian environment,[257] that spawned in his mind the figure of the redemptive Maiden and led to the emergence of the syncretistic cult that developed around his virgin daughter Eva at his court. Precisely by virtue of her being a woman, and of her status as a virgin—one whose human body, withheld from sexual contact with men, was available to receive the powers of the divine male[258] by way of the 'chiastic' matings of supernal and earthly beings—she could be conceived of as the incarnate divine female, who was the messiah of Israel, the ultimate, true redeemer.

This complex of heterodox ideas also represents a novel development in the Sabbatian doctrine of the incarnation. From the start—in Sabbatai Zevi's

[256] See Chs. 5 and 6 above.

[257] On the likelihood that some additional elements of Frank's messianic doctrine and cult were derived from other contacts with his Christian surroundings, see the next chapter.

[258] This is comparable to the traditional conceptualization of saintly men who abstain from sexual relations with their wives and thus become available for mating with the Shekhinah, the divine female—whether their abstention is permanent, on the mythical model of Moses after the revelation at the burning bush; or temporary, while embarking on long journeys, or on a life of itinerancy in pursuit of scholarly enlightenment; or in total isolation from society in preparation for prophetic, mystical, or magical experience, which required that the body be maintained in a state of 'holiness and purity'.

own mind, more markedly in the doctrinal formulations of Nathan of Gaza and some of his disciples, and with still greater emphasis in the conceptualizations of several of Sabbatai Zevi's messianic successors, such as Berukhyah of Salonica and Wolf Eybeschuetz—the Sabbatian messiah had been elevated to the rank of divinity. In some views, this was accomplished by means of apotheosis, that is, by the messiah's merging, after his death, with the male *sefirah* of Yesod or Tiferet, or even, in some views, with the female *sefirah* of Malkhut.[259] In others, however, it transpired by means of incarnation, that is, by one or the other of these *sefirot* donning the physical form of the messiah, transforming him, in his lifetime, into a flesh-and-blood, embodied divinity.[260] This radical version of the doctrine—though it was considered profoundly heretical not only by the opponents of the messianic movement but even by some of the more moderate Sabbatians, like Cardozo—allowed for the possibility that the incarnate divinity would reflect the androgynous nature of the kabbalistic godhead by becoming embodied, not necessarily in the single figure of the traditional male messiah, but as a messianic couple, a human male and female.

Unlike the Christian doctrine of the Incarnation, at whose centre, on both the human and the divine levels, stood an asexual, single, chaste male,[261] the Sabbatian doctrine of the messiah's divine incarnation had emerged in the context of the Jewish mystical tradition, which conformed to the universal Jewish norm of male and female sexual coupling, and had even discerned it, on the cosmic level, between the male and female aspects of the godhead. Consequently, the Sabbatian messiahs who were regarded as incarnate divinities were all, as far as we know, married men, and it is hardly surprising that their wives, and perhaps also other women of their households, should have been conceived of, like Sabbatai Zevi's own wives, as sharing in this dual aspect of their personalities. However, the status of these women was never fully or systematically worked out at the doctrinal level. Insofar as they feature in the sources that have come down to us, they appear to be fulfilling a second-

[259] For a discussion of the various sefirotic associations of the messianic figure in kabbalistic and Sabbatian thought see Liebes, 'Sabbatean Messianism', 101.

[260] See above, Ch. 5 n. 112, and this chapter, n. 150.

[261] Needless to say, this is an oversimplified representation of the Christian doctrine of the Incarnation, in which Mary, precisely because she is a woman and thus associated with the body, plays an indispensable role. Nevertheless, this oversimplification serves to define the basic distinction in this regard between the two religious traditions.

ary function, drawing such power and authority as they possess by extension from their husbands and in keeping with the conventions of the social and religious order within which they operated. Frank's fully articulated promotion of the female incarnation of divinity to the centre of the messianic stage stands in stark contrast to this Sabbatian background. It runs counter to the conventions that put other female consorts in the shadow of their messianic husbands. For surely, none of Frank's messianic predecessors ever set out to overturn the existing order with the same impetuous, subversive zeal that characterized his own revolutionary vision.

As the divine male in his messianic human embodiment, Frank was the first to frame explicitly the independent messianic role of the embodied divine female, a role he invested with unprecedented power and which he associated not with his wife—his natural consort, whose power, by all accounts, was viewed up to the end of her life as deriving entirely from his—but rather with his virgin daughter. As we have seen, at the outset of his career Frank did not diverge from the path set by his predecessors in their conception of the messianic couple. Notwithstanding the air of royalty that surrounded his wife —the Lady, as she was known at the court—he never attributed to her any messianic–divine powers of her own, and he certainly did not position her alongside himself, at the centre of the cult. The doctrine of the embodiment of the divinity as a woman took shape in his mind only after her death. Only then did he set at the heart of his vision the messianic Maiden in the form of his daughter. From that time on, it was this female figure that was destined to redeem the worlds, in her own right, by her own power, and not merely as the messiah's partner by virtue of her status as his wife.

This radical turn, though it placed the redemptive female at the centre of the messianic stage, did not go so far as to displace altogether the embodiment of the divine male; rather, it represented the concrete realization of the emergent, embodied messianic divinity as a male–female pair. This is evident from the continued appearances in Frank's statements of the Big Brother—his supernal counterpart—as the redemptive Maiden's companion, in the role either of her messianic agent, facilitating the accomplishment of her own mission, or of a sublime figure who is loftier than her, an esoteric male presence, for whose advent her own embodied manifestation was meant to prepare the world. Either way, the incarnate divine male and female are partners in the messianic enterprise:

For I and she would bring you there, and no one would protest.[262]

When I came out of jail, I would have sat with her in the carriage . . . and we would enter Warsaw, and the gold and silver would spill out everywhere we went . . . and we would sit upon the royal throne.[263]

That the emergent, embodied messianic divinity should take the form of a human couple is Frank's logical extrapolation from kabbalah's androgynous conception of the divinity, coupled with the zoharic tradition, on which he draws explicitly time and again, whereby the world will be redeemed with the advent of a latter-day Adam-and-Eve-like messianic couple. This couple was to 'pervert' and outwit the serpent and 'the one [Samael] who rides him'—the powers of the *sitra aḥra*—and so to rectify the misdeeds of the primordial couple, who had been 'perverted' by the serpent to bring down the curse of the original sin and its punishment upon the world: 'On this account, the world will continue to exist until a woman comes who is like Eve and a man who is like Adam, and they will pervert the evil serpent and outwit it.'[264] Frank quotes this statement from the Zohar on numerous occasions and in a variety of contexts.[265] For example, he describes his own messianic path as:

To act like the serpent, that is, to approach wisdom obliquely. This is [in fulfilment of the notion that the world will continue to exist] until there shall come a man in the form of Adam and a woman in the form of Eve. They will approach that snake obliquely and wisely.[266]

The same statement from the Zohar is cited in the 'Red Epistles' (which were written in red ink) circulated by Frank's followers in 1800, in which they called upon the Jews to join them in entering into the 'holy faith of Edom':[267]

For the time has come that Jacob [was referring to when he] promised 'I will come unto my Lord unto Seir' [Gen. 33: 14], for we know that until now he has not yet gone thither.[268] For our Holy Lord, who is Jacob, 'the most perfect of all'[269] . . . is the one who has led us on the true way in the holy religion of Edom . . . but he was still not done [with his task] at that time . . . and did not go to Seir, for all this was but to

---

[262] *Words of the Lord*, §1119.   [263] Ibid., §1118.

[264] Zohar, i. 145*b*–146*a*; and see above, at nn. 20–1, and n. 141.   [265] See n. 141 above.

[266] *Words of the Lord*, §666.   [267] On this concept in Frank's doctrine see n. 83 above.

[268] The Bible makes no mention of Jacob ever having fulfilled this promise to come to the place of Esau. The Jerusalem Talmud (*AZ* 2: 5) says that this will happen at the End of Days.

[269] Following the Zohar, ii. 23*a*: 'Rabbi Hiya said: "Jacob was the most praiseworthy of the Patriarchs, for he was perfect in everything."'

prepare the way for the [last] Jacob [Frank], the most perfect of all, at the End of Days. As the Zohar explains, 'Jacob, Jacob' [Gen. 46: 3]—the first [Jacob] is perfect, but the last [Jacob] is perfect in everything,[270] and he will complete [Jacob's mission in] everything. As it is said [in allusion to this] in the Zohar: 'Until a man comes who is like Adam and a woman who is like Eve, and they will pervert him [the serpent] and outwit him', and so forth. Therefore, we must follow in his path.[271]

Most of the epistle revolves around 'the first Jacob', that of the Bible and the Zohar, as a figure alluding—in the usual way of Frankist documents—to 'the last, more favoured Jacob' Frank who is perfect in everything. This epistle was composed and circulated some nine years after Frank's death, though it asserts that 'he certainly is not dead'[272] and will 'complete [his mission in] everything'. In that period, the court in Offenbach was being run by Frank's three children, headed by Eva, the central messianic cult figure. There can be no doubt that the statement from the Zohar is cited as an allusion to the messianic couple that was to be active 'at the End of Days'—namely, the male Jacob (Frank), who 'is like Adam', and the female 'Eva', his daughter, who 'is like Eve'.

[270] Zohar, i. 138*a*: '"Jacob, Jacob" [Gen. 46: 3]—the last [Jacob] is perfect, [but] the first is not perfect; for latterly he was told about Joseph [that he was still alive], and then the Shekhinah rested upon him.'

[271] This epistle was first published in [N.] Porges, 'La Lettre adressée par les Frankistes', 285–6. Scholem published and interpreted an excerpt from it, including this passage, in 'Redemption through Sin', 138–40. Scholem's translation is quoted here with some modifications. Another version of the same letter was published, with English translation, in Wacholder, 'Jacob Frank and the Frankists', 265–93.

[272] [N.] Porges, 'La Lettre adressée par les Frankistes', 285; Scholem, 'Redemption through Sin', 138. According to BT *Ta'an.* 5*b*:

> R. Yohanan said: 'Our forefather Jacob did not die.' [Someone else] responded: 'Does Scripture relate in vain how he was eulogized, embalmed, and interred?' He responded: 'I am bringing another scriptural passage to bear: "Then fear not, O Jacob my servant, says the Lord, nor be dismayed, O Israel; for lo, I will save you from afar, and your offspring from the land of their captivity" [Jer. 30: 10]. By analogy with his "offspring", we may infer that if his offspring are alive, he, too, is alive.'

In contrast to the Talmud, which does not deny the fact of Jacob's death, this Frankist epistle surely does intend to claim that Jacob Frank did not actually die but, evidently, disappeared until the time should come for his ultimate revelation. On the efforts made in the court at Offenbach to obscure the fact of Frank's death see above, Ch. 1 n. 98.

EIGHT

'The Mother of God': Frank and the Russian Sectarians

SCHOLARS OF HASIDISM, the school of spirituality initiated by Israel Ba'al Shem Tov (the Besht), have occasionally noted certain parallels—organizational, ritual, folkloric, and doctrinal—between the hasidic movement and the various sects that emerged in early modern Russia, either independently or out of the Old Believers' faction that seceded from the Russian Orthodox Church at the time of the schism (Raskol) of the second half of the seventeenth century.[1] These sects, and others whose origins are obscure and

[1] See Ysander, *Studien zum B'eštschen Ḥasidismus*, 372–92; Eliach, 'Russian Sects'; Weinryb, *Jews of Poland*, 237–8, 272–3, and 375 n. 4; and see the summary of M. Rosman in *Founder of Hasidism*, 58–60. Rosman (ibid. 58 and 232 n. 67) also counts Gershom Scholem among the scholars who have pointed to an affinity between hasidism and these sects, citing on this Scholem, 'The Historical Ba'al Shem Tov' (Heb.), 294. This claim requires clarification. Scholem points not to a possible relationship between hasidism and the Russian schismatics, or between it and any other local mystical sect, but rather to the close parallel between the hasidic institution of the tsadik and the ancient institution of the *starets* (pl. *startsy*) or 'elder' in the monastic tradition of the Eastern Church, which saw a revival in Russia beginning in the second half of the 18th century. This was not a dissident sect, but rather a phenomenon involving charismatic, mystically oriented individuals, like the Ba'al Shem Tov and his associates, who served as spiritual guides to the people around them. Scholem also noted that the Carpathian mountains of Moldavia, where according to *Shivḥei habesht*, the Ba'al Shem Tov withdrew for several years of solitary retreat in his youth, were also the region from which the *startsy* revival spread to Russia. However, that revival apparently began only in 1763—three years after the Ba'al Shem Tov's death in 1760—with the settlement of its initiator, the Russian monk Paisy Velichkovsky, in the Moldavian town of Neamţ, upon his return from his years of training in the monasteries of Mt. Athos in Greece. See e.g. Ware, *The Orthodox Church*, 129–30; Bolshakoff, *Russian Mystics*, 79–98; Smolitsch, *Russisches Mönchtum*, 488–9. Furthermore, the parallel pointed out by Moshe Idel (*Kabbalah*, 321 n. 137; id., *Ascensions on High*, 148–50, 160) between the ascensions of the soul practiced by the Ba'al Shem Tov and the non-Jewish practice, in the Moldavian Carpathians, of prophetic–ecstatic detachment of the soul from the body, has nothing to do with the dissident Russian Orthodox sects; it is related, rather, to a long shamanistic tradition in the region, and to the use of such techniques by local folk healers and sorcerers.

may be quite independent of the Raskol, proliferated in the course of the eighteenth century and spread primarily within the rural population of the Russian empire. Some of them—particularly those of the radical wing, which did not recognize the authority of the Orthodox clergy and were therefore labelled 'priestless' (Bespopovtsy)—were known for their antinomian inclinations and hostility towards both the civil and the ecclesiastical authorities. The Russian government endeavoured to suppress them, prompting several such groups, following a series of persecutions, to leave their districts of origin in northern Russia and flee to the border regions of the empire, far from the reach of the regime.

Some of the sectarians settled in the Ukraine, especially in south-eastern Poland—in the same region and at the same time that the hasidic movement was getting under way.[2] This geographical proximity, and the observation of some resemblance between the two religious phenomena, have led a number of scholars to conjecture about the possible influence of the Russian sectarians on Israel Ba'al Shem Tov and his associates in the early, formative stages of the hasidic movement. However, in the absence of any tangible evidence of contact between the two groups, the scholars who suggested the possibility of influence have mostly refrained from venturing firm conclusions. The only attempt so far to demonstrate the existence of such contacts, and to prove their decisive influence on the Besht and his doctrine, has been shown to be misconceived and utterly unfounded.[3] In fact, everything we know about the Russian sectarians and their settlements in Poland at that time—their secluded locations, their clandestine organization, their self-sufficient economy, and their tendency to avoid unnecessary contacts with the local Ukrainian population—would make

[2] For comprehensive studies of these sects, see Maude, *A Peculiar People*; Grass, *Die russischen Sekten*; Conybeare, *Russian Dissenters*; Bolshakoff, *Russian Nonconformity*; Klibanov, *Religious Sectarianism in Russia*; Crummey, *Old Believers and Antichrist*; Paert, *Old Believers*; Cherniasky, 'Old Believers'; Treadgold, 'Peasant and Religion'; Heard, *The Russian Church*, 208–97; and Tsakni, *La Russie sectaire*. For their distribution specifically in the Ukraine, see Popovych, *Narys istoriyi kul'tury Ukrayiny*, 180–1, and Taranets, *Kurenevskoe trimonastyr'e* (both cited in Turov, 'Hasidism and Christianity, 73 nn. 1 and 2). For a critical review of the scholarly literature on this subject, see Niqueux, *Vieux-croyants*, especially 'Vieux-croyants: Un chantier'; and Comtet, 'Karl Konrad Grass'.

[3] I am referring to Yaffa Eliach's article, 'Russian Sects'. See Scholem, 'Neutralization of the Messianic Element', 362 n. 37; Weinryb, 'Reappraisals in Jewish History', appendix, 971–4; and see Rosman's summary and references in *Founder of Hasidism*, 82–3.

it extremely unlikely that there existed any neighbourly relations between them and the Jews. Thus the notion of their possible influence on hasidism inevitably becomes even more far-fetched.[4]

Yet what could not be demonstrated for the early hasidic movement is eminently demonstrable for the Frankist messianic sect, which was also active at the same time and in the same regions as the founders of hasidism.[5] Moreover, the Russian sectarians had far more in common with the religious cult established by Frank—its doctrines, rituals, and modes of organization[6]—than with any feature of early hasidism, and this applies not least to their respective positions on the status of women.

Based on the most complete Polish version of Jacob Frank's collection of dicta, *Księga Słów Pańskich* (Book of the Words of the Lord), which was still available to him at the end of the nineteenth century but appears, at least so far, to have since been lost or destroyed,[7] Alexander Kraushar writes: '[Frank] describes a trip to a village, "where the *Filipons* [the Filippovtsy sectarians] lived", ruled by a woman. The people "who came to her, touched their forehead to the ground when facing her, and brought her gifts in the form of money".'[8] Before taking a closer look at this woman and the cult that, according to Frank, centred upon her, it is necessary to clarify the nature of the sectarian context in which she appears, and to show how Frank came to be associated with that context.

---

[4] See Crummey, *Old Believers and Antichrist*, 137; Heard, *The Russian Church*, 203, 211, 214–15, 218, 220, 222, 244–5; Hundert, 'The Context of Hasidism', 175; Turov, 'Hasidism and Christianity'; Popovych, *Narys istoriyi kul{'}tury Ukrayiny*, 180–1.

[5] To be sure, Michael Silver, in a still unpublished paper, has pointed out that the Sabbatian and Frankist centres in Podolia were not among the places where the Ba'al Shem Tov is said to have visited or sojourned during a lifetime spent in this region. He concludes from this that despite their close geographical and temporal proximity, and contrary to accepted scholarly opinion, there was no real geographical overlap between the two movements; rather, they seem to have had separate spheres of influence in the same general area (see Rosman's discussion of this issue in *Founder of Hasidism*, 82 n. 67). Nevertheless, the very geographical and temporal propinquity of the two movements cannot be denied.

[6] Scholars have already noted the relationship between the Polish Sabbatians, especially Frank and his circle, and the Russian sectarians; see Scholem, 'Redemption through Sin', 124–5; id., *Studies and Texts* (Heb.), 105–6, 119, and 127–8; and Weinryb, *Jews of Poland*, 237–8, 242–3, 248, 374–5 n. 4, and 377–8 n. 30; Davidowicz, *Jakob Frank*, 115, 117.

[7] See the remarks (in English) of Jan Doktór, the editor of the Polish edition of Frank's dicta: *Księga Słów Pańskich*, ii. 157–9. And see Scholem, *Kabbalah*, 305–6; Shmeruk, 'The Peregrinations' (Heb.), 87 n. 1; and Rachel Elior's summary in 'Jacob Frank and his Book' (Heb.), 473, and appendix 2, 544–5.   [8] Kraushar, *Jacob Frank*, i. 124.

The account attributed to him is undated, nor does it mention the name of the village he apparently visited. Kraushar conjectures that it refers to his sojourn in 1757 in Giurgiu or Gyurgevo in southern Romania, on the Bulgarian border[9] (that is, in the area then known as Wallachia). He connects Frank's visit to a 'Filipon' or Filippovtsy village with the presence there of one of the sect's leaders, a mysterious man called Moliwda, whose close relations with Frank are known from the Polish documentation of the disputation between the Frankists and the Jews held in Lvov during July and August 1759.[10] This Moliwda is described in the Polish sources as a former Orthodox Christian 'who had just re-embraced Roman Catholicism',[11] though this may have been a ruse; turning religious dissembling from a matter of exigency into a subversive principle was common among the persecuted sects (and in the Sabbatian tradition as well).[12] Moliwda, whose mother tongue was Polish (unlike Frank and most of his followers, whose command of the Polish language at that stage was poor), was one of the representatives of the Frankist side in the disputation with the rabbinic delegates of the Jews, and is described as 'Frank's interpreter and spokesman and as the translator of his comments . . . a zealous advocate of Frank's teaching among Jews'.[13]

A few months later, however, in January 1760, Frank and his apostate disciples were called in for an interrogation before the church authorities in Warsaw, 'in the presence of the eminent gentleman [Moliwda], the ever present companion of Frank, who was turned unexpectedly into a denouncer, accusing the master and his students of secret and magical activities and principles, among the latter a belief in metempsychosis, that is, the transmigration of souls'.[14] The circumstances in which Moliwda had changed sides, turning from advocate to prosecutor of Frank, are not entirely clear. Perhaps he really had returned to the bosom of the Catholic Church, and when he realized that the Frankists' conversion to Catholicism was merely a camouflage for their sectarian Judaism, he denounced them in the name of his old/new faith.[15] Be that as it

---

[9] See Ch. 7 n. 86 above.

[10] On the Lvov disputation and the blood libel levelled in the course of it by the Frankists against the Jews see Balaban, *Frankist Movement* (Heb.), 209–66.

[11] Ibid. 201, 208.   [12] See below, at n. 33.

[13] Kraushar, *Jacob Frank*, i. 123, and see Balaban, *Frankist Movement* (Heb.), 201–2, 206, 208, and 225.   [14] Kraushar, *Jacob Frank*, i. 161.

[15] Balaban suggests that Moliwda may initially have supported Frank in the expectation that he would encourage the conversion of his Jewish followers to Catholicism; see *Frankist Movement* (Heb.), 201–2.

may, Kraushar succeeded in identifying Moliwda with a Polish adventurer of noble birth by the name of Antoni Kossakowski, who 'married a country woman ... and ended up in Wallachia, as the leader of the *Bohomolcow* Sect[16] or the *Filipons*. Subsequently, under the name Moliwda, he declared that he ruled over one of the islands of the Greek archipelago.'[17] Further on, Kraushar quotes from his Polish source:

[This Kossakowski], a fellow filled with pleasantries, as well as inconsiderateness, ... was highly proficient in the Latin and Russian tongues. He was well versed in knowledge of the Holy Scriptures and the Church Fathers. With the appearance in Poland, near Lviv [Lvov], of Sects of Talmudists and anti-Talmudists,[18] he made his way under the name Moliwda to the Archbishop of Lviv, and had a hand in the public disputation among the Jews.[19]

It is difficult to identify with certainty the 'Filipons'—that is, the Filippovtsy sectarians—mentioned in the passage, though there can be little doubt that they were one of the sects that had split away from the Orthodox Church. Several of them appear to have been known by the same name, perhaps, as Weinryb supposes,[20] after Danila Filippov, the seventeenth-century founder of the Khlysty sect,[21] from which several offshoots emerged over the course of the eighteenth century.[22] This possibility is also suggested by the apparently contradictory descriptions of the Filippovtsy in different sources. In Frank's

[16] Kraushar's 'Bohomolcow' are the Bogomoltsy or Bogomoly, i.e. 'God-worshippers', one of the names by which the Khlysty sect was known (see n. 21 below). The Skoptsy, or 'self-castrators', who branched off from the Khlysty, were also called by the same name. See Grass, *Die russischen Sekten*, i. 485, 487; ii. 845, 849.   [17] Kraushar, *Jacob Frank*, i. 123.

[18] Already at the earlier public disputation between the Frankists and the delegates of the Jewish communities of Poland, held in Kamenets-Podolsky in June 1757, Frank and his followers identified themselves, and were perceived by the Polish clerics as 'kabbalistic', 'zoharite', or 'anti-talmudist' Jews, pitting themselves against the Talmud and its rabbinic defenders, who were labelled 'talmudists'. See Balaban, *Frankist Movement* (Heb.), 127, 133, 138, 159 n. 1, 160–2, 188, 197, 267–8, 281.

[19] Kraushar, *Jacob Frank*, i. 123–4, in English translation, quoted from Darowski, *Pamiętniki Józefa Kossakowskiego*, 53.   [20] Weinryb, *Jews of Poland*, 377–8 n. 30.

[21] The name 'Khlyst' is derived from 'Christ', as every leader of the sect who was viewed as the reincarnation of Jesus was called, but the name came to be mispronounced as the word meaning 'whip', on account of the sect's practice of self-flagellation.

[22] But there was also another radical sect known as the Philippons or Filippovtsy, named for its founder, a monk called Philip who was active in the northern Russian provinces in the first half of the 18th century and immolated himself, along with seventy of his disciples, in response to gov-

own statements, they are portrayed as a rather lowly sect of peasants, to whom Frank refers incidentally while upbraiding his own disciples for their stubborn cleaving to Judaism: 'You were and have remained Jews . . . You are even lower than the Filipowców; you are like simple peasants, servants.'[23] On the other hand, Jacob Emden, following the Lvov disputation, received a letter from the rabbis of Poland, which referred to rumours about the mass conversion to Judaism of an entire 'Greek' (that is, Orthodox) village in the province of Wallachia. From Emden's report of the letter's contents, it would seem that this comment was a reference to the Filippovtsy sect, whose members were said to include 'great merchants and men of fabulous wealth':

I continued to investigate this as well, and I enquired of several men of authority, and since the same truth was told by all, it can be written down and disseminated. That province was near the Ukraine, and its inhabitants were called Philiptsiv/Philiptsio. They would seem to have taken this name from that of one of Christ's apostles, who was called Philip, just as there are other sects called the Jacobieri [Jacobites?], the Thomasnir [Thomasites?], and so forth. Those who know them well say that there are among them great merchants and men of fabulous wealth. They also related that those who were converting to Judaism had promised that many more of their associates and others from their land, several hundred people, would yet come to take up the Jewish faith.[24]

Emden's conjecture about the origin of the name of the Filippovtsy sect is highly unlikely, as are his speculations on the names of other genuine or fanciful Christian sectarians, and the rumoured conversion of hundreds of the sect's members to Judaism is also doubtful.[25] However, it is clear from his account that some Jews in Poland had heard of the relationship between Frank and the Filippovtsy, whether their adherents fit more closely with Frank's

ernment persecution. See Bolshakoff, *Russian Nonconformity*, 77–8; Treadgold, 'Peasant and Religion', 87–8; Conybeare, *Russian Dissenters*, 155–6; Crummey, *Old Believers and Antichrist*, 181–3, 189; Paert, *Old Believers*, 42; and Heard, *The Russian Church*, 204, 238.

[23] Kraushar, *Jacob Frank*, ii. 277. See also Weinryb, *Jews of Poland*, 374 n. 4.

[24] Emden, *Sefer shimush*, 'Shevet musar', 84b.

[25] Weinryb speculates that these rumours may have stemmed from a misunderstanding: the Jews interpreted the sectarians' antipathy towards the ecclesiastical authorities and the clergy as indicating a predilection for Judaism (*Jews of Poland*, 375 n. 8). However, the rumours may have had a grain of truth: several of these sects, such as the Molokany ('Milk-drinkers'), took up customs drawn from the Jewish dietary laws, and some even observed the Jewish sabbath, on account of which they were called 'Subbotniki'. On the Russian Judaizing sects see e.g. Treadgold, 'Peasant and Religion', 91–2; Bolshakoff, *Russian Nonconformity*, 105; Klibanov, *Religious Sectarianism in Russia*, 45; Heard, *The Russian Church*, 281–2; and Conybeare, *Russian Dissenters*, 291, 324–5, and 330–1.

description of them as lowly peasants or with the report that reached Emden of a group that included wealthy merchants.[26]

These references leave no room for doubt that Frank had some contacts with the Filippovtsy sect—with their village, which he sought out and visited by his own account, and with Moliwda, their leader in Wallachia, with whom he maintained close relations, at least for a time. Moreover, Frank clearly was well aware of the numerous sects active in his vicinity, including not only the Slavic-Orthodox schismatics but also several sects of Protestant émigrés that had originated in Germany. In one of his addresses to his followers he declared: 'All the religions and nations . . . in general must join the Roman Catholic religion, including the *Filiponi*, the *Hernuci*,[27] the *Amonici*,[28] and all other such sects.'[29]

[26] It could be that these were not two different sects, both called Filippovtsy, but a single group whose members included both peasants and merchants. The Khlysty sect, for example, had originated within the rural population, but it was joined in the course of the first half of the 18th century by merchants and urban craftsmen, some of whom were wealthy. See Treadgold, 'Peasant and Religion', 96; Klibanov, *Religious Sectarianism in Russia*, 50–1, and 57–8; and Conybeare, *Russian Dissenters*, 361. Conybeare notes that of 300 members of the Khlysty sect who were tried and found guilty of heresy in Moscow in 1733, 100 were peasants, while 50 were merchants and craftsmen (the rest were listed as monks and nuns). The Molokany, from the sect's beginning, included both peasants and well-off urban merchants; see Klibanov, *Religious Sectarianism in Russia*, 154–5. See also Heard, *The Russian Church*, 210–13, 222–3. For a more general discussion of the development of commerce in Old Believers' settlements over time, see Crummey, *Old Believers and Antichrist*, 135–58.

[27] This was the 'Herrnhuter' sect, named after the village of Herrnhut in Saxony, where members of the Moravian Brothers sect settled in 1722. See Cross and Livingstone, *Dictionary of the Christian Church*, 643, s.v. 'Herrnhut', and 928–9, s.v. 'Moravian Brothers'. The sect was known for its missionary activities, and its members would seem to have had some connection with Sabbatians in the circle of Jonathan Eybeschuetz, in whom they discerned Christian leanings. See Scholem, *Studies and Texts* (Heb.), 109–10 and n. 116 on p. 110; Liebes, *On Sabbatianism* (Heb.), 212–37, who believes that Eybeschuetz's Sabbatian circle was, in fact, a secret Judaeo-Christian sect, and cf. Greisiger, 'Jüdische Kryptochristen', who questions the existence of such a sect, as well as Maciejko, 'Christian Elements', 24–36, who argues that the very notion of its existence arose from a series of missionary forgeries, although he, too, acknowledges that the Christian forgers must have had direct contacts with the secret Sabbatians and Frankists of their day.

[28] This would seem to refer to the Mennonites, another Protestant sect. An offshoot of the Anabaptists, it was called after its Dutch founder, Menno Simons. In the 1780s, the Mennonites of Danzig (Gdańsk) responded to the call of the Russian empress Catherine II, who offered land and easy terms of settlement to foreigners wishing to make their homes within her borders. The Mennonites settled in several of the undeveloped regions of the Russian empire, including the Ukraine. On this see Rowe, *Russian Resurrection*, 183; Durasoff, *The Russian Protestants*, 30–4; and Urry, *None but Saints*, 51–62.

[29] Quoted in Kraushar, *Jacob Frank*, i. 219, from one of the sections of Frank's collected dicta that have not come down to us.

Although all these are but shreds of evidence—distant echoes and vague rumours—they nevertheless point to a palpable, direct relationship between Frank and the sectarians, one that may well have been the source of some of his most bizarre and aberrant practices. This relationship goes well beyond the kind of parallelism that might be attributed to the inherent natures of analogous but discrete phenomena, to sheer coincidence or more generally to the 'spirit of the time'. Frank was quite unique in this respect, not only in relation to the Besht and his associates who, as we have seen, were most unlikely to have come in contact with any of the Orthodox schismatics, but also in relation to the other spiritual guides and prophets of Sabbatianism who were active in the vicinity of the Russian sectarians, but with whom they maintained no demonstrable contacts—direct or indirect, personal or doctrinal —as will become clear further on.

Several of these radical sects, which had seceded from the Orthodox Church, rejecting both its clergy and its rites, eventually split into distinct groups, each known for its own peculiar practices that often gave it its name, such as the castration of both men and women, practised by the Skoptsy sect—the 'self-castrators';[30] the ceaseless wanderings of the Stranniki ('nomads') sect;[31] or the drinking of milk throughout the forty days of Lent, which was the distinctive practice of the Molokany ('milk-drinkers').[32] But however much they differed from one another in their defining peculiarities, most of these groups shared a basic set of religious principles and modes of social organization. Some of these were the legacy of their common historical roots, arising from the circumstances in which they had originally split away from the Orthodox Church, while others were inherent in the clandestine frameworks they formed in consequence of persecution by the authorities. Undeniably, many of these common traits were also shared by the Sabbatian movement, particularly its radical, sectarian manifestations that emerged in the course of the eighteenth century. On the basis of this observation, Gershom Scholem remarked that the close parallel between

[30] See above, n. 16, and see also Bolshakoff, *Russian Nonconformity*, 92–4; Tsakni, *La Russie sectaire*, 76–9; Conybeare, *Russian Dissenters*, 363–70; Heard, *The Russian Church*, 264–73; and Engelstein, *Castration*.

[31] See e.g. Bolshakoff, *Russian Nonconformity*, 78–80; Tsakni, *La Russie sectaire*, 41–62; Treadgold, 'Peasant and Religion', 88; Conybeare, *Russian Dissenters*, 156–64; and Heard, *The Russian Church*, 242–6.

[32] See e.g. Bolshakoff, *Russian Nonconformity*, 105; Tsakni, *La Russie sectaire*, 150–9; Treadgold, 'Peasant and Religion', 91; and Heard, *The Russian Church*, 273–4.

the Polish Sabbatians and the Russian Orthodox sectarians who were active in their vicinity raises the possibility of some mutual contacts and influences:

One must allow for the possibility that there were contacts between the Sabbatian believers and the Russian sects that developed a strong presence in the Ukraine following the great schism in the Orthodox Church. . . . One should not overlook the emergence, from the early years of the eighteenth century, of sects whose antinomian spirit was quite similar to that of the radical Sabbatians, and which are known to have been very influential in Russia and the Ukraine. These parallels may have been coincidental, and the Podolian Sabbatians may have received all their doctrines exclusively from Salonica, but who can say which way the wind was blowing or tell us for certain that there were no breaches in the walls that separated the different faiths? For surely, both the Sabbatians and the antinomian offshoots of the Raskol (such as the Khlysty sect, which is most important in this respect, though it was by no means unique), entirely abandoned the dogmas of their respective religions. The 'Living Christ'— that is, any of the prophets of these [Russian] sectarians—was a figure entirely divorced from the Christology of the Greek Orthodox Church. Among them, anyone from whose throat the Holy Spirit spoke, and who stood at the centre of a sectarian community, was viewed as a new 'God-man', and the boundaries separating the mere prophet from the 'God-man' grew ever more blurred. This is precisely what happened to the Sabbatians: they, too, began to see in any prophet or leader a fresh spark of the messianic soul, a new vesture or reincarnation of Sabbatai Zevi. . . . In both cases, an unrestrained wave of emotionalism swept simple people to the position of leaders, and both were alike, to an extent, in the form taken by their organizational structures and in the clandestine rites practised by their adherents . . . the ecstatic dancing, the admission of women into the ritual, and the sexually deviant acts that were such an important part of it . . . The persecutions, aggravated when the germination of libertine practices became public knowledge . . . led in both cases to extreme secrecy and to a psychology born of duplicitous apostasy.[33]

All the parallels listed by Scholem, in the context specifically of this Polish–Ukrainian milieu, are indeed close and instructive. One might even add to them the eschatological–apocalyptic tension, which was a hallmark of various stages of Sabbatian messianism,[34] and which also prevailed, at least for a time, in most

---

[33] Scholem, *Studies and Texts* (Heb.), 105–6; and see also ibid. 119.

[34] Thus, for example, Jacob Frank expressed his sense that the End of Days was nigh, and that contemporary events could be interpreted as its dawn: 'In the year 1783, the End of Days began' (*Words of the Lord*, §75); 'On the night of 17 June, the Master declared: "You ought to have been happy when I heard that war had broken out in the world. That Foundation Stone, upon which the whole world will be established, shall begin to emerge and be revealed"' (ibid., §811); 'If you only knew of the good thing that transpired here on the three days of 19, 20, and 21 June

of the dissenting Russian sects.[35] However, without exception, all these parallels apply not only to the Polish Sabbatian sectarians of Podolia, but also to other Sabbatian centres, whether clandestine or overt, Jewish or apostate, in many other regions as well. For not only the Polish Sabbatian prophets, such as Heshel Tsoref and Hayim Malakh, but also the German, Moravian, and Bohemian prophets, such as Mordecai of Eisenstadt, Leibele Prossnitz, Jonathan Eybeschuetz and his son Wolf, as well as the Sephardi prophets from the Balkans and the Levant, such as Abraham Cardozo, Berukhyah of Salonica, and his successors in the apostate Doenmeh sect, were all viewed as prophets whose personality had acquired a messianic dimension of its own, and at least some of them were also elevated to the rank of living incarnations of the divine, 'God-men', as it were.[36] This blurring of the boundaries that allowed the messianic leader to be taken as a tangible manifestation of the divine had, of course, originated with Sabbatai Zevi himself. The persistence with which it recurred time and again throughout the various transmutations of the Sabbatian movement weakens the likelihood that the appearance in the Ukraine, from the early decades of the eighteenth century, of precisely this model of leadership in which the prophetic, the messianic, and the divine were combined, was necessarily a response, specifically of the Polish Sabbatians, to some external sectarian stimuli. It is much more likely that the idea had sprung from within the Sabbatian tradition itself. After all, we know that the disseminators of Sabbatianism in Podolia were in direct contact with Sabbatians abroad, particularly the Doenmeh sect, which maintained a belief in the messianic–divine status of its leader, Berukhyah.[37] On the other hand, nothing is known of any contacts between the Sabbatians of Podolia and the schismatic Russian sectarians, with the single exception of Jacob Frank, who alone can be shown to have had direct dealings with some of them.

[17]84. Though we are in the grip of suffering and poverty, you would grow plump with joy, because you would know what is about to emerge in the world' (ibid., §827).

[35] On the eschatological tension and the apocalyptic atmosphere that characterized most of the dissenting sects, which viewed the ecclesiastical schism in Russia as the onset of the wars of the End of Days, and their persecutors—the Orthodox Church and the Tsar—as personifications of the Antichrist and his henchmen, see e.g. Treadgold, 'Peasant and Religion', 83–5 and 89; Klibanov, *Religious Sectarianism in Russia*, 51; Conybeare, *Russian Dissenters*, 158; Paert, *Old Believers*, 31–3, 37–9; Heard, *The Russian Church*, 202–5, 269, 280; and Crummey, *Old Believers and Antichrist, passim.*   [36] See above, Ch. 1, at nn. 120–8.

[37] See Scholem, *Studies and Texts* (Heb.), 83, 98–105, 108, 110, 112, and 119.

It would seem, then, that the prototype of the prophet–messiah–god in the Sabbatian movement as a whole, and that of the 'Living Christ'—the constantly recurring human incarnation of the Christian God—in the Khlysty sect and its offshoots[38] were no more than parallel types of messianic leadership. The same is true of the other parallels listed by Scholem: the antinomian spirit; the wave of emotionalism that promoted even simple people to the positions of prophets and leaders; the ecstatic phenomena; the clandestine organization; the secret rites; and even the admission to them of women, and the consequent rumours of sexual depravity within the cult.[39] All these belonged to the common physiognomy of Russian sectarianism on the one hand, and Sabbatian sectarianism on the other. These features, which we have already encountered in other contexts,[40] were neither unique to Podolian Sabbatianism nor likely to have originated in it. It is more reasonable to suppose that they entered Poland with the dissemination of clandestine Sabbatianism from its Ottoman centres. The fact that the Slavic sects in the same region were displaying many similar characteristics, to the extent that the Polish Sabbatians could have been aware of this, might at most have made them more receptive to the novel Sabbatian notions being imported by their own brethren from across the Ottoman border.

We should also allow for the possibility of parallel but independent Muslim influence upon both sectarian phenomena in Podolia, Sabbatianism in the Jewish context and the Russian Orthodox schismatics in the Christian one. Muslim influence may have reached the Ukraine from the Ottoman areas of the Balkans, or from Podolia itself, which was annexed to the Ottoman empire from 1672 to 1699. One indicator of such a possibility may be the rumoured practice in both sectarian groupings of the orgiastic 'extinguishing of the lamps' ceremony, which is alleged to have had its origins in a secret ritual of the Bektashi Sufis, and to have spread from them to the Doenmeh in Salonica, from whom it reached Jacob Frank in Iwanie,[41] while at the same

[38] See e.g. Treadgold, 'Peasant and Religion', 93 and 95; Conybeare, *Russian Dissenters*, 273–4, 278, 340–5, 349, 357, 359, and 368; Klibanov, *Religious Sectarianism in Russia*, 46 and 70; Maude, *A Peculiar People*, 98–9, 118–20, and 129–31; Heard, *The Russian Church*, 252–5, 267–9; and Bolshakoff, *Russian Nonconformity*, 83–5.

[39] On all these phenomena, which characterized many of the dissenting Orthodox sects, see the references in n. 2 above.

[40] e.g. at the end of Ch. 2 above.   [41] See above, Ch. 2 n. 76.

time being reported independently in relation to the Russian Khlysty sect or some of its offshoots.[42]

In contrast to all these parallels, for which we have no evidence to make of them more than just that, Jacob Frank and his circle may be singled out by a number of peculiar customs, idiosyncratic rituals, and bizarre doctrines which have no precedent in any of the diverse and geographically diffuse Sabbatian centres, but which do have exact parallels among the schismatic Russian sects. Thus, for example, Frank called upon his followers over and over again to discard or destroy the old books and expunge all the dead laws inscribed on their pages:

You saw perfectly clearly that I commanded you to sell your ancient books for next to nothing. How is it that you have not understood that all those books and laws will be shattered like potsherds?[43]

And this, too, has come to your knowledge, that one must come to the desert without water [cf. Ps. 63: 1], that is, without the Torah.[44]

All of the teachings shall be obliterated.[45]

We have no need whatsoever of the kabbalistic books.[46]

Have I not told you long ago how I saw in my dream that all was erased, like paper that was written upon and then drenched with ink? Thus must everything be blotted out.[47]

All Israelites must be baptized and enter the place of Edom . . . The executioner will burn all their books and their ten commandments . . . even the kabbalist books and the Zohar—all will be burned! . . . All this will be for their own good.[48]

This call is totally foreign not only to Jewish tradition, but also to the Sabbatian tradition in which Frank had been reared. Sabbatianism never aspired to dispose of the sacred texts, doctrines, and laws of Judaism. On the contrary, even its wildest antinomian or a-nomian gestures were generally exegetical; that is to say, they were based on textual interpretations which, however contrary to Jewish law, were nevertheless anchored, following age-old practice, in the divine revelation to be found in the traditional texts. At the outside, the

[42] See e.g. Conybeare, *Russian Dissenters*, 353; Heard, *The Russian Church*, 262; and Bolshakoff, *Russian Nonconformity*, 90–1.   [43] Frank, *Words of the Lord*, §421.

[44] Ibid., §454.   [45] Ibid., §803.   [46] Ibid., §1088.

[47] Ibid., §798, and often elsewhere, throughout the book.

[48] Kraushar, *Jacob Frank*, ii. 323, §1775, which has not come down to us, except in Kraushar's transcription from the Polish manuscript of *Words of the Lord* available to him.

Sabbatians founded their more libertine views on the ancient notion that, at
the time of the redemption, the commandments of Judaism will be superseded
or transcended by a new messianic Torah, but they scarcely would have conceived of a world not subject to the authority of a Torah of some kind, as
altered or inverted as this might be. Even the most radical among them never
severed their traditional bond with the Holy Scriptures themselves, as attested
by the extensive homiletic and exegetical literature produced by the movement.

On the other hand, it is said of Danila Filippov, the supposed seventeenth-
century founder of the Khlysty (although the sect may in fact have its true
origins in the much more distant past, pre-dating the seventeenth-century
Raskol in which it was eventually subsumed)—who had declared himself the
exclusive incarnation of God—that he gave his followers twelve new commandments of his own devising, and the second of them abrogated all pre-
existing doctrines and texts. The compendium of spontaneous expressions
uttered by his disciples while in the throes of ecstatic prophetic fits, called 'The
Book of the Dove' (*Kniga golubina*) and said to comprise new revelations of
the 'living' Holy Spirit, was to take the place of both the New and the Old
Testaments—the dead truths. In order to substantiate his rejection of the
Holy Scriptures of the church, Filippov collected all the books he could find
and threw them into the Volga.[49] The leaders of the Dukhobor sect also exhib-
ited a tendency to reject the authority of Scripture and denounce the old books
as 'dead'.[50] This surprising affinity between the radical attitude taken by some
of the separatist Russian sects and the singular position adopted by Frank,
with his documented links to some of those same sects, would seem to go
beyond mere parallel; there must have been direct influence at play.

A further act of Frank's that was extremely anomalous, as alien to his
Jewish as to his Sabbatian tradition, and certainly unheard of in either the
Catholic or the Muslim faith that at one time or another he had 'entered' or
embraced, was closely paralleled by a well-documented practice that distinguished more than one of the schismatic Russian sects. This was his appointment from among his close associates of twelve 'apostles' who were also known

---

[49] See Conybeare, *Russian Dissenters*, 351 and 358; Maude, *A Peculiar People*, 98–9; Klibanov,
Religious Sectarianism in Russia, 49, 152; Bolshakoff, *Russian Nonconformity*, 83–4; and Heard,
The Russian Church, 254.

[50] See Maude, *A Peculiar People*, 118; and Heard, *The Russian Church*, 278.

as his 'brothers'. Picked out for this task already in Iwanie,[51] their designation as apostles was the product of Frank's fully conscious and explicit identification with Jesus and his twelve Apostles, according to the tradition of the New Testament:

Now I shall reveal to you what I had in mind to do when I first came from Lvov to Warsaw. Everyone saw that I appointed you as brothers. Your names were those of the apostles of yore.[52] You saw that I began doing supernatural deeds. I commanded that three horses be harnessed to the sleigh, in single file, and thus I rode through the streets of the royal city like a great lord. People would ask me, 'What are you doing?' I would reply: 'I, I am Jesus, and my brothers are the apostles.'[53]

This kind of identification with Jesus and his Apostles is unprecedented in the history of Sabbatianism. To be sure, Sabbatai Zevi had displayed a relatively positive attitude towards Jesus. According to Coenen's account of the events of December 1665 in Smyrna, he declared to the throng that had gathered on the sabbath in the Portuguese synagogue: 'What had Jesus of Nazareth done that you should have treated him so harshly? I shall yet endeavour to have him count as a prophet.'[54] Nathan of Gaza had even asserted a relationship of sorts between Jesus, the husk (kelipah) of the messiah, and Sabbatai Zevi, the messianic fruit.[55] From here, however, it is still a very long way to Frank's direct and explicit identification of himself and his twelve 'brothers' with Jesus and his twelve Apostles.[56] Admittedly, this declaration turns out to have had a

[51] See above, Ch. 6 n. 25.

[52] The Polish Kronika describes the occasion on which Frank selected twelve 'brothers' and gave them new names, several of which were among the names of Jesus' apostles: 'On 6 July 1758 [sic, though it should be 1759], at evening, the Master chose these twelve men as his brothers: Rabbi Moses, and he commanded him to be called Peter; Jakubowski, who [also] received the name Peter; Jacob Tyśmienicki, who received the name Big Jacob; Zwierzchowski, who received the name Bartholomew; Jacob Szymanowski, who received the name Little Jacob. Two men stood in the middle, and they were Franciszek Wołowski, who received the name Lucas, and beside him Matuszewski of sacred memory, who was called Matthew (Levine, Kronika, 50–2, §43; Doktór, Rozmaite adnotacje, 58–9).

[53] Frank, Words of the Lord, §1290 (§1291 in Fania Scholem's Hebrew translation, which is incomplete). See also above, Ch. 6 n. 25, as well as Doktór, 'Jakub Frank', 54–6.

[54] Coenen, False Hopes (Heb.), 56. Jesus counts as a messenger of God and a genuine prophet in the Islamic tradition (see Encyclopaedia of Islam, iv. 81–6, s.v. 'Īsā'), of which Sabbatai Zevi was most probably aware.   [55] See above, Ch. 7 n. 213.

[56] There may be a veiled allusion to Jesus and his twelve Apostles in the appointment in Gaza, in the summer of 1665, of twelve rabbis chosen to accompany Sabbatai Zevi to the Temple

subversive intent; further on, Frank hedges it with the scornful claim that the historical Jesus could not have been the true messiah–God, 'for if he was, how could he have been killed by Jews like himself?' However, the obvious conclusion to be drawn from this was that Frank himself was the 'true' Jesus, the invincible messiah–God, and his twelve apostles, too, could not be harmed by human might: 'All the soldiers in Warsaw with their weapons would not have had the power to overcome you.'[57]

These concepts and acts are unparalleled in Sabbatian sectarianism, but they are very closely analogous to some of those among the Orthodox schismatics. Hilarion Pobirokhin, one of the leaders of the Dukhobor sect in the last quarter of the eighteenth century and a contemporary of Frank's, declared himself to be the Son of God who would serve as the supreme arbiter of justice on the coming Judgement Day, and he appointed for himself twelve disciple-apostles, following the paradigm of Jesus' Apostles. Savely (Sabellius) Kapustin, who took his place, and his successors after him did the same. Ivan Timofeevich Suslov, spiritual heir and successor of Danila Filippov to the leadership of the Khlysty sect, was similarly declared the new incarnation of Jesus. He was raised to the rank of divinity at the age of 31 and thereupon appointed twelve apostles who disseminated his doctrines. According to the tradition of the sect, at the order of the Tsar and the heads of the Orthodox Church, he was put to death by

site in Jerusalem, where he intended to offer a sacrifice. See on this Scholem, *Sabbatai Sevi*, 240. It may also be possible to read the same allusion to Jesus and the Apostles into the etching printed on the back of the title page of the 1666 Amsterdam edition of *Tikun keriah lekhol yom vayom*, one of the penitential texts compiled by Nathan of Gaza which were widely distributed that year, in many editions; see the reproduction in Scholem, *Sabbatai Sevi*, opposite p. 546. The lower part of the etching shows thirteen figures seated at a round table. They clearly depict Sabbatai Zevi—a larger figure than the rest, seated on a throne—surrounded by twelve disciples, representing, according to Scholem's interpretation (ibid. 526) the twelve tribes of Israel (the caption to the reproduction for some reason has it that the seated figures of the disciples represent the *ten* tribes, but this is surely an error. The image is also interpreted correctly in the caption to the same etching in the original Hebrew edition of the work (*Shabetai tsevi*, ii, opposite p. 434). It is not impossible that this image of the messiah surrounded by twelve disciples was inspired by the Christian tradition of Jesus and his twelve Apostles, whose number is in any case said to represent the twelve tribes of Israel (cf. e.g. Rev. 21: 12–16). For other rumours linking either Sabbatai Zevi or Nathan of Gaza with the twelve companions who represent the twelve tribes, see Scholem, *Sabbatai Sevi*, 222–3 n. 69, 631, 709, 720, and 822.

[57] Frank, *Words of the Lord*, §1290.

crucifixion on a Friday and resurrected on a Sunday at least twice during his long life—thus accomplishing a feat even greater than that of the 'historical' Jesus.[58]

Frank also instituted in his circle an odd kind of ritual choreography, which involved lengthy sessions of standing in a circle with men and women in symmetrical formation opposite each other. These peculiar ceremonies were held 'outdoors, in public' and apparently were not obscene, unlike the notorious, clandestine 'extinguishing of the lamps' ceremony mentioned above. Descriptions of them have survived in the Polish *Kronika*,[59] and they are also mentioned in *Words of the Lord*.[60] There is nothing like them in any other Sabbatian tradition known to us, but they have close parallels in the practices of at least some of the dissenting Russian sects. For example, the English Quaker missionary Steven Grellet observed a Dukhobor ceremony during his visit to one of the sect's villages in the early nineteenth century, in which, according to his account, all the village's inhabitants came out of their houses and gathered in a central common. They stood there in a circle around an old man, who evidently was their leader, with the women to his right and the men to his left. An elderly woman stationed herself next to the old man and began to sing, and all the women joined in. After a time, one of the men approached the old man and bowed deeply before him, and the old man returned his bow. They did this three times, and then both turned to bow in unison to all the women, and the women, too, returned their bow. The old man returned to his place in the centre of the circle, and his companion once more bowed down to him, after which he again turned and bowed to the women, and then to the men. Then all the men, one after another, went up to the old man in the centre of the circle and kissed him, and when they had finished, the women, too, went up to him and kissed him, each in turn. When the women had finished, all the boys went up and kissed the old man, one after another, and when they had done, all the girls went up, and they, too, kissed him one after another.[61] While this ceremony and Frank's do not match in all their particulars, there is no denying the similarity of their general outlines. Ceremonies such as these, which Frank must almost certainly have observed on his journeys when, as we know from his own testimony, he visited

[58] See Conybeare, *Russian Dissenters*, 273 and 359; Bolshakoff, *Russian Nonconformity*, 83–4; Heard, *The Russian Church*, 254–5; and Maude, *A Peculiar People*, 98–9, 118, and 131.

[59] See above, Ch. 6, at nn. 26–30.   [60] See *Words of the Lord*, §§456 and 459.

[61] See Maude, *A Peculiar People*, 143. For another description see Conybeare, *Russian Dissenters*, 320–1.

some of the sectarian villages and witnessed their practices, may well have stimulated his ritualistic inclinations[62] and inspired the novel processions and ceremonies that he instituted in his own court.

Frank's divergence from the Sabbatian tradition in all its historic and regional variations extended to the status of women and the relations between the sexes at his court, and here, too, there is good reason to suppose that his most radical innovations were inspired by practices which were common among the dissenting Russian sects, to which his own practices bore a close resemblance. As we have seen, the equalization of the status of men and women within the sectarian organization, the incorporation of women in its spiritual life and the rituals practised within it, the central role played by women in the initiation of new members to its ranks, and the full recognition of their prophetic powers were all common to both the Russian schismatic sectarian communities and the Sabbatian movement from its inception.[63] With regard to these common features, then, there is no reason and no need to suppose that their analogous appearance in Frank's circle was a consequence of his exposure to external sectarian influence. But one of his most startling innovations, foreign to both the Jewish and the Sabbatian contexts to which he belonged, was his banning— at least at Offenbach, and possibly earlier—of all marriages amongst his followers.[64] As we have already argued, there are some indications that the Sabbatian movement, in which ascetic tendencies had always been interlaced with ritualized sexual licentiousness, broke through the traditional Jewish gender divide that recognized in sexual abstention on the part of men—within certain limits—a pietistic value, while denying any religious value to sexual abstention on the part of women.[65] However, the fragments of evidence for the existence of 'spinster' Sabbatian prophetesses, and the reports of prophesying by many young girls and virgins, in no way suggest the adoption of a universal precept of sexual chastity for women in Sabbatian circles, and chastity for all certainly was never a regular practice within the Sabbatian rank and file. The institution of marriage retained its validity within the sectarian Sabbatian

---

[62] See above, Ch. 6, at nn. 41–6.

[63] For discussions in this spirit of the status of women in the dissenting Russian sects see e.g. Conybeare, *Russian Dissenters*, 189–213; Tsakni, *La Russie sectaire*, 49, 73, 143–4, 153–4, 239–40, and 242–3; Treadgold, 'Peasant and Religion', 93–4; Paert, *Old Believers*, 26, 28–9, 40, 51 n. 34, 69, 109–45. The status of women in the Sabbatian movement is the subject of Chs. 1–5 above.

[64] See above, Ch. 1, at nn. 85–6.   [65] See above, Ch. 1, at nn. 64–81.

frameworks, even when it was intentionally violated by sexual transgressions; in fact, it was precisely the continuing validity of the traditional institution of marriage that gave these transgressions religious meaning in the Sabbatian world-view. Even the Catholic religion, into which Frank and his followers converted, though it set great store by celibacy on the part of the minority—both men and women—who were committed to the monastic vocation, could not have been a source of inspiration in this regard, since it recognized marriage as a universal and desirable framework for all the rest of humanity. Furthermore, Frank's court at Offenbach, notwithstanding its rigid separation between men and women, neither maintained nor aspired to maintain a monastic way of life.

In contrast, the abolition of the institution of marriage is among the most outstanding features of the radical faction of Old Believers seceding from the Orthodox Church, the faction known as 'priestless', which rejected the established Orthodox clergy as an agent of Satan. Most of the dissenting sects that branched off from this faction or fused with it—the Khlysty, the Skoptsy, the Dukhobory, the Filippovtsy, and the other sects mentioned above as possible sources of inspiration for Frank's bizarre practices—strictly forbade marriage as a direct consequence of their breach with the clergy. Without priests, it was impossible to carry out any of the Christian sacraments, including marriage. The apocalyptic tension that accompanied the ecclesiastical schism, marked by the expectation of an imminent End of Days, led at first to the radical solution of banning marriage and imposing a duty of sexual chastity on one and all, for what was viewed as the short period remaining until the final downfall of the Antichrist. As the years went by, however, the sects could not maintain this strict regimen, and other solutions were found: mating outside the framework of marriage; maintaining a mere pretence of chastity; celibate coupling; and so forth. One way or another, the problem of sex in the absence of marriage became a controversial issue that the sects themselves deliberated throughout the course of the eighteenth century, and on which account they were persecuted by the church and the civil authorities, which saw them as corrupt and licentious.[66]

---

[66] On the rejection of the institution of marriage, the deliberations over this issue, and the rumours of licentious living among the 'celibate' sectarians see Conybeare, *Russian Dissenters*, ch. 5: 'The Question of Marriage' (pp. 189–219), and also pp. 351, 358, and 363. On p. 358 Conybeare provides an English rendering of the ban on marriage issued as the sixth of the twelve new commandments that Danila Filippov, founder of the Khlysty sect, handed down to

It is not at all unlikely that Frank was inspired by these sects both in his ban on marriage and in his guidelines for the sexual relations between the 'brothers' and 'sisters' among his adherents. In fact, even his choice of the designations 'brothers' and 'sisters' may have been inspired by the prevalent use of these terms in many of the sectarian communities. For example, the Dukhobory, who maintained the equal status of all members of the sect, male and female, and intentionally obfuscated the familial hierarchy that more usually prevailed in the relations between husbands and their wives, and between parents and their children, forbade the use of the designations 'husband' and 'wife' and mandated in their stead the usage between couples of the designations 'brother' and 'sister'.[67]

Frank's greatest and most exotic innovation was his doctrine of the redemptive Maiden—the feminine aspect of the divinity, incarnated in his daughter Eva, who, in his last years and even more so after his death, came to be viewed as his messianic–divine mate and the focus of the cult at his court.[68] To be sure, this doctrine may have certain kabbalistic foundations, and the notion of the messianic couple did find some expression in the Sabbatian tradition that preceded Frank, but only in Frank's doctrine did it reach full development, in far more explicit formulations and in public proceedings that have no Sabbatian precedent. Frank himself, as we have seen, linked his doctrine of the redemptive Maiden especially with the Catholic cult of the icon of the Black Madonna at Częstochowa, and with the cult of Mary, mother of Jesus, in Christian tradition in general. However, his repeated emphasis on the concrete manifestation, in this world, of the Maiden concealed in the icon, and the identification of Eva, his flesh-and-blood daughter, with this divine manifestation, go far beyond the bounds of the official Christian cult—both Catholic and, for that matter, Orthodox—of Mary, mother of Jesus. At the same time, they point to the possibility of a link with the schismatic sectarians.

his followers: 'Marry not. He that is married shall live with his wife as with his sister, as is declared in the old scriptures. Let the unwedded wed not, the wedded separate.' See also Treadgold, 'Peasant and Religion', on the Pomortsy ('coast dwellers') sect, pp. 86–7; on the Fedoseevtsy sect (so named for its founder, Feodosy Vasiliev), p. 87; on the Filippovtsy sect, p. 88; and on the Khlysty sect, p. 94; and see Bolshakoff, *Russian Nonconformity*, 37–8, 77–8, 83–4, and 92–4; Tsakni, *La Russie sectaire*, 239–40; Maude, *A Peculiar People*, 98–101 and 125–6; Heard, *The Russian Church*, 201, 240–2, 247–9, 266; and Paert, *Old Believers*, 46–9.

[67] See Tsakni, *La Russie sectaire*, 143; Maude, *A Peculiar People*, 133; Heard, *The Russian Church*, 253; and Conybeare, *Russian Dissenters*, 281.   [68] See above, Ch. 7.

The Russian sects, from their inception, displayed a tendency to set beside the spiritual leader, who was seen as a reincarnation of Jesus, a female mate who usually was not his wife. She was seen as a reincarnation of Mary, mother of Jesus, and was called 'Mother of God'. Among the Khlysty, who were organized, in each of their settlements, into independent cells called 'ships' or 'naves', each cell was headed by a living 'Christ' who had beside him his own 'Mother of God', and both were viewed as possessing the Holy Spirit and as the source of divine authority.[69] The leaders of the Skoptsy sect, which branched off from the Khlysty sect and resembled it in its organizational structure, were also all viewed as the paired manifestation of the messianic divinity becoming flesh—the living 'Jesus' with the 'Mother of God' by his side. Conybeare, however, describes a slightly different situation in one of their centres, in the Tula district situated south of Moscow. In 1770 it numbered about a thousand members, divided into several 'ships', all of which were headed by a single 'Mother of God', the elderly Akulina (Aquilina) Ivanova, who had no living 'Jesus' with her at the time and held sole sway over her followers. She was known for her prophetic powers, and she directed a whole bevy of prophets and prophetesses who belonged to the sect.[70] Tsakni describes the ceremony at which a new female leader was chosen from among the venerated Skoptsy virgins, whose breasts and sexual organs had been amputated, and who were gifted with the power of prophecy. Once she had assumed her role, the woman was called 'Mother of God' and 'Queen of Heaven' as a consequence of her identification with the Holy Virgin, mother of Christ. From that time onward she was showered with gifts by the sect's members, who served her submissively and loyally.[71]

This portrayal accords well with the account of the veneration of the 'ruling' woman in the Filippovtsy village that Frank, by his own testimony, had visited.[72] We may assume that he was acquainted with this phenomenon and had encountered it more than once on his travels. His decision to bequeath his messianic mission to none other than his daughter Eva, who, after his death, bore the burden of this role to the best of her limited abilities, may also

[69] See Conybeare, *Russian Dissenters*, 341, 344–5, 349, 357, and 359; Treadgold, 'Peasant and Religion', 93; Bolshakoff, *Russian Nonconformity*, 84; Tsakni, *La Russie sectaire*, 73; Heard, *The Russian Church*, 204, 255, 262, 268, 285; and Maude, *A Peculiar People*, 98–9.

[70] Conybeare, *Russian Dissenters*, 363; Engelstein, *Castration*, 27–8. In the following generations the Skoptsy again came under the leadership of divine couples. See Conybeare, *Russian Dissenters*, 366 and 368.   [71] See Tsakni, *La Russie sectaire*, 83–4.   [72] See above, at n. 8.

have been inspired by another sectarian practice with which he was familiar. Among the Dukhobory, for example, the leadership, conceived of as the evolving incarnation of the divinity, was passed down not only from father to son but also from father to daughter, and some of those daughters wielded a great deal of power and influence.[73] The appointment of Eva as judge of the court, before whom the believers confessed their sins,[74] may also have been modelled on the tradition of these separatist sects: in each of the Khlysty 'ships', for example, the believers customarily confessed their sins before their leader, 'Jesus', or his mate, the 'Mother of God'.[75]

We have seen that Frank adopted Muslim sectarian practices that reached him by way of the apostate Salonican Sabbatians,[76] and that he drew Catholic inspiration from the cult of the Black Madonna at Częstochowa.[77] In the same way, in light of his awareness of the Russian sects active in his surroundings, and of the contacts he maintained for a time with at least one of their leaders, it seems entirely possible that he also wove into his doctrine certain beliefs and practices that had their origins in that sectarian milieu. The syncretism that always characterized Sabbatianism reached its peak in Frank's doctrine. His call for all faiths and religions to merge under the mantle of the Catholic Church[78] was but the obverse side of his subversive vision of the total demolition of them all.[79]

---

[73] See Treadgold, 'Peasant and Religion', 90; and Maude, *A Peculiar People*, 150.

[74] See above, Ch. 7, at n. 92.   [75] See Conybeare, *Russian Dissenters*, 356.

[76] See above, Ch. 2 n. 76.   [77] See Ch. 7 above.   [78] See above, Ch. 7, at nn. 74–83.

[79] Frank expressed this sentiment on many occasions. For example: 'I came to Poland only in order to abolish all the laws and all the religions' (*Words of the Lord*, §130). 'Jacob maintained the honour of his Lord even when he was in a place of other gods. So, too, must we maintain the honour of our Lord, and how shall we do this? By discarding every law and every religion' (ibid., §219). 'All the religions that have existed up to now, even that first and that second one you had [i.e. Judaism and Islam] . . . they all must be cut down, because they are but branches on a tree of death and when the branches are pruned away, they wither, as your own texts declare: "until the kingdom [of God] is transformed into heresy" [*ad tithapekh malkhut leminut*, BT *Sot.* 49*b* and BT *San.* 97*a*; the Hebrew words are transliterated in the Polish text as *At tissapech hamalches leminus*, reflecting the Ashkenazi pronunciation of the language], that is, all of them [i.e. all the kingdoms] will be cut down' (ibid., §708).

NINE

Conclusion: From Sabbatianism to Hasidism

THE EVIDENCE considered in the previous chapters suggests that throughout the century and a half of Sabbatianism's viable existence, both within Judaism and—in its apostate form—still in close association with it, the liberation of women from the 'curse of Eve' formed an integral part of its redemptive vision. That vision was marked from the outset by two opposing if intertwined trends. The first was egalitarian, holding women's status to be wholly analogous to men's, and thus beckoning women to partake equally—in their own right, albeit apart from the men—in every aspect of the ritual and spiritual life of the messianic community. While this trend may be viewed as conservative inasmuch as it preserved the traditional segregation of the sexes from one another, it was undoubtedly revolutionary in that it tacitly established a novel ontological parity between them: the formal separation of the women from the men was conducive to the enhancement of their spiritual stature; it released them from the bounds of materiality, physicality, and above all their inherent sexuality, to which tradition had always anchored them, and by which it defined female nature in terms of 'body' or 'matter' as against male nature—'soul' or 'form'.[1] The result was that women could engage on an equal footing in the same range of messianically charged religious activities as the men. Evidence for this can be found, for example, in Sabbatai Zevi's two 'coronation' ceremonies, held in Smyrna, in December 1665, in identical fashion on two consecutive days, one for men and the other for women; in the independent activity of his wife Sarah among the female messianic believers; in the sermons that Judah Hasid preached expressly in the 'women's synagogue', where

---

[1] For the Greek origins of this conceptualization of the male/female dichotomy, of which I believe there are some early intimations in the classical rabbinic sources, but which was imported into medieval Jewish philosophy and became ubiquitous in the literature of Jewish thought, see above, Ch. 3 n. 13.

he very likely also called them up to the reading from the Torah (as did Sabbatai Zevi in his day), for which he apparently brought them the traditional manuscript scroll; in the separate instruction of women in the Zohar; and in the symbolic juxtaposition at the Frankist court of the 'brothers' and 'sisters' in perfect symmetry, but always in two distinct groups and apart. We may conjecture that this trend could have drawn on eschatological traditions such as the Zohar's depiction of righteous women in Paradise, where—relegated to their own quarters, which are strictly off limits to righteous men (and even to angels!)—they occupy themselves with nothing other than the intellectual and spiritual pursuits of study and prayer.

The second trend was libertine. Its thrust was to cast off the burden of tradition and law, not least the laws of prohibited sexual unions. It set the relations between the sexes on an entirely new basis, drawing on midrashic traditions that envisage the 'slaying' of the evil impulse, the abrogation of the commandments, and the coming into effect of a new Torah in the messianic age. In kabbalistic tradition this idea was expressed in terms of progression from a world ordered by the Torah of Creation (*torah diberiah*), associated with the paradisal Tree of Knowledge and signifying the distinction between good and evil that engendered the restrictive system of halakhic prohibitions, to a state of perfected existence by order of the transcendent Torah of Emanation (*torah de'atsilut*), associated with the Tree of Life and free from all distinctions, oppositions, and restrictions.[2] This libertine trend, which subverted the highly gendered structure of Jewish ritual law, established parity between the sexes by way of blurring the distinction between them. Men and women would function interchangeably or together in situations in which tradition had normally kept them apart. This manifested itself, for example, in Sabbatai Zevi's calling up to the reading from the Torah of both men and women, in front of a mixed congregation, when in December 1665, he forced his way into the sabbath service at the Portuguese synagogue of Smyrna; in Jacob Frank's declaration that women should carry swords, and his proclivity for surrounding himself with an armed female guard; and in the mixed-sex Zohar study groups that apparently met in Prague at the turn of the eighteenth and nineteenth centuries. It was most evident in the series of 'bizarre' acts alluding to sexual transgression, which characterized Sabbatai Zevi's conduct almost from the start of his messianic career: his relations with his divorced wives, who were forbidden to him by Jewish law; the rumours of

---

[2] See above, Ch. 5, at nn. 48–9.

the virgins who were entrusted to him for mysterious purposes smacking of proscribed intimacy; and the affair of the 'sealed pouch' containing texts that called for the dissolution of the rules regulating sexual relations. This tendency persisted, and was even adopted as a sacred code of conduct, long after Sabbatai Zevi's demise, among those of the messianic sectarians who demonstrated their fealty to the 'Torah of Emanation' by consciously, deliberately, and ritually breaching the sexual restrictions of Jewish law.

The two trends, the egalitarian and the libertine, can be seen to have combined already in Sabbatai Zevi's personal address to women, as recorded by Thomas Coenen at the height of the messianic enthusiasm that erupted in Smyrna. In his address he promised to revoke the disabilities foisted upon women by the curse of Eve: to redeem them from the pain of childbirth, to free them from subjugation to their husbands, and so to make their wretched lot as happy as the lot of men. Thus far his egalitarian programme; but this was followed directly by the declaration that the messiah had come 'to annul the sin of Adam'—a promise which implied the libertine tidings of the abrogation of the restrictive Torah of good and evil. This Torah had come into effect only as a consequence of the primordial sin, and it was now becoming obsolete with the rescission of that sin and all its dire consequences.

It was precisely in this sense, and in reference expressly to the abolition of sexual prohibitions, that Moses Hagiz, sworn enemy of Sabbatianism, interpreted the claim that Sabbatai Zevi had 'rectified' the sin of Adam. This, he said, was one of the two most widespread notions among the Sabbatians of his time, by means of which they validated and even sanctified the act of sexual transgression. He denounced these attitudes as 'the gall of evildoers' and a 'wicked belief' upon which it was best not to dwell so as not to 'sully the air':

Since, with the advent of their filthy redeemer[3] Sabbatai Zevi, the sin of Adam and Eve has already been rectified, and [good] nourishment has been sifted from [evil] refuse,[4] a new Torah has gone forth from him, permitting the sexual prohibitions and all manner of admixture of [the permitted and] the forbidden, for [as they claim,] the

---

[3] The Hebrew for 'filthy', *mego'al*, plays on *go'el*, 'redeemer'.

[4] This is a reference to the kabbalistic doctrine, associated with Isaac Luria, whereby the 'rectification' or restoration of the world to a state of perfection is the long drawn-out process—culminating in the final redemption—of 'sifting', 'sorting', or extricating the world-sustaining vital particles of spiritual good ('nourishment') from the dead weight of material evil ('refuse') in which they are trapped.

very notion of admixture is no longer tenable, since that which was accursed has become blessed, 'and everything is prepared for the feast'.[5]

This, it seems, is why the Sabbatian call for the liberation of women was ultimately silenced. The sexual depravity, which had become a hallmark of the heretical messianic movement, was tacitly linked to the high visibility of women within its ranks. For the mere presence of women had always signalled the danger of unbridled sexuality;[6] their active participation in the licentious eschatological 'feast' was perceived as the eruption of dark forces which were inherent in women and had to be subdued in order for sober propriety to be restored. It was above all its association with rampant sexuality that discredited the messianic spirituality of women. It put an end to the activities of the Sabbatian prophetesses, and with it to the tradition from which they had emerged—that tradition of messianic prophecy by women, which pre-dated

---

[5] Hagiz, *Shever poshe'im* (published in London in 1714), 71, quoted in Scholem, *Researches* (Heb.), 349. The final sentence is a citation from *Pirkei avot*, 3: 17, referring—sarcastically, here—to the feast that awaits the righteous in the eschatological World to Come.

[6] For sexuality as the defining characteristic of women, see e.g. BT *Ber.* 24*a*, where a woman's little finger is likened to her genitals, and even an exposed 'hand's-breadth' of her body, her leg, her voice, or her hair are considered her 'nakedness', or *Derekh erets rabah*, 1: 13, where men are urged to refrain as much as possible from conversing with women, because 'a woman's conversation is nothing but lewd words [*divrei ni'ufim*]'. For the perception of female sexuality as an incontinent, menacing force, which presents a constant threat to the integrity of men, see Boyarin, *Carnal Israel*, 77–106, where he is at pains to distinguish the classical rabbinic sources' predominantly positive attitude towards women and sex from Philo's condemnation of female sexuality as the source of all evil. At the same time, however, he concedes the presence of sexually 'misogynistic' texts within the midrashic corpus, and points to the growing anxiety about women's sexuality that became prevalent in later Judaism. It is clearly not by accident that an obscure reference to 'the affair of Beruriah', which is offered in the Babylonian Talmud as a possible explanation for the shameful flight of her husband, R. Meir, from Palestine to Babylonia (see BT *AZ* 18*b*), is developed in a medieval tradition recorded by Rashi into an account of her ignominious suicide following her seduction by one of her husband's disciples (see Rashi ad loc.). Beruriah's exceptional learning, which challenged the rabbinic dictum (BT *Shab.* 33*b*; *Kid.* 80*b*) that 'women are light-headed' (understood as lewd), and clashed implicitly with the view whereby teaching women Torah is tantamount to teaching them lewdness (see BT *Sot.* 20*a*), is thus associated with transgressive sexuality as a matter of course. A poignant statement of this sensibility, which persists in traditionalist circles to the present day, can be found in the recent memoirs of an Orthodox upbringing by Naomi Seidman, who writes: 'A boy might conceivably become an *apikores*, a heretic, but transgression in a girl could only mean something sexual' (Seidman, 'Reflections', 55).

Sabbatianism by at least a century and a half but was quickly harnessed to the Sabbatian cause to be entirely subsumed in it.

For surely, the Sabbatian prophetesses did not spring up out of nowhere, and their emergence in virtually every corner of the Sabbatian world can hardly be attributed to the influence of this or that factor alone in any one of their many and diverse surroundings. The origins of the phenomenon in the early modern era would seem to go back to the expulsion of the Jews from Spain at the turn of the fifteenth and sixteenth centuries. The experience of the Conversos who remained on Iberian soil inevitably positioned their women at the heart of what became an illicit, covert, and above all domestic practice of residual Judaism. This seems to have spurred the emergence from their ranks of an array of messianic prophetesses, and it is reasonable to assume some degree of continuity between their prophetic activity and the comparable activity, equally driven by urgent messianic hopes, of the female visionaries with whom Hayim Vital came in contact in his Levantine milieu almost a century later. The women he describes, who all seem to have wielded considerable moral authority, were freely practising their prophetic craft in the Jewish communities of Safed, Jerusalem, and Damascus, where throughout this period, the local population was exposed to the overwhelming cultural influence of a large tide of immigrants originating, either directly or indirectly, in the Converso population of Iberia. This Iberian connection may well account for the natural ease with which prophetically inspired women could be accepted—as evidently they were, at least by Hayim Vital, who was himself of Calabrian descent, which put him within the Judaeo-Spanish orbit—as belonging to a long-established tradition of messianic prophecy by women. Vital's attitude to the female visionaries he encountered can be inferred from the fact that he never doubted or considered them in any way anomalous. His silence on this point suggests that he took their prophetic skill for granted, finding no need to hedge its credibility or to question its legitimacy. Rather, he seems to view the prophetesses of his acquaintance as in no way inferior, and in some cases decidedly superior to their male counterparts, such as himself.

Less than a century later, the appearance of hundreds or even thousands of Sabbatian prophetesses—once again in an Ottoman milieu which had absorbed large numbers of Iberian immigrants—was, admittedly, perceived as extraordinary by all, and by the movement's few ardent opponents as defying both reason and tradition. But the masses of Jews who believed in Sabbatai

Zevi did not doubt his female prophets any more than they doubted the male. It was above all the scale, not the nature of the phenomenon that appeared so remarkable to everyone who witnessed it. Fragments of evidence—such as reports that in Livorno, long before the outbreak of messianic frenzy in Smyrna, Sarah, who was eventually to marry Sabbatai Zevi, was well known and much sought after as a skilful prophetess—suggest that the professional practice of prophecy by individual women, as described by Hayim Vital, never died out but rather was temporarily overrun by the unprecedented surge of prophetic inspiration that engulfed men, women, and children, who all began to prophesy en masse in response to the messiah's call. But individual Sabbatian prophetesses resurfaced and continued to operate long after the tide of mass messianic prophecy had subsided.

Thus the visionary women in Vital's accounts seem to stand on a certain continuum that links them, at one end, with the Iberian prophetesses of the immediate aftermath of the expulsion, and at the other end with the women taking part in the Sabbatian eruption of mass prophecy.[7] When we view as contiguous all three apparently discrete manifestations of female prophetic spirituality, a tradition emerges of messianic prophecy by women that persisted for over 300 years, reaching its climax in the heyday of Sabbatianism, but surviving in one form or another right through to the last transmutations of the decaying messianic movement in the early 1800s.

One might have expected such a tradition to strike deep enough roots to ensure its future, and yet the demise of Sabbatianism coincided with the effective disappearance from the landscape of female visionaries and messianic prophetesses, or rather, as we shall see, with the delegitimization of any public display of female spirituality, which was now relegated to the domain of sorcery, spirit possession, or just plain madness.

That messianic prophecy as such should have subsided at this time is hardly surprising, given that the Sabbatian debacle, which had exposed the capacity of the messianic idea to undermine religious norms and morality, inevitably discredited, at least for a while, all manner of messianic agitation, and this applied to messianic prophecy by men and women alike.[8] Moreover, by the early nine-

---

[7] The first to bring together all these phenomena and to define them as a continuous thread of female mystical spirituality, whose existence had been overlooked by Jewish historiography, was Joseph Chajes, in his 1999 doctoral dissertation, 'Spirit Possession', 202–7, and subsequently in several of his published works. See e.g. Chajes, *Between Worlds*, 99–100.

[8] See e.g. the condemnation of all contemporary messianic prophecy by Leib b. Ozer, who

teenth century, in several western and central European centres of Sabbatianism, the Jewish community was undergoing a transformation brought about by acculturation, the Enlightenment, and emancipation, which eroded old frameworks of religious life and led to a crisis of traditional faith.[9] This was accompanied by a growing distaste for mystical religiosity and kabbalah, which were associated with the discredited Sabbatian heresy, and which could not be reconciled with the rationalist thinking that governed the processes of modernization.[10] Under these circumstances, kabbalistic messianism, whether championed by men or by women, was doomed to extinction.

But in eastern Europe, at the same time and in the same regions where Sabbatianism was waning, hasidism was in the process of becoming a mass movement. It shared the kabbalistic legacy of Sabbatianism, and adopted, or at least independently reproduced, its most distinctive mode of prophetic–charismatic leadership.[11] This gave rise to the still common perception that

concludes his 1718 account of the rise and fall of Sabbatai Zevi with the warning: 'We must not be impressed by those who perform awesome deeds, for they are all [driven] by the Other Side [Satan, the forces of evil], and we should keep as far away as possible from such people, since all they do is confound and disturb the worlds, causing nothing but adversity and leading to no good whatsoever. Rather, "Thou shalt be perfect with the Lord thy God" [Deut. 18: 13], for we can do without prophets, and let none other but Elijah the Prophet herald good tidings, salvations, and consolations' (*Story of Sabbatai Zevi* (Heb.), 209). See also below, at n. 61.

[9] See e.g. Kieval, *Languages and Community*, 26–34, 37–64; McCagg, *Habsburg Jews*, 22–6, 65–82; Scholem 'Sabbatian Will', 170–1; Duker, 'Polish Frankism's Duration', 297.

[10] On the aversion to the Zohar and kabbalah during this period, see Tishby, *Wisdom of the Zohar*, i. 43–50; Huss, 'Admiration and Disgust', 203–7. See also Meyer, *German-Jewish History*, i. 233–4, ii. 144. This is the sentiment to which Gershom Scholem referred as *Kabbala-Angst* (Scholem, 'Politik der Mystik', 2), and which, more recently, Mordecai Breuer described as 'Kabbalophobia' (Breuer, 'Fragments of Identity' (Heb.), 23). Notably, however, Rivka Horwitz has shown that some of the 18th- and early 19th-century maskilim, including Mendelssohn himself, were not altogether ignorant of or hostile to kabbalah, treating it as a metaphysical doctrine, which could be harmonized with rationalist Enlightenment values. She also highlights the survival of some strands of viable, if marginal, kabbalistic religiosity in 19th-century Germany, especially Bavaria, and the revival of interest in kabbalah by the turn of the 19th and 20th centuries. See Horwitz, *Multiple Faceted Judaism*, 11–235.

[11] Gershom Scholem, and following him, many other historians of kabbalah and hasidism, believed the institution of the tsadik—the charismatic leader in hasidism—to have evolved out of the Sabbatian 'ideal type' of the charismatic prophet-messiah. See e.g. Scholem, *Major Trends*, 333–4; id., *The Mystical Shape*, 124–6; id., 'The Two First Testimonies' (Heb.), 238–9; Weiss, 'Some Notes', 10–12; and id., 'Beginnings of Hasidism' (Heb.), 51–8. This view was challenged by Mendel Piekarz, who argued that much of the hasidic doctrine of the tsadik could

the hasidic movement was Sabbatianism's natural heir. Already in the late eighteenth century, the rabbinic opponents of hasidism denounced it as a latter-day offshoot of the messianic heresy, or else as its immediate successor within a long sectarian tradition, which had always been antithetical to rabbinic Judaism.[12] This was also the context in which the rise of hasidism was set by the Galician maskilim who campaigned against it in the early decades of the nineteenth century;[13] and the same view was still being echoed by some of the movement's early historians,[14] while others presented hasidism as a dialectical response to Sabbatianism, and thus, too, its product.[15]

Given this line of descent, hasidism might have been expected to preserve the inclusive, egalitarian attitude to women that was such a distinctive feature of Sabbatianism. It might have produced its own array of prophetically inspired women, enabling them to play a prominent role in the charismatic leadership of the movement. Indeed, within certain limits, the hagiographical tradition of nineteenth- and especially twentieth-century hasidism does acknowledge the prophetic insight of some distinguished women, whom it also credits with supernatural powers, considerable authority, and prestige. But this is almost exclusively confined to women who were related by family

have been drawn directly from the same kabbalistic sources that underlay the Sabbatian concept of the messiah, and thus that the emergence of charismatic leadership in hasidism could have altogether bypassed the discredited Sabbatian precedent. See Piekarz, *The Beginning of Hasidism* (Heb.), 299–302, and cf. Rubinstein, 'Between Hasidism and Sabbateanism' (Heb.).

[12] See Wilensky, *Hasidim and Mitnagedim* (Heb.), i. 62, 66–7, 116 n. 3, 156, 240–1, 245, 256, 258–64, 268, 276, 304, 328–9, 346; ii. 16, 45–6, 75, 104, 141–2, 179–80, 209, 268, 292, 296, 321. See also Werses, *Haskalah and Sabbatianism* (Heb.), 99–103.

[13] See Werses, ibid. 103–24.

[14] See e.g. Graetz, *History of the Jews*, v. 396–9; Kahana, *History of the Kabbalists* (Heb.), ii: *Even Ofel*, 65; Dubnow, *History of Hasidism* (Heb.), 1–2.

[15] This is implicit in the very presentation of Sabbatianism and hasidism as two consecutive chapters, representing two consecutive phases of the Jewish mystical tradition, in Gershom Scholem's influential *Major Trends in Jewish Mysticism*, where he also states this view explicitly (e.g. pp. 329–34), as he does elsewhere (e.g. 'Neutralization of the Messianic Element', 'The Two First Testimonies' (Heb.), 237–9, and '*Devekut*', 221). See also Buber, *Origins and Meaning*, 29–40; Tishby and Dan, 'The Doctrine and Literature' (Heb.), 251–3 and *passim*; Weiss, 'Some Notes', 11–13; id., 'Beginnings of Hasidism' (Heb.), 127–8, 133–4, 151, 169–70; and Rubinstein, 'Between Hasidism and Sabbatianism' (Heb.). But cf. Piekarz, *Beginning of Hasidism* (Heb.), 278–9, 299–302, as well as Idel, *Hasidism*, 1–17, and 'Martin Buber and Gershom Scholem', who reject this view of the relationship between the two movements on philological and methodological grounds respectively.

ties to the most famous male leaders of the movement: their mothers, widows, daughters or sisters, who derived from them such power and reputation as they possessed. This, after all, was no more than an extension of that ancient tradition in the rabbinical world, whereby the female relatives of illustrious men could acquire a reputation for piety, erudition, and even expert knowledge in certain fields of halakhah, particularly those pertaining to the lives of women. It is hardly surprising, therefore, that hasidism—a movement that places the charismatic personality of the leader at the heart of both its doctrine and social organization—should have exploited this tradition to the full, allowing the leader's supernatural aura to reflect on all those who were closest to him, including his female relatives. But the revolutionary novelty of Sabbatianism—its promotion of some women in their own right to positions of authority as inspired prophetesses, and its full incorporation of all women as a constituency of the messianic community—was conspicuously absent from the emergent hasidic movement. The early hasidic fraternities effectively excluded women from their ranks; even when some of the hasidic courts—and by no means all of them—admitted women for the purpose of seeking a personal blessing from the leader (tsadik or rebbe), they denied them access to his 'table', where he continued to address his teachings to the exclusively male gatherings of his disciples and followers. As for the reports of independent female leaders functioning as rebbes in their own right—while being grounded in the probable historical reality of one extraordinary 'holy virgin', the celibate Maid of Ludmir, who may have attracted for a while a grass-roots following of her own[16]—they testify above all that the phenomenon, perceived as an intolerable aberration, was suppressed so quickly and so thoroughly as to have left no more than a faint imprint on the collective memory of the movement. This was preserved in oral tradition but eradicated from the vast literary output of hasidism until the early twentieth century, when it was rescued from oblivion, not by any of the movement's authentic literary spokesmen, but rather by one of its renegades: the westernized historian S. A. Horodetsky, who, viewing hasidism as a traditionalist model for Jewish national revival, construed what he believed to be the equal rights it offered women in the religious sphere in terms that matched the utopian egalitarianism inherent in the secular ideology of Zionism. Subsequently, female leaders of hasidism continued to feature from time to time in various genres of popular literature, as a

[16] See above, Introd., n. 7.

mere curiosity at first, but eventually as an apologetic response to the challenges of modern feminism, and increasingly in our own time, as a focus for genuine spiritual stirrings and aspirations within feminist Orthodoxy and beyond.[17]

It is, perhaps, hardly surprising that, with the single, problematic, exception of the case of the Maid of Ludmir, the hasidic movement did not adopt the institution of holy virginity as a legitimate mode of female charismatic leadership. After all, even within Sabbatianism, this was never more than one—highly syncretistic and by no means universal—outlet for female prophetic spirituality, and it ran counter to a centuries-old tradition that rejected it in no uncertain terms. It is more surprising, however, that the hasidic call for the sanctification of the profane—the endeavour to spiritualize every aspect of corporeal life, which defined the movement and lay at its doctrinal core—did not extend to encompass women as full participants in the enterprise. Perceived as physical, and above all sexual, they became the objects of spiritual transformation without ever being allowed to engage in it actively as subjects.[18] For inasmuch as the hasidic doctrine, drawing on earlier strands of kabbalistic thought, may be reduced to a single overriding idea, it is that the godhead is a constant and all pervasive presence suffusing the whole of creation, reaching right down to its coarsest manifestations in man and in the base, material world that he

[17] For a critical evaluation of Horodetsky's interpretation of the tradition and its subsequent ramifications in the literature, see Rapoport-Albert, 'On Women in Hasidism'; ead., 'Emergence of a Female Constituency', 13*–14*, n. 15; Deutsch, *The Maiden of Ludmir*, 23–33. For the cluster of publications and women-led events in the summer of 2004, which celebrated the Maid of Ludmir as an inspirational model, and included a pilgrimage to her supposed burial place in the Mount of Olives cemetery in Jerusalem on what purports to be the anniversary of her death, see e.g. Levine Katz, 'In Memoriam Hannah Rachel' (Heb.); ead., 'Events of the *Yahrzeit*' (Heb.); Friedlander Ben Arza, 'Hannah Rachel' (Heb.).

[18] An exception may be found in the eschatological theme of the elevation of women, and the intensification of female power, that occurs from time to time in the homiletic literature of hasidism. When it does it echoes the kabbalistic notion of the inversion of gender hierarchies in the messianic future, and is invariably featured in contexts that are devoid of any live messianic tension. Far from advocating the spiritual empowerment of women in the here and now, it serves primarily to highlight the contrast between the promise of this empowerment in the utopian future and its absence from the mundane reality of the present. It is decidedly in that reality that hasidism grounds itself, providing men with the means of transcending it only temporarily, as a subjective experience or mental exercise, and without ever challenging the existing world order or toppling its gender hierarchies. See on this above, Ch. 5 n. 65.

inhabits.[19] Man's task is to harness his actions and thoughts to the enterprise of hallowing his mundane reality—converting the corporeal to the spiritual, 'matter' to 'form'[20]—which he does by stripping off its earthly exterior in order to expose the divine core that resides within it, animates and sustains it in existence. This transformation effectively disposes of the distinction between the sacred and the profane, since all existence is capable of being restored—albeit temporarily, until the final redemption—to its source in the undifferentiated unity and holiness of the godhead. Regardless of whether the material, the corporeal, and the mundane were sensed by the hasidic masters to exist in reality as such, or whether they held them to be merely an illusion that concealed the spiritual reality of the divine, which alone was truly existent,[21] the effect of this fundamental insight was to turn the domain of earthly life into hasidism's central arena for transformative action. Rather than preaching retreat from the world, as previous generations of kabbalists had done, hasidism generally advocated active engagement with it, since every aspect of mundane reality, even its basest material manifestations, presented itself as a ready vehicle for the holy.[22]

[19] See e.g. Elior, 'Spiritual Renaissance' (Heb.), 35; Tishby and Dan, 'The Doctrine and Literature' (Heb.), 258. For the kabbalistic sources of this idea, on which hasidism undoubtedly drew, see Idel, *Hasidism Between Ecstasy and Eros*, 17–18, 63–4, 215–18; Kauffman, *In All Your Ways Know Him* (Heb.), 44–84.

[20] e.g., 'The ultimate purpose of man's creation is that he should convert matter to form' (Jacob Joseph of Polonnoye, *Toledot ya'akov yosef*, 109*b*, and see also ibid. 124*c*, 135*b–c*, 142*b*); 'Man must purify himself to such an extent that he would turn matter into form' (Elimelekh of Lyzhansk, *No'am elimelekh*, ii. 401); 'Corporeality, namely eating and drinking and worldly affairs ... must be introduced into holiness' (ibid., i. 279); 'Earthliness, namely corporeality, must be raised ... to holiness ... that is to say, to the Upper World' (ibid., i. 14), and in many other places.

[21] For the view that hasidism consecrated and thus affirmed the reality of earthly existence—the 'here and now' as it is—to the exclusion of any other, transcendent reality, see Buber, *Origin and Meaning*, 114–49 and *passim*. For Scholem's rejection of this view, with the assertion that in consecrating the mundane, hasidism was effectively annihilating or denying its reality, see Scholem, 'Martin Buber's Interpretation', 238–45.

[22] Admittedly, some hasidic masters were concerned that the radical doctrine of 'worship through corporeality' might lend itself to vulgar interpretations by those who lacked the spiritual capacity for practising it authentically. Such people were liable to indulge in corporeal pleasures and worldly affairs while deluding themselves that they were thereby extracting the sacred from the profane. The solution to this problem lay in confining the practice of 'worship through corporeality' to the charismatic leaders of hasidism alone, while restricting the ordinary members of the community to normative devotional practices. See e.g. Meshulam Feivush Heller of Zbarazh, 'Yosher divrei emet', 118–19, §§16–17; Elimelekh of Lyzhansk, *No'am elimelekh*, ii. 428.

It stands to reason, therefore, that women, who were traditionally perceived as occupying precisely the domain of material existence, should have been incorporated in or even led the hasidic project of world sanctification, for who was better able than them to embody the transformation of the corporeal to the spiritual? Curiously enough, the sublimation of female sexuality, its transformation from physical to purely spiritual energy, does occur as a theme in hasidic writings, as, for example, in the following teaching by Dov Baer, the great Maggid of Mezhirech:

If one suddenly sees a beautiful woman, one must consider the origin of her beauty. For surely, were she dead, she would not possess this [beautiful] face but rather would be utterly ugly. Where, then, does her beauty come from? It must come from the power of the divine, which suffuses her and endows her face with its flush and beauty. It follows that the root of [physical] beauty is the power of the divine. Why, then, should I be drawn to a single instance of this power? It is better for me to cling to the origin and root of all worlds, where all beauty is to be found.[23]

And again, in another of the Maggid's teachings:

'Rachel came with her father's sheep' [Gen. 29: 9]. According to the *midrash*,[24] [Rachel came] in order [for Jacob] to cling to her [physical] beauty. On the face of it, this [interpretation] is untenable [since one can hardly attribute to Jacob such a base motive], but the real meaning is that it refers to the upper Rachel [namely, to the female aspect of the kabbalistic godhead, the *sefirah* Malkhut], since the beauty of the lower Rachel derives entirely from the upper one. And similarly, this is the meaning [in the case] of . . . the righteous Joseph, who did not desire [the physical] beauty [of Potiphar's wife].[25] Rather, through her [lower] beauty he became excited and desired the upper beauty, which is the beauty of his father [Jacob], the Beauty of Israel [who signifies the divine *sefirah* of Tiferet]. This is the meaning of 'and [he] fled and got him out' [Gen. 39: 15], that is to say, he [Joseph] fled her corporeal beauty and was eager to get out, [namely] out of this world, so as to cling to the upper beauty. And this is the meaning of the verse: 'Go forth and behold, O ye daughters of Zion' etc. [S. of S. 3: 11]. The meaning is: go forth out of corporeality, and behold nothing but the inner core of the matter, not its [external] corporeality. This is why Scripture says, 'and behold, O ye daughters of Zion'. It refers to the example of a woman's beauty, and it calls the corporeality of this beauty 'daughters of Zion', namely, [this beauty] is no more than a sign

[23] Dov Baer of Mezhirech, *Or ha'emet*, 31*b*. And see the parallel passages in id., *Or torah*, 105, and in *Tsava'at haribash*, 16*a*, §90.   [24] See *Yalkut shimoni*, i: *Deuteronomy*, 'Va'ethanan', §824.
[25] See Gen. 39, and cf. BT *Sot.* 36*b*.

and a *tsiyun*[26] [pointing to] the beauty above ... A man is [generally] not permitted to cling to this lower beauty, but if [a beautiful woman] suddenly comes towards him, by means of her beauty he should cling to the beauty above.[27]

Although in both examples the encounter with women triggers the encounter with the divine, the women are quickly discarded once the lust they have aroused by their 'lower' beauty has been converted to a desire for the 'upper' beauty of the godhead. Notably, it is the impact of their physical beauty on men and not their own physicality that is at stake here. The Maggid is not addressing himself to sexually arousing women, and certainly not to women who are themselves sexually aroused;[28] his teaching is targeted exclusively at his male audience. The sexuality of the women he refers to is being spiritualized only in the contemplative minds of the men who have been exposed to its potentially harmful effects.[29] The women themselves are oblivious of the

[26] The consonants of the Hebrew word *tsiyun*, meaning 'an indication' or 'a sign', are exactly the same as the consonants of the Hebrew name for Zion (*tsiyon*).

[27] Dov Baer of Mezhirech, *Magid devarav leya'akov*, 29–30, §15, and see also ibid. 331–3, §207. For the philosophical and kabbalistic sources of this theme, and its particular configuration in hasidic thought, see Idel, 'Female Beauty' (Heb.); id., *Kabbalah and Eros*, 153–78. For clear reverberations of the Maggid's homily in the teaching of Aaron of Apta (Opatów), see his *Or haganuz latsadikim*, 10b, cited in Idel, *Kabbalah and Eros*, 171.

[28] Women's experience of sexual arousal is hardly ever an issue in the classical rabbinic sources, which regularly focus on the sexual desire that women are assumed to arouse in men as a matter of course. For the construction of women as the embodiment of the sexual urge (*yetser*), to which all men are permanently susceptible, and the effective exclusion of women from the struggle to subdue it, in which the rabbis call on men alone to engage, see Ishay Rosen-Zvi, 'Do Women Have a *Yetzer*?' (Heb.), 'Sexualising the Evil Inclination', and 'Two Rabbinic Inclinations?'.

[29] As Idel points out ('Female Beauty' (Heb.), 317 and *Kabbalah and Eros*, 173), among the Orthodox opponents of hasidism, the mitnagedim, the hasidic teaching on the sublimation of erotic thoughts was perceived as the deliberate pursuit of women in order to stimulate erotic thoughts and then to 'elevate' them. Thus David of Maków, an arch opponent of hasidism, wrote: 'They walk idly, engaging in idle talk, saying that by walking in the marketplace and gazing at women they elevate their thought to God' (in Wilensky, *Hasidim and Mitnagedim* (Heb.), ii. 235). It is clear, however, that the Maggid generally disapproved of any eye contact with women. The sublimation technique he outlines is intended for unavoidable chance encounters, and he introduces it with the following warning: 'One should avoid looking at coarse, corporeal things, and even more so at beautiful women, for this would be driven by sexual desire and amount to idolatry' (*Or ha'emet*, 31a). The Maggid's disciple, Ze'ev Wolf of Zhitomir, reports in his name an incident dating back to his early life, apparently prior to his 'conversion' to the Ba'al Shem Tov's type of hasidism: 'I have heard from the Maggid ... that when he was a *melamed* [a

transformation and totally excluded from the experience. Far from being summoned in their own right to transcend their sexual nature, they continue to embody it even as they serve to enable the men to transcend their own—unwittingly constituting the means to the end of sublimating male desire. This is particularly striking in the second example cited above, where one of the scriptural passages from which the Maggid is drawing this lesson does, in fact, expressly address the 'daughters of Zion' themselves, calling upon *them* to 'go forth and behold King Solomon', who is taken here to represent a certain aspect of the godhead. But the Maggid instantly abandons the literal meaning by rendering the 'daughters of Zion' allegorically as 'corporeality' serving merely as 'a sign', a pointer to men in the direction that should lead to the spiritualization of their own desire. He clearly does not consider the possibility that the 'daughters of Zion' themselves might engage in the same spiritual exercise that he urges on his male adherents.

In fact, women are never addressed in the homiletical literature of hasidism. To the extent that they feature in it at all—either collectively, as the gender category 'female', or individually, in reference most commonly to female protagonists of the Hebrew Bible[30]—they are routinely allegorized. As such they may allude to one or the other of the female divine *sefirot*, to the restrictive, judgemental, or evil forces that emanate from the 'left-hand side', a feminine domain in the view of the kabbalists, or else they may signify one of the attributes traditionally marked by the philosophers as feminine—passivity, receptivity, and above all material corporeality—whereby as 'matter'

teacher to young children] in a certain village, while he was sitting there in some corner, a nobleman arrived, accompanied by a beautiful whore, with her chest exposed right down to her breasts, as is their custom. He suddenly looked [at her] inadvertently, and became greatly distressed. He then began to reject [this] evil in the following way: [by focusing his mind on the thought] that she was created out of her parents' sexual fluids, out of the abominable foods from which she draws her beauty . . . that semen is as repulsive as snakes . . . and that her beauty and charm arise from such an utterly repulsive thing. [He concentrated on this thought so intensely] that he began to vomit in front of them' (Ze'ev Wolf of Zhitomir, *Or hame'ir*, 'Ḥayei sarah', 11*b*; and see the discussion of this passage in Idel, 'Female Beauty' (Heb.), 319–20). As a method of extinguishing sexual desire, to focus on the 'repulsive' embryonic origins of the woman is comparable to focusing on her end as a decomposing corpse, but the next step, the transformation of the sexual desire she arouses into a vehicle for union with the divine, is absent here and must represent a later stage in the development of the Maggid's thinking.

[30] The portrayal of biblical women in hasidic literature is the subject of a doctoral dissertation by my student, Yaffa Aronoff.

or 'body' they are schematically juxtaposed with their standard male counterparts, 'form' and 'soul'.[31] To cite but a few formulaic examples: 'The female is
matter and the male is form';[32] 'Daughter is called body . . . and son is called
soul';[33] 'The soul is called Abraham, and the body is called Sarah';[34] 'It is
known that form, which is the soul, is called Abraham, while the body, which
is matter, is called Sarah';[35] 'This is why [Scripture says] "Then Jethro", having
been highly regarded as Moses' father-in-law, "took [Zipporah], Moses' wife,
after he had sent her back" [Exod. 18: 2]. This was the lesson of abasement,
which was learnt from the materiality of the body that Moses had sent back';[36]
'"If he has a wife" [Exod. 21: 3]—this alludes to the body, for he has rendered
his body fit for divine service—"then his wife shall go out with him" [ibid.],
that is to say, the body, too, will share in the pleasure of the soul';[37] '"If thou
know not, O thou fairest among women" [S. of S. 1: 8] . . . "women" alludes to
corporeality, which is feminine';[38] and so on. Even at the turn of the nineteenth and twentieth centuries, the fifth Lubavitcher Rebbe, Shalom Dovber,
was still allegorizing women in the same way when he called on the students of
the Tomekhei Temimim yeshiva, which he founded in 1897 as a means of com-
bating Haskalah (the Jewish Enlightenment), Zionism, and other secular
ideologies, to behave like soldiers on the eve of battle, of whom the rabbis had
said that, in order not to render their wives *agunot* (deserted) in the event that
they did not return home, "everyone who went out in the wars of the house of
David wrote a bill of divorcement for his wife" [BT *Shab.* 56a] . . . because to be
a soldier in the war of the house of David one must first divorce [oneself from]
all corporeal things in which worldly men engage'.[39]

[31] Very occasionally, the female may also signify 'soul'. See e.g. Ephraim of Sudyłków, *Degel*
maḥaneh efrayim, 'Tsav', 91: '"And if a man sell his daughter to be a maidservant" [Exod. 21: 7]
. . . "his daughter"—this is the soul, which descends to this world', or Elimelekh of Lyzhansk,
No'am elimelekh, i. 96: '"And he . . . took his two wives" [Gen. 32: 23]. This may be interpreted to
mean that a man has two wives, one is the wife whom the Creator . . . has commanded him to
take in order to be fruitful and multiply, and the other is his holy soul.' For this ambivalence in
the representation of women in hasidic homilies, see Rosman, 'Observations' (Heb.), 155–8.

[32] Dov Baer of Mezhirech, *Magid devarav leya'akov*, p. 180, §101, and see also ibid., p. 186,
§111.   [33] Menahem Mendel of Vitebsk, *Likutei amarim*, 37a–b, and see also ibid. 36a.

[34] Jacob Joseph of Polonnoye, *Toledot ya'akov yosef*, 109b.   [35] Ibid. 17b.

[36] Id., *Tsafenat pa'ne'aḥ*, 209.   [37] Elimelekh of Lyzhansk, *No'am elimelekh*, i. 233.

[38] Ibid., ii. 583.

[39] Yosef Yitshak Schneersohn [Shalom Dovber's son, the sixth Lubavitcher Rebbe], *Book of*
'Talks', 1942 (Heb.), 141–3, from a teaching addressed by his father to the yeshiva students on

Moreover, the hasidic masters often translate the ontological categories of male and female into a corresponding pair of anthropological categories, which are central to their view of society and their understanding of their relationship with their flock. These are, on the one hand, the minority category of 'men of form', of 'intellect' or 'spirit', also referred to as 'scholars', 'sages', 'priests', 'leaders', or 'heads', who eventually come to be designated consistently tsadikim, namely, the spiritual elite which constitutes the leadership of hasidism, and on the other hand, the majority category of 'corporeal' or 'material men' (literally: 'men of body' or 'men of matter')—the ordinary masses who make up the bulk of the hasidic following.[40] 'Masculinity' is attributed to the former and 'femininity' to the latter in numerous statements scattered, for example, throughout the writings of Jacob Joseph of Polonnoye: 'It is known that the men of matter are called woman, and the men of form are called man';[41] 'It is known that men of form are called man, and men of matter, who are as feeble as the female, are called woman. This explains the verse, "The woman shall not wear that which pertains unto a man" [Deut. 22: 5], that is to say, one who is like a woman, and who does not possess the quality and piety of man, should not assume them. And likewise the reverse, "neither shall a man put on a woman's garment" [ibid.], which is the quality of men of matter.

Simhat Torah in 1900. Notably, Yosef Yitshak Schneersohn, who succeeded his father in 1920, proceeded, from the 1930s on, to mobilize women as an active Habad constituency, and pioneered their initiation in the speculative teachings of hasidism. This was a radical departure from the norm, which was to revolutionize the status of women in Habad, especially under the leadership of Yosef Yitshak's successor, the last Lubavitcher Rebbe, Menachem Mendel Schneerson. The latter, without ever abandoning the traditional conceptualization of the female as material corporeality, was the first to incorporate, and even privilege women in the enterprise of hallowing the mundane. In this he followed the paradoxical line of thinking, so characteristic of Habad, whereby it is precisely the darkest corporeal 'matter' that has the capacity for being refined into the purest and most luminous manifestation of spiritual 'form'. This potentiality was being actualized in his own time—the final decades of the 20th century—which he believed to signal the inauguration of the messianic age. See on all this, Rapoport-Albert, 'Emergence of a Female Constituency', and 'Making a Home'.

[40] Each of the two classes has a much wider range of designations, usually suggested by the particular vocabulary of each of the biblical verses or rabbinic dicta in which the hasidic masters often anchor the distinction between them. The dichotomous complementarity of the two classes is the central theme of many hasidic homilies and constitutes a fundamental principle of hasidism. For a review of the range of contrasting designations in the seminal writings of Jacob Joseph of Polonnoye, see Nigal, *Leader and Congregation* (Heb.), 58–60.

[41] Jacob Joseph of Polonnoye, *Ketonet pasim*, 87.

Rather, each should act in accordance with his appropriate quality';[42] 'Adam was created with two faces ... male and female, one in front and the other behind,[43] and just as there are matter and form in every individual ... so there are in the world at large men of matter and [men] of form';[44] 'This is the meaning of "If any man's wife go aside" [Num. 5: 12]. ["Wife"] stands for men of matter, who are called woman, having turned aside and refused to listen to the scholar, who is called man';[45] 'The head of the city or of the generation is called man ... while the inhabitants of his city are called woman, [and they are] comparable to matter as against form.'[46]

While it highlights the conventional gender hierarchy, which makes the female inferior to the male, the construction of the hasidic leader as male in relation to his metaphorically female (but effectively male) flock serves above all to stress the need to maintain the crucial union between them. The charismatic leader must reach out to the masses, and they in turn must 'cleave' to him, in order for the flow of spiritual and material divine 'bounty' to engulf them both. Their mutual dependence and accountability are likened to the ties that bind together a male–female couple in sexual union:

Men of matter and men of form are partners inasmuch as each looks out for the other: the former provide for the material needs of the latter and sustain them, while the latter oversee and guide the former along the upright path. This is alluded to by Rabbah bar bar Hana, who referred to the place where earth and heaven touch each other.[47] Namely, the men of matter, who belong to the category of 'earth' [which in kabbalistic parlance refers to the female *sefirah* Malkhut], are united, by touching and kissing, with the men of form, who belong to the category of 'heaven' [kabbalistically alluding to Malkhut's male partner, the *sefirah* Tiferet].[48]

This vital connection between the tsadik and his flock is also often likened to the integrity of a single living organism in which both genders are combined: the tsadik as 'head', signifying the male 'form' or 'soul', is the spiritual component that animates the organism, while his followers are its female 'body',

---

[42] Id., *Toledot ya'akov yosef*, 188d.   [43] See e.g. BT *Ber.* 61a; *Gen. Rabbah* 8: 1.

[44] Jacob Joseph of Polonnoye, *Ketonet pasim*, 95.

[45] Id., *Toledot ya'akov yosef*, 121b, and see also id., *Tsafenat pa'ne'aḥ*, 394–5.

[46] *Toledot ya'akov yosef*, 153d.

[47] See BT *BB* 74a. The Aramaic for 'touch each other' here is *nashki*, which in Hebrew means primarily 'kiss'.   [48] Ephraim of Sudyłków, *Degel maḥaneh efrayim*, 'Tsav', 91–2.

comprising the material organs and parts.[49] In advocating the organic union between them and expressing it in gendered terms, hasidism is drawing on the ancient tradition that likened God as male, and the Jewish people as female, to a flesh-and-blood couple in marital union.[50] The male tsadik is coupled with his 'female' flock as the male God is coupled with his 'bride' Israel. This is one of many intimations that the status of the tsadik in hasidism is closely analogous to that of God,[51] but in the present context, it is important to note that femininity is being ascribed to the tsadik's male devotees, who are invested with the inherent materiality and corporeality that are traditionally attributed to women. Actual women never feature in the scheme and have clearly become redundant.

References to 'the female' become even further removed from any flesh-and-blood women when the categories of male and female are employed to distinguish between the two states of mind, or two alternative modes of operation, of the hasidic leader himself: 'When [the tsadik] engages in *torah* or prayer, then he is on the level of the male, but when occasionally he discusses matters relating to God-fearing and ethics, this is called female';[52] 'The divine service of the tsadik may take two forms. One is to serve spiritually, and the other is to renew and purify himself even by way of corporeality. The mode of spiritual service is called Abraham, namely, [it comes] from the male side, while the mode of corporeal service is called Sarah ... that is to say, the female side, which is called woman';[53] 'This may be what is alluded to by the verse "Live joyfully with the wife whom thou lovest" [Eccles. 9: 9]. For when [the tsadik] is on a high level, engaging in *torah* and prayer, he is called man, which

---

[49] See Nigal, *Leader and Congregation* (Heb.), 58–65; id., *Jacob Joseph of Polonnoye* (Heb.), 3–46; Dresner, *The Zaddik*, 136–41; Weiss, 'Beginnings of Hasidism' (Heb.), 82–8.

[50] See e.g. *Mekhilta derabi yishma'el*, 'Baḥodesh', 3: '"The Lord came from Sinai" [Deut. 33: 2], to receive Israel as a bridegroom comes forth to meet the bride.' This is a common theme, most prominently underlying the rabbinic interpretation of the Song of Songs as an allegory of the love between God and Israel.   [51] See Rapoport-Albert, 'God and the Zaddik', 319–23.

[52] Elimelekh of Lyzhansk, *No'am elimelekh*, ii. 315. When the tsadik prays or reveals his *torah* he is in direct contact with the Upper Worlds, from which he draws the divine 'bounty' to bestow it on the worlds below. This is his higher, 'male' mode of operation, as distinct from the lower 'female' mode, which consists of mere guidance on upright religious and moral conduct (*musar*). For a clear definition of *musar* as a lower level of instruction, in which *torah* may be 'clothed' in order to make it accessible to all, see Sternharz, *Life of Nahman of Bratslav* (Heb.), i. 'Nesiato le'erets yisra'el', 65, §19.   [53] Ibid., i. 27–8.

is not the case when he descends from this level to the level of the masses, at which point he is called woman. And when he accepts even this [lower level] joyfully and lovingly, uniting the two levels and raising them . . . this is alluded to by "Live joyfully with the wife whom thou lovest".[54]

'Male' and 'female' are also used to create a typology of hasidic leadership:

Everything holy has a male and a female aspect. The tsadik who bestows [the divine bounty on others] is called male, but the tsadik who is not at that level of bestowing is called female.[55]

There is the tsadik who, when he receives charity, does not intend it for his own pleasure and benefit but rather he intends that by means of it, abundant good will be bestowed on the whole of Israel . . . This tsadik is called male, for even though he receives, his intention and desire are only to bestow . . . And there is the tsadik who receives charity, and intends it also for his own benefit, to provide him with food and sustenance. This tsadik is called female, because his intention is also to receive.[56]

In articulating this psycho-anthropological theory, the hasidic masters confine themselves to the allegorical or metaphorical use of gender categories while appearing to be unconcerned with the relationship between men and women as such. Ostensibly, their category of 'male' is just as distant from the concrete reality of any man as is the category of 'female' remote from the reality of any woman; the two categories feature as a pair, operating on the same level of abstraction, and each acquires its meaning by contrast with the other. But the relationship of the concept to the reality it signifies is not quite the same in each case. For inasmuch as the tsadik is always a man, his maleness is both notional and concrete. He may possess a female 'aspect' or mode of operation, or else he may be ranked as a flawed 'female' tsadik, but as an ideal type he is always a male in terms of both gender and sex. His followers, on the other hand, are men who have been collectively classified as notional females. Their gender is at odds with their sex, but it is capable of being transcended. For their notional female state points above all, and in a language charged with erotic connotations, to the expectation that they will 'cleave' or 'adhere' to the male tsadik. By means of this they are integrated in him and restored to notional maleness. This, in turn, enables them, through him, to 'cleave' to a particular aspect of the godhead—one traditionally construed by the kabbalists as female. The situation of women is quite different. Their femaleness, which is

[54] Jacob Joseph of Polonnoye, *Toledot ya'akov yosef*, 36b.
[55] Elimelekh of Lyzhansk, *No'am elimelekh*, i. 168.   [56] Ibid. 283.

as notional as it is concrete, appears to be irredeemable. Although in principle they, too, might be included in the call for ordinary people—all notional females—to 'cleave' to the male tsadik, in reality, the speculative literature of hasidism never addresses them in these terms (or indeed, in any other; as argued above, this literature does not address women at all, at least not until the turn brought about by the crisis of secularization and modernity in the twentieth-century[57]); they are not present when the tsadik delivers his teachings to his assembled male hasidim, nor are they ever presumed to be reading it when it becomes available in print—always in Hebrew rather than Yiddish, the women's tongue. The female as an actual woman—or rather the notion of such a woman—concerns the hasidic masters only to the extent that her sexual allure is a threat to the spiritual integrity of men, who may or may not be able to rise to the challenge of sublimating it. In every other respect, she is effectively allegorized or metaphorized out of existence. Actual women do, of course, belong to the hasidic community, by virtue of family tradition and ties if not by independent affiliation, but from the doctrinal point of view, they are situated beyond its outer periphery. While they feature quite often in the hagiographical traditions, where they may be depicted in positive terms as pious, charitable, or steadfast in their faith in the tsadik,[58] the speculative teachings allow them to fall out of sight, since for all intents and purposes, they have been displaced as females by a 'feminized' fraternity of exclusively male hasidim.

The absence of women from the hasidic framework for the cultivation and enhancement of spiritual life might be taken to be self-evident—the natural consequence of having emerged within a tradition that always excluded women from its formal frameworks of intellectual and spiritual pursuit. But the scandalous precedent of Sabbatianism, which became notorious, as we have seen, not least on account of the sexual depravity associated with its inclusive attitude to women, suggests the probability that in erecting their own impermeable gender barriers, the hasidic masters were not just conforming to a traditional gender norm, but rather they were recoiling with horror from the spectre of its breached boundaries. For while the Sabbatian movement incorporated women, addressed them, and gave them agency and voice,

---

[57] On which see above, Introd., n. 9.

[58] See e.g. Nigal, 'Women in *Shivḥei habesht*' (Heb.); id., *Women in Hasidic Hagiography* (Heb.); Rosman, 'Observations' (Heb.), 162–3.

hasidic doctrine reduced them to the status of mute, irrelevant bystanders. This is particularly evident in the glaring contrast between the high profile and full legitimacy granted to the Sabbatian prophetesses, and the evident hasidic discomfort with the phenomenon of prophesying women.

Admittedly, prophetic revelation in general had been a problematic issue in rabbinic culture ever since the perceived cessation of ancient biblical prophecy. The rabbis of the early centuries CE reluctantly allowed it some limited outlets while always treating it with a certain measure of suspicion. They clearly valued the 'scholar' or 'sage' who interpreted God's word as revealed in the Law, over and above the visionary, who claimed to be revealing it afresh.[59] Among the medieval and early modern kabbalists, prophetic revelations, often mediated by heavenly messengers or mentors, were not uncommon but rarely publicized or based on any claim to the full prophetic title, which was generally reserved for the biblical prophets alone.[60] The Sabbatian eruption of mass prophecy, fully acknowledged and labelled as such, was an unprecedented popular revival of the ancient apocalyptic tradition. It brought to the fore a large number and great variety of prophets and prophetesses, who broadcast the gospel of the redemption, enhanced its credibility with supernatural feats, and in a number of cases also articulated it in complex metaphysical terms. However, in the aftermath of Sabbatai Zevi's apostasy and his eventual demise, recognition that his messianic movement had failed, coupled with its persistence as a subversive sectarian heresy, revived, and even intensified, the traditional reservations about prophetic revelation, which had proved to be so liable to delude and to lead the faithful astray.[61]

---

[59] See BT *BB* 12a, and the discussions in Urbach, *The World of the Sages* (Heb.), 9–49; Heschel, *Prophetic Inspiration*, 1–13. Cf. also above, beginning of Ch. 2.

[60] There were exceptions, usually in the context of local messianic agitation, e.g. 'the Prophet of Avila' in Spain at the end of the 13th century, and other such popular figures known as prophets in pre-expulsion Spain, on whom only fragments of information have survived (see Y. Baer, *A History of the Jews in Christian Spain*, i. 277–81; ii. 159–62, 356–8). Visionary–mystical activity is also known in pre-kabbalistic circles in Germany and France during the 12th and 13th centuries, e.g. Rabbi Trölstlin, the Prophet of Erfurt, or Ezra, the Prophet of Montcontour (see Scholem, *Origins of the Kabbalah*, 239–40). For a full review and discussion of the phenomenon, see Heschel, *Prophetic Inspiration*, 13–67.

[61] See n. 8 above. Mistrust of fresh prophetic revelation would seem to characterize the post-Sabbatian kabbalah generally. There is evidence for this in e.g. what has been termed the Lithuanian kabbalistic school, originating in Elijah, the Gaon of Vilna and persisting among

The hasidic movement shared these reservations and was equivocal about prophecy from the start. It certainly credited its charismatic leaders with insight into future and past events, with the ability to fathom secret actions and thoughts, and to commune with other-worldly domains; above all, it viewed their addresses to their followers as fresh revelations of nothing less than divinely inspired *torah*. All these attributes clearly belonged to the stock-in-trade of the classical prophet, and it is not surprising that many tsadikim identified themselves with the biblical Moses—master of all prophets.[62] Nevertheless, they generally refrained from appropriating the prophetic title (which was more commonly attached to them by their detractors),[63] and

his disciples and followers from the 18th right through to the early 20th century. On this see Schuchat, 'Lithuanian Kabbalah' (Heb.), 203–6.

[62] See Green, 'Typologies of Leadership', 146–9; Piekarz, *Hasidic Leadership*, 16–22. For a typology of mystical prophecy, and the rightful claim that despite their reluctance to acknowledge it by name, the hasidic masters displayed a range of prophetic powers rooted in a variety of earlier kabbalistic traditions, see Idel, 'On Prophecy and Early Hasidism'; id., 'The Besht as Prophet' (Heb.).

[63] For the ironic use of the designation *nevi'im* (prophets) or the downright derogatory *nevi'ei sheker* (false prophets) in the anti-hasidic polemical literature of the late 18th century, see Weiss, *Studies*, 39–40 n. 9, where he concludes: 'The conspicuous absence of any reference to this term in the Hasidic literature is no doubt due to the bad reputation of the word *navi* and has to be regarded as apologetical silence.' Weiss is not entirely accurate. Although the hasidic masters often endorse the classical rabbinic preference for the sage over the prophet, reiterating the notion that prophecy ceased with the last of the biblical prophets or the destruction of the Temple (see e.g. Epstein, *Ma'or vashemesh*, i. 'Mikets', 113, 'Rimzei purim', 283; Simhah Bunem of Pshiskha (Przysucha), *Kol mevaser*, iii. 'Teshuvah', 88, §16; Israel b. Shabbetai Hapstein of Kozienice, *Avodat yisra'el hashalem*, 'Likutim', 177; Alter, *Sefat emet*, iv: *Numbers*, 'Balak' 5649 (1889), 5650 (1890), and ibid., v: *Deuteronomy*, 'Shofetim' 5652 (1892), 5661 (1901)), and although at times they expressly disavow any claim to the prophetic title (see e.g. Menahem Mendel of Vitebsk's pastoral letters from the Land of Israel, in Barnai, *Hasidic Letters* (Heb.), 146 §31, 167 §39, and 238 §63), some are not averse to ascribing the status of prophecy to their own utterances (see e.g. Nahman of Bratslav in *Likutei moharan*, ii. §1: 8 and §8: 8, where—while acknowledging that there are no longer any prophets—he asserts that the 'spirit of prophecy' still rests upon every genuine 'leader', and he refers to the leader's prayer as prophecy, albeit without referring to himself as a prophet), or even to equating the tsadikim with prophets or with 'sons of prophets' (*benei hanevi'im*) by way of commentary on the biblical verses that mention these terms. See e.g. Tsevi Elimelekh of Dynów, *Agra dekhalah*, 'Shofetim', 198–9. Even Kalonymus Kalman Epstein (*Ma'or vashemesh*, i. 'Vayigash', 127) credits the 'great tsadikim', when they are attached to the supernal worlds, with the ability to prophesy and foretell the future, since the Shekhinah is speaking through their throats. Nevertheless, the claim to the title *navi* was rare and seems to

apparently regarded prophetic insight as being rooted in some form of pathology, while at the same time fully acknowledging the veracity of its claims. A clear example of this ambivalence, linked explicitly to the memory of the Sabbatian heresy, occurs in the 'writer's preface' to *Shivḥei habesht* (In Praise of the Ba'al Shem Tov), written in the final decade of the eighteenth century by Dov Baer of Linitz (Ilintsy), son-in-law of the Ba'al Shem Tov's personal scribe:

I myself have noticed as well that in the time between my youth and my old age, every day miracles have become fewer and marvels have begun to disappear. This happens because of our many sins. In earlier days when people revived after lying in a coma close to death, they used to tell about the awesome things they had seen in the upper world . . . Likewise my father-in-law . . . told about a man who had been lying in a coma in the holy community of Bershad. It was in the time when the sect of Shabbetai Tsevi, may his name be blotted out, was stirring. That man was shown several places in the books, in which some rabbis had erred and were almost led astray by that sect. He was ordered to tell the rabbis the exact meaning of those portions. In his days there were also mad people who injured themselves with stones during the reading of the Torah, and who used to reveal people's sins to them and tell them which of their sins would cause their soul to wander restlessly. I remember that in my youth, in the village where I studied with a teacher, poor people once came to the *ḥeder* and were given a meal. Among them there was a woman possessed by an evil spirit, but they did not realize it. The teacher began to study the portion of the Torah with the children, but when he had recited two or three verses the evil spirit threw the woman down, and her husband came and asked the teacher to stop his instruction because the contaminated spirit within her could not stand anything holy. When he stopped she rose and sat at her place. Because of all these things, many repented and the faith in the heart of each Jew was strengthened.[64]

have been viewed as problematic. Notably, the synonymous designation *ḥozeh* (seer), by which the founding father of Polish hasidism, Jacob Isaac Horowitz, the 'Seer of Lublin' (1745?–1815) became widely known, appears to be of late provenance and was not in use in the hasidic movement of his own lifetime (see D. Assaf, *Caught in the Thicket* (Heb.), 137 n. 1, 154 n. 72). For a hasidic controversy in the mid-1860s about the cessation or otherwise of the holy spirit and the gift of prophecy 'in our own time', see ibid. 235–54.

[64] Ben-Amos and Mintz, *In Praise*, 4 (with minor modifications to the translation), following the text of the first Hebrew edition (Kopys, 1814). The Berdichev edition of the work (1815) has the following additional sentence here: 'And now, because of our many sins, these things have disappeared. There were also, in our generation, righteous men who revealed the secrets of the future, and by means of this, faith in God and the Torah was strengthened.'

Genuine prophetic insight is being attributed here to the nearly dead 'after lying in a coma', or to self-harming 'madmen', whose pathology, alongside the pathology of spirit possession, is paradoxically prized for its power to instil faith, since the communications it conveys from the supernal worlds supply tangible proof of their existence. Given that the same type of prophetic insight is ascribed throughout the book to the Ba'al Shem Tov himself, as well as to some of his charismatic colleagues and associates,[65] it is clear that the proto-type of the hasidic tsadik shares the faculty of prophecy with marginal figures, caught up in the liminal states of near-death, possession, and madness.[66]

Another indication of hasidic ambiguity about the status of prophetic revelation occurs in Dov Baer of Linitz's account of the prohibition on prophesying in the circle of Nahman of Kosov, the Ba'al Shem Tov's fellow charismatic and sometime rival:[67]

I heard from the rabbi of our community that the famous rabbi, our teacher, Nahman of Kosov ... used to send messages to the members of the holy group in the city, telling each of them what sins they had to correct in this world. Everything that he said was true, but they were very annoyed with his prophecies, because they had an agreement among them not to prophesy.[68]

The 'holy group' sends one of its members to challenge Nahman on his failure to observe their collective decision to desist from the practice of prophecy, but Nahman denies the allegation: 'I was no prophet, neither was I a prophet's son [Amos 7: 14]', and he embarks on a lengthy explanation, from which it emerges that he had gained his awareness of his colleagues' (as well as his own) secret sins, not by exercising his faculty of prophecy but rather through communica-tions with a demonic figure—the impure soul of a deceased sinner, who had died while under the ban of excommunication.[69]

The explanation is bewildering. Why should the impure source of Nahman's prophetic insight render it more acceptable to the group than if it had originated in wholesome divine revelation? As Zvi Mark has observed:

[65] See e.g. *In Praise*, 234–5, §228; 63, §48 together with 67, §50, and time and again, *passim*.

[66] See Zvi Mark's analysis of madness as depicted in *Shivḥei habesht* (Mark, '*Dibbuk* and *Devekut*' (Heb.); id., *Mysticism and Madness* (Heb.), 18–46), which demonstrates that phenome-nologically, the madman and the tsadik are indeed closely analogous.

[67] For the relationship between Nahman of Kosov and the Besht, see Rapoport-Albert, 'Hasidism after 1772', 80–3

[68] Ben-Amos and Mintz, *In Praise*, 208, §209.   [69] Ibid. 208–10.

'A paradoxical attitude emerges from the story, whereby prophecy inspired by the holy spirit is "forbidden", while prophecy deriving from the demonic realm is "permitted" and perhaps even desirable.'[70] Joseph Weiss has already suggested that the key to understanding the problematics of prophecy in Nahman's 'circle of pneumatics' was the likely Sabbatian context from which the circle emerged:

Do these people fall into any already defined category of the religious history of eighteenth-century Judaism in Eastern Europe? The answer is that the members of the circle belong unmistakably to that pneumatic type of religious personality that was so abundantly represented in the history of the Sabbatian movement, i.e., to the type of the Sabbatian "prophet" ... Beyond the striking similarity between the religious phenomena of the Sabbatian prophets and of the circle to which Nahman belongs, the fact that the pneumatic figures in both societies are called by the very same name, i.e. *navi*, suggests a historical link ... One is tempted to suggest that he and his friends belonged to the last examples of a typically Sabbatian phenomenon in the religious history of later Judaism. G. Scholem ventured to trace back the historical origin of the Hasidic charismatic leader (*Ṣaddik*) to the Sabbatian prototype of the *navi*.[71] In this transformation of a Sabbatian type into a hasidic one, Nahman and his friends, belonging as they did, perhaps only peripherally, to both movements, have their place.[72]

Weiss goes on to conjecture that the circle's decision to stop prophesying was theologically motivated and 'marked the termination of their adherence to the Sabbatian belief', an interpretation, he argues, that 'would not be far-fetched in view of the historical transformation of Sabbatianism into hasidism'.[73] The suggestion that the circle might indeed have emerged from a covert Sabbatian background gains some support from the fact that Jacob Emden—that indefatigable campaigner against the messianic heresy—had implicated Nahman of Kosov in it[74] (although Emden's suspicions were not always justified, especially not when they were based on distant rumours from Poland). But even if neither Nahman nor his group had ever been involved with Sabbatianism,[75] the very fact that the practice of prophecy was itself so closely

[70] Mark, '*Dibbuk* and *Devekut*' (Heb.), 256; id., *Mysticism and Madness* (Heb.), 25.

[71] See Scholem, *Major Trends*, 333–4, *Studies and Texts* (Heb.), 115, 'The Two First Testimonies' (Heb.), 238–40, and cf. above at n. 15.   [72] Weiss, *Studies*, 29–30.

[73] Ibid. 30.   [74] See Emden, *Sefer hitabekut*, 80b; id. [David Avaz], *Petaḥ einayim*, 14b.

[75] Idel questions the Sabbatian background of the Kosov circle and its decision to desist from prophesying, in the context of his overall rejection of Scholem's (and consequently also Weiss's) claim that hasidism had emerged from and largely as a reaction to Sabbatianism. See Idel, 'On Prophecy and Early Hasidism', 44–5; id., 'The Besht as Prophet' (Heb.), 122–4.

associated with it may have been the inhibiting factor that prompted the circle at some point—perhaps in response to such suspicions as were being raised by Emden—to abandon their own prophesying. Nahman and his colleagues would have been aware that their prophetic activities were too close for comfort to the discredited practices of the heretical Sabbatian prophets. Invocation of the holy spirit was dangerous; it conjured up memories of the extravagant claims that had been falsely made in its name. By contrast, Nahman's insistence that he had gained his prophetic insight only as a result of being approached by a lost soul, who had been excluded from Paradise and was seeking restoration to holiness, redefined his experience in pastoral terms[76] while disavowing its prophetic dimension, thereby taking the edge off its unsavoury Sabbatian associations. For these associations between prophecy and heresy persisted long after the events that gave rise to them. This is evident, for example, in the following denunciation of the false Sabbatian prophets by the Galician hasidic master, Zevi Hirsch Eichenstein of Zhidachov (1763–1831), in the name of his teacher, Jacob Isaac, the 'Seer of Lublin' (1745?–1815):

I have heard my master, of blessed memory, say of those disciples, in the notorious event[77] in the days of the Taz,[78] who formed themselves into a separate sect and profaned the divine name. He attributed it to the fact that they desired to have the mystical experience of [a revelation of] Elijah and the holy spirit and prophecy by means of unifications.[79] But they failed to preserve a proper balance and they did not humble their physical matter and remained impure. They failed to take proper care of them-

---

[76] These terms are reminiscent of the Ba'al Shem Tov's mission to 'rectify' sinful souls and to secure their personal salvation as they seek admission to Paradise. Cf., e.g. the tale entitled 'The Besht and the Frog' in Ben-Amos and Mintz, *In Praise*, 24–6, §12, or the Ba'al Shem Tov's own report, in his letter to his brother-in-law, of his visionary encounter with innumerable souls pleading for his assistance in their endeavour to ascend to ever higher levels of the celestial worlds, in Jacobs, *Mystical Testimonies*, 150.

[77] An oblique reference to the appearance of Sabbatai Zevi and the mass messianic movement he inspired in the 1660s.

[78] The Taz is an acronymic reference to the celebrated talmudist and rabbi of Lvov, David b. Samuel Halevi (1586–1667), who became known by the title of his famous work *Turei zahav*, a commentary on a section of Joseph Caro's *Shulḥan arukh*. Swept up in the messianic frenzy which had erupted towards the end of his life, he appointed his two sons emissaries of his community, and in the spring of 1666, sent them to pay homage to Sabbatai Zevi, who was at that time imprisoned in Gallipoli. See Scholem, *Sabbatai Sevi*, 600–1, 620–7.

[79] A kabbalistic technique whereby mental images of intertwining divine names, representing sefirotic integration, are contemplated, and empower the practitioner to commune with the souls of the dead or with other supernal entities.

selves and walked in ways remote from their capacity. They performed unifications . . .
without refining their physical matter. And so they depicted for themselves the higher
forms from under the Chariot, with the result that lewd and adulterous forms got the
better of them, Heaven save us, and what happened happened, Heaven spare us. This
is what my master said in the name of the Baal Shem Tov, his soul is in Eden, that
these fools studied this science without having any capacity for and knowledge of the
awe and dread of Heaven, with the result that they took it all in a corporeal sense, and
so they went astray.[80]

   That hasidic anxieties surrounding prophecy were associated with its
prominence in the Sabbatian milieu becomes even more plausible if we take
into account the fact, first observed in this connection by Zvi Mark,[81] that
Israel Yoffeh, the Kopys printer who published the first edition of *Shivḥei*
habesht at the very end of 1814, had also published, earlier in the same year, and
apparently again in 1815, what may be termed the first Hebrew novel about
Sabbatai Zevi and his movement. The book, *Me'ore'ot tsevi* (The Events [in
the Life] of [Sabbatai] Zevi), also known as *Sipur ḥalomot vekets hapela'ot* (Tale
of Dreams, End of Wonders), was written anonymously by an author who had
assimilated Jewish Enlightenment values, and who set out to debunk the messianic movement as an entanglement with the demonic realm. It ascribed
Sabbatianism's success to the persuasive power of its prophets, who deluded
the people, exploiting their credulity with displays of miraculous feats, but
who had been empowered to perform them by the forces of 'the other side'—
the metaphysical source of evil.

   The prospect of publishing the first anthology of traditions 'in praise' of
Israel Ba'al Shem Tov—by now celebrated as the venerable founder of the
expanding hasidic movement—in such close proximity to the publication in
the same year of a damning account of Sabbatai Zevi, and the potential popularity of both works,[82] must have troubled the printer-cum-publisher Israel

---

[80] Eichenstein, *Turn Aside from Evil*, 83–4. The author goes on to guide the reader, basing
himself on Hayim Vital's prophetic manual, *Sha'ar hakedushah*, on how to avoid being deluded
by impure spirits and to attain the genuine holy spirit by means of Torah study, prayer, purification of the body's materiality, and the subduing of the evil inclination.

[81] See Mark, '*Dibbuk* and *Devekut*' (Heb.), 268–74, 282–4; id., *Mysticism and Madness* (Heb.),
35–40.

[82] The first edition of *Shivḥei habesht* (Kopys, 1814) was quickly followed in 1815 by two further editions, published in Berdichev and Łaszczów respectively, as well as by a Yiddish edition,
first published in Ostrog in the same year, and again in Korets in 1816. The publication history of

Yoffeh, who was himself a faithful follower of the Habad school of hasidism.[83] As Zvi Mark has observed, against the background of the publication of *Me'ore'ot tsevi*,

Israel Yoffeh faced a serious problem with the image of the Besht as it emerged from the manuscript writings of Dov Baer of Linitz . . . which he was eager to publish. From the very beginning of the work, the Besht was portrayed as a magician, endowed with supernatural powers, acknowledged by a possessed madwoman, and altogether uncomfortably reminiscent of the phenomenon of prophesying ignoramuses in the Sabbatian movement . . . What was to distinguish the Besht of *Shivḥei habesht* from the Sabbatian protagonists of *Me'ore'ot tsevi*?[84]

He goes on to propose the following solution:

The close proximity of the [two] books forced Israel Yoffeh to re-edit *Shivḥei habesht* and to reorganize its opening section in a way that would allay such anxiety as would arise from any comparison between the Ba'al Shem Tov's 'praises' and the narrative of *Me'ore'ot tsevi*. For Israel Yoffeh could assume with certainty that at least a substantial proportion of his customers who were going to read *Shivḥei habesht* would have earlier read *Me'ore'ot tsevi*, which he himself had published in the previous year, or else that they were bound to read the subsequent edition [of *Me'ore'ot tsevi*], which was due to be published in the same year in which he was also publishing *Shivḥei habesht*.[85]

Indeed, as he tells the reader in his preface to *Shivḥei habesht*, not only was Israel Yoffeh aware that the manuscript on which he was basing his edition 'had been copied over and over', so that 'errors would have increased in number until the meaning of the sentences would have been almost unrecognisable',[86] but he also makes the following declaration in the opening lines of the work itself:

Me'ore'ot tsevi is a little harder to establish. A Lvov edition purporting to have been published in 1804 (under the title *Sipur ḥalomot kets hapela'ot*), is taken by most bibliographers and scholars to have appeared only in 1824. Israel Yoffeh first published the work (under the title *Me'ore'ot tsevi*) in Kopys, apparently in two editions, 1814 and 1815, of which only the latter is extant. The title page of this edition refers, without supplying any details, to an earlier edition which has 'sold out', necessitating republication. There are several subsequent editions. See also Mark, '*Dibbuk* and *Devekut*' (Heb.), 270 n. 62; Werses, *Haskalah and Sabbatianism* (Heb.), 220–6.

[83] For Israel Yoffeh's affiliation with Habad, see Heilman, *Beit rabbi*, 75a [149]; Rosman, 'History of a Historical Source' (Heb.), 177–80.

[84] Mark, '*Dibbuk* and *Devekut*' (Heb.), 272–3; id., *Mysticism and Madness* (Heb.), 38–9.

[85] '*Dibbuk* and *Devekut*' (Heb.), 273–4; *Mysticism and Madness* (Heb.), 39.

[86] Ben-Amos and Mintz, *In Praise*, 'The Printer's Preface', 2.

The printer said: 'Since in the manuscripts from which I have copied these tales, the sequence of events and the revelation of the Besht—may his merit protect us, amen—are not in the right order, and because I heard everything in the name of *Admor*,[87] whose soul rests in heaven, in the proper order and with the correct interpretation, I will print it first as it was heard from his holy lips, and after that point in the story, I will include what has been written in the manuscripts.'[88]

Scholars have long been aware that the published edition of *Shivḥei habesht* contained several layers of recension,[89] and that Israel Yoffeh's intervention in the text was much more than a thorough proofreading exercise or a mere reorganization of the material, designed to establish, as he claims, the correct sequence of events. His contribution, evidently based on the Habad tradition on the Ba'al Shem Tov's early life, reflects a certain ideological agenda, aiming to attenuate the practical-kabbalistic, magical dimension of his personality, and to highlight instead his stature as a distinguished spiritual leader. To achieve this, Israel Yoffeh prefaced Dov Baer of Linitz's text with a cycle of some sixteen tales,[90] which he concluded with the following statement: 'Up to this point I heard the unfolding of these events in the name of *Admor*, may his soul rest in heaven. The other events and miracles that occurred I shall print according to the manuscripts that I obtained.'[91]

These two editorial units—Israel Yoffeh's tale cycle, with which he introduces the volume, and Dov Baer of Linitz's 'manuscript' text, representing an earlier and undoubtedly more authentic account transmitted by named individuals who were contemporaries and close associates of the Besht[92]—offer two ostensibly alternative versions of the Ba'al Shem Tov's prehistory and

[87] This is the honorific acronym of *adonenu, morenu verabenu* (our master, teacher, and rabbi), by which it is commonly assumed that Israel Yoffeh was referring to his late hasidic master, Habad's founder, Shneur Zalman of Lyady, who had died two years previously. See Mondshine, *Shivḥey Ha-Baal Shem Tov*, 19 n. 37; Rosman, 'History of a Historical Source' (Heb.), 179–80; and cf. Rubinstein, *Shivḥei habesht*, 25 n. 23.

[88] Ben-Amos and Mintz, *In Praise*, 6, with some modifications to the translation.

[89] See e.g. Reiner, '*Shivḥei habesht*' (Heb.); Rosman, 'History of a Historical Source' (Heb.); Rubinstein, 'Revelation Stories' (Heb.); Mondshine, *Shivḥey Ha-Baal Shem Tov*.

[90] It is difficult to establish their precise number, since the Kopys edition does not number the tales, and it is not always possible to decide where one ends and the other begins. Subsequent editors have introduced various divisions of the narrative into numbered paragraphs. The English edition lists 'The Beginning of the Writer's Manuscript' as tale 17 (Ben-Amos and Mintz, *In Praise*, 32), counting 16 discrete units in Israel Yoffeh's preceding cycle of tales.   [91] Ibid. 31.   [92] See Reiner, '*Shivḥei habesht*' (Heb.).

early life, during his years of anonymity, when he was disguised as an uncouth, uneducated brute, right up to the moment when he was ready to reveal his true nature in public. The relationship between the two units has been closely analysed by Rosman[93] who, following Mondshine,[94] has also demonstrated that the division between them is not clear-cut. Yoffeh's opening unit does, in fact, contain some sections, which he had clearly detached from their original position in Dov Baer of Linitz's manuscript, and introduced as bracketed additions to his own cycle of tales.[95] His version of the life was not a comprehensive or systematic alternative to the 'manuscript' text. Rather, it was intended to amend and complement it in order to account for the transformation of the Besht, in the course of the two generations that elapsed between his death in 1760 and the publication of *Shivhei habesht* in 1814, from a skilful manipulator of supernatural powers, which is how he was perceived by his contemporaries, and was still remembered by Dov Baer's informants when he produced his version in the mid-1790s, into the paragon of hasidic spiritual leadership that he became for Israel Yoffeh and his readership.[96]

A number of tales in Yoffeh's account closely parallel and suggest the possibility that they may be adaptations or direct responses to the tales that feature in the 'manuscript' text.[97] Consequently, the differences that nevertheless distinguish them may be taken to be particularly instructive as to Yoffeh's editorial intent. A striking example is the two parallel accounts of what is almost certainly a single occasion on which the Besht, while still disguised as an ignoramus, was revealed by a prophetically insightful person to be a holy man, endowed with supernatural powers.[98] Dov Baer of Linitz's 'manuscript' account—the earlier version of the two—directly follows a brief description of the Besht's life in a small village where, during the entire week, he would 'retire

---

[93] See Rosman, 'History of a Historical Source' (Heb.), 192–205.

[94] See Mondshine, *Shivhey Ha-Baal Shem Tov*, 20.

[95] See Rosman, 'History as a Historical Source' (Heb.), 183–92.

[96] See ibid. 202–5.   [97] See ibid. 193, 202–5.

[98] The relationship between the two tales was observed by Rubinstein ('Revelation Stories' (Heb.), 166), although following what is clearly an explanatory interpolation in the Korets Yiddish edition of *Shivhei habesht*, he treated them as referring to two consecutive events. The tales were rightly juxtaposed as alternative accounts of the same event by Zvi Mark ('*Dibbuk* and *Devekut*' (Heb.), 252–7; id., *Mysticism and Madness* (Heb.), 22–6), whose analysis I follow here, even though his main concern is to establish the affinity between madness and prophecy, while mine is to highlight the gender boundaries of each.

into seclusion in a house-like crevice that was cut into the mountain', return-ing home to his wife only on the sabbath's eve. Throughout this period, while he was still concealing his preoccupation with study and prayer, his brother-in-law, Gershon of Kuty (Kutow),[99] 'thought him to be an ignorant and boor-ish person, and he used to try to persuade his sister to obtain a divorce from him'.[100] At this point the account of his 'revelation' unfolds as follows:

Once the Besht came to a town[101] where there was a madwoman who revealed to everyone his virtues and vices. When the Besht, God bless his holy memory, came to the town, Rabbi Gershon asked the righteous rabbi, the head of the court of the holy community of Kuty, the righteous rabbi, the great light, our master and teacher, Moses, to take the Besht to this woman. Perhaps he would take to heart her reproaches and return to the proper path. And all of them went to her.[102]

The 'madwoman' of Kuty who can see through people's hearts and expose their secret actions or thoughts, who is moreover invested with the moral authority to reproach and return them 'to the proper path', is instantly recog-nizable as belonging to the type of the prophetically gifted woman we first encountered in Hayim Vital's accounts, and subsequently in numerous reports of the inspired Sabbatian prophetesses. The tale goes on:

When the rabbi of the holy community of Kuty entered, she said: 'Welcome to you who are holy and pure.' She greeted each one according to his merits. The Besht came in last and when she saw him she said: 'Welcome, Rabbi Israel', although he was still a young man. 'Do you suppose that I am afraid of you?' she said to him. 'Not in the least, since I know that you have been warned from heaven not to practise with holy names until you are thirty-six years old.'[103]

The madwoman, or rather—as we are led to understand—the spirit that possessed her and speaks from her mouth, sees through the Besht's disguise, and instantly recognizes that he is, in fact, a practitioner of 'holy names', namely a *ba'al shem* ('master of the name') a practical kabbalist who knows how to tap the magical power of the divine names and to manipulate it to good effect, engaging in such practices as exorcism, healing, and the production of talismanic objects. This, indeed, is how the Besht was perceived during his own lifetime, and how he was still being portrayed in much of Dov Baer's

---

[99] See on him, e.g., Heschel, *The Circle*, 44–112. [100] Ben-Amos and Mintz, *In Praise*, 34.
[101] The town in question is clearly Kuty, as becomes apparent directly below.
[102] Ben-Amos and Mintz, *In Praise*, 34. [103] Ibid.

'manuscript' text.[104] At the same time, however, the woman is aware that 'heaven' has forbidden the Besht to exercise his supernatural skills, and therefore the spirit within her—clearly the source of her 'madness', which is tantamount to her faculty of prophecy—should not be susceptible to his power. The tale proceeds to describe how the Besht, who had been urged to exorcize the spirit, strikes a mutual agreement with it, whereby the spirit will exit the woman's body so long as the Besht does not divulge its name. Once the spirit departs, and the woman is 'cured' of both madness and prophecy, she abruptly disappears from the narrative, and the tale concludes with the Besht subduing some 'impure spirits' elsewhere.

The portrayal of the woman in the tale is extremely ambiguous: on the one hand, her prophetic insights are celebrated and widely held to be true; she is clearly respected and trusted by such eminent men as Gershon of Kuty and Moses, the town's rabbi—both well known as scholars and kabbalistic adepts.[105] On the other hand, she is labelled 'mad' and described as being possessed—the passive medium of revelations communicated by an impure spirit. Her prophetic skills, as Mark rightly observes,[106] are closely analogous to the Besht's (although neither is ever referred to by the problematic title 'prophet'), but it is clear that her powers have been classified as symptomatic of a certain pathology, while his are presented throughout the book as wholesome and divinely inspired. Dov Baer of Linitz's 'manuscript' version depicts a late eighteenth-century environment in which the traditional type of prophetess (both Sabbatian and pre-Sabbatian) is evidently still present but is being relegated to the shady domain of spirit possession and madness. The privileged women who were at one time acknowledged as legitimate vehicles for revelations by the holy spirit are now perceived as tormented victims—mouthpieces of ghostly spirits seeking release from the grasp of the demonic realm. It is not by accident that the hagiographical literature of hasidism is so replete with exorcism narratives, in the vast majority of which the victims of possession are women or girls, who are being cured of their 'madness' by the tsadik acting as exorcist.[107]

---

[104] For the Besht's primary role as a *ba'al shem*, and the status of *ba'alei shem* in his day, see Scholem, 'The Historical Ba'al Shem Tov' (Heb.); Rosman, *Founder of Hasidism*, 11–26; Etkes, *The Besht*, 7–78.

[105] See Weiss, *Studies*, 34–8; Heschel, *The Circle*, 45–7.   [106] See above, at nn. 65–6.

[107] See Nigal, *"Dybbuk" Tales* (Heb.), 229–63; id., *The Hasidic Tale*, 208–11, 320–1; id., *Magic, Mysticism and Hasidism*, 67–133. For the ambivalent status of possession as 'religious madness'—

Israel Yoffeh's response to Dov Baer's 'revelation by madwoman' tale is to offer a comparable revelation tale of his own. With the exception of some variations in detail and one significant difference, it so closely resembles the basic structure and essential plot line of Dov Baer's tale that it is more than likely intended to function as its corrective.

Like Dov Baer's tale, Yoffeh's version is preceded by a description—more elaborate but essentially the same—of the Besht's life of covert piety during his residence 'in a certain village, where he . . . built a house of seclusion in the forest. He prayed and studied there all day and all night every day of the week, and he returned home only on the Sabbath.'[108] His outward behaviour, however, as in Dov Baer's version of the tale, was such that his brother-in-law, Gershon of Kuty, 'thought that the Besht was a simpleton' and despaired of him as 'good for nothing'.[109]

On one occasion, when he visited his brother-in-law in town during the festival of Sukkot, the Besht appeared to be adopting a wholly inappropriate and presumptuous manner for a man in his humble station—praying by the eastern wall of the synagogue, which was traditionally reserved for the dignitaries of the community, and following, as if he was a learned kabbalist, the Zohar's admonition not to don phylacteries (*tefilin*) on the intermediate days of the festival. At this, Gershon of Kuty was provoked into action:

He went with [the Besht] to the rabbi of the community[110] so that the rabbi would admonish him. They considered the Besht to be a pious man, but "an uncultured person is not sin-fearing [and neither is an ignorant person pious]."[111] The rabbi was a very righteous man. When they came to the rabbi's house, Rabbi Gershon kissed the mezuzah, but the Besht put his hand on the mezuzah without kissing it, and our master and rabbi, Rabbi Gershon, became angry with him over this as well. When they entered the rabbi's house, the Besht put aside his mask and the rabbi saw a great light. He rose up before the Besht. Then the Besht resumed the mask and the rabbi sat

a manifestation either of the holy spirit or of the demonic forces—see Chajes, *Between Worlds*, 119–38; Mark, *Mysticism and Madness* (Heb.), 18–46. By the 19th century, at least in the west, under the earlier impact of scepticism and the Enlightenment, this type of madness had been largely rationalized, psychologized, medicalized, and increasingly confined. On this see e.g. Foucault, *History of Madness*; Porter, *Madness*; Goldberg, *Sex, Religion and the Making of Modern Madness*; Szasz, *The Manufacture of Madness*.

[108] Ben-Amos and Mintz, *In Praise*, 27, §14.   [109] Ibid. 26–7, §13.

[110] The community in question is, again, Kuty, and the rabbi is the same Moses, head of the local rabbinical court. See Rubinstein, *Shivḥei habesht*, 55 n. 4.   [111] *Pirkei avot* 2: 5.

down. And this happened several times. The rabbi was very frightened, since he did not know who he was. Sometimes he seemed to be a holy person and at other times he seemed to be a common man. But when our master and rabbi, Rabbi Gershon, complained to him about the tefilin and the mezuzah, the rabbi took the Besht aside and privately said to him: "I command you to reveal the truth to me." And the Besht was forced to reveal himself to him. But the Besht commanded him in turn not to reveal anything that had transpired. When they came out the rabbi said to our master and rabbi, Rabbi Gershon: "I taught him a lesson, but I think he would not knowingly commit a fault against our customs. He has acted in innocence." Then the rabbi examined the mezuzah and they discovered that it had a defect.[112]

The essential contours of Yoffeh's plot are the same as Dov Baer's: both depict the unmasking of the Besht by an individual who was expected to chastise him; both locate the episode in Kuty and share most of their protagonists in common. Some of the differences between them are but mirror-reflections of each other, while others are no more than variations of nuance and stress. For example, the madwoman in Dov Baer's 'manuscript' text brazenly announces that she, or rather the possessing spirit that has invaded her, is not in the least afraid of the Besht; she has fathomed his true nature but feels immune to his power, which she knows to be constrained 'from heaven'. By contrast, the rabbi of Kuty—her counterpart in Yoffeh's tale—becomes very frightened on glimpsing the holiness of the Besht; he cannot reconcile it with the boorish behaviour of the man he has been charged to admonish. On the other hand, in Dov Baer's text, the woman and her spirit are soon subdued by the Besht, reduced to pleading for mercy and ultimately silenced, while in Yoffeh's version, the rabbi is allowed to maintain his authority and dignity throughout: he commands the Besht to reveal his true nature, and the Besht is forced to comply. Moreover, Yoffeh's rabbi is 'a very righteous man', flawed by no more than his defective *mezuzah*, while Dov Baer's madwoman, revealed to be drawing her power from the impure spirit of a deceased sinner, is entirely embroiled in the evil associated with his crime; once she is freed from its influence, she simply disappears from the tale. At the same time, however, her prophetic insight as depicted by Dov Baer is clearer and sharper than that of Yoffeh's rabbi: she can instantly see through the Besht's disguise, while the rabbi is puzzled by what he sees and cannot grasp it without the Besht's assistance. His prophetic faculty is inferior to the Besht's, while in Dov Baer's version, the madwoman is endowed with an insight that matches the Besht's

112 Ben-Amos and Mintz, *In Praise*, 27–8, §14.

and is distinguished from it only by its impure origin. This renders the confrontation between them a struggle between the powers of the holy and the profane, a polarity that is totally absent from the Besht's encounter with the rabbi.

The most significant difference, however, between the two versions of the tale is the very substitution of a mad female with a righteous and highly respected male. In both accounts, Rabbi Gershon—exasperated with his brother-in-law's antics—resorts to a resident of Kuty, whom he believes to be capable of admonishing the Besht and putting him 'on the proper path'. But while according to Dov Baer, he turns for help to a prophetically inspired woman, in Yoffeh's account the woman is nowhere to be found. She has been swept aside, her part in the plot ascribed instead to the town's rabbi—none other than the righteous Moses, who in the earlier version of the tale was instrumental in bringing the Besht to the woman whose role he now occupies himself. The capacity for genuine insight has been transferred from a deranged or possessed female to a traditional male figure of rabbinic authority. To Israel Yoffeh and his readers, this must have seemed a more appropriate setting for the first exposure of the Besht as a holy man.

The elimination of the woman from this version of the tale appears to represent the final stage of a process of displacement that must have begun as a reaction to the infamous Sabbatian prophetesses. In the first stage, captured by Dov Baer, a woman who, in the Sabbatian context (as in Hayim Vital's sixteenth-century milieu), would have been highly valued and even venerated as the voice of divine revelation, is reduced in stature by being labelled 'mad' and subsumed in the profanity of an impure spirit; her voice no longer communicates the holy but rather challenges and confronts it. Some twenty years later, when Yoffeh was adapting Dov Baer's tale to the hasidic sensibilities of his own generation, the displacement of the prophesying woman had become complete: she has now disappeared from the landscape altogether, to be replaced by a rabbi who alone is privileged to perceive the holiness of the Besht. Not only does Yoffeh's transposition of the scene dispose of the mad but insightful woman, it also has the effect of reconfiguring the Besht himself, most likely in the image of his own hasidic mentor, Shneur Zalman of Lyady.[113] His version of the tale implicitly aligns the Besht with the rabbinical world and its values (even though he outshines it with his unique brand of

[113] See Rosman, 'History of a Historical Source' (Heb.), 202–5.

charisma) by depicting him in collusion with the rabbi, to keep secret his true identity and nature. This collusion in Yoffeh's version echoes the collusion in Dov Baer's tale between the Besht and the woman, who agree to keep secret the identity and nature of her possessing spirit,[114] but the two collusions place the Besht in two diametrically opposed settings: rabbinic learning and authority on the one hand, spirit possession and madness on the other. Yoffeh's version transplants the Besht from the madwoman's world to the rabbi's, a world in which there is no longer any room for even a trace, however debased, of the prophetic spirituality of women.

Admittedly, hasidic literature does occasionally refer to women who experience prophetic visions without being labelled mad or possessed by spirits. In *Shivḥei habesht* itself, the 'manuscript' text of Dov Baer of Linitz relates in some detail the prophetic dreams of the wife of Abraham the Angel, son of the Maggid of Mezhirech. In one of her dreams, a 'supreme council [the Sanhedrin] of venerable elders' informs her that her husband is soon to die. She pleads with the elders to spare him, and is granted 'as a gift' the prolongation of his life by twelve more years. Her husband—himself prophetically aware of her dream—'congratulated her and blessed her for the true plea which prolonged his time', and 'indeed, this was what happened to him'.[115] Subsequently, her deceased father-in-law, the Maggid of Mezhirech, regularly appears in her dreams, to warn her whenever imminent danger threatens. When she first communicates the Maggid's warning to her husband he does not believe her. 'He said to her: "Why did he tell it to you and not to me?"' And yet his wife's dream comes true, and he suffers the consequences of ignoring her prophetic warning. On another occasion the Maggid again warns her in a dream against embarking on a journey, despite being urged by two eminent tsadikim to travel and rejoin her husband. When it transpires soon afterwards that her husband has just died, 'the tsadikim were ashamed to face Rabbi Abraham's wife, because she had perceived the future better than they had'.[116] The narrative is remarkably unsparing in its acknowledgement of the woman's prophetic insight, which is shown time and again to be superior to the insight of everyone else around her.

[114] See Ben-Amos and Mintz, *In Praise*, 35, §20.   [115] Ibid. 96–7, §75.
[116] Ibid. 97. For feminist readings of this tale, see D. Biale, 'A Feminist Reading' (Heb.), 139–43; Dvir-Goldberg, 'Voice of a Subterranean Fountain' (Heb.).

Another hasidic source which is unstinting in its acknowledgement of a woman's prophetic gift is Nathan Sternharz's description of Feyge, mother of Nahman of Bratslav and granddaughter of the Besht:

Towards the end of that year [1800], on the first day of Elul, his [Nahman's] daughter Odl was married. The wedding took place in Khmelnik, and the Rebbe was present together with his entire family. His mother, the righteous Feyge, of blessed memory, also attended, and during the marriage ceremony, she saw the [deceased] Ba'al Shem Tov, for like a tsadik, she possessed the holy spirit, and all the tsadikim held her to be in possession of the holy spirit and of great spiritual insight. In particular, her brothers, the famous tsadikim, namely the saintly rabbi [Ephraim] of Sudyłków and the saintly rabbi, our master Rabbi Barukh [of Międzybóż], held her to be like one of the prophetesses.[117]

Notably, in likening Feyge to 'one of the prophetesses'—by which he must be referring to the small cluster of biblical women thus described[118] and not to their more recent counterparts—the author does not flinch from invoking the prophetic title which the early hasidic sources were inclined to shun.[119] It may well be that by the time of writing, between 1824 and the author's death in 1845,[120] the designation 'prophet' had ceased to carry the Sabbatian associations it once conjured up, especially when used in reference to women. By the turn of the nineteenth and twentieth centuries, at any rate, such unsavoury associations must have long evaporated. Now, not only could a woman be likened to a full-fledged biblical prophetess, she could simply herself be known by that title. An example is Yente the Prophetess, mother of Isaac of Drohobycz—a contemporary of the Besht and one of his fellow charismatics— and grandmother of Yehiel Mikhl of Zolochev—disciple of both the Besht and the Maggid of Mezhirech, and a leading proponent of hasidism in Galicia. Although Yente is not mentioned in *Shivḥei habesht* or in any source close to her own, her son's, or even her grandson's lifetime, she features in a much later hagiographical source, tracing the family history of the grandson:

The wife of the saintly Rabbi Joseph Spravedliver,[121] mother of the saintly rabbi Isaac of Drohobycz, was called Yente the Prophetess. Once, while cleaning the house, she

---

[117] Sternharz, *Life of Nahman of Bratslav* (Heb.) (first published posthumously, Lvov, 1874), i. 'Mekom yeshivato unesi'otav', 54, §11.　　　　[118] See the start of Ch. 2 above.

[119] See above, at n. 63.　　[120] For the presumed time of writing, see Koenig, *Neveh tsadikim*, 76.

[121] A nickname of Slavonic derivation, meaning honest, truthful, just, fair.

recited the *kedushah* prayer [with its thrice holy response], and said that she had heard the angels say 'Holy' and therefore she said 'Holy' as well.[122]

Nevertheless, references to women endowed with prophetic insight remain extremely rare, and those that occur share one crucial feature in common: such women are invariably related to the most famous hasidic leaders of their day. As was suggested above,[123] their power is derived from their intimate association with illustrious male relatives, whose own charisma and reputation it serves to enhance. The singular tradition that ascribes this power to a woman who claimed it in her own right—the celibate Maid of Ludmir—demonstrates that she was viewed by her contemporary tsadikim as an aberration, or one possessed by an 'evil spirit', and at any rate a deviant who should be silenced, as indeed apparently she was, her career as a rebbe curtailed by marriage, and her memory effectively erased from the literary record of hasidism.[124]

Against the background of the bold Sabbatian redemptive vision which, as we have seen, had promised to deliver the equality and liberation of women—acknowledging their prophetic inspiration, investing them with power as autonomous agents, and fully engaging them en masse as an active constituency of the messianic movement—hasidism's disregard for women is particularly striking. It seems too regressive to be taken for granted as mere compliance with the gender norms that traditionally prevailed in the culture of rabbinic Judaism. The hasidic doctrine of hallowing the mundane, of rendering spiritual the corporeal and the material, simply begs to be interpreted as designed to facilitate the mobilization of women—as 'body' or 'matter'—to usher in the transformation into 'spirit' or 'form'. Indeed, it could be argued that there never was a theological framework more conducive to the promotion of women to the

---

[122] Donner, *Mayim rabim*, 137. See also Heschel, *The Circle*, 153; Rapoport-Albert, 'On Women in Hasidism', 519–20 n. 54; D. Assaf, 'Messianic Vision' (Heb.), 48 n. 36. Donner's brief reference to Yente the Prophetess which, to the best of my knowledge, is the earliest and only source for this tradition, gave rise to an elaborate Yiddish adaptation, which places Yente within an unbroken tradition of illustrious hasidic prophetesses, claims that she adopted an ascetic lifestyle, abstained from sexual relations with her husband, performed great miracles, and was proclaimed a prophetess by none other than the Besht himself. See Feinkind, *Froyen*, 20–5. All this is entirely fictional, and clearly inspired by the oral traditions about the Maid of Ludmir and other female hasidic leaders, first noted by Horodetsky (on which see above, at n. 17).

[123] See the text above at nn. 15 and 16.

[124] See the text above at nn. 16 and 17. Note, however, the possible allusion to her in a hagiographical source published in 1892 (above, Introd., n. 12).

privileged status of religious vanguard, for surely, they embodied the greatest potential for realizing the collective goal. Their total exclusion from the enterprise, therefore, appears to be wilful if not downright perverse, and calls for an alternative explanation.

It is not as if hasidism might have been expected to accomplish the gender revolution that Sabbatianism strove to effect. The source of the potential it held for women was quite different from the one on which the Sabbatians drew. The egalitarian vision that prompted the Sabbatians to blur the halakhic distinctions between the sexes was based on the notion that the world they inhabited was governed by a new Law—that messianic Torah, which transcended the halakhic framework, and where all differentiation and distinction ceased. At the same time, their empowerment of women, exemplified most tangibly in the elevation of Eva Frank to the position of female messiah, was driven by the kabbalistic dynamics of the redemptive process—essentially a divine drama, which the Sabbatians saw it as their mission to enact on earth. In that scenario, the power of the female increases as the process approaches its climax, when she rises from the bottom to the top of the sefirotic tree, adorning it as 'a crown to her husband' (Prov. 12: 4). The hasidim, for their part, did not share the Sabbatians' sense of living in messianic times. With few exceptions, they viewed themselves as situated in a world of 'exile'—primarily a state of mind, which could be transcended and transformed into a state of 'redemption' by way of mystical experience mediated by the tsadik. If they were to allow women to join in and even lead this transformation, it would have been on the basis that they conceived them as the very embodiment of earthly corporeality—base matter which concealed within it the capacity for soaring to the greatest spiritual heights. That hasidism shied away from engaging women in what was, after all, the logical conclusion of a principle that lay at its core might well be a measure of the bitter lesson it drew from the trauma of Sabbatianism. For the Sabbatian heretics had left behind a profound dread above all of the breached halakhic boundaries of sexual propriety. The sexual depravity imputed to their women was inextricably linked to their full engagement with the failed messianic project. It was an untimely eruption of female spirituality—a powerful force prematurely unleashed which was now to be stowed away, kept out of sight, and securely contained until the appointed time for its discharge, which was not to be until some unknown point in the distant messianic future.

APPENDIX

'Something for the Female Sex': A Call for
the Liberation of Women, and the Release of the
Female Libido from the 'Shackles of Shame', in an
Anonymous Frankist Manuscript from
Prague *c.*1800

I

INTRODUCTION

ONE of Gershom Scholem's most celebrated and controversial theses, a thesis he argued repeatedly over many decades, concerned the dialectical relationship between the kabbalistic-messianic heresy of Sabbatio-Frankism and the movements of Haskalah (Jewish Enlightenment) and Reform. At its root lay the proposition that the Sabbatian break from traditional Jewish institutions and values had prepared the ground for the collapse of religious frameworks and the transformation of much of Jewish society and culture in the context of late eighteenth- and nineteenth-century rationalism, secularization, and modernity. As early as 1937, in his first comprehensive essay on the history of Sabbatianism, Scholem stated his case as follows: 'In the onward course of the Sabbatian movement the world of traditional Judaism was shattered beyond repair. In the minds of those who took part in this revolutionary destruction of old values a special susceptibility to new ideas inevitably came to exist.'[1] And towards the conclusion of the same essay he elaborated the point further:

The hopes and beliefs of these last Sabbatians caused them to be particularly susceptible to the 'millennial' winds of the times. Even while still 'believers'—in fact, precisely because they were 'believers'—they had been drawing closer to the spirit of the Haskalah all along, so that when the flame of their faith finally flickered out they soon reappeared as leaders of Reform Judaism, secular intellectuals or simply complete and indifferent sceptics.[2]

A few years later, in his *Major Trends in Jewish Mysticism*, Scholem reiterated this view, illustrating it with a number of striking examples:

Around 1850, a consciousness of this link between Sabbatianism and reform was still alive in some quarters. In circles close to the moderate reform movement, a very

This appendix reproduces an abridged version of the introduction to, and a full English translation of, the Judaeo-German manuscript text, first published, together with a transcription of the original, in Rapoport-Albert and Merchan Hamann, 'Something for the Female Sex'.

[1] Scholem, 'Redemption through Sin' (first published in Hebrew as 'Mitsvah haba'ah ba'averah' in *Keneset*, 2 (1937)), in id., *Messianic Idea*, 126.

[2] Scholem, 'Redemption through Sin', 140; see also ibid. 90–1.

remarkable and undoubtedly authentic tradition had it that Aron Chorin, the first pioneer of reformed Jewry in Hungary was in his youth a member of the Sabbatian group in Prague. Prossnitz and Hamburg, both in the eighteenth century centres of Sabbatian propaganda and the scene of bitter struggles between the orthodox and the heretics . . . were among the chief strongholds of the reform movement in the beginning of the nineteenth century. The sons of those Frankists in Prague who in 1800 still pilgrimed to Offenbach, near Frankfort, the seat of Frank's successors, and who educated their children in the spirit of this mystical sect, were among the leaders, in 1832, of the first 'reform' organisation in Prague. The writings of Jonas Wehle himself, the spiritual leader of these Prague mystics around 1800, already display an astonishing mixture of mysticism and rationalism. Of his extensive writings, an extremely interesting commentary on the Talmudic *Aggadoth* is extant in manuscript[3] from which it is clear that his particular pantheon had room for Moses Mendelssohn and Immanuel Kant side by side with Sabbatai Zevi and Isaac Luria. And as late as 1864 his nephew, writing in New York, lengthily praises in his testament[4] his Sabbatian and Frankist ancestors as the standard-bearers of the 'true Jewish faith', i.e. of a deeper spiritual understanding of Judaism.[5]

By far the most colourful illustration of the progression from sectarian kabbalistic messianism to Enlightenment, accompanied in this case by integration into non-Jewish European society and active involvement in its revolutionary politics, was the career of Moses Dobruschka, alias Franz Thomas von Schoenfeld, alias Junius Frey, which Scholem had painstakingly reconstructed. Dobruschka was a second cousin of Jacob Frank, who embraced Catholicism in 1775 without renouncing his family's ties to Sabbatianism.

[3] In a footnote Scholem identifies this as the '*perush le'ein ya'akov* [commentary on *Ein ya'akov*]' manuscript in the Schocken Library in Jerusalem, from which he was eventually to publish one section. See Scholem, 'Frankist Commentary' (Heb.) (all references are to the reprinted edition in id., *Studies and Texts* (Heb.), 422–52). On this manuscript, its authorship, and its relation to the present manuscript, see below.

[4] This is a reference to the testament of Gottlieb Wehle, a member of the leading Sabbatian Wehle family of Prague, who emigrated to America and settled in New York in 1849. Scholem subsequently published an annotated English translation of this testament in his 'Sabbatian Will' (all references are to the reprinted edition in id., *Messianic Idea*, 167–75).

[5] Scholem, *Major Trends*, 304. See also ibid. 299–300 and 320. Scholem notes that Leopold Löw, a leading figure in the Jewish Reform movement of 19th-century Hungary, had himself remarked on the association of the Moravian Sabbatians with the new rationalist movement, and he acknowledges that Sigmund (Shai) Hurwitz and Zalman Rubashov (Shazar) were the first to suggest, however impressionistically, the possibility of the link between the inner crisis of Jewish messianism as manifested in Sabbatianism and its offshoots, and the encroachment of modernity on the traditional modes of Jewish life (see ibid. 301–2; *Messianic Idea*, 85).

Following Frank's death in December 1791, he was apparently expected to succeed him as leader of the sect at its headquarters in Offenbach, but he declined to take up this role, pursuing instead his career as a prolific German Enlightenment-inspired author and leading figure in the Jewish–Christian, kabbalistically orientated Masonic order of the Asiatic Brethren, ending his life at the guillotine in 1794 as a Jacobin revolutionary in Paris.[6]

For a variety of religious and historiosophical considerations, Scholem's thesis, and more generally the importance with which his presentation of the dynamics of kabbalistic messianism had invested the Sabbatian debacle, aroused considerable opposition in both Orthodox and academic circles,[7] most notably in Baruch Kurzweil's critical essays published in the Israeli press.[8] But it was Jacob Katz, Scholem's colleague and friend who, having previously defended him (and himself) against Kurzweil's vituperative attacks in the press,[9] eventually took it upon himself to assess the validity of the thesis by way of rigorous historical investigation. In a paper first published in Hebrew in 1979,[10] but completed and submitted for publication some three years earlier,[11] he presented

[6] See Scholem, 'Career of a Frankist' (Heb.) (all references are to the reprinted edition in id., *Studies and Texts* (Heb.), 141–216).

[7] See the discussion of this in D. Biale, *Gershom Scholem*, 159–65, 171–4; Werses, *Haskalah and Sabbatianism* (Heb.), 9–20; Maciejko, 'Scholem's Dialectic'; Zadoff, 'The Debate' (Heb.). See also e.g. Werblowsky, 'Reflections' (Heb.); Schweid, *Judaism and Mysticism*, 85–6, 133–9.

[8] These were collected and published in several volumes. For Kurzweil's critique of Scholem, see Kurzweil, *Our New Literature* (Heb.), 78–109; *The Struggle* (Heb.), 99–240; and *Facing Perplexity* (Heb.), Schwarcz's introduction, 25–33, and *passim*. See also the discussions in D. Biale, *Gershom Scholem*, 172–4; Myers, *Re-Inventing the Jewish Past*, 172–5; id., 'The Scholem–Kurzweil Debate'; and Zadoff, 'The Awl and the Sack' (Heb.), 73–8.

[9] The exchange between Katz and Kurzweil appeared in *Haaretz*, 16 Apr. 1965, 5; 14 May 1965, 10–11; and 28 May 1965, 10–11. Kurzweil's attacks were reprinted in his volumes of collected essays listed in n. 8 above). Katz's response was republished in his *Jewish Nationalism*, 213–24.

[10] See Katz, 'The Possible Connection' (Heb.). Unless otherwise stated, all subsequent references are to the 1998 English version, published under the title 'The Suggested Relationship'.

[11] See Katz's unpublished letter to Scholem, sent from Columbia University, New York, and dated 8 March 1976, in which he states that, shortly before his departure from Jerusalem, he submitted the paper to S. Stein, one of the two editors of the Altmann Festschrift, where it was to be published for the first time three years later. The unpublished correspondence between Scholem and Katz is held at the Jewish National and University Library, Department of Manuscripts and Archives, Gershom Scholem Archive 4° 1599. We are grateful to the library for permission to quote from this correspondence, and to Noam Zadoff and Jonatan Meir for bringing it to our attention.

findings that challenged Scholem's thesis on several counts. His conclusions may be summarized as follows.

(*a*) The indisputable geographical and chronological overlap of central European Sabbatianism on the one hand, and Jewish Enlightenment or Reform on the other, especially in Hamburg and a small number of Bohemian–Moravian communities, was not necessarily indicative of any inherent continuity or connection between the two movements.

(*b*) Some of the individuals singled out by Scholem as examples of the progression from Sabbatianism to Haskalah or Reform were either lacking in any real Sabbatian 'credentials' or else had been drawn towards the Berlin Haskalah prior to, rather than following and as a result of, their involvement with sectarian Sabbatianism.

(*c*) It is plausible that in response to communal censure and social marginalization, some Sabbatians, who were persecuted by the rabbinic authorities, might have chosen to free themselves altogether from the yoke of rabbinic authority and halakhah, but this sociological factor does not in itself constitute proof of any ideological affinities between their heretical messianism and their estrangement from Orthodox Jewish practice. Nevertheless, some disillusioned Sabbatians might well have been drawn towards the liberating ideology of Haskalah specifically in those communities where both Sabbatianism and the Haskalah movement had struck roots, such as Prossnitz (Prostějov) and Prague.

(*d*) A clear distinction should be drawn between Haskalah and Reform—terms that Scholem had used interchangeably in this context. While a Sabbatian legacy might have facilitated the transition to Haskalah, with which it shared the impulse to undermine traditional religious authority, it could hardly have pointed in the direction of Reform, which sought to revitalize the religious principles of Judaism and to refresh the sources from which it drew its authority.

(*e*) If any demonstrable connection existed between Sabbatianism and Haskalah or Reform, it was in the personalities and strategies of their chief Orthodox opponents, who regarded both movements as equally subversive, and who set out to combat both with equal passion and zeal.[12]

[12] See Katz, 'The Suggested Relationship'.

In the letter in which he announced to Scholem that he had submitted his paper for publication,[13] claiming that it was time to review the issues 'from the other side of the barricade' (*min hatsad hasheni shel hamitras*), Katz reported that news had reached him that Scholem himself had not long since readdressed the same issues in a lecture delivered in New York and again in Boston. He went on to enquire:

> I have been told that you presented some new material, but I am not clear whether this was a reference to an as yet unpublished manuscript in your possession or whether my informant was wrong, and what you meant was the material you have already published in the Baron Festschrift.[14] Be that as it may, I assume that this 'oral *torah*' is but a prelude to the 'written *torah*' to follow, and that your lecture will be published. When and where? Is there a chance that I might still make use of it when proofreading [my own paper], or would you prefer to see first what I have managed to dig up? . . . In any case, it would be odd and unproductive if the two papers were to appear simultaneously without their authors having taken account of each other's work.[15]

Scholem must have surmised the critical position his friend was adopting from the title of his paper, 'On the Supposed Connection between Sabbatianism and Haskalah and Reform' ('Al hakesher hamesho'ar bein hashabeta'ut levein hahaskalah vehareformah'), as Katz himself had reported it to him in the opening lines of his letter. He underlined the offensive element, *hamesho'ar* ('the supposed'), while annotating Katz's reference to himself as one who observed things from 'the other side of the barricade' with more indignant underlining and two exclamation marks.[16] He was clearly irritated and unwilling

---

[13] See above, n. 11. In this letter Katz refers to his paper by what had clearly been its original title: *Al hakesher hamesho'ar bein hashabeta'ut levein hahaskalah vehareformah* (On the Supposed Connection between Sabbatianism and Haskalah and Reform). Notably, by the time the paper was published in 1979, the word *hamesho'ar* (supposed) had been dropped from the title and replaced, in Hebrew, by *Lishe'elat hakesher bein* . . . (On the Question of the Connection between . . .), and in English translation—as printed in the English table of contents of the book—by 'The Possible Connection . . .', somewhat attenuating the openly polemical tone of the original. A milder version of it survives, however, as 'The Suggested Relationship . . .' in the title of the 1998 English version of the paper (see above, n. 10), published long after Scholem was no longer alive. For Scholem's response to the original title as the probable reason for the change, see below, at nn. 16–18.

[14] This is a reference to Scholem, 'Frankist Document', on which see more below.

[15] Scholem–Katz correspondence, Gershom Scholem Archive 4° 1599. The English translation of all excerpts from the original Hebrew of this correspondence is our own.

[16] See above, nn. 11 and 13.

to co-operate, as his prompt reply from Jerusalem, dated 19 March 1976, makes quite clear:

Your paper to which you refer will deal with the <u>supposed</u> (!)[17] connection between Sabbatianism and Haskalah [as viewed] from 'the other side of the barricade'. Since from that other side there never was much interest in taking the issue into consideration, as I have demonstrated on the basis of the little that is known about this, and since the attitude of the Haskalah to Sabbatianism is clear beyond any doubt, I, for my part, have never found anything to consider here. I concerned myself exclusively with the question, which was indeed important to me, of the relation of the last Sabbatians to Haskalah, not the other way round. This relation is not 'supposed'; it is well documented.[18]

Scholem goes on to confirm that his lecture was indeed based, in addition to materials previously published by himself and by others, on 'unknown material' in manuscript, which he hopes eventually to publish in full, but on which for the time being he can speak only in outline and by way of 'oral *torah*'. Having thus refused to send the text of his New York and Boston lecture to Katz, he concludes by declining the offer to see Katz's own paper in advance of publication, and insists that his sole concern is that his published argument as formulated in *Major Trends* and 'Redemption through Sin' should not be misrepresented.[19]

Scholem's unpublished lecture, delivered in English in New York and in Hebrew in Boston,[20] is entitled 'Frankism and Enlightenment'. It is preserved in English in the Scholem Archive at the Jewish National and University Library in Jerusalem,[21] on twenty-two sides: ten numbered pages, with the addition of a two-sided page numbered 5*b* inserted between 5 and 6, on approximately A5-sized paper, in double-sided capital letter typescript, including underlining, corrections, and annotations in the author's hand. The lecture begins with a brief statement of the connection between Frankism and Enlightenment as formulated in Scholem's earlier writings. This connection,

---

[17] The double underlining and bracketed exclamation mark are in the original. Scholem's evident indignation, focused on the one element of the paper's title that betrayed its critical approach, must explain the deletion of 'supposed' from the published Hebrew version of 1979. See above, n. 13.

[18] Scholem–Katz correspondence, Gershom Scholem Archive 4° 1599.   [19] Ibid.

[20] See ibid., Scholem's reply to Katz dated 19 March 1976.

[21] Gershom Scholem Archive 4° 1599/156. We are grateful to Dr Paweł Maciejko, who drew our attention to the existence of this lecture, and to the library for permission to quote from it.

he argues, has been ignored by Jewish historians, not only on account of their sheer distaste for the 'unsavoury' phenomenon of Frankism, but also since much of the relevant evidence was deliberately suppressed or even destroyed, either in the hands of the sectarians themselves or by their numerous opponents. In spite of this, Scholem insists, the connection must be recognized as paralleling and belonging in the same context as the generally acknowledged connection between mysticism and Enlightenment in European history, especially with regard to such radical sects as the Quakers, the Pietists, and the Bohemian Brethren. There follows a section entitled rather awkwardly 'Story of my Researches', in which Scholem discerns three distinct branches of Frankism: the Polish branch, largely baptized and centred in Warsaw; the Bohemian–Moravian branch, overwhelmingly Jewish and centred in Prague; and the common ground shared by both branches, originating in the periods when the Frankist 'court' was based in Brünn (Brno) and Offenbach during 1773–86 and 1788–1816 respectively. This section is followed by a survey of the evidence on the remarkable combination of Frankist belief and *Aufklärung* (Enlightenment) ideas, much of which had escaped the attention of earlier scholars but which, according to Scholem, was either attested or rumoured in connection with both the Polish Frankists and their German-speaking brethren in Bohemia-Moravia. Following these preliminaries, the bulk of the lecture is devoted to a description and analysis of the fresh evidence contained in what Scholem introduces as 'two newly discovered manuscripts in Jerusalem', to which he refers as 'popping up' in the Jewish National Library in 1934 and 1960 respectively.[22] He characterizes both as 'letters, notes and explanations of biblical books (Esther, איכה [Lamentations]) and passages [*sic*], and talmudic and midrashic [*agadot*] (*Ein Jacob*), written about 1800–

---

[22] 'Frankism and Enlightenment', 3ᵛ–4ʳ. The dates of the discovery as reported here do not match those supplied by Scholem elsewhere. See his 'Frankist Commentary' (Heb.) where, in the 1974 reprint of the original 1961 version (p. 422, end of n. 2), he inserts a remark in square brackets to the effect that one of the two manuscripts was 'discovered in 1950 in the National Library in Jerusalem', a fact of which he was clearly unaware when he published the original version of the paper. A similar claim with regard to the same manuscript appears in Scholem's introduction to his edition of 'Frankist Letter' (Heb.), 634 (all references here and below are to the reprinted edition in id., *Researches* (Heb.), 634–50), where he refers to the manuscript as 'one of the unexpected discoveries following the upheavals of the Holocaust . . . an important anthology which found its way in the 1950s to the National Library in Jerusalem'. See also below, n. 26.

1805 (possibly partly even a little earlier)', in a language which he calls 'Hochdeutsch (mixed with Jiddish and Hebrew), all, of course, written in Hebrew letters'.[23]

This brief characterization of the two manuscripts somewhat blurs the distinction between them. It is clear that Scholem considered their provenance, probable authorship, and linguistic features to be similar if not identical, but their contents, as we learn even from his own descriptions elsewhere,[24] are quite distinct: one comprises a wide diversity of discrete compositions ranging from personal letters, addresses, and notes to long homilies and biblical commentaries, while the other is an exposition primarily of the talmudic *agadot* (from most, but not all of the chapters in tractates *Berakhot* and *Shabat*) contained in the popular midrashic anthology *Ein ya'akov*. It was from this latter manuscript (fos. 47a–57a)[25] that Scholem had published the Frankist commentary on Psalms 113–18 (Hallel), which was embedded in the text of the commentaries on the talmudic *agadot*.[26] At the time of publication, in 1961,

[23] 'Frankism and Enlightenment', 4ʳ.

[24] Scholem published two relatively short treatises, one from each of the two manuscripts, both of which he described in some detail in the introduction to each. See his 'Frankist Commentary' (Heb.), 422–8, and 'Frankist Letter' (Heb.), 634–8. In 1976, when he was preparing his lecture 'Frankism and Enlightenment' for Boston and New York, the former treatise, excerpted from the first manuscript, had long been published (in 1961), but the latter, excerpted from the second manuscript, was to appear only subsequently, in 1977. It is clear that at the time of writing his lecture Scholem was working on and preoccupied exclusively with the second of the two manuscripts. The lecture, which promises to report on both manuscripts—*'their* history', *'their* character', *'their* language', and *'their* author' (3ᵛ–4ʳ; emphasis added)—switches abruptly to a detailed discussion of 'the manuscript' in the singular (4ʳ), and from that point on deals exclusively with the manuscript from which the 'Frankist Letter' (Heb.) was to be published two years later. On this manuscript, see below, n. 29.

[25] The manuscript, which runs to 203 folios, contains three successive pagination sequences, marked—probably in the author's hand—at the top left-hand corner of each folio. In addition, a single pagination sequence, running consecutively from 2 to 203, was inserted by another hand in the middle of the bottom margin of each folio. The commentary on Hallel appears on 47a–57a at the conclusion of the author's second pagination sequence, corresponding to 92a–102a in the consecutive pagination sequence.

[26] See his 'Frankist Commentary' (Heb.), 423. Scholem describes the route by which this precious manuscript eventually found its way to Jerusalem from Prague where, in the early part of the 20th century, an old female descendant of one of the Bohemian Frankist families had given it to the then chief rabbi of Prague, Dr Hayim Brody (who, as Scholem notes, refused to disclose her identity, presumably in order to protect her reputation from unsavoury sectarian associations). Dr Brody in turn gave the manuscript to Salman Schocken in whose famous

he still considered that manuscript to be the sole remnant of a large collection of unpublished Frankist 'treasures' which, during the nineteenth century, had been in the possession, first of Wolfgang Wessely (himself of Moravian, probably Frankist descent), and later of Adolf Jellinek,[27] each of whom had published a version of the same 1803 New Year homily on the 'Aleinu' prayer, originating in what Scholem clearly believed to be one of the lost manuscripts the collection had once contained.[28]

library it was deposited, and it was there that Scholem must have found it, apparently as soon as the library was transferred from Berlin to Jerusalem in 1934, the date of the discovery suggested in his lecture 'Frankism and Enlightenment' (see above, n. 22). This manuscript (now catalogued as Schocken Institute 14610) is written in an Ashkenazi Hebrew hand in Judaeo-German strewn with explanatory notes in Hebrew and full of quotations in the original language of the biblical, rabbinic, and kabbalistic sources. On the basis of occasional acronymic references in the text to ר״י and מו״ח שי״נ, which Scholem deciphered as ר' יונה (Rabbi Jonas) and מורי וחמי שיאיר נרו (my teacher and father-in-law, may his light shine) (see 'Frankist Commentary' (Heb.), 424, and cf. below, n. 32), he suggested that the anonymous author and/or copyist of the Schocken manuscript might have been Jonas Wehle, who headed the circle of Frank's devotees in Prague during the final decade of the 18th century and the first two decades of the 19th, possibly with the assistance of his brother Aaron Ber Wehle, or else with either Aaron Ber's son-in-law, Barukh Patschotsch, or Jonas's own son-in-law, Arieh Löw Enoch Hönig Edler von Hönigsberg, acting as his amanuensis. For the latter's eventual identification as the author of the manuscript, see below, at and around nn. 35–40.

[27] See Scholem, 'Frankist Commentary' (Heb.), 422–3.

[28] The Judaeo-German New Year homily on the 'Aleinu' prayer (fos. 1a–8b of the manuscript) was first published by W. Wessely in 1845 anonymously, in an annotated German transcription, heavily edited to modernize the rather awkward German vocabulary and syntax, under the title 'Aus den Briefen eines Sabbatianers'. Six years later he republished an identical version of the same text, this time under his own name. The beginning of the same homily, evidently taken from the same manuscript (fos. 1a–3b), was published again by Adolph Jellinek, to whom, as Jellinek reports in the introduction to his edition, Wessely had bequeathed his entire collection of Frankist manuscripts. Jellinek's version ('Eines Anhängers'), restored to the original German in Hebrew characters so as to preserve the authentic character of the text, appeared in two short instalments in the periodical *Hakol* in 1885. The second instalment (issue no. 287, col. 61), like the first, concludes with the bracketed Hebrew formula *hemshekh yavo* (sequel to follow), leading to the expectation of at least one further instalment in a subsequent issue. However, issue no. 292, col. 143, contains an editorial announcement to the effect that publication of this text is being discontinued on the grounds that it is written in 'jargon', namely Judaeo-German, rather than in Hebrew, the preferred language of *Hakol* and its readers. See on this, Werses, *Haskalah and Sabbatianism* (Heb.), 151–3. For a hostile reaction to the publication of this heretical Frankist text in *Hakol*, which may well have prompted the editor, Michael Levi Frumkin-Rodkinson, to discontinue it, see Meir, 'Mikhael Levi Rodkinson' (Heb.), 268 and n. 197.

As it turned out, this apparently lost manuscript was the one that eventually surfaced at the Jewish National and University Library in 1950 or thereabouts,[29] and it was from this manuscript, previously in the possession of both Wessely and Jellinek, that Scholem himself was to publish in 1978 'A Frankist Letter on the History of the Faith' (fos. 46*b*–49*b*).[30] It was also to this manuscript, on which he was clearly working at the time, that he devoted the bulk of his unpublished 'Frankism and Enlightenment' lecture in 1976.[31]

In 1961, when he published 'A Frankist Commentary on Hallel' (Heb.) from MS Schocken 14610, Scholem was still uncertain of its authorship and speculated that it was 'connected' to 'the two brothers Jonas and Aaron Ber Wehle, who belonged to a distinguished Prague family, and who headed the [Bohemian] Frankist fellowship in the early years of the nineteenth century'. In addition, he considered the possibility that the copyist or scribe who produced the manuscript, and who frequently referred to what Scholem had deciphered as his father-in-law by the acronym שי"נ ח מו",[32] was either Baruch Patschotsch, who had married Aaron Ber Wehle's daughter Amalia, or Arieh Löw Enoch Hönig Edler von Hönigsberg, who was married to Jonas Wehle's daughter, Deborah.[33] But while he could not decide between these two sons-in-law, Scholem was able to establish with confidence that the manuscript was produced in Prague during the early years of the nineteenth century, between approximately 1805 and, at the latest, the death in 1816 of Jacob Frank's daughter Eva, who is referred to in the manuscript without the accompany-

---

[29] See above, n. 22. The manuscript—Jewish National and University Library 8° 2921—was acquired from an Austrian Jew who had immigrated to Israel and brought it with him after the war. See Scholem, 'Frankist Letter' (Heb.), 634. See also Liebes' editorial comment (ibid., n. 1) pointing out that Mr Shlomo Zucker of the library's department of manuscripts was the one who identified and, at Scholem's request, transcribed the entire manuscript for him. Mr Zucker's transcription, in 300 pages of typescript corresponding to the manuscript's 121 folios, is held at the National Library's Gershom Scholem Archive 4° 1499/155.1 and 155.2. Although we have occasionally emended his readings, Mr Zucker's generally accurate transcription has greatly facilitated our work on the present edition of 99*a*–103*a*—the treatise entitled 'Something for the Female Sex', translated below.

[30] See above, n. 22.   [31] See above, n. 24.

[32] See above, n. 26, although it is clear from the closely related MS National Library 8° 2921 that the correct decipherment of the acronym שי"נ is not שיאיר נרו, as Scholem had suggested, but rather שיחיה נצח, a formula whose German counterpart ל"ע [לעבע עוויג—*lebe ewig*, 'may he live eternally'] occurs time and again throughout that manuscript interchangeably with שי"נ. See below, p. 345 n. 34.   [33] See above, n. 26.

ing acronym ז״ל (of blessed memory), a formula which would have been appended to her name had she no longer been alive at the time of writing.[34]

By 1976, however, when he wrote his 'Frankism and Enlightenment' lecture, Scholem, who was previously aware only of MS Schocken 14610, had become acquainted with the second extant Frankist manuscript from Prague, National Library 8° 2921. On the basis of this, he was able to conclude that the author of both manuscripts was one and the same, and that he was none other than Jonas Wehle's son-in-law Arieh Löw Enoch Hönig Edler von Hönigsberg.[35] In fact, some six years earlier, Scholem had already intimated that there was evidence pointing to von Hönigsberg as the main author of both manuscripts,[36] and by 1974 he had become sufficiently confident of this identification to publish it as his unqualified conclusion in the introduction to his edition of von Hönigsberg's petition to the Prague police commissar, submitted on 9 November 1800, as a protest against the persecution to which he was being subjected at the time by the leading rabbis of Prague.[37] The petition was discovered in the late 1930s in the archive of the Czechoslovakian Ministry of the Interior, within a file containing some remnants of what had clearly once been a voluminous collection of documents relating to the Prague Frankists. Václav Žáček reported on the discovery, described the contents of the file, and published two other documents from it in 1938.[38] On the basis of his description, and with the assistance of Salman Schocken, Scholem was able a year later to obtain a copy of the petition,[39] but he did not publish it until 1974, by which time he had reached the conclusion that the petition and its author should be linked to the two anonymous Frankist manuscripts from Prague, Schocken 14610 and National Library 8° 2921.

If Scholem's conclusion is correct—and, with some qualifications, we are inclined to accept it—that von Hönigsberg, who wrote the petition to the

---

[34] See Scholem, 'Frankist Commentary' (Heb.), 425–6.

[35] See id., 'Frankism and Enlightenment', 4^r.

[36] See id., 'Career of a Frankist' (Heb.), 175 n. 103.

[37] See Scholem, 'Frankist Document', 788–9. As regards the 1803 New Year homily published by both Wessely and Jellinek in the 19th century (see above, n. 28), which was eventually recognized as the opening section of the newly discovered National Library 8° 2921 Prague manuscript, Scholem had already identified 'Jonas Wehle's son-in-law' as the author when he first published, in 1948, his English translation of Gottlieb Wehle's 'Sabbatian Will from New York'. See the 1971 reprint edition of this paper in Scholem, *Messianic Idea*, 170.

[38] Žáček, 'Zwei Beiträge', 343–410.   [39] See Scholem, 'Frankist Document', 787.

police commissar, also produced the two anonymous Prague manuscripts,[40] then the petition provides valuable biographical information about our author, supplementing what can be gleaned about his life from a number of other sources. He was born in 1770 or 1771[41] to a wealthy Jewish family involved in the Habsburg administration of the tobacco monopoly. His grandfather, Israel Hönig, was among the first Jews of the empire to be ennobled (in 1789) without undergoing baptism.[42] In 1787 the young von Hönigsberg was married off to Deborah, daughter of Jonas Wehle—the leading light of the Bohemian Frankists, who was at the same time an admirer of Moses Mendelssohn and a

[40] The identification of von Hönigsberg as the author of all three is indeed plausible (on their common linguistic features, see below, 'A Note on the Language of the Manuscript'), but the precise nature of his relationship to the two manuscripts is not entirely clear. There is no doubt that the anonymous manuscripts share many characteristics and are closely related to one another, but—leaving aside their distinct contents and disparate organizational structures (on which see above, at and around n. 24)—Schocken 14610 contains considerably more Hebrew than does National Library 8° 2921, and it appears to be the work of a copyist rather than an autograph (as is suggested, for example, by the numerous scored-through dittographies that occur throughout it (see e.g. 6*b*, 8*b*, 16*a*, 23*a*, 28*a*, 37*b*, 42*a*, 44*a*, 45*a*, 80*a*, 80*b*, 83*a*, 84*a*, 86*a*, 90*b*, 138*b*, 144*b*, 145*b*, 148*a*, 158*a*, 158*b*, 163*b*, 173*a*, 176*b*, 179*b*, 180*b*, and 184*b* in the consecutive pagination sequence), in contrast to National Library 8° 2921, which is virtually free of dittography but contains minor deletions, insertions, and corrections that seem to reflect an author's decision to rephrase a sentence or substitute one word with another for the sake of clarity and out of stylistic considerations (see e.g. 11*b*, 43*b*, 46*b*, 54*b*, 71*b*, 80*b*, 93*a*, 100*a*, 101*a*, 102*a*, 109*a*, and 115*b*)). Moreover, the two manuscripts appear to have been written by two distinct hands. Scholem himself, in his early speculations about the authorship of Schocken 14610, was undecided on the question whether the manuscript was the product of a 'writer' (*kotev*) or a 'copyist' (*ma'atik*), concluding with the proposition that while authorship should be ascribed to Jonas Wehle and his son-in-law Löw von Hönigsberg, the manuscript itself might be a copy made by one of their fellow-sectarians (see Scholem, 'Frankist Commentary' (Heb.), 424–5). By the time he published, some seventeen years later, the excerpt from National Library 8° 2921, he was confident that von Hönigsberg was the author of 'most, if not quite all' of that manuscript (see id., 'Frankist Letter' (Heb.), 635), but did not address the question of the manuscript hand or its relationship to that of Schocken 14610, a question which, for the lack of conclusive evidence, must, for the time being, remain unresolved.

[41] See Scholem, 'Frankist Letter' (Heb.), 635, and cf. id., 'Frankist Document', 788. As regards the end of his life, the sources conflict: according to some he died in 1811, but others note his death on 2 February 1828 (see ibid.). The later date is more plausible, since von Hönigsberg was listed among the signatories to an appeal, published in the summer of 1818, advocating the republication of selections from past volumes of *Hame'asef*, whose regular publication had ceased in 1811. See on this Werses, *Haskalah and Sabbatianism* (Heb.), 94.

[42] See Scholem, 'Frankist Document', 788; McCagg, 'Austria's Jewish Nobles', 163–83, esp. 172.

subscriber to the publication of his German translation of the Pentateuch.[43] In his petition to the police commissar, von Hönigsberg reports on his educational background as follows:

In my youth, my dear parents had me instructed in Bible, Hebrew grammar, Talmud, and the German language, and I acquired some general familiarity with Jewish as well as German literature. My parents also had me study logic and metaphysics, and I developed a strong inclination towards philosophy.[44]

He goes on to acknowledge the subsequent influence on his intellectual development of his father-in-law, Jonas Wehle who, as he argues, was a highly respected member of the Jewish community of Prague until the present outbreak of the misguided rabbinic campaign against him and his family:

He was formerly considered in the city as a paragon of religious piety, known to be a great theologian, and an authority on the Kabbalah and Jewish literature in general. We soon became friends, indeed the most intimate of friends, and we engaged in mutual instruction and friendly exchanges of ideas. Thus I would read out to him some instructive philosophical writings, and he would read and explain to me some theological and kabbalistic principles, some obscure passages in the Talmud, the [doctrinal] system of our Sages, and the Spirit of Judaism.[45]

It is clear from this that von Hönigsberg was the greater expert of the two in philosophy, in which he had been instructed from his youth, and towards which he confessed his 'strong inclination'. He was thus in a position to introduce the literature of European philosophy to his father-in-law. The latter, in turn, was better acquainted with the traditional sources of Judaism; he could enhance his young protégé's understanding of rabbinic literature, and above all introduce him to the mysteries of kabbalah—a subject that was conspicuously absent from von Hönigsberg's account of his early curriculum of study. It seems likely that Wehle, who was born in 1752,[46] still received an exclusively Jewish religious education, and that it was from within this traditional intellectual background that he was drawn towards the heretical messianic kabbalah. Only later in life did he encounter the Haskalah ideology and began to explore European philosophy under his son-in-law's guidance. By contrast, von Hönigsberg, who was born some twenty years later, had acquired from the

---

[43] See Scholem, 'Frankist Document', 788; id., 'Frankist Commentary' (Heb.), 424.

[44] Id., 'Frankist Document', 810–11. The English translation of the original German here and below is our own. See also Werses, *Haskalah and Sabbatianism* (Heb.), 82–3.

[45] Scholem, 'Frankist Document', 811.   [46] See Scholem, *Kabbalah*, 306.

outset a broader and more modern education which included, in addition to the classical rabbinic sources, the study of Bible and Hebrew grammar, as well as the German language and its literature, and philosophy, all of which point to the Haskalah orientation to which, during the 1780s, his generation of young upper-crust Prague Jews was the first to be fully exposed.[47]

There is little doubt that the kabbalistic doctrines imparted by Jonas Wehle to his young son-in-law bore a distinctive Sabbatio-Frankist character, and it was probably under the impact of his initiation into the esoteric teachings of the sect that von Hönigsberg accompanied his father-in-law on a pilgrimage to its headquarters in Offenbach on at least one occasion, in 1793— a little over a year after the death of Jacob Frank in December 1791.[48] Although he is said to have been bitterly disappointed by his experience of the Offenbach 'court'—run at that time by Frank's two sons, Josef and Rochus, and his daughter Eva, who functioned as its messianic figurehead[49]—von Hönigsberg's subsequent writings, as the two Prague manuscripts clearly testify, remained saturated with Frankist phraseology and ideas[50] while at the same time betraying his early acquaintance with European Enlightenment literature, and his evident admiration for Mendelssohn and the Berlin Haskalah.[51] It would seem, however, that unlike his father-in-law, Jonas Wehle, who may serve to illustrate Scholem's thesis on the connection between sectarian kabbalistic messianism and the modern ideology of Haskalah, inasmuch as he seems to have graduated from the former to the latter, von

[47] See Kieval, *Languages of Community*, 45–53; Kestenberg-Gladstein, *Neuere Geschichte*, 115–33.

[48] See Guttmann, 'Lazarus Bendavid', 206; Gelber, 'Di zikhroynes fun moses porges', appendix 1, col. 292.

[49] According to Lazarus Bendavid, who met von Hönigsberg in Prague sometime after his return from Offenbach, he had been looking forward to the 'bliss' of his encounter with Eva Frank, but was forced 'to leave without accomplishing his goal, despite having passed the difficult test to which she had subjected him, because, as she admitted, she did not consider him holy enough for her to demean herself by conversing with him' (Guttmann, 'Lazarus Bendavid', 206), and according to Wolf Lipmann Hamburger's testimony of November 1800 he returned to Prague 'almost deranged' with disappointment, having very nearly lost his Frankist faith (Gelber, 'Di zikhroynes fun moses porges', appendix 1, col. 292).

[50] For examples of these, see the annotated English translation below.

[51] For evidence of his acquaintance with European Enlightenment literature, see the discussion at pp. 340–2, nn. 7, 9, 10, 11, and 13 in the translation below. On his Haskalah connections, see below, at nn. 61–70.

Hönigsberg, despite the Frankist connections of at least some members of his distinguished family[52] (connections that would account for his marriage into the Wehle family, which was prominent in the Bohemian leadership of the sect), had been exposed to Enlightenment philosophy and Haskalah some years prior to his initiation into the sectarian kabbalah of his father-in-law, and may thus be seen as having progressed from one ideology to the other in precisely the opposite direction. This, indeed, is how his intellectual progression (or rather his regression, from the critical point of view) is portrayed in a number of thinly disguised references to von Hönigsberg that appear in the anonymously published, Haskalah-inspired Hebrew satire entitled *A Conversation between the Year 1800 and the Year 1801*.[53] The author of this pamphlet, written in Prague in 1800 at the height of the controversy surrounding the activities of the sectarians in the city, appears to subscribe to a moderate version of the Haskalah vision. He mocks the heretics' preoccupation with kabbalah at the expense of both talmudic study and the pursuit of modern science and philosophy, and he aims his sharpest arrows at one amongst them whom he depicts as a renegade from the camp of Enlightenment and Reason to the ranks of the 'deranged' kabbalistic sectarians. Although von

---

[52] See Scholem, 'Frankist Document', 788, where he describes the Hönig family as 'connected by many links with other outstanding Frankist families from Moravia and Bohemia such as the Dobruschkas of Brünn and the Wehles of Prague', and id., 'Frankist Commentary' (Heb.), 425, where he states that 'his family belonged, at least in its greater part, to the circle of the Frankists'. It seems that the father of the family, von Hönigsberg's grandfather Israel Hönig, had married into the Sabbatian (later Frankist) Wehle-Landsofer family of Prague (see id., 'Career of a Frankist' (Heb.), 175 n. 103). In addition, one of von Hönigsberg's uncles, Wolf Hönig, was married to a sister of Moses Dobruschka (see ibid. 145 n. 11, 150 n. 29, 158 n. 54, 168), and Wolf's father, von Hönigsberg's great-uncle Benjamin Hönig, who was the younger brother of his grandfather Israel Hönig, was a close associate of Jacob Frank's first cousin and mother of Moses Dobruschka, Schöndl Hirschl-Dobruschka, with whose husband, Solomon Zalman, he was involved in the tobacco monopoly administration. In 1775, a year after the death of Solomon Zalman (who—it should be noted—remained Jewish to the end of his life and may not have shared his wife's well-attested affiliation with the sect; see above, Ch. 4, at nn. 24–7), Benjamin Hönig was resident in Schöndl Dobruschka's house in Brünn, where he converted to Catholicism and assumed (without royal authorization) the titled name of von Bienenfeld. See McCagg, *Habsburg Jews*, 34–5. On the history of the Hönig family, see also Kestenberg-Gladstein, *Neuere Geschichte*, 409, s.v. Hönig v. Hönigsberg.

[53] For a detailed discussion of this satire, and the plausible suggestion that its author was Baruch Jeiteles (1773–1813), see Kestenberg-Gladstein, *Neuere Geschichte*, 184–91; ead., 'Who Is the Author?' (Heb.); Werses, *Haskalah and Sabbatianism* (Heb.), 74–81.

Hönigsberg is never mentioned by name, what we know about him from other sources, especially from his petition to the police commissar, exactly matches the descriptions of the renegade in the satire:

There is among these believers a man who was formerly a follower of Reason—well versed in booklore and languages, pursuing the paths of human enquiry, adept in philosophy and an accomplished scholar, yet he is one of those who stubbornly cling to this fallacy! Is it possible for a man who has been even briefly illuminated by the light of Reason to become implicated in such folly?! . . . It is undeniable that he is a man of insight and understanding, learned and adept in philosophy. Moreover, prior to his affiliation with this kabbalistic sect he was a lover of Reason and had a fine intellect. But the cause of his departure from the path of Reason is the cause of his derangement now . . . And afterwards, when the man became intimately connected to this family of kabbalistic sectarians,[54] they endowed him with the spirit of their kabbalah, [teaching him] to gaze at the speculum that shines,[55] [to see] the visions of the Zohar and kabbalah. And the man, who was deranged by this heavenly philosophy, saw that the knowledge [he had gained] was good and proceeded liberally to derange himself with it. In this knowledge—allusions, letter permutations, computations of their numerical values and the like—his mind had found the means by which to make straight that which was crooked and which could not be made straight by means of any other knowledge at his disposal. All the difficulties and doubts that he did not manage to resolve by recourse to other sciences were resolved for him by the principles of kabbalah . . . This man proceeded to abandon both Reason and sense, his father and mother, and he clung to this worthless notion, becoming deranged like one of them.[56]

It is indeed as a man of Reason turned kabbalistic sectarian (and not the other way round), that Jacob Katz presents von Hönigsberg, making him an important test case for his critique of Scholem's thesis.[57] Reviewing the evi-

[54] This would seem to be a reference to von Hönigsberg's marriage into the Wehle family, which was prominent in the leadership of the sectarians in Prague.

[55] Namely, to experience prophetic vision.

[56] *A Conversation*, 19–23, quoted in the original Hebrew in Werses, *Haskalah and Sabbatianism* (Heb.), 92–3. The English translation is our own.

[57] Katz, 'The Suggested Relationship', 517–21. Another of Katz's test cases, illustrating his claim that the direction of the movement proposed by Scholem between Frankism and Enlightenment must be reversed, is Ephraim Joseph Hirschfeld, who had lived for some years as a maskil near Moses Mendelssohn in Berlin, only later in life becoming involved, together with Jacob Frank's cousin, Moses Dobruschka (known at the time as Franz Thomas von Schoenfeld), in the syncretistic kabbalistic theosophy of the Asiatic Brethren Masonic order, and eventually establishing contact with the Frankist sect when he settled at its headquarters in Offenbach (see ibid. 517, and the references cited there to the detailed studies of Hirschfeld by both Scholem and Katz).

dence of his petition to the police commissar in light of *A Conversation*'s depiction of the 'deranged' renegade, Katz concludes his analysis of von Hönigsberg's case as follows:

No doubt the author of 'The Conversation Between the Years 1800 and 1801' was right in claiming that by grafting his kabbalistic inspiration to his philosophical knowledge, he removed himself from the circle of *maskilim*, both in social and intellectual terms. A link between Sabbatianism and Haskalah was forged in his personal identity—not by Sabbatianism forming the background to the Haskalah, but in the opposite direction.[58]

While diverging in their interpretations of the direction of the turn from one orientation towards the other, Scholem and Katz, as well as Werses, who has also addressed himself to the same issue, all acknowledge the incontrovertible fact that von Hönigsberg's writings display ideas drawn from both ideological camps,[59] although on this, too, their interpretations diverge. All three agree that, in his petition to the police commissar, von Hönigsberg was appealing to the authorities' sympathy by presenting himself as an enlightened, civilized, modern Jew who was the victim—like the champions of the Berlin Haskalah in their day—of the obscurantist bigotry of the Prague rabbinate, in whose estimation Enlightenment was tantamount to heresy. He therefore emphasized his Haskalah orientation while suppressing altogether his sectarian beliefs—the real cause of the rabbinic persecution about which he was protesting. This evident ploy led Katz to conclude that von Hönigsberg's enlightened self-representation was totally insincere, namely, that by 1800, when he wrote his petition, he had long abandoned the Haskalah orientation of his early youth and—as the satirical *A Conversation* (Heb.) implies—had consequently been rejected by, or else severed all his social and intellectual ties to the Prague maskilim, having made, during the late 1780s, a clear-cut and irreversible transition to the camp of the kabbalistic sectarians under his father-in-law's influence.[60] Werses, on the other hand, who examined in detail von Hönigsberg's involvement with the Haskalah movement, was able to show that, not only did he subscribe and contribute some writings

[58] Ibid. 521. Werses, who refers to Katz's conclusions, seems to share them, albeit without posing an explicit challenge to Scholem's thesis. See his *Haskalah and Sabbatianism* (Heb.), 9–20, 92 n. 116.

[59] See Scholem, 'Frankist Commentary' (Heb.), 424, and see more below; Katz, 'The Suggested Relationship', 517–21; Werses, *Haskalah and Sabbatianism* (Heb.), 81–2, 84, 88.

[60] See Katz, 'The Suggested Relationship', 519–21.

to the chief literary organ of the Berlin Haskalah—the periodical *Hame'asef*—
some ten years after his marriage into the Frankist Wehle family, and at least
four years after his well-attested pilgrimage to the headquarters of the sect in
Offenbach,[61] but he was also proudly introduced by the editors of *Hame'asef* as
the member of a most distinguished and noble family, 'an honourable and
highly esteemed man, upright and pure of heart'.[62] It is clear that they did not
suspect him of any involvement with the unsavoury kabbalistic sect, and that
they considered his Haskalah credentials to be impeccable. Moreover, his
contributions to the journal (in which he explicitly acknowledged his debt to
his father-in-law and sectarian kabbalistic mentor, Jonas Wehle![63])—ethical
expositions of several aggadic passages drawn from the talmudic tractate
Berakhot—appeared to be in tune with the Haskalah posture of *Hame'asef*, and
contain no intimation of what must by then have been von Hönigsberg's
well-entrenched heretical kabbalistic convictions.[64] Werses' analysis of von
Hönigsberg's contribution to *Hame'asef* points to a number of possible hints at
his sectarian affiliation,[65] but these are confined to ostensibly innocuous statements, such as the urgent call to pursue every opportunity to acquire true
wisdom and insight,[66] which, as Werses suggests, may be read as a veiled

[61] See von Hönigsberg, 'Wise Letters' (Heb.). See also the discussion in Werses, *Haskalah
and Sabbatianism* (Heb.), 84–91. Scholem had already noted von Hönigsberg's contribution to
Hame'asef (see Scholem, 'Frankist Document', 788 n. 8), but, as Werses observes, he referred
only to one of its two instalments, and did not discuss its contents at all.

[62] Editorial introduction (*Divrei hame'asefim*), *Hame'asef*, 7 (1797), issue no. 1, p. 22. The
English translation here and below is our own. See also Werses, *Haskalah and Sabbatianism*
(Heb.), 85–6.

[63] The 'Letters' are addressed 'to my master and teacher, my father-in-law, my close friend
and relative' (*la'adoni mori hami alufi umoda'i*), and they are presented as the product of his
instruction: 'Behold, my master! Your words have borne fruit, and this is their fruit!' (*Re'eh na
adoni! Devareikha asu peri, vezeh piryam!*). See von Hönigsberg, 'Wise Letters' (Heb.), 7/1, p. 25.

[64] Notably, five out of the seven aggadic passages from tractate *Berakhot* which he expounds
in his Hebrew contributions to *Hame'asef* are expounded also in the Judaeo-German manuscript commentary on *Ein ya'akov* (MS Schocken 14610), yet most of the interpretations
offered in *Hame'asef* differ considerably from those found in the manuscript commentary,
which tend to draw out of the talmudic material a distinctly messianic or characteristic Frankist
lesson rather than the purely ethical lessons taught in the 'Wise Letters'. Cf. 'Wise Letters', 7/1,
letter 1, pp. 27–8; letter 3, pp. 30–2; 7/3, letter 5, pp. 196–8; letter 6, pp. 198–9, and letter 7, pp. 199–
203 with MS Schocken 14610, 11*b* §39, 8*a–b* §27, 5*a* §15, 12*b* §43, and 10*a–b* §36 respectively.

[65] See Werses, *Haskalah and Sabbatianism* (Heb.), 88–90.

[66] See von Hönigsberg, 'Wise Letters' (Heb.), 7/1, letter 3, pp. 30–2.

reference to the esoteric kabbalah of the heretics, or the advocacy of tolerance and compassion, accompanied by admonitions against the violent persecution of wrongdoers,[67] as well as the advice to be cautious about the expression of opinions that are liable to be misunderstood and to attract derision or censure,[68] which may conceivably echo the author's experience of mounting hostilities towards the sectarians in Prague. There is, however, nothing in von Hönigsberg's Hebrew 'Wise Letters' that alludes to any kabbalistic or heretical point of doctrine.[69] Werses concludes from all this that

It is impossible to determine with certainty to what extent von Hönigsberg remained sincerely faithful to these two spiritual worlds simultaneously, or whether he merely donned the Haskalah mantle [in his petition to the police commissar] as a disguise and a subversive ploy . . . It should be taken into account that the chronological gap between his Haskalah and his Frankism periods was relatively small; one period appears to stretch right up to the other, and it is impossible to point to a clear dividing line between them.[70]

Surprisingly, given his long-standing commitment to the notion of progression from sectarian kabbalism to Haskalah, it was Scholem who gauged von Hönigsberg's position—contrary to Katz's interpretation, and without any of Werses' equivocations—as a genuine integration or fusion of his two intellectual worlds. While Katz perceived a clear dividing line between von Hönigsberg's early Haskalah period and his subsequent transformation into a fully fledged kabbalistic sectarian, and while Werses found it difficult to determine whether this transformation was ever clear-cut and complete, in his 1976 unpublished lecture entitled 'Frankism and Enlightenment' (rather than, as

---

[67] Ibid., letter 1, pp. 26–7.   [68] Ibid., letter 4, pp. 32–3.

[69] A possible exception is the author's emphasis in letter 1 (ibid., pp. 27–8), which illustrates the merit of forgiveness and compassion with a famous passage from BT *Ber.* 10*a*, on the crucial role played by Beruriah, R. Meir's wife, in persuading her husband to forgive his wicked neighbours, who had been oppressing him, and to pray for their repentance rather than for their demise. Von Hönigsberg makes a special point of praising 'this upright woman', who 'turned her husband's heart towards good', and concludes his exposition of the passage with the call to 'accept the truth from whomsoever has declared it, be they young or old; to that person you should hearken'. This injunction to heed the truth even if it is revealed by a woman, highlighting her superior capacity to serve as its authoritative source, may echo the author's preoccupation with the status of women, which was inspired as much by his kabbalistic sectarianism as by his acquaintance with certain European Enlightenment tracts, and which is fully evident throughout his manuscript, especially in 'Something for the Female Sex'.

[70] Werses, *Haskalah and Sabbatianism* (Heb.), 84 and 88. The translation is our own.

one might have expected, *From* Frankism *to* Enlightenment), Scholem intro-duced his analysis of von Hönigsberg's Prague Judaeo-German manuscripts (or rather, as we have seen, essentially of only one of the two—National Library 8° 2921) as follows:

[There exists] the closest connection and alliance between the two factors: heretical kabbalism and Haskala. On the one hand, the author defends all the paradoxical tenets of Frankism, and on the other hand he takes up a vigorous tendency permeated by doctrines of Enlightenment. He uses alternatively and sometimes on the same page the terminology of Kabalah in its several forms and of Enlightenment as expounded by great men like Leibniz, Kant, Moses Mendelssohn and Naphtali Herz Wessely.[71]

It must be noted that both Katz and Werses appear to have based their respective interpretations of von Hönigsberg only on those of his writings that were available to them in print: his German petition to the police commissar and the two short excerpts, one from each of his two Judaeo-German manu-scripts, that were published by Scholem,[72] as well as, in the case of Werses, von Hönigsberg's Hebrew contributions to *Hame'asef*, all of which they juxtaposed with the depiction of the man generally taken to be von Hönigsberg in the satirical *A Conversation* (Heb.). Scholem, on the other hand, had acquainted himself in addition with the full text of von Hönigsberg's two extensive Prague manuscripts, and it was this that enabled him to assess more accurately the nature of the ambivalence they presented. When we compare von Hönigs-berg's published autobiographical statements with the bulk of his manuscript sectarian writings, it becomes clear that he did not graduate, as Scholem's famous thesis had stipulated, from the heretical kabbalah of the Frankists to the rationalist ideology of the Enlightenment any more than he abandoned, as Katz had argued, the Haskalah orientation of his youth in favour of the hereti-cal messianic kabbalism of the sectarians. Rather, he genuinely combined the two discrete sources of his spiritual and intellectual inspiration, clearly view-ing them as being mutually corroborative and in perfect harmony with each other. Indeed, it is precisely in these terms that *A Conversation* (Heb.) ridicules

[71] Scholem, 'Frankism and Enlightenment', 4ᵛ.

[72] But not, it seems, the excerpt from the Prague manuscript that eventually became National Library 8° 2921, which was published twice in the course of the 19th century, first by Wessely and later by Jellinek (see above, n. 28). Katz does not refer to it at all, and Werses, who describes the circumstances of its publication (see his *Haskalah and Sabbatianism* (Heb.), 151–3, 168–9), does not address its contents.

the man who is almost certainly to be identified as von Hönigsberg:[73] 'He combined many philosophical ideas, both ancient and modern, together with the doctrines of kabbalah. He took some of the teachings of the philosopher Kant and dressed them up in the garb of the Zohar and the kabbalistic teachings of the Ari [Isaac Luria].'[74]

In his unpublished lecture Scholem illustrates this remarkable fusion of ideas in reference to the paradoxical notion of the true 'faith'—the sectarians' repeatedly frustrated but nonetheless persistent hope of imminent redemption. As von Hönigsberg argues in one section of the manuscript,[75] which may well echo his own bitter disappointment with the pilgrimage to Offenbach he undertook only a few years earlier,[76] this 'faith' defies all reason; it is verified and sustained precisely by the fact that it clashes, time and again, with the evidence of reality.[77] And yet, Scholem observes, von Hönigsberg was capable of couching this quintessentially Frankist doctrine of paradoxical faith in rationalist terms inspired by the Enlightenment thinkers he admired:

We have thus before us an apology and even an apotheosis of the intrinsically paradoxical character of the faith. This term is used sometimes in a sense depending on its

[73] Scholem had originally identified him as Jonas Wehle, who at that time he also considered to be the author of the Frankist commentary on *Ein ya'akov* preserved in MS Schocken 14610. See his 'Redemption through Sin', 140–1. As we have seen, this identification was more compatible with his thesis on the late Sabbatians' turn from sectarian kabbalism to Haskalah, but he subsequently came to the conclusion that the author of the manuscript commentary, and the man depicted in *A Conversation* (Heb.) as combining rational philosophy and kabbalah, was none other than von Hönigsberg. This identification precluded the notion of a turn from one ideology to the other and suggested instead the 'closest connection and alliance' between the two, as described in the passage quoted above from the lecture 'Frankism and Enlightenment'.

[74] *A Conversation* (Heb.), 23.

[75] This is the section that Scholem was to publish two years later as 'A Frankist Letter on the History of the "Faith"' (Heb.).

[76] See above, n. 49, and see Scholem, 'Frankist Letter' (Heb.), 637, on the personal experience underlying von Hönigsberg's argument.

[77] For some stark statements of faith in precisely the opposite of what appears to be the evidence of reality, see e.g. MS National Library 8° 2921, 25*b*–26*a*:

וואס מאן זיהט דארף מאן ניכט גלויבן דס הייסט אין ווראהייט אמונה . . . בקיצור, כל אמונות א"י [אלוהי יעקב] הוא להאמין בהיפך הראות . . . וא"כ [ואם כן] מאז והלאה שזכה אדם לאמונת א"י יודע שעיקר אמונה להאמין דווקא היפך הראות, גראס פיר קליין קלייין פיר גראס אנצווישן etc. . . .

('What one sees one must not believe; this, in truth, is what faith is . . . In short, all faith in the God of Jacob [Frank] is to believe in the opposite of what is apparent . . . Therefore, from the moment that one merits to believe in the God of Jacob, one knows that the essence of the

rationalistic usage and explanation in the writings of Wessely on Ethics,[78] but at other times in the sense given to it in the Sabbatian sects. The 'religion of reason' whose main tenets are God, liberty, and immortality (as defined by Leibniz and Kant) becomes closely bound to the religion of paradox, a characteristic of the Frankists. The 'weakness of theoretical reason'—obviously a phrase borrowed from Kant—gives way to the strength of the religion of paradoxical belief.[79]

Scholem proceeds to present what he terms 'the nexus between Frankism and the Prague Enlightenment'[80] that is attested throughout von Hönigsberg's manuscript, and he concludes his lecture with one other, particularly striking example. This is the author's passionate call for the 'emancipation of women', a topic to which he devotes a whole treatise, and to which Scholem refers—apparently from memory and at any rate quite inaccurately—as 'Letter to the Feminine Sex'—'Brief fürs weibliche Geschlecht',[81] whose actual title as it appears in the heading of this section of the manuscript is: 'Something for the female sex, who hope for what God will do, and, more specifically, what concerns his sacred help!' (עטוואס פיר דס וייבליכע גשלעכט דיא האפּען אויף דס ווס ג׳[אטט] מאכען ווירד, אונד זיינע היי ליגע היילפּע נעהער אנגעהעט!).[82] So radical is this extraordinary call for the liberation of women from the 'shackles' of marital 'enslavement' and conventional morality that Scholem is prompted to raise the possibility that our author may have been exposed to the influence of one of the earliest and boldest 'manifestos' of modern European feminism: 'The question arises whether the Frankist writer was possibly influenced by the earliest English writings of an anarchist character like Goodwin [*sic*][83] and his wife Mary Goodwin-Wollstonecraft, the authoress of *The Vindication of the Rights of Women* [*sic*] (1792).'[84]

faith is to believe precisely in the opposite of what is apparent, to take big for small, small for big … etc.')

[78] N. H. Wessely, *Book of Ethics* (Heb.) (first published in Berlin 1786?–8). For Wessely's discussion of the nature of faith, see ibid., pt. 2, ch. 5, 53*b*–65*a*.

[79] Scholem, 'Frankism and Enlightenment', 5^r–v.   [80] Ibid. 5^v.   [81] Ibid. 8^v.

[82] MS National Library 8° 2921, 99*a*–103*a*, translated below. For the ambiguities of the title, see p. 338 n. 1 to our English version.

[83] The correct name is Godwin. Scholem is referring to the English political philosopher and author William Godwin (1756–1836).

[84] Scholem, 'Frankism and Enlightenment', 8^r. The correct title of Wollstonecraft's book concludes with the singular 'Woman'. On Mary Wollstonecraft, her book, and its reception, see e.g. Godwin (Wollstonecraft's widower), *Memoirs*; Janes, 'On the Reception of Wollstonecraft's *Vindication*'; and C. Johnson, *Cambridge Companion*, which contains an extensive bibliography.

Scholem acknowledges the fact that 'already Sabbatai Zwi had made a speech in the synagogue of Izmir in December 1665, announcing the forthcoming . . . liberation of women from masculine domination and its burden of sufferings',[85] a fact which may now be firmly placed in the context of Sabbatianism's egalitarian tendencies and its promotion of women to positions of prophetic and even messianic–divine authority. This was a unique feature of the movement, underpinned by certain kabbalistic traditions on the inversion of gender hierarchies at the time of the redemption. It emerged at the very inception of Sabbatianism and persisted in one form or another throughout its history, culminating in the veneration in Frankist circles of Eva Frank as the female messiah and the living incarnation of the divine *sefirah* Malkhut.[86] In von Hönigsberg's manuscript treatise, this kabbalistic legacy of sectarian 'feminism' is fused together with some of the pioneering calls for the liberation and equal rights of women that were beginning to be heard in Europe in the course of the eighteenth century.

There is little doubt that our author was acquainted—either directly or through German epigones—with the works of such French Enlightenment authors as Montesquieu and Rousseau, whose pronouncements on female nature, and on the status of women in society, can be read between the lines of his treatise on the 'elevation' and liberation of the female sex.[87] He does not, however, appear to have used *A Vindication of the Rights of Woman*, as Scholem himself rightly points out just as soon as he raises—if only to reject—the possibility of such an influence by Mary Wollstonecraft's famous work: 'The term emancipation of women, which was made widely known by her writings, recurs in our letters [i.e. the manuscript treatise], but the development of the idea shows no use of this source.'[88]

Wollstonecraft's book, first published in London in 1792, could conceivably have reached our author, especially since it was immediately translated and published in German in 1793.[89] However, not only is it difficult to trace its impact on contemporary German readers,[90] but the thrust of the book's

---

[85] Scholem, 'Frankism and Enlightenment', 8[v].

[86] On all this, see Chapter 7 above. See also our annotated translation below.

[87] For evidence of this, see pp. 340–2 nn. 7, 9, 10, 11, and 13 and p. 345 n. 35, to the translation below.   [88] Scholem, 'Frankism and Enlightenment', 8[r].

[89] The German edition appeared as Maria Wollstonecraft, *Rettung der Rechte des Weibes* (Schnepfenthal, 1793). The translator was the prolific German author and educationalist Christian Gotthilf Salzmann.   [90] See Dawson, *Contested Quill*, 283.

revolutionary feminism is totally at odds with von Hönigsberg's. While he celebrates what he regards as the innate qualities of female nature—sensitivity, intuition, an instinctive sense of morality, practical good sense, wit, tenderness, volatility, compliance, the desire to please and to be loved, and above all sensuality—in terms that echo strongly Rousseau's characterization of the female in *Émile*,[91] Wollstonecraft dismisses this perception of the female as a disabling social construct,[92] and her book is full of diatribes against Rousseau, who had given it such a wide currency.[93] She rejects the prevalent attribution of what was often referred to at the time as 'sensibility'[94] to all women by default, arguing that it is not innate but arises simply from their lack of educational opportunities, and she insists that the female intellect's capacity for reason is in every way equal to the male's.[95] Admittedly, both our author and Wollstonecraft condemn the social order of their day in similar terms: it oppresses women and subjects them as slaves to the tyranny of men or their 'despotism' (a term which both probably derive from Montesquieu[96]); it warps and stifles their true nature, preventing them from realizing their full human potential. But the remedies they prescribe and their ultimate aspirations could hardly differ more from one another. Wollstonecraft advocates political and educational reforms, looking forward to the incorporation of women in the liberty, fraternity, and equality from which the French Revolution had continued effectively to exclude them.[97] Von Hönigsberg, on the other hand, argues above all for the release from 'captivity'—understood in the sense of 'shame', 'modesty', or in other words, the constraints of conventional sexual morality—of the full force of female sensuality. He expects this to be inaugurated by the emergence from concealment of the messianic Virgin or Maiden, whom he believes (paradoxically, of course, despite or rather precisely on account of his disappointing personal encounter with her) to be embodied in the figure of Eva Frank. According to him, the creative vitality of female sensuality has

[91] See below, p. 340 n. 9 to the translation.
[92] See e.g. Wollstonecraft, *Vindication*, 88–9, 108, 101, 121 n. 1, 123, 165, and *passim*.
[93] See ibid. 83–4, 90–4, 96, 100, 102, 107–9, 111, 131, 142, 147–59, 172–3, 203, 216, 221, 246.
[94] For the rise and fall of 'sensibility' (in the sense of intuitive emotional intelligence, which by the end of the 18th century came to be regarded as excessive sentimentality) in 18th- and early 19th-century discourse, and for Wollstonecraft's critique of its manifestation in women who were denied the opportunity to cultivate the mitigating faculty of reason, see e.g. Todd, *Sensibility*; Barker-Benfield, *Culture of Sensibility*, esp. 351–95.
[95] See Wollstonecraft, *Vindication*, 91–3, 101, 104–5, 121–2, 187–8, and *passim*.
[96] See below, p. 341 n. 11 to the translation.   [97] On this see Proctor, *Women*, 110–85.

long been subdued or repressed within societies that seclude and enslave their women, relegating them to the passive role of gratifying men's sexual urges. Once it is unleashed, the innate sensuality of the female will in turn revitalize the sensuality of the male, which has been dormant or reduced to base lust in the 'corrupt nature' of this world, but is bound to revert to the full glory of its true nature at the time of the redemption.

If there exists some possible affinity between von Hönigsberg's vision of the liberation of female sensuality and any strand of European Enlightenment or revolutionary thought, it is to be found not in the treatises advocating women's education and civil rights, but rather in that earlier intellectual shift, which may be seen as one of the 'unsettling ramifications of philosophical naturalism and Spinozism, as well as [Pierre] Bayle's radical separation of morality from religion', that eroded traditional notions of virtue, and generated 'a growing impulse not just towards the emancipation of women but of the human libido itself'.[98] As Jonathan Israel observes, already in the second half of the seventeenth century, a number of radical European thinkers had begun to call for the liberation of the sexual impulse, which they recognized as inherent in men and women alike. They were particularly concerned with the repression of sexuality in women by the inculcation of the traditional female virtues of modesty and chastity, and they condemned it as self-imposed imprisonment or forced imprisonment by men.[99]

It is impossible to tell how much of this literature—some of it originally published in Latin, considered scandalous or banned (although becoming available in both French and German in the course of the eighteenth century)[100]—would have been accessible to von Hönigsberg and may have merged in his mind with the kabbalistically informed vision of the release and 'elevation' of female sensuality in the perfected new order of the messianic world. What is clear, however, is that far from denying the inherent differences dividing female nature from male, as did most radical European advocates of equal rights for women, he envisaged the ultimate manifestation of their true natures as being clearly distinct, albeit evenly matched, and combined through the free flow of their complementary sensualities in blissful sexual union.

[98] Israel, *Radical Enlightenment*, 82–3.
[99] See ibid. 86–7; id., *Enlightenment Contested*, 572–89; Porter, *Flesh*, 144–5.
[100] See Israel, *Radical Enlightenment*, 87–9; id., *Enlightenment Contested*, 583.

A NOTE ON THE LANGUAGE OF THE MANUSCRIPT

In his unpublished lecture 'Frankism and Enlightenment' Scholem describes the language of both Prague manuscripts, Schocken 14610 and National Library 8° 2921, as 'Hochdeutsch (mixed with Jiddish and Hebrew), all, of course, written in Hebrew letters'.[101] This summary characterization requires some qualification: while the language clearly aims to be *Hochdeutsch*, namely standard literary German, it falls short of this time and again throughout the two manuscripts. Scholem acknowledges our author's linguistic limitations when he describes elsewhere another sample of his writing—his petition to the police commissar of Prague, which is the only fully extant specimen of his writing in German characters.[102] As an official document addressed to the non-Jewish authorities, von Hönigsberg composed it—admittedly in haste and in a state of considerable agitation, as he confesses[103]—in the best standard literary German he could muster (unlike the two anonymous manuscripts, for which he employed Judaeo-German, written in Hebrew characters and clearly intended for clandestine internal circulation). Nevertheless, the document displays the same shortcomings as are evident in the two Judaeo-German manuscripts. Scholem evaluates the quality of this language as follows: 'He writes a very ungrammatical and often barbarian German full of mistakes in spelling and syntax. It is evident that the text did not undergo a stylistic revision on the part of somebody better acquainted with correct German style.'[104]

His verdict seems somewhat harsh. At least some of von Hönigsberg's linguistic shortcomings were not uncommon among his contemporaries, whether Jewish or not, especially in the provincial territories of the Austro-Hungarian empire, where universal education in the German language had only recently been established.[105]

---

[101] See 'Frankism and Enlightenment', 4ʳ.

[102] To the best of our knowledge, only fragments of two other samples of von Hönigsberg's German writing survive. These are his translations from Eleazar Fleckeles' collection of anti-Frankist sermons, *Ahavat david*, and the ban of excommunication issued in Prague against the Sabbatians in 1726, both of which he submitted to the police commissar together with his petition. Fragments of both are quoted by Žáček in 'Zwei Beiträge', 372–3, 398–9 nn. 34 and 36.

[103] See von Hönigsberg's 'Petition' in Scholem, 'Frankist Document', 810.   [104] Ibid. 789.

[105] For the introduction of elementary German education throughout the empire during the 1780s, see below, n. 110. To gauge the quality of von Hönigsberg's German, cf., on the one hand,

These observations are compatible with what is known about von Hönigs-berg's educational background from his petition to the police commissar.[106] Although he was clearly fluent in German, he is unlikely to have acquired it through formal schooling, but was in all probability tutored in the language at home, as was customary among the wealthier Jewish families of Prague,[107] and as his own account of his upbringing clearly implies. Admittedly, the first school to offer Jewish children a primary education in German, the *Normal-schule*, was established in Prague in 1782, following Joseph II's bestowal of his Toleranzpatent on the Jews of Bohemia in 1781, and the proclamation in the same year of his decree of compulsory elementary German education throughout the empire.[108] As a result of negotiations between government officials and the rabbinic leadership of Prague, the school did not admit its Jewish students prior to their tenth birthday, to ensure that they would acquire a firm grounding in traditional religious studies before becoming exposed to German instruction in secular subjects. Von Hönigsberg, who was born in 1770 or 1771,[109] would have been at just the right age of 11 or 12 to be sent to the *Normalschule*, but it is most unlikely that he was, since the school served exclu-sively the children of the poor, while the middle and upper classes continued to educate their sons at home.[110]

Von Hönigsberg's imperfect command of German mars both his petition to the police commissar and his two Prague manuscripts. This is evident in a range of grammatical errors, syntactical flaws, orthographic inconsistencies,

'Franzens des Zweyten Römischen Kaisers Gesetze und Verfassungen im Justitzache ... in den ersten vier Jahren seiner Regierung' (Prague, 1819), which is written in flawless German and may serve as a benchmark for the highest linguistic standard of imperial documents dating from the 1790s, and, on the other hand, the official reports written during the 1770s by Count Carol Friedrich von Zollern, the provincial Prefect of the Brünn (Brno) district of Moravia, which display similar linguistic flaws to von Hönigsberg's. His reports were published in Rabinowicz, 'Jacob Frank in Brno', 435–40. For a discussion of this issue, see Emeliantseva, 'Die Wehles', 62–3, who rejects Scholem's characterization of von Hönigsberg's German on the grounds that it is not in any way inferior to von Zollern's language. We are grateful to Ekaterina Emeliantseva for allowing us to consult the relevant section of her dissertation.

[106] See above, at nn. 44–7.   [107] See Kieval, *Languages of Community*, 58.
[108] Ibid. 54–5.   [109] See above, n. 41.
[110] On this, see Kestenberg-Gladstein, *Neuere Geschichte*, 34–66; Kieval, *Languages of Com-munity*, 56–7. For an assessment of von Hönigsberg's education, see Emeliantseva, 'Zwischen Tradition und Mystik', 561–3.

lexical incongruities, and many stylistic infelicities.[111] Some of these may be due to underlying interference from either Yiddish or local German dialect, which often share common characteristics, but others must arise simply from his lack of formal education in the German language.[112]

In the translation below, footnotes cued with symbols are the author's own, while our comments, cued with numerals, appear as endnotes on pp. 338–45. All explanatory insertions enclosed in square or, within them, in angle brackets are the translators'; those enclosed in parentheses are by the author, as is all underlining. Where the author incorporates in his Judaeo-German text Hebrew or Yiddish terms originating in Hebrew, these appear in Hebrew characters, followed by our English translations. We have tried to remain as faithful as possible to the original German, retaining some of its awkward stylistic features (notably the inconsistency of subject number, e.g. frequent switches between 'woman' and 'women', 'she' and 'they' in the same sentence or paragraph), but were forced at times, for the sake of intelligibility, to break up particularly long sentences, to modify the punctuation, and to opt for one out of several alternative translations of ambiguous phrases and terms. Where our choices or occasional departures from the literal sense might affect the meaning significantly, we have supplied the literal translation ('lit.') or the italicized German in square brackets immediately following our English rendering. Thanks are due to Hugh Denman, and to professors Erika Timm and Dovid Katz, whose helpful observations and comments on the Judaeo-German language of the original manuscript underlie the present English translation.

[111] For illustrations of all these, see Rapoport-Albert and Merchan Hamann, 'Something for the Female Sex', 105–7.

[112] Cf., however, Kestenberg-Gladstein's observations, based on a personal communication from the late Chone Shmeruk, on a contemporary sample of Judaeo-German writing by Israel, son of Ezekiel Landau, rabbi of Prague: 'He makes no effort to write pure German, as is evidenced especially in his irregular use of the dative and the accusative, as well as in his word order. One may perhaps refer to this as Bohemian Jewish-German, used both orally and in writing. It must have had at its root a certain linguistic self-consciousness, of which one can find other attestations. One should not underestimate this conscious desire to legitimize and maintain the linguistic status quo, the desire not to imitate the educated German of the surrounding milieu. In that situation, the author, who was in any case educated in Hebrew, was able to express his sense of solidarity with the uneducated masses' (*Neuere Geschichte*, 164; the translation of the German original is our own).

[99a]

Something for the female sex, who hope for what God will do, and, more specifically, what concerns His sacred help![1]

[The prophet] Jeremiah [31: 22] said the following verse about the new [thing] to come: 'How long will you veil and hide yourself, O you suffering daughter?[2] G[od] has made (created) a new thing in <u>the world</u>:[3] the female [shall] compass the male'[4] or the maiden [shall] compass the youth! What does this mean? What is this welcome news? What consequences does it have for the salvation of the world? What are the happy consequences of so solemn a proclamation? Has G[od] created something new in the world?

This is a very great thing, the beginning of everything good in <u>the world</u>, without which [this good] will not come about [lit. it is impossible]. You will be well aware that the personification of שכינה [Shekhinah—the tenth, female aspect of the kabbalistic godhead], from now on better called the H[oly] Virgin, the בתולה [virgin], is the gateway to G[od] and to all divine treasures. All capacity for Him is in her; all the keys to His treasures are with her; everything apparent, manifest, and revealed in the world is to be revealed through her; <u>she</u> is the first step and the <u>gateway</u>;[5] she is also the true <u>sensuality</u>[6] of [lit. for] G[od], just as every good wife is her husband's sensuality. Since we are able to grasp only that which we perceive on the evidence [lit. examples] of our senses,[7] let us begin by considering the status and nature of the female sex, in order thereby to surmise the nature of things godly.

Both the physical and the mental constitution of the female are entirely disposed to <u>sensuality</u> [*Reizbarkeit*] (whereas the male's are more [disposed] to firmness). Her[8] outward appearance is obviously designed to this end, and the qualities of her soul—her tenderness, her love, her patience, her desire to please, her submissiveness, and to a certain extent even her frailty contribute to it—even her more practical understanding of trivial matters, her ability to grasp 1,000 minor circumstances—to order and judge them correctly, her fine feelings and taste, her appreciation of all that is decent, beautiful, proper, and moral without having been taught, her sensitive soul, her sensibility, her need for company, her wit, her capacity for knowing at once what to do in changing circumstances, her lighter and more volatile disposition, in short—everything is in keeping with sensuality [*Reizbarkeit*].[9] But greater even than all these are her need to love and be loved, [her need for] faithfulness and warm-heartedness!—I can more readily imagine 100 cases of men who are happy without being loved than a single [case of an] unloved [and yet happy] woman! [99b] A man must be educated in order to feel that a world filled with love, warm-heartedness, and affection is true Paradise, but a woman who is not entirely bereft of her femininity will sense this at once. What primarily moves and prompts men to love is nothing other than their sexual drive [*sinnlicher Trieb*]. On the other hand, the whole essence of woman is to be loved, kissed, etc. The mere absence of love and warm-heartedness is liable to make her feel unhappy and empty, while a single loving man is sufficient for her so long as she is attached to him and he to her. Women who do not, through fear of G[od], deny or pervert their natural instincts from early child-hood, who have not been badly brought up, and who therefore follow their hearts more readily, can demonstrate this even better.[10] This is the lesson of experience, and it is how women are universally described.

To love and have tender feelings for children, a sentiment to which women are capable of yielding, is the second part of their character and happiness, and it is closely connected to the first. A solitary man is far less unnatural than a [solitary] woman. But while love, and being loved, and sensuality [*Reizbarkeit*], and behaving in such a way as to make herself attractive [*reizbar*] (which is quite distinct from vanity and worldliness) are the basis and essence of a woman's soul,* she in turn has shackles within her own character, and even

---

* That is why no quality in a man is as attractive to a woman as his love and affectionate faithfulness to her (which the man does not always feel). As the חכמים [Sages] said, a woman prefers the most miserable existence, getting by on no more than bare necessities but with her husband by her side, to a life of great riches but with her husband far away on many journeys [see BT *Ket.* 62b: 'A woman prefers one kab <a scanty measure, namely scanty living> with <sexual> licence to ten kabs with abstinence']. And the חכמי[ם] [Sages] further say that a woman is [designed] for virtually nothing other than to adorn and beautify herself, that is to

more so in the world at large. <u>As she can hardly live in accordance with her character,</u> how much less than a man is she able to satisfy her own desires. In most countries of the world, in the whole of Asia and Africa, the women are mere slaves, treated despotically and oppressed. They are forbidden to go out, must walk about veiled, and are guarded by eunuchs like תפוסים [prisoners].[11] They are effectively and ממש [actually] in lifelong detention, cut off from society, which is their life, and from any [opportunity of] allowing themselves to be seen, which is their basic instinct. In many countries of the world, among the savages, [**100a**] they are condemned, ממש [quite literally], to slave labour on behalf of men, even carrying loads and working in the fields and the like, while the men stay idle. She is a total slave, treated by her husband with despotism and contempt, and she has <u>no will of her own</u> (so that they curse their lives and hold themselves to be the most unfortunate creatures). <u>Is not her entire character being slain here?</u> Certainly! And so it was in the ancient world (until the rule of the Germans and the C[atholics],[12] and in part also among the Greeks and the Romans[13]), almost as far as the then civilized world extended.

In Judaism similarly—though not in the same way, albeit mostly—everything in the female sex that arouses sensuality [*Reizbarkeit*] is called ערוה [nakedness, genitalia, lewdness]. It must be covered and not seen in women. Beautiful hair in a woman must be covered; the sweet voice of women must not be heard; their luring power in singing melodies, in which their gentleness, delicacy, and sensuality [*Reizbarkeit*] develop fully, may not be displayed; [and] a bared שוק יד ורגל אפי׳[לו] [leg, hand, and foot is even] more of an ערוה in women.[14] With no male, towards whom her soul is truly drawn, may she be [alone] together. This is precisely what is called יחוד [prohibited seclusion with a member of the opposite sex who is not one's spouse]. If any of the above things were to happen, her husband could send her away in disgrace, without her dowry. Her greatest praise is: she sits locked up at home <u>honourably</u>

say, she takes great care to be attractive [*reizbar*]; a woman is [designed] for nothing other than a man, for nothing other than children, for nothing other than beauty and clothes. [See ibid. 59*b*: 'R. Hiyya taught: A wife <should be taken> mainly for the sake of her beauty, mainly for the sake of children. And R. Hiyya further taught: A wife is mainly for the wearing of a woman's finery.' See also BT *Ta'an.* 31*a*: 'Set your eyes on beauty, for woman has been created for nothing but beauty ... Look out for a <good> family, for woman has been created for nothing other than <to produce> children.'] In short—everything [springs] from the same ground.

כל כבודה בת מלך פנימה ['The king's daughter is all glorious within'].[15] Eagerness to go out and run about is reckoned a great flaw [in her], as if she must be kept in prison, where one cannot go out without a guard. If she has a husband then she is subject to his will almost like a slave! And she has only her husband's morality to thank for such freedom as remains to her. By dint of the laws, no one would look at her with an adoring eye, not even at her fine clothes. She may not greet anyone except through her husband. She must avoid even the slightest suspicion or else she will be rightly exposed to his greatest jealousy. He can divorce her, [but] she cannot [divorce] him except by being seen as a female rebel.[16] And finally, as regards the finest sentiment of the soul, [sexual] love—here, too, she is not her own master. If the husband desires it—she must obey to avoid being liable to severe punishment by law. If, [however], she feels inclined to [make] love, if her sensuality [*Reizbarkeit*] reaches its highest levels, she cannot hint at this with [as much as] a <u>word</u>. In [what concerns] the finest sentiment, flowing from the most tender [source] and subject mostly to the mood and caprice of the inner soul—**[100b]** to be treated so much like a slave! Effectively to suppress both desire and distaste! Does this not mean that her whole feminine character is to be slain and stifled?[†] Of course, she lives and

---

[†] This is the meaning alluded to by way of סוד [secret] [in the statement]: the לויתן [Leviathan, the primordial sea monster] was created זכר ונקיבה [male and female], but [had they gone on to procreate] the world would have had no קיום [lasting existence]. [Therefore] הרג את הנקיבה, וסירס או צינן את הזכר [He <God> slew the female and castrated or chilled the male]. [See BT *BB* 74*b*; Zohar, ii. 34*a*–*b*. For an analysis of this talmudic myth, see Fishbane, *The Exegetical Imagination*, 41–55. For an analysis of its kabbalistic adaptations, see Idel, 'Leviathan and its Consort' <Heb.>, 145–86. Our author is not entirely faithful to his source, which has God chilling the female's flesh, not the male's, in order to preserve it for the future banquet where it will be served to the righteous in the World to Come. He does, however, acknowledge correctly <see below> the alternative mode—salting—by which God preserves for the banquet the female's, not the male's flesh. Following a long kabbalistic tradition, our author proceeds to allegorize the male and female Leviathans, but as becomes evident directly below, the concepts to which he takes them to allude are entirely his own.] This is [to be] understood as follows: לויתן means man and woman in respect of their souls' qualities of love. Were this [namely, the presence in the world of procreating Leviathans] to occur within corrupt Nature just as it will in the [messianic] future, then the world would have no existence. That is why הרג את הנקיבה [He slew the female]—the feminine nature was slain, and צינן את הזכר או סירס [He chilled or castrated the male]—the masculine nature was cooled off. For as soon as the sensuality [*Reizbarkeit*] of the female is no more, the masculine nature is no longer its true self. All this was undertaken by the ס'[טרא] דקדושה [the Side of Holiness], so that the result would be לקיום העולם [for the lasting existence of the world] within corrupt Nature.

has some pleasures, but her inner, her true femininity is stifled. A king's son in captivity can have a number of pleasures and live, but his royal disposition is frozen, stifled. So also here.

Furthermore, the female sex, created to be so receptive to bliss, able to taste the honey of all joys, created to kiss, to adore, to give and receive happiness, to love and be loved—whose very tongue has a finer [capacity to] taste, whose hand has a more sensitive touch, whose eye and ear are keener—sensing the root of all that is fine and itself the root of all spiritual sensations—this female sex is, at the same time, [afflicted] with pain = toil and tribulations, which entirely crush and agitate her spirit! Childbearing, which is such a joy for a woman, is embittered by strenuous pregnancy, by a dejected and low spirit during that time, and by birth pangs and frailty thereafter. When a mother plays tenderly with her children, her delicate feelings are lightened to a certain extent, but this is dissipated and embittered by her strenuous and menial labours in the first years of childhood. [1o1a] And then [there are also] the domestic chores which numb her sensations and to which she is confined, as well as being subject to the power of her husband. In short, all this embitters women's sense of bliss.

Indeed, she is constrained by [lit. has] shackles within her very character, that is to say, her great <u>modesty</u>—a virtue so great, which considerably enhances [lit. heightens] [her] charms [*Reize*], but [one] which shackles her will and her being. Golden shackles are still shackles. Everything that propriety, custom, and convention forbid externally is precisely what her modesty forbids internally. Perhaps one must call this by another name, but I simply do not know another word [for it]. This stirring in her character even determines [lit. makes] her whole being. No matter how much she wants to be loved, how eager she is to make herself attractive, and however much these [desires of hers] are necessary even to her lover—if they could, if it were possible for them to be concealed ... to withdraw, as it were, into themselves and be hidden from her lover, even from her husband, and how much more so from the world at large—[this] is her whole being.

But all this was necessary, and [put in place] for the salvation of the world,

ומסכים עם הסוד כולו [And this is entirely consistent with the esoteric meaning]. **Even the image of** ומלחה לצדיקים לעתיד לבוא [and He salted her for the righteous in the messianic future]—**that the female is salted for the** צדיקים לע"ל [righteous in the messianic future] **is a fine image for the sensuality** [*Reizbarkeit*] [of women], **which is heightened through being held back for so long.**

[a world] in which, in its present [lit. this] state, there is good and evil, and where—on the one hand—such a detriment, a lack of loving kindness and love, and—on the other hand—slavery for half of humanity [i.e. womankind] have caused this. It was necessary for as long as sin and carnal [lit. animal] excess, namely corrupt Nature, א"ז [אשה זרה, lit. 'foreign' or 'strange woman', traditionally understood as loose/adulterous woman, or, alternatively, אשת זנונים —'wife of whoredom']¹⁷ and the שפחה [handmaid] reigned.¹⁸ What calamity has come into the world through female seduction? And what charming [*reizende*] enticements to everything that is sensuous [*alle Sinnlichkeit*], [to] corrupt תענוגים [pleasures], [to] vanity and fashions do female seduction and charms [*Reize*] themselves contain? What would it have been like if, right from the start, women had possessed full freedom, power, and leisure? What if they had been able to show their inner character, to spread their nets without shame? What if they had not been restricted by suffering, dependence, confinement at home, the pains of pregnancy, childbirth and upbringing, and finally by the shame which the concealment of their sensuality [*Reize*] demands? The good part of the female sex, and the ח"א [אשת חיל—Woman of Valour]¹⁹ herself, placed this constraint upon themselves so that, at the very least, the corrupt ערוה [lewd] nature of the [other] half would be subject to the same constraint.

This is evident, but so long as the h[oly] stock [lit. stem—*Stamm*] of womanhood remains subject to this state [of affairs], the world will not be capable of being healed. If the true female nature is confined and, so to speak, slain, **[101b]** and if the true sensual power [*Reizkraft*] of the males is stifled, then the male sex, too, is not truly alive, because the vitality of the male is on the same level as the sensuality [*Reizbarkeit*] of the female. Life and sensuality [*Reizbarkeit*] are most intimately related. ([If] the female nature is confined, how can the true nature of the male show itself?) Consider the difference between, [on the one hand], the pleasure of the savage, whose wife must obey him in every respect and whom he treats despotically, and, [on the other hand], the pleasure of two lovers or a husband and wife who are each in possession of free will and who agree with each other, where the wife arouses the love of her husband with her charms [*Reizen*]. From this you can see that as soon as the husband treats his wife despotically, and she is no longer a <u>woman</u>, he is no longer a true <u>man</u>, despite appearances. This may rightly be compared to the difference between, [on the one hand], the man who is self-aroused and, [on the other hand], the kind of sensuality [*Reizbarkeit*] that causes him to be aroused externally. In the former case, his own energy constitutes [both] the sensuality [*Reizbarkeit*] and the object of its arousal, and it exhausts itself, [while] here, [in the latter case], the full energy of sensuality [*Reizbarkeit*] affects him from without and acts upon him, so that he is able to do nothing other than submit to it completely. [This is the case] wherever the female sex is sought out with love and zeal, where often it is the object of male devotion and adoration. Of course, in this case the female nature comes out of slavery exalted and free, but the male sex becomes effeminate and stands beneath it. The male sex is then aroused through its love for and notion of women's charms [*Reize*], but it is still not aroused and excited externally, by the female sex [itself]. It is the way of the world that the youth strives to seek out the maiden, to be pleasing to her and to earn her love. This, of course, is already an <u>elevation</u> of the female sex and proof of its rightful <u>appreciation</u>; it is also the beginning of culture, marking out the customs of Europe and Edom.[20] But in these circumstances the female is the centre point and the male sun revolves <u>around her.</u>

The חכמים [Sages] illustrated this more aptly with an example. During marital intercourse, if the husband's lust **[102a]** for his wife is gratified [lit. expressed] first, then the fruit [of intercourse] is female. But if the wife's sensual arousal [*Reiz*] is gratified [lit. expressed] first, then the fruit is <u>male</u>.[‡] So long as the youth pursues the maiden—and the more confined and concealed she is, whether through modesty, conventional propriety, or external circumstances, the [more the] youth wishes to be pleasing to her and to expose her sensuality [*Reize*]—then the fruit of such intercourse is <u>female</u>. But when the time comes for the female to compass the male[21] and the maiden to pursue the youth, that is to say, [when] the maiden goes out freely, she may and she will display her [sensuality] without shame. [This is] in order that she may unfold

[‡] In Hebrew:

איש מזריע תחלה יולדת נקיבה; אשה מזרעת תחלה יולדת זכר. כמ״ש [= כמו שכתוב], אשה כי תזריע ויולדת [!] זכר. ותזריעה [!] מרמז גם כן לעתיד, שאומרת "<u>ממני פריך</u> נמצא"

[If the man produces seed first, she gives birth to a female; if the woman produces seed first, she gives birth to a male. As Scripture says: 'If a woman have conceived seed, and born a man child' <Lev. 12: 2, and see BT *Nid.* 31a>. And <the imperfect tense of the Hebrew verb for> 'have conceived' also alludes to the future, as she says: 'From me is thy fruit found' <Hos. 14: 9>.]

all her charms [*Reize*] and her femininity, so as to excite the youth. Oh, then will the fruit [of intercourse] be <u>male</u>! So long as <u>woman</u> is concealed, so long as the sensuality [*Reizbarkeit*] of the female is not apparent, so long as the female character is not open to such an extent [that would enable a woman] to exhibit outwardly her inner desire for a man, all true male powers and true life remain hidden. Therefore, it is clear that above all the female must be elevated, that above all the holy Maiden and holy femininity must be borne on high, so to speak, [so that] finally, [the female will be raised] to such an extent that she will thereby be able to excite and attract the male, and show [herself] openly, and the whole world will be מתוקן [restored to perfection], and the maidens will pursue the youths. But then the reign of the א"ז [אשה זרה—loose/adulterous woman, or אשת זנונים—'wife of whoredom'] and the שפחה [handmaid][22] must come to an end, because, as the H[oly] F[ather] [Jacob Frank] says, so long as the reign of the שפחה endures, the א"ח [אשת חיל—Woman of Valour],[23] the true power of h[oly] femininity, remains hidden, concealing itself so as not to be seen by her [the handmaid], as Scripture says, 'how much longer will you, suffering daughter, with all your suffering, veil and hide yourself?'[24] That is to say, how much longer will you, H[oly] Maiden, refrain from coming out in your majestic beauty, with your true godly charms [*Reize*]? **[102b]** How much longer [will you] remain veiled? The time of your rival's reign, when everything in Nature remained as of old and nothing new came forth—this time is over: G[od] has created a new thing in the world.[25] Shame—the shackles of the א"ז—is no longer necessary; the maiden compasses and pursues the youth; the male sun is the centre point around which femininity revolves, with all its charms unfolding; the <u>woman</u> is a complete <u>woman</u>, developing ever more in order to excite the man and to expose his vitality, and thus the man is a true <u>man</u>, and the woman [is] the ornament and crown of her husband![26]

This new thing is the basis of all that is new. As soon as she is revealed, everything will and can be revealed through her.§ If [on the other hand] she is

§ Such a statement is to be found in the holy words of O[ffen]b[ach] [These might be Jacob Frank's 'words', either those recorded specifically during his period of residence in Offenbach, from 1786 until his death in 1791, or, perhaps, a more comprehensive collection of his dicta, which our author would have associated with Offenbach since this was the centre of the Frankist cult at the time when he himself became associated with it. He might have had access to some manuscript compilation of the 'words', such as has come down to us in the Polish versions of *Words of the Lord*, or he could have been instructed in them orally by his father-in-law,

concealed [lit. confined] then this means that regardless of what you know, of what your view might be, of what you have searched for and brought to light, everything will remain as concealed as before!

This is why ש"ה [שיר השירים—the Song of Songs] begins with what <u>she</u> wants: ישקני מנשיקות פיהו ['Let him kiss me with the kisses of his mouth'].[27] It is not he [the male lover of the Song] who initiates [the love act], since [this, namely, the scene described in the Song of Songs] is already [a] reflection of the new [i.e. the messianic future]. The words of T[he] H[oly] F[ather] [Jacob Frank] now become so vividly clear: only in <u>Edom</u>[28] can one exalt <u>her</u>, since, behold, woman is confined everywhere; especially in the Asiatic and Turkish lands she is a <u>slave</u>. How, then, can one exalt her there (and how is it possible there to deliver the world from the curse)? For wherever woman is confined, everything else must be confined as well. How, then, is knowledge, [i.e.] דעת[29] possible here? She, the H[oly] Virgin, is the <u>head of the world</u>, the head of all powers.[30] There, in Turkey, the head is concealed, and amongst the Jews one may not go about בקלות ראש [light-headed],[31] but here, in <u>Edom</u>, one goes about bareheaded—(if the head is uncovered, everything else can be uncovered). Here the females are free to go out, here they enjoy **[103a]** the true esteem of men, here one deals with the Virgin respectfully, and even the שררות [noblemen] stand before her politely[32] and with respect.¶ Here the <u>shell</u>

Jonas Wehle <see introduction above>, but he is not likely to have heard them directly from Frank, since as far as we know he visited the Offenbach court only after Jacob Frank's death, by which time the court was being run by his two sons and his daughter Eva <see Guttmann, 'Lazarus Bendavid', 206; Gelber, 'Di zikhroynes fun moses porges', appendix 1, col. 292>. A record of at least some of Frank's 'words' known to have been compiled at the Offenbach court survives in Polish in the Lublin manuscript of *Words of the Lord* and was published as an appendix to Jan Doktór's edition of the text, *Księga Słów Pańskich*, ii. 122–33. Another body of Frankist texts associated with Offenbach in the period following Frank's death is the Polish work known by the title of *Isaiah's Prophecies*. The work itself is not extant but Kraushar described and quoted from it extensively <see Kraushar, *Jacob Frank*, ii. 375–94, and 545 n. 1>. The particular Offenbach statement quoted here does not, however, appear among any of these Offenbach materials], **that as soon as one thing is revealed, everything that he says will be revealed.**

¶ So it says in the h[oly] words of O[ffen]b[ach] [see above, author's footnote §], **that when he came into** <u>the</u> **world, and saw women and maidens go out in the street, he believed that he was in** [גן עדן ג"ע—the Garden of Eden, Paradise] [This statement, attributed to Frank, could well echo the sense of surprise he might have experienced on returning from his long sojourn in the Islamic territories of the Ottoman empire to the Christian environment of Poland, where women were readily visible in public places]. **And in the h[oly] account of the birth and the begetting** [or, possibly: in the account of the holy birth and the begetting] **is found** [the state-points to the presence of the fruit,[33] which is to be elevated here (so as to release the world from the curse, as our dear ע״ל ב״ל[34] has said). In Russia woman is even more exalted—she can be a reigning <u>monarch</u>, which indeed she has often been.[35] In the religion of the C[atholics], false though it is, the name Virgin is revered as being divine. Thus here she may be exalted as being human, become queen, and be crowned as goddess—the H[oly] Virgin of God.

ment] **that it was a** חידוש [an extraordinary thing; a marvel] **also for the great king to see bare-breasted maidens, etc.** [We are grateful to Prof. Erika Timm for her comments on the original Judaeo-German of this passage, whose syntax is ambiguous and whose precise meaning still eludes us. It clearly refers to specific statements by Frank, which we have not been able to locate, although the theme of bare-breasted virgins or maidens does occur more than once in his extant dicta. See *Words of the Lord*, §2, and especially the collection of his dreams, *Widzenia Pańskie* <The Lord's Visions>, preserved in the Lublin manuscript of the work and published in Jan Doktór's Polish edition, *Księga Słów Pańskich*, ii., where bare-breasted maidens are mentioned in §§2254 and 2264. It may be that the 'Paradise' where Frank imagines 'women and maidens' to be walking about freely, and especially his reference in the same context to 'bare-breasted maidens', springs from his acquaintance with the tradition of Islam, which keeps women out of men's sight during life on earth, but populates the heavenly Paradise it promises to the righteous after death with full-breasted female virgins who attend to their needs. The reference to the 'holy birth and the begetting', with its apparent Christian associations, is obscure, but may have its echo in one of the 'prophecies' of Frank's leading disciples recorded in Offenbach after his death and quoted by Kraushar from the book of *Isaiah's Prophecies*. The 'prophecy' seems to allude to the rebirth or Second Coming of Frank, in reference to Isa. 9: 6 and its standard Christological interpretation: 'For unto us a child is born, unto us a son is given: and the government shall be upon his shoulder: and his name shall be called Wonderful, Counseller, The mighty God, The everlasting Father, The Prince of Peace.' It reads as follows: 'At that time a holy child will be born to us. We will be given a Lord who has already carried us afar on his shoulders. He will be the true Lord of the whole world, and his name, now hidden, will be revealed and made known. Until now, he appeared to us as wonderful because he wrought miracles for us and for himself. As a counsellor, he counselled us to follow him so he could rescue us from the claws of evil. As the source of power, all nations came happily, and he always shielded us from evil and protected us; as a hero, in a blink of an eye he could shatter and destroy the whole world, but he did not do it and he holds his power in limits and bounds, which is a sign of a true knight; as eternal, he alone, this holy Adam from whom all children were born, will remain our father eternally; as Prince of Peace, he will be returned to the human race once the entire world recognizes him as the true head and prince of the whole earthly kingdom' <Kraushar, *Jacob Frank*, ii. 381–2, (translation slightly modified)>]

וזה הסוד ג״כ [= גם כן] במפתחות שלגאולה וכדי שיתודע הדבורא צריך שיהי׳[ה] כמו ויגש אליו יהוד׳[ה] שפעל למטה התודעות יוסף ולעילא התודעו׳[ת]—ויגש אליו יהוד׳[ה] נגשה בו שיתודעו וע״כ [= ועל כן] ואל יחר אפך—שהוא נגד הטבע והחק בטבע הלזו: וזה ג״כ כי ברא ה׳ חדשה בארץ נת״ג [= נקבה תסובב גבר] כי לעילא לית ערוה ותצא לאה לקראתו וכאן בארץ.

[And this mystery <namely, the public display of women, and the exposure of the maidens'

You will remember all too well that, closely bound up with this is the fact that the whole of the seed [*Stamm*] of David made its appearance in this

breasts referred to above, which presumably allude to the full revelation of the Maiden—the divine female, the tenth *sefirah* Malkhut>, too, is of the keys to the redemption <for the probable source of the expression 'keys to the redemption', which may or may not represent here a more specific, if obscure, Frankist technical term, see *Gen. Rabbah*, 70: 6, p. 803 in Albeck's edition>. And in order for the male to become <similarly> known, it should be in the manner of 'Then Judah came near unto him' <Gen. 44: 18—the beginning of the account of the encounter in Egypt between Jacob's sons, with Judah as their spokesman, and their brother Joseph whom they did not recognize in his Egyptian guise until he 'made himself known' to them, as is related in Gen. 45: 2. 'Joseph' is a common designation of the ninth *sefirah* Yesod, the sexual organ of the divine male who joins the female *sefirah* Malkhut in sexual union. Midrashic tradition interprets Joseph's 'becoming known' to his brothers as his exposure of his circumcised organ, to convince them that he was not an Egyptian prince but their long-lost Jewish brother. See *Gen. Rabbah*, 93: 8, 11, p. 1170 in Albeck's edition. If this is the association of ideas intended here, then the author is referring to the complete exposure or revelation of the divine male, which corresponds to the complete exposure or revelation of the divine female>. This effected the 'making known' of Joseph below, and above <it effected> a 'making known' <by way of> 'Then Judah came near unto him.' She <? If the sudden switch to the feminine here is not a slip, then this is a possible reference to Tamar, Judah's daughter-in-law, who seduced him into making her his own rather than his son's wife by way of levirate marriage. See Gen. 38> 'drew near unto him' <see Deut. 25: 9, in the context of the laws of levirate marriage> in order that they should know each other <'know' here, as elsewhere in biblical Hebrew, meaning sexual intercourse>. For this reason <Judah said to Joseph>, 'and let not thine anger burn' <Gen. 44: 18>, for it <presumably the unnatural, incestuous relations between Judah and his daughter-in-law; see Lev. 18: 15, 20: 12> is against Nature and the law of this Nature. This is <the significance> also of 'For the Lord hath created a new thing in the earth, a woman shall compass a man' <Jer. 31: 22, and see above, p. 327 at nn. 3–4>, for 'in the world above there is no incest' <*Tikunei hazohar*, §56, 90*b*>, 'and Leah went out to meet him' <Gen. 30: 16, which continues: 'and said, Thou must come in unto me . . . And he lay with her that night.' This may refer to both Jacob's incestuous marriage to Rachel and Leah, who were sisters, and to Leah's active sexual pursuit—'compassing'—of Jacob>, here, on earth.]

Yet another רמז [allusion, here pointing to the messianic future] within Judaism is that it is a good time when maidens, young girls, go out freely—although one finds that, as חז"ל [חכמינו זכרונם לברכה—Our Sages of Blessed Memory] said, no days were as happy for Israel as ט"ו באב [the fifteenth day of the month of Av] and מוצאי יו"כ [the night following the Day of Atonement], when the Jewish maidens go out to dance in (borrowed, since the true ones are [as yet] unknown) white clothes [see BT *Ta'an.* 26*b* and 31*a*; *BB* 121*a*, and with variations, Mishnah *Ta'an.* 4: 8; JT *Ta'an.* 4: 7; *Lam. Rabbah*, Petihta 32]. The חכמים [Sages] also speak about the innocent wiles [*Reizungen*] which they [the maidens] employed to lure the young men, the beautiful ones boasting of their beauty, the מיוחסים [well born] of their יחוס [high birth], the rich ones of their wealth, the pious of their piety! [See BT *Ta'an.* 31*a*, and JT *Ta'an.* 4: 7.]

manner;[36] that the female sex, belying its present natural inclination to shame, acting [at that time] under the greatest compulsion, dangerously and in disguise, exposing itself to [malicious] gossip, had [nevertheless] gone out freely; the maiden—the female sex—had aroused and pursued the youth—the male. This had been the case with the daughters of Lot[37]—the maternal line in Moab from which David descended;[38] this had been the case with Tamar and Judah,[39] designed to launch David's paternal line, even though Tamar was forced to adopt a false image, כבי'/כויל [as it were], and to go out furtively, yet freely, to seduce Judah; and finally, <u>Ruth with Boaz</u>: she had laid herself at his feet, begging and entreating him to take her, so much so that she moved him to entreat her![40] If this was the case then, how much more so [will it be] the case at the time of שלמות [perfection]. At that time it was a trial, a great transgression and self-denial that nevertheless yielded its reward, but at [the future time of] שלמות it will be natural and the greatest of pleasures.

TRANSLATORS' NOTES

1   Alternative translations might be: 'Something for the female sex, who hope for what God will do, and [for?] what more closely pertains to His sacred help!' or, just possibly, 'Something for the female sex, who hope for what God will do, whose [lit. and His] sacred help is drawing nearer!' The ambiguity arises from our author's proclivity for joining his sentences together by conjunction rather than subordination, and from the fact that the German verb *angehen* can mean both 'to concern', 'relate', or 'pertain to', and 'to come on' (as does the cognate Yiddish *ongeyn*, which may underlie our author's German usage, and which similarly means both 'to concern' and 'to appear', 'arrive' or 'arrive unexpectedly'). The German adverb *näher*, meaning 'more closely', is often used in the sense of 'in greater detail' or 'more specifically', which is adopted here. We are grateful to professors Erika Timm, Dovid Katz, and Jerold Frakes for their comments on the range of possible readings of this title.

2   The Hebrew original of Jeremiah, here rendered unusually as 'suffering daughter', is הבת השובבה which the traditional commentators and all the versions—both ancient and modern—take to mean 'backsliding', 'wavering', 'rebellious', or even 'repentant daughter', deriving שובבה from the root שוב meaning 'turn' or 'return'. However, our author may well derive the word from the root שבה meaning 'capture' (even the text of Jeremiah seems to exploit the proximity of the two roots, שוב and שבה, when it juxtaposes them in the next verse: בשובי את שבותם), in which case he would take הבת השובבה to mean the 'captive daughter' and from this presumably arrive at 'suffering daughter'. We are grateful to Dr Joanna Weinberg for this suggestion, to Dr Gillian Greenberg for reviewing the ancient versions on the verse, and to professors Chava Turniansky

and Marion Aptroot for verifying that both the German and the Yiddish Bible translations accessible to our author agree with the traditional understanding of the verse
and could not have suggested to him the rendering of השובבה as 'suffering'. This is particularly notable since elsewhere (in his German petition to the Prague police commissar, for which see our introduction above at nn. 36–7), our author clearly relies on
the German Bible translation by Mendelssohn and his collaborators; see e.g.
Scholem, 'Frankist Document', 794 and 795, where Deut. 21: 23, and Prov. 17: 5 respectively are quoted faithfully from that translation. Suffering through captivity or
enslavement is precisely how our author goes on to describe the universal condition of
women in the 'corrupt nature' of this world, a condition which he considers, as will
become evident below, to both parallel and reflect the state of the divine female, the
kabbalistic *sefirah* Malkhut or Shekhinah, to whom he goes on to refer as the Holy
Virgin. This designation suggests the strong likelihood that his rendering of
הבת השובבה was inspired by Jacob Frank's characterization of the redemptive Virgin
or Maiden—the term by which he consistently refers to the human manifestation of
the divine female, and to whom our author clearly takes Jer. 31: 22 to be alluding.
Throughout Frank's collection of dicta, tales, visions, and dreams he describes the
Maiden as wretched and suffering (a fate he often claims to be sharing with her) on
account of his adherents' failure to trust him and to follow his directives to the letter
(see e.g. Frank, *Words of the Lord*, §§566, 622, 634, 668, 1118). This 'betrayal', he claims,
has obstructed the realization of the Maiden's messianic mission, preventing her from
revealing herself to the world and bringing about the redemption. On the sufferings
of the Maiden in Frank's teaching, see above, Ch. 7, at nn. 182–5.

3   The author's underlining of 'the world' or 'this world', both here and further below,
may well be an allusion to yet another element of Jacob Frank's doctrine. Frank had
turned on its head the long-standing eschatological tradition, originating in the
classical rabbinic sources and developed during the Middle Ages in both rationalistic
philosophical and kabbalistic circles, whereby the messianic future would be experienced as a refinement of every aspect of corporeal existence—a spiritualization or
intellectualization of material reality, including the sublimation of the body and its
physical appetites. By contrast, Frank's vision of the redeemed world entailed the concrete substantiation of the spirit, including the full physical materialization of the
divine, and it laid particular emphasis on this transformation taking place 'here', 'on
earth', 'in this world' and not in any rarefied, other-worldly, or heavenly domain. See
e.g. *Words of the Lord*, §§327, 1001, and see the discussion above, Ch. 7, at nn. 233–45.

4   Jer. 31: 22: עד מתי תתחמקין הבת השובבה, כי ברא ה' חדשה בארץ, נקבה תסובב גבר ('How long wilt
thou go about [Rashi: 'hide yourself from me'], O thou backsliding daughter? For the
Lord hath created a new thing in the earth, a woman shall compass a man.')

5   All these references to the Shekhinah, identified with the kabbalistic *sefirah* Malkhut
(one of whose common designations in the kabbalistic sources is 'gate' or 'gateway',
associated also with the 'keys' to the 'storehouse of divine treasures') and the redemptive Holy Virgin or the Maiden, echo Jacob Frank's numerous statements on the same
subject. See e.g. 'Without her it is impossible to seek God and to draw near to Him,

and whoever finds Him will lose Him, Heaven forbid, for she is the gateway to God' (*Words of the Lord*, §516); 'She is the first gate by which to enter' (ibid., §580); 'She is the gateway to God. Only through her is it possible to come to God and reach Him' (ibid., §620); 'In a certain place there are palaces, and in them is the Maiden. Surrounding the palaces are innumerable treasures … whoever holds out to obey her is given a great treasure' (ibid., §627); 'All the power is with her and in her hands' (ibid., §778), and so on. For Frank's concept of the redemptive Maiden see above, Ch. 6, and Ch. 7, at n. 145.

6   The German original is *Reizbarkeit*—a key term in our text—which usually means (and meant already at the time of composition) sensitiveness, sensitivity, or—in a medical, neurological context—irritability. However, our author clearly invests it with another, perhaps idiosyncratic, meaning. This seems to derive from the related noun *Reiz*, which can mean a physiological stimulus, but also sensual allure, appeal, attraction, or charm. Gershom Scholem, in his unpublished lecture 'Frankism and Enlightenment' (on which see our introduction above), referred to the author's use of the term *Reizbarkeit* and translated it, without qualification or explanation, as 'sensuous nature' or 'sensuality' (see Scholem, 'Frankism and Enlightenment', 9ʳ, 10ʳ). While this rendering seems to fit the context better than any alternative translation, it is difficult to justify in terms of the available lexicographical data. We have nevertheless decided to follow Scholem's intuition, but have drawn attention to the ambiguities of the original by supplying it in square brackets immediately following each of its English renderings. We have also supplied the German original following the translation of a few other terms closely related to *Reizbarkeit* either etymologically or semantically.

7   This remark betrays our author's familiarity with the philosophical currents of his time. By the middle of the 18th century, most Enlightenment thinkers had come to reject René Descartes' doctrine of innate ideas in favour of John Locke's sensationalist theory of knowledge, whereby all ideas are acquired through the experience of the physical senses. See e.g. Gay, *The Enlightenment*, 176–8, 181–5; Rousseau, *Émile*, p. xxviii; Israel, *Radical Enlightenment*, 477–501.

8   In the original German the sentence begins with *ist* (is) rather than *ihr* (her), but this is clearly a slip.

9   Much of this characterization of women would seem to be inspired, either directly or indirectly, by Rousseau's *Émile* (first published in 1762), which, though highly controversial, was extremely influential, especially on German Enlightenment literature. (There were at least six German translations of *Émile* between 1762 and 1799, with two German editions of his philosophical works and his novels published in Prague, in 1779–89 and 1788–94 respectively. For the reception of Rousseau's work in German, see Süssenberger, *Rousseau*, 316–18, and Mousnier, *La Fortune des écrits de Jean-Jacques Rousseau*, 314–15.) Book V of *Émile* is devoted to the education of Sophie—Émile's ideal female partner. It is replete with observations contrasting the 'innate' female nature with that of the male, which are reminiscent of our author's observations both here and further below. For example: 'His virtue is in his strength … her strength is in

her charms' (p. 385); 'For nature has endowed woman with a power of stimulating man's passions in excess of man's power of satisfying those passions ... In this respect the woman's mind exactly resembles her body' (p. 387); 'He can do without her better than she can do without him' (p. 302); 'Every woman desires to be pleasing in men's eyes, and this is right' (p. 393); 'A woman's real resource is her wit' (p. 401); 'Ideas of propriety and modesty are acquired earlier in girls than in boys' (p. 405); 'A woman's reason is practical, and therefore she soon arrives at a given conclusion' (p. 407); 'The man teaches the woman what to see, while she teaches him what to do. If women could discover principles and if men had as good a head for detail, they would be mutually independent' (p. 407); 'The obedience and fidelity which she owes to her husband, the tenderness and care due to her children, are such natural, self-evident consequences of her position that she cannot honestly refuse her consent to the inner voice which is her guide' (p. 414); 'Woman should discover, so to speak, an experimental morality, man should reduce it to a system. Woman has more wit, man more genius; woman observes, man reasons' (p. 419); 'Her mind is keen rather than accurate, her temper pleasant but variable' (p. 426), and so on. For the discourse on the nature of woman in European Enlightenment literature in general, and Rousseau's influence in particular, see e.g. Hoffmann, *La Femme*; Proctor, *Women*.

10 This, too, would seem to echo Rousseau's revolutionary educational theory, which advocated the cultivation of natural instinct and was critical of formal religious education for suppressing it. See e.g. Dame, *Rousseau on Adult Education*, 65–71; 89.

11 The concept of 'despotism' gained currency in 18th-century political discourse initially through the writings of Thomas Hobbes and John Locke, but it was Charles de Secondat, Baron de Montesquieu, who invested it with the unequivocally negative connotations evident in our author's repeated use of the term both here and below. Moreover, Montesquieu was the first to associate despotism specifically with the control over women commonly exercised by men, which he exposed most vividly in his fictional work, *The Persian Letters*. The book, first published anonymously in 1721, created an immediate sensation and remained popular throughout the 18th century. It is constructed as a collection of 161 letters, written or received by two Persian travellers who are contrasting the European way of life with the Oriental customs and manners of their own land. Some 40 per cent of the letters concern the behaviour or treatment of women. While clearly designed as a thinly disguised critique of European society and its manners, the letters highlight the oppressive condition of women in the Oriental harem where, precisely in the terms employed here by our author, they are confined, isolated, and guarded by eunuchs, subject to the despotic authority of their husbands. For a discussion of Montesquieu on the oppression of women as an essential component of his notion of despotism, see Schaub, *Erotic Liberalism*. These ideas, first expressed in the exotic fictional framework of *The Persian Letters*, were later elaborated theoretically in Montesquieu's *The Spirit of the Laws*, first published in 1748. Here the concept of despotism is often associated with the condition of women in a variety of political regimes, including—as in our text—those of 'Asia and Africa' (see e.g. Montesquieu, *The Spirit of the Laws*, VII. 9 (p. 104), XV. 12 (p. 255), XV. 19 (pp.

262–3), XVI. 4 (p. 266), XVI. 9 (p. 270), XVI. 10 (p. 270), XIX. 12 (p. 314), XIX. 15 (p. 316), XXVIII. 22 (p. 561); both *The Spirit of the Laws* and *The Persian Letters* were translated and available in German soon after their first publication in French (see Herdmann, *Montesquieurezeption*, 86–7, 312). Admittedly, our author might have gained his acquaintance with the setting and theme of *The Persian Letters* only indirectly, through the numerous epigones of the work in both French and German literature during the latter part of the 18th century. It had even left its imprint on the Hebrew Haskalah literature of the time, with which our author was certainly familiar (see our introduction above), in the form of Isaac Euchel's anonymously published satire, 'The Letters of Meshulam, son of Uriah the Eshtemoite' (Heb.), which appeared in several instalments in *Hame'asef*, 6 (1790) and was clearly modelled on Montesquieu's *The Persian Letters*. (For Euchel's work see the annotated edition in Friedlander, *Studies* (Heb.), 19–61, and the bibliographical references to earlier studies cited there.)

12 The original has, here and elsewhere throughout the manuscript, the letter 'ק' signifying *Katholiken*, as is evident from the context. The contrast between European Catholicism and the religions of 'the whole of Asia and Africa', including—as our author goes on to argue immediately below—Judaism, echoes Jacob Frank's promotion of Catholicism (which he and some of his followers had embraced) as superior to both Judaism and Islam inasmuch as within it, and within it alone, the redemptive figure of the Maiden, in her exterior guise of the Holy Virgin—Mary, mother of Christ—is fully acknowledged and venerated openly. This, in turn, according to Frank, is reflected in the chivalrous conduct—the gallantry, honour, and respect accorded to women by men—which characterizes Christian (for him, primarily Catholic) society, and contrasts favourably with the attitude to women prevailing in Judaism (where women are excluded from the cult, and the holy Maiden is no more than an allusion to the female *sefirah* of Malkhut–Shekhinah in the symbolic language of the kabbalists), and especially within Islam, where women are altogether confined, secluded, and oppressed. Islam was the religion of Sabbatai Zevi's conversion, within which, as Frank has it, he tried but inevitably failed to find the route to the messianic Maiden. See above, Ch. 7, at nn. 74–83 and p. 335 nn. 31–2.

13 The source, either direct or indirect, of this observation on the condition of women in ancient Greece and Rome might well have been Montesquieu, *The Spirit of the Laws*, VII. 9–14 (pp. 104–9).

14 See BT *Ber.* 24a: 'R. Isaac said: an [exposed] handbreadth in a woman is lewdness [ערוה] ... Rav Hisda said: an [exposed] leg in a woman is lewdness ... Samuel said: a voice in a woman is lewdness ... Rav Sheshet said: hair in a woman is lewdness.'

15 Ps. 45: 14.

16 Underlying the term 'female rebel' (*Empörerin*) is the halakhic term *moredet* ('rebellious wife')—the wife who refuses to discharge her marital duties to her husband. See e.g. Mishnah *Ket.* 5: 7.

17 For אשה זרה (strange woman) see Prov. 2: 16 and 7: 5, traditionally contrasted with the אשת חיל (Woman of Valour) of Prov. 12: 4 and 31: 10, as indeed our author proceeds to

do immediately below. אשה זרה (in Polish 'Ta cudza kobieta') is also the term by which Jacob Frank often refers to the evil counterpart of the redemptive Maiden. She is the seductress who entraps those pursuing the Maiden and prevents them from reaching her. See e.g. *Words of the Lord*, §§198, 397, 888, 891, 1135. For אשת זנונים (wife of whoredom) see Hos. 1: 2. The Zohar refers to both the 'strange woman' and the 'wife of whoredom' as representatives of the forces of evil (see e.g. Zohar, i. 73*b*, 148*a*) and at times conflates them, as at i. 38*b*: "A woman of valour is a crown to her husband" [Prov. 12: 4]. This is the secret of the faith, for a man to adhere to his Master and fear Him, constantly, without straying right or left. Surely, we have already established that a man should not pursue another [object of] fear, called "wife of whoredom" [Hos. 1: 2]. For this reason it is written: "To deliver you from the strange woman, from the stranger who flatters with her words" [Prov. 7: 5].'

18   See Prov. 30: 23: ושפחה כי תירש גברתה ('and a handmaid that is heir to her mistress'). For the kabbalistic background of this reference to the reign of the handmaid, who has usurped the power of her mistress, the Matronita—the *sefirah* Malkhut—and who governs the world for the duration of the exile, but who will be deposed with the restoration of the mistress to her rightful place at the redemption, see e.g. the exposition of the same verse in Zohar, iii. 69*a*. Jacob Frank was fond of this theme and often referred to it in his dicta, identifying the mistress with the holy Maiden—the human incarnation of Malkhut. See e.g. *Words of the Lord*, §§190, 397, 1228.

19   Prov. 12: 4, 31: 10. See above, p. 342 n. 17.

20   The biblical name of Edom traditionally refers to Christendom, and this may well be all that is meant here. However, in Frankist parlance 'the holy faith of Edom' came to signify Jacob Frank's own syncretistic faith, which combined the overt Catholicism that he and his Polish followers had embraced, with the sectarian messianic cult he constructed around himself, ultimately envisaging the total eradication of all established religions, including Christianity. See Scholem, 'Redemption through Sin', 131, 138–41, *Kabbalah*, 284, 293–4, and 'Sabbatian Movement in Poland' (Heb.), 132; and above, Ch. 7 n. 83.

21   See above, p. 339 n. 4.

22   See above, p. 342 n. 17, and n. 18.

23   See above, n. 19.

24   See above, p. 338 n. 2 and p. 339 n. 4.

25   Jer. 31: 22.

26   See Prov. 12: 4: 'A virtuous woman is a crown to her husband.' In kabbalistic literature, this verse is often cited to allude to the inversion of gender hierarchy at the time of the redemption, when the female *sefirah* Malkhut will rise from the lowest to the highest point of the divine emanation.

27   S. of S. 1: 2.

28   See above, n. 20.

29   דעת ('knowledge') is the term by which Frank usually referred to his new religion—

'knowledge of Edom' attained by conversion to Catholicism in order to subvert it from within, in anticipation of the collapse of all religions and the redemption to be inaugurated by the Maiden. On this see Scholem, 'Redemption through Sin', 131 and id., 'Sabbatian Movement in Poland' (Heb.), 132; and above, p. 343 n. 20. In the Polish recension of Frank's *Words of the Lord*, the term always appears in transliterated Hebrew as *Das* (see e.g. *Księga Słów Pańskich*, §§229, 245, 256, 263, 500, 516, 624, 715, 1200, 1295, 1304), reflecting the Ashkenazi pronunciation of the original Hebrew, but also giving rise to the alternative reading דת ('religion'), an ambiguity which Frank and his followers might well have intended. See e.g. Scholem, *Studies and Texts* (Heb.), 64; 'Redemption through Sin', 139.

30   'Head' or 'Head of all the worlds', who possesses 'all the power', is how Frank often refers to the redemptive Maiden. See e.g. *Words of the Lord*, §§766, 1140, 1175, and see above, Ch. 7 n. 78.

31   בקלות ראש means 'with lightness of head', namely 'frivolously', rather than 'with a bare head' (בגילוי ראש), which would seem to be what our author had meant to say, perhaps associating the 'lightness' of the head with its exposure, although he must have had in mind such rabbinic censure of 'lightheadedness' in the sense of frivolity, and its clear association with lewdness, as: שחוק וקלות ראש מרגילין לערוה ('laughter and light-headed-ness turn lewdness into a habit', *Pirkei avot* 3: 12). The author is clearly echoing Jacob Frank's repeated stress on the advantage of the Christian custom of baring the head in a posture of reverence or respect over the Jewish, and especially the Islamic, practice of covering it up at all times. In this context he denigrates Islam as the religion of Sabbatai Zevi's futile conversion, a conversion that failed to bring about the exposure of the 'Head', namely the revelation of the redemptive Maiden, symbolized by the head. See also n. 32 below.

32   Throughout this passage our author rightly attributes to Jacob Frank the preference he expresses for 'Edom' (Christianity), the religion of 'bareheadedness' in which men take off their hats in the presence of ladies or on entering a place of worship (the exposed head symbolizing the revelation of the divine female in all her glory), over 'Turkey' or 'the Asiatic and Turkish lands' (representing Islam), as well as Judaism, where the head (and thus the divine female) must be covered, namely concealed, at all times. The advantage of 'Edom' is its open veneration of the divine female embodied in the Holy Virgin, as well as its concomitantly respectful attitude to women, in con-trast with the 'covering up', the confinement and seclusion of women in Islamic soci-ety, and the concealment in Judaism of all references to the divine female within the arcane language of the kabbalists. For this recurrent theme in Frank's dicta, see e.g. *Words of the Lord*, §§530, 1107, 1175, 1195, and see above, Ch. 7, at nn. 74–83.

33   This is another recurrent theme in Jacob Frank's teaching. See e.g. *Words of the Lord*, §§397, 725, 917, and see above, Ch. 7, at nn. 130 and 213. The 'shell' is the Holy Virgin Mary of Christianity, who leads to the 'fruit' contained within it, the redemptive Maiden—the embodiment of the *sefirah* Malkhut. In order to bring about the redemption, the believers must expose the true Maiden who is concealed beneath her

exterior guise of the Virgin Mary. In other words, the believers must proceed, by way of conversion to Christianity, from the outer 'shell' to the redemptive 'fruit' within.

34   The acronym is clearly a reference to a fellow member of the sect, but we have not been able to decipher it and to establish his identity. The first element, ל"ב, must represent the initial letters of his name, and the second, ל"ע, which occurs time and again throughout the manuscript, in comparable acronymic references to fellow sectarians, may well represent the formula לעבע עוויג (*lebe ewig*—'may he live eternally') as a German equivalent of the Hebrew שי"נ or יחי"נ (נצח שיחיה or יחיה נצח), which similarly occurs throughout the manuscript as an alternative second element of similar, and at times identical, acronymic references. Cf. e.g. the use of ל"ע in such instances as ר"פ ל"ע (ר"פ ל"ע וואר היר ר"ה ויו"כ' was here for the New Year and the Day of Atonement) or ר"פ ל"ע (ר"פ ל"ע הביא שמועה טובה מארץ מרחק' brought good news from a distant land) (both on fo. *1a* of the manuscript), ל"ע (מייני קינדער ל"ע' my children, ל"ע) (fo. *9a*), יחי"נ (רמ"ב ל"ע (ווֹיא רמ"ב ל"ע זאגט' as says) (fo. *10b*) and so on, with the equivalent use of שי"נ or שי"נ in such instances as פאלגנדר בריף וואַרד גשריבן אן ר"א יחי"נ' (the following letter ר"פ (and was written to ר"א יחי"נ (ר"א יחי"נ) (fo. *1a*), ור"פ שי"נ אמר כי לא היה כ"כ אויף פאללנד בדרך נס' (fo. *8a*), מן האגרות שכתב מחמד לבנו' שי"נ said that it was not so noticeably miraculous) ר"ל יחי"נ' (from the letters written by our beloved ר"ל יחי"נ) (fo. *8b*) and so on.

35   The paradox of the enslavement of women in the home, where they are subject to the despotic authority of men, as against the experience of effective government by women in those societies (including 'Muscovy') that allow women to serve as monarchs, is discussed by Montesquieu in his *The Spirit of the Laws* (VII. 17 (p. 111)), which was probably familiar to our author. Here, however, he abandons his condemnation of what he had earlier presented as the virtually universal oppression of women, to promote—in line with his Frankist convictions—the superiority of Christianity (Edom) over both Islam and Judaism, in respect of the greater deference it accords to women, as is evidenced, among other things, by the supreme authority exercised, for much of his own lifetime, by such female rulers as Anna, Elizabeth, and Catherine the Great, empresses of Russia.

36   This may also be an allusion to the Davidic descent of Christ, who is introduced in the opening lines of the New Testament as 'Jesus Christ, the son of David, the son of Abraham', and whose full genealogy follows directly. See Matt. 1: 1–16.

37   See Gen. 19: 7–16.

38   For David's maternal descent from Ruth the Moabite, see Ruth 4: 17. For the Moabites' descent from the incestuous sexual relations between Lot and his elder daughter, see Gen. 19: 36–7; *Gen. Rabbah*, 41: 5; *Num. Rabbah*, 20: 22–3; *Midrash tanḥuma*, 'Balak', 17; *Zohar*, i. 110a–b. The descent of the messiah specifically from a succession of incestuous relations is explored in Rut Kara-Ivanov Kaniel, 'The Seed' (Heb.). I am grateful to the author for making her paper available to me in advance of publication.

39   See Gen. 38.

40   See Ruth 3.

Bibliography

AARON OF APTA (OPATÓW), *Or haganuz latsadikim* (Żółkiew, 1800).

ABOAB, SAMUEL, *Devar shemu'el* (Venice, 1702).

ABRAHAMS, ISRAEL, *Jewish Life in the Middle Ages* (London, 1896).

ABRAVANEL, ISAAC, *Yeshu'ot meshiḥo* (Königsberg 1861; facsimile edn. Jerusalem, 1967).

AESCOLY, AARON ZEEV, 'A Flandrian Newsletter Concerning the Sabbatian Movement' (Heb.), in Yitzhak Baer et al. (eds.), *Dinaburg Jubilee Volume* [Sefer dinaburg] (Jerusalem, 1949), 215–36.

—— *Jewish Messianic Movements* [Hatenu'ot hameshiḥiyot beyisra'el] (Jerusalem, 1956).

ALLEN, PRUDENCE, *The Concept of Woman: The Aristotelian Revolution 750 BC–AD 1250* (Grand Rapids, Mich., 1985).

ALTER, JUDAH LEIB OF GER (GÓRA KALWARIA), *Sefat emet al hatorah*, 5 vols. (Jerusalem, 1997).

AMARILLO, ABRAHAM, 'Sabbatean Documents from the Saul Amarillo Collection' (Heb.), *Sefunot*, 5 (= Isaiah Sonne Memorial Volume [Sefer zikaron liyshayahu zoneh]) (Jerusalem, 1961), 235–74.

ANDERSON, GARY A., *The Genesis of Perfection: Adam and Eve in Christian and Jewish Tradition* (Louisville, Ky., 2001).

ASSAF, DAVID, *Caught in the Thicket: Chapters of Crisis and Discontent in the History of Hasidism* [Ne'eḥaz basevakh: pirkei mashber umevukhah betoledot haḥasidut] (Jerusalem, 2006).

—— 'A Messianic Vision among Volhynian Hasidim' (Heb.), *Gal-ed*, 20 (2006), 39–54.

ASSAF, SIMHA, *Penalties after the Redaction of the Talmud* [Ha'onashin aḥarei ḥatimat hatalmud] (Jerusalem, 1922).

ATKINSON, CLARISSA W., *The Oldest Vocation: Christian Motherhood in the Middle Ages* (Ithaca, NY, 1991).

ATTIAS, MOSHE (ed. and trans.), GERSHOM SCHOLEM (commentary), and ISAAC BEN-ZVI (introd.), *Songs and Hymns of the Sabbatians* [Shirot vetishbaḥot shel hashabeta'im] (Tel Aviv, 1947).

AVAYOU SHLOMO, and AVRAHAM ELQAYAM, 'A Critical Edition of *Mirat bereshit tovah*' (Heb.), *Kabbalah: Journal for the Study of Jewish Mystical Texts*, 8 (2003), 184–280.

AZMON, YAEL (ed.), *A View into the Lives of Women in Jewish Societies* [Eshnav leḥayeihen shel nashim baḥavarot yehudiyot] (Jerusalem, 1995).

AZULAI, ABRAHAM, *Or haḥamah* (Przemyśl, 1896).

BACK, SAMUEL, 'Aufgefundene Aktenstücke zur Geschichte der Frankisten in Offenbach', in *Monatsschrift für Geschichte und Wissenschaft des Judentums*, 26 (1877), 189–92, 232–40, 410–20.

BADALANOVA, FLORENTINA, 'Notes on the Cult of the Virgin Mary in Slavia Orthodoxa: The Interpretation of Folk and Christian Themes', in Irina Sedakova and Tatyana Tsivyan (eds.), *Slavyanskoe i balkanskoe yazykoznanie. Chelovek v pros-transtve Balkan: Povedencheskie stsenarii i ku'lturnye roli* [Slavonic and Balkan Linguistics. Man in the Balkan Landscape: Behavioural Scenarios and Cultural Roles] (Moscow, 2003), 159–203.

BAER, RICHARD A., Jr., *Philo's Use of the Categories of Male and Female* (Leiden, 1970).

BAER, YITZHAK (Fritz), *Die Juden im christlichen Spanien*, 2 vols. (Berlin, 1936).

—— 'The Forged *Midrashim* of Raymond Martini and their Place in the Religious Controversy of the Middle Ages' (Heb.), in *Studies in Memory of Asher Gulak and Samuel Klein* [Sefer zikaron le'asher gulak ushemu'el klein] (Jerusalem, 1942), 28–49.

—— *A History of the Jews in Christian Spain*, 2 vols. (Philadelphia, 1966).

—— 'The Messianic Movement in Spain in the Period of the Expulsion' (Heb.), *Me'asef Zion*, 5 (1933), 61–74.

BALABAN, MEIR, *On the History of the Frankist Movement* [Letoledot hatenu'ah hafrankit] (Tel Aviv, 1935).

BALI, RIFAT N., 'Memoirs and Interviews of Sabbatians' (Heb.), *Kabbalah: Journal for the Study of Jewish Mystical Texts*, 9 (2003), 313–27.

BAR-LEVAV, AVRIEL, 'Ritualisation of Jewish Life and Death in the Early Modern Period', *Leo Baeck Institute Year Book*, 47 (2002), 69–82.

BARKER-BENFIELD, G. J., *The Culture of Sensibility: Sex and Society in Eighteenth-Century Britain* (Chicago, 1992).

BARNAI, JACOB, 'Christian Messianism and the Portuguese Marranos: The Emergence of Sabbateanism in Smyrna', *Jewish History*, 7/2 (1993), 119–26.

—— 'Congregations in Smyrna in the Seventeenth Century' (Heb.), *Pe'amim*, 48 (1991), 66–84.

—— *Hasidic Letters from Erets Yisrael* [Igerot ḥasidim me'erets yisra'el] (Jerusalem, 1980).

—— 'The Jews in the Ottoman Empire (1650–1830)' (Heb.), in Yosef Tobi, Jacob Barnai, and Shalom Ben-Asher, *History of the Jews in the Islamic Countries* [Toledot hayehudim be'aretsot ha'islam], ed. Shmuel Ettinger (Jerusalem, 1981), i. 118–73.

—— 'The Jews of the Ottoman Empire in the Seventeenth and Eighteenth Centuries', in Haim Beinart (ed.), *Moreshet Sepharad: The Sephardi Legacy* (Jerusalem, 1992), ii. 134–65.

—— 'The Origins of the Jewish Community in Smyrna in the Ottoman Period' (Heb.), *Pe'amim*, 12 (1972), 47–58.

—— 'The Portuguese Marranos in Smyrna in the Seventeenth Century' (Heb.), in M. Stern (ed.), *Nation and History* [Umah vetoledoteiha] (Jerusalem, 1983), i. 289–98.

—— 'R. Hayim Benveniste and the Rabbinate of Smyrna in his Time' (Heb.), in Minna Rozen (ed.), *The Days of the Crescent* [Yemei hasahar] (Tel Aviv, 1996), 151–91.

—— 'R. Yosef Escapa and the Rabbinate of Izmir' (Heb.), *Sefunot*, 18 (1985), 53–81.

—— *Sabbatianism: Social Perspectives* [Shabeta'ut: heibetim ḥevratiyim] (Jerusalem, 2000).

BARUKH B. GERSHON OF AREZZO, 'A Memorial Unto the Children of Israel' (Heb.), in A. Freimann (ed.), *On the Subject of Sabbatai Zevi* [Inyenei shabetai tsevi] (Berlin, 1923), 43–69.

BASHAN, E., 'The Political and Economic Crisis in the Ottoman Empire from the End of the XVIth Century, as Reflected in the Responsa Literature' (Heb.), in *Proceedings of the Sixth World Congress of Jewish Studies* [Divrei hakongres ha'olami hashishi lemada'ei hayahadut] (Jerusalem, 1975), ii. 107–15.

BEINART, HAIM, 'Almadén: Conversos in a La Mancha Village' (Heb.), *Zion*, 47 (1982), 17–55.

—— 'The Conversos of Agudo, a Village in La Mancha' (Heb.), *Tarbiz*, 50 (1981), 423–49.

—— 'Conversos of Chillón and Siruela and the Prophecies of Mari Gómez and Inés, the Daughter of Juan Esteban' (Heb.), *Zion*, 48 (1983), 241–72.

—— 'The Conversos of Halia and the Movement of the Prophetess Inés of Herrera' (Heb.), *Zion*, 53 (1988), 13–52.

—— 'The Exodus of Conversos from the Iberian Peninsula in the Fifteenth to Seventeenth Centuries' (Heb.), in *Commemorative Volume for Shelomo Umberto Nakhon* [Sefer zikaron lishelomo umberto nakhon] (Jerusalem, 1978), 63–106.

—— 'A Prophesying Movement in Cordova in 1499–1502' (Heb.), *Zion*, 44 (1980), 190–200 (Yitzhak Baer Memorial Volume).

—— 'The Prophetess Inés and her Movement in her Home Town, Herrera' (Heb.), in *Studies in Jewish Mysticism, Philosophy, and Ethical Literature Presented to Isaiah Tishby on his Seventy-Fifth Birthday* [Meḥkarim bekabalah, befilosofyah yehudit uvesifrut hamusar vehahagut, mukdashim liyshayah tishbi bimlot lo shivim veḥamesh shanim] (Jerusalem, 1986), 459–506.

—— 'The Prophetess Inés and her Movement in Puebla de Elcocer and Talarubias' (Heb.), *Tarbiz*, 51 (1982), 633–58.

BEN-AMOS, DAN, and JEROME R. MINTZ (eds. and trans.), *In Praise of the Baal Shem Tov*. See *Shivḥei habesht*

BENAYAHU, MEIR, 'The Great Apostasy in Salonica (Heb.), *Sefunot*, 14 (= *The Book of Greek Jewry*, iv: *The Shabbatean Movement in Greece* [Sefer yavan 4: Hatenu'ah hashabeta'it beyavan]) (Jerusalem, 1971–8), 77–108.

—— 'The "Holy Brotherhood" of R. Judah Hasid and their Settlement in Jerusalem' (Heb.), in Isaac Ben-Zvi and Meir Benayahu (eds.), *Sefunot*, 3–4 (= *S. Z. Shazar Jubilee Volume* [Sefer hayovel lishneur zalman shazar]) (Jerusalem, 1960), 131–82.

—— 'A Key to Understanding the Documents on the Sabbatian Movement in Jerusalem' (Heb.), in *Studies in Mysticism and Religion Presented to Gershom G. Scholem on his Seventieth Birthday* [Meḥkarim bekabalah uvetoledot hadatot mugashim legershom shalom bimlot lo shivim shanah] (Jerusalem, 1967), 35–45.

—— *Rabbi Hayim Yosef David Azulai* (Heb.), ii (Jerusalem, 1959).

—— 'Sabbatai Zevi's Marriage to the Daughter of R. Joseph Filosoff' (Heb.), *Sefunot*, 14 (= *The Book of Greek Jewry*, iv: *The Shabbatean Movement in Greece* [Sefer yavan 4: Hatenu'ah hashabeta'it beyavan]) (Jerusalem, 1971–8), 27–32.

BEN-NAEH, YARON, 'Response to Ruth Lamdan' (Heb.), *Zion*, 66/4 (2001), 533–5.

—— 'Same-Sex Sexual Relations among Ottoman Jews' (Heb.), *Zion*, 66/2 (2001), 171–200.

BEN-ZVI, ISAAC, 'Kabbalistic Tracts from Berukhia's Circle' (Heb.), in Isaac Ben-Zvi and Meir Benayahu (eds.), *Sefunot*, 3–4 (= *S. Z. Shazar Jubilee Volume* [Sefer hayovel lishneur zalman shazar]) (Jerusalem, 1960), 349–94.

BERGER, A., '*Ayalta*: From the Doe in the Field to the Mother of the Messiahs', in S. Lieberman and A. Hyman (eds.), *Salo Wittmayer Baron Jubilee Volume*, English section, i (Jerusalem, 1974), 209–17.

BIALE, DAVID, 'A Feminist Reading of Hasidic Texts' (Heb.), in Renée Levine Melammed (ed.), *"Lift Up Your Voice": Women's Voices and Feminist Interpretation in Jewish Studies* [Harimi bako'ah kolekh: al kolot nashiyim ufarshanut feministit belimudei hayahadut] (Tel Aviv, 2001), 124–44.

—— *Gershom Scholem: Kabbalah and Counter-History* (Cambridge, Mass., 1979).

BIALE, RACHEL, *Women and Jewish Law* (New York, 1984).

BILU, YORAM, 'Dybbuk and Maggid: Two Cultural Patterns of Altered Consciousness in Judaism', *Association for Jewish Studies Review*, 21 (1996), 341–66.

BIRGE, JOHN KINGSLEY, *The Bektashi Order of Dervishes* (1937; facsimile edn. London, 1994).

BIRKENTHAL, DOV BER OF BOLECHÓW, *Divrei binah*, selections published by A. Y. Brawer in *Galician Jewry* [Galitsyah viyhudeiha] (Jerusalem, 1965), 210–74.

BOLSHAKOFF, S., *Russian Mystics* (Kalamazoo, Mich., 1977).

—— *Russian Nonconformity* (Philadelphia, 1950).

BORNSTEIN-MAKOVETSKI, LEA, 'Social Relations between Jews and Non-Jews in the Ottoman Empire in the Sixteenth and Seventeenth Centuries' (Heb.), *Mikedem umiyam*, 6 (1995), 13–33.

BOWMAN, STEVEN, 'Messianic Expectations in the Peloponnesos', *Hebrew Union College Annual*, 52 (1981), 195–202.

BOYARIN, DANIEL, *Carnal Israel: Reading Sex in Talmudic Culture* (Berkeley, Calif., 1993).

BREUER, MORDECAI, 'Fragments of Identity and Memory' (Heb.), in Haviva Pedaya and Ephraim Meir (eds.), *Judaism: Topics, Fragments, Faces, Identities. Jubilee Volume in Honour of Rivka* [Yahadut: sugiyot, keta'im, panim, zehuyot. Sefer rivkah] (Be'er Sheva, 2007), 21–5.

BROWN, PETER, *The Body and Society* (London, 1989).

—— 'The Notion of Virginity in the Early Church', in B. McGinn et al. (eds.), *Christian Spirituality: Origins to the Twelfth Century* (New York, 1985), 427–43.

BRÜLL, N., *The History of Sabbatai Zevi* [Toledot shabetai tsevi] (Vilna, 1879).

BUBER, MARTIN, *The Origin and Meaning of Hasidism* (New York, 1960).

BUCHAN, MORAG, *Women in Plato's Political Theory* (New York, 1999).

CARDOZO, ABRAHAM, 'Letter' (Heb.), in A. Freimann (ed.), *On the Subject of Sabbatai Zevi* [Inyenei shabetai tsevi] (Berlin, 1923), 87–92.

—— *Selected Writings*, trans. and introd. David J. Halperin (New York, 2001).

CARLEBACH, ELISHEVA, *The Pursuit of Heresy: Rabbi Moses Hagiz and the Sabbatian Controversies* (New York, 1990).

CARY, MARY, *A New and More EXACT Mappe or Description of the New Jerusalem's Glory* (London, 1651).

CHAJES, JOSEPH H., *Between Worlds: Dybbuks, Exorcists, and Early Modern Judaism* (Philadelphia, 2003).

—— 'City of the Dead: Spirit Posession in Sixteenth Century Safed', in Matt Goldish (ed.), *Spirit Possession in Judaism: Cases and Contexts from the Middle Ages to the Present* (Detroit, 2003), 124–58.

—— 'Spirit Possession and the Construction of Early Modern Jewish Religiosity', Ph.D. diss., Yale University, 1999.

CHERNIASKY, M., 'The Old Believers and the New Religion', *Slavic Review*, 25 (1966), 1–39.

CHRISTIAN, W. A., JR., *Apparitions in Late Medieval and Renaissance Spain* (Princeton, NJ, 1981).

COENEN, THOMAS, *The False Hopes of the Jews as They Came to Light in the Figure of Sabbatai Zevi* [Tsipiyot shav shel hayehudim kefi shehitgalu bidemuto shel shabetai tsevi], trans. into Hebrew by Arthur Lagawier and Efraim Shmueli, with introduction and notes by Yosef Kaplan (Jerusalem, 1998), from Coenen, *Ydele verwachtinge der Joden getoont in den Persoon van Sabetai Zevi* (Amsterdam, 1669).

COHEN, A., and B. LEWIS, *Population and Revenue in the Towns of Palestine in the Sixteenth Century* (Princeton, NJ, 1978).

COHEN, MORTIMER J., *Jacob Emden: A Man of Controversy* (Philadelphia, 1937).

COHN, NORMAN, *The Pursuit of the Millennium* (London, 1970).

COMTET, ROGER, 'À propos du livre de Karl Konrad Grass, *Die russischen Sekten* (Dorpat, 1907, 1909, 1914)', in Michel Niqueux (ed.), *Vieux-croyants et sectes russes du XVII*ᵉ *siècle à nos jours* (= *Revue des études slaves*, 69/1–2) (Paris, 1997), 183–200.

A Conversation between the Year 1800 and the Year 1801 [Siḥah bein shenat taf-kuf-samekh uvein shenat taf-kuf-samekh-alef] (Prague, 1800).

CONYBEARE, F. C., *Russian Dissenters*, Harvard Theological Studies 10 (Cambridge, Mass., 1921).

CORDOVERO, MOSES, *Pardes rimonim* (Munkács, 1906; facsimile edn. Jerusalem, 1962).

CROSS, F. L., and E. A. LIVINGSTONE (eds.), *The Oxford Dictionary of the Christian Church* (London, 1974).

CRUMMEY, ROBERT O., *The Old Believers and the World of Antichrist* (Madison, Wis., 1970).

DAICHES, S., *Babylonian Oil Magic in Later Jewish Literature*, Jews College Publications 5 (London, 1913).

DAME, FREDERICK WILLIAM, *Jean-Jacques Rousseau on Adult Education and Revolution: Paradigma of Radical Pedagogical Thought* (Frankfurt am Main, 1999).

DAN, JOSEPH, 'Archons of the Cup and Archons of the Toenail' (Heb.), in id., *Studies in Ashkenazi Hasidic Literature* [Iyunim besifrut ḥasidei ashkenaz] (Ramat Gan, 1975), 34–43.

—— 'Armilus: The Jewish Antichrist and the Origins and Dating of the Sefer Zerubbavel', in P. Schäfer and M. Cohen (eds.), *Toward the Millennium* (Leiden, 1998), 73–104.

—— *The Hasidic Story: Its History and Development* [Hasipur haḥasidi] (Jerusalem, 1975).

—— *Hebrew Ethical and Homiletical Literature* [Sifrut hamusar vehaderush] (Jerusalem, 1975).

DAN, JOSEPH, *On Sanctity: Religion, Ethics and Mysticism in Judaism and Other Religions* [Al hakedushah] (Jerusalem, 1997).

DANKOFF, ROBERT, 'An Unpublished Account of *Mum Sondurmek* in the Seyahatname of Evliya Chelebi', in Alexandre Popovic and Gilles Veinstein (eds.), *Bektachiyya: Études sur l'ordre mystique des Bektachis et les groupes relevant de Hadji Bektach* (Istanbul, 1995), 69–73.

DAROWSKI, ADAM, *Pamiętniki Józefa Kossakowskiego, biskupa Inflanckiego* ['Memoirs of Józef Kossakowski, Bishop of Livland] (Warsaw, 1891).

DAVID, ABRAHAM, *Immigration and Settlement in Erets Yisrael in the Sixteenth Century* [Aliyah vehityashvut be'erets yisra'el bame'ah ha-16] (Jerusalem, 1993).

—— 'Safed as a Centre for the Resettlement of Conversos in the Sixteenth Century' (Heb.), in Abraham Haim (ed.), *Society and Community: Proceedings of the Second International Congress for Research on the Sephardi and Oriental Jewish Heritage, 1984* [Ḥevrah ukehilah: midivrei hakongres habein-le'umi hasheni leḥeker yahadut sefarad vehamizraḥ, 5745] (Jerusalem, 1991), 183–204.

—— 'The Spanish Exiles in the Holy Land', in Haim Beinart (ed.), *Moreshet Sepharad: The Sephardi Legacy* (Jerusalem, 1992), ii. 77–108.

DAVIDOWICZ, KLAUS S., *Jakob Frank, der Messias aus dem Ghetto* (Frankfurt am Main, 1998).

DAVIES, NORMAN, *God's Playground: A History of Poland*, 2 vols. (Oxford, 1981).

DAWSON, RUTH P., *The Contested Quill: Literature by Women in Germany, 1770–1800* (Newark, NJ, 2002).

DEUTSCH, NATHANIEL, *The Maiden of Ludmir: A Jewish Holy Woman and her World* (Berkeley, Calif., 2003).

DOKTÓR, JAN, 'Jakub Frank, a Jewish Heresiarch and his Messianic Doctrine', *Acta Poloniae Historica*, 76 (1997), 53–74.

—— (ed.), *Księga Słów Pańskich*. See Frank

—— (ed.), *Rozmaite adnotacje, przypadki, czynności i anekdoty pańskie* [Various Notes, Events, Activities, and Anecdotes Concerning the Lord] (Warsaw, 1996).

DONNER, NATHAN NATA, OF KOLOBEEL (KOŁBIEL), *Butsina kadisha* (Piotrków, 1912; Benei Berak, 2001).

—— *Mayim rabim* (Warsaw, 1899), repr. in *Holy Books by the Disciples of the Ba'al Shem Tov* [Sefarim kedoshim mitalmidei ba'al shem tov], vol. xviii (Brooklyn, 1984).

—— *Menorat zahav* (Warsaw, 1904; Benei Berak, 2001).

DOV BAER (THE MAGGID) OF MEZHIRECH, *Magid devarav leya'akov*, annotated critical edn. by Rivka Schatz-Uffenheimer (Jerusalem, 1976).

—— *Or ha'emet* (Zhitomir, 1900).

—— *Or torah* (Jerusalem, 1968).

DRESNER, SAMUEL, *The Zaddik: The Doctrine of the Zaddik According to the Writings of Rabbi Yaakov Yosef of Polnoy* (London, 1960).

DUBNOW, SIMON, *The History of Hasidism* [Toledot haḥasidut] (Tel Aviv, 1960).

DUKER, A. G., 'Polish Frankism's Duration', *Jewish Social Studies*, 25 (1963), 287–333.

DURASOFF, S., *The Russian Protestants: Evangelicals in the Soviet Union, 1944–1964* (Rutherford, NJ, 1969).

DVIR-GOLDBERG, RIVKA, 'Voice of a Subterranean Fountain: The Image of a Woman through the Hasidic Tale' (Heb.), *Jerusalem Studies in Jewish Folklore*, 21 (2001), 27–44.

DYNNER, GLENN, 'How Many *Hasidim* Were There Really in Congress Poland? A Response to Marcin Wodziński', *Gal-ed*, 20 (2006), 91–104.

—— *Men of Silk: The Hasidic Conquest of Polish Jewish Society* (Oxford, 2006).

EICHENSTEIN, ZEVI HIRSCH, OF ZHIDACHOV, *Turn Aside from Evil and Do Good: An Introduction and a Way to the Tree of Life*, trans. with annotations and introd. Louis Jacobs (London, 1995); first published in Hebrew as *Sur mera va'aseh tov* (Lvov, 1832).

ELBAUM, JACOB, *Repentance and Self-Flagellation in the Writings of the Sages of Gemany and Poland 1348–1648* [Teshuvat halev vekabalat yisurim] (Jerusalem, 1993).

ELIACH, Y., 'The Russian Dissenting Sects and their Influence on Israel Baal Shem Tov, Founder of Hasidism', *Proceedings of the American Academy for Jewish Research*, 36 (1968), 57–83.

ELIMELEKH OF LYZHANSK, *No'am elimelekh*, ed. Gedalyah Nigal, 2 vols. (Jerusalem, 1978).

ELIOR, RACHEL, 'Jacob Frank and his Book, *Words of the Lord*: Religious Anarchism as a Restoration of Myth and Metaphor' (Heb.), in ead. (ed.), *The Sabbatian Movement and its Aftermath: Messianism, Sabbatianism and Frankism* [Hahalom veshivro: hatenu'ah hashabeta'it usheluhoteiha: meshihiyut, shabeta'ut, ufrankizm], Jerusalem Studies in Jewish Thought 17 (Jerusalem, 2001), ii. 471–548.

—— 'The Lubavitch Messianic Resurgence: The Historical and Mystical Background, 1939–1996', in P. Schäfer and M. Cohen (eds.), *Toward the Millennium* (Leiden, 1998), 383–408.

—— 'Spiritual Renaissance and Social Change in the Beginnings of Hasidism' (Heb.), in Moshe Hallamish (ed.), *Alei Shefer: Studies in the Literature of Jewish Thought Presented to Rabbi Dr Alexandre Safran* [Alei shefer: mehkarim besifrut hahagut hayehudit mugashim likhevod harav doktor aleksander safran] (Ramat Gan, 1990), 29–40.

ELLINSON, GETSEL, *Woman and the Mitzvot: A Guide to the Rabbinic Sources*, i: *Serving the Creator* (Jerusalem, 1986); ii: *The Modest Way* (Jerusalem, 1992); iii: *Partners in Life* (Jerusalem, 1998).

ELMALEH, ABRAHAM, *Sabbatai Zevi, the Sabbatian Sects and the Remnants of his Messianic Movement in the Present Day* [Shabetai tsevi, kitotav useridei tenu'ato hameshihit beyameinu eleh] (Jerusalem, 1927).

ELON, MENACHEM, *Jewish Law: History, Sources, Principles*, 4 vols. (Philadelphia, 1994).

ELQAYAM, AVRAHAM, 'The Absent Messiah: Messiah Son of Joseph in the Thought of Nathan of Gaza, Sabbatai Zevi, and Abraham Miguel Cardozo' (Heb.), *Daat*, 38 (1997), 33–82.

—— 'Başım tacı Şabbetai: A Sabbatian Hymn from the Kapancılar Community' (Heb.), *Kabbalah: Journal for the Study of Jewish Mystical Texts*, 7 (2002), 225–35.

—— '"Bury My Faith": A Letter of Sabbatai Zevi in Exile' (Heb.), *Pe'amim*, 55 (1993), 4–37.

ELQAYAM, AVRAHAM, 'The Mystery of Faith in the Writings of Nathan of Gaza' [Sod ha'emunah bekhitvei natan ha'azati], Ph.D. diss., Hebrew University (1993).

—— 'Sabbatai Zevi's Zohar' (Heb.), *Kabbalah: Journal for the Study of Jewish Mystical Texts*, 3 (1998), 345–87.

—— 'To Know Messiah: The Dialectics of Sexual Discourse in the Messianic Thought of Nathan of Gaza' (Heb.), *Tarbiz*, 65 (1996), 637–70.

EMDEN, JACOB, *Akitsat akrav* (Altona, 1753).

—— *Beit yehonatan hasofer* (Altona, 1763).

—— *Edut beya'akov* (Altona 1754).

—— *Ma'aseh nora bepodolia*, printed in id., *Sefer hapedut vehapurkan* (Altona, 1769); reprinted in the appendices to M. Balaban, *On the History of the Frankist Movement* [Letoledot hatenu'ah hafrankit] (Tel Aviv, 1935), pt. 2, 296–305.

—— *Megilat sefer* (Warsaw, 1897).

—— *Mitpahat sefarim* (Altona, 1768).

—— [DAVID AVAZ], *Petah einayim*, printed at the end of id., *Shevirat luhot ha'aven* (Żółkiew [Altona], 1756 [1759]).

—— *Sefer hitabekut* (Lvov, 1877).

—— *Sefer shimush* (Amsterdam [Altona]), 1758–63).

—— *Zot torat hakena'ot* (Lvov, 1870).

—— (ed.) *Seder olam rabah, Seder olam zuta*, and tractate *Ta'anit* (Hamburg, 1757).

EMELIANTSEVA, EKATERINA, 'Die Wehles. "Häretische" Bildungselite zwischen jüdischer Tradition und frankistischer Mystik, 1700–1849', MA diss., Albert Ludwigs University, 1999.

—— Zwischen jüdischer Tradition und frankistischer Mystik. Zur Geschichte der Prager Frankistenfamilie Vehle: 1760–1800', *Kwartalnik Historii Żydów*, 4/200 (2001), 549–65.

Encyclopaedia Judaica, 16 vols. (Jerusalem, 1972).

Encyclopaedia of Islam New Edition, 12 vols. (Leiden, 1960–2009).

ENGELSTEIN, LAURA, *Castration and the Heavenly Kingdom: A Russian Folktale* (Ithaca, NY, 1999).

EPHRAIM OF SUDYŁKÓW, *Degel mahaneh efrayim* (Zhitomir, 1875).

EPSTEIN, A., 'Une lettre d'Abraham ha-Yakhini a Nathan Gazati', *Revue des Études Juives*, 26 (1893), 209–19.

EPSTEIN, KALONYMUS KALMAN, *Ma'or vashemesh*, 2 vols. (Jerusalem, 1986).

ETKES, IMMANUEL, *The Besht: Magician, Mystic, and Leader*, trans. from the Hebrew by Saadya Sternberg (Waltham, Mass., 2005).

EUCHEL, ISAAC, 'The Letters of Meshulam, son of Uriah the Eshtemoite' (Heb.), in Yehuda Friedlander (ed.), *Studies in Hebrew Satire* [Perakim basatirah ha'ivrit], i: *Hebrew Satire in Germany (1790–1797)* [Beshilhei hame'ah hayod-het begermanyah], (Tel Aviv, 1979), 19–61.

EVEN-SHEMUEL, JUDAH, *Midrashim of Redemption* [Midreshei ge'ulah] (Jerusalem, 1953).

FAIERSTEIN, MORRIS M. (trans. and introd.), *Jewish Mystical Autobiographies: Book of Visions and Book of Secrets* (New York, 1999).

FEINKIND, M., *Froyen rabbonim un barimte perzenlekhkaytn in poylen* [Female Rabbis and Famous Personalities in Poland] (Warsaw, 1937).

FENTON, PAUL, 'Shabbetay Sebi and his Muslim Contemporary Muhammed an-Niyazi', in D. R. Blumenthal (ed.), *Approaches to Judaism in Medieval Times*, (Atlanta, Ga., 1988), iii. 81–9.

FINE, LAWRENCE, *Physician of the Soul, Healer of the Cosmos: Isaac Luria and his Kabbalistic Fellowship* (Stanford, Calif., 2003).

FISHBANE, MICHAEL, *The Exegetical Imagination: On Jewish Thought and Theology* (Cambridge, Mass., 1998).

FISHMAN, TALYA, 'A Kabbalistic Perspective on Gender-Specific Commandments: On the Interplay of Symbols and Society', *Association for Jewish Studies Review*, 17 (1992), 199–245.

FLECKELES, ELEAZAR, *Ahavat david* (Prague, 1800).

—— *Teshuvah me'ahavah*, pt. 1 (Prague, 1809).

FOUCAULT, MICHEL, *History of Madness*, ed. Jean Khalfa, trans. Jonathan Murphy and Jean Khalfa (London, 2006).

FRANCES, IMMANUEL, 'Sipur ma'aseh shabetai tsevi venatan ha'azati bekitsur' [A Brief Account of Sabbatai Zevi and Nathan of Gaza], *Kobez al yad*, 1 (1885), 133–6.

—— and JACOB FRANCES, *Tsevi mudah*, *Kobez al yad*, 1 (1885), 101–28.

FRANK, JACOB, *Book of the Words of the Lord* [Sefer divrei ha'adon], trans. into Hebrew by Fania Scholem from the Polish Kraków manuscript; interim edition/working draft (unpublished) prepared by Rachel Elior (Jerusalem, 1997).

—— *Księga Słów Pańskich* [Book of Words of the Lord], ed. Jan Doktór, 2 vols. (Warsaw, 1997).

FREELY, JOHN, *The Lost Messiah* (London, 2001).

FREIMANN, A. (ed.), *On the Subject of Sabbatai Zevi* [Inyenei shabetai tsevi] (Berlin, 1923).

FRIEDLANDER BEN ARZA, SARAH, 'Hannah Rachel of Ludmir' (Heb.), *Kolekh: Forum nashim datiyot*, 95 (1 Tamuz 2004), 3–4.

FRIEDLANDER, YEHUDA (ed.), *Studies in Hebrew Satire* [Perakim basatirah ha'ivrit], i: *Hebrew Satire in Germany (1790–1797)* [Beshilhei hame'ah hayod-ḥet begermanyah] (Tel Aviv, 1979).

GALANTÉ, ABRAHAM, *Nouveaux documents sur Sabbetaï Sevi: Organisation et us et coutumes de ses adeptes* (Istanbul, 1935).

GAY, PETER, *The Enlightenment: An Interpretation*, ii: *The Science of Freedom* (London, 1973).

GELBER, NATHAN MICHAEL, 'Di zikhroynes fun moses porges' [Memoirs of Moses Porges], in A. Tscherikover (ed.), *YIVO—Historishe shriftn*, i (Warsaw, 1929), cols. 253–96. *See also* Porges (cols. 265–88 only).

—— *The History of the Jews in Brody* [Letoledot yehudei brodi] (Jerusalem, 1955).

GELLER, YAAKOV, 'Inter-Ethnic Relations in the Ottoman Empire' (Heb.), *Mikedem umiyam*, 2 (1986), 29–54.

GERBER, HAIM, *Economic and Social Life of the Jews in the Ottoman Empire in the Sixteenth and Seventeenth Centuries* [Yehudei ha'imperyah ha'otomanit bame'ot ha-16–17: kalkalah vehevrah] (Jerusalem, 1982).

GIL, MOSHE, *In the Kingdom of Ishmael: Studies in Jewish History in Islamic Lands in the Early Middle Ages* [Bemalkhut yishma'el bitekufat hage'onim], 4 vols. (Tel Aviv, 1977).

GINSBURG, E. K., *The Sabbath in the Classical Kabbalah* (New York, 1989).

GINZBERG, LOUIS, *Legends of the Jews*, 7 vols. (Philadelphia, 1968).

GODWIN, WILLIAM, *Memoirs of the Author of Vindication of the Rights of Woman* (London, 1798).

GOITEIN, S. D., 'A Report on Messianic Troubles in Baghdad in 1120–21', *Jewish Quarterly Review*, 43 (1952–3), 57–76.

GOLDBERG, ANN, *Sex, Religion, and the Making of Modern Madness: The Eberbach Asylum and German Society 1815–1849* (Oxford, 1999).

GOLDISH, MATT, *The Sabbatean Prophets* (Cambridge, Mass., 2004).

GRAETZ, H., *History of the Jews from the Earliest Times to the Present Day*, 5 vols. (London, 1901).

GRASS, K. K., *Die russischen Sekten*, 2 vols. (Leipzig, 1907; repr. 1966).

GREEN, ARTHUR, 'Shekhinah, the Virgin Mary, and the Song of Songs: Reflections on a Kabbalistic Symbol in its Christian Context', *Association for Jewish Studies Review*, 26/1 (2002), 1–52.

—— 'Typologies of Leadership and the Hasidic Zaddiq', in id. (ed.), *Jewish Spirituality*, ii: *From the Sixteenth-Century Revival to the Present* (New York, 1987), 127–56.

GREISIGER, LUZ, 'Jüdische Kryptochristen im 18. Jahrhundert? Dokumente aus dem Archiv der Evangelischen Brüderunität in Herrnut', *Judaica*, 60 (2004), pt. 1, 204–23, pt. 2, 325–39.

GRIES, ZEEV, *Conduct Literature: Its History and Place in the Life of Beshtian Hasidism* [Sifrut hahanhagot: toledoteiha umekomah behayei hasidav shel habesht] (Jerusalem, 1989).

—— 'The Copying and Printing of Kabbalistic Books as a Source for the Study of Kabbalah' (Heb.), *Mahanayim*, 6 (1993), 204–11.

—— 'The Fashioning of *Hanhagot* (Regimen Vitae) Literature at the End of the Sixteenth Century and During the Seventeenth Century, and Its Historical Significance' (Heb.), *Tarbiz*, 56 (1987), 527–81.

GROSSMAN, ABRAHAM, *The Early Sages of Ashkenaz* [Hakhmei ashkenaz harishonim] (Jerusalem, 1981).

—— *Pious and Rebellious: Jewish Women in Europe in the Middle Ages* [Hasidot umoredot: nashim yehudiyot be'eiropah biymei habeinayim] (Jerusalem, 2001); English trans. Jonathan Chipman (Waltham, Mass., 2004).

GRUNWALD, MAX, 'MATTERSDORF', *Jahrbuch für jüdische Volkskunde* (Berlin, 1925), 402–503.

GUTTMANN, JACOB, 'LAZARUS BENDAVID', *Monatsschrift für Geschichte und Wissenschaft des Judentums*, 61[25] (1917), appendix 3, 205–6.

GUTWIRTH, E., 'The "World Upside-Down" in Hebrew', *Orientalia Suecana*, 30 (1981), 141–7.

HACKER, JOSEPH, 'Pride and Depression: Polarity of the Spiritual and Social Experience of the Iberian Exiles in the Ottoman Empire' (Heb.), in M. Ben-Sasson, R. Bonfil, and J. R. Hacker (eds.), *Culture and Society in Medieval Jewry. Studies Dedicated to the Memory of Haim Hillel Ben-Sasson* [Tarbut vehevrah betoledot yisra'el biymei habeinayim: kovets ma'amarim lezikhro shel hayim hilel ben-sason] (Jerusalem, 1981), 541–86.

—— 'Rabbi Jacob b. Solomon Ibn Habib: An Analysis of Leadership in the Jewish Community of Salonica in the XVIth Century' (Heb.), in *Proceedings of the Sixth World Congress of Jewish Studies* [Divrei hakongres ha'olami hashishi lemada'ei hayahadut] (Jerusalem, 1975), ii. 117–26.

—— 'The Sephardim in the Ottoman Empire in the Fifteenth through Eighteenth Centuries' (Heb.), in M. Abitbol et al. (eds.), *The Sephardi Jewish Diaspora after the Expulsion from Spain* [Hapezurah hayehudit hasefaradit aharei hagerush] (Jerusalem, 1993), 27–71.

—— 'The Sephardim in the Ottoman Empire in the Sixteenth Century' (Heb.), in Haim Beinart (ed.), *Moreshet Sepharad: The Sephardi Legacy* (Jerusalem, 1992), ii. 109–33.

—— 'The *Sürgün* System and Jewish Society in the Ottoman Empire during the Fifteenth to Seventeenth Centuries', in Aron Rodrigue (ed.), *Ottoman and Turkish Jewry: Community and Leadership* (Bloomington, Ind., 1992), 1–65.

HAGIZ, MOSES, *Mishnat hakhamim* (Wansbeck, 1733).

—— *Shever poshe'im* (London, 1714; facsimile edn. Jerusalem, 1970).

HAHN, SCOTT, *Hail Holy Queen: The Mother of God in the Word of God* (New York, 2001).

HAKOHEN, ASHER (OF TIKTIN), 'Keter rosh: orhot hayim' (Volozhin, 1819), in *Sifrei haga'on rabi eliyahu* (Jerusalem, n.d.).

HAKOHEN, ELIJAH, *Sefer merivat kodesh*, in A. Freimann (ed.), *On the Subject of Sabbatai Zevi* [Inyenei shabetai tsevi] (Berlin, 1923), 1–40.

HALBERTAL, MOSHE, 'Nahmanides' Conception of Death, Sin, Law, and Redemption' (Heb.), *Tarbiz*, 71/1–2 (2001–2), 133–62.

HALPERIN, DAVID J., *Sabbatai Zevi: Testimonies to a Fallen Messiah* (Oxford, 2007).

HAMILTON, ALASTAIR, *The Family of Love* (Cambridge, 1981).

—— *Heresy and Mysticism in Sixteenth-Century Spain: The Alumbrados* (Cambridge, 1992).

HAPSTEIN, ISRAEL B. SHABBETAI, OF KOZIENICE, *Avodat yisra'el hashalem* (Jerusalem, 1956).

HASENFELD, GALIA, 'Women's Roles in a Marginal Community: The Case of the Moriscos According to Inquisition Trials in Cuenca (1560–1610)' (Heb.), *Historia*, 3 (1999), 33–53.

HEARD, ALBERT F., *The Russian Church and Russian Dissent* (New York, 1887).

HEILMAN, HAYIM MEIR, *Beit rabi* (Berdichev, 1902).

HELLER, MESHULAM FEIVUSH, OF ZBARAZH, 'Yosher divrei emet', in *Likutim yekarim* (Jerusalem, 1974), 109–44.

HELLNER-ESHED, MELILA, 'A River Issues Forth from Eden: The Language of Mystical Inspiration in the Zohar' (Heb.), *Kabbalah: Journal for the Study of Jewish Mystical Texts*, 2 (1997), 287–310.

—— *A River Issues Forth from Eden: On the Language of Mystical Experience in the Zohar* [Venahar yotse me'eden: al sefat hahavayah hamistit bazohar] (Tel Aviv, 2005).

HERDMANN, FRANK, *Montesquieurezeption in Deutschland im 18. und beginnenden 19. Jahrhundert* (Hildesheim, 1990).

HESCHEL, ABRAHAM JOSHUA, *The Circle of the Baal Shem Tov: Studies in Hasidism*, ed. Samuel H. Dresner (Chicago, 1985).

—— *Prophetic Inspiration After the Prophets: Maimonides and Other Medieval Authorities*, ed. Morris M. Faierstein (Hoboken, NJ, 1996).

HEYD, MICHAEL, 'The "Jewish Quaker": Christian Perceptions of Sabbatai Zevi as an Enthusiast', in Allison P. Coudert and Jeffrey Shoulson (eds.), *Hebraica Veritas? Christian Hebraists and the Study of Judaism in Early Modern Europe* (Philadelphia, 2004), 234–65.

HOFFMANN, PAUL, *La Femme dans la pensée des Lumières* (Paris, n.d.).

HORODETSKY, SHMUEL ABBA, *Hasidism and the Hasidim* [Hahasidut vehahasidim], 4 vols. (Tel Aviv, 1953).

—— [as 'S.A.G.': Shmuel Abba Gorodetsky], 'Ludmirskaya deva (Die Ludmirer moid)' [The Ludmir Maid], *Evreiskaya starina*, 1/4 (1909), 219–22.

HOROWITZ, MARYANNE CLINE, 'Aristotle and Woman', *Journal of the History of Biology*, 9 (1976), 183–212.

HORWITZ, RIVKA, *Multiple Faceted Judaism* [Yahadut rabat hapanim] (Be'er Sheva, 2002).

HUNDERT, GERSHON, 'The Context of Hasidism', in W. Kowalski and J. Muszyńska (eds.), *Żydzi wśród chrześcijan w dobie szlacheckiej Rzeczypospolitej* [Jews among Christians in the Days of the Noble Republic] (Kielce, 1996), 171–84.

HUSS, BOAZ, 'Admiration and Disgust: The Ambivalent Re-Canonisation of the *Zohar* in the Modern Period', in H. Kreisel (ed.), *Study and Knowledge in Jewish Thought* (Be'er Sheva, 2006), 203–37.

—— 'Sabbatianism and the History of the Acceptance of the Zohar' (Heb.), in Rachel Elior (ed.), *The Sabbatian Movement and its Aftermath: Messianism, Sabbatianism, and Frankism* [Hahalom veshivro: hatenu'ah hashabeta'it usheluhoteiha: meshihiyut, shabeta'ut, ufrankizm], Jerusalem Studies in Jewish Thought 16 (Jerusalem, 2001), i. 53–73.

—— 'Zohar Translations' (Heb.), in Ronit Meroz (ed.), *New Developments in Zohar Studies* [Hidushei zohar: mehkarim hadashim besifrut hazohar] (= *Te'udah*, 21–2) (Tel Aviv, 2007), 33–107.

IDEL, MOSHE, *Ascensions on High in Jewish Mysticism: Pillars, Lines, Ladders* (Budapest, 2005).

—— 'The Attitude to Christianity in the *Sefer hameshiv*' (Heb.), *Zion*, 46 (1981), 77–91.

—— 'The Besht as Prophet and Talismanic Magician' (Heb.), in Avidov Lipsker and Rella Kushelevsky (eds.), *Studies in Jewish Narrative Presented to Yoav Elstein*

[Ma'aseh sipur: meḥkarim basifrut hayehudit mugashim leyo'av elshtein] (Ramat Gan, 2006).

—— 'Female Beauty: A Chapter in the History of Jewish Mysticism' (Heb.), in Immanuel Etkes et al. (eds.), *Within Hasidic Circles: Studies in Hasidism in Memory of Mordecai Wilensky* [Bema'agelei ḥasidim: kovets meḥkarim lezikhro shel profesor mordekhai vilenski] (Jerusalem, 2000), 317–34.

—— *Hasidism between Ecstasy and Magic* (New York, 1995).

—— *Kabbalah and Eros* (New Haven, 2005).

—— *Kabbalah: New Perspectives* (New Haven, 1988).

—— 'Leviathan and its Consort: From Talmudic to Kabbalistic Myth' (Heb.), in I. Gruenwald and M. Idel (eds.), *Myth in Judaism: History, Thought, Literature* [Hamitos bayahadut: historyah, hagut, sifrut] (Jerusalem, 2004), 145–86.

—— 'Martin Buber and Gershom Scholem on Hasidism: A Critical Appraisal', in Ada Rapoport-Albert (ed.), *Hasidism Reappraised* (London, 1996), 389–403.

—— *Messianic Mystics* (New Haven, 1998).

—— 'On the History of the Interdiction against the Study of Kabbalah before the Age of Forty' (Heb.), *Association for Jewish Studies Review*, 5 (1980), Hebrew section, 1–20.

—— 'On Prophecy and Early Hasidism', in Moshe Sharon (ed.), *Studies in Modern Religions, Religious Movements and the Bābī-Bahā'ī Faiths* (Leiden, 2004), 41–75.

—— 'On Prophecy and Magic in Sabbateanism', *Kabbalah: Journal for the Study of Jewish Mystical Texts*, 8 (2003), 7–50.

—— '"One from a Town, Two from a Clan". The Diffusion of Lurianic Kabbalah and Sabbateanism: A Re-examination', *Jewish History*, 7 (1993), 79–104.

—— 'Particularism and Universalism in Kabbalah', in D. Ruderman (ed.), *Essential Papers on Jewish Culture in Renaissance and Baroque Italy* (New York, 1992), 324–44.

—— 'Types of Redemptive Activities in the Middle Ages' (Heb.), in Z. Baras (ed.), *Messianism and Eschatology* [Meshiḥiyut ve'eskhatologyah] (Jerusalem, 1983), 253–79.

ISRAEL, JONATHAN I., *Enlightenment Contested: Philosophy, Modernity, and the Emancipation of Man, 1670–1752* (Oxford, 2006).

—— *Radical Enlightenment: Philosophy and the Making of Modernity, 1650–1750* (Oxford, 2001).

JACOB IBN NA'IM, *Mishkenot ya'akov* (Salonica, 1721).

JACOB JOSEPH OF POLONNOYE, *Ketonet pasim*, ed. Gedalyah Nigal (Jerusalem, 1985).

—— *Toledot ya'akov yosef* (Korets, 1780; repr. Jerusalem, 1966).

—— *Tsafenat pa'ne'aḥ*, ed. Gedalyah Nigal (Jerusalem, 1989).

JACOBS, LOUIS, *Jewish Mystical Testimonies* (New York, 1977).

JACOBSON, Y., 'The Aspect of the Feminine in the Lurianic Kabbalah', in P. Schäfer and J. Dan (eds.), *Gershom Scholem's Major Trends in Jewish Mysticism: 50 Years After* (Tübingen, 1993), 239–55.

JAKOBSON, R. AND M. HALLE, 'The Term *Canaan* in Medieval Hebrew', in L. Dawidowicz, A. Erlich, and R. Erlikh (eds.), *For Max Weinreich on his Seventieth Birthday* (London, 1964), 147–72.

JANES, R. M., 'On the Reception of Mary Wollstonecraft's *A Vindication of the Rights of Woman*', *Journal of the History of Ideas*, 39/2 (1978), 293–302.

JASTROW, M., *A Dictionary of the Targumim, the Talmud Babli and Yerushalmi, and the Midrashic Literature* (New York, 1971).

JELLINEK, ADOLF, 'Eines Anhängers von Jakob Frank, nach der einzingen Handschrift', *Hakol*, 6/286 (22 Jan. 1885), cols. 40–2; 6/287 (4 Feb. 1885), cols. 59–61.

—— '*Seder gan eden*, Version B' (Heb.), in id., *Beit hamidrash* (Leipzig, 1853–78; 3rd facsimile edn. Jerusalem, 1967), i, pt. 3, 131–40.

JELSMA, A., *Frontiers of the Reformation: Dissidence and Orthodoxy in Sixteenth Century Europe* (Aldershot, 1998).

JOHNSON, CLAUDIA L. (ed.), *The Cambridge Companion to Mary Wollstonecraft* (Cambridge, 2002).

JOHNSON, ELISABETH A., 'Marian Devotion in the Western Church', in Jill Raitt (ed.), *Christian Spirituality*, ii (London, 1987), 392–414.

KAGAN, R. L., *Lucrecia's Dreams: Politics and Prophecy in Sixteenth Century Spain* (Berkeley, Calif., 1990).

KAHANA, DAVID, *A History of the Kabbalists, the Sabbatians and the Hasidim* [Toledot hamekubalim, hashabeta'im vehaḥasidim], 2 vols. (Tel Aviv, 1926–7).

KAPLAN, YOSEF, 'Attitudes towards Circumcision among the Early Modern Western Sephardim' (Heb.), in Joseph R. Hacker, Yosef Kaplan, and B. Z. Keder (eds.), *From Sages to Savants: Studies Presented to Avraham Grossman* [*Rishonim ve'aharonim: mehkarim betoledot yisra'el mugashim le'a vraham grosman*] (Jerusalem, 2010), 353–89.

—— *From Christianity to Judaism: The Story of Isaac Orobio de Castro*; English trans. Raphael Loewe (Oxford, 1989).

—— '"Karaites" in Early Eighteenth Century Amsterdam', in D. S. Katz and J. I. Israel (eds.), *Sceptics, Millenarians and Jews* (Leiden, 1990), 196–236.

—— 'The Social Function of the *Herem* in the Portuguese Jewish Community of Amsterdam in the Seventeenth Century', *Dutch Jewish History*, 1 (1984), 111–55.

—— 'The Struggle against Travellers to Spain and Portugal in the Western Sephardi Diaspora' (Heb.), *Zion*, 54 (1999), 65–100.

—— 'The Travels of Portuguese Jews from Amsterdam to the "Lands of Idolatry" (1644–1724)', in id. (ed.), *Jews and Conversos* (Jerusalem, 1985), 197–224.

KARA-IVANOV KANIEL, RUT, '"The Seed that Comes from Another Place": The Affair of Lot's Daughters in the Biblical, Rabbinic, and Zoharic Sources' (Heb.), Jerusalem Studies in Jewish Thought 22 (forthcoming).

KARAMUSTAFA, AHMET T., *God's Unruly Friends* (Salt Lake City, 1994).

KATZ, JACOB, *Jewish Nationalism: Essays and Studies* [Le'umiyut yehudit: masot umehkarim] (Jerusalem, 1979).

—— 'The Suggested Relationship between Sabbatianism, Haskalah, and Reform', in id., *Divine Law in Human Hands: Case Studies in Halakhic Flexibility* (Jerusalem, 1998), 504–30; 1st pub. as 'The Possible Connection of Sabbatianism, Haskalah and Reform Judaism' [Lishe'elat hakesher bein hashabeta'ut levein hahaskalah vehareformah], in S. Stein and R. Loewe (eds.), *Studies in Jewish Religious and Intellectual*

History Presented to Alexander Altmann on the Occasion of his Seventieth Birthday (University, Ala., 1979), Hebrew section, 83–100, repr. in id., *Halakhah in Straits: Obstacles to Orthodoxy at its Inception* [Hahalakhah bameitsar: mikhsholim al derekh ha'ortodoksyah behithavutah] (Jerusalem, 1992), 262–78.

KAUFFMAN, TSIPPI, *In All Your Ways Know Him: The Concept of God and Avodah Be-Gashmiyut in the Early Stages of Hasidism* [Bekhol derakheikha de'ehu: tefisat ha'elohut veha'avodah begashmiyut bereshit haḥasidut] (Ramat Gan, 2009).

KESTENBERG-GLADSTEIN, RUTH, *Neuere Geschichte der Juden in den böhmischen Ländern. Erster Teil. Das Zeitalter der Aufklärung 1780–1830* (Tübingen, 1969).

—— 'Who Is the Author of the "Dialogue between the Years 1800 and 1801"?' (Heb.), *Kiryat sefer*, 40 (1965), 569–70.

KHOTSH, TSEVI HIRSH (B. YERAHMIEL), *Naḥalat tsevi* (Frankfurt am Main, 1710–11).

KIEVAL, HILLEL J., *Languages of Community: The Jewish Experience in the Czech Lands* (Berkeley, Calif., 2000).

KIMELMAN, R., *The Mystical Meaning of 'Lekhah dodi' and Kabbalat Shabbat* [Kavanot 'lekhah dodi' vekabalat shabat] (Los Angeles, 2003).

KLAUSNER, J., *The Messianic Idea in Israel*, trans. from Hebrew by W. F. Steinspring (London, 1956).

KLEIN, DR, 'Zuschrift an Herrn Moses Mendelson in Hamburg. Die Zusammenstellung der rabbinischen Autoritäten im vorigen Jahrhundert betreffend', *Literaturblatt des Orients*, 33 (1848), cols. 524–8, 540–4.

KLEIN-BRASLAVY, SARA, *Maimonides' Interpretation of the Adam Stories in Genesis* [Perush harambam lasipurim al adam befarashat bereshit] (Jerusalem, 1986).

KLIBANOV, A. I., *History of Religious Sectarianism in Russia* (Oxford, 1982).

KNOHL, ISRAEL, '"The Friend of the King": The Messiah of the Qumran Sect' (Heb.), *Kabbalah: Journal for the Study of Jewish Mystical Texts*, 3 (1998), 243–58.

—— *The Messiah Before Jesus: The Suffering Servant of the Dead Sea Scrolls*, trans. David Maisel (Berkeley, Calif., 2000).

KNOX, R. A., *Enthusiasm: A Chapter in the History of Religion* (Notre Dame, Ind., 1994).

KOCHOWSKI, WESPAZJAN, *Annalium Poloniae Climacter Secundae* (Kraków, 1688); published in Polish translation as *Lata Potopu 1655–7* [The Years of the Deluge], ed. L. Kukulski et al. (Warsaw, 1966).

KOENIG, NATHAN TSEVI, *Neveh tsadikim* (Benei Berak, 1969).

Kol bo (Lvov, 1860).

KOREN, SHARON FAYE, 'A Christian Means to a *Conversa* End', *Nashim*, 9/1 (2005), 27–61.

KRAUSHAR, ALEXANDR, *Frank i frankiści polscy, 1726–1816*, 2 vols. (Kraków, 1895). Hebrew edn. (vol. i only) trans. N. Sokolow: *Frank and his Following* [Frank va'adato] (Warsaw, 1896). English edn. (2 vols. bound in 1), trans. Stanley Bergman: *Jacob Frank: The End to the Sabbataian Heresy*, ed. Herbert Levy (Lanham, Md., 2001).

KRAUSS, SAMUEL, 'Schöndl Dobruschka', in *Festschrift Armand Kamina zum siebzigsten Geburtstage* (Vienna, 1937), 143–8.

Kronika. See Levine

KUNTZ, MARION L., *Guillaume Postel, Prophet of the Restitution of All Things: His Life and Thought* (The Hague, 1981).

KURZWEIL, BARUCH, *Facing the Spiritual Perplexity of Our Generation* [Lenokhaḥ hamebukhah haruḥanit shel dorenu], edited with an introduction by Moshe Schwarcz (Ramat Gan, 1976).

—— *In the Struggle over Jewish Values* [Bama'avak al erkhei hayahadut] (Jerusalem, 1969).

—— *Our New Literature: Continuity or Revolution* [Sifrutenu haḥadashah: hemsekh o mahapekhah] (Tel Aviv, 1965).

KUSHNIR-ORON, MICHAL, 'The *Sefer ha-peli'ah* and the *Sefer ha-kanah*: Their Kabbalistic Principles, Social and Religious Criticism, and Literary Composition' [Hapeliah vehakanah: yesodot hakabalah shebahem, emdatam hadatit ḥevratit vederekh itsuvam hasifrutit] Ph.D. diss., Hebrew University of Jerusalem, 1980.

KUZMACK, LINDA, 'Aggadic Approaches to Biblical Women', in E. Koltun (ed.), *The Jewish Woman: New Perspectives* (New York, 1976).

LACOMBE, OLIVIER, 'Ascèse de chasteté et mystique érotique dans l'Inde', in C. Baudouin et al. (eds.) *Mystique et continence: Travaux scientifiques du VIIe Congrès international d'Avon*, Études carmélitaines 31a (Bruges, 1952), 61–9.

LAMDAN, RUTH, 'Notes on Yaron Ben-Naeh's Article: Same-Sex Sexual Relations among Ottoman Jews' (Heb.), *Zion*, 66/4 (2001), 531–2.

—— *A Separate People: Jewish Women in Palestine, Syria and Egypt in the Sixteenth Century* (Leiden, 2000).

LANDAU, EZEKIEL, *She'elot uteshuvot noda biyhudah* (Prague, 1776).

LANDAU, ISAAC, *Zikaron tov* (Piotrków, 1892).

LEIB B. OZER, *The Story of Sabbatai Zevi* [Sipur ma'asei shabetai tsevi], trans. from original Yiddish manuscript (*Beshraybung fun shabbsai tsvi*), with introd. and notes, Zalman Shazar (Jerusalem, 1978).

LENOWITZ, HARRIS, *The Jewish Messiahs* (New York, 1998).

LERNER, ROBERT, *The Heresy of the Free Spirit in the Later Middle Ages* (Notre Dame, Ind., 1972).

LEVIN, SHMARYA, *Childhood in Exile*, trans. Maurice Samuel (London, 1929).

LEVINE, HILLEL, 'Frankism as Worldly Messianism', in P. Schäfer and J. Dan (eds.), *Gershom Scholem's Major Trends in Jewish Mysticism: 50 Years After* (Tübingen, 1993), 283–300.

—— (ed.), *The Kronika: On Jacob Frank and the Frankist Movement* [Hakhronikah: te'udah letoledot ya'akov frank utenu'ato], dual-language Hebrew/Polish edn., trans. from an unpublished Polish manuscript (Jerusalem, 1984).

LEVINE KATZ, YAEL, 'The Events of the *Yahrzeit* of Hannah Rachel Verbermacher' (Heb.), *Mabu'a*, 43 (2004/5), 65–74.

—— 'In Memoriam Hannah Rachel, 1806–1888' (Heb.), *Hatsofeh* (16 July 2004), 12.

—— 'Seven Prophetesses and Seven Sefirot: A Consideration of Kabbalistic Interpretation' (Heb.), *Daat*, 44 (2000) 123–30.

—— 'The Voice of the Bride in the Future' (Heb.), in Simha Raz (ed.), *The Religious Zionist Anthology in Memory of Zerah Warhaftig* [Kovets hatsiyonut hadatit lezekher zeraḥ varhaftig] (Jerusalem, 2001), 365–8.

LEVINE MELAMMED, RENÉ, *Heretics or Daughters of Israel? The Crypto-Jewish Women of Castile* (New York, 1999).

—— 'Women in Post-1492 Spanish Crypto-Jewish Society' (Heb.), in Yael Azmon (ed.), *A View into the Lives of Women in Jewish Societies* [Eshnav leḥayeihen shel nashim beḥavarot yehudiyot] (Jerusalem, 1995).

LIBERMAN, HAIM, 'The Book *Naḥalat tsevi* by Rabbi Hirsh Khotsch of Kraków, with a False Title Page' (Heb.), in id., *Ohel Raḥel* (New York, 1980), i. 417–23.

LIEBERMAN, SAUL, *Sheki'in* (Jerusalem, 1939).

—— 'Raymond Martini and his Alleged Forgeries', *Historia Judaica*, 5 (1943), 87–102.

LIEBES, YEHUDA, 'The Messiah of the Zohar: On R. Simeon bar Yohai as a Messianic Figure', in id., *Studies in the Zohar* (New York, 1993), 1–84.

—— 'Michael Cardozo: Author of *Raza demeheimanuta*, Attributed to Sabbatai Zevi and the Erroneous Attribution of *Igeret magen avraham* to Cardozo' (Heb.), in id., *On Sabbatianism*, 35–48.

—— *On Sabbatianism and its Kabbalah: Collected Essays* [Sod ha'emunah hashabeta'it] (Jerusalem, 1995).

—— 'Sabbatean Messianism', in id., *Studies in Jewish Myth and Messianism* (New York, 1999), 93–106.

—— 'Sections of the Zohar Lexicon' [Perakim bemilon sefer hazohar], Ph.D. diss., Hebrew University of Jerusalem, 1976.

LOEWENTHAL, NAFTALI, 'Women and the Dialectic of Spirituality in Hasidism', in Immanuel Etkes et al. (eds.), *Within Hasidic Circles: Studies in Hasidism in Memory of Mordecai Wilensky* [Bema'agelei ḥasidim: kovets meḥkarim lezikhro shel profesor mordekhai vilenski] (Jerusalem, 1999), English section, 7–65.

MACIEJKO, PAWEŁ, 'Christian Elements in Early Frankist Doctrine', *Gal-ed*, 20 (2006), 13–41.

—— 'Gershom Scholem's Dialectic of Jewish History: The Case of Sabbatianism', *Journal of Modern Jewish Studies*, 3/2 (2004), 207–26.

—— 'The Literary Character and Doctrine of Jacob Frank's *The Words of the Lord*', *Kabbalah: Journal for the Study of Jewish Mystical Texts*, 9 (2003), 175–210.

MACK, HANANEL, 'The Source and Development of the Sabbatian Exposition on the Rescission of the Mitsvot' (Heb.), *Sidra*, 11 (1995), 55–72.

MACK, P., *Visionary Women: Ecstatic Prophecy in Seventeenth-Century England* (Berkeley, Calif., 1992).

MAIMON, SOLOMON, *The Autobiography of Solomon Maimon*, trans. from German, with additions and notes, J. Clark Murray (London, 1954).

MAIMONIDES, MOSES, *Guide of the Perplexed*, trans., with introd. and notes, Shlomo Pines, 2 vols. (Chicago, 1963).

MANDEL, ARTHUR, *The Militant Messiah* (Atlantic Highlands, NJ, 1979).

—— 'Some Marginalia to the Later History of the Frankist Movement' (Heb.), *Zion*, 43 (1978), 68–74.

MANEKIN, RACHEL, 'The Development of the Idea of Religious Education for Girls in Galicia in the Modern Era' (Heb.), *Massekhet*, 2 (2004), 63–85.

MANN, JACOB, 'A Messianic Excitement in Sicily and Other Parts of Southern Europe', in id., *Texts and Studies*, i (Cincinnati, 1931), 34–44.

MARK, ZVI, '*Dibbuk* and *Devekut* in *In Praise of the Baal Shem Tov*: Notes on the Phenomenology of Madness in Early Hasidism' (Heb.), in Immanuel Etkes et al. (eds.), *Within Hasidic Circles: Studies in Hasidism in Memory of Mordecai Wilensky* [Bema'agelei ḥasidim: kovets meḥkarim lezikhro shel profesor mordekhai vilenski] (Jerusalem, 1999), 247–86.

—— *Mysticism and Madness in the Work of R. Nahman of Bratslav* [Mistikah veshiga'on biytsirat r. naḥman mibratslav] (Tel Aviv, 2003).

MAUDE, A., *A Peculiar People: The Doukhobors* (London, 1905).

MCCAGG, WILLIAM O., JR., 'Austria's Jewish Nobles, 1740–1918', *Leo Baeck Institute Year Book*, 24 (1989), 163–83.

—— *A History of Habsburg Jews 1670–1918* (Bloomington, Ind., 1992).

MÉCHOULAN, HENRY, 'Au dossier du Sabbatisme: Une relation italienne du XVIIème siècle', in D. S. Katz and Jonathan I. Israel (eds.), *Sceptics, Millenarians, and Jews* (Leiden, 1990), 185–95.

MEIR, JONATAN, 'Mikhael Levi Rodkinson: Between Hasidism and Haskalah' (Heb.), *Kabbalah: Journal for the Study of Jewish Mystical Texts*, 18 (2008), 229–86.

MEISELMAN, MOSHE, *Jewish Woman in Jewish Law* (New York, 1978).

MÉLIKOFF, I., 'La Cérémonie du Ayni-i-Djem (Anatolie Centrale)', in Alexandre Popovic and Gilles Veinstein (eds.), *Bektachiyya: Études sur l'ordre mystique des Bektachis et les groupes relevant de Hadji Bektach* (Istanbul, 1995), 65–8.

—— 'Recherche sur une coutume des Alevis: Musahip, "Frère de l'au-delà"', in Alexandre Popovic and Gilles Veinstein (eds.), *Bektachiyya: Études sur l'ordre mystique des Bektachis et les groupes relevant de Hadji Bektach* (Istanbul, 1995), 75–83.

MENAHEM MENDEL OF VITEBSK, *Likutei amarim* (Lvov, 1911).

Me'ore'ot tsevi [Events [in the Life] of [Sabbatai] Zevi] (Kopys, 1814, 1815); also published under the title *Sipur ḥalomot kets hapela'ot* [Tale of Dreams, End of Wonders] (Lvov, 1804 [1824]).

MEROZ, RONIT, 'Redemption in Lurianic Teaching' [Ge'ulah betorat ha'ari], Ph.D. diss., Hebrew University of Jerusalem, 1988.

MEYER, MICHAEL A. (ed.), *German-Jewish History in Modern Times*, 4 vols. (New York, 1996–8).

Midrash tehilim, ed. S. Buber (Vilna, 1891).

MIZRAHI, HAYIM, 'Evidence of Messianic Agitation on Corfu from a Christian Source' (Heb.), in Isaac Ben-Zvi and Meir Benayahu (eds.), *Sefunot*, 3–4 (= *S. Z. Shazar Jubilee Volume* [Sefer hayovel lishneur zalman shazar]) (Jerusalem, 1960), 537–40.

MOLKHO, ISAAC R., and ABRAHAM AMARILLO, 'Autobiographical Letters of Abraham Cardozo' (Heb.), in Isaac Ben-Zvi and Meir Benayahu (eds.), *Sefunot*, 3–4 (= *S. Z. Shazar Jubilee Volume* [Sefer hayovel lishneur zalman shazar]) (Jerusalem, 1960), 183–241.

MONDSHINE, YEHOSHUA (ed.), *Shivhey Ha-Baal Shem Tov.* See *Shivḥei habesht*

MONTESQUIEU, CHARLES LOUIS DE SECONDAT, *The Spirit of the Laws*, trans. and ed. Anne M. Cohler, Basia Carolyn Miller, and Harold Samuel Stone (Cambridge, 1989).

MOPSIK, CHARLES, *Sex of the Soul: The Vicissitudes of Sexual Difference in Kabbalah*, ed. Daniel Abrahams (Los Angeles, 2005).

MOSELEY, MARCUS, *Being for Myself Alone: Origins of Jewish Autogiography* (Stanford, Calif., 2005).

—— 'Jewish Autobiography in Eastern Europe: The Pre-History of a Literary Genre', D.Phil. diss., University of Oxford, 1990.

MOSES, LEOPOLD, 'Inschriften und Urkunden aus den Siebengemeinden', *Jahrbuch der Jüdisch-Literarischen Gesellschaft*, 18 (Frankfurt am Main, 1927).

MOUSNIER, JACQUES, *La Fortune des écrits de Jean-Jacques Rousseau dans les pays de langue allemande de 1782 à 1813* (Paris, 1980).

MYERS, DAVID N., *Re-Inventing the Jewish Past: European Jewish Intellectuals and the Zionist Return to History* (New York, 1995).

—— 'The Scholem–Kurzweil Debate and Modern Jewish Historiography', *Modern Judaism*, 6 (1986), 261–86.

NACHT, JACOB, *The Symbolism of the Woman: A Study in Folklore with Reference to Jewish and World Literature* [Simlei ishah bimekoroteinu ha'atikim, besifrutenu haḥadashah uvesifrut ha'amim] (Tel Aviv, 1959).

NADAV, YAËL, 'A Kabbalistic Treatise of R. Solomon Ayllion' (Heb.), in Isaac Ben-Zvi and Meir Benayahu (eds.), *Sefunot*, 3–4 (= *S. Z. Shazar Jubilee Volume* [Sefer hayovel lishneur zalman shazar]) (Jerusalem, 1960), 301–47.

NAHMAN OF BRATSLAV, *Likutei moharan* (New York, 1966).

NELLI, RENÉ, 'La Continence cathare', in C. Baudouin et al. (eds.), *Mystique et continence: Travaux scientifiques du VIIe Congrès international d'Avon*, Études carmélitaines 31a (Bruges, 1952), 139–51.

NEUBAUER, A., 'Excerpts from the Writings of R. Joseph b. Isaac Sambari' (Heb.), in id., *Medieval Jewish Chronicles and Chronological Notes* [Seder haḥakhamim vekorot hayamim], i (Oxford, 1887; facsimile edn. Jerusalem, 1967), 62–115.

NIGAL, GEDALYAH, *"Dybbuk" Tales in Jewish Literature* [Sipurei "dibuk" besifrut yisra'el], 2nd edn. (Jerusalem, 1994).

—— *The Hasidic Tale* (Oxford, 2008).

—— *Leader and Congregation* [Manhig ve'edah] (Jerusalem, 1962).

—— *Magic, Mysticism and Hasidism: The Supernatural in Jewish Thought* (Northvale, NJ, 1994).

—— *Rabbi Jacob Joseph of Polonnoye (Polna): Selected Writings* [Torot ba'al hatoledot] (Jerusalem, 1974).

—— 'Women in the Book *Shivḥei habesht*' (Heb.), *Molad*, 31[241] (1974), 138–45; repr. in id., *Studies in Hasidism* [Meḥkarim baḥasidut], ii (Jerusalem, 1999), 365–78.

—— *Women in Hasidic Hagiography* [Nashim basiporet haḥasidit] (Jerusalem, 2005).

NIQUEUX, MICHEL (ed.), *Vieux-croyants et sectes russes du XVIIe siècle à nos jours* (= *Revue des études slaves*, 69/1–2) (Paris, 1997).

NIQUEUX, MICHEL, 'Vieux-croyants et sectes russes: Un chantier pour la recherche', in id. (ed.), *Vieux-croyants et sectes russes*, 7–19.

O'FAOLAIN, J., and L. MARTINES, *Not in God's Image* (New York, 1973).

PACHTER, MORDECHAI, 'The Concept of Devekut in the Homiletical Ethical Writings of Sixteenth Century Safed', in Isadore Twersky (ed.), *Studies in Medieval Jewish History and Literature*, ii (Cambridge, Mass., 1984), 171–230.

PAERT, IRINA, *Old Believers, Religious Dissent and Gender in Russia, 1760–1850* (Manchester, 2003).

PALERMO, GIUSEPPE, 'The Settlement of Sicilian Jews in Baronial Lands (1470–1493)' (Heb.), *Sefunot*, 7[22] (1999), 83–138.

PARUSH, IRIS, *Reading Jewish Women: Marginality and Modernization in Nineteenth-Century Eastern European Jewish Society*, trans. from the Hebrew by Saadya Sternberg (Waltham, Mass., 2004).

PATAI, RAPHAEL, *The Hebrew Goddess* (New York, 1967).

PELIKAN, JAROSLAV, *Mary through the Centuries* (New Haven, 1996).

PERL, JOSEPH, *Revealer of Secrets*, trans. from Hebrew, with introd. and notes, Dov Taylor (Boulder, Colo., 1997); first published as *Megaleh temirin* (Vienna, 1819).

—— *Uiber das Wesen der Sekte Chassidim*, ed. Avraham Rubinstein as *The Essence of the Sect of the Hasidim* [Al mahut kat haḥasidim]: German manuscript with introduction and annotations in Hebrew (Jerusalem, 1977).

PERLMUTTER, M. A., *Jonathan Eybeschuetz and his Relationship to Sabbatianism* [Yonatan eibeshuts veyaḥaso el hashabeta'ut] (Jerusalem, 1947).

Pesikta rabati, ed. M. Friedmann (Ish Shalom) (Vienna, 1880).

PIEKARZ, MENDEL, *The Beginning of Hasidism* [Biymei tsemiḥat haḥasidut] (Jerusalem, 1978).

—— *The Hasidic Leadership: Authority and Faith in Zadicim as Reflected in the Hasidic Literature* [Hahanhagah haḥasidit: samkhut ve'emunat tsadikim be'ispaklaryat sifrutah shel haḥasidut] (Jerusalem, 1999).

Pirkei derabi eli'ezer (Warsaw, 1852).

POLEN, NEHEMIA, 'Miriam's Dance: Radical Egalitarianism in Hasidic Thought', *Modern Judaism*, 12 (1992), 1–21.

POPKIN, R. H., 'Christian Interest and Concern about Sabbatai Zevi', in Matt D. Goldish and Richard H. Popkin (eds.), *Millenarianism and Messianism in Early Modern European Culture: Jewish Messianism in the Early Modern World* (Dordrecht, 2001), 91–106.

—— 'Jewish–Christian Relations in the Sixteenth and Seventeenth Centuries: The Conception of the Messiah', *Jewish History*, 6 (1992) (= *Frank Talmage Memorial Volume*, ii), 161–77.

—— 'Jewish Messianism and Christian Millenarianism', in P. Zagorin (ed.), *Culture and Politics in Puritanism and Enlightenment* (Berkeley, Calif., 1980), 67–90.

—— 'Three English Tellings of the Sabbatai Zevi Story', *Jewish History*, 8 (1994), 43–54.

POPOVYCH, M., *Narys istoriyi kul'tury Ukrayiny* [An Essay on the History of the Culture of the Ukraine] (Kiev, 1998).

PORGES, MOSES, 'Eine Wallfahrt nach Offenbach', *Frankfurter israelitisches Gemeindeblatt*, 6 (Feb. 1932), 121–3; 7 (Mar. 1932), 150–1; Yiddish trans.: N. M. Gelber, 'Memoirs of Moses Porges' [Di zikhroynes fun moses porges], in A. Tscherikover (ed.), *YIVO—Historishe shriftn*, i (Warsaw, 1929), cols. 265–88: English trans.: Arthur Mandel, *The Militant Messiah* (Atlantic Highlands, NJ, 1979), 155–70.

PORGES, [N.], 'Texte de la lettre adressée par les Frankistes aux communautés juives de Bohème', *Revue des Études Juives*, 29 (1894), 282–8.

PORTER, ROY, *Flesh in the Age of Reason: The Modern Foundations of Body and Soul* (New York, 2004).

—— *Madness: A Brief History* (Oxford, 2002).

PROCTOR, CANDICE E., *Women, Equality, and the French Revolution* (New York, 1990).

RABINOWICZ, O. K., 'Jacob Frank in Brno', in A. Newman and S. Zeitlin (eds.), *The Seventy-Fifth Anniversary Volume of the Jewish Quarterly Review* (Philadelphia, 1967), 429–45.

RAPOPORT-ALBERT, A., 'The Emergence of a Female Constituency in Twentieth-Century HaBaD', in David Assaf and Ada Rapoport-Albert (eds.), *Let the Old Make Way for the New: Studies in the Social and Cultural History of Eastern European Jewry Presented to Immanuel Etkes* [Yashan mipenei ḥadash: meḥkarim betoledot yehudei mizraḥ eiropah uvetarbutam. Shai le'imanu'el etkes], 2 vols. (Jerusalem 2009), i: *Hasidism and the Musar Movement* [Ḥasidim uva'alei musar], English section, 7*–68*.

—— 'God and the Zaddik as the Two Focal Points of Hasidic Worship', in Gershon D. Hundert (ed.), *Essential Papers on Hasidism: Origins to Present* (New York, 1991), 299–329.

—— 'Hasidism after 1772: Structural Continuity and Change', in ead. (ed.), *Hasidism Reappraised* (London, 1996), 76–140.

—— 'Making a Home for the Divine on Earth: Women in the Teaching of the Last Lubavitcher *Rebbe*' (forthcoming).

—— 'A Maskilic Tract in Defence of Hasidism in an Anonymous Manuscript from the Circle of E. Z. Zweifel' (Heb.), in David Assaf et al. (eds.), *Studies in East European Jewish History and Culture in Honor of Professor Shmuel Werses* [Mivilnah liyrushalayim: meḥkarim betoledoteihem uvetarbutam shel yehudei mizraḥ eiropah mugashim leprofesor shemu'el verses] (Jerusalem, 2002), 71–122.

—— 'On Women in Hasidism: S. A. Horodecky and the Maid of Ludmir Tradition', in A. Rapoport-Albert and S. J. Zipperstein (eds.), *Jewish History: Essays in Honour of Chimen Abramsky* (London, 1988), 495–525; revised Hebrew version in D. Assaf (ed.), *Zaddik and Devotees: Historical and Sociological Aspects of Hasidism* [Tsadik ve'edah: heibetim historiyim veḥevratiyim beḥeker haḥasidut] (Jerusalem, 2001), 496–527.

—— and César Merchan Hamann, '"Something for the Female Sex": A Call for the Liberation of Women, and the Release of the Female Libido from the "Shackles of Shame", in an Anonymous Frankist Manuscript from Prague *c*.1800', in Joseph Dan (ed.), *Gershom Scholem (1897–1982): In Memoriam* [Sefer zikaron legershom shalom bimlot esrim veḥamesh shanim lemoto], Jerusalem Studies in Jewish Thought 21 (Jerusalem, 2007), ii, English section, 77–135.

RASHI (R. SOLOMON B. ISAAC), *Responsa* [Teshuvot rashi], ed. Israel Elfenbein (New York, 1943).

The Records of the Council of the Four Lands [Pinkas va'ad arba aratsot], 2nd edn. of *Acta Congressus Generalis Judaeorum Regni Poloniae (1580–1764)*, compiled and annotated, Israel Halpern (Jerusalem, 1945); rev. edn., Israel Bartal (ed.), introd. by Shmuel Ettinger, i (1580–1792) (Jerusalem, 1990).

REINER, ELCHANAN, 'Shivḥei habesht: Transmission, Editing, Printing' (Heb.), in *Proceedings of the Eleventh World Congress of Jewish Studies* (Jerusalem, 1994), division c, vol. ii, pp. 145–52.

RIEMER, NATHANAEL, 'Beer und Bila Perlhefters Schrift "Beer Schewa". Der Handschriftenbefund, Struktur und Charakter des Werkes', MA diss., University of Potsdam, 2002.

—— 'Zwischen christlichen Hebraisten und Sabbatianern. Der Lebensweg von R. Beer und Bila Perlhefter', *Aschkenas*, 14/1 (2004), 163–201.

RIVLIN, BRACHA, 'Guidelines on the History of the Jewish Family in Greece in the Sixteenth and Seventeenth Centuries' (Heb.), in Michel Abitbol, Yom Tov Assis, and Galit Hasan Rokem (eds.), *Hispano-Jewish Civilization after 1492: The Fourth International Congress for Research on the Sephardi and Oriental Heritage, 1992* [Ḥevrah vetarbut: yehudei sefarad le'aḥar hagerush—midivrei hakongres habeinle'umi harevi'i leḥeker moreshet yahadut sefarad vehamizraḥ, 1992] (Jerusalem, 1997), 79–104.

ROBINSON, JAMES T., 'Some Remarks on the Source of Maimonides' Plato in *Guide of the Perplexed* I. 17', in Shlomo Berger, Michael Brocke, and Irene Zwiep (eds.), *Zutot: Perspectives on Jewish Culture* (Dordrecht, 2003), 49–57.

ROSANES, S., *The History of the Jews of Turkey and the Levant, iv: 1640–1730* [Korot hayehudim beturkyah ve'aretsot kedem] (Sofia, 1933–4).

ROSEN-ZVI, ISHAY, 'Do Women Have a *Yetzer*? Anthropology, Ethics, and Gender in Rabbinic Literature' (Heb.), in Howard Kreisel, Boaz Huss, and Uri Ehrlich (eds.), *Spiritual Authority: Struggles over Cultural Power in Jewish Thought* [Samkhut ruḥanit: ma'avakim al ko'aḥ tarbuti bahagut hayehudit] (Be'er Sheva, 2010), 21–34.

—— 'Sexualising the Evil Inclination: Rabbinic "Yetzer" and Modern Scholarship', *Journal of Jewish Studies*, 60/2 (2009), 264–81.

—— 'Two Rabbinic Inclinations? Rethinking a Scholarly Dogma', *Journal for the Study of Judaism*, 39 (2008), 513–39.

ROSENTHAL, JUDAH M., 'The Idea of the Abrogation of the Commandments in Jewish Eschatology' (Heb.), in *Meyer Waxman Jubilee Volume* (Jerusalem, 1966), Hebrew section, 217–33.

ROSMAN, MOSHE, *Founder of Hasidism: A Quest for the Historical Ba'al Shem Tov* (Berkeley, Calif., 1996).

—— 'The History of a Historical Source: On the Editing of *Shivḥei habesht*' (Heb.), *Zion*, 58/2 (1993), 175–241.

—— 'Observations on Women and Hasidism' (Heb.), in David Assaf and Ada Rapoport-Albert (eds.), *Let the Old Make Way for the New: Studies in the Social and Cultural History of Eastern European Jewry Presented to Immanuel Etkes* [Yashan mipenei ḥadash: meḥkarim betoledot yehudei mizraḥ eiropah uvetarbutam. Shai le'imanu'el etkes], 2 vols. (Jerusalem, 2009), i: *Hasidism and the Musar Movement* [Ḥasidim uva'alei musar], 151–64.

ROUSSEAU, JEAN-JACQUES, *Émile*, trans. Barbara Foxley, introd. P. D. Jimack (London, 1993).

ROWE, M., *Russian Resurrection* (London, 1994).

ROZEN, MINNA, *A History of the Jewish Community of Istanbul: The Formative Years, 1453–1566* (Leiden, 2002).

Rozmaite adnotacje. See Doktór

RUBINSTEIN, AVRAHAM, 'Between Hasidism and Sabbatianism' (Heb.), in id. (ed.), *Studies in Hasidism* [Perakim betorat haḥasidut uvetoledoteiha] (Jerusalem, 1977), 182–97.

—— 'The Revelation Stories in *Shivḥei habesht*' (Heb.), *Alei sefer*, 6–7 (1977), 157–86.

—— (ed.) *Shivḥei habesht.* See *Shivḥei habesht*

SAFRAN, B., 'Rabbi Azriel and Nahmanides: Two Views of the Fall of Man', in I. Twersky (ed.), *Rabbi Moses Nahmanides (Ramban): Explorations in his Religious and Literary Virtuosity* (Cambridge, Mass., 1983), 75–106.

SAMBARI, JOSEPH B. ISAAC, *Sefer divrei yosef: Eleven Hundred Years of Jewish History Under Muslim Rule* [Sefer divrei yosef: elef ume'ah shenot toladah yehudit betsel ha'islam], ed. Shimon Shtober (Jerusalem, 1994).

SASPORTAS, JACOB, *Tsitsat novel tsevi*, ed. Isaiah Tishby (Jerusalem, 1954).

SCHACTER, JACOB J., 'History and Memory of Self: The Autobiography of Rabbi Jacob Emden', in Elisheva Carlebach et al. (eds.), *Jewish History and Jewish Memory: Essays in Honour of Yosef Hayim Yerushalmi* (Hanover, 1998), 428–52.

SCHÄFER, PETER, 'Daughter, Sister, Bride: Images of the Femininity of God in the Early Kabbalah', *Journal of the American Academy of Religion*, 68/2 (2000), 221–42.

—— *Mirror of His Beauty: Feminine Images of God from the Bible to the Early Kabbalah* (Princeton, NJ, 2002).

SCHATZ[-UFFENHEIMER], RIVKA, '"Mystic Visions of King Messiah": An Early Document by an Apostate Sabbatean' (Heb.), *Sefunot*, 12 (= *The Book of Greek Jewry*, ii [Sefer yavan 2]) (Jerusalem, 1971–8), 217–52.

—— 'Portrait of a Sabbatian Sect' (Heb.), in Isaac Ben-Zvi and Meir Benayahu (eds.), *Sefunot*, 3–4 (= *S. Z. Shazar Jubilee Volume* [Sefer hayovel lishneur zalman shazar]) (Jerusalem, 1960), 395–431.

SCHAUB, DIANA J., *Erotic Liberalism: Women and Revolution in Montesquieu's Persian Letters* (Lanham, Md., 1995).

SCHECHTER, SOLOMON, 'Safed in the Sixteenth Century', in id., *Studies in Judaism* (New York, 1958), 231–97.

SCHIMMEL, ANNEMARIE, *Mystical Dimensions of Islam* (Chapel Hill, NC, 1975).

SCHNEERSOHN, YOSEF YITSHAK, *Book of 'Talks', 1942* [Sefer hasiḥot heh-taf-shin-bet] (Brooklyn, 1973).

—— *Divrei yemei harabanit rivkah* [The History of *Rebbetsn* Rivkah] (Brooklyn, 2003).

SCHOLEM, GERSHOM, 'Abraham Michael Cardozo: Homily on "Israel was holiness unto the Lord"' (Heb.), in id., *Researches in Sabbatianism*, 425–52.

SCHOLEM, GERSHOM, 'The Career of a Frankist: Moses Dobruschka and his Meta-morphoses' (Heb.), *Zion*, 35 (1970), 127–81; repr. in id., *Studies and Texts*, 141–216.

—— 'The Crypto-Jewish Sect of the Dönmeh (Sabbatians) in Turkey', in id., *The Messianic Idea in Judaism*, 142–66.

—— '*Devekut*, or Communion with God', in id., *The Messianic Idea in Judaism*, 203–27.

—— *Explications and Implications: Writings on Jewish Heritage and Renaissance* [Devarim bego: pirkei morashah uteḥiyah] (Tel Aviv, 1975).

—— 'Frankism and Enlightenment', unpublished lecture, Jewish National and University Library, Gershom Scholem Archive 4° 1599/156.

—— 'A Frankist Commentary on Hallel' (Heb.), in *Yitzhak F. Baer Jubilee Volume* [Sefer hayovel leyitshak ba'er] (Jerusalem, 1961), 410–30; repr. in id., *Studies and Texts* (Heb.), 422–52.

—— 'A Frankist Document from Prague', in S. Lieberman and A. Hyman (eds.), *Salo Wittmayer Baron Jubilee Volume*, English section, ii (Jerusalem, 1974), 787–814.

—— 'A Frankist Letter on the History of the "Faith"' (Heb.), in Shmuel Werses, Nathan Rotenstreich, and Chone Shmeruk (eds.), *The Dov Sadan Volume* [Sefer dov sadan] (Tel Aviv, 1977), 346–60; repr., with editorial additions, in id., *Researches in Sabbatianism*, 634–50.

—— '*Gilgul*: The Transmigration of Souls', in id., *On the Mystical Shape of the Godhead* (New York, 1991), 197–250.

—— 'The Historical Ba'al Shem Tov' (Heb.), in id., *Explications and Implications*, 287–324.

—— *In the Footsteps of Messiah* [Be'ikevot mashiaḥ] (Jerusalem, 1944).

—— 'Information on Sabbatians in Books by Missionaries from the Eighteenth Century' (Heb.), in id., *Researches in Sabbatianism*, 609–30.

—— *Kabbalah* (Jerusalem, 1974).

—— 'A Letter of Abraham Cardozo to the Rabbis of Smyrna' (Heb.), in id., *Studies and Texts*, 298–331.

—— *Major Trends in Jewish Mysticism* (New York, 1965).

—— 'Martin Buber's Interpretation of Hasidism', in id., *The Messianic Idea in Judaism*, 227–50.

—— 'The Meaning of the Torah in Jewish Mysticism', in id., *On the Kabbalah and its Symbolism* (London, 1965), 32–86.

—— *The Messianic Idea in Judaism and Other Essays on Jewish Spirituality* (New York, 1971).

—— 'The Neutralization of the Messianic Element in Early Hasidism', in id., *The Messianic Idea in Judaism*, 176–202.

—— 'Notes from Italy on the Sabbatian Movement in 1666' (Heb.), in id., *Researches in Sabbatianism*, 491–509.

—— *On the Mystical Shape of the Godhead* (New York, 1991).

—— *Origins of the Kabbalah* (Princeton, NJ, 1987).

—— 'Politik der Mystik: Zu Isaac Breuers "Neuem Kusari"', *Jüdische Rundschau*, 57 (17 July 1934), 1–2.

—— 'Redemption through Sin', in id., *The Messianic Idea in Judaism*, 78–141.

—— *Researches in Sabbatianism* [Meḥkerei shabeta'ut], ed. Yehuda Liebes (Tel Aviv, 1991).

—— *Sabbatai Sevi: The Mystical Messiah, 1626–1676* (Princeton, NJ, 1976). English trans. by R. J. Zwi Werblowsky of *Shabetai tsevi vehatenu'ah hashabeta'it biymei ḥayav*, 2 vols. (Tel Aviv, 1957).

—— 'The Sabbatian Movement in Poland' (Heb.), in id., *Studies and Texts*, 68–140.

—— 'A Sabbatian Will from New York', *Miscellanies of the Jewish Historical Society of England*, 5 (1948), 193–211; repr. in id., *The Messianic Idea in Judaism*, 167–75.

—— 'Shekhinah: The Feminine Element in Divinity', in id., *On the Mystical Shape of the Godhead* (New York, 1991), 140–96.

—— 'The Sources for the "Story of Rabbi Gadiel the Child" in Kabblistic Literature' (Heb.), in id., *Explications and Implications*, 270–83.

—— *Studies and Texts Concerning the History of Sabbatianism and its Metamorphoses* [Meḥkarim umekorot letoledot hashabeta'ut vegilguleiha] (Jerusalem, 1974).

—— 'Toward an Understanding of the Messianic Idea in Judaism', in id., *The Messianic Idea in Judaism*, 1–36.

—— 'The Two First Testimonies on the Relations between Hasidic Groups and Ba'al Shem Tov' (Heb.), *Tarbiz*, 20 (1949), 228–40.

SCHUCHAT, RAPHAEL, 'Lithuanian Kabbalah as an Independent Trend of Kabbalistic Literature' (Heb.), *Kabbalah: Journal for the Study of Jewish Mystical Texts*, 10 (2004), 181–206.

SCHWARTZ, DOV, *Messianism in Medieval Jewish Thought* [Hara'ayon hameshiḥi bahagut hayehudit biymei habeinayim], (Ramat Gan, 1997).

—— *The Philosophy of a Fourteenth-Century Jewish Neoplatonic Circle* [Yashan bekankan ḥadash: mishnato ha'iyunit shel haḥug hane'oplatoni bafilisofyah hayehudit bame'ah ha-14] (Jerusalem, 1996).

SCHWARZ, BARUKH, *Hayai* (Jerusalem, 1930).

SCHWEID, ELIEZER, *Judaism and Mysticism According to Gershom Scholem: A Critical Analysis and Programmatic Discussion*, trans. from the Hebrew and introd. D. A. Weiner (Atlanta, Ga., 1985).

'Sefer divrei ha'adon'. See Frank, *Words of the Lord*

Sefer divrei yosef. See Sambari

Sefer habahir, ed. R. Margaliot (Jerusalem, 1978); ed. D. Abrams (Los Angeles, 1994).

Sefer hakanah (Kraków, 1894; facsimile edn. Jerusalem, 1974).

Sefer ḥasidim, ed. J. Wistinezki and J. Freimann (Berlin, 1891; Frankfurt am Main, 1924).

Sefer toledot ha'ari, ed. M. Benayahu (Jerusalem, 1967).

Sefer zerubavel, in Judah Even-Shemuel, *Midrashim of Redemption* [Midreshei ge'ulah] (Jerusalem, 1953), 55–88.

SEIDMAN, NAOMI, 'Reflections on a Belated Apostasy', *Contemplate: The International Journal of Cultural Jewish Thought*, 3 (2005/6), 52–7.

SHAROT, STEPHEN, *Messianism, Mysticism and Magic* (Chapel Hill, NC, 1982).

Shivḥei habesht [In Praise of the Ba'al Shem Tov] (Kopys, 1814); English edn., trans. and ed. Dan Ben-Amos and Jerome R. Mintz: *In Praise of the Baal Shem Tov*

(Bloomington, Ind., 1970); facsimile edn.: *Shivhey Ha-Baal Shem Tov: A Facsimile of a Unique Manuscript, Variant Versions, and Appendices* [Sefer shivḥei habesht: faksimil miketav hayad hayeḥidi hanoda lanu veshinuyei nusaḥav le'umat nusaḥ hadefus], ed. Yehoshua Mondshine (Jerusalem, 1982); *In Praise of the Ba'al Shem Tov (Shivhei Ha-Besht) with Introduction and Annotations* [Shivḥei habesht: mahadurah mu'eret umevo'eret], ed. Avraham Rubinstein (Jerusalem, 1991).

SHMERUK, CHONE, 'The Peregrinations of Jacob Frank's *Sefer divrei ha'adon* from Yiddish to Polish' (Heb.), *Gal-ed*, 14 (1995), 23–36; repr. in id., *The Call for a Prophet* [Hakeriah lenavi] (Jerusalem, 1999), 87–100.

—— *Yiddish Literature: Aspects of its History* [Sifrut yidish: perakim letoledoteiha] (Tel Aviv, 1978).

SHMUELI, EPHRAIM, *With the Last Generation of Jews in Poland* [Bador hayehudi ha'aḥaron bepolin] (Tel Aviv, 1986).

SHOHET, AZRIEL, *Beginnings of the Haskalah among German Jewry* [Im ḥilufei tekufot: reshit hahaskalah beyahadut germanyah] (Jerusalem, 1960).

SIMHAH BUNEM OF PSHISKHA, *Kol mevaser*, 3 vols. (Ra'anana, 1991).

SISMAN, CENGIZ, 'A Jewish Messiah in the Ottoman Court: Sabbatai Sevi and the Emergence of a Judeo-Islamic Community (1666–1720)', Ph.D. diss., Harvard University, 2004.

SMOLITSCH, I., *Russisches Monchtum* (Amsterdam, 1978).

SONNE, ISAIAH, 'New Material on Sabbatai Zevi from a Notebook of R. Abraham Rovigo' (Heb.), in Isaac Ben-Zvi and Meir Benayahu (eds.), *Sefunot*, 3–4 (= *S. Z. Shazar Jubilee Volume* [Sefer hayovel lishneur zalman shazar]) (Jerusalem, 1960), 39–70.

SPECK, PAUL, 'The Apocalypse of Zerubbabel and Christian Icons', *Jewish Studies Quarterly*, 4/2 (1997), 183–90.

SPIEGEL, JACOB S., 'R. Jacob ibn Na'im and his Attitude to the Kabbalah and Sabbatianism' (Heb.), *Maḥanayim*, 6 (1993), 198–203.

STEIN, LEOPOLD, 'Mittheilung über die Frankistensekte', *Achawa*, 3 (1870), 154–60.

STERNHARZ, NATHAN, *The Life of Nahman of Bratslav* [Ḥayei moharan], 2 vols. (New York, 1965).

SÜSSENBERGER, CLAUS, *Rousseau im Urteil der deutschen Publizistik bis zum Ende der Französischen Revolution. Ein Beitrag zur Rezeptionsgeschichte* (Berne, 1974).

SZASZ, THOMAS S., *The Manufacture of Madness* (London, 1971).

TAMAR, DAVID, *Studies in the History of the Jews in the Land of Israel and the Middle East* [Meḥkarim betoledot hayehudim be'erets yisra'el uve'aretsot hamizraḥ] (Jerusalem, 1981).

TARANETS, S., *Kurenevskoe trimonastyr'e: Istoriya russkogo staroobryadcheskogo tsentra v Ukraine* [Three Monasteries in Kurenevka: History of the Russian Centre of 'Old Believers' in the Ukraine] (Kiev, 1999).

TA-SHMA, ISRAEL, 'Where Were the Books *Hakanah* and *Hapeliah* Composed?' (Heb.) in Immanuel Etkes and Yosef Salmon (eds.) *Studies in the History of Jewish Society in the Middle Ages and in the Modern Period, Presented to Professor Jacob Katz on his Seventy-Fifth Birthday* [Perakim betoledot haḥevrah hayehudit biymei habeinayim

Printed and bound by CPI Group (UK) Ltd, Croydon, CR0 4YY

09/06/2025

14685796-0002

uva'et haḥadashah mukdashim leprofesor ya'akov kats bimlot lo shivim veḥamesh shanah] (Jerusalem, 1980), 56–63.

TELENBERG, AHARON, 'The Sabbatian Theology in Judah Levi Tovah's *Commentary to Genesis*' (Heb.), *Kabbalah: Journal for the Study of Jewish Mystical Texts,* 8 (2003), 151–83.

—— SHLOMO AVAYOU, and AVRAHAM ELQAYAM, 'A Translation of *Mirat bereshit tovah* from Ladino to Hebrew' (Heb.), *Kabbalah: Journal for the Study of Jewish Mystical Texts,* 8 (2003), 281–368.

THOMAS, KEITH, 'Women and the Civil War Sects', in T. Aston (ed.), *Crisis in Europe 1560–1660* (London, 1965), 317–40.

TISHBY, ISAIAH, *Messianic Mysticism: Moses Hayim Luzzatto and the Padua School,* trans. Morris Hoffman (Oxford, 2008).

—— *Paths of Faith and Sectarianism* [Netivei emunah uminut] (Ramat Gan, 1964).

—— and JOSEPH DAN, 'The Doctrine and Literature of Hasidism' (Heb.), in A. Rubinstein (ed.), *Studies in Hasidism* [Perakim betorat haḥasidut uvetoledoteiha] (Jerusalem, 1977), 250–315. (Originally published as 'Hasidism' [Ḥasidut] in *Encyclopaedia Hebraica,* xvii (Jerusalem, 1965), 756–821.)

—— and FISHEL LACHOWER (eds.), *The Wisdom of the Zohar: An Anthology of Texts* (English trans. David Goldstein), 3 vols. (London, 1991).

TODD, JANET, *Sensibility: An Introduction* (London, 1986).

TRACHTENBERG, JOSHUA, *Jewish Magic and Superstition: A Study in Folk Tradition* (New York, 1974).

TREADGOLD, W., 'The Peasant and Religion', in W. S. Vicinich (ed.), *The Peasant in Nineteenth-Century Russia* (Stanford, Calif., 1986), 72–107.

TSAKNI, N., *La Russie sectaire* (Paris, 1888).

Tsava'at haribash, ed. J. I. Sochet (Brooklyn, 1975).

TSEVI ELIMELEKH OF DYNÓW, *Agra dekhalah* (New York, 1964).

TUROV, IGOR, 'Hasidism and Christianity of the Eastern Territory of the Polish–Lithuanian Commonwealth: Possibile Contact and Mutual Influences', *Kabbalah: Journal for the Study of Jewish Mystical Texts,* 10 (2004), 71–105.

UFFENHEIMER, B., 'From Prophetic to Apocalyptic Eschatology' (Heb.), in Zvi Baras (ed.), *Messianism and Eschatology* [Meshiḥiyut ve'eskhatologyah] (Jerusalem, 1984), 27–72.

URBACH, EPHRAIM E., *The Sages: Their Concepts and Beliefs,* trans. from the Hebrew by Israel Abrahams (Cambridge, Mass., 1987).

—— *The World of the Sages: Collected Studies* [Me'olamam shel ḥakhamim: kovets meḥkarim] (Jerusalem, 1988).

URRY, J., *None but Saints: The Transformation of Mennonite Life in Russia, 1789–1889* (Winnipeg, 1989).

VITAL, HAYIM, 'Book of Visions', in *Jewish Mystical Autobiographies: Book of Visions and Book of Secrets,* trans. and introd. Morris M. Faierstein, preface by Moshe Idel (New York, 1999); original Hebrew edn.: *Sefer haḥezyonot,* ed. A. Z. Aescoly (Jerusalem, 1954).

VON HÖNIGSBERG, LEIB [as 'L.v.H.': the Hebrew initials *lamed-feh-heh* = Leib von Hönigsberg], 'Wise Letters' (Heb.), *Hame'asef*, 7/1 (1797), 22–37; 7/3 (1797), 196–203.

WACHOLDER, BEN ZION, 'Jacob Frank and the Frankists' Hebrew Zoharic Letters', *Hebrew Union College Annual*, 53 (1982), 265–93.

WALDEN, MOSHE MENAHEM, *Nifle'ot harabi* (Warsaw, 1911).

WARE, T., *The Orthodox Church* (Harmondsworth, 1964).

WARNER, MARINA, *Alone of All Her Sex: The Myth and the Cult of the Virgin Mary* (New York, 1983).

WEINRYB, B. D., *The Jews of Poland* (Philadelphia, 1973).

—— 'Reappraisals in Jewish History', in S. Lieberman and A. Hyman (eds.), *Salo Wittmayer Baron Jubilee Volume*, English section, ii (Jerusalem, 1974), 939–74.

WEISS, JOSEPH, 'The Beginnings of Hasidism' (Heb.), in A. Rubinstein (ed.), *Studies in Hasidism* [Perakim betorat hahasidut uvetoledoteiha] (Jerusalem, 1977), 122–81.

—— 'Some Notes on the Social Background of Early Hasidism', in id., *Studies in Eastern European Jewish Mysticism*, 3–25.

—— *Studies in Eastern European Jewish Mysticism* (Oxford, 1985).

WEISSBERG, ISAAC JACOB, *Ga'on vashever*, pt. 2 of Mikhl b. Aaron David Gordon, *Shever ga'on* (Warsaw, 1884).

WEISSLER, CHAVA, *Voices of the Matriarchs* (Boston, 1998).

—— 'Women in Paradise', *Tikkun*, 2 (1987), 43–6, 117–20.

WEISSMAN, D., 'Bais Yaakov: A Historical Model for Jewish Feminists', in E. Koltun (ed.), *The Jewish Woman* (New York, 1976), 263–300.

WERBLOWSKY, R. J. Z., 'Reflections on Gershom Scholem's "Sabbatai Zevi"' (Heb.), *Molad*, 15 (1957), 539–46.

WERSES, S., *Haskalah and Sabbatianism: The Story of a Controversy* [Haskalah veshabeta'ut: toledotav shel ma'avak] (Jerusalem, 1988).

—— 'Women in Hasidic Courts as Reflected in Mitnagdic Polemics and Maskilic Satire', *Gal-ed*, 21 (2007), 29–47.

WESSELY, NAPHTALI HERZ, *Book of Ethics* [Sefer hamidot] (Berlin, 1786?–8).

WESSELY, WOLFGANG, 'Auf den Briefen eines Sabbatianers', *Zeitschrift für die historische Theologie*, 15 (1845), 136–52; repr. in *Orient*, 12 (1851), 534–43, 568–74.

WILENSKY, MORDECAI, 'Four English Pamphlets on the Sabbatian Movement in the Years 1665–6' (Heb.), *Zion*, 15–17 (1950–2), 150–72.

—— *Hasidim and Mitnagedim* [Hasidim umitnagedim], 2 vols. (Jerusalem, 1970).

WILHELM, K., and GERSHOM SCHOLEM, 'The Proclamation against the Sabbatian Sect' (Heb.), *Kiryat sefer*, 30 (1954–5), 99–104; repr. in Gershom Scholem, *Researches in Sabbatianism* [Mehkerei shabeta'ut], ed. Yehuda Liebes (Tel Aviv, 1991), 600–8.

WILLIAMS, G. H., *The Radical Reformation*, 3rd edn. (Kirksville, Mo., 1992).

WINSTON, D., 'Philo and the Rabbis on Sex and the Body', *Poetics Today*, 19 (1998), 41–62.

WIRSZUBSKI, CHAIM, *Between the Lines: Kabbalah, Christian Kabbalah and Sabbatianism* [Bein hashitin: kabalah, kabalah notsrit, shabeta'ut], ed. Moshe Idel (Jerusalem, 1990).

—— 'On Spiritual Love: From the Writings of Nathan of Gaza' (Heb.), in id., *Between the Lines*, 210–20.

—— 'The Sabbatian Kabbalist R. Moses David of Podhajce' (Heb.), in id., *Between the Lines*, 189–209.

—— 'The Sabbatian Theology of Nathan the Prophet' (Heb.), in id., *Between the Lines*, 152–87.

WODZIŃSKI, MARCIN, 'How Should We Count *Hasidim* in Congress Poland? A Reply to Glenn Dynner', *Gal-ed*, 20 (2006), 105–20.

—— '"Sprawa chasydymów": Z materiałów do dziejów chasydyzmu w Królestwie Polskim' ['"The Case of the Hasidim": From Materials on the History of Hasidism in the Kingdom of Poland'], in Krystyn Matwijowski (ed.), *Z historii ludności żydowskiej w Polsce i na Śląsku* [History of the Jews in Poland and Silesia] (Wrocław, 1994), 227–42; trans. into French, 'L'Affaire des "Chasydymów": Materiaux pour l'histoire des Hassidim dans le Royaume de Pologne', *Tsafon: Revue d'études juives du Nord*, 29 (1997), 35–58.

WOLFSON, ELLIOT R., *Circle in the Square* (Albany, NY, 1995).

—— 'Constructions of the Shekhinah in the Messianic Theosophy of Abraham Cardoso, with an Annotated Edition of *Derush ha-Shekhinah*', *Kabbalah: Journal for the Study of Jewish Mystical Texts*, 3 (1998), 11–143.

—— 'Coronation of the Sabbath Bride: Kabbalistic Myth and the Ritual of Androgynisation', *Journal of Jewish Thought and Philosophy*, 6 (1997), 301–43.

—— 'The Engenderment of Messianic Politics: Symbolic Significance of Sabbatai Sevi's Coronation', in P. Schäfer and M. Cohen (eds.), *Toward the Millennium* (Leiden, 1998), 203–58.

—— 'Gender and Heresy in the Study of Kabbalah', *Kabbalah: Journal for the Study of Jewish Mystical Texts*, 6 (2001), 231–62.

—— 'Hebraic and Hellenic Conceptions of Wisdom in *Sefer ha-Bahir*', *Poetics Today*, 19 (1998), 147–73.

WOLLSTONECRAFT, MARY, 'A Vindication of the Rights of Woman', in *The Works of Mary Wollstonecraft*, ed. Janet Todd and Marilyn Butler, 7 vols. (London, 1989), v. 61–266.

Words of the Lord. See Frank

WYNTIJES, SHERRIN MARSHALL, 'Women in the Reformation Era', in R. Bridenthal and C. Koonz (eds.), *Becoming Visible: Women in European History* (Boston, 1977), 167–91.

YERUSHALMI, Y. H., *From Spanish Court to Italian Ghetto* (Seattle, 1971).

YSANDER, T., *Studien zum B'eštschen Ḥasidismus in seiner religionsgeschichtlichen Sonderart* (Uppsala, 1933).

ŽÁČEK, VÁCLAV, 'Zwei Beiträge zur Geschichte des Frankismus in den böhmischen Ländern', *Jahrbuch der Gesellschaft für Geschichte der Juden in der Čechoslovakischen Republik*, 9 (Prague, 1938), 343–410.

ZADOFF, NOAM, '"The Awl and the Sack": Joseph Weiss, Baruch Kurzweil, and Gershom Scholem's Historical Vocation' (Heb.), in Y. Hotam, M. Schmidt, and N. Zadoff (eds.), *History as Vocation: A Collection of Essays in Honour of Moshe Zimmermann on the Occasion of his Sixtieth Birthday* [Historyah kisheliḥut: asufat ma'amarim likhevodo shel moshe zimerman bimlot lo shishim] (Jerusalem, 2006), 73–8.

ZADOFF, NOAM, 'The Debate between Baruch Kurzweil and Gershom Scholem on the Research of Sabbatianism' (Heb.), *Kabbalah: Journal for the Study of Jewish Mystical Texts*, 16 (2007), 299–360.

ZE'EV WOLF OF ZHITOMIR, *Or hame'ir* (Warsaw 1883).

ZELDES, NADIA, 'A Magical Event in Sicily: Notes and Clarifications on the Messianic Movement in Sicily' (Heb.), *Zion*, 58/3 (1993), 347–63.

The Zohar, trans. and commentary Daniel C. Matt, 4 vols. (Pritzker edn., Stanford, Calif., 2004–7).

Index